THE ILLUSTRATED HISTORY OF BOXING

Franklin

THE ILLUSTRATED HISTORY OF BOXING

HARRY MULLAN

Crescent Books
New York

Photographic acknowledgments
All black and white photographs supplied by the author, Harry Mullan. Colour photographs supplied by the following:
Front cover: Marvin Hagler v. Sugar Ray Leonard (All-Sport Photographic, London/Mike Powell)
Back cover: Muhammad Ali v. Joe Frazier (Focus on Sports, New York)
Title page: Sugar Ray Leonard (All-Sport Photographic, London/Duomo)
All-Sport Photographic, London 103, Simon Bruty 311 bottom, Dave Cannon 243, Chris Cole 176, 311 top, Tony Duffy 447 bottom, Duomo 141 bottom, 277, Bob Martin 121, 124 top, Mike Powell 244 bottom, Steve Powell 70, 122–3, 175, 379 top & bottom; The Associated Press, London 413; Focus on Sports, New York 69; John Jacobs 124 bottom; Linda Platt, Las Vegas 104, 209, 210 top, 244 top, 278, 312, 345 bottom, 346 top & bottom, 380 top & bottom, 414 top & bottom, 447 top; Popperfoto, London 35 top & bottom, 36; Sporting Pictures, London 141 top, 142, 210 bottom, 345 top, 448.

Front jacket: *Sugar Ray Leonard and Marvin Hagler in April 1987. Leonard won on points.*
Back jacket: *Muhammad Ali – 'The Greatest'.*
Title page: *Sugar Ray Leonard before his fight with Hagler.*

First English edition published by
The Hamlyn Publishing Group Limited
Bridge House, Twickenham, Middlesex TW1 3SB, England

This 1987 edition published by Crescent Books
Distributed by Crown Publishers, Inc.
225 Park Avenue South
New York, New York 10003

ISBN 0-517-62953-4
h g f e d c b a

Printed in Italy

Contents

For my parents, Pat and Maureen, with love.

INTRODUCTION

WHEN Nat Fleischer and Sam Andre first published *A Pictorial History of Boxing* in 1959 there were eight weight divisions and eight champions. The book deservedly became a standard work, but boxing has changed dramatically in the near-30 years since then.

We now have 16 divisions and (at last count) 43 'world champions' and the balance of power, at least from light-welterweights downwards, has shifted from West to East.

Hence this new attempt to chronicle the ever more complicated history of world championship boxing from a late 1980s viewpoint. It is not intended to replace *Pictorial History*, but rather to accompany it.

Wherever possible I have tried to avoid using the standard illustrations, those which have been seen many times already. In this aim I have been greatly assisted by my friend Jim Jacobs of New York, who owns the world's largest collection of fight films and photos and also directs the careers of world champions Mike Tyson and Edwin Rosario.

Some of the early photos in this book are in fact stills which Jim has taken from moving pictures, and which appear here on the page for the first time.

As always, my American friends and colleagues responded to requests for help with the kind of generosity which is typical of their country. Debbie Munch of Caesars Palace merits special thanks: I phoned her one Monday evening (London time) to request a fairly large selection of action photos from major fights which the hotel has hosted. With breathtaking American efficiency, they were on my desk on Wednesday morning, via air courier.

World Boxing, *KO* magazine, and the venerable *Ring* were all extremely helpful. Nigel Collins of *Ring* supplied many early photos, while the *Ring Record Book and Encyclopedia* was a constantly invaluable source of reference.

Stanley Weston and Peter King, respectively the Publisher and Editor-in-Chief of *KO* and *World Boxing*, gave freely from their picture files, as did Bert Blewett and his photographer associates on *South African Boxing World.*

Makoto Maeda and the Japanese monthly *World Boxing* provided most of the photographs of Oriental fights.

Other material was supplied by my many friends amongst the Danish sporting press, as well as by private collectors like the ever-obliging Derek O'Dell.

I could not have written this book without the back-up of my colleagues on *Boxing News*, Anthony Connolly, Daniel Herbert and Tim Mo, who virtually took over the production of the paper in order to free me to concentrate on the book during the months of research and writing.

Finally, I want to record my gratitude to my wife Jessie and children Siobhan, Kevin and Ian, who endured my frequent absences and bad-tempered presence while the work was in progress.

Harry Mullan
London, 1987

HEAVYWEIGHTS

THE ORIGINS of professional boxing cannot be pinpointed with quite the precision of, say, rugby football, which was born in 1823 when a rebellious Rugby schoolboy, William Webb Ellis, picked up the ball during a football match, tucked it under his arm, and ran. Prize-fighting had existed, in varying degrees of savagery, since gladiators clubbed each other to death wearing iron-studded hand bindings called *caesti.* Homer's *Iliad*, written around 1100 BC, describes a prize-fight between Epeus and Euryalus.

Although bare-knuckle fighting peaked in popularity during the free-wheeling days of the late 18th to mid-19th centuries, the legitimate starting point for a history of boxing in its modern, gloved form is probably the challenge which John L. Sullivan – or, more likely, his press agent – issued in 1891 'for a purse of $25,000 and a bet of $10,000... to James J. Corbett, who has uttered his share of bombast'. Sullivan was a brawling, hard-living and hard-drinking Irish-American who had earned recognition as world champion with a series of brutal bare-fist battles against Charlie Mitchell, Paddy Ryan, and Jake Kilrain.

But by the time Sullivan issued his famous challenge to the one-time bank clerk from San Francisco he was a dissipated 32-year-old, who had not been tested in a serious fight for more than

Contemporary illustration of the Corbett v Sullivan fight in New Orleans, showing Corbett landing one of the innumerable straight lefts which so confused, bewildered and eventually demoralized the one-time 'Boston Strong Boy'. Corbett's victory, and the style with which it was achieved, marked the beginning of the game's modern era.

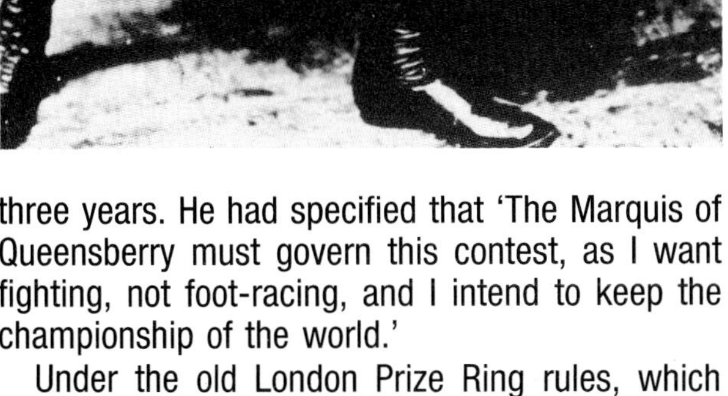

Above left: *John L. Sullivan, who lost the first gloved fight for the heavyweight title.*

Above: *James J. Corbett, the boxing bank clerk who shocked Sullivan.*

three years. He had specified that 'The Marquis of Queensberry must govern this contest, as I want fighting, not foot-racing, and I intend to keep the championship of the world.'

Under the old London Prize Ring rules, which had governed his previous 34 contests, the veteran might have had a chance, but when they met at the Pelican Athletic Club in New Orleans on 7 September 1892, he found himself faced for the first time by an opponent who played the game by different rules. The 26-year-old Corbett preached and practised the heresy that it was permissible to hit without being hit, and that four accurately delivered left jabs could count for more than a single roundhouse right in the style which Sullivan personified.

By modern standards, Corbett was too light even to box for the cruiserweight title, scaling a mere 3 lb over the modern light-heavyweight limit of 12 st 7 lb (175 lb) against Sullivan's 15 st 2 lb (212 lb). But in this new style of boxing, where skill and technique counted for more than brute strength and raw courage, that was no disadvantage. Long before the halfway stage the outcome was inevitable. Sullivan, paying the price of three years of good living and late nights, found his challenger as elusive as a handful of fog. Time and again, Corbett laughed in his face as he made him miss with swings and swipes, and then countered with sharp, stinging, demoralizing and accurate jabs.

The 21st round was one of the pivotal moments in boxing history. Corbett at last took the initiative against the exhausted champion, pummelling him with a series of rights to the head before a final right to the ear and left to the jaw dropped him face-first onto the sand-covered floor of the ring. As the referee, Professor John Duffy, completed the count, Sullivan's followers in the gallery showered the ring with the green bands which they had carried to denote their support for him. When the

Corbett (left) in preparation for his only successful defence, against England's Charlie Mitchell in 1894.

old champion had recovered sufficiently he walked to the edge of the ring, held up his hands for silence and said (with more than a touch of the chauvinism which marked American attitudes to world boxing until Muhammad Ali finally internationalized the sport in the 1960s): 'I'm glad it was an American who beat me, and that the championship stays in this country.'

Corbett, a high-society dandy who relished his nickname of 'Gentleman Jim', had revolutionized the sport, but he never enjoyed anything like the degree of popularity held by Sullivan. The boxing world never quite forgave him for having toppled an idol; it was a reaction with which, in the decades ahead, champions such as Ezzard Charles, Gene Tunney and Larry Holmes would become familiar.

Corbett made only one successful defence, knocking out England's Charlie Mitchell in 1894, but his contribution to the development of boxing in its modern form can never be under-valued. He changed the face of boxing as surely as Ali did seven decades later, and even if his impact on the world stage was not nearly as significant as Ali's, his place in history is just as secure.

Corbett earned a footnote in the history books by knocking out Peter Courtney of Trenton, New Jersey, two years to the day after beating Sullivan. The Courtney fight, which was scheduled for the unusual distance of two-minute rounds, was staged at the Edison Laboratory in Orange, New Jersey, and marked the first time that moving picture cameras had been used to record a fight. However, the film lasted for only 90 seconds at most, so as soon as it ran out 'Time' would be called, and the between-rounds intervals extended to two minutes or more until the cameras had been reloaded.

Apart from a three-round knockout of Jim McVey in an exhibition match in New Orleans in January 1895, Corbett spent most of the year trying

Joe Choynski (left) and Corbett had a long-lasting feud, but they finally made peace years after they had both retired. James J. Jeffries, then the heavyweight champion, supervises the peacemaking.

Above: *Cornish-born Bob Fitzsimmons developed his extraordinary punching power through his work in a smithy.*

unsuccessfully to arrange a defence against the English-born Bob Fitzsimmons. They were matched three times, first in New York for $10,000 a side, then in Dallas for $41,000 and a $10,000 sidestake, and finally in Hot Springs for $10,000, but each proposed meeting fell through. Ten months later, Corbett announced his retirement and 'presented' his championship to Galway-born Peter Maher, after the Irishman's 63-second knockout of Steve O'Donnell at Long Island.

Maher's claim to the championship was shaky enough at best, for he had been beaten in 12 rounds by Fitzsimmons at New Orleans in March 1892, but it vanished entirely when Fitzsimmons kayoed him again, this time in 95 seconds, on 21 February 1896. Corbett, like Sullivan before him, had not had a serious contest for more than three years but public opinion – and a faltering stage career – now forced him to announce that he was reclaiming the championship. He fought Fitzsimmons at Carson City, Nevada, on St Patrick's Day, 1897, in the first open-air arena ever erected specifically for a boxing match.

Fitzsimmons, born in Helston, Cornwall, was one of the game's freaks. In his fighting prime he rarely

Below: *Rare glimpse of a late 19th-century training camp, as Fitzsimmons prepares for his 1897 clash with Corbett.*

MECHANICS
PAVILLION
DEC. 20-1905
ED
GRANBY
REF.
WILLIE
FITZGERALD
"PHILA"
JACK
O'BRIEN
BOB
FITZSIMMONS
BILLY
JORDAN
ANNOUNCER

FITSSIMMONS V LANG
ROUND. 1.

scaled more than 12 st 2 lb (170 lb). His weight for the Corbett match was announced as 167 lb, although it was widely believed that he had been even lighter, and that the promoters had concealed the fact lest the announcement of his true weight affect the gate takings.

Fitzsimmons already held the middleweight title, which he had won from the original Jack Dempsey ('Nonpareil' Jack) on a 13th-round knockout in 1891. He was probably the least athletic looking heavyweight contender of all time, with spindly legs, freckles and a rapidly receding hairline which made him look even older than his 33 years. But his years of hard physical work in a smithy in New Zealand (where his family had emigrated when he was nine) had given him tremendous upper-body development and better punching power than any other heavyweight of his generation.

There was no love lost between the rivals. Fitzsimmons bitterly resented the way Corbett had (in his view) avoided him for five years so depriving him of his peak earning potential. And the handsome, arrogant Corbett was so contemptuous of his unprepossessing challenger that he made a point of snubbing him whenever they met in public.

For six rounds, the champion's arrogance seemed justified. He outboxed Fitzsimmons with ease, dominating the smaller man with elegant left jabs and flooring him with a left hook in the sixth. Fitzsimmons fell heavily, barely beating referee George Siler's count at 'nine', and clung on desperately to survive the round.

But this was Corbett's last chance of victory – from the seventh round onwards Fitzsimmons took over, boring inside Corbett's jab and hammering punches into the fading champion's body. At the end of the 13th round Fitzsimmons called down to Rose, his wife and manager, to bet everything she could on his victory in the 14th. He was as good as his word: early in that round he jabbed two lefts at

Fitzsimmons squares off with Philadelphia Jack O'Brien (top left) *before the December 1905 fight which cost Bob the light-heavyweight title. Eight years earlier, Fitzsimmons had defeated Corbett for the heavyweight championship* (right) *and also won the middleweight title in 1891. He was the first three-time champion in boxing history. His last major fight came in 1909, when at the age of 46 he was knocked out in 12 rounds by Bill Lang for the Australian heavyweight title* (left).

Corbett's head, feinted a right to the jaw and, as the champion's guard came up, switched his weight to fire a right under the heart and a left to the pit of the stomach. Corbett sank to his knees, gasping. He was conscious, but unable to force enough air into his lungs to raise himself to his feet as Siler counted him out.

It was a stunning result, but at least one spectator was unimpressed. James J. Jeffries, a bulky 21-year-old of Scotch-Dutch extraction, had been Corbett's sparmate and claimed to have floored him. Whatever the truth, the youngster's performance against the champion after only five professional fights gave him the confidence to climb to the top. By late 1898 he had established himself as a leading championship contender, with wins over the durable Irishman Tom Sharkey and the great black heavyweight Peter Jackson, the man against whom even the great John L. Sullivan had 'drawn the colour line'.

In August 1898 Jeffries' manager Bill Brady brought him east to New York and conceived the publicity gimmick of matching him with two men on the same night, Bob Armstrong and Steve O'Donnell. It was designed to whip up interest in a possible title fight with Fitzsimmons, but the plan went awry in the first round of his 10-rounder with Armstrong, when Jeffries smashed his right hand on the black man's head.

Not for the first time, Jeffries revealed the extraordinary degree of courage and endurance which became his trademark. Although he hung on for nine more rounds to win the decision, he left the ring to jeers from the disappointed crowd when it was announced that he could not go through with the O'Donnell fight. He returned, somewhat sheepishly, to his San Francisco home, while the indefatigable Brady remained in New York, trying to salvage the Fitzsimmons fight.

Shrewdly, he turned the Armstrong debacle to his advantage, using it as evidence to convince the champion that the cumbersome, almost muscle-

The badly winded James J. Corbett struggles unsuccessfully to rise after Fitzsimmons' 14th-round body punch ended the Californian's reign at Carson City, Nevada on 17 March 1897. James J. Jeffries (below), *the man who was destined to dethrone Fitzsimmons two years later, watched from the ringside.*

Jeffries was an assiduous trainer, and he needed to be in supremely good condition for his gruelling title defence against the Irishman Tom Sharkey in 1899. The heat from the overhead lights was so intense that Jeffries lost 20 lb, and referee George Siler had to wear a hat to protect himself.

bound Jeffries would be a slow and easy target. The ploy worked and Fitzsimmons took him on at Coney Island on 25 July 1902. But Jeffries was not quite as optimistic as his manager – he bet $5,000 on Fitzsimmons at odds of 10-6, explaining that if he was beaten he would need the money, and that if he won he would not miss it.

When Jeffries' bet became public knowledge, the odds on Fitzsimmons rose even higher. Tommy Ryan, the former world welterweight champion who had been engaged to train Jeffries, came up with a psychological master-stroke which virtually ensured that his client would lose his bet but win the title: he instructed Jeffries to visit Fitzsimmons' dressing room before the fight, ostensibly to discuss the rules, and then to demonstrate his strength by giving the champion a bearhug. He did so, and this first-hand experience of the power his 38lb heavier opponent possessed sapped the veteran's morale. Although the fight went into the 11th round, it had long since ceased to be a contest. Jeffries had floored Fitzsimmons as early as the second round, and put him down twice more in the tenth before finally despatching him with a single left hook.

By the lethargic standards of his predecessors, Jeffries was a busy champion with seven defences over the next five years. His first, against the former sailor Tom Sharkey (a native of Dundalk, Ireland), was one of the most brutal fights ever seen even in an era that was distinctly unsqueamish. It went the scheduled 25 rounds, and the damage they inflicted on each other was

Tom Sharkey, from Dundalk, settled in America after service in the Navy and became one of the toughest contenders of his time. Note the cauliflower ear, common in those days.

horrific. Sharkey suffered two broken ribs and severe facial cuts, while Jeffries dislocated his elbow. The heat from the overhead lights, which had been installed so that the contest could be filmed (the first time that artificial lighting had been used for this purpose) was so intense that Jeffries lost 20 lb during the fight, but the Irishman was too weary to capitalize on the champion's exhaustion and was clearly outpointed.

Jeffries' reputation as the ring's 'Iron Man' was enhanced with a 23-round knockout of Corbett in his next defence in May 1900. For more than 20 rounds Corbett's boxing was a delight, and the cumbersome Jeffries was made to miss repeatedly. But the distance was too long for the almost 34-year-old challenger, and between the 21st and

Marvin Hart (left) *is probably the least-known heavyweight champion of them all: he was never accorded universal recognition, and his reign lasted only seven months before Tommy Burns* (below) *outpointed him in Los Angeles in February 1906. Burns and Hart were two of the smallest men ever to contest the title – Burns was 5 ft 7 in, Hart 5 ft 11 in.*

23rd rounds Jeffries' immense natural strength began to tell until, late in the 23rd, he feinted a right and met Corbett coming off the ropes with a left hook that knocked him cold.

On 25 July 1902 Bob Fitzsimmons got another chance at the title. For eight rounds he pounded Jeffries, breaking his nose, and opening deep cuts on both cheeks and over each eye. It had been rumoured before the fight that Fitzsimmons had planned to 'doctor' his hands with plaster of Paris, which prompted the laconic reply from Jeffries that 'If he wants to use that, then let him – I'll flatten him anyway.'

It took Jeffries eight rounds to keep his word. As Fitzsimmons broke from a clinch, smiled, and spoke to him the champion moved in and kayoed him with a single left hook to the jaw. His remaining defences, against Jack Munroe and Corbett again, were not quite so arduous, and by 1904 Jeffries had run out of challengers. He announced his retirement as undefeated champion and, as was the custom at that time, claimed the right to appoint his successor.

Marvin Hart, a small (5 ft 11 in) heavyweight from Kentucky who had not taken up boxing until he was 23, was matched with Jack Root, who two years previously had become the first holder of the world light-heavyweight title. (The remarkable

Fitzsimmons, incidentally, won the light-heavyweight title in 1903 and held it for over two years, thus becoming the first man in history to win world titles at three weights.)

Hart and Root met at Reno, Nevada, where Jeffries attempted to confer a degree of validity on the fight by acting as referee and presenting Hart with the belt after he had survived a seventh-round knockdown to kayo Root in the 12th. But even Jeffries' seal of approval was not enough to convince the boxing public and Hart, despite a fine record highlighted by a 20-rounds decision over the formidable Jack Johnson in March 1905, was never fully recognized as world champion.

Hart's reign, such as it was, lasted a mere seven months during which he made only one appearance in the ring, knocking out Pat Callahan in the second round of a non-title fight. His tenuous claim to the championship was disputed by many of the leading heavyweights of the day, most vociferously by the improbable figure of Noah Brusso, a stumpy 5 ft 7 in French-Canadian who scaled around the light-heavyweight limit of 175 lb and boxed professionally as Tommy Burns. Burns had overcome his physical disadvantages with a gutsy, aggressive style of fighting that had carried him through 38 fights with only three defeats, and with a flair for self-publicity which earned him recognition as a contender without having to go through the tiresome formalities of beating some of the division's proven quality men.

Burns secured a match with Hart in Los Angeles on 23 February 1906, despite having lost his previous fight on a 20-rounds decision to Jack 'Twin' Sullivan. It was one of the few occasions when the world heavyweight title was contested by two men who were each less than 6 ft tall.

Burns won decisively on points, and then set about consolidating his claim to the title by taking the championship 'on the road'. He became the first truly *international* champion, taking on anyone who could find a backer for a challenge, regardless of the opponent's qualifications or lack of them. Some of his challengers were a long way short of contender status: Jem Roche, for example, was despatched inside a round in Dublin, while English challengers Jack Palmer and Gunner Moir were little better.

Nonetheless, Burns' 11 successful defences did include some respectable victories over decent performers such as Jim Flynn, light-heavyweight champion Jack O'Brien, and Bill Squires (whom he

Publicity shots could be just as corny in 1907 as in 1987: this is Burns allegedly trying his hand at cab-driving in Hampstead, London prior to his defence against Gunner Moir.

Jem Roche (below) *qualified for the record books by getting knocked out in just 88 seconds by Tommy Burns in Dublin on St Patrick's Day, 1908. It remained the fastest heavyweight title fight until Mike Dokes stopped Mike Weaver 74 years later.*

Burns flattened Bill Squires (above, *on the left*) *three times, in America, France and Australia, . . . but the shadow of Jack Johnson* (below) *hung over him until they met in 1908.*

knocked out successively in California, Paris, and Sydney, thereby qualifying Squires for the unenviable distinction of being the only title challenger in history to have been knocked out by the same man in three different continents.)

American historians are still dismissive of Burns' ability. Bert Randolph Sugar, for example, wrote in *100 Years of Boxing* that: '...his dubious claim to the championship was greeted by an overwhelming apathy that rivalled the sound of one hand clapping'. Such comments are, though, a shade unfair to a man who, by bringing the title to England, France, Ireland, and Australia, did much to make it a *world* title rather than just the American championship. By 1908, the Canadian had earned universal acceptance as champion, but there was a long, black shadow hanging over him – Jack Johnson.

John L. Sullivan had drawn the colour line nearly 20 years previously with the ignoble statement that 'I've never fought a nigger, and I never will', since when the great black heavyweights had struggled for recognition. None of them had been allowed to fight for the championship, and craftsmen such as Sam Langford, Joe Jeanette, Sam McVey, and Johnson himself had been forced to spend their peak years fighting each other in seemingly interminable series across America.

Langford, for example, met Harry Wills 23 times, McVey 15, Jeanette 14, Jim Barry 12, and Jeff Clarke 11. The best that they could hope for was to become the 'Negro heavyweight champion', which Johnson did in 1904 by knocking out Denver Ed Martin in Los Angeles. Yet most of them were also 'businessmen', who were not averse to letting the local white ticket-seller beat them for a consideration. But Johnson was not prepared to play that game. He had a well-founded belief in his own ability which, in the racist parlance of those times, made him 'an uppity nigger'. His self-confidence was interpreted as mere arrogance, which was intolerable to those who then ran boxing.

Johnson made no concessions to white sensitivities, and his womanizing outraged white America. His great contemporary (and future opponent), middleweight champion Stanley Ketchel, was eulogized as 'a man's man' for precisely the sort of sexual behaviour which Johnson practised, only in his Caucasian case it was considered forgiveable. Johnson's preference, however, was for white women, and thus he was pilloried while Ketchel was lionized.

These were times when contemporary fight reports used terms such as 'nigger', 'coon', 'blackie', and 'Sambo' as a matter of course. No black fighter, and least of all one who, like Johnson, actively courted unpopularity, could expect favours or sympathy from an exclusively white-owned and dominated press. But in the end Johnson's magnificent ability outweighed all other considerations, and forced his acceptance as the division's leading contender.

Burns, a shrewd businessman who never knowingly undersold himself, knew that a fight with Johnson would bring him his biggest ever purse and misled the ever-gullible fight public into believing that he was scared of meeting the black man. Johnson played along, chasing Burns across Europe and on to Australia, continuously hurling taunting and provocative challenges at him. Public

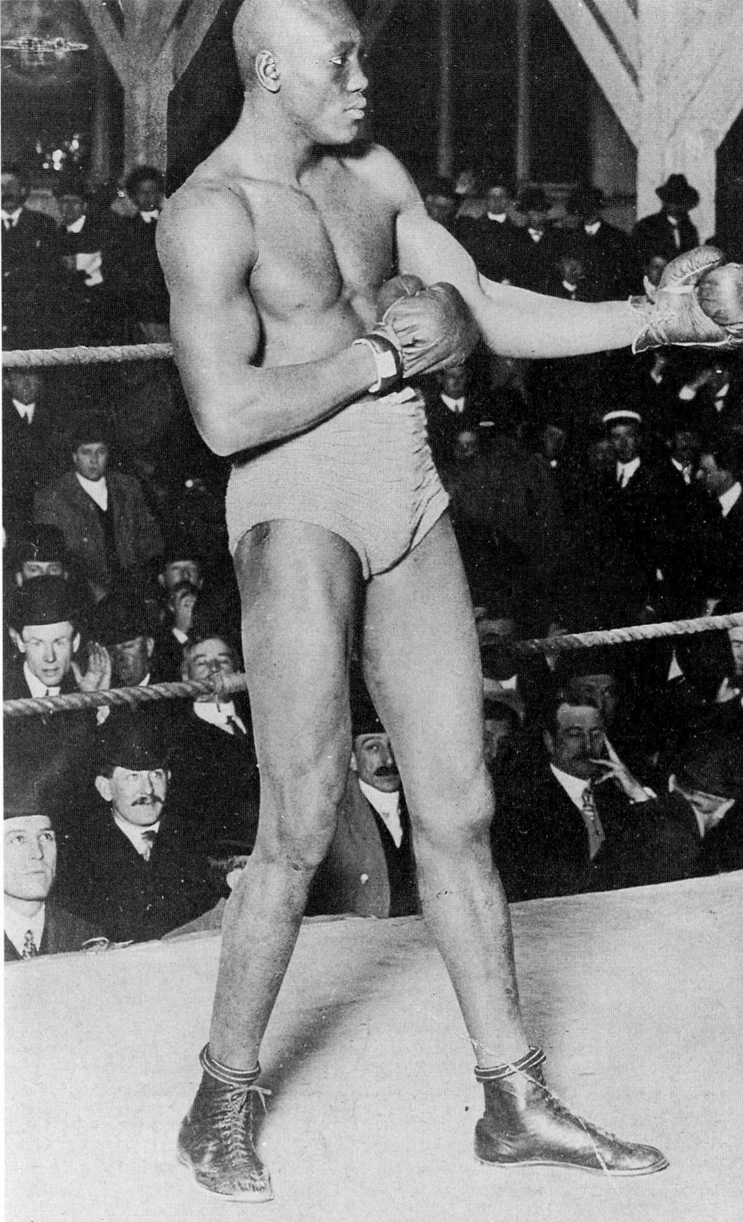

Above: *Sam McVey (right) was one of the blacks whose careers suffered because of Johnson's conduct.*

Johnson's great weakness was for women – or to be specific, for white women. He married three of them, including Etta Duryea (above left) *and Irene Pineau* (above right)*, and scandalized America by keeping a string of mistresses. His womanizing outraged the establishment, and ensured that no other black fighter would get a chance at the heavyweight title for more than 20 years.*

Below: *Tommy Burns, looking every inch the shrewd businessman he was, exploited Johnson's notoriety to ensure a big purse.*

Above and below: *When Johnson at last got Burns into the ring at Rushcutter's Bay, Sydney, on Boxing Day 1908, he made him pay dearly for keeping him waiting so long: Burns took a one-sided beating before the police stopped the fight.*

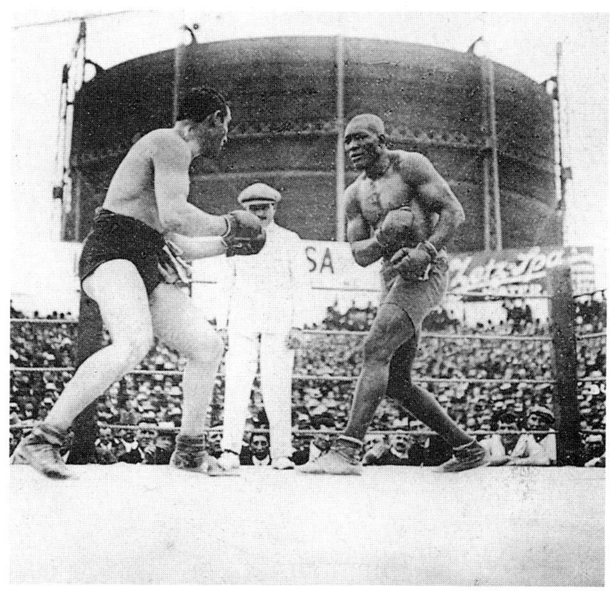

demand for the fight became irresistible, just as Burns had calculated. Finally, the champion accepted an astonishing (for those times) $30,000 purse from Australian promoter Hugh D. McIntosh to defend his title against Johnson at Rushcutter's Bay, Sydney, on 26 December 1908.

Although the fight proved just as one-sided as Johnson had predicted, Burns' performance in defeat was so heroic that it ended, once and for all, the speculation that he had been scared to meet a man who outweighed him by 20 lb and who towered over him by seven inches. It was not an edifying spectacle; Johnson toyed with the champion, taunting him, talking to him, bullying him, and doing everything within his power to humiliate him.

He could, almost certainly, have ended the fight whenever he chose, but there were too many debts to be called in, too many slights and snubs to be avenged. He made Burns pay dearly for what had been done to all the great black heavyweights who had been denied the chance which Johnson was now grasping. To Johnson, this was more than a simple boxing match, and the ferociously racist press coverage ensured that the public at large would also see it in terms of black versus white.

When the police finally entered the ring in the 14th round to stop the fight, the news that the world had a black heavyweight champion sparked a wave of race riots and lynchings across America. There were pious hopes expressed in some quarters that, having become champion, Johnson might sufficiently modify his behaviour to make it acceptable to white opinion – but the one-time dock labourer from Galveston, who had been born a mere 15 years after the abolition of slavery, was very much his own man. Johnson married four times, three of his wives being white women, and scandalized America not only by his own sexual mores but by those of the clientele of the saloon he opened in Chicago, the Café de Champion. But his performances in the ring, more than in the bedroom, marked him as a formidable champion. His total dominance of the heavyweight stage caused the writer Jack London, in an infamous piece, to urge the old champion James J. Jeffries to 'emerge from his alfalfa farm and remove that golden smile from Jack Johnson's face.' He concluded: 'Jeff, it's up to you. The White Man must be rescued!' While Jeffries pondered the wisdom of such a move, the world's white heavyweights virtually conceded the field to Johnson and competed instead for a nebulous title called the 'White Heavyweight Championship'.

Gunboat Smith, Georges Carpentier and Battling Levinsky each claimed the dubious distinction at one time, while others like Al Palzer, Frank Moran, Carl Morris, and Luther McCarthy (who died tragically after a knockout by Arthur Pelkey) were all billed as 'Great White Hopes'. It was a peculiarly undignified period in boxing history, lasting for as long as the hated Johnson occupied the heavyweight throne.

Johnson's accession to the title launched one of boxing's most shameful chapters – the frantic search for a 'White Hope' who could dethrone him. Luther McCarthy (pictured above right, *with Arthur Pelkey) looked the part until Pelkey knocked him out in the first round. McCarthy, tragically, died on the arena floor. Gunboat Smith* (left) *knocked out Pelkey in 15 rounds in January 1914 to claim the 'White Heavyweight Championship', but defeats by Georges Carpentier, Sam Langford and Jim Coffey removed him from contention. Even middleweight Stanley Ketchel* (right) *was pushed into challenging Johnson, and lasted into the 12th round.*

Johnson did nothing to enhance his popularity when he kayoed middleweight champion Stanley Ketchel in his first defence in October 1909. According to legend Johnson had agreed to 'carry' the challenger into the 12th round for the benefit of the moving picture cameras, and duly did so for 11 lazy rounds until, in the 12th, Ketchel tried to double-cross Johnson and floored him with a heavy right. The outraged Johnson bounced up at once and flattened Ketchel with a right that was so savage that five of Ketchel's teeth were afterwards found embedded in Johnson's glove.

By now the demand for Jeffries to come out of retirement had grown deafening, although with hindsight the white public's confidence in the

veteran was hopelessly misplaced. The old champion was 35 years old, weighed a bloated 21½ st (300lb) and had not boxed for five years, and yet he was expected to beat a man whom even the most strident racist had to acknowledge was a fighter without apparent flaw. But Jeffries, who was rumoured to be burdened with a $12,000 gambling debt, was soon persuaded to take the fight.

Johnson's high living – he rarely travelled anywhere without an entourage that included several exotic white prostitutes – meant that he was also in dire need of ready cash. Tex Rickard, who was to establish himself as the most innovative and imaginative promoter in boxing history, secured the match by reportedly settling both parties' debts and guaranteeing a combined purse of $101,000, plus an under-the-table bonus of $10,000 each on contract signature.

Rickard was a master publicist, and carefully-planted stories about every possible aspect of the fight raised public interest to an unprecedented high. No ticket-selling angle was left untried; there were rumours that the writer H. G. Wells would referee, and even Sir Arthur Conan Doyle, creator of Sherlock Holmes, was sent a solemn invitation by the editor of the *New York Morning Telegraph* to officiate. 'The fact is', he wrote to Conan Doyle, 'that when the articles were signed recently your name was suggested for referee, and Tex Rickard, promotor of the fight, was greatly interested, as were many others. I believe it will interest you to know that the opinion was unanimous that you would do admirably in the position. In a voting contest several persons sent in your name as their choice. Believe me, among sporting men of the best class in America you have very strong admirers, and your avowed admiration for the great sport of boxing has made you thousands of friends.' It was, of course, a brilliant publicity ploy: it had already been agreed that Rickard himself would referee.

Ex-champion James J. Corbett was hired to stoke the publicity fires, which he did with unabashedly racist statements such as: 'Take it from me, the black boy has a yellow streak and Jeff will bring it out when he gets him into that ring.' The hysteria grew until even the men who fixed the betting odds were carried away by it. Absurdly,

Al Kaufman (left), a moderate white heavyweight, boxing an exhibition with Johnson at Reno. They also met in 1909.

The wave of white fervour behind James J. Jeffries swept away even the bookmakers' better judgement, and the veteran ex-champion was a 10–6 betting favourite when he challenged Johnson at Reno on 4 July 1910. But their confidence was hopelessly misplaced, and the fight proved one of Johnson's easiest. He taunted the pathetic 'White Hope' for round after round, before he finally put him out of his misery in the 15th round.

Jeffries was installed as betting favourite, and Johnson promptly wired his brother Claude in Chicago to 'Bet your last copper on me.'

The closer they got to the fight, the deeper Jeffries went into depression. Even a visit from the legendary John L. Sullivan, the man who had introduced the colour bar into boxing, failed to lift his sagging spirits – and yet, when they entered the ring at Reno, Nevada, at 1.30 pm on 4 July, 1910, Jeffries was a 10-6 betting favourite. The crowd of 15,760 even included curtained boxes occupied by women, who for the first time were attending a fight in substantial numbers. They witnessed a championship contest that was every bit as one-sided as Johnson's rout of Tommy Burns 18 months before. Johnson taunted Jeffries endlessly, smiling at him and saying 'Come on, Mr Jeff – show us what you've got. Do something, man, this is for the championship.'

It went like this for round after round, with Jeffries growing increasingly weary, desperate, and demoralized, his face bruised and swollen. By the 13th, there were shouts of 'Stop it, don't let him be knocked out', but the challenger plodded on gamely until, in the 15th, Jeffries went sprawling through the ropes for the first knockdown of his career. Friends helped him to climb back, although

His enforced exile in Paris was no great hardship for Johnson, one of life's natural boulevardiers. He financed his taste for good times and expensive clothes (below) *with the occasional ring appearance, including this 20-round win over the one-time Pittsburgh dentist, Frank Moran.*

they would have done him more of a service by leaving him where he was. Johnson moved in and floored him again with a burst of left hooks. Sam Berger, in Jeffries' corner, threw in the towel, but Rickard ignored it and counted him out.

Once again, race riots exploded across America. There were deaths, lynchings, and disturbances in Pennsylvania, Maryland, Ohio, Mississippi, Virginia, Missouri, Georgia, Arkansas, and Colorado. On the night of 4 July, 11 people died, two whites and nine blacks.

It had been the most publicized and the richest event in boxing history. Johnson took away $60,000, plus his $10,000 advance, and an additional $50,000 for his share of the motion picture rights. Jeffries' share was $40,400, with $50,000 for the film rights. Their sale of the film rights proved a shrewd move, as state after state banned its showing, for fear that it might lead to more riots.

Johnson now became the target of official displeasure. The Mann Act, which prohibited the transportation of women across state lines for 'immoral purposes', was invoked against him on the testimony of Belle Schrieber, a white prostitute whom Johnson had taken to California to keep him entertained while training for the Jeffries fight. He was convicted, sentenced to a year and a day in prison, and fined $1,000.

Released on bail to settle his affairs, Johnson went on the run. He raised some ready cash by defending his title against Jim Flynn in New Mexico for $30,000, and then took off for Paris where he was mainly based for the next three years. He defended the championship there three times: André Sproul was knocked out in two rounds, but fellow-American Jim Johnson (no relation) held him to a ten-round draw in December 1913 – the first time that two blacks had contested the heavyweight title. Six months later he trounced the latest 'White Hope', Frank Moran, on a 20-round decision.

But by now Johnson, nearly 37, was homesick and in debt. An unscrupulous promoter called Jack Curley promised him $35,000 to defend his title against Jess Willard, a hulking farm-hand from Kansas, at Havana racetrack in Cuba. Curley also convinced Johnson that he had persuaded the United States government to grant him a free pardon, although of course no such arrangement had been made.

Above: *Jess Willard was one of the few early champions who could match the 'super-heavies' of the modern era. The former Kansas farmhand was 6 ft 6½ in, and 230 lb.*

Below: *The scene at Oriental Park race-track, Havana on 15 April 1915: 16,000 spectators – including around 1,000 women – watch Willard and Johnson.*

Willard, a giant of 6 ft 6½ in and 16 st 6 lb (230 lb), was a man of limited accomplishment who had not even boxed professionally until he was 29 years old. He had, however, built up a decent enough record against fellow 'White Hopes' such as Arthur Pelkey, Luther McCarthy, Gunboat Smith, and Carl Morris. The fight was scheduled for 45 rounds, the longest agreed distance under modern rules.

It was fought in a sapping 103°F (39.5°C) heat, with the fading skills of the veteran champion never enough to see him through such a demanding distance against one of the biggest and strongest heavyweights of the decade. For 25 long rounds Johnson survived – and then a left to the body and an overhand right in the 26th ended his six-year reign. Johnson later claimed that he had taken a dive, and cited as evidence a famous photograph of the finale, which shows him lying on his back, his right arm seeming to shield his eyes from the sun and his legs drawn up to protect them from the scorching canvas. Less frequently seen, however, is the next shot in that sequence, which shows Johnson prostrate with both arms and legs in full contact with the canvas.

The episode was a typically graceless end to a sour and scarred championship reign, and it would

The aging Johnson did well enough in the early rounds (left), *and at 37 would probably have retained the title on points had the fight been scheduled for 15 rounds. But the younger, fresher Willard wore him down, and knocked him out in the 26th round. Johnson afterwards used this photo* (below) *as evidence that he had 'thrown' the fight.*

Willard's moment of triumph in Havana (above). *Only ten days earlier, on 5 April 1915, young Jack Dempsey* (left) *had been outpointed in a meaningless four-rounder at Salt Lake City by the long-forgotten Jack Downey.*

be more than 20 years before a black man would again fight for the heavyweight title.

The new champion was a moody, bland individual whose lumbering and uninspired ring style matched his personality. However unpopular his predecessor had been, Johnson had at least kept the championship in the public eye, but Willard now put it into cold storage. He made one lacklustre defence in New York against the veteran contender Frank Moran in March 1916, having first stipulated that Moran would have to knock him out to win. Moran could not do so, and the result was duly recorded as 'No Decision'.

For the next three years, the world heavyweight champion virtually disappeared from the boxing scene. When he next surfaced, in July 1919, it was to face the man who would become one of the most spectacular champions of them all – the 'Manassa Mauler', Jack Dempsey.

Dempsey and the Golden Years

THE First World War had recently ended, leaving America hungry for excitement, entertainment, and exhilaration. Jack Dempsey was the man for the moment. His savage style of fighting, which he had mastered during hard years as a bar-room brawler scuffling for a few dollars in the saloons of Colorado and Utah, sent him streaking up the heavyweight ratings with a succession of dramatic knockout victories.

He despatched 26 opponents inside a round in his first four years as a professional, including an 18-second kayo of the 6 ft 5 in Fred Fulton and a four-second faster demolition of the one-time 'White Hope' Carl Morris in December 1918. A fortnight after beating Morris, he knocked out the former 'White Heavyweight Champion' Gunboat Smith in two rounds, and set up the Willard fight on 4 July 1919 with five consecutive one-round knockouts.

There was no love lost between his manager, Jack 'Doc' Kearns, and promoter Tex Rickard, whom Kearns had accused of stealing his top Australian middleweight, Les Darcy. Kearns was determined to make Rickard pay, and did so by

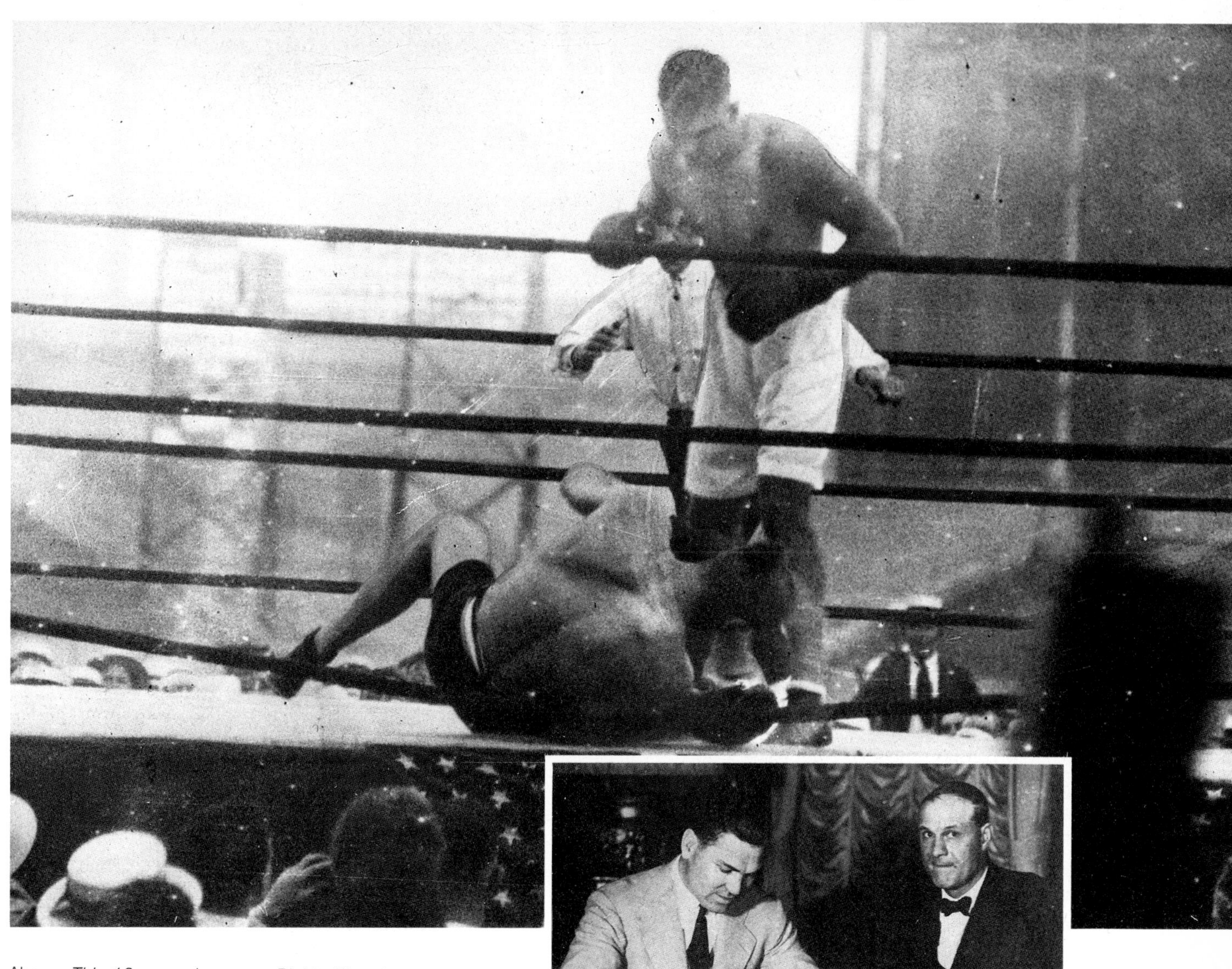

Above: *This 18-second knockout of the giant Fred Fulton at Harrison in July 1918 moved Dempsey closer to a title fight with Willard. It was Dempsey's ninth first-round victory that year.*

Right: *The shrewd Tex Rickard paid Dempsey $27,500 to face Willard; it proved a sound investment, and launched a most successful boxer–promoter partnership.*

forcing him to part with a guarantee of $27,500 for Dempsey's services. Willard proved even harder to satisfy: he demanded, and got, a guarantee of $100,000.

It was the most talked-about fight since Johnson had beaten Jeffries, nine years before to the day. Rickard built an 80,000-seat arena, with standing room for 20,000 more. But despite the public interest it was not a sell-out. Rickard had, for once, overdone the hard sell by announcing that 'seats are going fast'; potential customers stayed away rather than make the journey to Toledo, Ohio, and risk disappointment on arrival.

Dempsey conceded a massive 58 lb to the hulking Willard, but the weight advantage was no help to the champion. The superbly conditioned challenger (left) destroyed him, flooring him seven times and inflicting appalling facial damage before Willard retired at the end of the third round.

The heat on that Independence Day afternoon was fierce, with the temperature touching 112°F (44°C). Willard, the 37-year-old champion, had all the physical advantages at 6 ft 6½ in and 17½ st (245 lb) against Dempsey's 6 ft 1 in and 13 st 5 lb (187 lb), but it proved to be one of the most ill-matched championship fights ever seen. The Kansas giant was floored seven times in the first round, and Dempsey, who had instructed Kearns to bet $10,000 to $100,000 on a first-round finish, had already left the ring and was heading for the dressing room as Willard's seconds attempted to revive him from the final knockdown at the end of the round.

Although referee Ollie Pecord had counted Willard out as he sat slumped in a corner, an official explained that the bell had sounded to end the round before the count had been completed, so Dempsey was recalled to the ring. The photo taken at the moment of the supposed finish was later cited as evidence to support Willard's theory that Dempsey's gloves had been 'doctored'. According to Willard, the object which is clearly visible in the photo, on the canvas by the fallen champion's left knee, was an iron weight which Dempsy had clutched in his fist for added punching power. In reality, it was probably only a cigar which an over-

The dazed, bewildered Willard reels from Dempsey's snarling attack in the opening round.

Above: *Willard was convinced that Dempsey's gloves had been 'doctored' in Toledo, but despite his bitterness he was always civil to Dempsey when, years later, they met socially.*

excited ringsider had thrown into the ring.

Dempsey's bet on his first-round kayo had been lost, but the title was nearly his. Yet, incredibly, Willard survived another two rounds despite fearsome physical damage. His jaw was broken in two places, two of his ribs were smashed, five teeth were missing, one eye was closed, his nose was squashed, and the hearing in his left ear permanently impaired. His courage was beyond measure, but it was utterly pointless. At the end of the third round Willard retired on his stool, telling his cornermen that he could not continue. Dempsey was champion, and the most exciting period in the division's history had begun . . . but Willard would go to his grave 49 years later still a bitter and unforgiving old man who was convinced that he had been the victim of shady tactics.

Dempsey's first defence was against his friend and one-time sparmate Billy Miske, who was terminally ill with Bright's Disease. Miske begged Dempsey to give him a title shot in order that he might provide for his family, and Jack obliged by putting his title at stake at Benton Harbour, Michigan, on 6 September 1920. The fight drew $143,904: Miske was paid $25,000 and Dempsey $55,000. In view of Miske's medical condition it could hardly be classed as a serious contest, and Dempsey duly knocked him out in three rounds.

This was one of only two occasions on which Dempsey would fight for a promoter other than Rickard. The Triple Alliance of Dempsey, Kearns, and Rickard became the most significant combination in boxing history. Their first venture, a defence against the useful Bill Brennan in New York on 14 December 1920, drew a capacity crowd of 15,000, paying $162,760, with the champion on a guarantee of $100,000. But Dempsey's perform-

Above: *Billy Miske, Dempsey's first challenger, goes down for the count in the third in September 1920.*

Below: *The champ clowns in a New York gym with Packey O'Gatty, a New York bantamweight.*

ance was a distinct letdown, and he was well behind on points after 11 rounds before at last catching up with his elusive challenger in the 12th.

It was a disappointing show by the champion, but worse was to come. An enterprising newspaperman unearthed a publicity photograph of Dempsey allegedly aiding the war effort by hammering in rivets in a New York shipyard. Unfortunately for Jack, the photograph showed him wearing patent leather shoes at the time, and he was duly labelled a 'slacker' (a draft dodger). Although Dempsey was indicted by a Federal Grand Jury for draft evasion, he was acquitted.

Rickard, though, was always ready to explore the commercial potential of any angle, however discreditable. Over in Europe Georges Carpentier, a handsome, matinee-idol Frenchman with a distinguished war record, had emerged as the dominant figure in European boxing. He was everything that Dempsey was not – a suave, debonair and sophisticated figure compared to the usually scowling, unshaven ex-hobo Dempsey. It was a contest between the war hero and the 'slacker'; the Old World and the New.

Once more, Rickard manipulated the press brilliantly, with the fight capturing the public imagination like no other before it. Dempsey v Carpentier became boxing's first million-dollar gate: receipts for their 2 July 1921 clash at Boyle's Thirty Acres, New Jersey, were a staggering $1,789,238, of which Dempsey was guaranteed $300,000.

By modern standards the pair were small – the Frenchman, who held the world light-heavyweight title, scaled under that division's limit at 12 st 4 lb (172 lb), while Dempsey came in at 13 st 6 lb (188 lb). A record 700 pressmen covered the event which was also the first title fight to be broadcast.

More than 80,000 packed in for one of the most dramatic fights in championship history. Dempsey won the first round, then Carpentier almost knocked the champion out with a stunning right hand in the second. But Dempsey clinched, held, and mauled his way to the end of the round, and

Boxing's first million-dollar gate: 80,000 fans watch Jack Dempsey (right) knock Georges Carpentier out in the fourth round at Boyle's Thirty Acres, New Jersey.

the Frenchman's chance was gone. He had smashed his right thumb on Dempsey's head, and no heavyweight in history could have beaten the 'Manassa Mauler' with one hand. In the third round the challenger took a brutal beating, and the crowd, recognizing that the tide had turned irrevocably, were silent. A hard left hook floored Carpentier for eight in the fourth, and then a right to the body dropped him on his right side to be counted out by referee Harry Ertle.

It was two years almost to the day before Dempsey was back in the ring in serious competition, outpointing Tommy Gibbons over 15 rounds at Shelby, Montana, on 4 July 1923. The town had sought to put itself on the map – at Rickard's prompting – by staging a world heavyweight title fight, guaranteeing the champion $300,000. But only 7,000 attended, and all four of the town's banks went broke by meeting Dempsey's guarantee.

Above: *Dempsey and referee Harry Ertle help the stricken Carpentier to his feet. The gesture was untypical of Dempsey, and boosted his popularity with the hitherto hostile public.*

Below: *The man who broke the banks in Shelby, Montana . . . Dempsey (right) outpoints Tommy Gibbons in the title defence which bankrupted a town.*

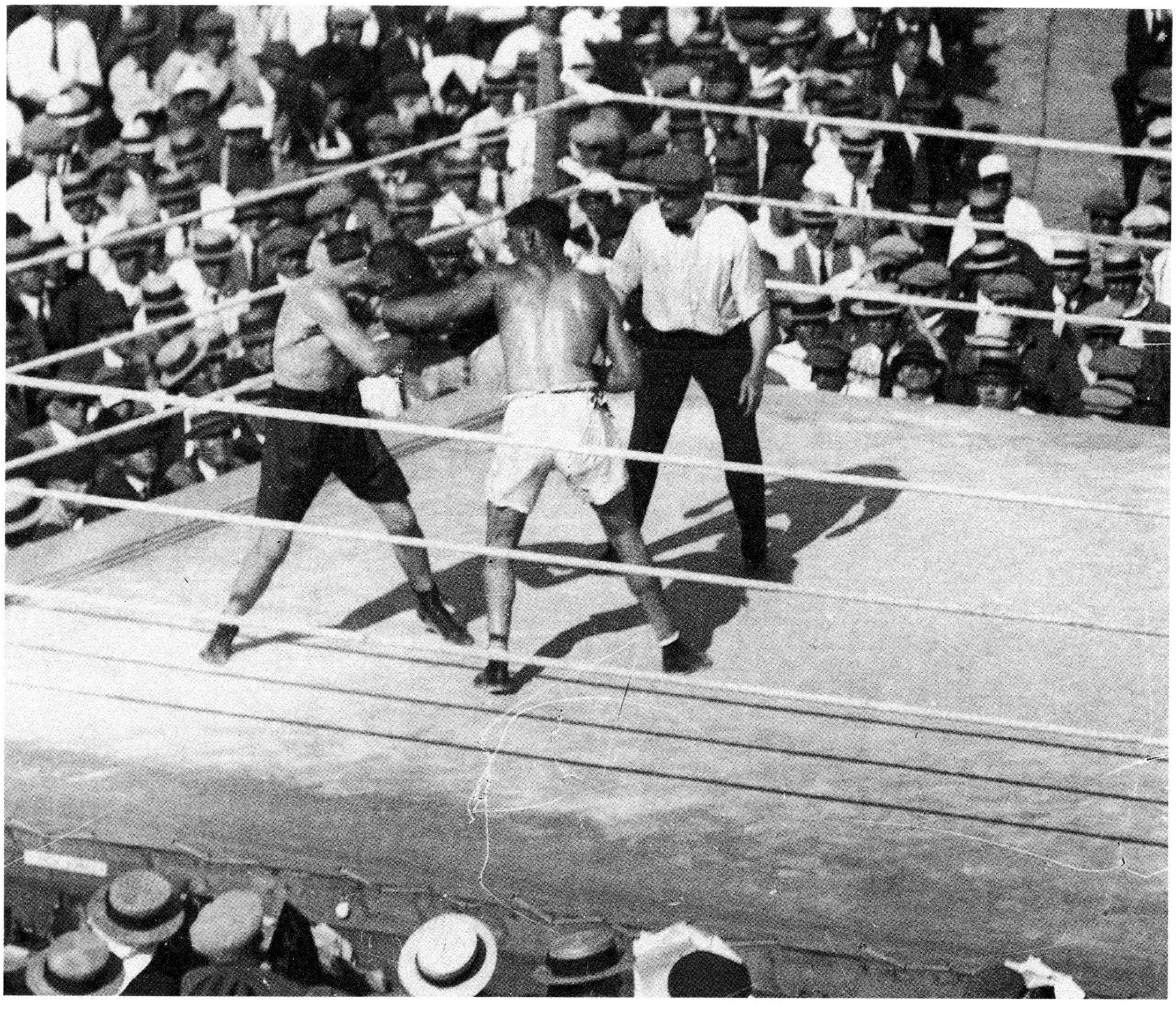

Gibbons, a hard, seasoned professional from St Paul, Minnesota, did not earn a cent from the biggest event of his boxing life. It was the last anti-climactic night in Dempsey's career; his subsequent appearances were all occasions of high drama, each with its own place in boxing legend.

Just over two months after his disappointing win over Gibbons (when Kearns had to hire a special train to get the pair out of town with the takings) he was in the ring at the New York Polo Grounds

Left: *Luis Firpo (on the right, before his July 1923 fight with ex-champ Jess Willard) was a crude but dangerous puncher, as he proved by knocking Dempsey out of the ring.*

Floyd Patterson (above) *and Ernie Terrell* (right) *both refused to acknowledge Muhammad Ali's change of name, and insisted on calling him 'Cassius Clay'. Ali/Clay made them pay for their impertinence. Patterson, whom he called 'The Rabbit', took a merciless beating for 12 rounds, during much of which he was half-crippled by a back injury. Terrell was taunted endlessly with 'What's my name? What's my name?', as the normally gracious and sporting Ali gave the most vicious performance of his long career. It was an unedifying spectacle, and it finished the once-useful Terrell as a top-level fighter.*

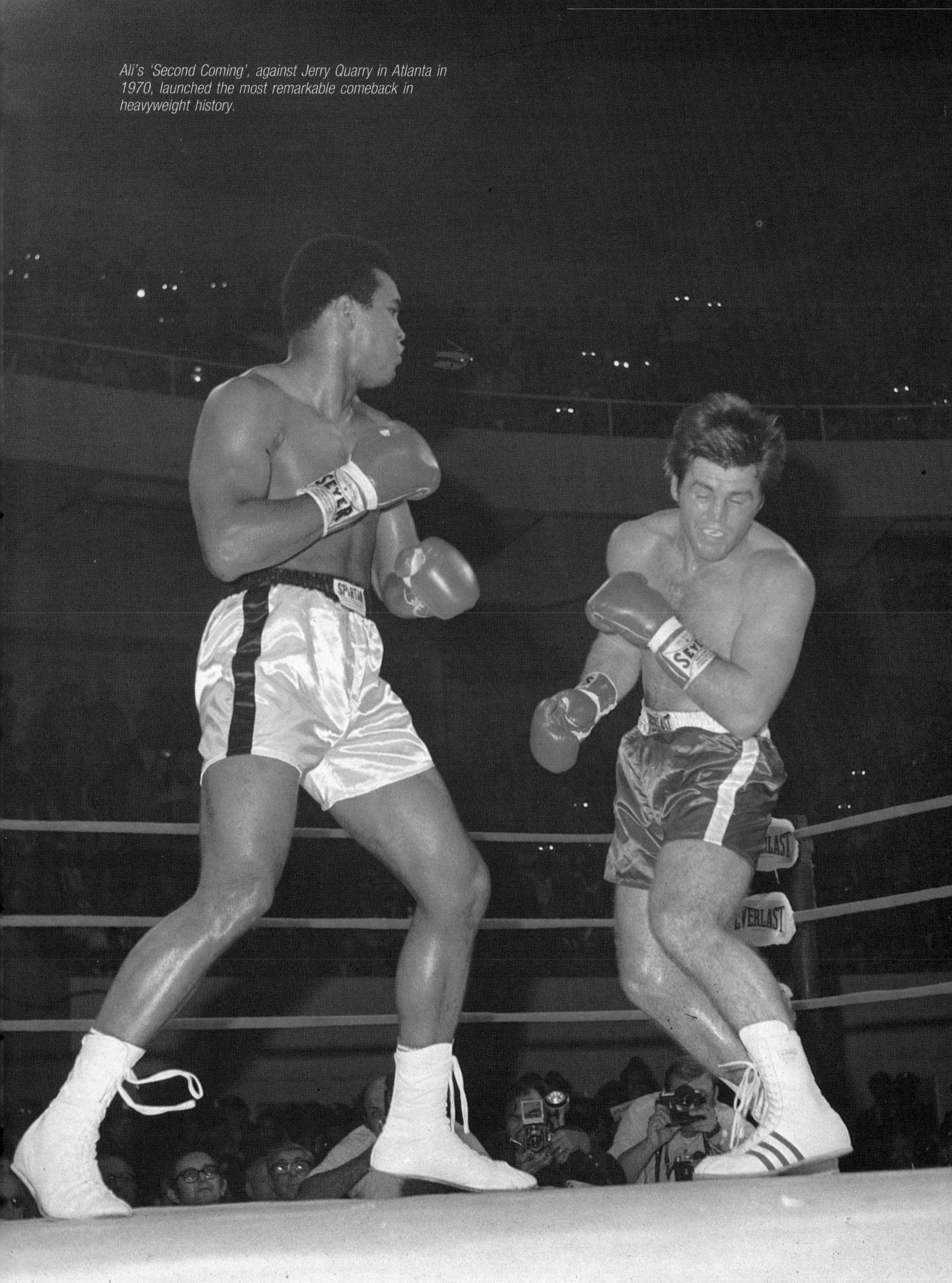

Ali's 'Second Coming', against Jerry Quarry in Atlanta in 1970, launched the most remarkable comeback in heavyweight history.

defending against the Argentinian Luis Firpo, who was billed – with every justification – as 'the Wild Bull of the Pampas'. The 6 ft 3 in Firpo had a prodigious right-hand punch but little or no technique. His best-known victim was Dempsey's predecessor Jess Willard, who was 41 at the time, but such was Dempsey's mass appeal that a crowd of 125,000 packed the Polo Grounds on 14 September 1923 to give Rickard his second million-dollar gate, with receipts totalling $1,188,603.

It is the end of the road for former champion Jess Willard, 41, as Luis Firpo knocks him out in seven rounds at Jersey City on 12 July 1923.

The fight lasted just three minutes 57 seconds, but it contained a lifetime of drama. Firpo was floored seven times in the first round and three times in the second, including the knockout, but he still came within moments of the biggest upset yet seen in the ring. Dempsey came out at the first bell, fired a left hook, and missed, and Firpo's countering right caught him flush on the chin.

Dempsey fell forward, but bounced up without a count. He lashed back with two left hooks that dropped Firpo, and then a right to the jaw had the challenger down again. Firpo again jumped up without a count, and rocked Dempsey with a right, but the champion retaliated with body punches that floored the Argentinian for the third time. Firpo spent almost as much of that unforgettable round on the floor as he did on his feet. He was down four more times before, suddenly, he fired over a straight right that knocked Dempsey through the ropes and out of the ring, his feet flailing the air as he landed on the press benches. Eager hands shoved him back through the ropes – in complete disregard of the rules, which stipulated that a fallen fighter must regain his feet unaided – but before the near-unconscious champion could be floored

Firpo goes down for the seventh time in what was, perhaps, the most exciting heavyweight title fight of all.

again the bell came to his rescue.

Dempsey was in just as bad shape as his challenger, but he knew that as long as Firpo remained upright he was potentially dangerous. Left hooks at the start of the second put Firpo down for the eighth time, for a count of two, and then a right to the body and a following left dropped him again for four. He was defenceless when he got up, and Dempsey – one of the game's most merciless finishers – ended it with two more hooks after just 57 seconds of the round. Firpo did not stir for a couple of seconds, and then started to writhe convulsively. He rolled onto his back, drew up his knees in agony, but this time he could not rise.

It was Dempsey's last serious contest for almost four years. He made his money instead in films, exhibitions, and personal appearances, while the rest of a fairly undistinguished heavyweight field scuffled amongst themselves for the right to challenge him. There was, though, one outstanding practitioner whom Dempsey was careful to avoid – Harry Wills, a classy black fighter who was probably a better boxer than any of his contemporaries. Wills, in common with every black contender from Johnson to Joe Louis, fell victim to the colour bar. Dempsey, like Sullivan before him, had drawn the colour line in a public statement the day after dethroning Willard, and his refusal to defend against the eminently qualified Wills remains the only blemish on his otherwise distinguished record as champion.

Wills and his ever-persistent manager Paddy Mullins campaigned for four years, from 1922 to 1926, for a match with Dempsey. According to Dempsey's version, published in his autobiography *Dempsey*, he was personally willing to meet Wills, but Kearns was strongly opposed to black v white fights on principle. And Rickard, in common with most other promoters, was reluctant to get involved in the racial tensions which the fight would inevitably provoke, and in the subsequent search for another 'White Hope' which would ensue if Wills were to be given the chance he deserved and won.

But under pressure from the New York Commission, a contract for the fight was duly signed on 11 July 1922. The shrewd Kearns, however, had inserted a 'get-out' clause to the effect that the date for the fight 'be set within 60 days after a reliable promoter undertook to stage the fight.' Kearns knew very well that no such promoter would emerge, and when the 60-day period had elapsed Wills was once more shunted to the rear of the championship queue, while Dempsey went ahead with the defence against Tommy Gibbons.

Dempsey busied himself with his stage and film career in the years after the Gibbons fight, while his detractors hinted that one very sound reason for his reluctance to face Wills was the damage that reduction to the status of ex-champion might do to his show-business earnings – his 'marquee value', in the modern idiom.

The Wills affair surfaced again in 1925 when Dempsey – who by now had split acrimoniously from Kearns and was being advised by Rickard – tried to set up a fight in New York only to find that the New York Commission, under pressure from Paddy Mullins, had suspended him for his failure to fight Wills. Rickard had his own views on the champion's ideal opponent, but it proved to be one of the few mistakes he ever made – and probably the costliest. The man he wanted was Gene

Above: *Handsome, sophisticated Gene Tunney was nobody's idea of a heavyweight boxer . . . but he was destined to end the Dempsey Era.*

Right: *Like every black contender since Jack Johnson, Harry Wills was denied a chance at the title, though many felt he could have beaten Dempsey.*

The only man to beat Gene Tunney was the marvellous middleweight champion Harry Greb, but when they met in this February 1923 rematch Greb was floored and outpointed. Tunney was a gifted performer, but unlike the gregarious Dempsey (pictured right with his wife Estelle at the Kentucky Derby) the one-time Marine never courted popularity.

Tunney, the former American light-heavyweight champion and a handsome, classy box-fighter who had lost only once in a long career. That solitary loss, to the former world middleweight champion Harry Greb, was soon reversed, and Tunney then confirmed his high ranking by trouncing quality heavyweights including Tommy Gibbons, Bartley Madden, and Johnny Risko.

The 28-year-old ex-marine was a press agent's dream – and unusually the material with which the newspapers were bombarded was all true. He actually *was* a well-educated, well-read, and literate man whose autobiography *A Man Must Fight*, written entirely unaided by ghost writers, remains one of the classics of ring literature. He was as familiar with the works of Shakespeare and Plato as he was with the records and styles of his heavyweight contemporaries, whom he studied with a clinical, analytical intelligence. Dempsey, like the rest, had been put under Tunney's microscope, and was judged wanting.

Socially, Tunney shunned the fast-living, free-spending set who patronized and lionized Dempsey. In every way, in ring style and personality, he and Dempsey were at opposite ends of the spectrum. Rickard and Dempsey appreciated the fight's commercial potential, but the Wills controversy refused to go away. Rickard finally tried to get around the problem by matching Tunney with Wills, being confident that the stylish Tunney had the measure of the veteran black contender. But the plan fell apart when Wills priced himself out of the fight, so Rickard was free to announce that Dempsey would defend against Tunney in Yankee Stadium, New York.

According to Dempsey's autobiography, he was assured that his New York licence would be returned to him if he made the appropriate official an under-the-table payment of $25,000. But Dempsey had negotiated a guarantee of $475,000 from Rickard who, prompted by Gene Normile (who was doing Dempsey's business at the time), switched the fight to Philadelphia.

A crowd of 120,000 packed the open-air stadium on 23 September 1926, but Dempsey, now 31, could not reproduce the fire and venom which had made him such an irresistible force in his previous defences. Tunney outboxed him easily in round after round, many of them fought in driving rain, and the once-formidable Dempsey was made to look like a crude plodder. By the end of round ten (the longest distance permissable

Johnny Risko (right) *was outscored by Tunney in November 1925. In his next fight, Tunney took the championship from Dempsey.*

Dempsey's left hook accounts for Jack Sharkey in the seventh round in July 1927 (left). *The win earned Dempsey a rematch with Tunney, which took place in Chicago two months later. For seven rounds, it went the way of their first meeting, with Tunney* (below) *easily outboxing the aggressive challenger . . . but then, a minute into the seventh, came the most controversial and discussed knockdown in history – the Long Count.*

under Philadelphia law) there was no doubt about the outcome: the title had changed hands.

Dempsey was so disappointed with his own performance that he determined to give it one more try. On 21 July 1927 he knocked out Jack Sharkey in the seventh round to qualify for a rematch with Tunney. (Sharkey, who had at last removed Wills from the title picture by beating him in October 1926, went on to become champion himself five years later.)

The Tunney rematch took place on 22 September 1927 at Soldiers Field, Chicago, and is immortalized as 'The Battle of the Long Count'. Tunney, although never a popular hero in the Dempsey mould, demanded and got a record purse of almost one million dollars: according to his own account, he wrote Rickard a cheque for the few thousand dollars difference between his purse and the million, so that Rickard could then write *him* a cheque for the magical seven figures. The cancelled cheque was later framed, and hung in Tunney's office as a tangible and dramatic reminder of his unique place in boxing's history. Dempsey's purse was a more modest $450,000, though still an exceptional sum for a challenger.

The fight was boxing's first two-million-dollar gate, drawing $2,658,660. Referee Dave Barry instructed both men before the start that, in the event of a knockdown, the man scoring the knockdown had to go to the farthest neutral corner (in all Dempsey's previous title fights he had been allowed to stand directly over his fallen opponent, thus giving him no real chance to recover).

For six rounds, it was a rerun of their first meeting with Tunney's left jab dictating the action.

Above: *Referee Dave Barry tried to usher Dempsey to a neutral corner before taking up a count on Tunney, but five seconds elapsed before Dempsey obeyed.*

Then, a minute into the seventh, Dempsey caught him with a right over the top of the champion's jab and followed with a series of short two-handed hooks until the dazed Tunney sank to the canvas, his left arm clutching the middle rope. The title was within Dempsey's grasp but, in the excitement of the moment, he forgot the rule which Dave Barry had stressed would be enforced and stood over Tunney, his arms on the top rope.

Barry grabbed the challenger around the waist and hauled him to the centre of the ring, pointing to the neutral corner. Four or five seconds had elapsed before the message finally penetrated, and when Dempsey had at last obeyed his instruction Barry commenced the count. These vital seconds gave Tunney time to recover sufficiently to get to one knee, and he took the count in that position, rising at 'nine'. The crisis was past, and for the remaining two-and-a-half rounds he did not let Dempsey near him, and even floored the fading ex-champ briefly in the eighth on the way to a clear-cut points win.

In total, Tunney was on the floor for 14 seconds in that eventful seventh round. He insisted that he could have beaten the count even without the 'bonus' five seconds, but wrote in his autobiography *A Man Must Fight:*

> Realizing, as do all professional boxers, that the first nine seconds of a knockdown belong to the man who is on the floor, I never had any thought of getting up before the referee said 'nine'. Only badly dazed boxers who have momentarily lost consciousness, and show-offs, fail to take the nine seconds that are theirs. No boxer that I have ever known has carried a stopwatch on his wrist going into the ring. Boxers always go by the referee's timing; whether 25 seconds or nine seconds had elapsed when the referee said 'nine' would have made no difference to me. My signal to get off the floor was the count 'nine'.

Even in the supreme crisis of his boxing career, Tunney's cool brain was still calculating the odds.

It was the end of Dempsey's serious ring career, although he did make a comeback of sorts some

Tunney recovered so completely from the knockdown that he even floored Dempsey briefly (below) *in the eighth round. Their two fights marked the beginning of a lifelong friendship, and they are pictured* (top right) *on one of their frequent appearances together.*

years later, mainly in exhibitions. But for Tunney, there was only one more fight, when he stopped the rugged New Zealander Tom Heeney in 11 rounds at Yankee Stadium on 23 July 1928. He retired the following year and married a society heiress, Polly Lauder, although by then he was independently wealthy, and (unlike many other ex-champions) there was never a hint of a comeback in his career.

The Tunney v Heeney fight was also Tex Rickard's last promotion – he died in Florida in

Below: *The last of Tunney's 65 victories: after stopping Tom Heeney in 11 rounds at Madison Square Garden in July 1928, he quit at the top, as undefeated champion.*

January 1929. With his death, Dempsey's defeat, and Tunney's retirement, the most colourful and exciting period that the sport had yet known was over. For the next seven years their successors were a string of near-anonymous mediocrities, and it took the blazing talent of a young black puncher from Detroit, called Joe Louis, to restore to the heavyweight title the status and esteem it had enjoyed in its glory days.

Gene Tunney's son John, a Kennedy-style Democrat, once regarded as Presidential material, became a senator.

Louis Bridges the Eras

JOE Louis was so superior to his immediate predecessors, that, as A.J. Liebling noted in *The Sweet Science:* '...he knocked out *five* of these world champions – Schmeling, Sharkey, Carnera, Baer, and Braddock, the last of whom happened to be holding the title when Louis hit him. A decade later he knocked out Jersey Joe Walcott, who nevertheless won the title four years afterwards.'

These 'interim' champions were not actually *bad* fighters – indeed the first of them, Max Schmeling of Germany, knocked out Louis in 12 rounds in June 1936, the only setback Louis experienced on an otherwise serene and untroubled road to the title. Schmeling's reign could not have begun on a more undistinguished note. He remains the only world heavyweight champion to have been crowned while sitting on the canvas, where he had been deposited by a low blow thrown by Jack Sharkey, a talented but temperamental fighter of Lithuanian extraction whose real name was Josef Paul Cukoschay.

There was nothing glorious about Max Schmeling's coronation as Gene Tunney's successor – he won the title sitting on the canvas, after a low blow from Jack Sharkey. But the German was actually a fine fighter, as he proved by knocking out Joe Louis in 12 rounds in June 1936.

Schmeling's victory, on 12 June 1930, made him the biggest name in European sport and he spent the next year exploiting that status in various forgettable films. He found the time in 1931 to make a solitary ring appearance, stopping the 'Georgia Peach', Young Stribling, in the 15th round at Cleveland in July 1931. Sharkey, meantime, had re-established himself with a draw against middleweight champion Mickey Walker and a decision over Primo Carnera, and was clamouring for a rematch with Schmeling.

It took place at Long Island Bowl on 21 June 1932, and this time it was the German's turn to feel aggrieved. Sharkey won an unpopular verdict after 15 fairly forgettable rounds, and Schmeling's manager Joe Jacobs was moved to coin an immortal phrase for a radio interviewer's benefit: 'We wuz robbed! We shoulda stood in bed!'

Sharkey was an unremarkable fighter whose volatile and emotional nature tended to negate whatever fighting qualities he had. 'Whenever something didn't please me in the ring I'd go into

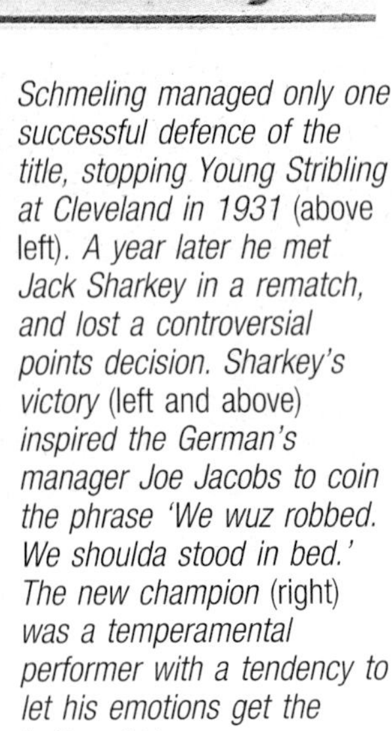

Schmeling managed only one successful defence of the title, stopping Young Stribling at Cleveland in 1931 (above left). *A year later he met Jack Sharkey in a rematch, and lost a controversial points decision. Sharkey's victory* (left and above) *inspired the German's manager Joe Jacobs to coin the phrase 'We wuz robbed. We shoulda stood in bed.' The new champion* (right) *was a temperamental performer with a tendency to let his emotions get the better of him.*

GENE TUNNEY
WILLIE MICHEL
NO SMOKING

Primo Carnera, the one-time circus strongman from Italy, was groomed to succeed Sharkey with a string of wins over hand-picked opposition.

tantrums', he confessed in a London *Sunday Times* interview in the early 1970s. Such was not the stuff of greatness.

But even while Sharkey enjoyed his brief 12 months at centre stage, his successor was being groomed by the powerful and often sinister men who ran the sport in those shady days. A former circus strongman called Primo Carnera, an Italian from Sequals, had been persuaded on account of his size, 6 ft $5\frac{3}{4}$ in and 18 st 8 lb (260 lb), to take up the sport. He had minimal natural aptitude for it,

Below: *Harry Wills, the veteran black contender who had been carefully avoided by Jack Dempsey, was finally removed from the championship picture by this 1926 loss to Jack Sharkey.*

Right: *George Godfrey, pictured after his retirement, was another outstanding black fighter of the period whose colour denied him the opportunities which his talent merited.*

Larry Gains, the Empire champion from Canada, had to settle for winning the 'Black Heavyweight Championship'.

Gains outclassed Carnera in London in May 1932, taking an easy 10-round points decision, but that result was not allowed to interfere with the Italian's build-up. Two months later, Carnera knocked out Jack Gross (above) *in seven rounds in New York, and in November he beat Jose Santa* (left) *in six rounds, also in New York. In all, Carnera had 26 fights that year, including seven in December.*

and had been beaten by Young Stribling, Jim Maloney, Sharkey, Stanley Poreda, and Larry Gains, the elegant black Canadian who, in an echo of the pre-Jack Johnson era, had been awarded something called the 'Coloured Heavyweight Championship' after beating another great black contender, George Godfrey, in 1929. Four years earlier, Gains had kayoed Schmeling in two rounds, but despite an outstanding record Gains never got the title chance which his talent merited. 'Like every man who ever laced on gloves, I dreamed of becoming heavyweight champion of the world', he wrote in his autobiography *The Impossible Dream*, 'but, for me, it was always the impossible dream, the unreachable star. The politics of the day were against it. The bar was up.'

The boxing business in America had grown tired of the unexciting individuals who now populated the heavyweight rankings, and a month after his defeat by Gains (which had attracted an official attendance of 62,000 to London's White City Stadium) Carnera was back in America. Boxing's string-pullers had decided that he would be the man to revitalize the industry, and they had the power to ensure that there would be no further embarrassments on his way to the championship. A succession of knockover victories were arranged

Below: *This fifth-round knockout of Isidoro Gastanaga in New York in March 1936 was the last of Carnera's 88 victories. He went home to Italy penniless, but returned to America after the war and had a successful second career as a wrestler.*

Carnera's fifth-round knockout of Ernie Schaaff (left) *ended in tragedy, but there was a happier ending to his next appearance, when he knocked out Jack Sharkey* (below) *in six rounds to become world champion.*

for him, after one of which (against Ernie Schaaf) his opponent died. It has been generally assumed, although never proven, that most of the big Italian's American victories were fixed results, and Budd Schulberg later based his classic *The Harder They Fall* on the Carnera story.

By mid-1933 Carnera's management decided that the public had been sufficiently prepared for his coronation, and he duly knocked out Sharkey in six rounds at Long Island on 29 June. He was champion – but no amount of careful stage-management could conceal the fact that Carnera was not a world-class fighter. And the public were

The moment of Carnera's coronation, as referee Arthur Donovan counts Jack Sharkey out.

Max Baer was the most colourful heavyweight since Jack Dempsey, and had all the physical assets necessary to become one of the game's great champions. But he could never take his profession too seriously, and his carefree attitude often cost him fights which he should have won. On form, though, as in this 1933 defeat of Max Schmeling (below and top right) *he was a formidable fighter. Dempsey had high regard for him, and even refereed his final victory – a first-round knockout of Pat Comiskey at Jersey City in September 1940* (bottom right).

not as gullible as the new champion's manipulators had expected. They wanted to see a *real* fighter as champion, and 24-year-old Max Baer fitted the bill.

Baer was a thunderous punching playboy whose wise-cracking and womanizing provided sports-writers with reams of colourful copy. He was also a much better than average fighter, as he proved with his tenth round battering of Max Schmeling in June 1933. He had also given Ernie Schaaf a severe beating before Schaaf's fatal fight with Carnera, and it was probably this, rather than anything the relatively light-hitting Carnera did, that was responsible for his death. Baer too had had first-hand experience of a ring tragedy when Frankie Campbell, a promising young heavyweight, died after Baer had knocked him out in five rounds in August 1930. Those close to Baer said that the incident had a profound effect on him, preventing the fighter from realizing his full potential.

Baer, whose brother Buddy was a competent heavyweight who later faced Joe Louis twice for the championship, tried to cash in on the Jewish market by wearing the Star of David on his trunks. In fact he was of German Catholic extraction, and his trainer Ray Arcel settled the matter of his ethnic origins with the marvellous line that 'I seen the guy in the shower, and believe me he ain't Jewish!'

But Jewish or Catholic, the public wanted Baer rather than Carnera at the top, and the fight was arranged for 14 June 1934 in New York. Carnera

Max's brother Buddy (top left) *was a useful heavyweight, who twice challenged Joe Louis for the title – but Max was the one destined to become champion. He had to wait for his chance while Carnera retained the title against the 86 lb lighter Tommy Loughran* (left). *When Baer met Carnera in June 1934, the combination of the challenger's clowning and the champion's natural clumsiness turned it into a farce, with Carnera sometimes pulling Baer down with him* (below) *as Baer floored him a total of 11 times. Finally, after the 11th knockdown* (right) *Carnera himself appealed to referee Arthur Donovan to stop the fight.*

had, in the meantime, retained his title twice, outpointing the Basque Paolino Uzcudun in the only all-European heavyweight title fight and then outscoring the great light-heavyweight Tommy Loughran, over whom he enjoyed an 86 lb weight advantage. 'The big bum kept standing on my feet', Loughran grumbled afterwards.

As expected, Baer easily defeated the lumbering Italian in a fight so one-sided that, at times, it threatened to degenerate into farce. Carnera was floored 11 times, sometimes even dragging Baer over with him. Baer wisecracked his way through the fight, talking to the champion, plucking at the hairs on his opponent's chest and, at the start of the tenth, walking over to the Italian's corner to shuffle in his resin box while Carnera gazed at him in total bewilderment.

The 52,268 fans who paid over $428,000 hardly got value for their money, but at least they could console themselves with the thought that they had

been present at the coronation of a man who looked set for a long reign. Carnera, who finally appealed to referee Arthur Donovan to stop the fight in the 11th, was officially paid $152,870 for his pains, but it is doubtful if he saw even a fraction of that sum. Within two years the sadly exploited ex-champ was penniless, although it is pleasant to record that he later returned to America as a professional wrestler and made, and kept, a small fortune.

Baer was a colourful and charismatic figure with the potential to become one of the better heavyweight champions, but his great flaw was that he could never take the game too seriously, so that when, after a year's layoff, he defended the title against James J. Braddock in New York, he frittered the championship away through poor preparation and sloppy performance.

Braddock's late-career success was an inspiring story, particularly in a country which was still enduring the long, bleak years of the Great Depression. He had been a useful light-heavyweight in the late 1920s, and lasted the distance in a world title challenge against Tommy Loughran in 1929. But after that his career went into rapid decline, and he won only 11 of his subsequent 32 fights.

By September 1933 he was in virtual retirement, having smashed his right hand on his opponent's head in his last fight. Unable to box or find work, the 28-year-old had to resort to state benefits of

While Baer (above, *pictured stopping Tony Galento) enjoyed a year's inactivity after becoming champion, ex-champ Max Schmeling put himself high in the ratings with this revenge knockout of Steve Hamas* (below left) *in Hamburg in 1935, but turned down the chance to challenge Baer. Instead, James J. Braddock* (below right) *was chosen.*

Few gave the veteran Braddock a chance against Baer, but he outboxed the ill-prepared champion (right) in round after round to take a clear points win, and upset odds of 10–1.

$24 per month to feed his wife and three children. However, when his hand had healed sufficiently, he offered himself as 'the opponent' for Corn Griffin, an unbeaten prospect, on the under-card of Carnera's title fight with Baer.

Griffin, a 5-1 favourite, was confidently expected to sweep the veteran aside and go on to challenge the new champion, but Braddock survived a first-round knockdown to flatten Griffin in the third. He was paid a mere $250: six fights later he would earn $293,660 to risk the world title against Joe Louis. The upset win earned Braddock a ten-rounder with John Henry Lewis, a classy 20-year-old whose sole loss had been to the light-heavyweight champion Maxie Rosenbloom, whom Lewis had subsequently beaten twice in non-title fights. Once more, Braddock upset the odds – but Lewis, too, went on to become world light-heavyweight champion less than a year later.

When Braddock outboxed the dangerous left-hooking Art Lasky in March 1935 he found himself, unbelievably, at the head of the heavyweight queue. Max Schmeling had turned down the chance to challenge Baer, and the two other reasonably marketable contenders, Lasky and Steve Hamas, had been eliminated by Braddock and Schmeling respectively. The press did their best to exploit the rags-to-riches angle in Braddock, building him up as the 'Cinderella Man', but the firmly unsentimental odds-makers had him a 10-1

outsider when he entered the ring with Baer on 13 June 1935.

One hour later they were counting their losses. Braddock had outboxed the sluggish champion to win in a canter, and there would not be a bigger upset in heavyweight boxing until Cassius Clay demoralized the 'unbeatable' Sonny Liston nearly 30 years later. It was a heart-warming, tear-jerking

Two weeks after Braddock outpointed the crude-swinging Baer (left), *the division's new sensation Joe Louis hammered Primo Carnera to defeat in six rounds. Louis was already regarded as the uncrowned champion – but then Max Schmeling* (right) *shocked him with a 12th-round knockout.*

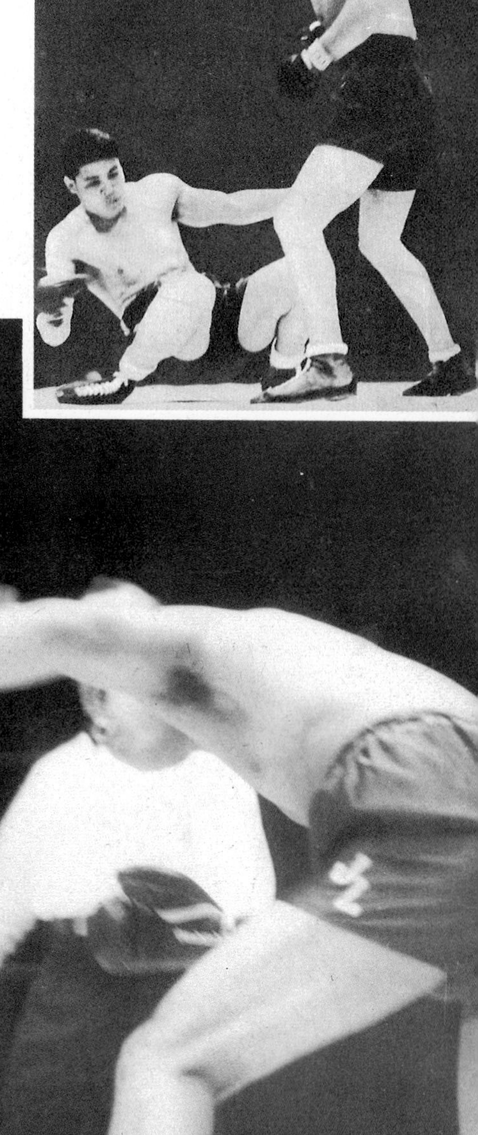

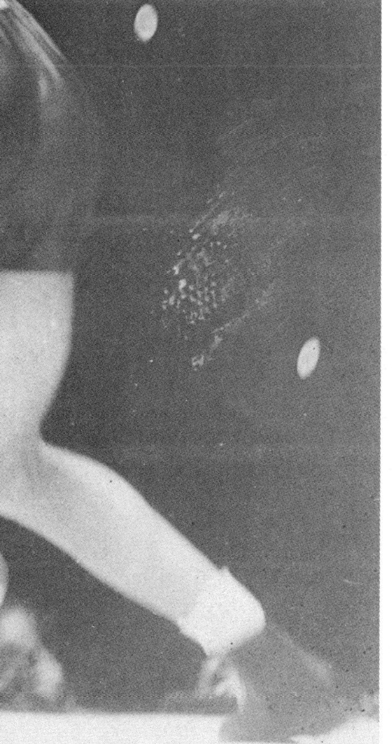

Many of Louis' early opponents performed as if they were beaten before they climbed into the ring. King Levinsky (left) *was swept aside in the opening round in Chicago in August 1935, while the former champion Jack Sharkey* (above) *offered little opposition in his third-round defeat in New York in August 1936. It was Louis' first fight after the Schmeling setback, and it confirmed that no lasting damage had been done by the German.*

story, but Braddock's day in the sun was brief. While the new champion savoured his status as a symbol of hope for the countless victims of the Depression, the dramatically talented young Joe Louis was decimating the rest of the division as he surged irrestistibly towards the title.

The former national amateur champion from Detroit had virtually cleared the field of contenders in a little under three years, with quick wins over Carnera and Baer as well as quality men such as Lee Ramage, King Levinsky, and Paolino Uzcudun. Max Schmeling temporarily interrupted his progress with a surprise 12th-round knockout in June 1936, but while Braddock lingered in semi-retirement Louis quickly re-established himself with a string of seven wins, including a merciless three-round destruction of Jack Sharkey. His electrifying performances drew the sort of crowds that boxing had not seen since Dempsey's day, and he had been marked for greatness since his debut on Independence Day (4 July) 1935, when he

knocked out Jack Kracken in a minute and a half at the quaintly named Bacon Casino in Chicago.

By the sheer weight of his talent, Louis battered down the barriers which Jack Johnson had erected two decades earlier. His public demeanour was everything that Johnson's was not. By modern standards Louis would be considered an 'Uncle Tom', but he must be judged against the background of his times. Chris Mead, in his definitive biography *Champion – Joe Louis* wrote that:

> During his career Louis did not speak out against racism. He did make mild appeals for equal opportunity and actively opposed segregation in the army during and after World War Two, but he was always careful to avoid offending whites. His black managers consciously tailored his public image that way. No other strategy was possible during the 1930s and 1940s.

Louis' spectacular climb up the ratings made him the idol of the black ghettos, and particularly the children (top left). *After his sixth round knockout of Primo Carnera* (left and below) *he commanded international attention. Carnera took an even worse beating from Louis than he did from Baer, and Louis' victory – only days after Braddock had taken the championship from Baer – established Joe as the top contender.*

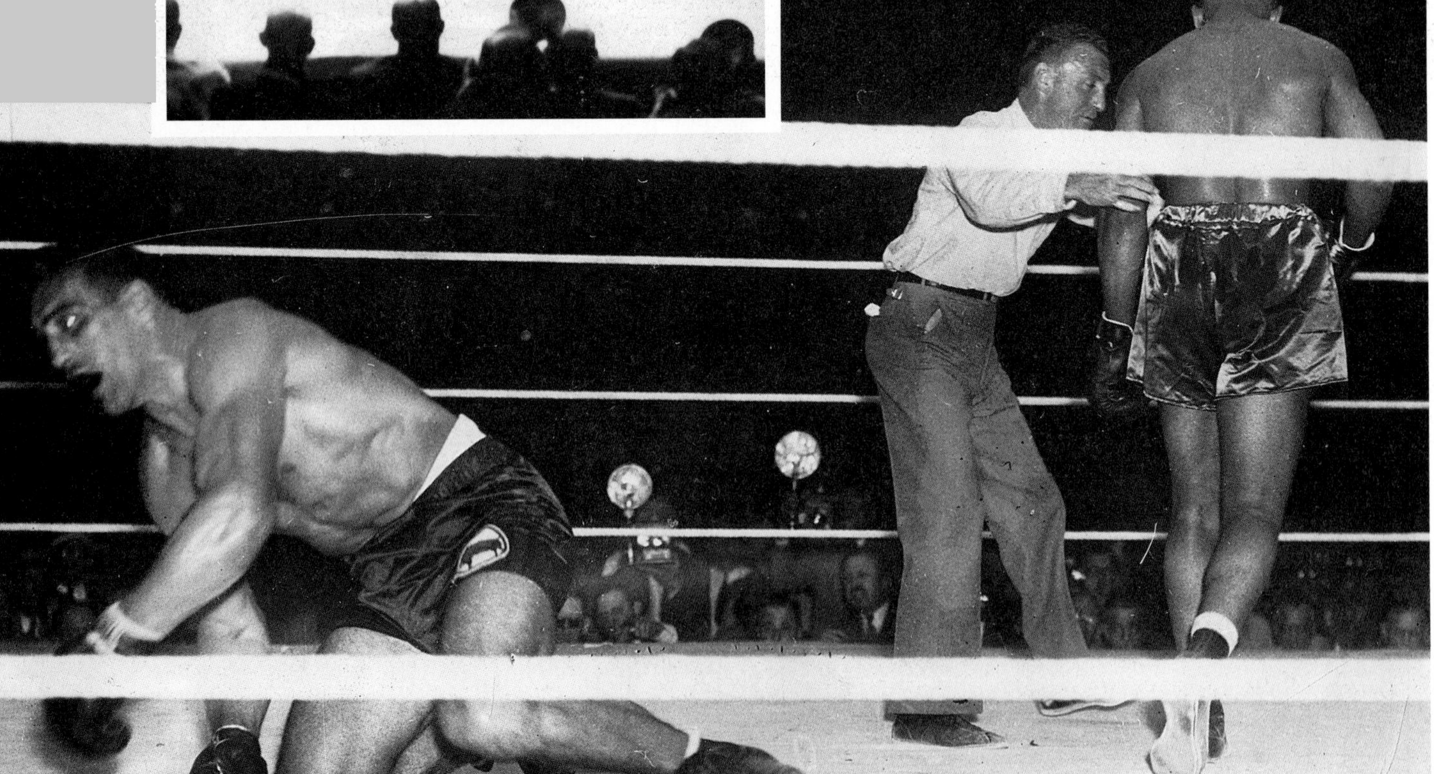

Above and below: *According to a patronizing caption which accompanied these agency pictures, Louis' big ambition was to visit London, have an ice cream with George Bernard Shaw and stand on the balcony of Buckingham Palace with the King and Queen. The agency, with some smart montage work, made the absurdity seem a reality.*

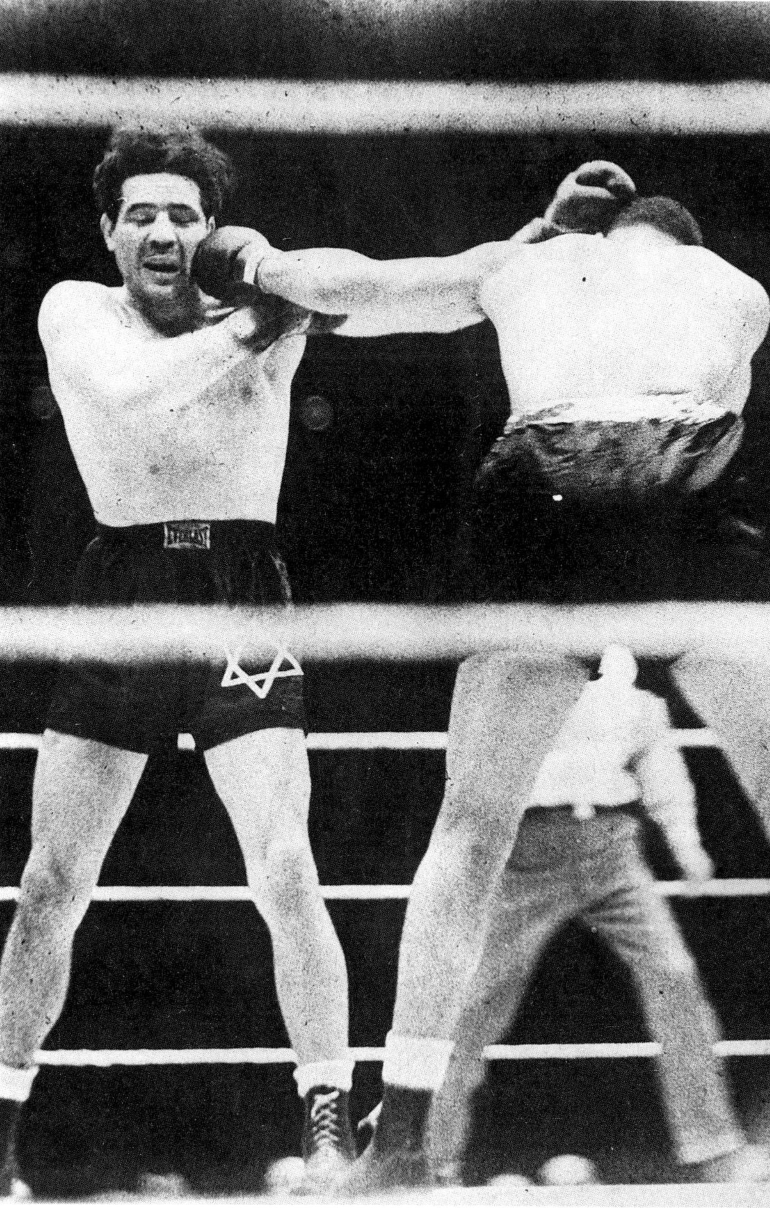

Above: *The erratic Max Baer (left) had one of his bad nights against Louis in September 1935, and was crushed in four rounds.*

In a period when it was unprecedented for a black man to be accepted on his own terms and for his own worth by white society, Louis forced America to assess him on his talents rather than his pigmentation. It was a major breakthrough, for America itself as much as for boxing, and blacks throughout the continent benefitted from Louis' success. As Mead put it: 'Not only did (Louis) have to establish himself as a dominant athlete to get a shot at the heavyweight title; he also had to prove that blacks could compete on equal terms with dignity and without exacerbating racial antagonism. Louis accepted that responsibility and performed so well that he became a challenge to segregation, the challenge that began to crack the system.'

Much of the publicity that Louis attracted was insufferably patronizing, and was, in its own way, just as racist as any of Jack London's anti-black diatribes. He was portrayed as an inarticulate but docile creature, his speech reported in what the white press, in Europe even more than America, imagined was typical Deep South 'nigger talk', with liberal sprinklings of 'dese', 'dem', and 'honeychile' to give it authentic flavour. All of which, of course, ignored the fact that Louis had been taken north to Detroit by his step-father when he was 12 years old, and had grown to maturity on that city's tough streets, a world away from the cotton fields of Alabama where he had been born on 13 May 1914.

However, if Louis was going to get a title chance white America had first to be convinced that he did not represent a social threat in the way that the fiercely independent and proudly black Johnson had done. Eventually, the racial objections were overcome . . . but the business problems posed by Braddock's astute manager Joe Gould proved almost as difficult to surmount.

Louis' rise to prominence had been engineered by Mike Jacobs, a man-about-boxing in his sixties who had learned his trade working under Tex Rickard during the Dempsey era. He had been an established promoter long before Louis emerged, but his alliance with Joe made him the single most influential figure in the business.

The Louis v Braddock showdown took months of negotiating, and at one time it seemed that Jacobs might have been outmanoeuvred and that Braddock would instead defend against the former champion Max Schmeling. The German even signed a contract for the fight, to take place at Madison Square Bowl in Long Island, and he solemnly weighed in on that day for a fight which the whole world knew would not take place.

Gould and Braddock had struck an extraordinary deal with Jacobs, one which left Schmeling out in the cold. The champion would get almost $300,000 – a huge guarantee for those times – plus ten per cent of Jacobs' net profits from heavyweight title promotions for the next decade should Louis win. It proved a better deal than they could ever have imagined, and Braddock's percentage from Louis' fabulous title reign exceeded even the purse he got for the fight itself.

Gould, naturally, did not want this potentially unethical arrangement to be widely known, so he announced instead that he had opted for Louis rather than Braddock because of public opposition to the prospect of Schmeling, who since his

Louis' unimpressive 10-round points win over the elusive Bob Pastor (right) *in Madison Square Garden in January 1937 raised a ripple of uncertainty about his chances of dethroning Braddock. For a while it seemed that the Louis camp had been outmanoeuvred, and that Max Schmeling might get the first crack at the new champion. But there was opposition to the idea of having the Nazis' most valuable propaganda symbol* (below) *installed as heavyweight champion and Schmeling was quietly side-tracked*

Braddock and Louis met in Chicago on 22 June 1936, a year and three days after Louis' loss to Max Schmeling. For a few moments in the opening round, history threatened to repeat itself: the veteran champion caught Louis with a right uppercut, and dropped him (right). *He was up before referee Tommy Thomas could start the count, and took charge of the fight from the second round onwards.*

knockout of Louis was the Nazis' most valuable propaganda asset, endowing Hitler's master race theory with a degree of credibility by becoming the first man to regain the championship. No one was fooled, of course, but the superbly courageous and wholehearted display which Braddock gave against Louis dispelled any unease that even the most cynical observers might have felt about a contract which actually made it worth a champion's while to lose his title.

Gould and Braddock knew that there was little chance of retaining the title – which was why they had held out for such a remarkable deal – but the ever-gullible public were led to believe (in cheerful contradication of all they had been told before) that Louis was not such a man-eater after all. Promoter Jacobs had planted stories about Louis' poor condition and loss of fighting edge, and the papers duly printed them. Much was made of Louis' difficult ten-round win over Bob Pastor, a smart-boxing type in the Braddock mould, a few months earlier. The Madison Square Garden crowd had actually booed Louis from the ring that night, disappointed by his failure to dispose of Pastor inside the distance. Pastor, though, could not have cared less, collecting $6,000 on a $2,000 bet that he would complete the course.

Jacobs' con-trick worked so well that 45,500 paid $715,470 to pack Chicago's Comiskey Park on the night of 22 June 1937, with at least the whites in the crowd half-believing that Braddock could keep the title. For three minutes it seemed they might be right: Braddock floored Louis with a right uppercut in the opening round, and even though Louis bounced up without a count he had clearly been hurt.

But it was the only point in the fight when Braddock had a hope. From then on Louis took him apart with clinical precision until, at the end of the seventh round, Gould looked at his battered champion as he slumped onto the stool and said 'Jimmy, I'm going to tell (referee Tommy) Thomas to stop it.' Braddock, with a bad cut over his left eye, his right eye swollen almost shut and his lip split, replied with one of boxing's immortal quotes: 'If you do, I'll never speak to you again.'

It is the end for Braddock, 70 seconds into the eighth round, but it is the beginning of the greatest reign in championship history. Louis held the title for 11 years and 25 successful defences.

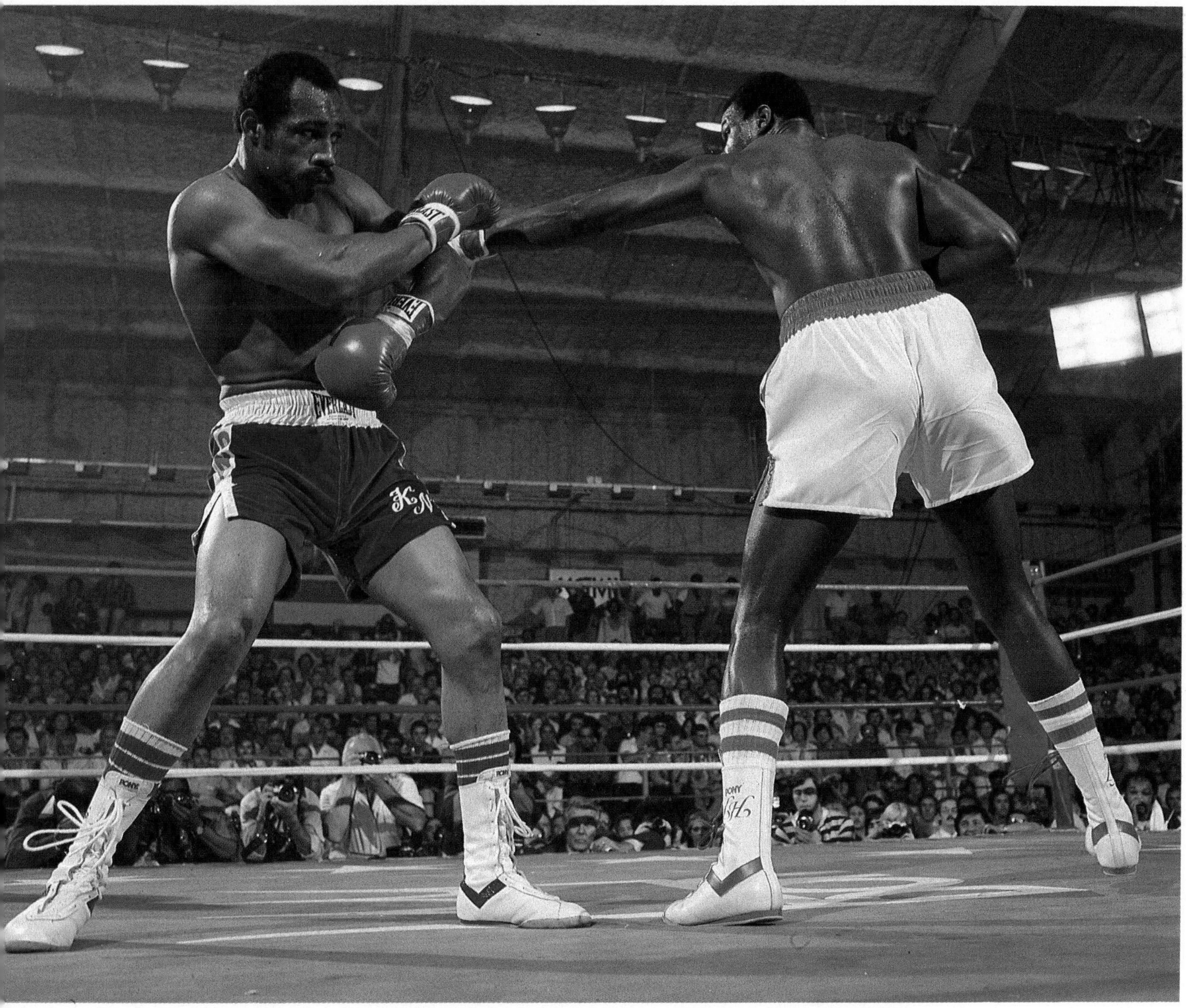

Ken Norton (above, *on the left*), *the only heavyweight champion to have won his title in a committee room rather than the ring, lost it on his first defence to Larry Holmes, but their Las Vegas 15-rounder in 1978 ranks with the division's great fights. Gerrie Coetzee* (left, *knocking out Michael Dokes*) *had an undistinguished spell as WBA champion, losing on his first defence to Greg Page.*

Such was the magic of Muhammad Ali's name that when, at the tail-end of his career, he made an ill-advised bid for Larry Holmes' title, many normally sound judges actually gave him a chance of winning. But in a fight which echoed Charles v Louis, Holmes gave his one-time idol a sustained beating before Ali's cornermen pulled him out after 10 rounds.

One minute and 10 seconds later it was over. Braddock missed with a right, Louis feinted a left and threw an overhand right that caught Braddock on the jaw. The champion toppled onto his right side, almost in slow motion, landing face first. When Tommy Thomas had counted him out, he was hustled back to his dressing room to have 23 stitches inserted in his various facial cuts. The title was gone, but he had not sold it cheaply.

Jacobs shopped around for a 'safe' opponent for Louis' first defence and then, as now, the surest

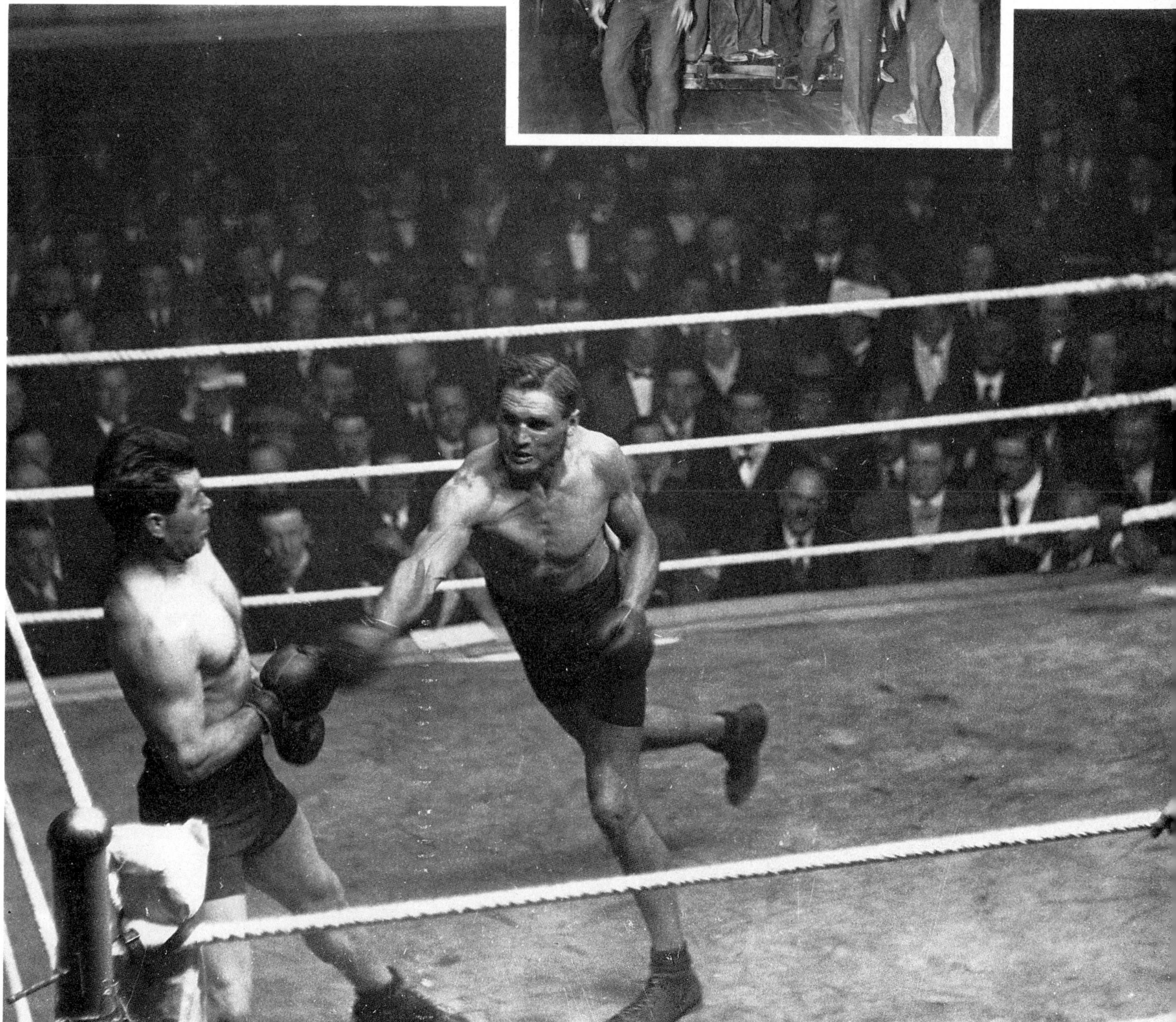

Below: *Phil Scott (right, beating Tom Berry in 1925) was remembered in America as the archetypal British heavyweight – but Tommy Farr was to change all that.*

Right: *Harlem went wild the night Louis beat Braddock – for the first time since Jack Johnson's defeat 22 years previously, there was a black champion to cheer.*

place to look was Britain. At that time British heavyweight boxing was, in American eyes, personified by Phaintin' Phil Scott, who had tried to make a career out of sitting on the canvas, clutching his groin and shouting 'foul'. Sometimes it worked, as when the Norwegian giant Otto Von Porat was disqualified in their semi-final eliminator for the world title which Gene Tunney had vacated. But when Scott faced Jack Sharkey in the final eliminator, referee Lou Magnolia was not so easily fooled when he went down from a right which landed on the hip. He gave the Englishman every chance to recover, but then declared Sharkey the

Scott's peculiar contribution to boxing was the no-foul rule, which was instituted in America chiefly as a consequence of his defeat by Jack Sharkey in 1930 (left).

Farr was made of sterner stuff, as his wins over Red Burman (above) *and Max Baer* (below) *proved – although Baer looks more like the winner.*

winner and thereby contributed substantially towards the acceptance throughout America of the 'no foul' rule, which made it impossible for a man to win a major fight on disqualification. (It was applied as recently as December 1962, when welterweight champion Emile Griffith was declared a ninth-round knockout winner over Jorge Fernandez of Argentina, who had been hit low in their Las Vegas championship battle. Referee Harry Krause allowed Fernandez five minutes in which to recover, and then ruled that Griffith had retained his title by a knockout.)

Jacobs opted for Tommy Farr, the one-time coal miner from Tonypandy, but any ideas Jacobs may have had that Farr shared Scott's fragility were soon dispelled. The Welshman, who boxed his first 10-rounder a fortnight after his 13th birthday, was a strong, stubborn performer who had earned his right to a title fight with wins over Tommy Loughran, Bob Olin, and Max Baer, all world champions. But since he was a *boxer* rather than a puncher the Americans did not give him a chance. The British certainly did though, and the blow-by-

The Welshman's stubborn stand against Louis established him as a national hero in Britain.

blow commentary which the BBC transmitted live, in the small hours of 31 August 1937, held the nation's attention like no other sporting event before.

Farr's performance was so unexpectedly good, so stubborn and so brave that over the decades it grew in the telling until, even 50 years after the event, there are those who claim that the Welshman was robbed. The reality is, as always, rather different. Louis won comfortably on points and

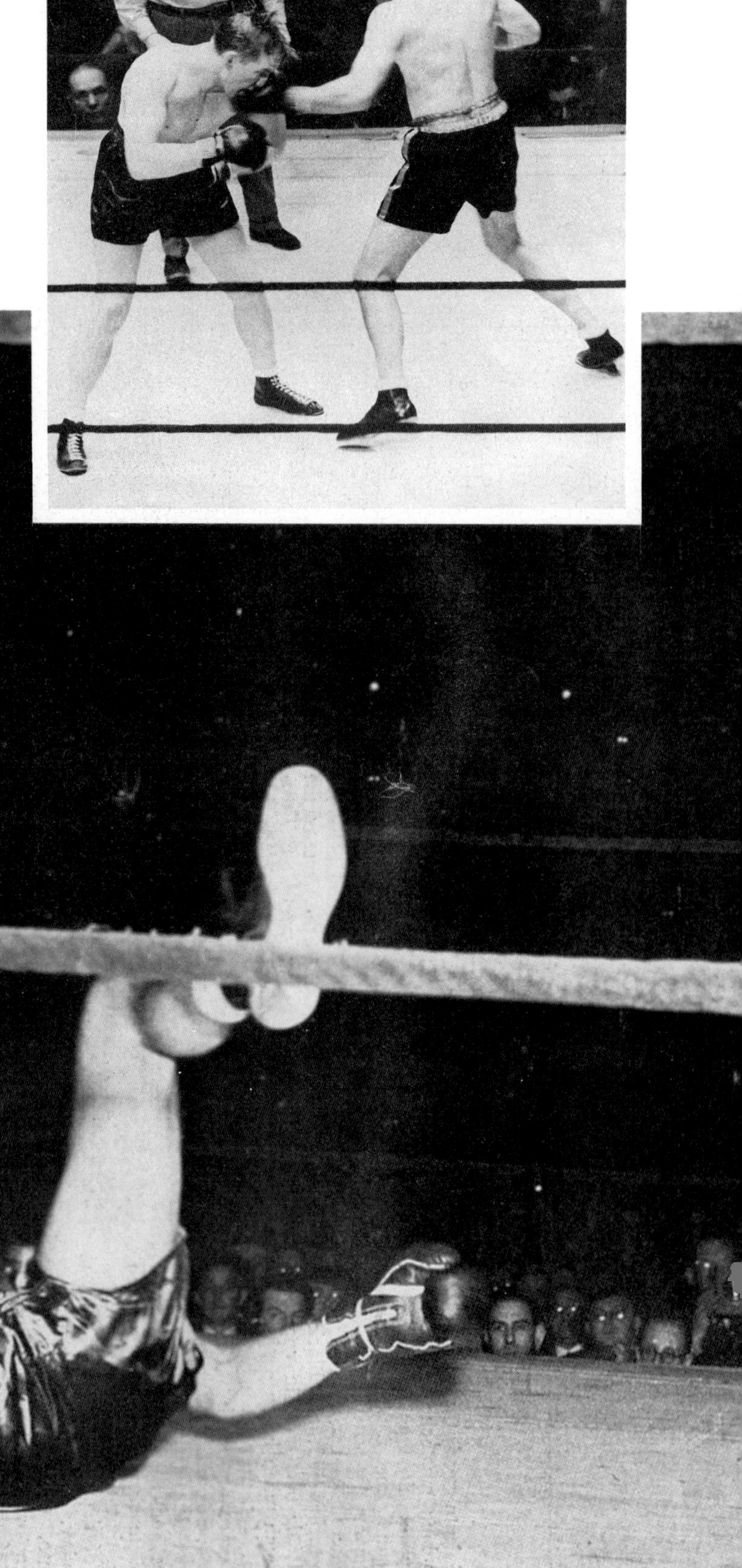

Below: *Louis looked for easier pickings after his unexpectedly tough match with Farr, and his second defence was this three-knockdown, third-round kayo of Nathan Mann in New York.*

Right: *Farr (left) was out of luck in each of his five American fights, and was generally thought to have outpointed James J. Braddock in their 1938 New York 10-rounder.*

Farr, an amiable and attractive personality who had no delusions about himself, never claimed otherwise. Farr went on to box four more times in America without a solitary win, although by popular consensus he *was* robbed against James J. Braddock and Max Baer in New York in 1938.

However, Europe's interest in the heavyweight title did not end with Farr's defeat. While Louis chalked up easy defences against Nathan Mann (kayo 3) and Harry Thomas (kayo 5), Schmeling continued to press his claims for a rematch with the man whom he had once knocked out. Wins over Harry Thomas, Ben Foord, and Steve Dudas kept him in the picture, and Schmeling's value to the Third Reich as a propaganda symbol ensured that America was not allowed to forget that he already held a knockout victory over Louis, and that what he had done once he could certainly do again. Schmeling, in fairness, never revelled in his role as Nazi figurehead, but he did not go out of his way to discourage Dr Goebbels' associates from depicting him as such.

As anti-German feeling grew in America, influenced by its powerful Jewish lobby, the pressure mounted on Louis to erase the sole blemish on his record and, at the same time, humiliate Adolf Hitler and his self-styled 'Master Race'. When Schmeling returned to America to pursue his claim for a title fight, the press whipped

Max Schmeling kept himself in contention for a Louis rematch with a series of good wins, including this points defeat in Hamburg of the South African, Ben Foord.

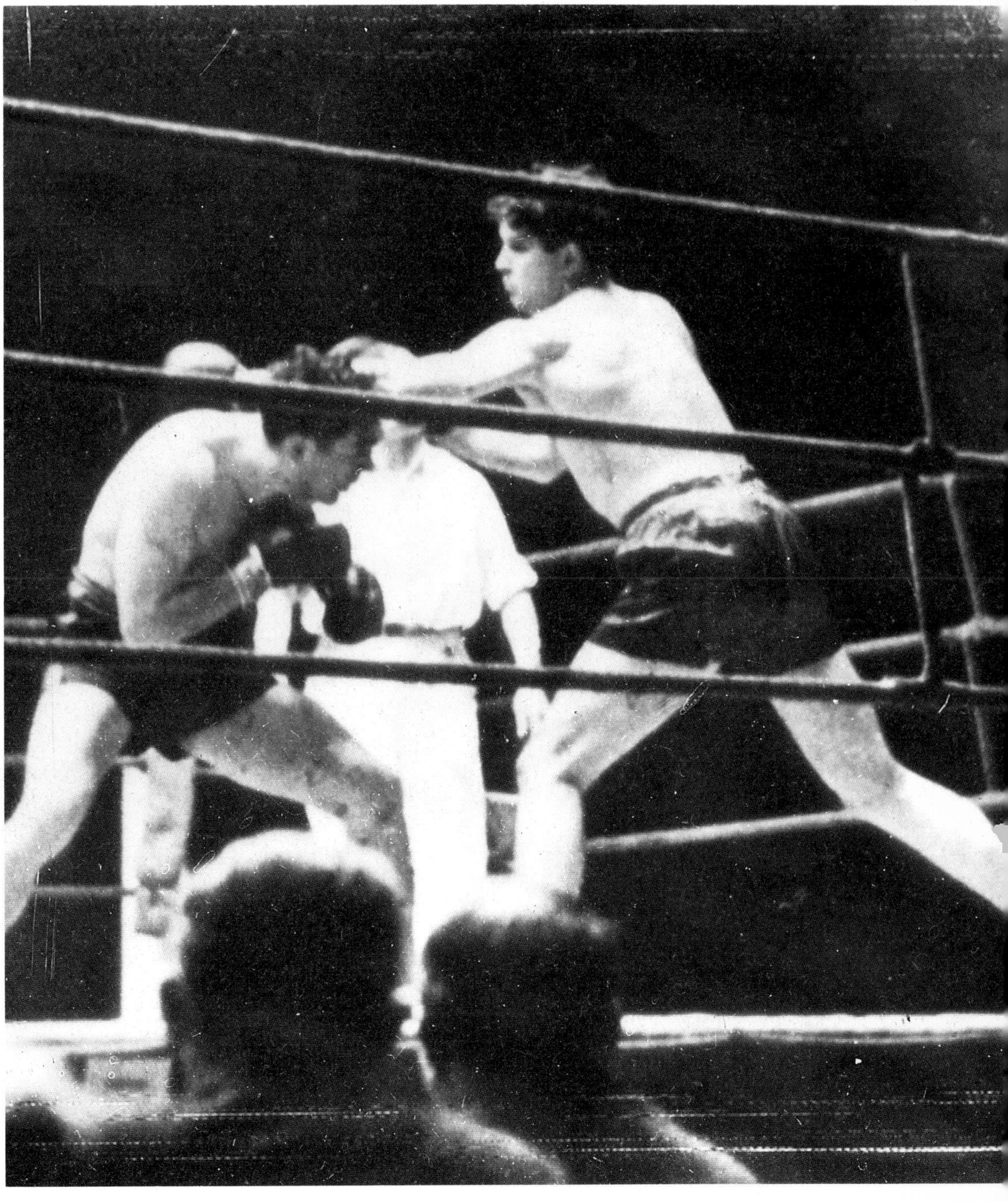

Despite the press build-up, there was never any genuine animosity between Louis and Schmeling, who is pictured (left) *on a visit to the champion's training camp. But in the ring* (above and top right), *Louis showed him no mercy: his 124-second destruction of the only man to have beaten him was the supreme moment of Louis' long career.*

up 'patriotic' hysteria to the point where the fight was depicted as some kind of holy war between rival ideologies. All kinds of fiery, flowery speeches were attributed to both principals in the build-up to their rematch at Yankee Stadium, New York on 22 June 1938 (exactly a year since Louis had become champion).

A syndicated article on the day of the fight, for example, credited Louis with the unlikely sentiments that: 'Tonight I not only fight the battle of my life to revenge the lone blot on my record, but I fight for America against the challenge of a foreign invader, Max Schmeling. This isn't just one man against another or Joe Louis boxing Max Schmeling; it is the good old USA versus Germany'. One detects the hand of promoter Jacobs there: more than 70,000 fans responded by paying $1,015,012 to pack the famous baseball arena and witness history in the making.

Schmeling and Louis were, despite the lurid press releases, just two honest professionals who wanted to get on with their work. Pride, as much as patriotism, demanded that Louis do a convincing job on the German, and he rose to the challenge with the finest performance of his career. It took him exactly 124 destructive seconds, during which time Schmeling was floored three times and the live German radio transmission was pulled off the air as Schmeling screamed in pain after a right to the back broke two vertebrae. It was the night when Louis touched the heights of ring genius – the masterwork for which, above all others, he deserves to be remembered.

The defeat finished Schmeling as a contender, although he had one more fight before the outbreak of the war (during which he served as a paratrooper) and even made a brief comeback in 1947-48, finally retiring at the advanced age of 43.

Below: *The German's 24 years in the ring ended in Berlin on 31 October 1948 with a points loss to Richard Vogt (right). Schmeling was a month past his 43rd birthday.*

The annihilation of Schmeling removed the last doubts that existed about Louis' right to be regarded as the finest fighting man since Jack Dempsey, and it would be nine years before his dominance was seriously challenged by the veteran Jersey Joe Walcott. During that period Louis defended the title more times than any of his predecessors. Between 25 January 1939, when he knocked out his friend John Henry Lewis, the light-heavyweight champion, inside a round, until 1 March 1949, when he announced his retirement as undefeated champion, Louis successfully defended the title 20 times, with only Arturo Godoy and Walcott taking him the full 15 rounds.

The credentials of some of his challengers were shaky, but they did not all deserve the collective title of 'Bums of the Month', by which history

The ups and downs of a champion's life ... Louis flattens John Henry Lewis in the first round (top right) *but suffers a shock knockdown by the remarkably unathletic Tony Galento* (right), *whom he stopped in the fourth. His defence against glamorous Billy Conn* (below, *pictured at the weigh-in) was even tougher. Louis was behind on points until he caught up with Conn in the 13th* (opposite, top).

remembers them. The 'fat freak' Tony Galento, for example, who reportedly trained on beer and cigars in his New Jersey saloon, floored the champion in their June 1939 title fight in New York before being cut to pieces and kayoed in the fourth. And the smart-boxing light-heavyweight champion Billy Conn had a good points lead when Louis finally caught up with him and knocked him out in the 13th round of their 1941 title fight at the Polo Grounds, New York, in front of a large crowd.

Bob Pastor, who had taken Louis the distance in a difficult ten-rounder in 1937, was beaten in 11 rounds in a rematch while Godoy, the tough Chilean who had survived the 15-round course in February 1940, did not make it past the eighth in the return fight four months later.

Right: *The rugged Chilean Arturo Godoy proved a worthy challenger, taking Louis the full 15 rounds in their first meeting and into the eighth second time around.*

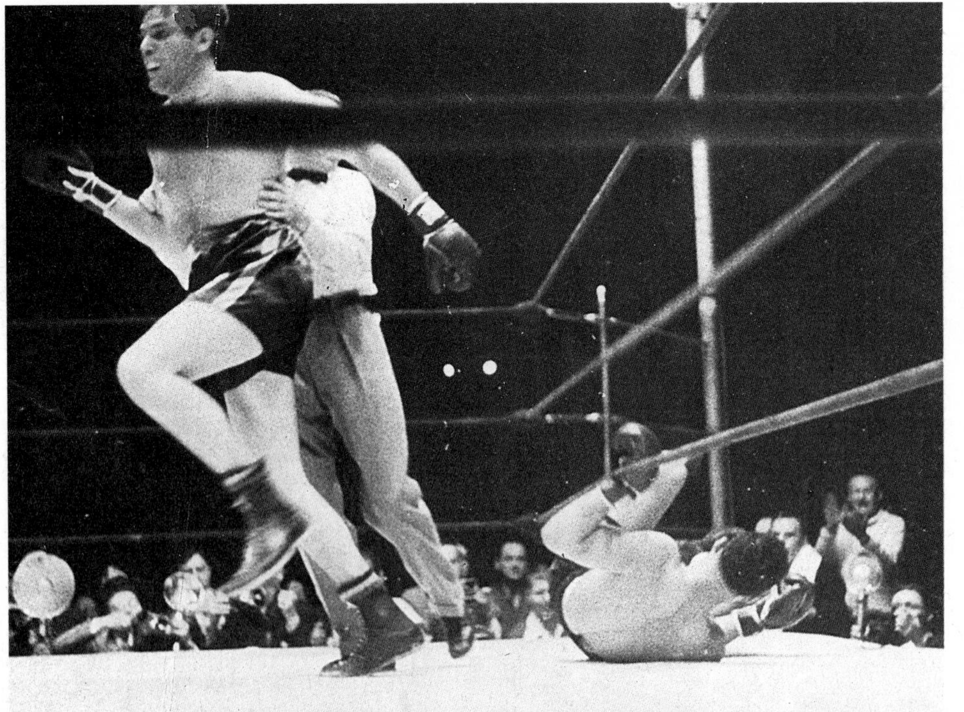

Max Baer's brother Buddy enjoyed a glimpse of glory when he knocked Louis out of the ring in their first meeting, in May, 1941. Baer was eventually disqualified in the seventh round, but was easily beaten in the rematch in January 1942. Louis knocked him out in the opening round, and donated his entire purse to the Naval Relief Fund. Louis' behaviour during the war, most of which he spent in uniform (above, *with Billy Conn) endeared him to the American public.*

Above: *Conn (left) proved a much less serious threat when he challenged Louis again in June 1946, and was beaten in the eighth.*

But it was Louis' behaviour during America's involvement in World War Two, most of which he spent in uniform, that clinched his place as American folk hero. He defended his title against Buddy Baer (who had taken him into the seventh round in a previous title bid) and knocked him out in the first, donating his entire purse to the Naval Relief Fund, and then ten weeks later kayoed Abe Simon in six rounds for the benefit of the Army Relief Fund. Even Mike Jacobs, a man with a deep-rooted love for a dollar, was moved by Louis' example to donate his profits of $37,229 from the Baer fight to the fund, while Baer himself contributed $4,078.

In Chris Mead's biography of Louis he quotes a *New York Daily News* writer, Jimmy Powers, who argued that: 'You don't see a shipyard owner risking his entire business. If the government wants a battleship, the government doesn't ask him to donate it. The government pays him a fat profit... The more I think of it, the greater a guy I see in this Joe Louis.'

Louis spent most of the war years touring the various theatres of war, giving exhibitions and doing what he could to maintain the troops' morale. By 1946, when he was rematched with Billy Conn, Louis was 32 and past his prime, but he shook off over four years of ring rust to kayo the handsome Irish-American in the eighth. A first-round knockout of Tami Mauriello in September 1946 set up the June 1947 fight with the New Jersey veteran Joe Walcott, an undistinguished 34-year-old who had lost two of his previous five fights, to Joey Maxim and Elmer Ray. Walcott was given such little chance that the New York Commission originally insisted that the fight be billed merely as an exhibition.

The Commission relented under pressure from Jacobs and, indirectly, from Louis himself, who had spent all but $500 of the $100,000 he had earned from the Mauriello fight on good living and bad investments. Walcott's record was, at best, mediocre – he had been knocked out by Al Ettore and Abe Simon, both of whom had in turn been flattened by Louis, and he had also lost at least eight other fights in a decidedly sketchy list which could be traced back to 1930, when he was just 16 years old. According to the form book Walcott did not have a chance, yet he came closer to beating Louis than anyone since Max Schmeling.

Louis was floored in the first and fourth rounds, and Walcott easily avoided the ponderous champion's counter-attacks. By the end of the 15th both champion and challenger were convinced that the title had changed hands, and the disheartened

Tami Mauriello did not survive the first round with Louis in their September 1946 title fight . . . but look at the damage inflicted in that time (right).

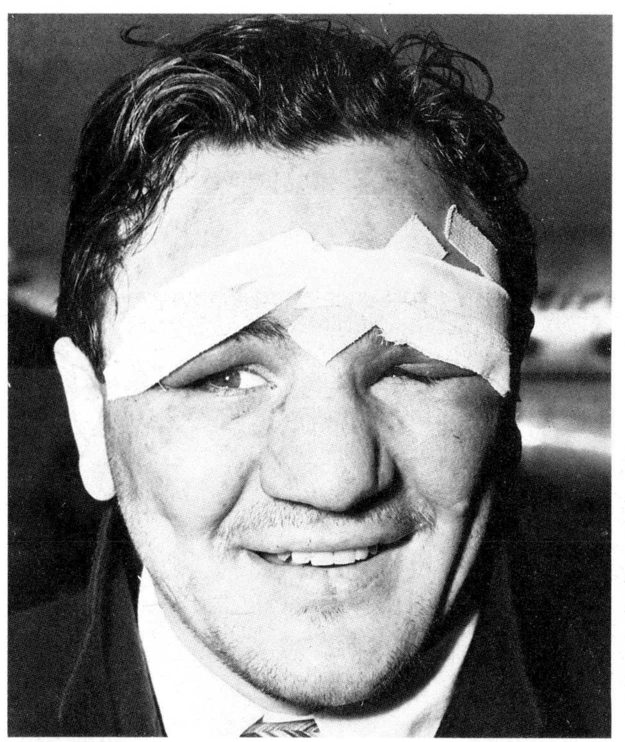

Louis even ducked through the ropes on his way to the dressing room before the decision had been announced. His cornermen ordered him back – to hear the announcement that he had retained his title on a split decision by scores of 8-6-1, 9-6, and 7-6-2 (in Walcott's favour). For the first time in an unrivalled championship career, Louis left the ring to jeers.

Below: *Jersey Joe Walcott was at first not considered good enough to meet Louis, but when he was allowed to do so he floored the champion twice.*

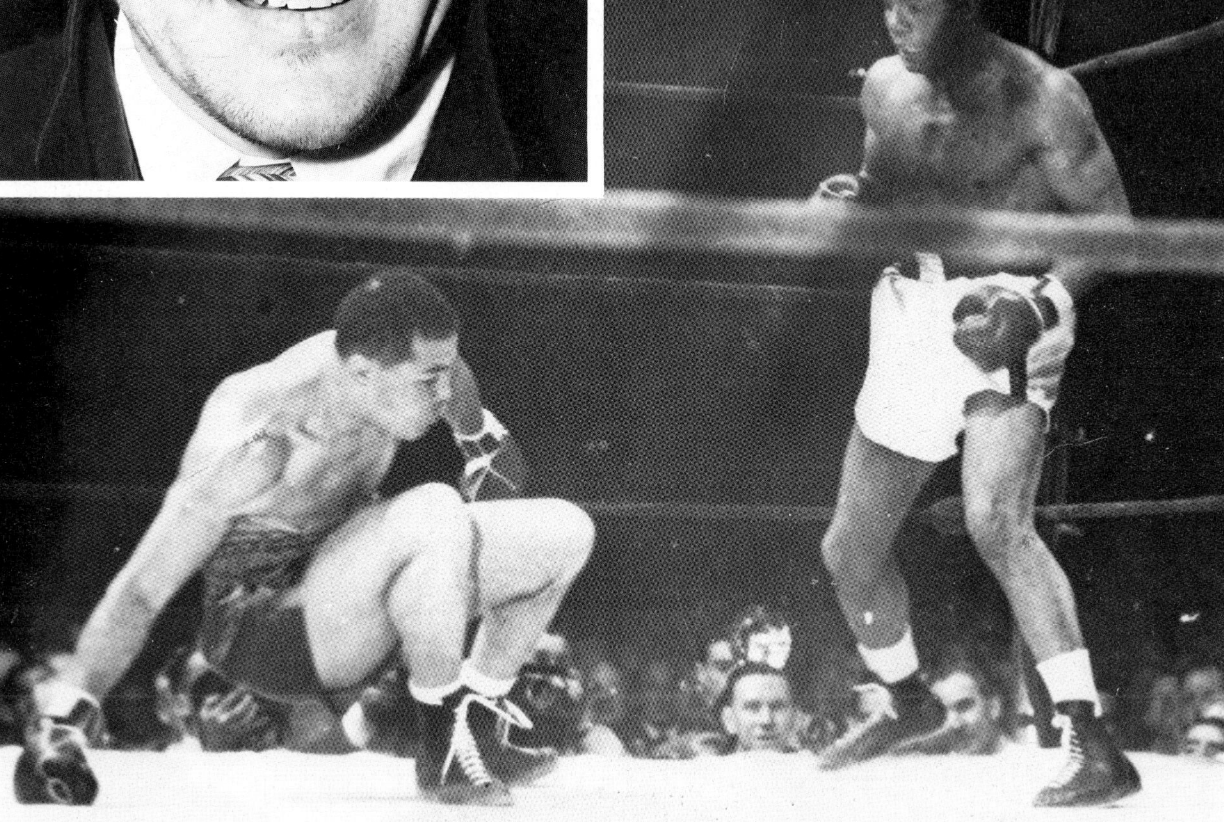

Right: *Walcott appeared to have outpointed Louis, and Joe himself was so sure he had been beaten that he even left the ring before the official announcement. But the judges thought otherwise, and Louis retained the title on a booed split decision. Walcott would have to wait more than three years before he, at last, became world champion.*

Louis recognized that he was not anything like the man he had been in his prime, but his pride – and a spiralling income tax bill – would not let him retire on such a sour note. He granted Walcott a return fight in Yankee Stadium on 25 June 1948 and, although Walcott floored him again in the third round, the old champ found enough reserves to kayo his most troublesome challenger in the 11th. The time had come to quit, but Louis was incapable of walking away from the sport he had graced for 15 years. On the very evening that he announced his retirement, 1 March 1949, he was in the ring at Nassau boxing an exhibition with Ed Crawley, and the round of exhibition tours went on virtually without let-up until he announced his comeback to serious competition in August 1950.

Walcott's performance against Louis earned him a rematch six months later . . . but Louis despatched him in 11 rounds.

When Louis retired for the first time he seemed to have made his financial future reasonably secure. With the help of a lawyer friend, Truman Gibson, he negotiated a package under which he would give up the title, sign the leading contenders to exclusive contracts, and sell the rights in the ensuing tournament to a promoter. The promoter he chose was Jim Norris who, with his associate Arthur Wirtz, formed the International Boxing Club (IBC) that was to control the heavyweight title until Floyd Patterson became champion in 1956. Louis' move effectively put his old backer Mike Jacobs out of business, but Norris' offer had been too attractive to decline – a lump sum of $350,000 plus $20,000 a year and stock in the new company.

Louis duly notified Abe Greene, the president of the National Boxing Association (the NBA) of his retirement, and the NBA (an American-based federation of state commissions, which eventually evolved into the World Boxing Association) nominated Walcott to meet Ezzard Charles, a small but accomplished stylist, for the vacant title. The pair had, of course, already been signed up by the IBC to meet in June 1949.

Charles, born in Lawrenceville, Georgia (but now based in Cincinnati, Ohio) had long been considered one of the outstanding fighters of his generation. In an amateur career which commenced in 1937, he had had 42 fights, winning them all, including every championship for which he had ever entered. He probably reached his peak as a light-heavyweight in the mid-1940s when he thrice beat Archie Moore, who later became one of the great 175 lb champions, and scored three wins over Joey Maxim, also a future light-heavyweight king. In his early days Charles was billed as the 'Cincinnati Cobra' because of the smooth delivery and stunning power of his punches, but in 1948 Sam Baroudi failed to regain consciousness after

Ezzard Charles (above) *took over when Louis retired as undefeated champion. With his victory, control of the heavyweight title passed to the International Boxing Club, headed by Jim Norris* (right). *Norris and the IBC monopolized the championship until the independent-minded Cus D'Amato steered Floyd Patterson to the title in 1956.*

Charles' career was shadowed by tragedy when Sam Baroudi (above) *died after being knocked out by him in 1948.*

Action from the first of Charles' four title fights with Jersey Joe Walcott, who lost the first two but finished level.

Charles had knocked him out in 10 rounds in Chicago.

Charles never really got over the tragedy. His ring style changed and he became a cautious, even hesitant performer. He had by then outgrown the light-heavyweight division, although he never became a big heavyweight and, in fact, scaled 6 lb under the present *cruiserweight* limit for most of his heavyweight championship fights. Wins over the dangerous Joe Baksi (kayo 11), Johnny Haynes (kayo 8) and Maxim again (on points over 15 rounds) earned him the Walcott fight. He outscored the aging Walcott in a dull 15-rounder, and became a busy champion with defences against Gus

Big Joe Baksi was a dangerous contender, but Charles dismissed him in 11 rounds.

Lesnevich, Pat Valentino, and Freddie Beshore.

By 1950 Louis, then 36 years old and in financial chaos, had been forced into an inevitable comeback. The Internal Revenue Service had billed him for $500,000 in unpaid tax, and were not interested in any of the compromise offers made by the former champion and his advisers. There was only one way that Louis could make enough to clear the debt, so in August 1950 he signed to fight Charles on 27 September in New York. The various commissions around the world which had withheld recognition from Charles agreed to recognize the winner as the undisputed champion. It was an emotional night, for Charles as much as for the once-formidable Louis and his millions of admirers. Louis had been Charles' boyhood idol, but now in order to reach the pinnacle of the profession which Louis had inspired him to pursue, Charles was expected to destroy a legend. He did so, with cold professionalism but no pleasure.

Louis was too slow, ponderous, and old to trouble the younger man, and Charles won 12 of the 15 rounds. He could almost certainly have knocked Louis out in the final round, but allowed the veteran to finish out of respect for the man's unique contribution to boxing. It should have been the end for Louis, but of course it was not – he had earned only $100,458 from the fight, and now he owed tax on that sum as well as on the balance of the original $500,000 debt. The debt spiralled out of control as interest was added to the total, and eventually it grew to such an absurd figure that, in belated practical recognition of Louis' achievements, the American Government wrote off the entire sum in his final years. But in the meantime

Light-heavyweight champion Gus Lesnevich lasted into the seventh round when he tried for Charles' NBA title in 1949.

LOUIS		CHARLES
36	AGE	29
6 FT. 2 IN.	HEIGHT	6 FT.
216 LBS.	WEIGHT	182 LBS.
17 IN.	NECK	16 ½ IN.
76 IN.	REACH	74 IN.
42 IN.	CHEST NORMAL	39 IN.
45 IN.	CHEST EXPANDED	42 IN.
12 ¼	FOREARM	12
11¾ IN.	FIST	12 IN.
37 IN.	WAIST	33 IN.
15 ¼ IN.	BICEPS	15 ½ IN.
22¾	THIGH	20
14¼ IN.	CALF	13 IN.
10 IN.	ANKLE	8 ½ IN.

Charles took no pleasure in trouncing Joe Louis, his boyhood idol, when the old champion attempted to regain the title he had never lost in the ring. Charles gave the 36-year-old veteran a steady pounding, closing his left eye and outscoring him by a wide margin. It should have been the end of the line for Louis, but his tax problems kept him in the ring for another year.

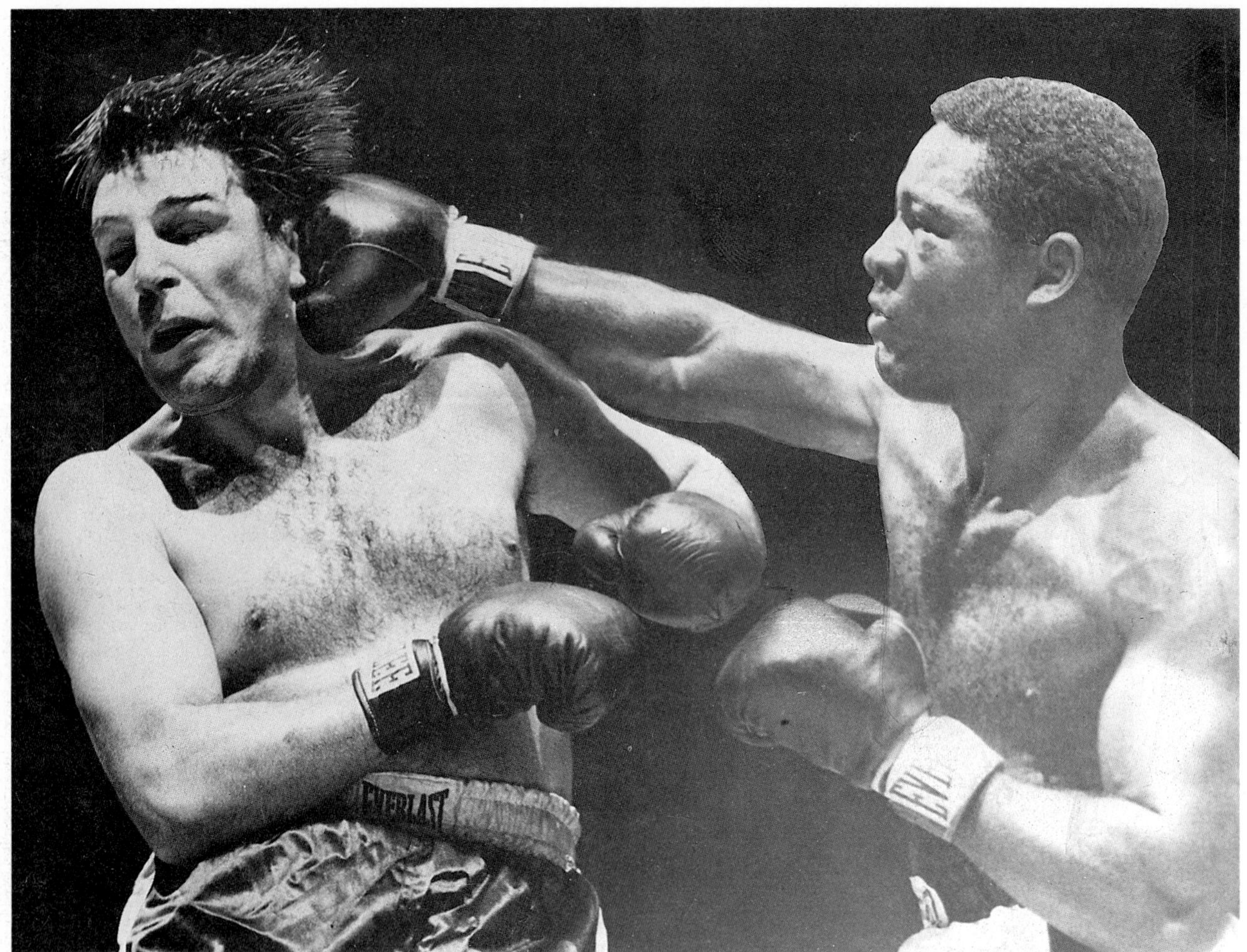

Left: *Jersey Joe Walcott got a second chance at Charles' title in March 1951, but the result was the same – a points loss.*

Above: *Charles made eight successful defences, including this 10th-round win over Lee Oma in New York in January 1951.*

Louis had to carry on trying to pay the bill, and that meant fighting younger and harder men long after he should have been enjoying honourable retirement. Within two months of losing to Charles he was back in the ring, outpointing the Argentinian Cesar Brion over 10 rounds in Chicago.

Six days later Charles made his first defence of the now undisputed title, kayoing Nick Barone in 11 rounds in his hometown of Cincinnati, and he kept busy in 1951 with defences against Lee Oma (kayo 10), Walcott again (on points), and his old rival Joey Maxim, whom he also outpointed. He then signed for yet another meeting with the perennial challenger Walcott at Pittsburgh on 18 July 1951, but by now public interest was minimal in this third meeting. Few gave the 37-year-old Walcott a chance, but a single left hook in the seventh round made Jersey Joe the oldest heavyweight champion in history. He may even have been older than his

Opposite: *Oma had disgraced himself in a 1948 fiasco in London against Bruce Woodcock, but he won 15 of his subsequent 17 fights to earn this crack at Charles.*

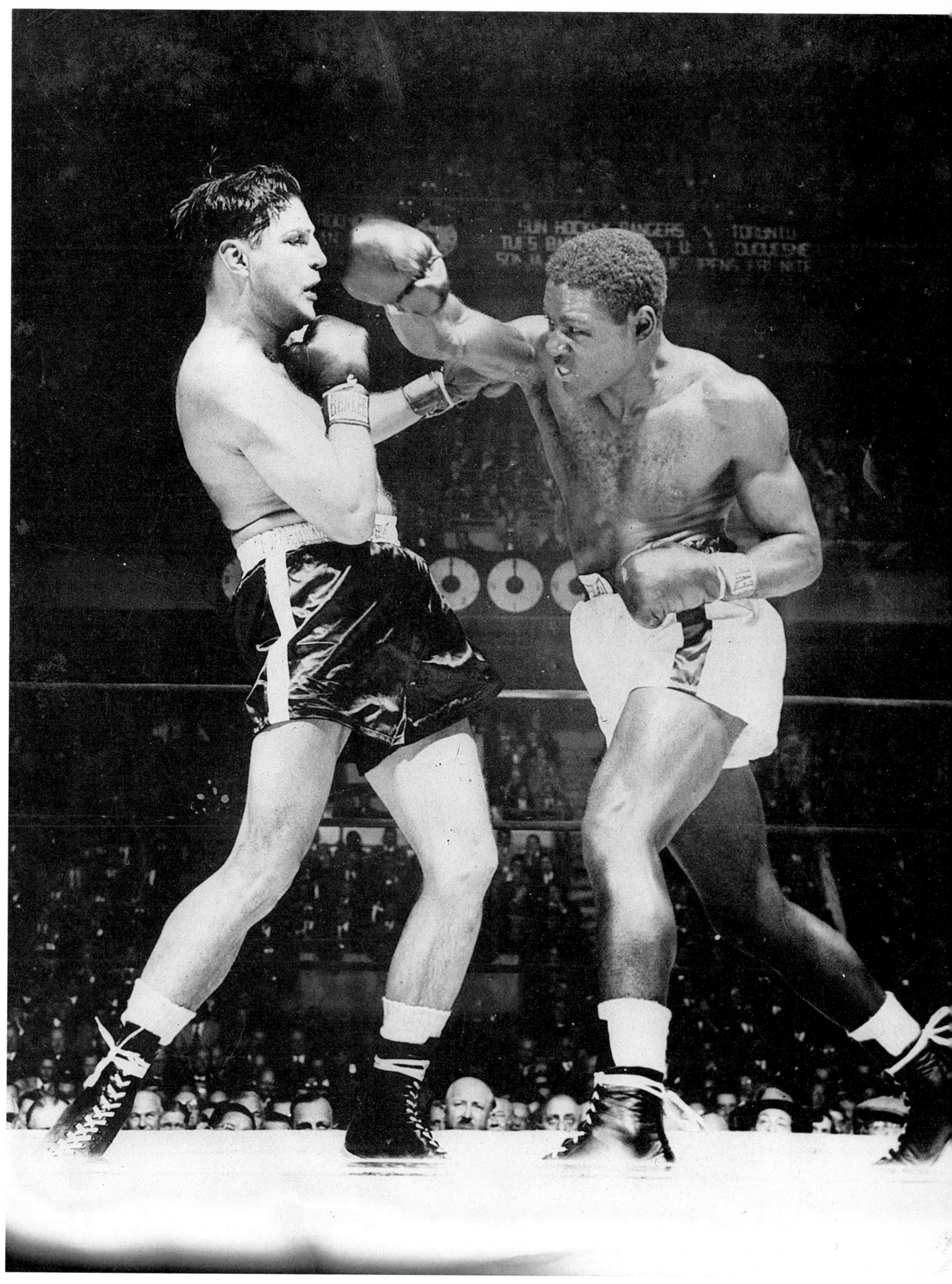

Walcott's left hook (above) *made him the oldest man ever to win the heavyweight title when he knocked out* Ezzard Charles (left) *in seven rounds in July 1951. It was Jersey Joe's fifth championship bid.*

official age, but whatever the truth it was still a remarkable achievement by a man who had failed in four previous title challenges. The veteran's success, in defiance of logic, history and the betting odds, was a tribute to his persistence and professionalism.

Walcott's win echoed James J. Braddock's 'Cinderella' story 16 years earlier in more ways than one. Braddock had been a caretaker champ whose reign was shadowed by a powerful young challenger in Joe Louis. Now Walcott filled the same role: his Nemesis, who was destined to become the world's first white heavyweight champion since Braddock, was a squat, crude, but immensely powerful slugger from Brockton called Rocky Marciano.

Marciano: the Rock Rolls Up

ROCKY Marciano, the son of a poor immigrant shoemaker from a village near Naples, was a throwback fighter who would have flourished in a less refined era. He relied on heart, durability, and raw power to overcome his many technical shortcomings. His trainer, a former bantamweight called Charlie Goldman, tried hard to add skill to Marciano's savagery but had to settle instead for capitalizing on his protege's formidable natural assets.

Goldman recalled the first time he put the novice Marciano in the sparring ring against an experienced professional: 'He was so awkward we just stood there and laughed. He didn't stand right, he didn't throw a punch right, he didn't do anything right. Then, all of a sudden, he throws a roundhouse right and the big guy is out like a mackerel.' That terse account could serve, with only minor adjustments, as a description of most of Marciano's 49 professional engagements.

Rocky's amateur career had been brief but spectacular, winning eight contests, mostly by clean knockout, and losing four. He won the State AAU title, which qualified him to go on to box Coley Wallace in the trials for America's 1948 Olympic team, but since he had injured his hand in his semi-final he had to withdraw. Marciano was pushing 25, which is late to launch a pro career, but his close friend and next door neighbour Allie Colombo persuaded him to try it. Marciano signed with a local manager, Gene Caggiano, but the relationship was short-lived and sour, and in 1948 Colombo wrote a letter that changed Marciano's life. The letter was to Al Weill, a powerful New York

Rocky Marciano, the only heavyweight champion with a perfect record: 49 fights, 49 wins.

Below and right: *The three key figures in Marciano's entourage were Al Weill (seated, with top British promoter Jack Solomons), Allie Colombo and the bespectacled trainer Charlie Goldman, with the champ.*

fight figure who, in addition to being matchmaker for the ubiquitous IBC, was also a friend and associate of gangsters Frankie Carbo and 'Blinky' Palermo, who were later exposed by the Kefauver Commission on Organized Crime as being the under-cover controllers of American boxing.

Colombo wrote: 'Your name was recommended to me...in regards to your handling a future heavyweight champion. Rocco Marchegiano is 23 years old (he was actually almost 25) 190 lb and one of the greatest prospects in the country . . . He is rough and tough and has shown in his amateur fights a tremendous punch in either hand. He has the necessary foundation to become a great fighter. If you are interested, contact me soon.'

Weill did, and invited the pair to New York where, after watching him spar, he agreed (on Goldman's advice) to take over his career. Because the New York Commission's rules prohibited

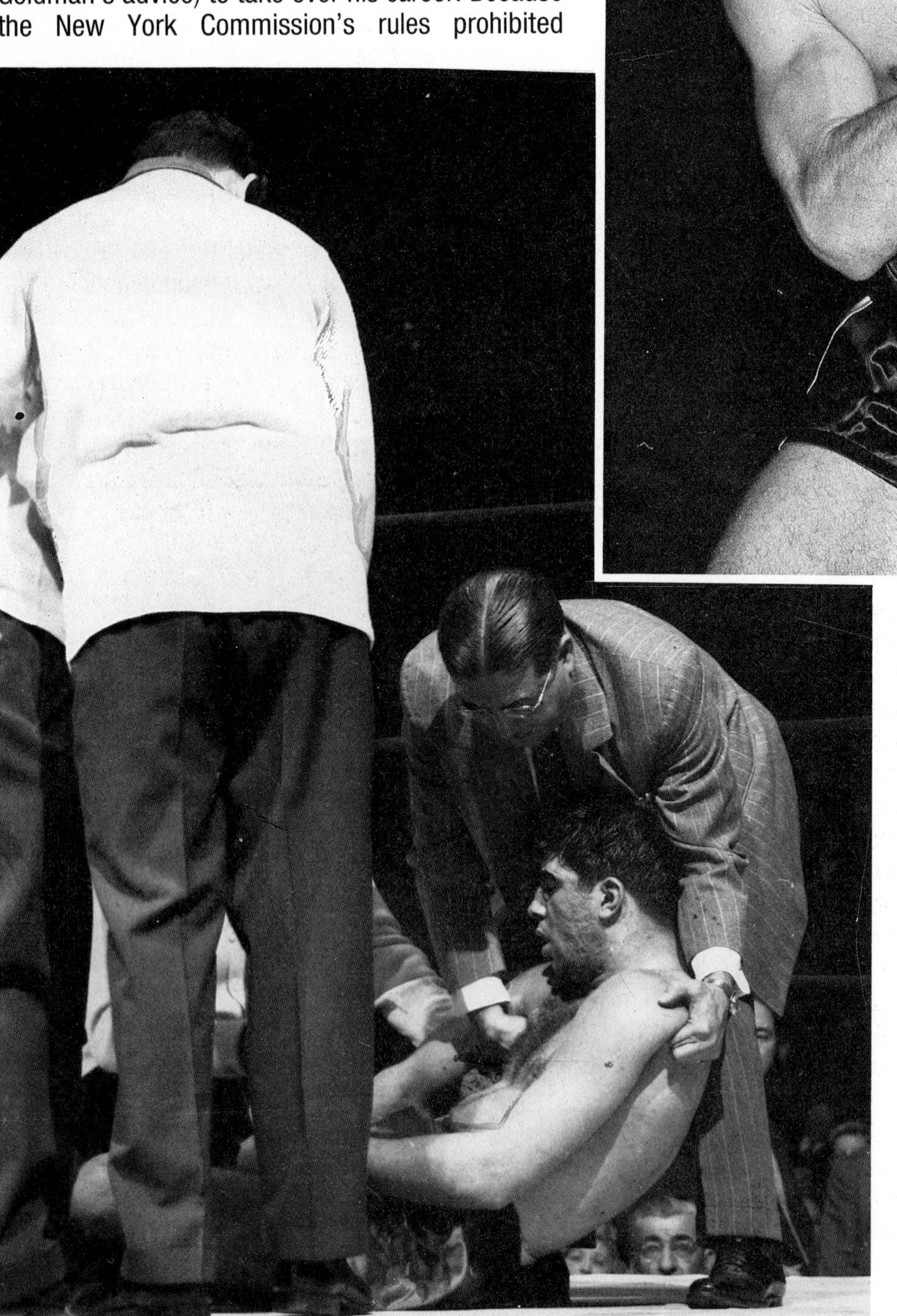

Roland LaStarza (above on the left, winning a tough 10-round decision over Fred 'Rocky' Jones) and Carmine Vingo were two of Marciano's most significant victims. He beat them in consecutive fights, hospitalizing Vingo (left) after a brutal six-round war in December 1949 and then edging out LaStarza on a split verdict three months later. It was the closest that the Rock ever came to defeat.

matchmakers from acting as managers, Marciano's official manager was Weill's stepson Marty, but it was Al who held the reins. (The Kings, Don and son Carl, have virtually monopolized the heavyweight title since the early 1980s by the same device.) The triumvirate of Weill, Marciano, and Goldman would have an impact on heavyweight boxing as potent as the famous 'Triple Alliance' of Dempsey, Kearns, and Rickard 30 years previously.

Marciano's rise through the ranks was spectacular. Only two of his first 24 opponents – Don Mogard and Ted Lowry – took him the distance, and 19 of his victories were gained inside three rounds. By December 1949, Weill judged him ready for his first big-time test, against a rugged Italian-American from the Bronx, Carmine Vingo.

The pair clashed in Madison Square Garden on 30 December in a fight full of fierce Italian pride. Vingo, who had celebrated his 20th birthday the previous day, had won 27 of his 30 fights. Marciano had the edge in punching power, as he showed by flooring Vingo for counts of nine in each of the first two rounds, but Vingo rallied strongly from the second knockdown and traded punches head-to-head.

It was wildly exciting: the *New York Times* reported next morning that there had been 'torrid slugging during the third, fourth, and fifth rounds, until it seemed human endurance could stand no more; one or the other must drop from the combination of punches and exhaustion.' Marciano almost went over in the fifth, but Vingo was too far gone to follow up and a round later the gallant New Yorker, his nose smashed, fell heavily, the back of his head bouncing off the canvas. The referee counted to three, and then waved the fight over. Vingo was taken, unconscious, to hospital where he lingered in a coma for a week before starting the long road to recovery. Marciano later befriended his old rival, and helped pay his hospital bills.

The near-tragedy was a traumatic experience for Marciano, whose personality was the complete reverse of the primitive, rough, uncaring near-savage he became in the ring. But at least the fight had been so thrilling that he was now established as a major force in heavyweight boxing, a position he consolidated with a string of good wins in 1950. His first appearance since the Vingo affair was the Garden's second biggest draw of 1950, when 13,658 watched him win a controversial split decision over Roland LaStarza, a handsome 22-year-old New Yorker who had won all his previous 37 fights. It was the closest Marciano had come to defeat: the judges scored it 5-4-1 Marciano and 5-4-1 LaStarza, and the third judge had them level at 5-5, but made Rocky ahead on the supplementary points system by 9-6.

The rest of Marciano's opponents in 1950 and early 1951 were less demanding, but in July of that year the ultra-cautious Weill was persuaded to take another chance, this time against the heavy-punching Mormon from Utah, Rex Layne. Five years younger than Marciano, Layne had lost only once in 36 fights which included 24 wins inside the distance. Weill had not been keen to take the match, but Jim Norris, who headed the IBC, gave Marciano 30 per cent of the gate takings. Since Layne had already beaten Jersey Joe Walcott, Marciano's sixth-round knockout was a significant step forward. Six weeks later Rocky knocked out the former NBA title challenger Freddie Beshore in four rounds, setting up an October date with the faded but still formidable Joe Louis.

Louis had won eight in a row since the Ezzard Charles defeat. The opposition was of mixed quality but a few, like Lee Savold (who had been recognized as world champion by the British Board of Control after beating Bruce Woodcock in June 1950), were good enough to prove that the old Brown Bomber could not yet be written off. Louis, now 37, was seen as the perfect launch-pad for Marciano towards a crack at Walcott's title, but for five rounds his still-elegant left jab kept him in the fight and split Marciano's eyebrow.

But Louis could not withstand the relentless pressure the younger man was applying, and by the end of the seventh Marciano had moved into a clear points lead by 5-2, 4-3, and 4-2-1. The end was not long in coming. Louis was floored for an eight count early in the eighth, and was then knocked through the ropes onto the ring apron, one leg stretched under the bottom rope. Referee Ruby Goldstein began the count, but waved his arms at 'three' to signal the end, so sparing the old champion the indignity of a knockout defeat.

This final gesture was the least that the boxing world owed to the man who had been perhaps the sport's finest exponent. The sight of the battered wreck who had once been the marvellous Joe Louis made a deep and lasting impression on Marciano, who wept as he visited Louis in the dressing room afterwards. 'What's the use of

Lee Savold, whom Britain briefly (and absurdly) recognized as world champion, took a fearful beating from Joe Louis (left) *in June 1951 – but it was a different story when Louis faced Marciano* (below) *four months later. Rocky was ferocious in the ring: if the hook missed, the following elbow didn't.*

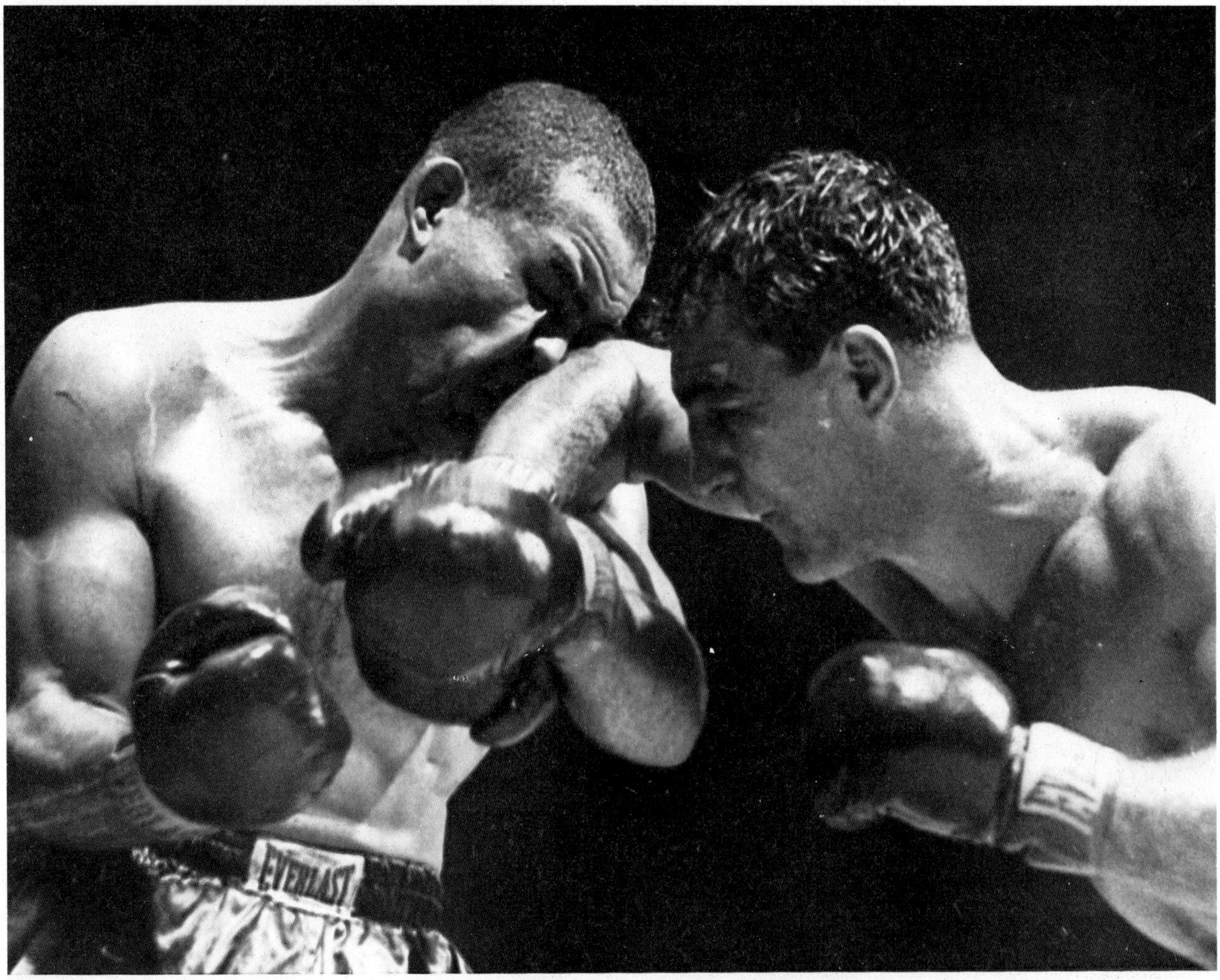

crying?' asked the ever-dignified Louis. 'The better man won, that's all. Marciano is a good puncher and he is hard to hit. I'm not too disappointed. I only hope everyone feels the same way I do about it. I'm not looking for sympathy. I guess everything happens for the best.'

Marciano was now the hottest name in boxing, but he knocked a little of the gloss off his drawing power with a clumsy and unimpressive win over Louis' victim Lee Savold in his first fight of 1952. Savold absorbed a frightful beating; his nose was flattened, his lips split, and both eyes cut before his manager Bill Daly called it off at the end of the sixth. But despite the punishment he had inflicted, the crowd were unhappy with Marciano's per-

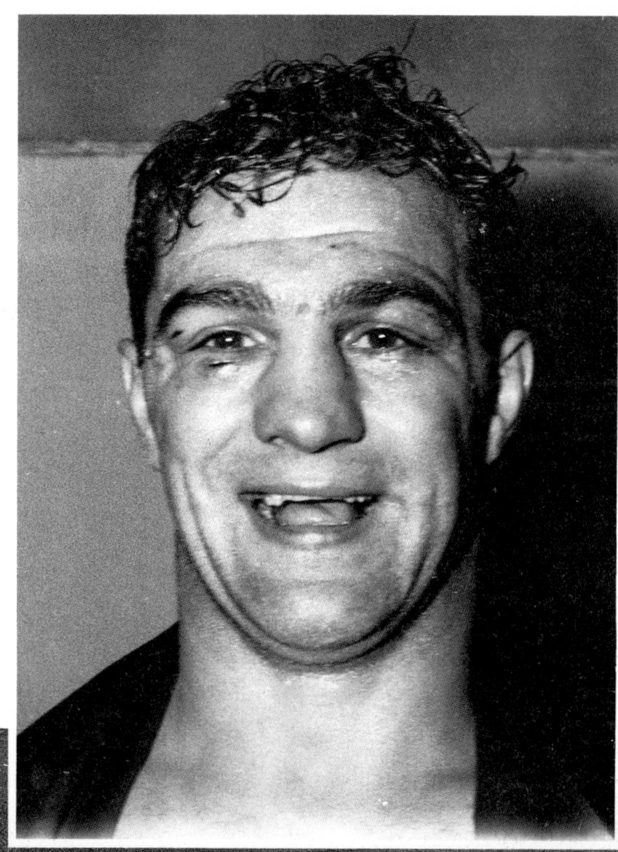

No wonder Marciano looks elated . . . he has just scored the biggest win of his career, knocking Joe Louis out of the ring and out of boxing in the eighth round at New York in October 1951.

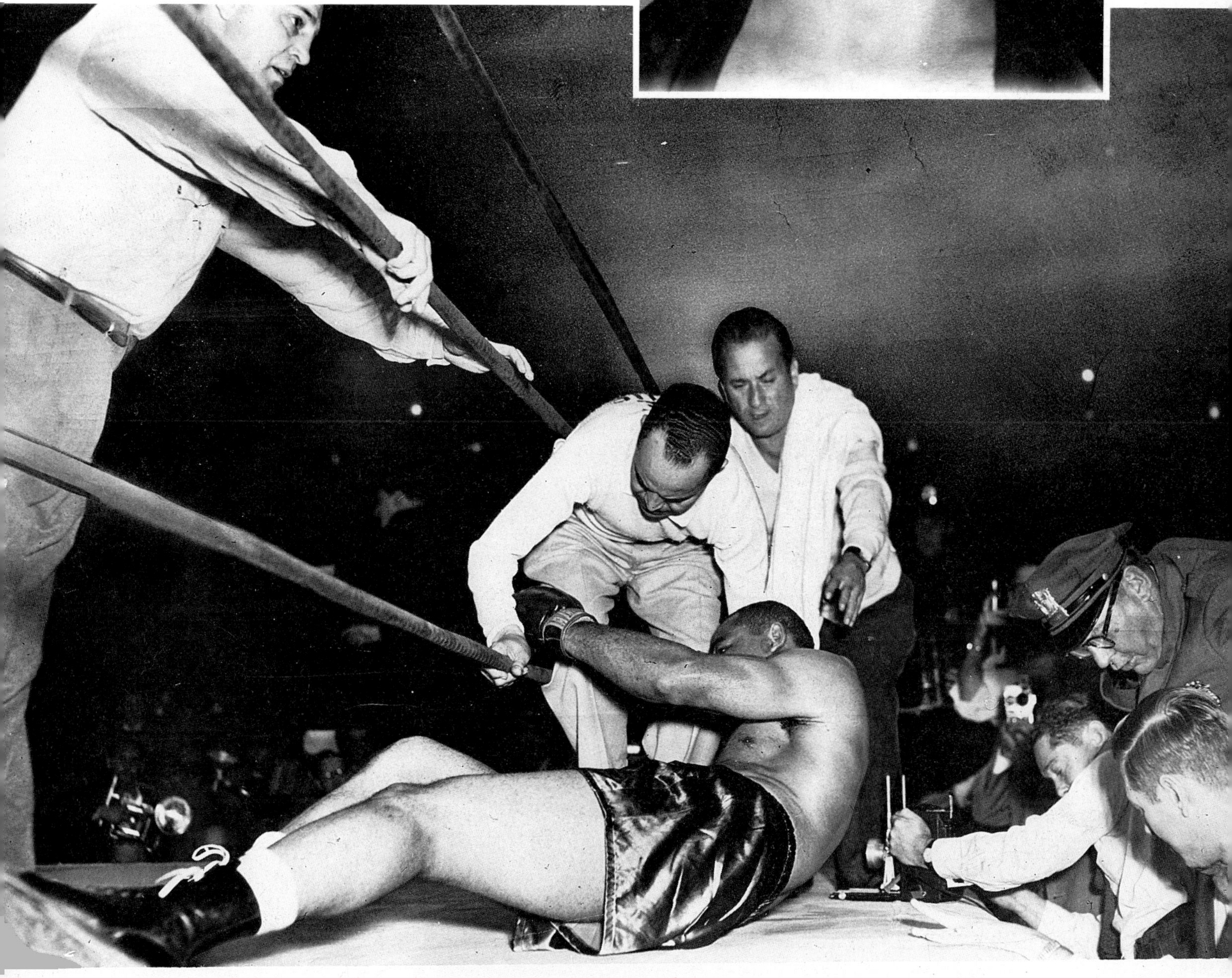

formance and laughed derisively as he frequently swung himself off balance.

A couple of quick knockouts over modest opposition in Gino Buonvino and Bernie Reynolds restored the gloss to Marciano's image, but it was his two-rounds demolition of Harry 'Kid' Matthews in July 1952 that clinched his title chance. Matthews had lost just three out of 87 fights, but at only 12 st 11 lb (179 lb) was not heavy enough to trouble Marciano. Two left hooks in the second swept Matthews off his feet, his head jarring off the bottom rope.

The defeat of Matthews removed the last obstacle from Marciano's path to the title fight, but the Walcott match took longer than expected to negotiate because the champion's manager, Felix Bocchicchio, had a criminal conviction in New York and could not get a licence there. The contracts were finally signed for 23 September 1952 at Municipal Stadium, Philadelphia. Walcott would get 40 per cent of the take against the challenger's 20 per cent, giving the New Jersey veteran a career-best payday of $138,070, plus $140,000 for the motion picture rights.

It was Braddock v Louis all over again, the aging champion against the seemingly unbeatable young contender, the old pro who had paid his dues against the media darling who had been manoeuvred into the title shot by a combination of shrewd matching and good publicity work. The Braddock v Louis parallel continued when Walcott floored Marciano with a perfect left hook in the first round, just as Braddock had done to Louis 15 years before. The knockdown left Marciano more embarrassed than hurt, and from the second to the sixth it was the challenger's fight as his crude, clubbing but hurtful blows slowed Walcott and sapped his strength. By the sixth both men were bleeding, Walcott from a cut over the left eye and Marciano from the scalp – but then, in the seventh,

The second-round destruction of Harry Matthews (inset) *in July 1952 set up Marciano's title fight with Walcott, but it took the aging champion less than a round to show Marciano that he would not be disposed of quite so easily.*

Marciano v Walcott developed into one of the classic title fights, with Marciano later claiming that for a long period he could not see out of his left eye, as a result of a heat-producing substance (allegedly smeared on the champion's neck and shoulder) rubbing into his eye whenever the pair came to close quarters.

Marciano began to fade.

He claimed later that he could not see out of his left eye, and Bocchicchio was accused of rubbing capsicum Vaseline, a heat-producing petroleum jelly, into Walcott's gloves so that it would affect his opponent's eyes. However Marciano claimed that the Vaseline was on the champion's body, between his neck and shoulder, so that every time the boxers came together, it rubbed into his eyes. But there were other theories – Sam Silverman, a New England fight figure who had promoted many of Rocky's early contests, told Everett M. Skehan, author of *Rocky Marciano*, that he blamed Marciano's own corner team for the problem:

> I was sitting ringside, right next to them. I think it was poor work, a mistake by his own handlers, that blinded Rocky. Whatever they used on his head got into his eyes. Al Weill had everybody crazy in the corner. Everybody got nerved up. Instead of using towels and pads, they hit the kid with a sponge and the cut stuff went right into his eyes. The poor kid couldn't see. He was getting the shit punched out of him.

Above and right: *The punch that launched a legend . . . Marciano's devastating right in the 13th round sends Walcott 'flowing down like flour out of a chute.' Walcott had staged a magnificent defence of his title, but that blow would perhaps have floored any champion in history, and the veteran never looked likely to beat the count.*

The judges agreed with Silverman's assessment of events; at the start of the 13th round they had Walcott in front by margins of 8-4, 7-5, and 7-4-1. Even if the champion lost the last three rounds, he could still save the title with a majority draw. He had only to carry on with the clever, cagey, countering battle he had been waging for 12 rounds, but then, not for the first time, one punch rewrote the record books. After 33 seconds of the 13th, as Walcott gave ground towards the ropes, he started to throw a right. Marciano launched his own, marginally faster, right, and it exploded on the veteran's jaw with devastating results.

It may well have been the single most telling punch in heavyweight history. Walcott went down as if he had been filletted, his body slithering down the ropes until it came to rest with his left arm hooked around the middle strand and his forehead touching the canvas. In A.J. Liebling's marvellous phrase, 'he flowed down like flour out of a chute', without a hope of beating referee Charley Daggert's count.

They were rematched in May 1953 in Chicago, but like so many return fights it proved a huge anti-climax as Walcott folded in just two minutes 25 seconds of the opening round. Marciano did the damage with a left hook followed by a right uppercut, but because Walcott's back had been towards the television cameras when the punches were thrown (in those days before multi-angled and instant replay pictures) the millions of television viewers, and many of the 'live' attendance of 16,034, assumed that the near 40-year-old

There was a rematch, of course, but this time Walcott collapsed in the opening round (left). The challenger's self-disgust is evident as he kicks disconsolately at the ropes, but the 16,034 spectators were even more unhappy, having paid $331,795 to watch just 145 seconds of action.

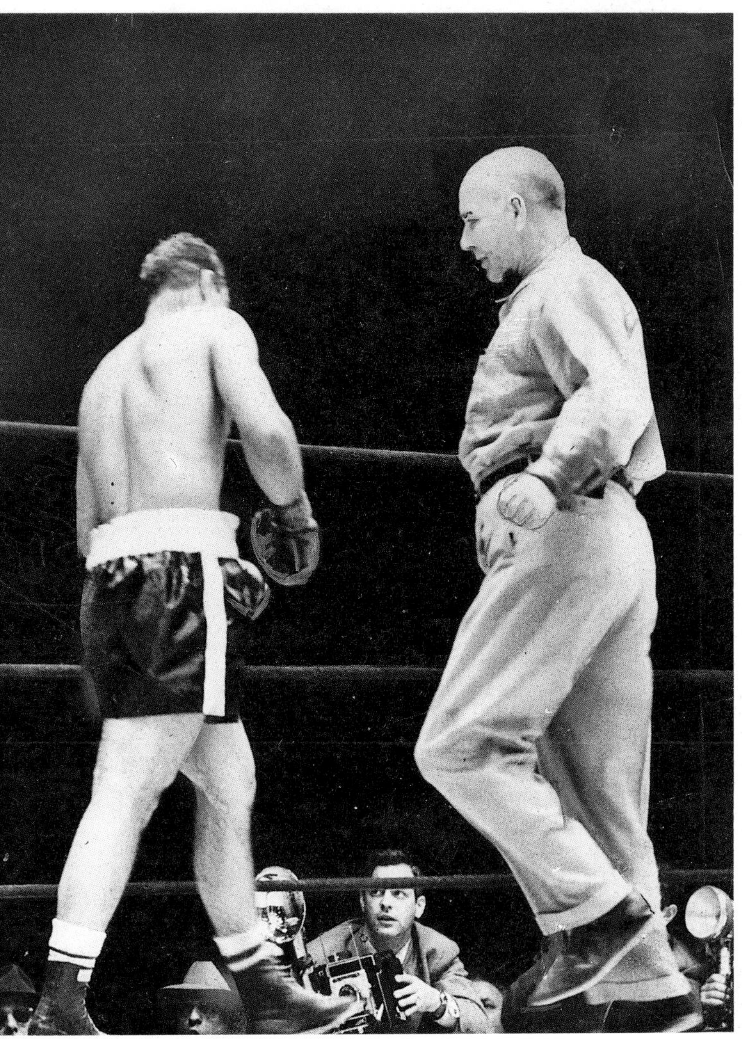

challenger had merely looked for a comfortable place to fall. Suspicions were not allayed by the curious revelation that Walcott, the knocked-out loser in their first fight, had been paid $250,000 for the rematch against the champion's $166,038.60. But at least the money cushioned Walcott's retirement; to no one's surprise he announced he would not box again.

Marciano needed a convincing win over a challenger with unquestionable credentials to restore his credibility, and Roland LaStarza, the man who had taken him to a desperately close and controversial split decision in 1950, got the job. A crowd of 44,562 came to the Polo Grounds, New York, on the night of 24 September 1953 to see if LaStarza could do it again. For six rounds he could; his smart boxing, coupled with Marciano's repeated fouling which caused referee Ruby Goldstein to penalize him the sixth round, moved LaStarza into a clear points lead.

The title was slipping away, but Marciano responded in the seventh with an assault of a sustained ferocity rarely seen in the ring. For three-and-a-half rounds he punched, battered, and

clubbed at any available target until at last, in the 11th the weary LaStarza was knocked through the ropes and onto the ring apron. He got to his knees at five and, unbelievably, was up at nine, but referee Ruby Goldstein had seen enough. After-

After his hard-earned win over Roland LaStarza (above left and right) *in his second title defence, Marciano opted for ex-champ Ezzard Charles as his next challenger. It seemed a safe match – but Charles fought superbly* (below). *It was the sixth and final time that Marciano was taken the full distance in his 49-fight career.*

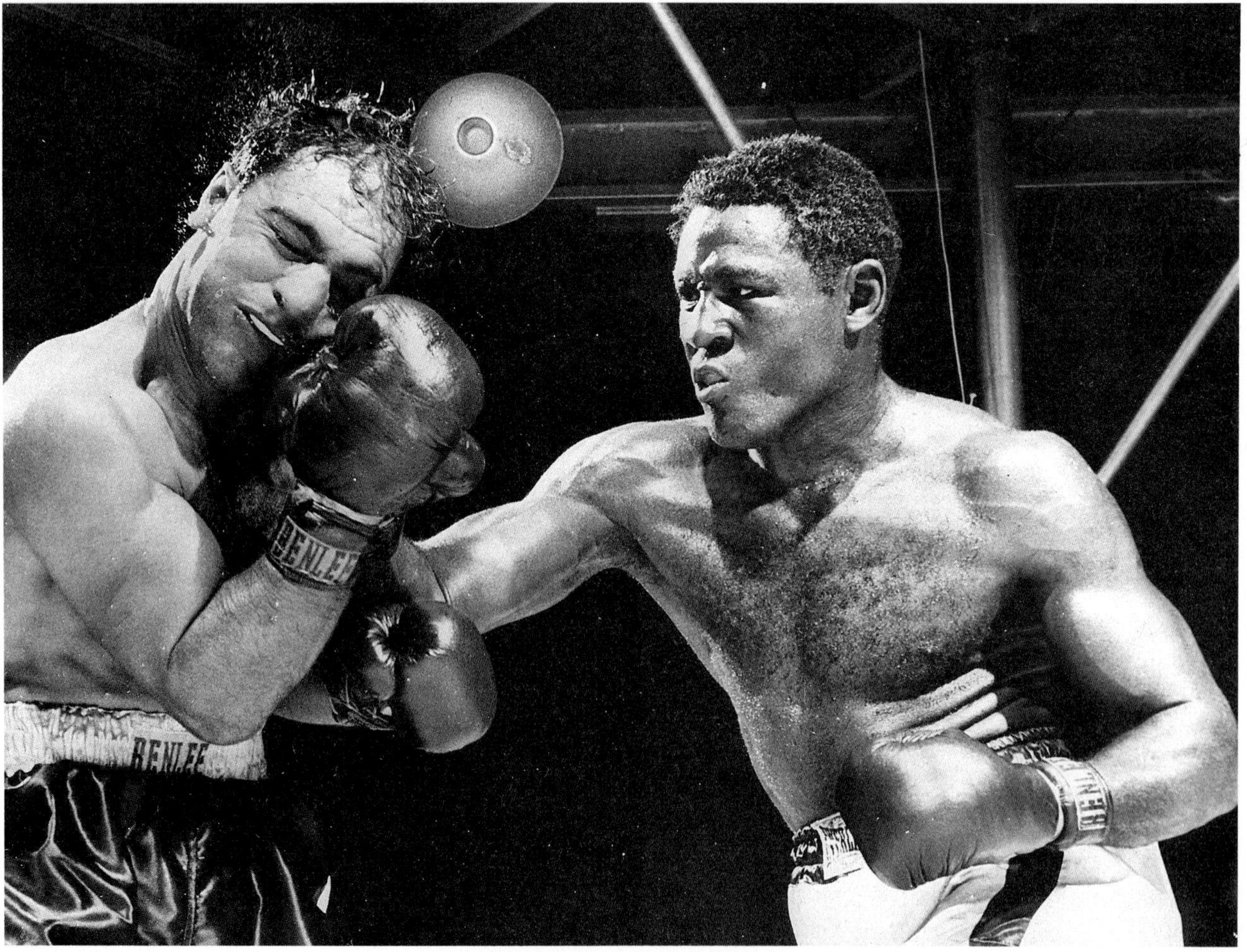

Marciano, bleeding from a bad cut over the left eye, fought himself to a standstill but could not force the stubborn 33-year-old veteran to surrender. Charles was exhausted at the final bell (above right) *but Marciano had nothing left either. It was Rocky's toughest challenge.*

wards, LaStarza was found to have broken bones and blood vessels in his arms, where Marciano had been hammering at them to bring down the guard. Wherever Marciano's blows landed, they inflicted damage.

It had been a tougher fight than expected, and Weill now looked around for a less demanding opponent. Ezzard Charles, the near 33-year-old ex-champion, had the right qualifications – he had been beaten in two of his previous four fights by the huge Cuban Nino Valdes, and by light-heavyweight Harold Johnson, who nine years later took the world title at that weight. Although his last two fights had brought respectable wins over Coley Wallace, who was beaten in the tenth, and Bob Satterfield, a heavy-hitting but vulnerable type who was stopped in the second round, Charles looked a 'safe' opponent. But he turned out to be anything but 'safe', and gave Marciano one of the most gruelling fights of his career.

Charles cut him by the left eye in the fourth, a wound that was two inches long and an inch deep. Liebling quotes Freddie Brown, Marciano's over-worked 'cuts man', as saying that 'With a cut like that, you got to be nervous – a quarter of an inch further in and it would of run like a faucet'.

But from the half-way stage Marciano's immense natural strength and ruggedness began to wear down Charles, and in the eighth it was Charles' turn to bleed, from a cut on the right eyelid. The challenger was in trouble in each of the rounds from the tenth to the 13th, but somehow found the heart and resilience to share the 14th. It was his last stand: Rocky drove him around the ring in the final round, but by now was so arm-weary himself that he could not summon up a final knockout punch, and the combination of Marciano's exhaustion and Charles' memorable courage ensured that the challenger survived the full course. Marciano won on a unanimous decision with scores of 8-5-2, 9-5-1, and 8-6-1. The crowd of 47,585 in Yankee Stadium on that June night in 1954 had witnessed one of the decade's great heavyweight fights – but many of them felt that they had also witnessed the start of Marciano's decline, for he had been unable to dispose of a stubborn but aging challenger inside the distance.

There had to be a rematch, and the Marciano doubters needed to wait only three months for their answer. Charles was floored by a right in the second, and thereafter clinched and mauled his way through the next three rounds, allowing Marciano to compile a wide points lead. But, in the sixth, the champion suffered perhaps the worst cut of an often gory career. Charles' right elbow caught Marciano's nose, splitting it as cleanly as if he had hit it with a hatchet. Blood geysered from the wound, as the blood vessels in his left nostril split.

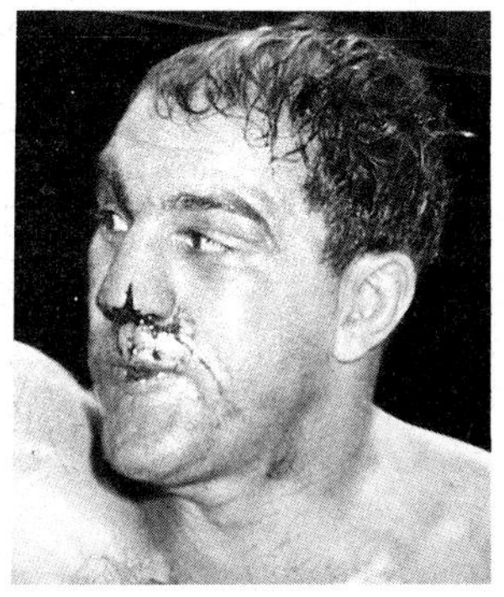

When the pair met again three months later, Marciano once more had to cope with a gory injury, this time to his nose. The cut was so bad that the champion's cornermen had to plead with the New York Commission's doctor not to stop the fight.

Marciano's cornermen pleaded with the Commission doctor not to stop the fight, and he reluctantly agreed to let it continue. With his title hanging by a bloody thread, Marciano went flat out for victory in the seventh. Charles somehow survived, but not for long. Trainer Charlie Goldman urged Marciano between rounds to 'Go after him now or you'll bleed to death', but when he resumed his onslaught in the eighth he ran onto a countering right which opened another cut in the corner of the left eye. But Marciano, fighting now with desperation, ignored the blood to smash a right to the head that dropped Charles for four. The challenger got up and staggered along one side of the ring; Marciano swung a wide left, and a right that grazed him as he fell again. This time, Charles stayed down on one knee until referee Al Berl had counted him out.

Charles never recaptured the fire of his first fight with Marciano, and was knocked out in the eighth in the rematch (above). *As with most ex-champs, the wins became harder to find when the title was gone, but Charles still managed some impressive results such as his second-round knockout of the dangerous Bob Satterfield* (right), *and his points win over the rugged Argentinian Cesar Brion* (below).

Opposite: *The last of the modern Great White Hopes, Gerry Cooney, fought aggressively and well against Larry Holmes in the richest championship fight in the division's history, but Holmes won in 13 rounds.*

The defeat finished Charles as a title contender, but like so many before him he could not accept that his career was in decline. He struggled on for another five years, losing 13 of his subsequent 23 fights against increasingly mediocre opposition before retiring, at 38, in September 1959.

Marciano's ninth-round pummelling of the immensely brave but outpunched Englishman Don

EVERLAST
PONY
PONY

Jerry 'The Bull' Martin (left) was a tough and persistent light-heavyweight challenger in the early 1980s, but found WBC title-holder Dwight Muhammad Qawi too good for him in this 1982 encounter. Qawi stopped him in the sixth.

Cockell at San Francisco in May 1955 earned the champion $130,124, but also a lasting reputation in Britain as a rough and even dirty fighter. Cockell was subjected to all kinds of foul tactics, so much so that radio commentator Eamonn Andrews was moved to say that: 'Marciano is one of the toughest champions who ever rubbed a foot in resin, but he has never read the rule books. He played a different sport from the one Cockell was taught. He butted unmercifully, he hit with the elbows, he hit low. A British referee would have sent him to his corner after three rounds.'

The catalogue of fouls was horrific: in the first round, Cockell was kidney-punched; in the third, he was hit after the bell; in the fourth, a butt split open a cut on his forehead; he was hit low in the fifth and again in the sixth, when he was also punched three times after the bell; in the seventh, he was butted and hit low again, and was hit in the ninth while on the floor – yet referee Frankie Brown, whose fee of $1,000 (then £357) was the highest ever paid to a championship official in California, did not issue a solitary caution.

With Cockell's defeat, Marciano had virtually cleaned up the heavyweight division. The only man who could conceivably have given him a worthwhile test, Nino Valdes of Cuba, had been outsmarted in an open-air 15-rounder in Las Vegas by light-heavyweight champion Archie Moore, who kept moving the bigger man around so that the desert sun was constantly in his eyes.

That win had given some validity to Moore's ambition to challenge for the heavyweight title. He was one of the most astonishing characters the game had ever produced. Even his age was a mystery: he said that he was born on 13 December 1916, but his mother (who was there at the time) insisted that he had been born three years earlier, which made him 41 years old when he started campaigning for the Marciano fight. He had been a professional for nearly 17 years before he finally got a chance at the light-heavyweight title, then held by Joey Maxim, and in his three years as champion had tightened his grip on the title with two defences against Maxim, a 14th-round stoppage of Harold Johnson, and a third-round

Above: *Archie Moore, the ancient light-heavyweight champion, established his right to meet Marciano with this 15-round points win over the Cuban, Nino Valdes (left) in May 1955.*

Below and right: *The roly-poly Englishman Don Cockell showed commendable courage in his ninth-round defeat by Marciano in May 1955, but had to contend with some extraordinarily lenient refereeing as Marciano was allowed to commit foul after foul, including this blatant head-butt.*

knockout of middleweight champ, Carl 'Bobo' Olson.

Between fights, Moore used to bloat to 30–40 lb above the championship limit, but being a supreme self-publicist he convinced sports writers that he had acquired a secret weight-reducing formula from the Australian aborigines while he was boxing there in 1940. The formula, according to Moore, was distilled from the bark of the eucalyptus tree and helped melt the pounds away magically. No one, apparently, thought to ask him why he was not marketing the miracle formula commercially, which would have made him considerably more money than he was earning from the demanding but not especially rewarding business of being light-heavyweight champion. The truth, however, was much more mundane: Moore simply chewed the goodness from meat and discarded the pulp, thereby obtaining the nourishment without the bulk.

Since Moore was in the same predicament as Marciano, having no attractive challengers in his own division, he began applying his publicity talents towards the pursuit of a fight with the heavyweight champion. For months he bombarded sports editors and writers with letters, clippings, poems, cartoons, and anything else that he thought might stir interest in the proposition. Marciano was happy to play along, and let the interest gradually build – he was confident that he could beat 'Ancient Archie', but it was in both their interests to milk the publicity for all it was worth. The fight really sold itself, making even Moore's promotional genius unnecessary. The light-heavyweight champion had won 21 in a row, and had either knocked out or stopped 120 of his 190 opponents. (Before he retired in 1963, Moore disposed of a further 25 assorted heavies and light-heavies, thereby setting a record of 145 victories inside the distance. It is inconceivable that, in these days of 40-fight 'veterans', Moore's total will ever be equalled.)

Only the Battle of the Long Count, nearly 30 years previously, drew higher receipts. It grossed $2,248,117, and the 61,574 fans who turned up at Yankee Stadium on the evening of 21 September 1955 represented the largest crowd of Marciano's career. The fight had been postponed for 24 hours because of fears that Hurricane Ione, which had been threatening the New York area, might strike. In fact, it was a dry autumn evening, and the only storms would be in the ring. As with all Marciano's fights, the thrills were not long in coming: early in the second Marciano missed with a right and started to throw a left, but Moore stepped inside it with a classically short right, and the champion was down.

The astonishing Moore took on all-comers, from middleweight champion Carl 'Bobo' Olson (right, *en route to a third-round knockout defeat in a 1955 light-heavyweight title bid) to heavyweights like Bert Whitehurst* (below), *whom Archie hammered in 10 rounds in 1958.*

The standing eight count, normally operative in New York, had been waived for this fight, but referee Harry Kessler apparently forgot. When Marciano rose groggily at two, clutching the top rope and gazing out at the crowd, Kessler continued the count to four and then wiped the champion's gloves. In all, eight seconds had elapsed before Moore was allowed to resume the attack, and in that time Marciano's head had cleared sufficiently to enable him to survive. Those extra six seconds probably cost Moore the title. His record shows him to have been the greatest

Moore's brush with immortality . . . Marciano goes down in the first round, but though he got up at 'two', referee Harry Kessler restrained Moore from attacking again until a further six seconds had elapsed. The heavyweight title was within Moore's reach, but in boxing, more than any other sport, the difference between glory and obscurity can be slight . . . as slight as six seconds.

From the third round onwards Marciano took charge, rocking the 41-year-old Moore with a barrage of hooks and uppercuts.

finisher of them all, and the dazed, near-defenceless Marciano would have been an easy target.

Moore was scathing about Kessler (whom he had first encountered during his amateur career, 20 years earlier) in his autobiography *The Archie Moore Story:*

> I was so furious at Kessler I thought I'd better hit him first and get that obstacle out of the way. But as it was, I turned to fight Rocky and I was blind and stupid with rage. And my rage wasn't directed at Marciano, because so far he was the only one cooperating with me... I felt I now had to fight two men.

Archie's chance was gone, and even though the fight lasted into the ninth it had become, from the third onwards, a grim struggle for survival as Marciano steam-rollered through Moore's skills, pounding at any available inch of target area. By the sixth Moore was almost spent – he was floored twice, once for four and then, in the round's dying moments, for eight. He came back to win the seventh, with a champion's pride and flourish, but he had nothing left and was on the canvas again as the bell ended the eighth. The Commission doctor, Vincent Nardiello, asked him between rounds if he wanted to quit. Moore's reply was memorable: 'I too am a champion', he said, 'and I'll go down fighting.'

One minute into the ninth, Marciano ended it. A stream of hooks drove Moore across the ring, and he sagged to the canvas against the ropes, grabbing at the middle strand as he went down. He almost rose at eight, but then sat back heavily, his left arm hooked over the rope, and was counted out in that position. After the fight, according to Moore, a sportswriter encountered Charley Johnston, the challenger's manager, in the corridor leading to the dressing room. 'He asked Charley if he was going to see how I was,' Moore recalled. 'Charley's answer was my moment of truth. He said he didn't care how I was, he was going to see how much we had gotten on the losing end'. Johnston's misplaced priorities cost him a world champion – Moore said he never spoke to him again, 'aside from necessity' – but since Archie's total purse had come to $241,187 the manager's eagerness was understandable.

Floyd and the Hammer of Thor

MARCIANO never fought again. On 21 April 1956 he announced his retirement, bowing out with what remains the only perfect record of any of the 26 men who, up to the time of writing in early 1987, have held the undisputed heavyweight championship of the world – 49 fights, 49 wins, 43 inside the distance. Such was the magnetism of the Marciano name that even into his forties he was being propositioned to make a comeback, but common sense prevailed.

Marciano's retirement virtually ended the stranglehold which Jim Norris and the IBC had enjoyed on the heavyweight title. Two days before Rocky's announcement, the Federal Government started proceedings against the IBC under the 'anti-trust' (anti-monopoly) laws, claiming that the IBC had staged 36 of the 44 championship fights between 1949 and 1953.

The IBC was on the ropes, and was dealt a further blow by the decision to nominate Floyd Patterson, the 1952 Olympic middleweight champion, to fight Archie Moore for the vacant title. Patterson was managed by Cus D'Amato, a fiercely independent New Yorker who had guided Patterson up the ratings without any help from Norris, and who was determined that he alone would remain the master of his fighter's future. Patterson's sole defeat was a disputed points loss to the former light-heavyweight champion Joey Maxim, and he had earned his chance at the vacant championship by outscoring the eccentric Tommy 'Hurricane' Jackson in an eliminator six weeks after Marciano's retirement.

On 30 November 1956, Patterson's distinctive leaping left hooks accounted for Moore in the fifth round at Chicago. Patterson, who at 21 years and 10 months had become the youngest man to win the heavyweight title, was a little over half his opponent's age. D'Amato stubbornly resisted all attempts to draw him into the IBC fold, so instead Patterson defended against non-IBC connected

The young Floyd Patterson (right) scores a fifth-round win over Willie Troy in New York in January 1955.

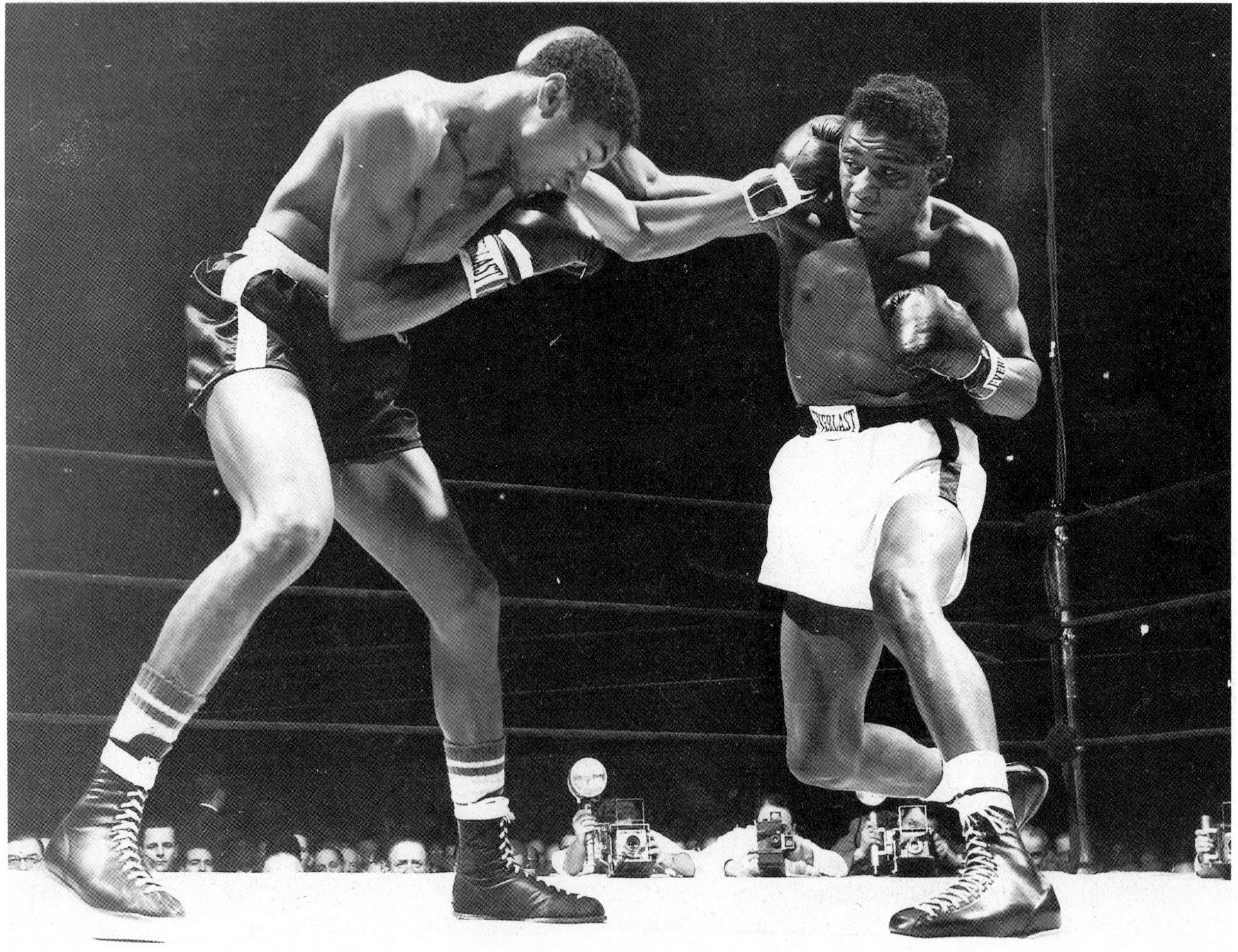

challengers such as Pete Rademacher, the 1956 Olympic heavyweight champion who was having his first professional fight; Roy Harris, a schoolteacher from the gloriously named town of Cut 'N'Shoot, Texas; Hurricane Jackson, in a rematch; and the former British champion Brian London, who defied the British Board of Control to meet Patterson in Indianapolis in 1959 and was fined

Above: *Tommy 'Hurricane' Jackson (left) took Patterson the distance in this 12-round final eliminator for the title.*

Having won the vacant title by knocking out Archie Moore, Patterson and his mentor Cus D'Amato took no chances on losing it. Floyd defended it against safe opponents like Peter Rademacher (below, *who was having his first pro fight) and Roy Harris* (right), *who floored him.*

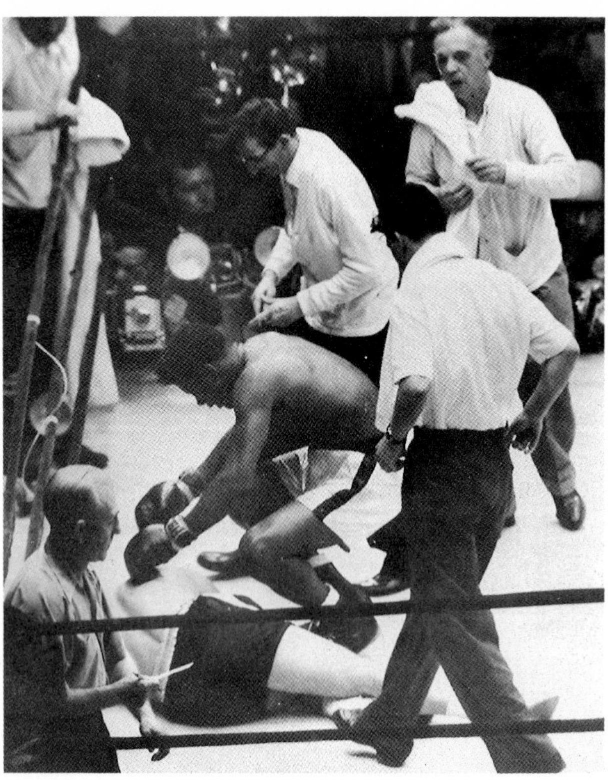

Patterson, apologetic as ever, flattened English challenger Brian London in May 1959 (left) *and then signed to meet the hard-hitting Swede Ingemar Johansson* (above) *the following month. It was a rare mistake by Cus D'Amato, and it proved costly.*

£1,100 for his impudence. London was not complaining, though: he was knocked out in 11 rounds, but after paying the fine he still walked away with over £20,000.

Patterson and D'Amato were pilloried for avoiding the leading contenders like Zora Folley and Eddie Machen, but Floyd's opponents were handpicked for political as much as professional reasons. D'Amato did his best for Patterson, enabling the one-time problem teenager to gross over eight million dollars in a long and lucrative career. However, his champion's place in the heavyweight merit list is perhaps lower than it need have been because of D'Amato's ultra-cautious and ultra-independent approach to management.

When Patterson signed to defend against Sweden's dimple-chinned Ingemar Johansson at Yankee Stadium in June 1959, it was thought to be just another routine assignment for him. European heavyweights have never enjoyed a high reputation in America, and *Swedish* heavyweights even less so. Although the 26-year-old challenger was ranked No. 1 by the influential *Ring* magazine, whose ratings were accepted in those days as quasi-official, Johansson was better known for his debacle in the 1952 Olympic heavyweight final, when he was disqualified for 'not trying' against the giant American, Ed Sanders.

According to A. J. Liebling, 'Sanders was so big that his final opponent, a Swede, simply ran away. The judges disqualified the Swede, who said afterwards that it had suddenly occurred to him he might be killed.' Johansson's version, published in

his autobiography *Seconds Out of the Ring* was predictably different:

> I knew that I neither had the condition nor the knowledge to take the American by attacks without taking risks simultaneously. I intended not to try attacking him in the first two rounds and to save myself for the last to try to snatch a points advantage.

French referee Roger Vaisberg, however, was not prepared to wait for the planned third-round explosion and instead disqualified Johansson at the end of the second.

'I can see through what happened now', Johansson wrote with astonishing self-delusion. 'I fought badly because I was badly trained. Sanders did just as badly for his part. The referee could have put life into the struggle if he had been a more experienced referee. The fault was with him more than anyone else.' It was certainly an original interpretation of a fight in which, on the Swede's own admission, he did not even attempt a single blow.

Johansson had disgraced himself in the 1952 Olympic final, when he was disqualified against American Ed Sanders (above). *Sanders had a brief pro career, but died after a fight in Boston in 1952. Johansson lived down his Olympic fiasco with a string of impressive pro wins, including this fifth-round defeat of Karl Schiegl* (left) *in 1955 – although his unorthodox training methods, featuring all the comforts of home, raised a few eyebrows.*

Such a history did nothing to inspire American confidence in Johansson's chances of upsetting Patterson, particularly as the champion – then a dazzling 17-year-old middleweight – had been considered one of the star performers of the same Olympics in which Johansson had disgraced himself.

Johansson had an eccentric approach to training. To the horror of traditionalists, he installed his gorgeous girl friend Birgit in the training camp, and his exercises were rumoured to be more horizontal than vertical in the weeks leading up to the title fight. The couple were pictured dancing in the hotel attached to his training quarters at Grossingers,

outside New York, and the Swede did nothing to dispel the image created for him of a playboy.

'My training was incomparably better than Floyd's', he argued. 'He was put in a closed-in unhealthy gymnasium under artifically ascetic conditions. He slept in a cubicle-type room in the training barn, far from his wife and children, and chewed sadly the monotonous beef diet which superstition prescribes for American boxers'.

The press thought him an amiable fool, but Johansson and his shrewd adviser Edwin Alquist knew what they were doing. Johansson had tremendous one-punch hitting power, especially with the right, and the American trade did not take sufficient note of the first-round knockout he had scored in his previous fight over the top-ranked Eddie Machen, a man whom Patterson had avoided. Johansson had also flattened good European opposition including Henry Cooper, Joe Erskine and Heinz Neuhaus, but this did not cut much ice in American circles. He had become European champion in 1956 by kayoing the Italian Franco Cavicchi and had retained the title against Cooper and Erskine. Johansson's overall record showed 20 wins in 20 fights, with only seven going the full distance.

The Americans should have taken more note of Johansson's knockouts of good-class heavyweights like Eddie Machen (inset) *and Henry Cooper.*

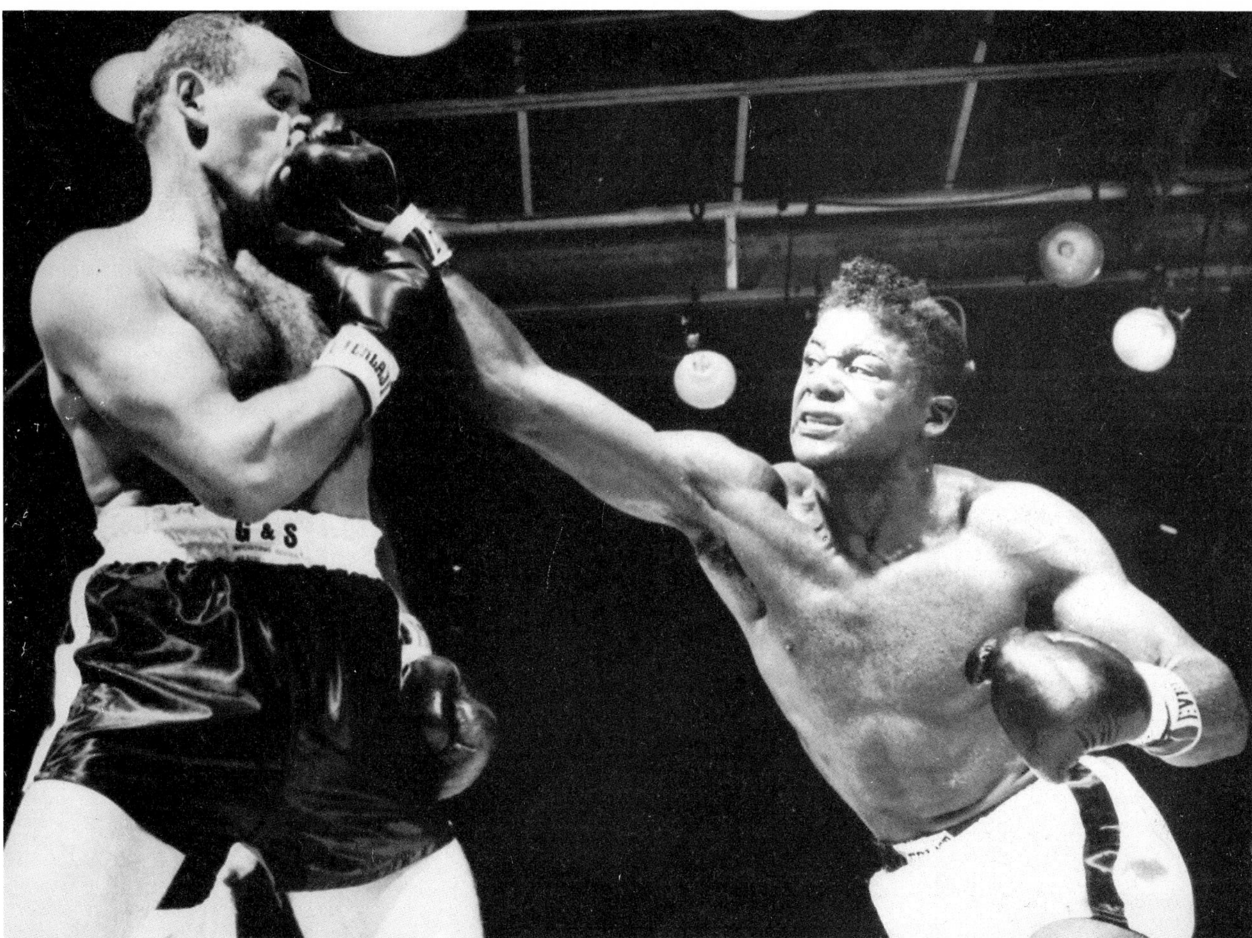

With hindsight, Johansson should have been given much more chance than he was of beating the brittle Patterson, who took a total of 17 counts during his championship career and had even been dropped by Pete Rademacher, who was having his first professional outing. What Rademacher could do, surely the hardest hitting heavyweight to come out of Europe since Max Schmeling could match?

The American public thought not, and only 18,215 turned up at Yankee Stadium on 26 June 1959 to watch him try. The attendance was 3,500 fewer than for Patterson's Los Angeles defence against Roy Harris ten months earlier, although the champion's pay for the Johansson fight was more than six times what he had grossed from the Harris fight.

For two rounds it looked as though the press had got it right: Johansson had not landed a worthwhile blow, and Patterson seemed to have matters well under control. But then, in the opening minute of the third, Johansson clipped him with a left hook and followed with the right – the much-publicized but so far invisible 'Ingo's Bingo'. It landed flush on Patterson's mouth: a few inches lower, on the jaw, and the fight might have ended there and then. Patterson went over for a count of 'nine', and was so dazed when he arose that he walked towards a neutral corner. (He explained afterwards that he

The Swede was dismissed as a no-hoper when he faced Patterson at Yankee Stadium, New York on 26 June 1959. Patterson controlled the early exchanges (above), *but once 'Ingo's Bingo' connected in the third round* (below) *it was a different story. Seven knockdowns later, the world had a new heavyweight champion.*

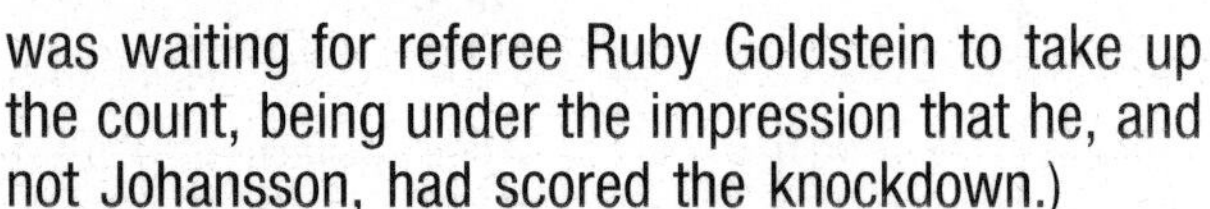

was waiting for referee Ruby Goldstein to take up the count, being under the impression that he, and not Johansson, had scored the knockdown.)

Johansson put him down six more times in the most one-sided round since Louis had destroyed Schmeling in their rematch, and when Patterson fell for the seventh time Goldstein waved the challenger away without bothering to take up the count. It had taken the man who only six and a half years previously had been accused by the Swedish Boxing Association's chairman of 'bringing shame to the Swedish name' a mere eight minutes and three seconds to become Scandinavia's greatest ever sporting idol.

But Ingo's victory did not make him any more professional in his approach to the business: it merely meant that he now had the funds to have an even better time than he had enjoyed as challenger. He spent a happy 12 months wringing every last kroner from the championship and the contrast between his year and Patterson's could not have been more striking. Patterson, complex and obsessive, was so ashamed of his performance that he immediately went into seclusion, trying to remedy the flaws that had caused his downfall, and honing his mind and body into the finest shape of his life, in preparation for the return fight.

It took place at the Polo Grounds on 20 June 1960 and Patterson, already the youngest holder of the title, became the first man to regain it. He did so with the greatest display of his career, in a manner graphically recorded by George Whiting, the most stylish boxing writer of his generation, in the London *Evening Standard:*

The moody and reclusive Patterson lived like a hermit (above left) *while he trained for the rematch with Johansson, and when it took place (359 days later) the American's left hook made him the first man in history to regain the heavyweight title* (below).

Here comes sweet and savage revenge – born of despair, cradled in determination and fashioned in sweat.

America's Floyd Patterson, the fighting man they said could never come back, is once again heavyweight champion of the world – the first of his rough profession ever to regain the title in sixty years of boxing. He did it with two murderous left hooks in New York's perspiring Polo Grounds – delivered in 1 min 51 secs of the fifth round on the head of Ingemar Johansson, the dimpled Swede who toppled him off the summit almost exactly a year ago.

Rarely have fighting fortunes switched so suddenly, so dramatically, so savagely. With the shattered Swede lying flat and lifeless near his frantic corner, the triumphant Patterson flung his arms to the heavens, waved joyously to the crowd, and then, remembering that gallantry is called for in the moment of victory, ran smartly to the assistance of his crumpled opponent.

In fact, Patterson believed that he had seriously injured Johansson, and the sight of the Swede lying unconscious, blood trickling from the corner of his mouth and his leg twitching in spasms, disturbed the new champion so profoundly that he was never again able to recapture the cold, controlled ferocity of that historic performance.

Patterson retained the title in a third meeting with Johansson in March 1961, in a wild brawl which saw the champion on the floor twice in the first round. Yet he came back to drop Johansson near the end of the round, and then knocked him out in the sixth. With the tiresome Swede finally out of the way, Patterson and D'Amato picked up where they had left off before Johansson interrupted them. A white, crew-cut ex-footballer from Boston called Tom McNeeley was selected as the next challenger, on the basis of a 23-0 record which, predictably, did not include any wins over worth-

The third Patterson v Johansson fight was an up-and-down affair, with Patterson on the floor twice in the first round (right) *before knocking out the Swede in the sixth. His next challenger, Tom McNeeley, was less threatening and was beaten inside four rounds* (below).

while opposition. McNeeley, hopelessly outclassed, was floored ten times and kayoed in four rounds at Maple Leaf Gardens, Toronto in December 1961 – but even he managed to score a knockdown over the vulnerable champion.

While Patterson and D'Amato were working their way through the lower reaches of the division, an upheaval was in progress at the top. The brooding, menacing figure of Sonny Liston, a former hoodlum and strike breaker from Arkansas, was clubbing his way up the ratings with a series of chillingly destructive victories over some of the best men around. Cleveland Williams, perhaps the hardest punching heavyweight of the decade, was beaten twice inside three rounds; Mike De John went in six; Nino Valdes in three; and Roy Harris, the Texan who had taken Patterson into the 12th round and even floored him, was dismissed contemptously inside a round. By May 1960 Liston was ranked No.

Mean and menacing Sonny Liston (above) *was regarded as the uncrowned king for at least two years before he won the title. While Patterson and Johansson tossed the championship back and forth, the powerful ex-convict was consolidating his position at the top of the rankings with stunning performances like this third-round demolition of the once formidable Cuban, Nino Valdes. The knockout, in Chicago in August 1959, was Liston's 18th consecutive win. In his previous fight, Liston had flattened the big-hitting Cleveland Williams in three rounds.*

1 and when in the space of two and a half months in late 1960 he defeated Zora Folley and Eddie Machen the demand for Patterson to face the man whom many already regarded as the uncrowned champion grew deafening.

Patterson had always been careful to avoid both Folley and Machen, each of whom had fully deserved a title chance during either of Patterson's tenures. Yet Liston flattened Folley in three rounds and then, as if to prove that he was not just a crude slugger, comfortably outpointed the skilful Machen (at the time ranked No. 2) in a 12-round eliminator.

In the more liberal 1980s possession of a criminal record is virtually a prerequisite for recognition as a heavyweight contender, to the point where it is considered worthy of attention if the fighter concerned has *not* been in trouble with the law. But things were very different in the moralistic climate of 1960. Liston was condemned outright as a 'jailbird', with few bothering to explore the appalling social background which had moulded him. Liston's father had married twice, and Sonny (real name Charles) had 24 half-brothers and sisters. When he was 13 he ran away from the family home in Arkansas to live with his mother in

Much of Liston's consuming aggression derived from his tough and unhappy childhood, in Arkansas and then in St Louis.

St Louis, but because his childhood had been spent working in the fields instead of the schoolroom the hulking youngster was put in a class with children five years his junior, who mocked the illiterate, withdrawn, and unhappy boy. He endured it for a year, and then fled to the streets where he ran wild, eventually finishing up in prison for armed robbery.

The prison's Catholic chaplin, Father Charles Stephens, took an interest in Liston, encouraging him to take up boxing, which he did professionally after being paroled in 1953. Like so many delinquents before and since, Liston found salvation in the ring. Only one man had beaten him, the seasoned old professional Marty Marshall, who broke Liston's jaw in the second round of his eighth fight. Despite this setback Sonny survived another six rounds to lose on points, and he trounced Marshall twice in rematches. By the end of 1961 Liston's record stood at 33 wins in 34 fights, 23 inside the distance.

Patterson's position was becoming untenable for a man who, whatever his technical deficiences, never lacked courage or pride. At last, tired of being called a 'cheese champion' and 'a pretender', Floyd ignored D'Amato's advice and signed to meet Liston in Chicago on 25 September 1962. The contest was projected as 'Beauty v the Beast'.

It took Liston only 126 seconds to annihilate the thoroughly intimidated Patterson in Chicago. Patterson had been so sure of the outcome that he had even brought a false beard and glasses with him to the stadium, to enable him to escape in disguise afterwards.

Patterson had a carefully burnished image as the sport's 'Mr Clean', a self-effacing, hard-working, church-going family man. The image suited the mood of the times – John F. Kennedy was then in the White House, and his brother Robert, the Attorney General, was engaged in the biggest attack yet launched on organized crime in America. Liston, the one-time convict, had a list of friends and associates which included many of the names being investigated by Robert Kennedy's Justice Department. When the squeaky-clean Patterson was summoned for an audience with the President, it seemed to elevate the fight almost to a Holy War, a Crusade – but this time it would have paid to put your money on the infidels.

Joseph D. O'Brian summed up the fight succintly in a *Ring* magazine feature in February 1987:

> Floyd Patterson was the Hope of the Civilized World. John F. Kennedy was counting on him. Eleanor Roosevelt was counting on him. Every parlour liberal who ever attended a Pete Seeger concert or voted for Adlai Stevenson was counting on him. Every middle-class black who figured Sonny Liston would give the race a bad name was counting on him. And after two minutes, the referee was counting on him, all the way to ten.

Patterson had been so thoroughly demoralized by Liston's vast, intimidating presence that he had even brought a false beard and glasses to the stadium to enable him to escape in disguise after his humiliation. (Patterson, an obsessively private man whom one wit dubbed 'Freudian Floyd', was reported to spend $3,000 a year on theatrical make-up.) He performed like a man in a trance, mesmerized like a stoat by a snake. Liston needed only 126 seconds to show the world that he was not merely a media creation, but a fighter of formidable, even frightening, talent and power.

The new champion was a man of mystery – even his age was a matter of dispute. He claimed to have been born on 8 May 1932, but had a daughter who was in her late teens. Liston discouraged probing questions with an icy stare, and consequently the known details about his life are sketchy. He remains the only major figure in heavyweight history who has not been the subject of at least one biography.

There was the usual rematch, in the Las Vegas Convention Hall on 22 July 1963, but Floyd's dreams of beating the odds disappeared in exactly 130 seconds as Liston floored him three times and knocked him out. 'I know the public isn't with me but that's their bad luck', Liston told the press afterwards. 'They'll just have to swing along with me until somebody else comes along'.

The rematch, in Las Vegas, took only four seconds longer. Liston looked unbeatable – but Cassius Clay (below) *had other ideas.*

But that 'somebody else' had already arrived, and was sitting comfortably in the No. 1 contender spot in the ratings, even though no one seriously believed he could dethrone the mighty Liston. He was the descendant of a slave, with the pride and arrogance of an emperor, and he had the improbable name of Cassius Marcellus Clay.

'Float Like a Butterfly'

CASSIUS CLAY'S name derived from his ancestors' 'owner', a southern Senator of some minor significance in American history. As was the custom in those days, slaves were given their owner's name to signify that they were his property. Yet it was the black Cassius Clay, the son of a sign-painter from Louisville, Kentucky, who was destined to make an impact on American and even world history far greater than that achieved by his white namesake. Clay had been introduced to boxing as a skinny 8 st (112 lb) 12-year-old by a Louisville policeman, Joe Martin. He first attracted international attention at the Rome Olympic Games in 1960 when his bombastic, boastful, clowning personality – which fortunately was matched by a dazzlingly original talent in the ring – made him the Games' outstanding discovery. He beat the best that Europe and Australia had to offer, winning the light-heavyweight gold medal, but while his exuberant style filled acres of newsprint, no one really took him seriously when he announced that he was destined to become the greatest heavyweight champion the sport had known.

However, a syndicate of white businessmen from his hometown were sufficiently impressed by his commercial possibilities to offer him a professional contract, engaging the vastly experienced and knowledgeable Angelo Dundee as his trainer and nominally his manager. Clay was a product of an era when successful sportsmen did *not* brag or boast, least of all if they were Americans, who invariably attributed their success to Mom, apple pie, and the 'American Way'. Clay was wildly and boisterously different: basing his act on that of the wrestler 'Gorgeous' George, his 'I am the Greatest' quickly became an international catch-phrase.

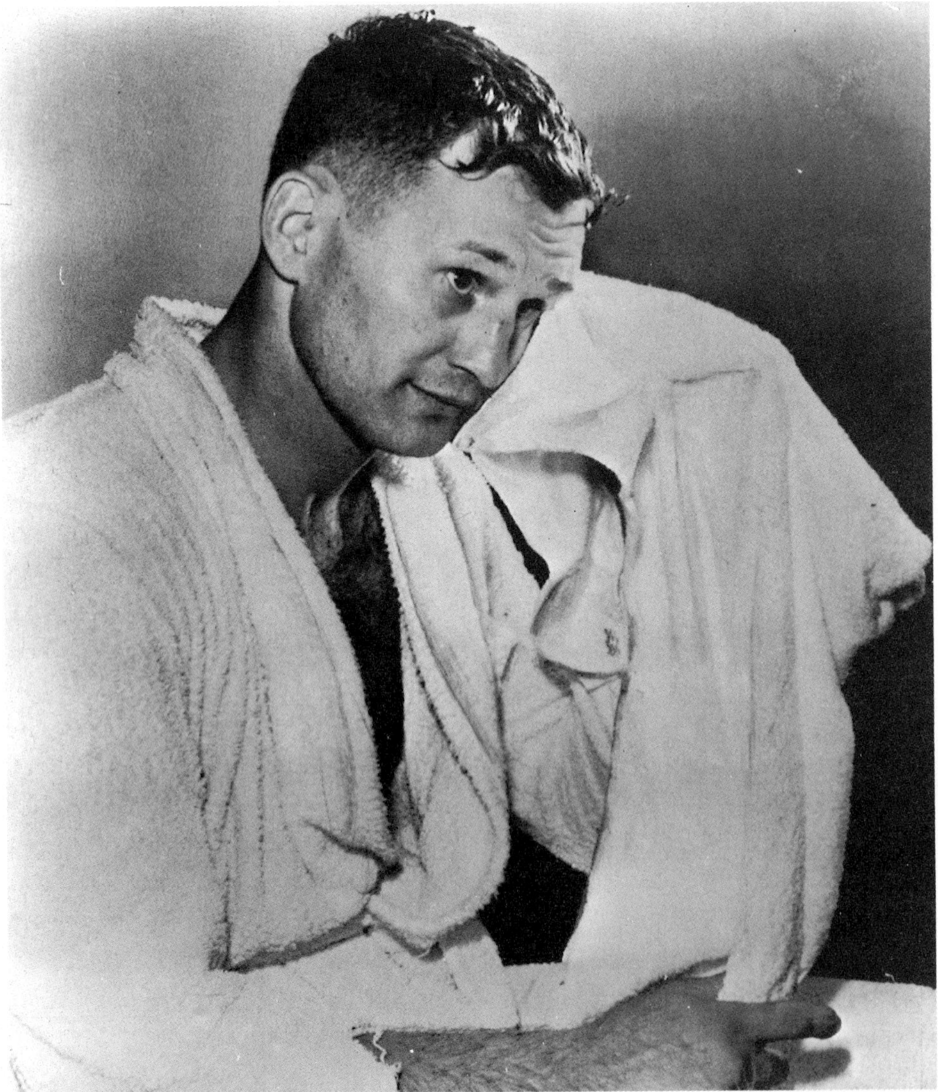

He is not instantly recognizable, but Tunney Hunsaker has his own niche in the record book. The ex-policeman and part-time fighter from West Virginia was Cassius Clay's first professional opponent, losing on points over six rounds in Clay's hometown of Louisville on 29 October 1960.

Right: *Britain's popular Frank Bruno (on the right) flattered to deceive in the early rounds of his WBA title bid against Tim Witherspoon at Wembley in 1986, but the American ground him down in 11 rounds.*

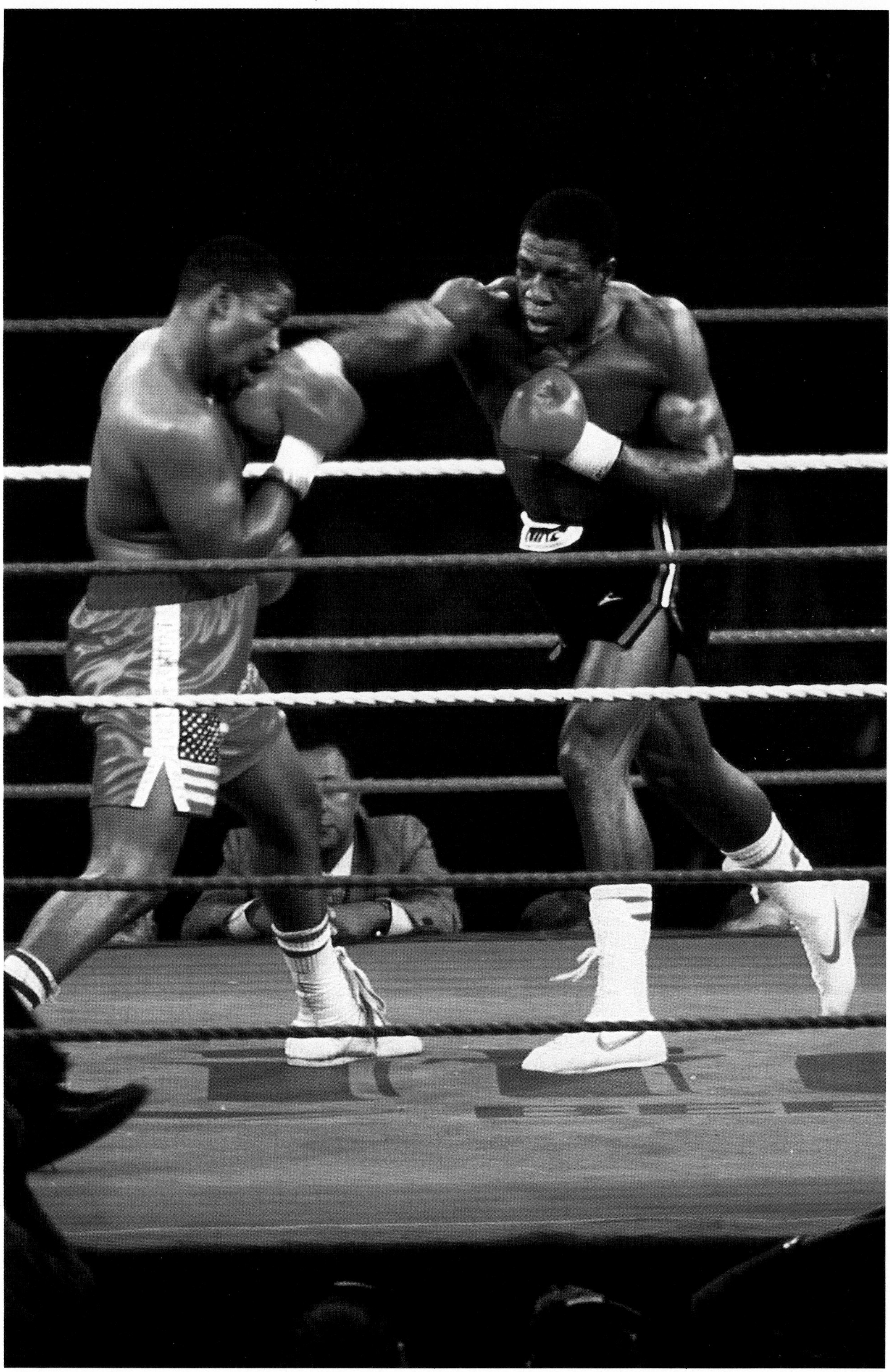

CAESARS
PALACE

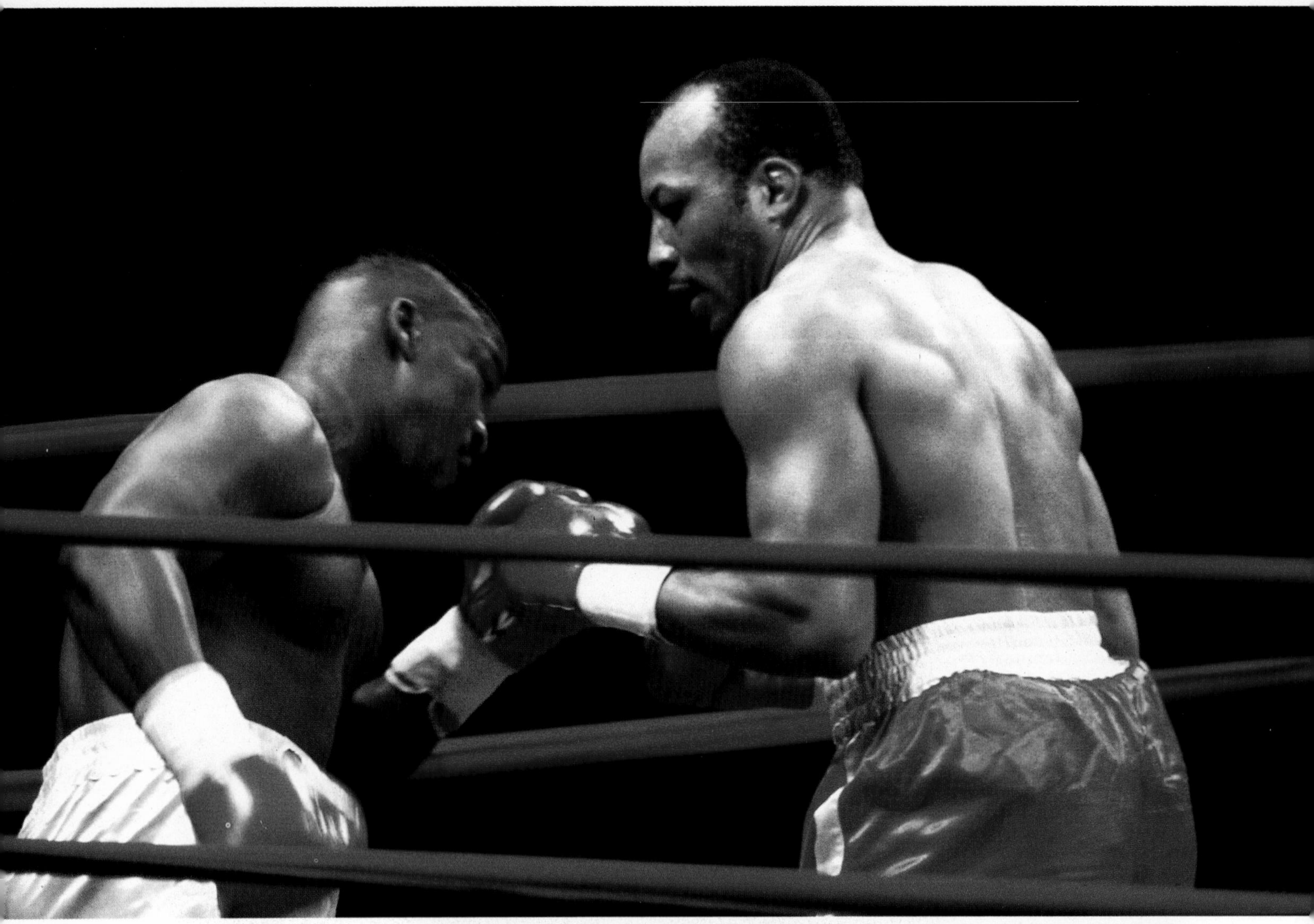

Previous pages: *a breathtaking panoramic view of Fight Night at Headquarters, Caesars Palace.* Above: *James 'Bonecrusher' Smith became the first college graduate to win a heavyweight title when he crushed Tim Witherspoon inside a round at Madison Square Garden in December 1986, and he fought a smart fight to frustrate Mike Tyson* (right) *three months later in their unification match. Tyson won an overwhelming points victory, but at least Smith avoided the usual fate of Tyson rivals.*

After this fourth-round win over his one-time trainer Archie Moore in November 1962, the boxing world was forced to take the boisterous youngster seriously. It was Clay's big breakthrough, but Moore's farewell: the veteran never fought again in a genuine contest.

Clay began predicting the rounds in which his opponents would be beaten, couching the predictions in doggerel (but often very funny) verse. The world had never seen anything quite like Cassius Clay, and could not get enough of him – especially when he fulfilled his predictions to the minute. His early opponents included the usual share of soft touches, but there were some worthwhile men amongst them such as Alonzo Johnson, George Logan, Alejandro Lavorante, and Alex Miteff. By late 1962 Clay had talked himself into a fight with the seemingly eternal Archie Moore, now stripped of his light-heavyweight title but still, at nearly 50 years old, a top-grade performer. In his three previous fights in 1962 Moore had had good results: he knocked out Lavorante in the tenth round; Howard King, a good-class second division heavyweight went out in the first; and he then boxed a ten-round draw with the Angelo Dundee-managed Willie Pastrano, who became light-heavyweight champion only seven months later.

There was an element of 'needle' attached to the match. Moore had been hired in the early days of Clay's career to provide coaching assistance, but the two massive egos were mutually incompatible and Moore was discharged, amidst some bitterness. Clay announced the prediction in the usual way:

When you come to the fight
Don't block the halls
And don't block the door,
For y'all may go home
After round four.

And they did. Apart from a semi-exhibition victory over a wrestler called Mike DiBiase the elderly Moore never boxed again.

Clay's predictions went wrong next time, when he had a real struggle beating former light-heavyweight contender Doug Jones on a ten-round decision in Madison Square Garden. He had forecast:

> Jones likes to mix
> So I'll let it go six.
> If he talks jive
> I'll cut it to five.
> And if he talks some more
> I'll cut it to four.

But the irrepressible Cassius was unrepentant: 'First I said six, then I said four', he told reporters. 'Six and four is ten, and the fight went ten, so I called it right again!' The win moved Clay into the No. 2 position, behind Patterson, and while he waited for Liston to dispose of Floyd in their rematch, Clay looked around for another, preferably rated, opponent whose defeat could ensure that he took over the No. 1 slot. He settled on the British champion Henry Cooper as the man most likely to afford him a win with the minimum risk or

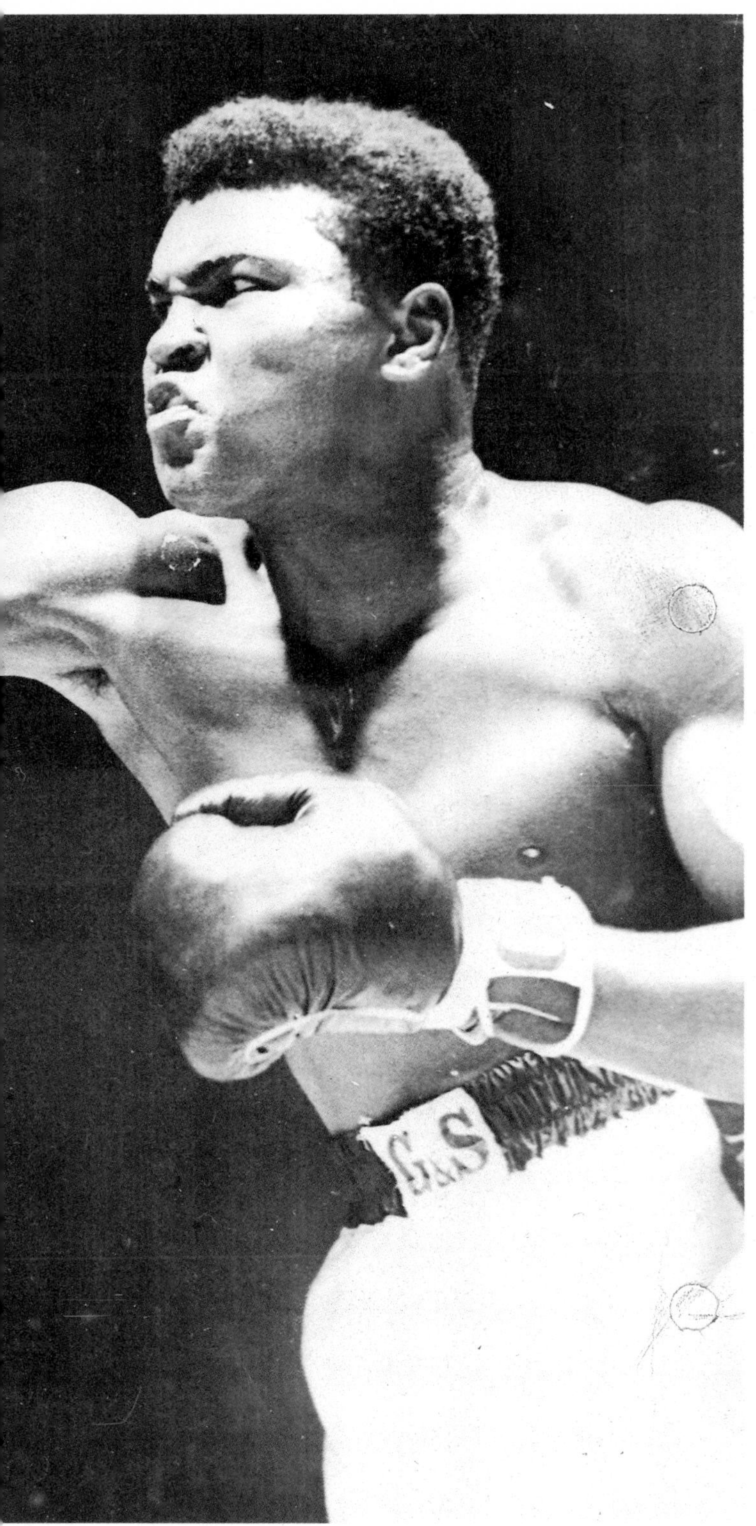

A hard-earned points win over the former light-heavyweight contender Doug Jones (left) *moved Clay up the rankings, but he needed one more worthwhile win to clinch the top spot. British champion Henry Cooper* (above, *with his three Lonsdale Belts) was selected as the sacrificial victim – but 'Our 'Enry' was not prepared to oblige.*

inconvenience. Cooper was a likeable but somewhat fragile fighter who had been knocked out by Joe Bygraves, Ingemar Johansson, and Zora Folley, and stopped on cuts by Uber Bacilieri and Peter Bates. He had won a Lonsdale Belt outright, but his overall record was a modest 27 wins and a draw in 36 fights and at 29 he was considered to be past his prime.

Jack Solomons, still Britain's leading promoter, paid Clay somewhere between the figure of £100,000 (reported in the British press at the time) and the more precise, and therefore more convincing, figure of $56,098 reported in Clay's ghosted autobiography *The Greatest*. Clay's brilliant showmanship drew a crowd of around 30,000 to Wembley Stadium to see whether the brash 21-year-old could fulfil his prediction that:

> London Bridge is falling down
> And so will Cooper in London Town.

For three-and-three-quarter rounds the fight went according to Clay's script. Cooper had

Cooper v Clay was a box-office winner from the moment the pair met at a pre-fight lunch (inset, *flanked by promoter Jack Solomons and Clay's brother, Rudi). The fight lived up to its hype, with one left hook from the Englishman in the fourth round almost rewriting heavyweight history. Had Cooper found the target earlier in the round, boxing's next 15 years would have been considerably duller.*

pressed forward doggedly, even bloodying Clay's nose in the first round, but generally played straight man to the clowning, bouncy, flashy Clay. It seemed almost as if Clay was holding him up so as not to spoil the prediction, which stipulated a fifth-round finish. The cut-prone Englishman was already leaking from several injuries around the eyes. But then, in the dying moments of the fourth, Clay got careless. Cooper backed him into the ropes, Clay's arms hanging loosely by his sides in the style that had rewritten boxing's textbooks. Cooper stepped in with a perfect left hook and the American crashed to the floor, his right arm hooked over the middle strand of the ropes.

He was on his feet, badly dazed, at four, but the bell rang before Cooper could hit him again. A split had opened in Clay's left glove during the third round, and during the interval Angelo Dundee summoned referee Tommy Little to the corner to inspect the damage, which had mysteriously worsened in the meantime. The ploy earned his client valuable extra seconds in which to recover, and by the time the fifth round finally got underway Clay's head had cleared. Seventy-five seconds

The gory finale as referee Tommy Little pulls Cooper out of the fight in the fifth round . . . as Clay had predicted.

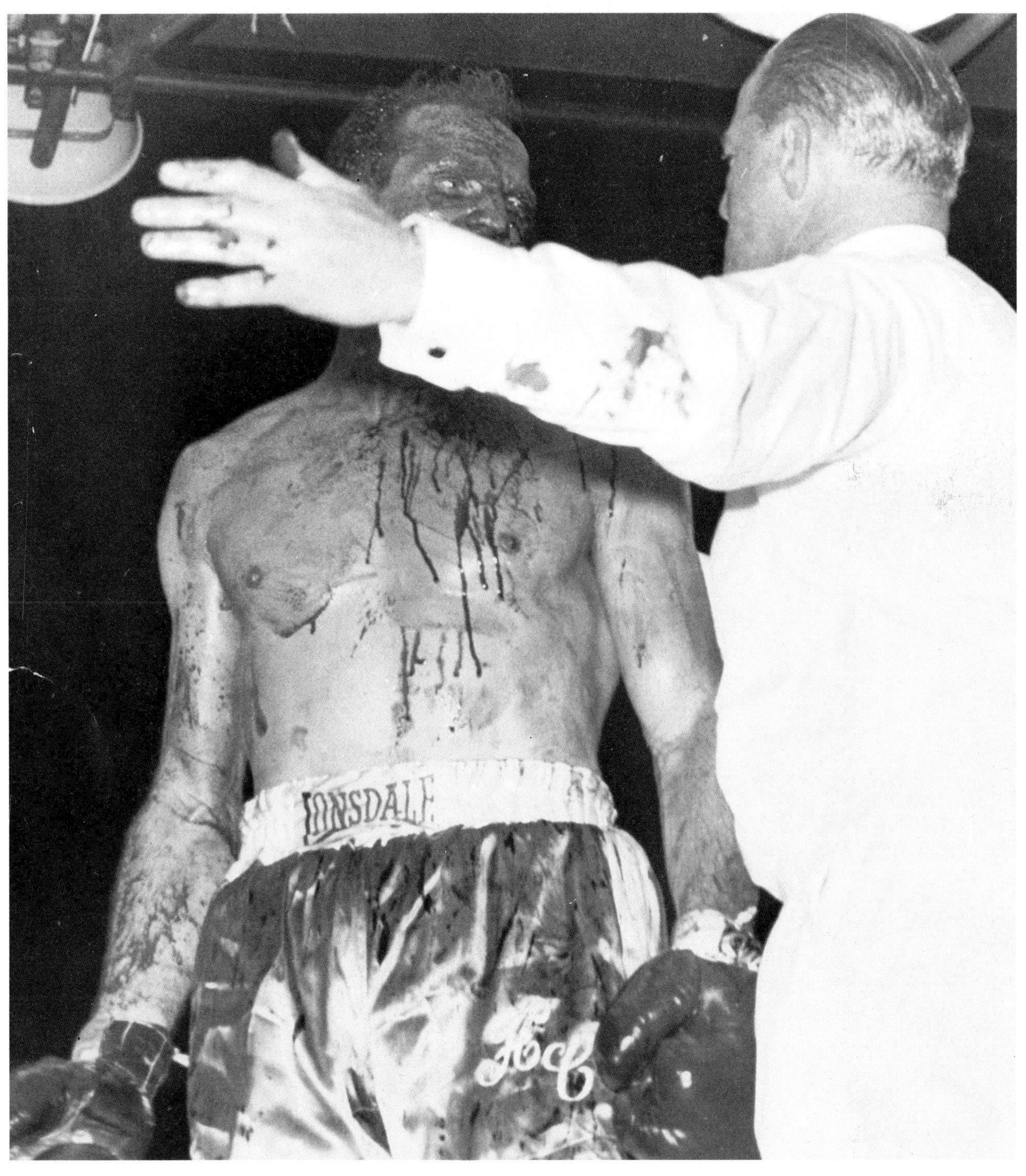

later, his slashing blows had brought blood spraying from four different cuts around Cooper's left eye, and forced Mr Little to call a halt. It would be the closest brush with defeat that Clay would have for eight years, and that single glorious punch transformed Cooper from journeyman heavyweight to national hero.

At least Clay had the victory he needed, and what he called 'Bear-Hunting season' was now open. For the next six months Clay and his camp-followers made Sonny Liston's life a misery as he whipped up demand for the title fight. He followed the champion everywhere, issuing endless taunts and challenges, and making wisecracks which the slow-witted Liston could neither match nor counter:

King Liston will stay
Only until he meets Cassius Clay.
Moore fell in four,
Liston in eight.

Clay's prediction was as outrageous as ever. Despite his glittering credentials, including 19 straight wins, when the fight was finally scheduled for Miami Beach on 25 February 1964, it was viewed more as an *event* than as a serious sporting contest. No one really gave the youngster a chance of victory, and the fight's attraction lay in seeing how long it would take Liston to close the braggart's mouth. Unbelieveably, big bad Sonny Liston had become the 'good guy', and the man whom boxing's establishment had tried for years to keep away from the championship now found himself in the unaccustomed role of sentimental favourite. Liston was a 7-1 betting favourite, while virtually the only expert to predict a Clay victory was the challenger himself.

At the weigh-in Clay caused pandemonium. He screamed, yelled, and danced around until the Miami Commission became so exasperated with his antics that they fined him $2,500 for 'unseemly conduct'. The Commission doctor, Alexander Robbins, said that 'Clay's acting like a man scared to death. He is emotionally unbalanced, liable to crack up before he enters the ring.'

As a psychological ploy, it worked. Liston was now in a state of hopeless mental confusion, and when Clay reappeared shortly afterwards, quite calm and controlled, Liston must have begun to think that he had been matched with a madman.

That night Liston fought like a zombie, plodding

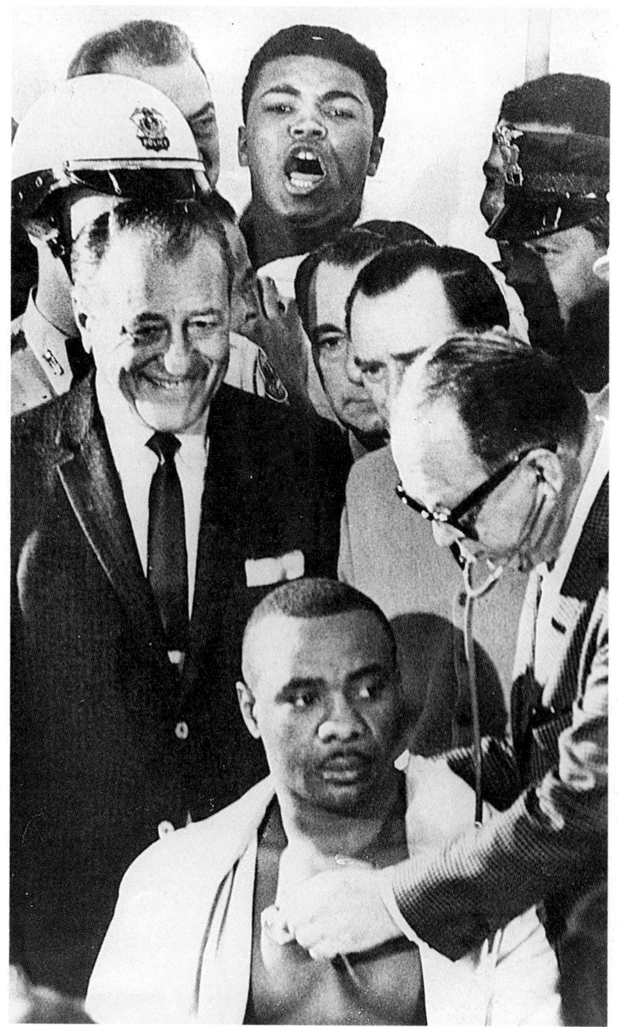

Clay caused such uproar at the weigh-in for his first title fight with Liston that he was fined $2,500 for outrageous conduct. In the ring that night, though, Clay dominated the man he called 'The Big Ugly Bear'.

after the elusive challenger and being picked off by whiplash jabs and hooks that raised a swelling under his right eye and opened a cut under his left. In the fourth, the medication which Liston's corner was using on the cut found its way into the challenger's eye, temporarily blinding him to the point where Clay panicked, asking Dundee to cut off the gloves and retire him between rounds. But Dundee shoved him out for the fifth with orders to run away until the eye had cleared, which Clay did unashamedly in an extraordinary round. By the sixth Clay had so fully recovered that the now demoralized, weary and bleeding Liston could not come out for the seventh round. He claimed a shoulder injury, and although X-rays did indeed show some damage, in reality the once-unbeatable champion had been embarrassed into defeat.

The day after his coronation, Clay caused another sensation by renouncing his 'slave' name of Clay in favour of Cassius X, since he had recently become a follower of the Black Muslim leader Malcolm X. Shortly afterwards, however, he adopted the Muslim name of Muhammad Ali, although it would be many years before his new name would be used by the same boxing writers who had readily accorded his predecessors Tommy Burns, Jack Sharkey, Joe Louis, Jersey Joe Walcott, and Rocky Marciano the privilege of changing *their* names. It was a courageous and principled step for Clay/Ali to take, but in the right-wing America of 1964 it was commercial suicide. His decision cost him millions of dollars in lost earnings from endorsements, personal appearances, and sponsorship deals.

The Muslims' radical stance and apparent hatred of all whites alienated America, even a substantial section of its black population. Ali was no longer an amusing eccentric, but had become instead the figurehead for a dangerous and increasingly influential ideology.

When Ali faced Liston again in the rematch at Lewiston, Maine, 15 months later, Liston was both the betting and the sentimental favourite. (Ali gleefully recalled hearing a redneck in the crowd shout 'Kill the nigger, Sonny!'). But Liston's spell as

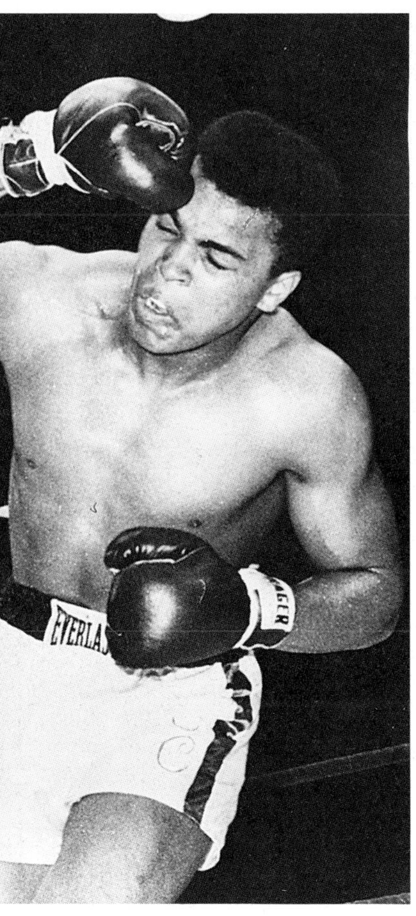

The day after winning the title, Clay stunned white America with the announcement that he had joined the Black Muslims (above) *and would henceforth be known as Cassius X, and later as Muhammad Ali. Public opinion swung against him, so that Liston was forced into the unaccustomed and undeserved role of sentimental favourite when the pair were rematched in May 1965. It did not help Sonny any: he was knocked out in one round in history's most chaotic heavyweight championship fight.*

a public favourite was short-lived, and in the most chaotic and controversial heavyweight title fight of all, he was knocked out in the first round by a punch which virtually nobody saw. Liston went down, spreadeagled, and after referee Jersey Joe Walcott had finally got Ali to a neutral corner he moved in to start the count. But the timekeeper, Francis McDonough, called Walcott over to the ropes and told him that Liston had already been down for 22 seconds, and that he himself had counted the challenger out twice.

Ali, meantime, had resumed his attack on the now upright Liston, forcing Walcott to jump between them to signal that the fight was over. Officially, it had lasted 60 seconds, a new record for a heavyweight title fight, but timing of the film showed that in fact Liston went down after one minute 42 seconds, and that Walcott had signalled the end after two minutes 12 seconds.

The truth of what happened that night will probably never be known. Liston said that he was waiting for Ali to be pulled away before he got up, and that in any case since Walcott had not taken up a count over him, how could he have been counted out? There were even rumours that snipers planned to assassinate Ali, and that Liston had been frightened into a quick surrender. But given Liston's background and violent record, it seems highly unlikely that he would have been scared into

Liston won 15 out of 16 fights after the second Ali fiasco, but the lingering suspicions surrounding that affair prevented the former champion from ever getting close to another title chance.

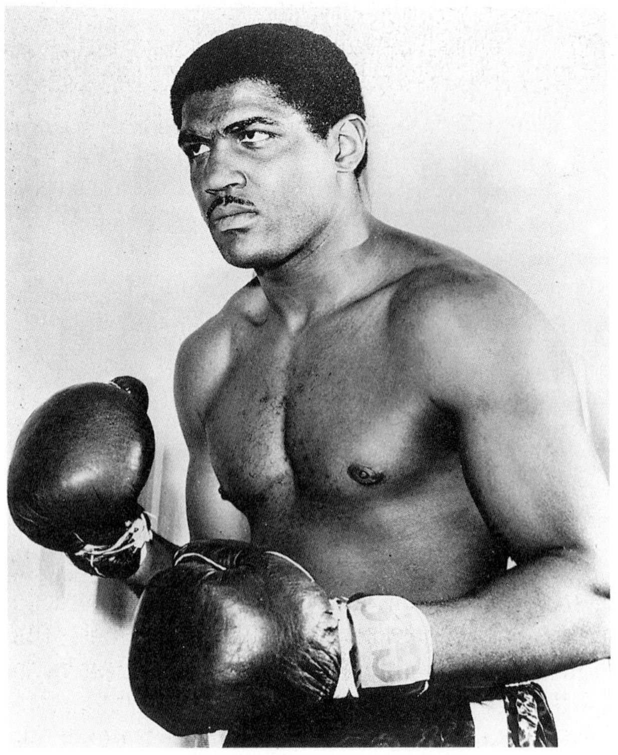

The competent but unglamorous Ernie Terrell, whom the World Boxing Association installed as champion after they stripped Ali of the title ostensibly because he had signed for the Liston rematch.

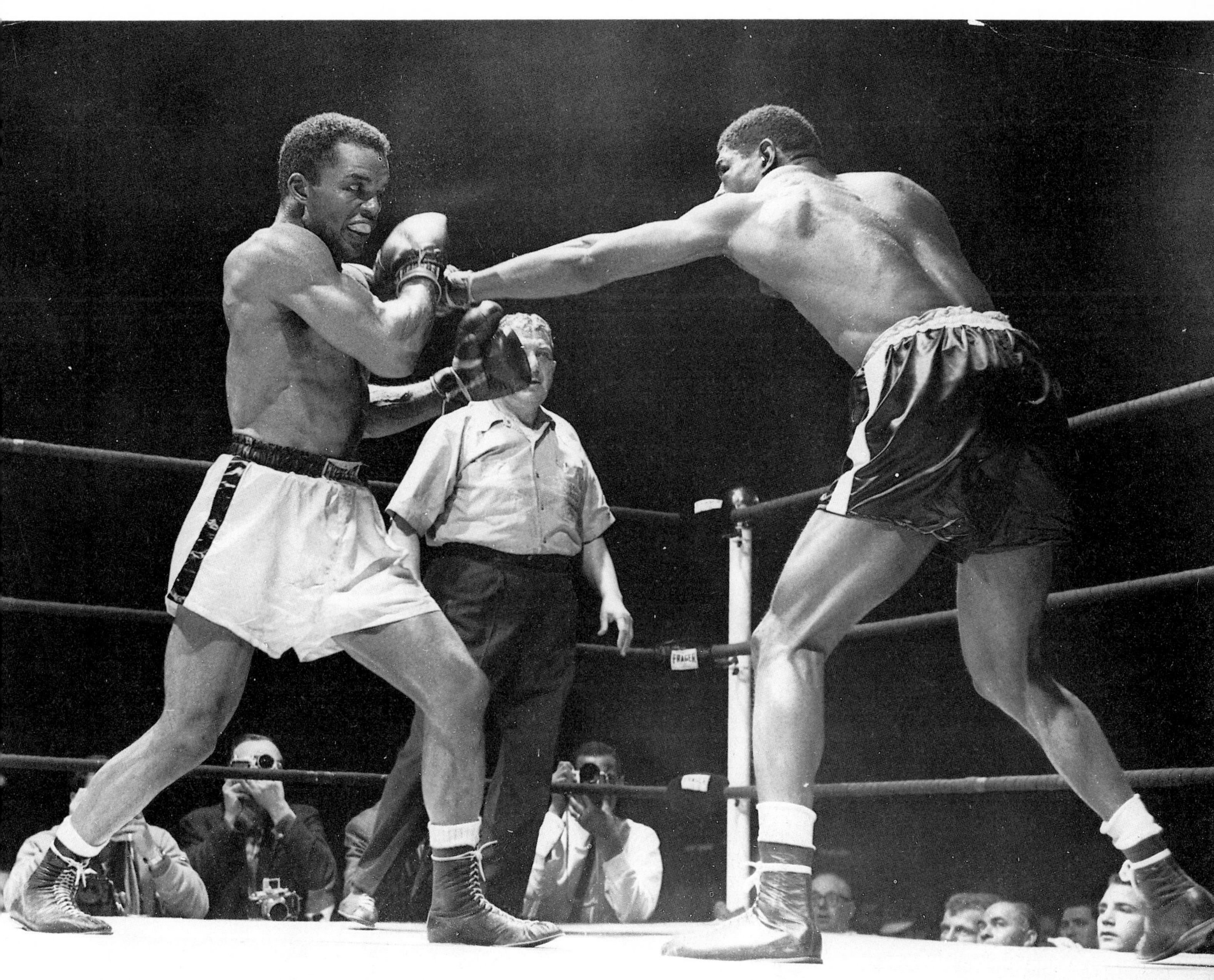

Terrell (right) *outscores Eddie Machen for the vacant WBA title. His third defence was a unification match with Ali.*

submission. Ali insisted that his 'corkscrew punch', a chopping right to the head, had despatched the challenger. The film does indeed show the punch landing, but not with the force which would have been considered necessary to knock out the tough and experienced Liston.

The truth went with Liston to his grave when, after a moderately successful comeback between 1966 and June 1970 during which he won 15 out of 16 fights, he was found dead of a drug overdose at his Las Vegas home on 30 December. The former champion maintained his air of mystery to the very end. The man for whom no birth record existed is also without an official date of death, for the coroner could only establish that he had died some time during that week.

The Liston rematch did not carry universal recognition as a title fight since the World Boxing Association (formerly the National Boxing Association) had declared the title vacant on 14 September 1964, ostensibly because Ali had signed for the rematch but in reality as part of the backlash against the champion's alignment with the Black Muslims. Ernie Terrell, a lanky Chicago boxer with a dull style and some unsavoury underworld connections, won their version of the title by outpointing Eddie Machen in March 1965, but attempts to match Ali and Terrell collapsed when first New York and then Chicago banned it, the former because of Terrell's dubious connections and the latter because of Ali's declared opposition to US involvement in Vietnam.

Ali had originally been classified 1-Y by his local

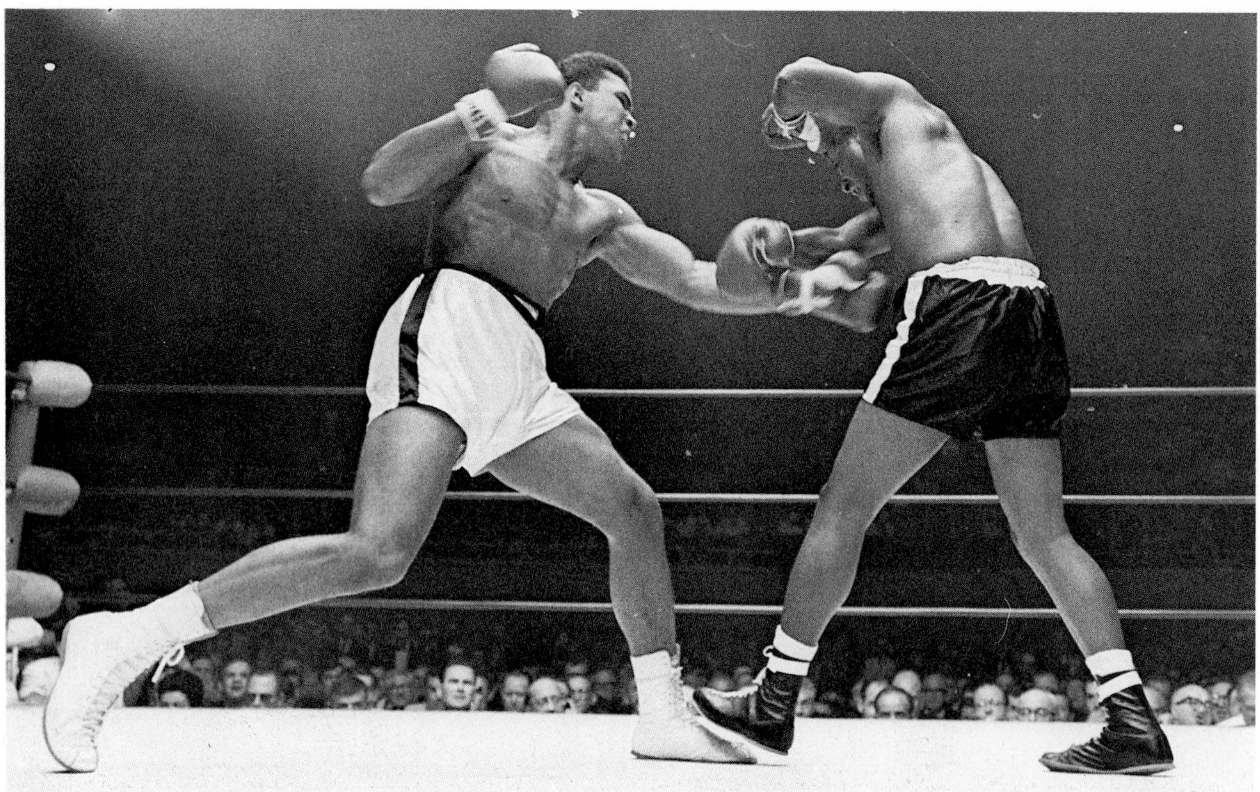

Between 22 November 1965, when he stopped Floyd Patterson in 12 rounds in Las Vegas (above) *and 14 November 1966, when he kayoed Cleveland Williams in three rounds in Houston, Ali risked the title six times. He appeared twice in England, cutting Henry Cooper to a bloody sixth-round defeat* (left) *and kayoing Brian London in the third* (opposite).

Army Draft Board, after failing their intelligence test, but when in February 1966 he was passed and reclassified as 1-A, he immediately applied for exemption from military service as a minister of religion (Islam) and a conscientious objector. While feeling grew that the champion should either be drafted or jailed, Ali undertook the busiest schedule of any title-holder since Louis. In November 1965 he battered Floyd Patterson (who insisted on calling him Cassius Clay) into a painful 12th-round defeat in Las Vegas, having contemptuously dismissed Patterson as an 'Uncle Tom' and a 'white man's nigger'. Four months later he outclassed the Canadian strongman George Chuvalo in Toronto, and then in 1966 he took the title on the road for the first time since Primo Carnera had outpointed Paolino Uzcudun in Rome in 1933.

In the space of six breath-taking months, Ali risked his title four times. Henry Cooper was cut to defeat in six rounds of an anti-climactic rematch at Highbury football stadium in May, then Brian London, one of his least qualified challengers, was destroyed in three rounds at Earls Court in August by a bewildering 14-punch combination. Less than five weeks later Ali was in Frankfurt, where the

Stubborn German southpaw Karl Mildenburger gave Ali a tough time before being stopped in the 12th round (above), *but the dangerous Cleveland Williams was easily swept aside in three rounds in what many regard as the greatest performance of Ali's career.*

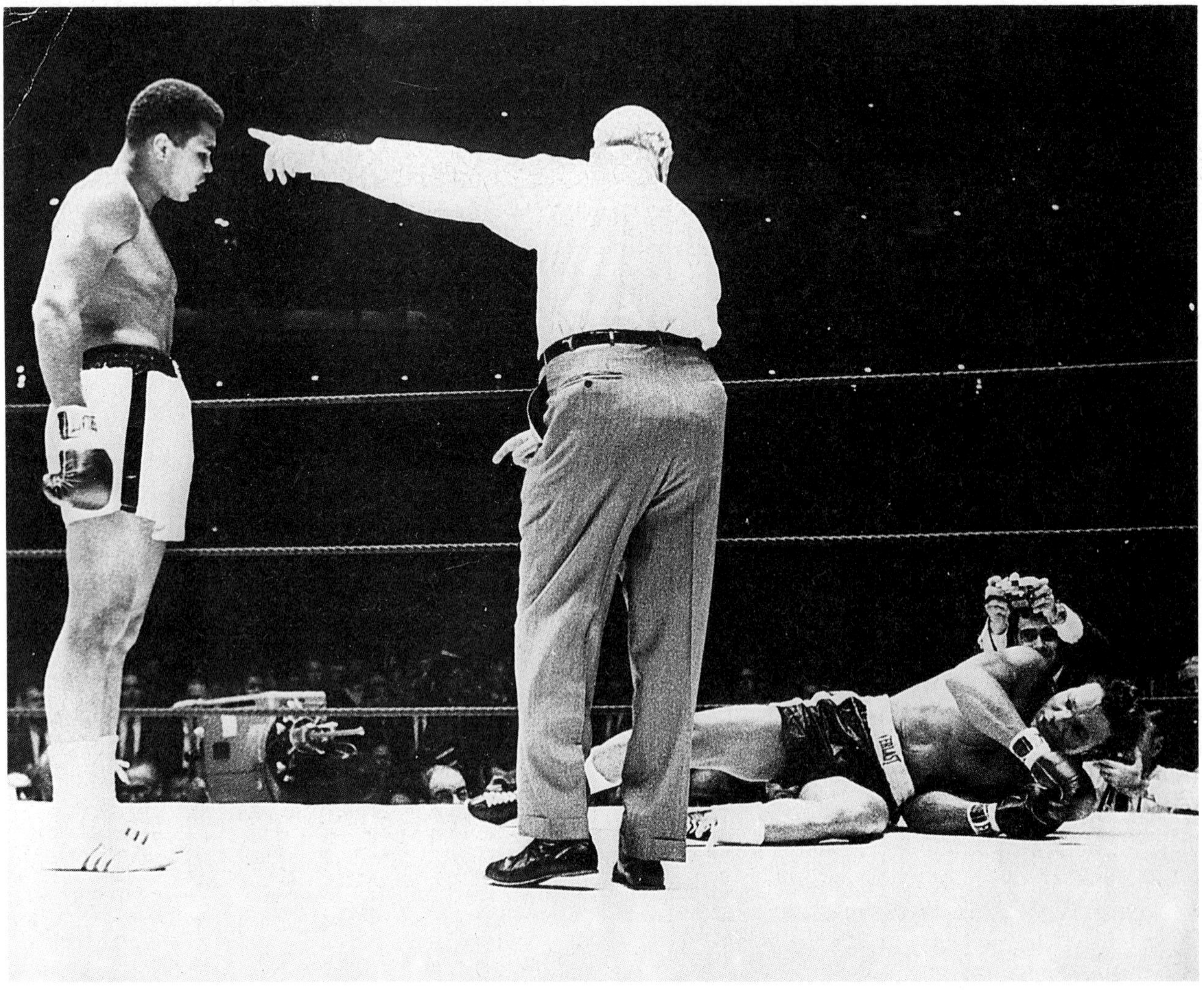

capable and awkward German southpaw Karl Mildenburger gave him problems before being stopped in the 12th round, and then, in November, Ali rounded off the year with what many regard as his finest performance, a three-round, four knock-down demolition of the dangerous Cleveland Williams.

Ali reclaimed the undisputed title with a brutal 15-rounds win over WBA champion Terrell at Houston on 6 February 1967. It was a sour, cruel, vicious display by Ali, and it repelled many of his sympathizers. Terrell, like Patterson, had refused to acknowledge Ali's name change, so Ali taunted him endlessly during the fight with 'What's my name? What's my name?' as he battered the brave but limited pretender. By the end Terrell was almost blinded, but Ali seemed unwilling to finish him off and instead exacted the last second of punishment from the man whom, in a post-fight television interview, he gracelessly dismissed as 'a dog'.

It was a new and ugly face that Ali was showing to the world: he knew that the boxing establishment was about to rob him of the best years of his career, and he worked out his resentment on the hapless Terrell. Six weeks later the veteran Zora

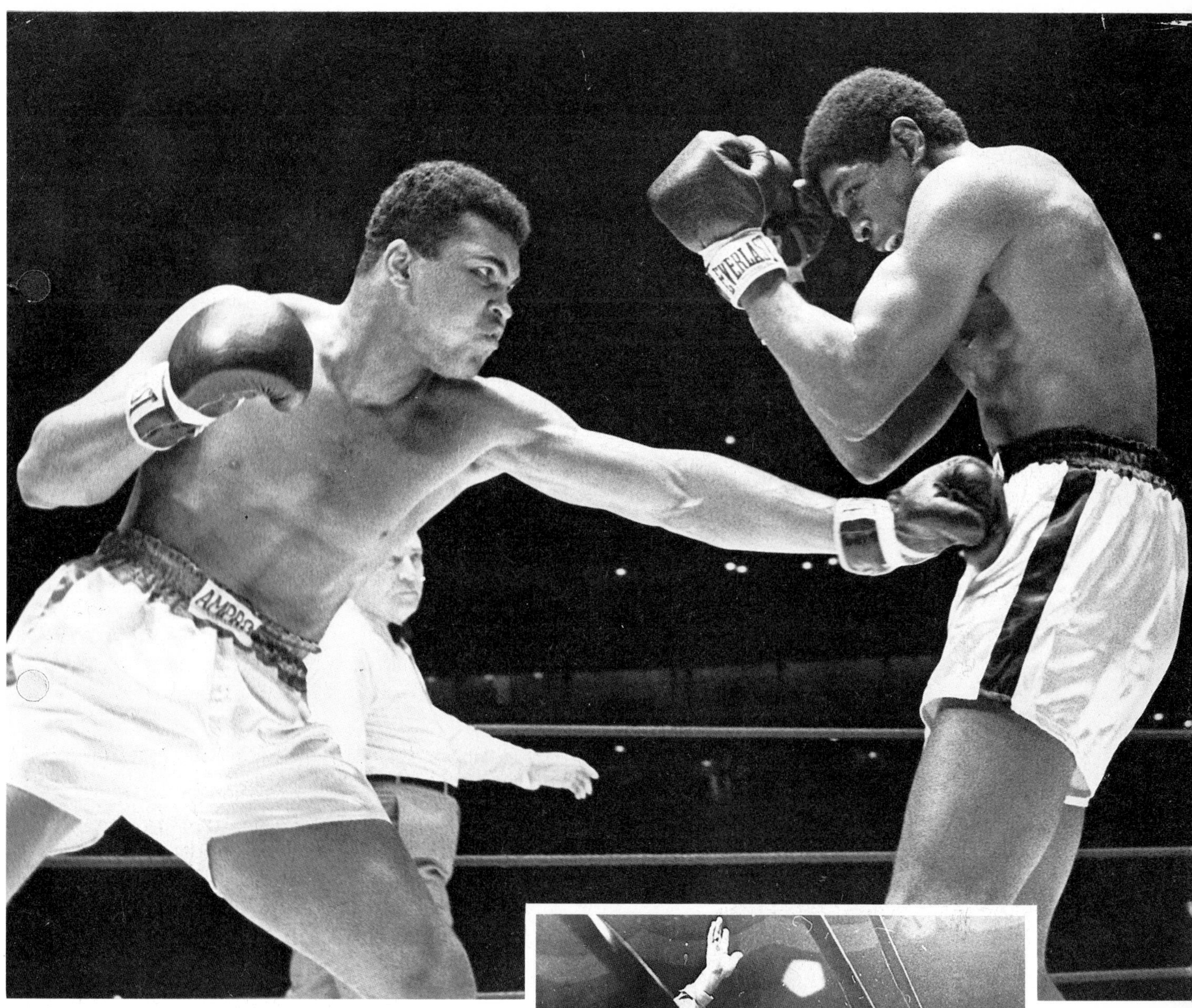

Ernie Terrell had made two successful defences of his WBA title before facing Ali in a 'unification' match in February 1967. He took a cruel and one-sided beating from the ill-tempered Ali (above), *who retained the undisputed title on a seventh-round knockout just six weeks later against the veteran Zora Folley* (right).

Folley at last got a world title chance, though six years past his prime, and was knocked out by Ali in seven rounds at Madison Square Garden. (Poor Folley never had much luck in his life. He wasted his best years in pursuit of champions whom he could have beaten, in Patterson and Johansson, and then had to face the unbeatable Ali when he finally got his opportunity.) A few years after his retirement, Folley was killed in a freak swimming pool accident at his home. It was the last time Ali was seen in the ring for three and a half years: on 28 April 1967, the WBA and the New York Commission stripped him of the heavyweight title for refusing to join the US Army.

Ali's one-time sparring partner Jimmy Ellis crushed Leotis Martin (above on the left) *on the way to winning the vacant WBA version of the title, but his claim to the title was overshadowed by the formidable talent of Joe Frazier* (right), *whom New York recognized as the new champion.*

The WBA now set up an elimination tournament to find a new 'champion' and as if to underline the paucity of the division it was won by Ali's sparring partner, Jimmy Ellis. New York, and several other American states, opted out of the WBA plan and instead nominated a blubbery 17 st 5 lb (243 lb) boxer from Grand Rapids, Michigan, Buster Mathis, to contest their version of the vacant title with the man whose name would, in years to come, be linked to Ali's as inextricably as Dempsey's is to Tunney's – Joe Frazier.

Frazier, the 1964 Olympic heavyweight champion from Philadelphia, had won 37 of his 39 amateur fights before turning professional under the management of a syndicate of 40 shareholders, each of whom contributed $250 for their share of the fighter whose snorting, bulling aggression and total commitment to attack soon earned him the nickname 'Smokin' Joe'. It was to prove a spectacularly good investment – Frazier's left hooks had brought him 19 wins in a row, 17 of them inside the distance, and his match with Mathis (who was also unbeaten in 23 fights) drew 18,096 fans to watch them inaugurate the new Madison Square Garden.

Frazier battered Mathis to an 11th-round defeat, thereby reversing his two amateur losses. Under the guidance of Yank Durham, Frazier became a busy champion, defending against an assortment

Frazier had battered his way to the Olympic gold medal in 1964 (right) *and was an instant sensation as a pro with performances like this fourth-round stoppage* (below) *of the Canadian 'Iron Man' George Chuvalo.*

Ellis and Frazier met for the undisputed title (below) *in February 1970. It was Ellis' first fight since his close win over Floyd Patterson* (above) *in September 1968, and Frazier easily beat him in four rounds.*

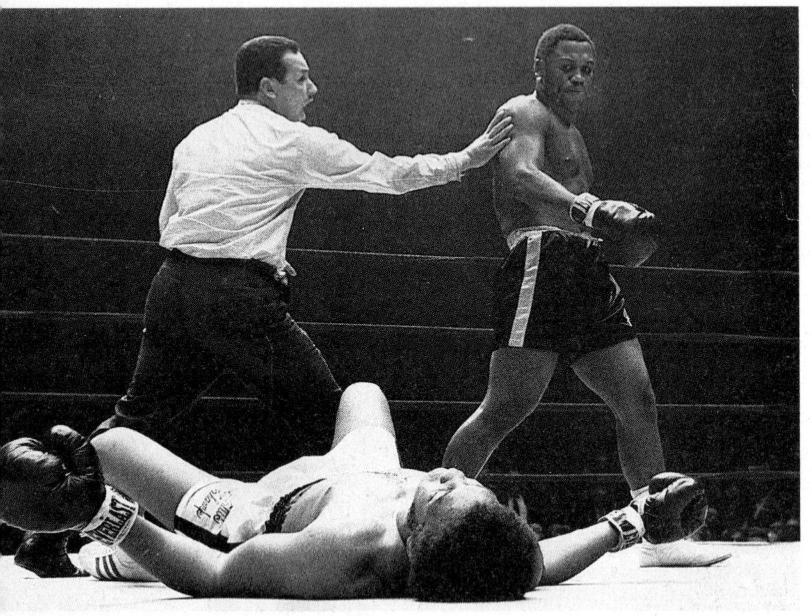

of moderate fighters and top-flight contenders. Manuel Ramos, Mexico's only challenger for a heavyweight title, was beaten in two rounds in June 1968, and two months later Frazier outpointed the durable Oscar Bonavena, who had floored him twice and come close to defeating him in his 12th fight. Dave Zyglewicz took almost as long to pronounce as to knock out in April 1969, and in June Frazier crushed the rugged Irish-American from California, Jerry Quarry, in seven rounds.

Ellis, meanwhile, had struggled to retain his WBA title when Floyd Patterson, making one last determined bid to win the title for an unprecedented third time, took him to a close decision in Stockholm in September 1968.

The world's other governing bodies, including the World Boxing Council and the British Boxing Board of Control, had stood aloof from the scramble, choosing instead to continue to recognize Ali as champion. But in March 1969, the WBC declared the title vacant because of Ali's continued inability to defend it due to his involvement in court proceedings. They announced that they would recognize the winner of a match between the rival claimants Frazier and Ellis as the new champion. The pair met in Madison Square Garden on 16 February 1970, when Frazier fought like the 6-1 favourite the bookies had made him to floor Ellis twice and force his retirement after four rounds. The world at last had an undisputed champion, and an outstandingly good one.

But popular sentiment in America during the years of Ali's exile had swung against involvement in the Vietnam conflict, and gradually the attitude and views which had cost Ali his championship and his peak earning years came to be shared by a majority of young Americans. Ali v Frazier had been one of those hypothetical matches, like Dempsey v Louis, that offered endless possibilities for argument and discussion since the winner could never be known. But then suddenly, from the most improbable area, Ali had support: Georgia, once the heartland of American racism, agreed to give him a licence. State Governor Lestor Maddox, once a club-swinging civil rights basher, had thrown a lifeline to this most potent symbol of black activism. It showed how far America had progressed since 1966, although the cynics noted that Maddox probably needed the black vote.

Jerry Quarry, a gifted but erratic fighter who could usually be relied upon to lose when it mattered most, was Ali's comeback opponent in Atlanta on 26 October 1970. For the first time there were almost as many blacks as whites at a major fight in America; black personalities including Coretta King, Whitney Young, and Dr Ralph Abernathy were at the ringside, and Ali did not let them down. For two rounds he moved and danced as if he had never been away, and in the third he chopped open a cut on Quarry's left eye to force a stoppage. The win put Ali back in contention, and when on 7 December he did what Frazier had not achieved in 25 bitter rounds, flooring the diamond-hard Argentinian Oscar Bonavena three times for a 15th-round stoppage, he proved that he was ready to tackle Frazier. Such was his magnetism that

This was the night when Mike Tyson proved he was as good as his publicity claimed. Trevor Berbick was a well-respected WBC champion, but Tyson smashed him to defeat in less than six minutes to become the youngest man ever to hold a version of the championship.

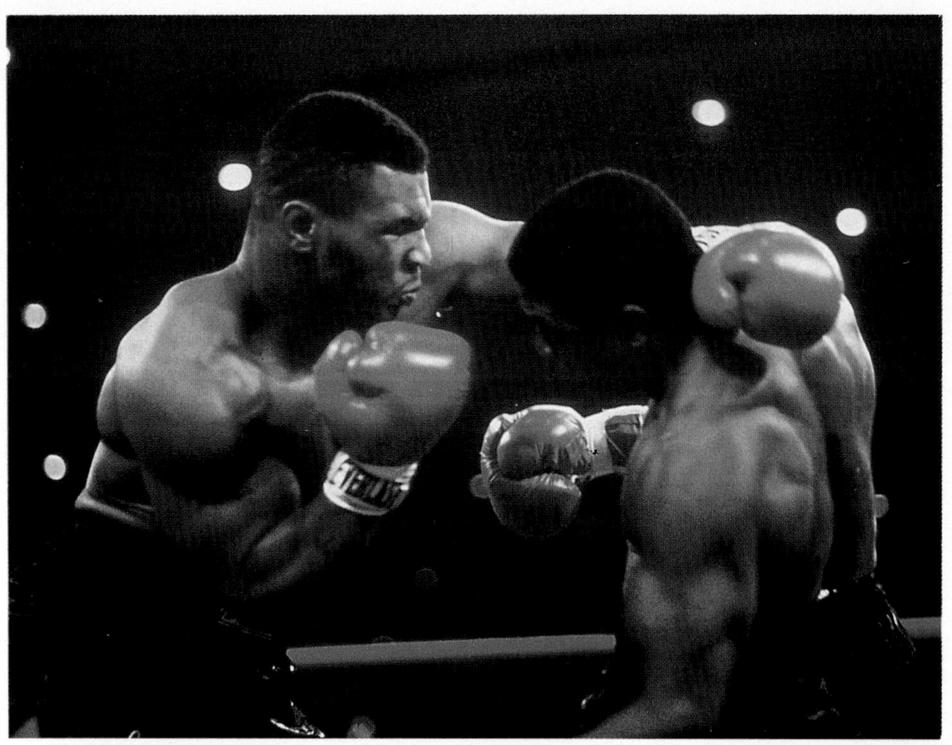

EVERLAST
EVERLAST
U.S.A

even after only two fights in nearly four years he had convinced the public that he was as powerful a force as he had been in 1966.

Teddy Brenner, matchmaker at Madison Square Garden, summed up Ali's love-hate relationship with a world far beyond the narrow confines of boxing when he said: 'I could announce that tomorrow Muhammad Ali will walk across the Hudson River and charge $20 admission, and there would be 20,000 down there to see him do it. And half of them would be rooting for him to do it and the other half would be rooting for him to sink'.

The match was irresistible and it was soon made: 23 days after Ali had beaten Bonavena, the Frazier fight was announced for the Garden on 8 March 1971. They would earn $2½ million apiece for a fight which was watched by 300 million

Ali's long exile ended with a cut-eye stoppage of Jerry Quarry (above) *in the unlikely setting of Atlanta, Georgia.*

Opposite: *Mike Tyson oozing menace and what he likes to call 'bad intentions'.*

Public demand for an Ali v Frazier showdown grew after Ali halted the previously unstoppable Argentinian Oscar Bonavena in the 15th round at Madison Square Garden in December 1970, and Muhammad could always be relied on to keep the publicity bubbling with his clowning and taunting whenever the pair met publicly. In private, though, the two men shared a mutual respect even if they were never friends.

television viewers in 46 countries, and which was piped into 337 closed circuit outlets. It was billed as the 'Fight of the Champions', the first time that two undefeated champions had contested the heavyweight title. Between them, they had won 17 title fights, and Frazier had whetted the appetite even further by a spectacular two-round knockout of the respected light-heavyweight champion Bob Foster four months earlier, in his first defence of the undisputed championship.

It was the perfect pairing, the genuine fight of the century. Their styles offered an intriguing blend of aggression with skill, power with grace. Their personalities, too, offered dramatic contrast. Frazier was an uncomplicated family man who had been born into poverty in Beaufort, South Carolina, and had been raised in the tough black ghetto in Philadelphia. He had no time for Ali's theatricals and political posturing, being a straightforward fighting man of the highest quality, who was fiercely proud of his title and resentful of any suggestion that he held it by default. There was another aspect to their rivalry, too, which Phil Pepe brought out in his biography of Frazier, *Come Out Smokin'*:

Frazier was a fighting man, pure and simple, who did not share Ali's love of theatricals. He had the last laugh on the man who had taunted and teased him so unmercifully, flooring Ali in the last round to ensure his points win.

Public sentiment seemed to side with Ali. He was an idol among blacks and liberals, a hero among college students and hippies and yippies, a martyr among Muslims and peaceniks. Frazier unwillingly carried the colors of the establishment, the patriot groups, the silent majority, the hardhats and the hard-nosed corps of boxing authorities. He was the white man's champion. He was boxing's 'white hope'.

For once, a fight lived up to the hype. For 15 unforgettable rounds, they provided bitter, skilful, passionate and unrelenting action, with the lead changing frequently. Frazier won it with a blazing finish, flooring Ali in the final round with a crushing left hook, but Ali added a new dimension to his legend by the manner in which he accepted and acknowledged defeat: the great fighters have to know how to lose, too.

There had to be a rematch, but before it could take place the huge and intimidating George Foreman, who had succeeded Frazier as Olympic heavyweight champion, made his own spectacular intervention. Before facing Foreman, though, Frazier made two easy defences in 1972 against overmatched, lowly-rated white challengers, Terry Daniels and Ron Stander. Ali, meantime, having won his appeal against his draft conviction was able at last to concentrate on his boxing and ran up a string of ten wins in places as distant as Switzerland, Japan, Canada and Ireland. The return with 'Smokin' Joe' looked certain to take place in 1973, but before the year was a month old Frazier was an ex-champion.

George Foreman, who had succeeded Frazier as Olympic champion, followed him onto the professional throne as well when he halted Frazier in the second at Kingston, Jamaica.

Ali rebuilt his career after the Frazier setback with a string of 10 wins, including this 11th-round stoppage of Al 'Blue' Lewis in Croke Park, Dublin, in July 1972.

Foreman had won 37 fights in a row, 34 inside the distance, going into his title challenge at Kingston, Jamaica, on 22 January – his 25th birthday. The statistics were impressive, but Frazier's performance against Ali had been so breathtakingly good that few gave Foreman a chance of victory. But Frazier badly underestimated the Texan, and had spent as much time performing with his pop group *The Knockouts* as in serious preparation. He paid the price when Foreman floored him six times, three in each round, before referee Arthur Mercante stopped the contest after 95 seconds of the second round.

Ali had his own problems. A magnificently built former Marine, Ken Norton, broke his jaw and hustled him to a points defeat in San Diego in March 1973. The loss cost Ali the North American title, which he had won from his friend and former sparmate Jimmy Ellis in 1971.

The intimidating presence of George Foreman (above, with Frazier) *did not deter Ali from his quest for another world title. He won the North American title by stopping his close friend Jimmy Ellis in 12 rounds* (below).

Foreman looked awesome as he battered Frazier to the canvas six times to force the second round stoppage.

He took quick revenge with a thrilling win over Norton in his next fight, but needed a surging last round rally to clinch victory. An easy win over Rudi Lubbers of Holland, in the unlikely setting of Djakarta, set up a rematch with Frazier which was widely seen as an eliminator for the right to meet Foreman. (Frazier had regained some prestige by outpointing Joe Bugner in London.)

The second meeting of the two ex-champions did not touch the heights of their first, but it was close and hard-fought, and Ali's narrow win meant that he had now beaten both of the men who had beaten him. Foreman, meantime, had enhanced his aura of invincibility with chilling destructions of Joe 'King' Roman in Tokyo, and Ken Norton in Caracas, in one and two rounds respectively. Even devoted Ali admirers such as Hugh McIlvanney of the *Observer* newspaper feared for the 32-year-old's well-being when the fight was made in Kinshasa, Zaire, on 30 October 1974. McIlvanney expressed the fairly general view of the champion when he wrote, in comment on Angelo Dundee's claim that 'Ali knows how to handle him': 'I too know a way to beat George Foreman, but it involves shelling him for three days and then sending in the infantry.'

The Kinshasa affair, the first heavyweight title fight ever staged on the African continent, was put together by Don King, a flamboyant black impresario who over the next decade would gain a near-monopoly on the heavyweight title. Ali had promised to shock the world again, and he did so with a battle plan of almost suicidal bravery, allowing Foreman virtually to punch himself out on his arms and rib cage for seven rounds before

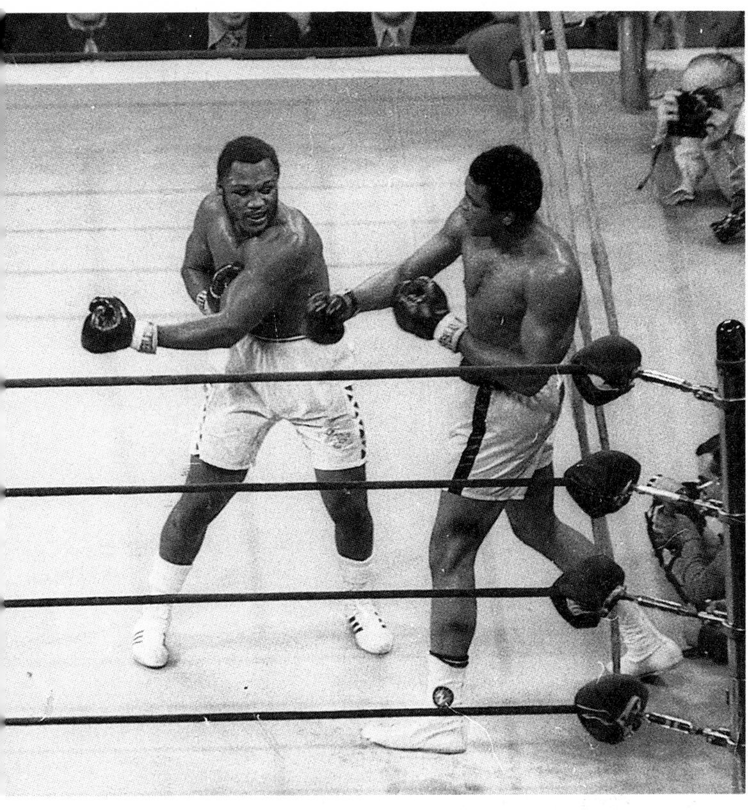

Ali took revenge over Frazier in their rematch (left)*, but few gave him a chance of beating the formidable Foreman, who destroyed Joe Roman inside a round in his first defence of his championship* (above).

knocking out the exhausted champion in the eighth. Ali notched up ten successful defences in a busy three-year span, some of them routine wins over the likes of Chuck Wepner (thus providing Sylvester Stallone with the idea for the *Rocky* films), Jean-Pierre Coopman, Joe Bugner, and Alfredo Evangelista. But there were also more demanding defences against Ron Lyle, Jimmy Young, Earnie Shaver and his old rival Ken Norton, as well as a heroic 14th-round retirement win over Joe Frazier in a fight which was so draining that it

Yet again, Ali amazed the world by regaining the title with an eighth-round knockout of Foreman in Zaire (below left). *Britain's safety-first challenger Joe Bugner* (below) *lasted the distance in July 1975.*

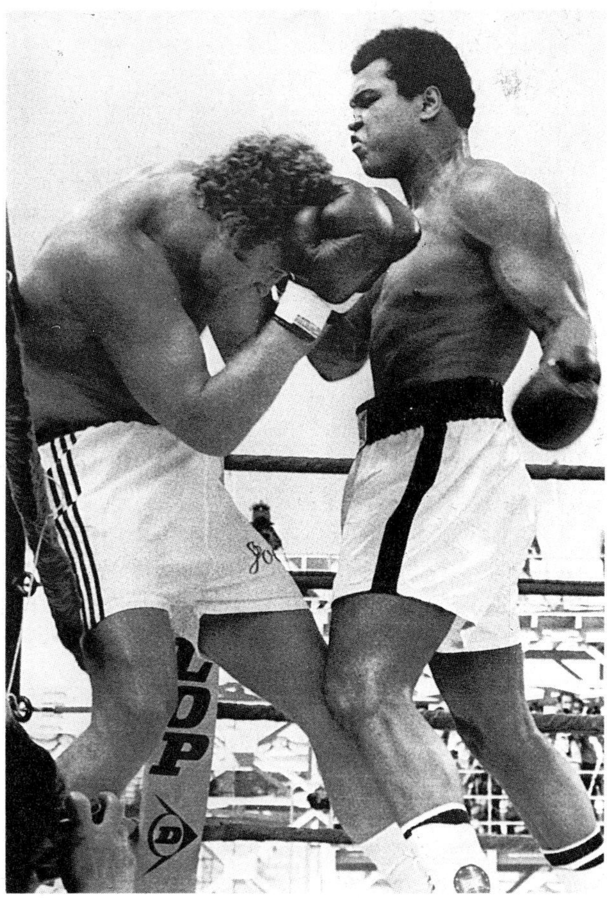

Earnie Shavers (above) *and three-time rival Ken Norton* (left) *gave Ali life-or-death battles in New York, and by now the evidence of Ali's decline was clear.* Bottom: *The Thrilla in Manila – Ali's magnificent third clash with Frazier.*

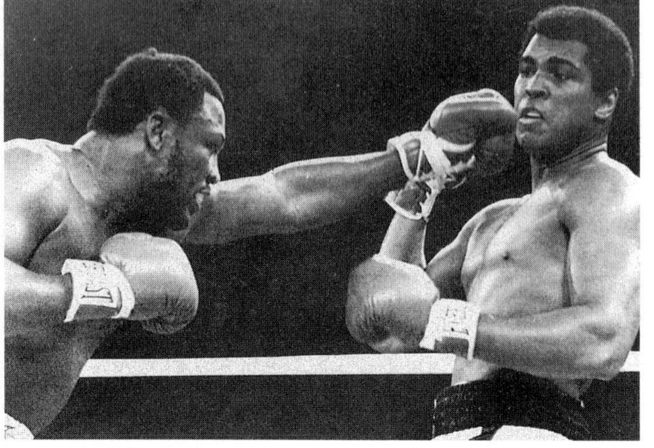

effectively finished them both.

In February 1978, Ali faced the 1976 Olympic light-heavyweight champion Leon Spinks, a gap-toothed eccentric from Detroit, who had had only seven professional fights. Ali fought sluggishly and listlessly, allowing the hard-working, almost frenetic Spinks to bustle him out of the championship. Spinks' victory, as a 10-1 outsider, was the biggest upset since Ali had shocked Sonny Liston nearly 14 years previously. Spinks, though, did not enjoy his undisputed title for long.

Just over one month later the WBC stripped him for agreeing to a rematch with Ali instead of meeting their top contender Ken Norton, and then 'declared' Norton champion on the strength of his 15-round points win over Jimmy Young in November 1977, in a fight which had been recognized at the time as a final eliminator for Ali's title. But the world at large still saw Spinks as the real champion, until Ali ended his brief reign with the last great performance of his fabulous career at New Orleans in September 1978. The 36-year-old veteran turned back the years with a dazzling 15-round exhibition to take a lop-sided decision.

It should have been the perfect moment for Ali's exit. No one else, especially in these days of

Leon Spinks' upset win over Ali in February 1978 (left) *was the last contest for the undisputed title. The WBC stripped Spinks for signing a rematch with Ali* (right) *and installed Ken Norton as champion on the strength of his win over Jimmy Young* (above). *After Ali had retired as undefeated WBA champion, the vacant title was won by John Tate, who outscored Gerrie Coetzee* (below).

fragmented titles, is likely to match his achievement of winning the championship three times. But, weighed down by the demands of his own ego as much as by the financial strains imposed by his army of camp followers, he first relinquished the WBA title in September 1979 and then made a pathetic attempt to come back a year later. The greatest career in sports petered out with two fumbling losses, to Larry Holmes and Trevor Berbick. Ali, of all champions, deserved better.

John Tate, a bulky but soft-chinned black from Tennessee, won the vacant WBA title in October

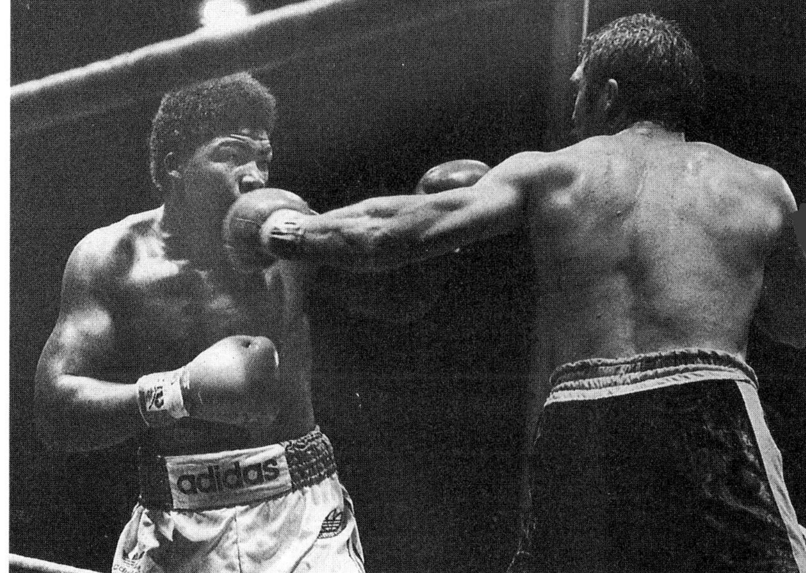

1979, and thereafter it passed with bewildering rapidity to Mike Weaver (who at least managed two successful defences), Mike Dokes, Gerrie Coetzee, Greg Page, Tony Tubbs, Tim Witherspoon and James 'Bonecrusher' Smith.

While the WBA title was being steadily devalued by the relentless mediocrity of its holders, the talented and under-valued Larry Holmes was imposing his own authority and credibility on the WBC version. He won it from Ken Norton in June 1978 in a magnificent 15-rounder in Las Vegas, thereby earning Norton the unhappy distinction of

Mike Dokes (above) *took the WBA title from Mike Weaver on a controversial first-round stoppage, but then lost it to South Africa's Gerrie Coetzee* (left). *Coetzee was kayoed in his first defence by Greg Page, pictured* (below on the right) *beating James Tillis on an eighth-round knockout.*

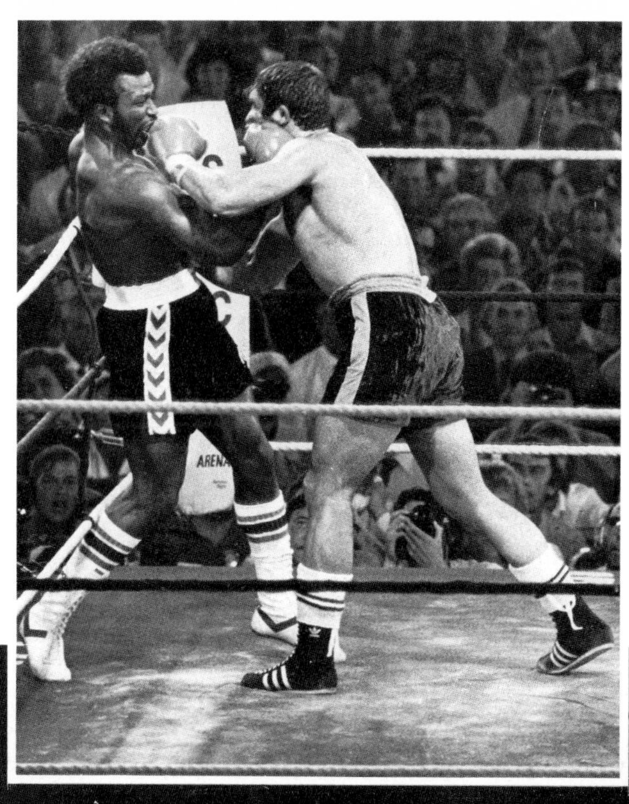

The WBA title has had an undistinguished series of holders. Mike Weaver kayoed Gerrie Coetzee to retain it (left) *in 1980, while Tony Tubbs* (right), *outpointing another short-term tenant, Bonecrusher Smith (nearest camera) had a brief spell in the hot seat. Tim Witherspoon took it from Tubbs, and held it against Britain's Frank Bruno* (below) *before losing it to Smith in a major upset in December 1986.*

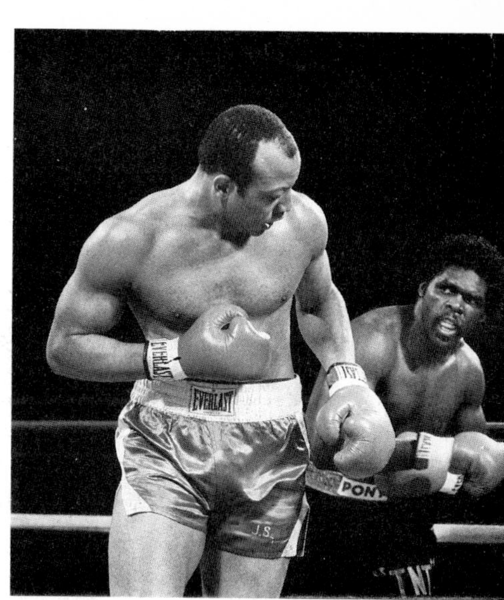

Larry Holmes had served a long apprenticeship against the likes of Young Sanford (above right) *before getting his WBC title chance against* Ken Norton (above) *in June 1978. He went on to make 16 defences, including this stoppage of David Bey* (below).

being the only heavyweight champion who never won a single fight for the title. Holmes, who had learned his trade as sparring partner to most of his immediate predecessors, dominated the division with a string of 16 defences against challengers of such varied quality as Ossie Ocasio, Lorenzo Zanon, Earnie Shaver, Trevor Berbick, Gerry Cooney, and Tim Witherspoon. But, like Ezzard Charles and Gene Tunney before him, he suffered by following one of the sport's legends, and he was never accorded the respect that his ability and record merited.

The parallel with Charles and Louis continued when, in October 1980, Holmes trounced the faded Muhammad Ali in an embarrassingly one-sided title

Gerry Cooney, the best of the modern 'White Hopes', earned a fortune in defeat by Holmes in June 1982 (right). *Two years earlier, Big Bad Leroy Jones* (below) *had inaugurated the era of the fat heavyweights when he took Holmes into the eighth round of a title bid in Las Vegas. Tony Tubbs, Tim Witherspoon, Greg Page, and the rest looked equally unathletic.*

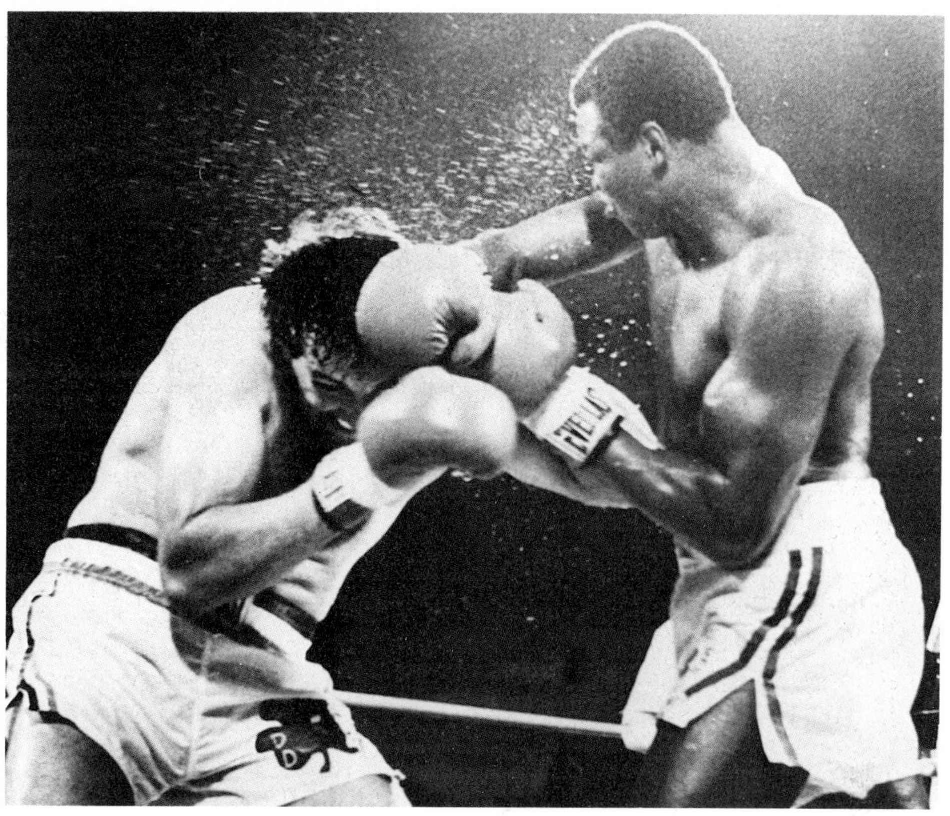

fight in Las Vegas. Ali, at 38, had nothing left, and to his credit Holmes frequently stood back rather than punish him. Long before Ali's corner retired their man at the end of the 10th, Holmes had been looking appealingly to the referee to intervene.

Holmes was the true champion, a fact underlined when Mike Weaver, a powerful but limited Californian, won the WBA title a year after being

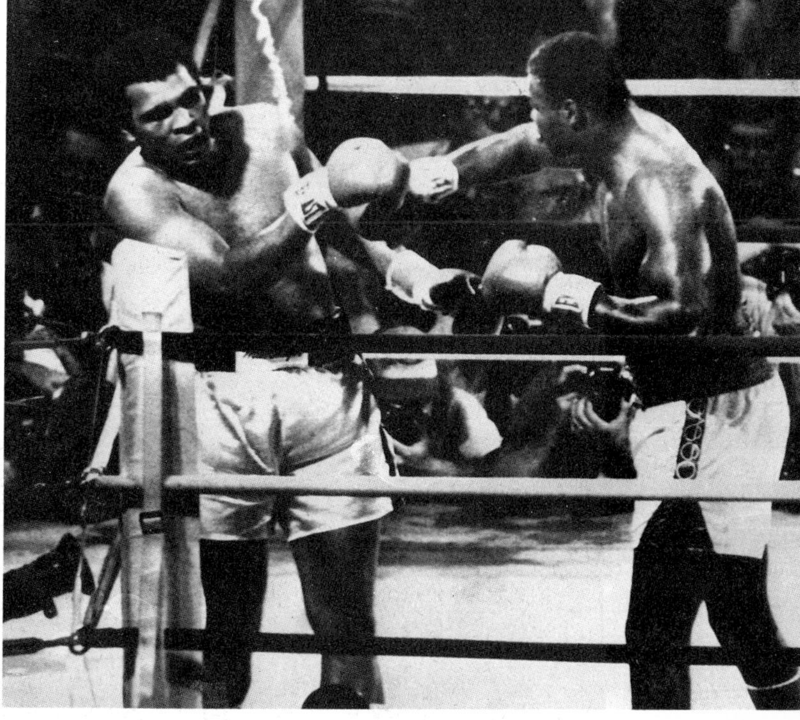

The saddest sight in modern heavyweight history . . .Muhammad Ali, half-blinded, in the fight he should never have taken. But even this humiliating defeat failed to convince Ali that enough was enough: he made one more pathetic attempt to come back, when Trevor Berbick outpointed him in Nassau.

stopped by Holmes in a bid for the WBC version. The Pennsylvanian cemented his claim to be the world's top heavyweight with a brilliant 13th-round stoppage of the unbeaten Gerry Cooney, the most capable of the various 'White Hopes' to emerge during the 1980s, but when in late 1983 Holmes and the WBC fell out he accepted recognition from the newly formed International Boxing Federation. It was a powerful coup for the IBF, and the weakness of the rival claims were emphasized when Tim Witherspoon, whom Holmes had beaten only ten months earlier, won the vacant WBC title. In his first defence of the IBF crown Holmes stopped James 'Bonecrusher' Smith, who went on to take the WBA title in December 1986.

Holmes made two more defences of the IBF title before losing it on a close and controversial decision to Mike Spinks, Leon's brother. It was his first defeat, just one win short of matching Rocky Marciano's perfect 49-0 record, and when Holmes lost a second narrow verdict in the rematch seven months later he retired in disgust.

The WBC title passed, on Holmes' abdication, to Witherspoon, Pinklon Thomas, Trevor Berbick and Mike Tyson

The confusion and the splintering of what was once the most valuable and prestigious title in all sport threatened to do lasting damage to the game's credibility – until the explosively talented Mike Tyson emerged from the pack. He destroyed Berbick in two rounds in November 1986 to become, at 20, the youngest title claimant in

Marvis Frazier made an ill-advised attempt to emulate his famous father, but Holmes destroyed him inside a round.

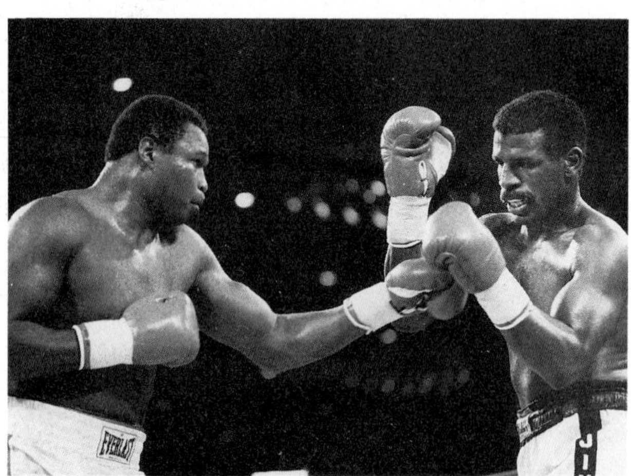

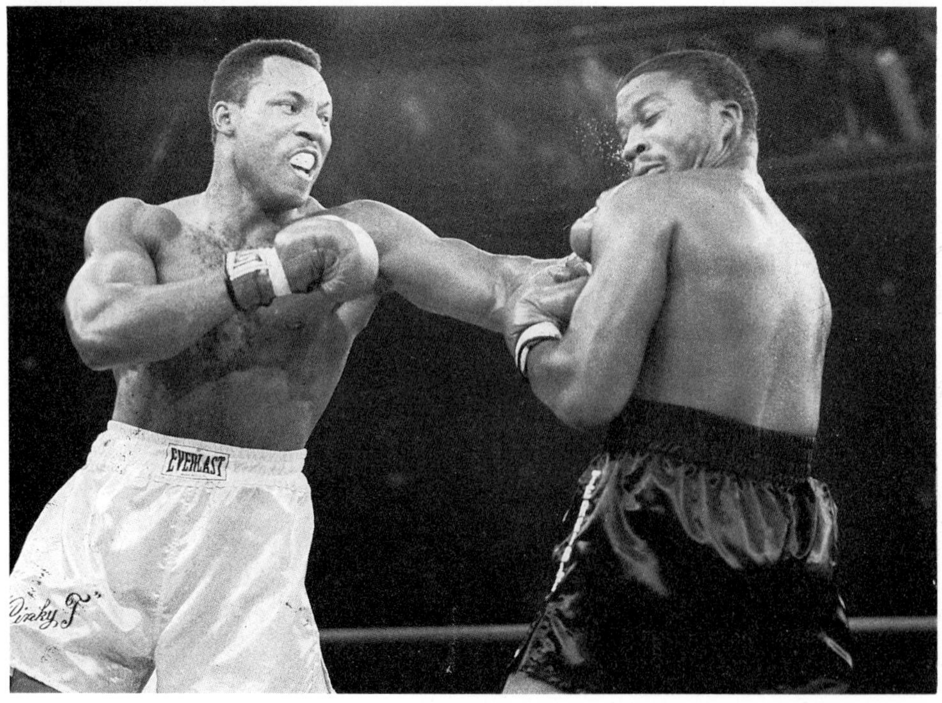

Holmes relinquished the WBC title, which passed from Tim Witherspoon to Pinklon Thomas (left, *outscoring Witherspoon*)*. Holmes claimed the IBF title, but lost it after three defences to Mike Spinks* (above) *on a close verdict in Las Vegas. Mike and Leon are the only brothers to have won the heavyweight title.*

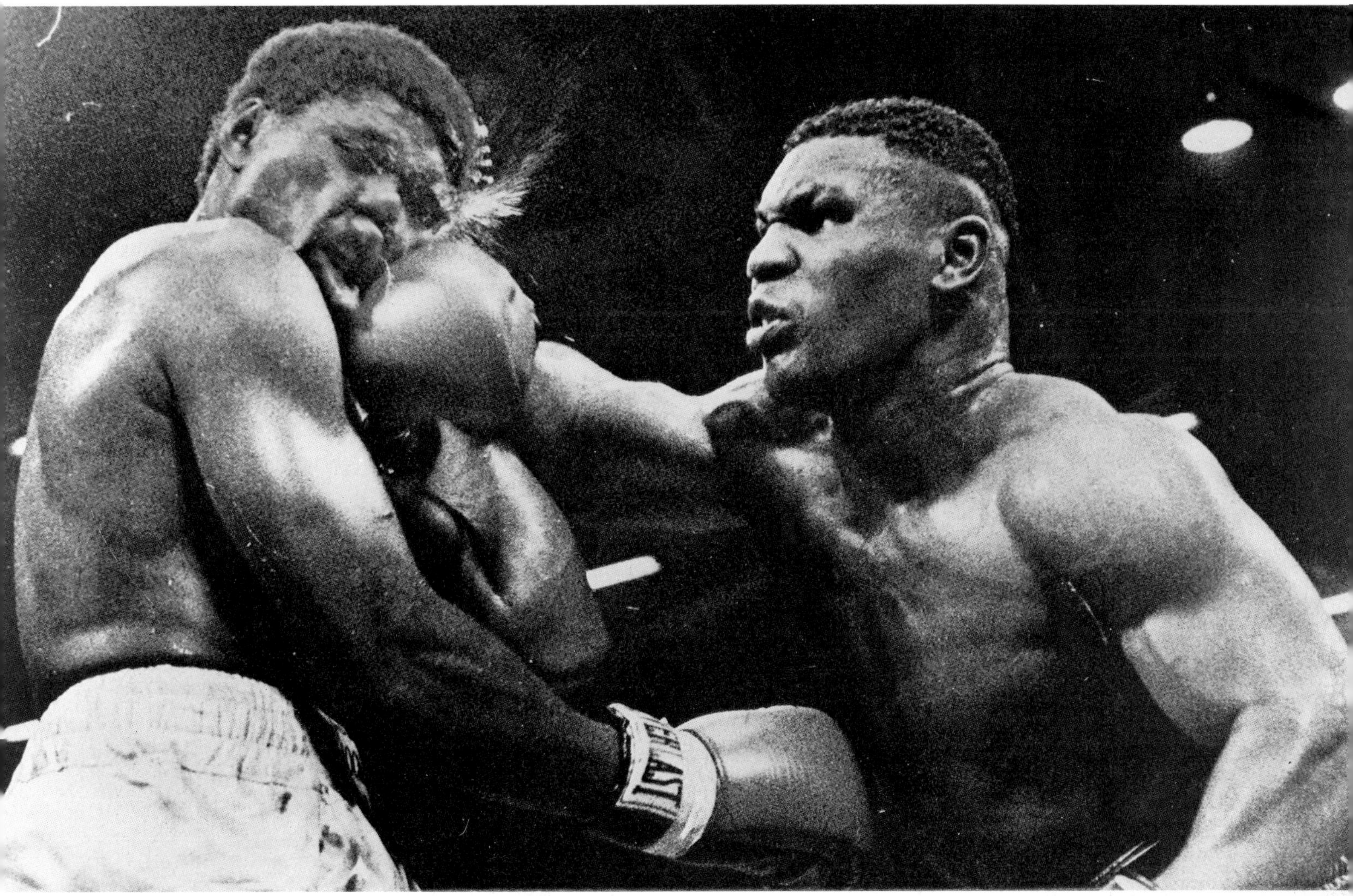

Graphic illustrations of the frightening punching power of Mike Tyson, the man who now controls the destiny of the richest prize in sport . . . the heavyweight championship.

heavyweight history. A protégé of Floyd Patterson's Svengali, Cus D'Amato, Tyson had crammed 28 fights (26 won inside the distance) into less than two years of pro competition.

In March 1987 he easily outpointed Bonecrusher Smith to add the WBA title to his collection, a few weeks after the IBF had stripped Mike Spinks of their title for his failure to defend it against their leading contender Tony Tucker. When Tyson smashed Pinklon Thomas into sixth-round defeat in Las Vegas two months later, Tucker stopped James 'Buster' Douglas in ten rounds on the same show to take over the vacant IBF championship and set up a final unification match with Tyson.

After almost ten years and a host of forgettable pretenders – with the splendid exception of Larry Holmes – the heavyweight title was at last poised to regain its lost status.

The division is boxing's flagship. It needs a believeable champion, and Tyson looks to have the stamp of potential greatness. But then nothing is ever certain in boxing, and it is that very unpredictability that gives heavyweight boxing its unique and enduring appeal.

ALL THE WORLD HEAVYWEIGHT TITLE FIGHTS

1882–1900

*07 Feb 82 John L. Sullivan w.ko.9 Paddy Ryan at Mississippi City

*10 Mar 89 John L. Sullivan drew 39 Charlie Mitchell at Chantilly

*08 Aug 89 John L. Sullivan w.rsf.75 Jake Kilrain at Richburg
**Under London Prize rules (bare-knuckle)*

07 Sep 92 James J. Corbett w.ko.21 John L. Sullivan at New Orleans

25 Jan 94 James J. Corbett w.ko.3 Charlie Mitchell at Jacksonville

17 Mar 97 Bob Fitzsimmons w.ko.14 James J. Corbett at Carson City

09 Jun 99 James J. Jeffries w.ko.11 Bob Fitzsimmons at Coney Island

03 Nov 99 James J. Jeffries w.pts.25 Tom Sharkey at Coney Island

1900–

11 May 00 James J. Jeffries w.ko.23 James J. Corbett at Coney Island

15 Nov 01 James J. Jeffries w.rtd.5 Gus Ruhlin at San Francisco

25 Jul 02 James J. Jeffries w.ko.8 Bob Fitzsimmons at San Francisco

14 Aug 03 James J. Jeffries w.ko.10 James J. Corbett at San Francisco

26 Aug 04 James J. Jeffries w.ko.2. Jack Munroe at San Francisco
Jeffries announced retirement

03 Jul 05 Marvin Hart w.rsf.12 Jack Root at Reno

23 Feb 06 Tommy Burns w.pts.20 Marvin Hart at Los Angeles

02 Oct 06 Tommy Burns w.ko.15 Jim Flynn at Los Angeles

28 Nov 06 Tommy Burns drew 20 Phil Jack O'Brien at Los Angeles

08 May 07 Tommy Burns w.pts.20 Phil Jack O'Brien at Los Angeles

04 Jul 07 Tommy Burns w.ko.1 Bill Squires at Colma, California

02 Dec 07 Tommy Burns w.ko.10 Gunner Moir at London

10 Feb 08 Tommy Burns w.ko.4 Jack Palmer at London

17 Mar 08 Tommy Burns w.ko.1 Jem Roche at Dublin

18 Apr 08 Tommy Burns w.ko.5 Jewey Smith at Paris

13 Jun 08 Tommy Burns w.ko.13 Bill Squires at Paris

24 Aug 08 Tommy Burns w.ko.13 Bill Squires at Sydney

02 Sep 08 Tommy Burns w.ko.6 Bill Lang at Melbourne

26 Dec 08 Jack Johnson w.rsf.14 Tommy Burns at Sydney

16 Oct 09 Jack Johnson w.ko.12 Stanley Ketchel at Colma, California

04 Jul 10 Jack Johnson w.rsf.15 James J. Jeffries at Reno

04 Jul 12 Jack Johnson w.rsf.9 Jim Flynn at Las Vegas, New Mexico

28 Nov 13 Jack Johnson w.ko.2 Andre Spoul at Paris

19 Dec 13 Jack Johnson drew 10 Jim Johnson at Paris

27 Jun 14 Jack Johnson w.pts.20 Frank Moran at Paris

05 Apr 15 Jess Willard w.ko.26 Jack Johnson at Havana

25 Mar 16 Jess Willard no dec.10 Frank Moran at New York

04 Jul 19 Jack Dempsey w.rtd.3 Jess Willard at Toledo

06 Sep 20 Jack Dempsey w.ko.3 Billy Miske at Benton Harbour.

14 Dec 20 Jack Dempsey w.ko.12 Bill Brennan at New York

02 Jul 21 Jack Dempsey w.ko.4 Georges Carpentier at Jersey City

04 Jul 23 Jack Dempsey w.pts.15 Tom Gibbons at Shelby, Montana

14 Sep 23 Jack Dempsey w.ko.2 Luis Angel Firpo at New York

23 Sep 26 Gene Tunney w.pts.10 Jack Dempsey at Philadelphia

22 Sep 27 Gene Tunney w.pts.10 Jack Dempsey at Chicago

23 Jul 28 Gene Tunney w.rsf.11 Tom Heeney at New York
Tunney announced retirement

12 Jun 30 Max Schmeling w.dis.4 Jack Sharkey at New York

03 Jul 31 Max Schmeling w.rsf.15 Young Stribling at Cleveland

21 Jun 32 Jack Sharkey w.pts.15 Max Schmeling at Long Island NY

29 Jun 33 Primo Carnera w.ko.6 Jack Sharkey at Long Island NY

22 Oct 33 Primo Carnera w.pts.15 Paulino Uzcudun at Rome

01 Mar 34 Primo Carnera w.pts.15 Tommy Loughran at Miami

14 Jun 34 Max Baer w.rsf. 11 Primo Carnera at Long Island, NY

13 Jun 35 James J. Braddock w.pts.15 Max Baer at Long Island, NY

22 Jun 37 Joe Louis w.ko.8 James J. Braddock at Chicago

30 Aug 37 Joe Louis w.pts.15 Tommy Farr at New York

23 Feb 38 Joe Louis w.ko.3 Nathan Mann at New York.

01 Apr 38 Joe Louis w.ko.5 Harry Thomas at Chicago

22 Jun 38 Joe Louis w.ko.1 Max Schmeling at New York

25 Jan 39 Joe Louis w.rsf.1 John Henry Lewis at New York

17 Apr 39 Joe Louis w.ko.1 Jack Roper at Los Angeles

28 Jun 39 Joe Louis w.rsf.4 Tony Galento at New York

20 Sep 39 Joe Louis w.ko.11 Bob Pastor at Detroit

09 Feb 40 Joe Louis w.pts.15 Arturo Godoy at New York

29 Mar 40 Joe Louis w.rsf.2 Johnny Paychek at New York

20 Jun 40 Joe Louis w.rsf.8 Arturo Godoy at New York

16 Dec 40 Joe Louis w.rtd.6 Al McCoy at Boston

31 Jan 41 Joe Louis w.ko.5 Red Burman at New York

17 Feb 41 Joe Louis w.ko.2 Gus Dorazio at Philadelphia

21 Mar 41 Joe Louis w.rsf.13 Abe Simon at Detroit

08 Apr 41 Joe Louis w.rsf.9 Tony Musto at St Louis

23 May 41 Joe Louis w.dis.7 Buddy Baer at Washington

18 Jun 41 Joe Louis w.ko.13 Billy Conn at New York

29 Sep 41 Joe Louis w.rsf.6 Lou Nova at New York

09 Jan 42 Joe Louis w.ko.1 Buddy Baer at New York

27 Mar 42 Joe Louis w.ko.6 Abe Simon at New York

19 Jun 46 Joe Louis w.ko.8 Billy Conn at New York

18 Sep 46 Joe Louis w.ko.1 Tami Mauriello at New York

05 Dec 47 Joe Louis w.pts.15 Jersey Joe Walcott at New York

25 Jun 48 Joe Louis w.ko.11 Jersey Joe Walcott at New York
Louis announced retirement

22 Jun 49 Ezzard Charles w.pts.15 Jersey Joe Walcott at Chicago *(NBA title)*

10 Aug 49 Ezzard Charles w.rsf.7 Gus Lesnevich at New York

14 Oct 49 Ezzard Charles w.ko.8 Pat Valentino at San Francisco

15 Aug 50 Ezzard Charles w.rsf.14 Freddy Beshore at Buffalo

27 Sep 50 Ezzard Charles w.pts.15 Joe Louis at New York
(Undisputed title)

05 Dec 50 Ezzard Charles w.ko.11 Nick Barone at Cincinnati

12 Jan 51 Ezzard Charles w.rsf.10 Lee Oma at New York

07 Mar 51 Ezzard Charles w.pts. 15 Jersey Joe Walcott at Detroit

30 May 51 Ezzard Charles w.pts.15 Joey Maxim at Chicago

18 Jul 51 Jersey Joe Walcott w.ko.7 Ezzard Charles at Pittsburgh

05 Jun 52 Jersey Joe Walcott w.pts.15 Ezzard Charles at Philadelphia

23 Sep 52 Rocky Marciano w.ko.13 Jersey Joe Walcott at Philadelphia

15 May 53 Rocky Marciano w.ko.1 Jersey Joe Walcott at Chicago

24 Sep 53 Rocky Marciano w.rsf.11 Roland La Starza at New York

17 Jun 54 Rocky Marciano w.pts.15 Ezzard Charles at New York

17 Sep 54 Rocky Marciano w.ko.8 Ezzard Charles at New York

16 May 55 Rocky Marciano w.rsf.9 Don Cockell at San Francisco

21 Sep 55 Rocky Marciano w.ko.9 Archie Moore at New York
Marciano announced retirement

30 Nov 56 Floyd Patterson w.ko.5 Archie Moore at Chicago

29 Jul 57 Floyd Patterson w.rsf.10 Tommy Jackson at New York

22 Aug 57 Floyd Patterson w.ko.6 Pete Rademacher at Seattle

18 Aug 58 Floyd Patterson w.rtd.12 Roy Harris at Los Angeles

01 May 59 Floyd Patterson w.ko.11 Brian London at Indianapolis

26 Jun 59	Ingemar Johansson w.rsf.3 Floyd Patterson at New York
20 Jun 60	Floyd Patterson w.ko.5 Ingemar Johansson at New York
13 Mar 61	Floyd Patterson w.ko.6 Ingemar Johansson at Miami
04 Dec 61	Floyd Patterson w.ko.4 Tom McNeeley at Toronto
25 Sep 62	Sonny Liston w.ko.1 Floyd Patterson at Chicago
22 Jul 63	Sonny Liston w.ko.1 Floyd Patterson at Las Vegas
25 Feb 64	Cassius Clay w.rtd.6 Sonny Liston at Miami *(Clay announced he would henceforth be known as Muhammad Ali)*
14 Sep 64	*WBA withdrew recognition of Ali because he signed for return bout with Sonny Liston*
05 Mar 65	Ernie Terrell w.pts.15 Eddie Machen at Chicago *(Vacant WBA title)*
25 May 65	Muhammad Ali w.ko.1 Sonny Liston at Lewiston, Maine
01 Nov 65	Ernie Terrell w.pts.15 George Chuvalo at Toronto *(WBA title)*
22 Nov 65	Muhammad Ali w.rsf.12 Floyd Patterson at Las Vegas
29 Mar 66	Muhammad Ali w.pts.15 George Chuvalo at Toronto
21 May 66	Muhammad Ali w.rsf.6 Henry Cooper in London
28 Jun 66	Ernie Terrell w.pts.15 Doug Jones at Houston *(WBA title)*
06 Aug 66	Muhammad Ali w.ko.3 Brian London in London
10 Sep 66	Muhammad Ali w.rsf.12 Karl Mildenberger at Frankfurt
14 Nov 66	Muhammad Ali w.rsf.3 Cleveland Williams at Houston
06 Feb 67	Muhammad Ali w.pts.15 Ernie Terrell at Houston *(Undisputed title)*
22 Mar 67	Muhammad Ali w.ko.7 Zora Folley in New York
28 Apr 67	*Ali stripped of title by WBA and New York State Athletic Commission for refusing to join US Army.*
04 Mar 68	Joe Frazier w.rsf.11 Buster Mathis at New York *(New York State version of vacant title)*
27 Apr 68	Jimmy Ellis w.pts.15 Jerry Quarry at Oakland *(WBA version of vacant title)*
24 Jun 68	Joe Frazier w.rtd.2 Manuel Ramos at New York *(New York State title)*
14 Sep 68	Jimmy Ellis w.pts.15 Floyd Patterson at Stockholm *(WBA title)*
10 Dec 68	Joe Frazier w.pts.15 Oscar Bonavena at Philadelphia *(New York State title)*
22 Apr 69	Joe Frazier w.ko.1 Dave Zyglewicz at Houston, Texas *(New York State title)*
23 Jun 69	Joe Frazier w.rsf.7 Jerry Quarry at New York *(New York State title)*
16 Feb 70	Joe Frazier w.rtd.4 Jimmy Ellis at New York *(Undisputed title)*
18 Nov 70	Joe Frazier w.ko.2 Bob Foster at Detroit
08 Mar 71	Joe Frazier w.pts.15 Muhammad Ali at New York
15 Jan 72	Joe Frazier w.rsf.4 Terry Daniels at New Orleans
25 May 72	Joe Frazier w.rsf.4 Ron Stander at Omaha
22 Jan 73	George Foreman w.rsf.2 Joe Frazier in Kingston, Jamaica
01 Sep 73	George Foreman w.ko.1 Joe Roman in Tokyo
26 Mar 74	George Foreman w.rsf.2 Ken Norton in Caracas
30 Oct 74	Muhammad Ali w.ko.8 George Foreman in Kinshasa
24 Mar 75	Muhammad Ali w.rsf.15 Chuck Wepner at Cleveland
16 May 75	Muhammad Ali w.rsf.11 Ron Lyle at Las Vegas
01 Jul 75	Muhammad Ali w.pts.15 Joe Bugner in Kuala Lumpur
01 Oct 75	Muhammad Ali w.rtd.14 Joe Frazier in Manila
10 Feb 76	Muhammad Ali w.ko.5 Jean-Pierre Coopman in San Juan, Puerto Rico
30 Apr 76	Muhammad Ali w.pts.15 Jimmy Young in Landover, Maryland
25 May 76	Muhammad Ali w.rsf.5 Richard Dunn in Munich
28 Sep 76	Muhammad Ali w.pts.15 Ken Norton in New York
16 May 77	Muhammad Ali w.pts.15 Alfredo Evangelista in Landover, Maryland
29 Sep 77	Muhammad Ali w.pts.15 Earnie Shavers in New York
15 Feb 78	Leon Spinks w.pts.15 Muhammad Ali in Las Vegas
18 Mar 78	*Spinks stripped by WBC for failure to defend against Ken Norton. The WBC then proclaimed Norton champion on the basis of his 15-rounds points win over Jimmy Young in their final eliminator in Las Vegas on 5 November 1977*
10 Jun 78	Larry Holmes w.pts.15 Ken Norton in Las Vegas *(WBC title)*
15 Sep 78	Muhammad Ali w.pts.15 Leon Spinks in New Orleans *(WBA title)*
10 Nov 78	Larry Holmes w.ko.7 Alfredo Evangelista in Las Vegas *(WBC title)*
24 Mar 79	Larry Holmes w.rsf.7 Osvaldo Ocasio at Las Vegas
22 Jun 79	Larry Holmes w.rsf.12 Mike Weaver in New York
28 Sep 79	Larry Holmes w.rsf.11 Earnie Shavers in Las Vegas
Sep 79	*Muhammad Ali announced his retirement as WBA champion*
20 Oct 79	John Tate w.pts.15 Gerrie Coetzee at Pretoria *(Vacant WBA title)*
03 Feb 80	Larry Holmes w.ko.6 Lorenzo Zanon in Las Vegas
31 Mar 80	Larry Holmes w.rsf.8 Leroy Jones at Las Vegas
31 Mar 80	Mike Weaver w.ko.15 John Tate in Knoxville *(WBA title)*
07 Jul 80	Larry Holmes w.rsf.7 Scott LeDoux at Bloomington
02 Oct 80	Larry Holmes w.rtd.10 Muhammad Ali in Las Vegas
25 Oct 80	Mike Weaver w.ko.13 Gerrie Coetzee at Sun City
11 Apr 81	Larry Holmes w.pts.15 Trevor Berbick at Las Vegas
12 Jun 81	Larry Holmes w.rsf.3 Leon Spinks at Detroit
03 Oct 81	Mike Weaver w.pts.15 James Tillis at Rosemount, Ill.
06 Nov 81	Larry Holmes w.rsf.11 Renaldo Snipes at Pittsburgh
11 Jun 82	Larry Holmes w.rsf.13 Gerry Cooney at Las Vegas
26 Nov 82	Larry Holmes w.pts.15 Randy 'Tex' Cobb at Houston
10 Dec 82	Mike Dokes w.rsf.1 Mike Weaver at Las Vegas
27 Mar 83	Larry Holmes w.pts.12 Lucien Rodriguez at Scranton
20 May 83	Larry Holmes w.pts.12 Tim Witherspoon at Las Vegas
20 May 83	Mike Dokes drew 15 Mike Weaver at Las Vegas
10 Sep 83	Larry Holmes w.rsf.5 Scott Frank at Atlantic City
23 Sep 83	Gerrie Coetzee w.ko.10 Mike Dokes at Richfield
Dec 83	*Larry Holmes relinquished WBC title and accepted recognition from the newly formed International Boxing Federation*
09 Mar 84	Tim Witherspoon w.pts.12 Greg Page at Las Vegas *(Vacant WBC title)*
31 Aug 84	Pinklon Thomas w.pts.12 Tim Witherspoon at Las Vegas
09 Nov 84	Larry Holmes w.rsf.12 James 'Bonecrusher' Smith at Las Vegas
01 Dec 84	Greg Page w.ko.8 Gerrie Coetzee at Sun City
15 Mar 85	Larry Holmes w.rsf.10 David Bey at Las Vegas
29 Apr 85	Tony Tubbs w.pts.15 Greg Page at Buffalo
20 May 85	Larry Holmes w.pts.15 Carl Williams at Reno
15 Jun 85	Pinklon Thomas w.ko.8 Mike Weaver at Las Vegas
22 Sep 85	Mike Spinks w.pts.15 Larry Holmes at Las Vegas
17 Jan 86	Tim Witherspoon w.pts.15 Tony Tubbs at Atlanta *(WBA title)*
22 Mar 86	Trevor Berbick w.pts.12 Pinklon Thomas at Las Vegas *(WBC title)*
19 Apr 86	Michael Spinks w.pts.15 Larry Holmes at Las Vegas
19 Jul 86	Tim Witherspoon w.rsf.11 Frank Bruno in London
06 Sep 86	Michael Spinks w.rsf.4 Steffen Tangstad at Las Vegas
22 Nov 86	Mike Tyson w.rsf.2 Trevor Berbick at Las Vegas *(WBC title)*
12 Dec 86	James 'Bonecrusher' Smith w.rsf.1 Tim Witherspoon in New York *(WBA title)*
Feb 87	*Michael Spinks stripped of IBF title for refusal to defend against their leading contender, Tony Tucker*
07 Mar 87	Mike Tyson w.pts.12 James 'Bonecrusher' Smith at Las Vegas *(WBC and WBA titles)*
30 May 87	Mike Tyson w.ko.6 Pinklon Thomas at Las Vegas
30 May 87	Tony Tucker w.rsf.10 James 'Buster' Douglas at Las Vegas *(Vacant IBF title)*

CRUISERWEIGHTS

TODAY, when any heavyweight under 16 st (224 lb) is at a distinct disadvantage, the recent introduction of the cruiserweight division has been one of the more far-sighted decisions taken by boxing's often myopic governing bodies.

Prior to 1979, boxers scaling more than 12 st 7 lb (175 lb) were officially classed as heavyweights, but were expected to concede 50 or 60 lb and still compete on level terms. This patent absurdity was at last rectified first by the WBC and then the WBA and IBF when, in 1979, 1982, and 1983 respectively they introduced the new 'in-between' category. But even in this thoroughly sensible move they were incapable of agreement. The WBC initially set the weight limit at 13 st 8 lb (190 lb) but increased it by 5 lb at their 1981 Convention. The WBA, who inaugurated their version of the title in 1982, did so at the limit of 190 lb as did the IBF a year later.

Furthermore, the authorities have not even been able to agree on a title for this new division. The WBC opted for 'cruiserweight', thus reviving the term that had been used (particularly in Britain) 50 years earlier as an alternative name for the light-heavyweight class. The WBA went for the more ponderous 'junior heavyweight' title, while the IBF

Below: *Marvin Camel achieved a unique double by being the first winner of both the WBC and IBF versions of the cruiserweight title.*

Right: *Carlos DeLeon, a Puerto Rican protégé of the veteran American fight figure Bill Daly, was a three-time WBC title winner.*

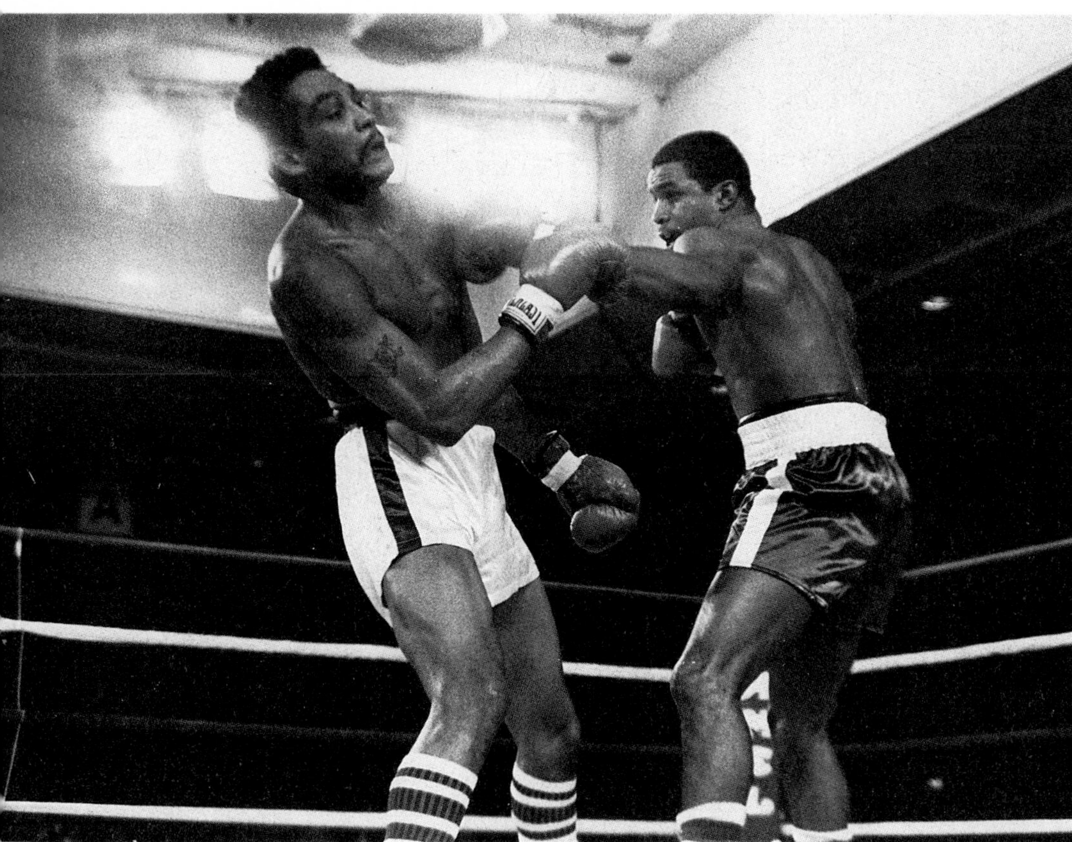

DeLeon (left, *on the right) took the title from Marvin Camel and then stopped him in seven rounds in a rematch. Between them DeLeon and Camel have had more cruiserweight title fights than anyone else, and are two of the most dominant figures yet produced by the division. S. T. Gordon* (below) *was a dangerous but unpredictable type whose victims included future WBC heavyweight champion Trevor Berbick.*

chose the same name as that used by the WBC, even though they disagree by 5 lb on the division's weight limit. It is no wonder that world boxing is in such a state of administrative chaos.

The boxing press and public, however, favour 'cruiserweight' and the term 'junior heavyweight' is rarely used even by WBA personnel except in official announcements and ratings.

Since this is one of boxing's newest categories it has yet to produce any outstanding holders of any of the three versions of the title. Some of its handful of champions, though, have been colourful and interesting individuals, such as the WBC's first winner Marvin Camel, a part-black, part-Flathead Salish Indian, and Piet Crous, the South African who became the first 'bank clerk' since James J. Corbett to win a world title (Crous actually worked for a building society, but that is close enough.)

Camel, one of a family of 14, boxed a draw in Yugoslavia with the former light-heavyweight champion Mate Parlov in the division's inaugural title fight in December 1979, but outscored Parlov in the Las Vegas rematch in March 1980. He held the title for less than one year, losing it in November to Carlos DeLeon of Puerto Rico in a bloody 15-rounder. DeLeon retained it in a rematch with Camel before losing it, on a second-round stoppage, to a hard-hitting but lightly regarded fighter from Los Angeles called S.T. Gordon, in June 1982.

The new champion revealed startling un-

Below: *Gordon hammers Carlos DeLeon in two rounds to take the title.*

Alfonzo Ratliff (above, *on the right) had a brief spell as WBC champion in 1985. He switched between the cruiserweight and heavyweight divisions, until beaten by Mike Tyson.*

professionalism when he told newsmen that he was not aware, until just before the fight, that the WBC had raised the limit from 190 to 195 lb, and that had he known he would have come in heavier than the 191 lb to which he had reduced in training.

Gordon, who had never boxed as an amateur, managed one successful defence before DeLeon reclaimed the championship in July 1983. The Puerto Rican at last brought some consistency to the title, retaining it against Alvaro Lopez, Anthony Davis, and Bashiru Ali, but in June 1985 he was outpointed by a Chicagoan called Alfonzo Ratliff, whose nickname 'Big Foot' derived from his size 17 shoes. (Promoter Don King cracked 'You can't knock this guy out – however hard you hit him, he can't fall – he just sways back and forth on those feet like a cartoon character.')

Ratliff did not enjoy a long reign: he was an ex-champ within four months, losing in Las Vegas to a strong but crude former Marine, Bernard 'The Bull' Benton, who had lost his two fights prior to the title chance. But 'The Bull', too, failed to survive his first defence, and in March 1986 the WBC title was back in the hands of DeLeon.

The WBA title has had a rather more settled history. Ossie 'Jaws' Ocasio, a Puerto Rican stablemate of DeLeon's, disappointed 25,000 South Africans by winning a split decision over their man, Robbie Williams, at Rand Stadium to take the vacant championship in February 1982. He was a worthy champion, with three successful defences between then and his return trip to Africa in

'Big Foot' Ratliff (below, *on the right) in action against Elijah Tillery. Former heavyweight champ Leon Spinks also tried his luck in the new division, but was halted with a cut eye after six rounds by Carlos DeLeon* (above).

Ossie Ocasio (above), *once an unsuccessful heavyweight title challenger (against Larry Holmes), won the vacant WBA title on a split decision* (below) *over the South African Robbie Williams in front of a 25,000 crowd in Johannesburg.*

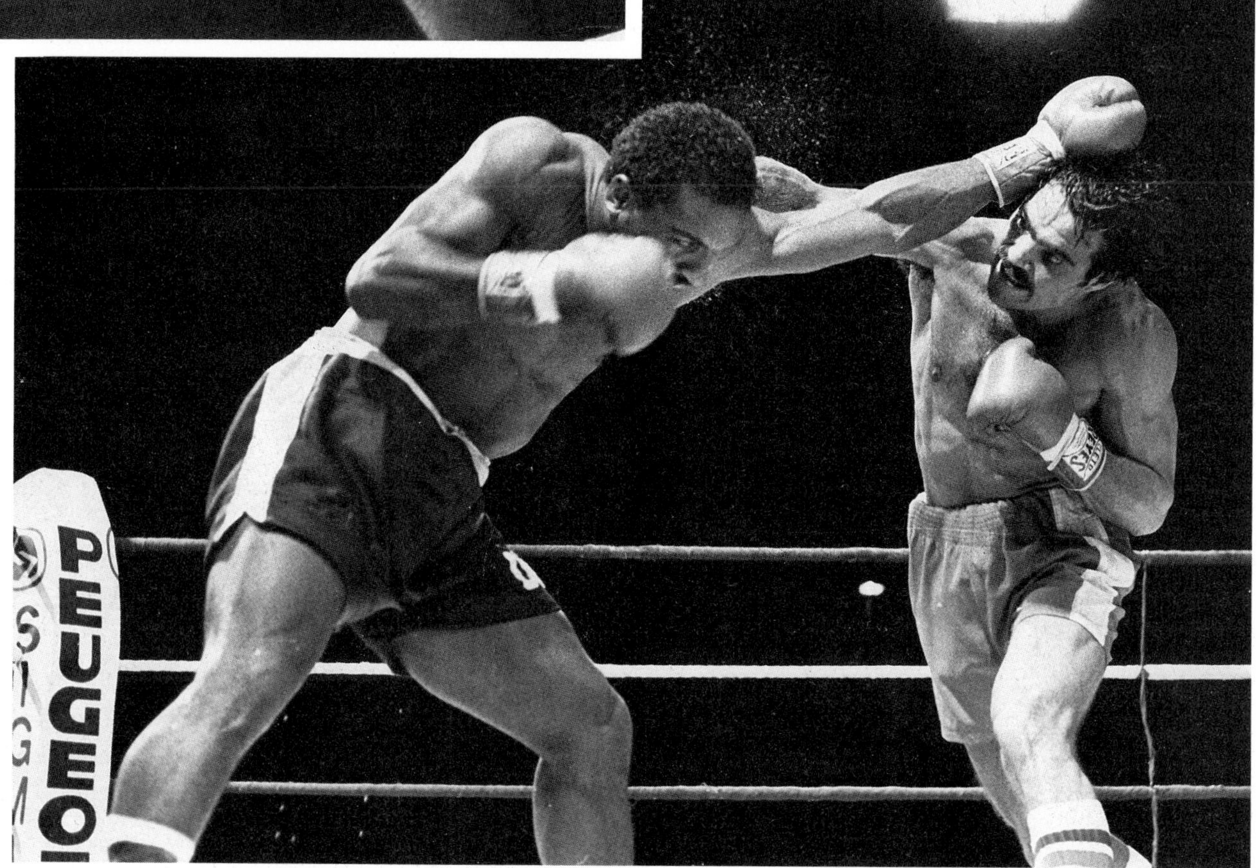

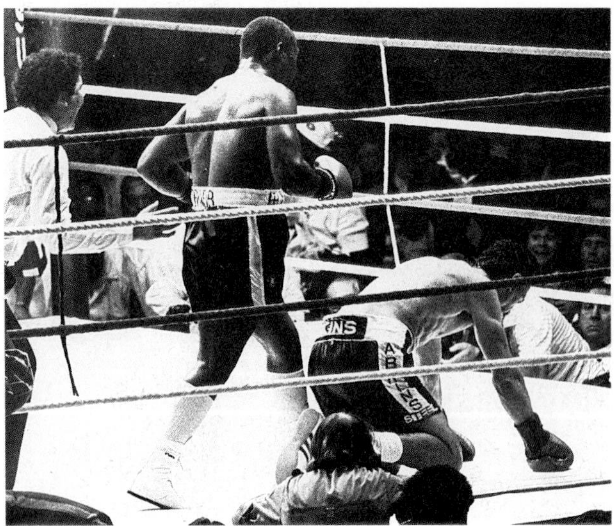

Piet Crous avenged Williams' defeat by taking the WBA title from Ocasio (above), *but lost* (right) *to former WBC light-heavyweight champion Dwight Muhammad Qawi.*

December 1984, when Piet Crous outscored him in a big upset. The South African clerk had not been beaten in 22 fights, and he took no chances with his choice of opponent for his first defence. American Randy Stephens had boxed only once in the previous 18 months, and was well into the veteran stage of his career – yet he floored Crous in the third round of their March 1985 clash in Sun City, only for Crous to fire back and stop him later in the same round.

Dwight Muhammad Qawi, the former light-heavyweight champion, battered Crous to an 11th-

Left: *Veteran American Randy Stephens trades blows with Crous in their 1985 thriller. Both were floored.*

Below: *Evander Holyfield (right, taking the WBA title from Qawi) has developed into a formidable champion.*

LeeRoy Murphy (far left) *was rather lucky to win the IBF title from Marvin Camel, but made three successful defences including this 12th round knockout of Commonwealth champion Chisanda Mutti in Monaco in 1985.*

round defeat in Sun City four months later and then promptly announced that he would refuse to defend the title there until apartheid had been abolished, a principle which had not prevented him from challenging for it in the South African puppet state. However, the question became academic when Qawi lost his first defence to the former Olympic light-heavyweight semi-finalist Evander Holyfield, who beat his gold medal-winning team-mates in the race to become a professional world champion.

Marvin Camel, who had been the WBC's first champion, achieved a unique double by also becoming the inaugural IBF champion when he knocked out the inexperienced Canadian Roddy McDonald in five rounds at Halifax, Novia Scotia, in December 1983. Camel was in a commanding points lead in his first defence against the former amateur star Lee Roy Murphy of Chicago in Billings, Montana, in October 1984 when the ringside doctor stopped the fight at the end of the 14th round because of cuts over both the veteran's eyes. Murphy was a lucky winner, but he proved a solid champion with three defences before Ricky Parkey, a 30-year-old from Tennessee who had been beaten by Bernard Benton in 1984 for the United States title, floored him three times and stopped him in the 10th round. It was Murphy's first loss in 24 fights, and the fact that the two black Americans fought in Marsala, Sicily, was an eloquent comment on the extent to which boxing had, by late 1986, become so internationalized and also dominated by television networks. Lower labour costs in Europe make it cheaper for American networks to arrange title fights in Europe and screen them back to the United States, than to hold them in America itself.

In May 1987 Holyfield outclassed Parkey and stopped him in three rounds at Caesars Palace to add the IBF title to his WBC crown, and raise hopes that the cruiserweights might soon have a single champion. Assuming that he does not fight himself out of competition and be forced to chase the heavyweight title, Holyfield may be the man who will earn for the unglamourous and relatively new division the public acceptance which has so far eluded it.

HOW THE CRUISERWEIGHT TITLE HAS CHANGED HANDS

08 Dec 79	Marvin Camel drew 15 Mate Parlov in Split *(Vacant WBC title)*
31 Mar 80	Marvin Camel w.pts.15 Mate Parlov in Las Vegas *(Vacant WBC title)*
26 Nov 80	Carlos De Leon w.pts.15 Marvin Camel in New Orleans
13 Feb 82	Ossie Ocasio w.pts.15 Robbie Williams in Johannesburg *(Vacant WBA title)*
27 Feb 82	S. T. Gordon w.rsf.2 Carlos De Leon at Cleveland
17 Jul 83	Carlos De Leon w.pts.12 S. T. Gordon at Las Vegas
13 Dec 83	Marvin Camel w.ko.5 Roddy McDonald at Halifax, NS *(Vacant IBF title)*
01 Dec 84	Piet Crous w.pts.15 Ossie Ocasio at Sun City
06 Oct 84	LeeRoy Murphy w.rsf.14 Marvin Camel at Billings
06 Jun 85	Alfonzo Ratliff w.pts.12 Carlos De Leon at Las Vegas
27 Jul 85	Dwight Muhammad Qawi w.rsf.11 Piet Crous at Sun City
21 Sep 85	Bernard Benton w.pts.12 Alfonzo Ratliff at Las Vegas
22 Mar 86	Carlos De Leon w.pts.12 Bernard Benton at Las Vegas *(WBC title)*
12 Jul 86	Evander Holyfield w.pts.15 Dwight Muhammad Qawi at Atlanta *(WBA title)*
25 Oct.86	Rickey Parkey w.rsf.10 LeeRoy Murphy at Marsala, Italy *(IBF title)*
15 May 87	Evander Holyfield w.rsf.3 Ricky Parkey at Las Vegas *(WBA and IBF titles)*

LIGHT HEAVYWEIGHTS

ANY PROJECT devised by a man who combined the professions of boxing writing and boxing management has to be viewed with a degree of scepticism, so it should be no surprise to learn that the early days of the light-heavyweight class are swathed in scandals and rumours of fight-fixing.

The division was the brainchild of a Chicago sports writer, Lou Houseman. He was looking after the affairs of a talented but small-framed fighter called Jack Root, who had a weight problem. He could not get down to the middleweight limit, but at 11 st 11 lb (165 lb) he could not compete successfully with the heavyweights – especially as the title was then in the hands of the 216 lb James J. Jeffries. The enterprising Houseman, however, had the solution: he matched Root with the former middleweight champion Kid McCoy, and persuaded some of his newspaper friends to report the fight as being for the 'light heavyweight' title.

McCoy, a colourful individual who married eight women and murdered a ninth, was duly outpointed in Detroit on 22 April 1903, and the world had a new champion. But not for long. In July George Gardner, a 26-year-old from Lisdoonvarna in County Clare, knocked Root out in 12 rounds. The division's first year of existence saw its third champion crowned when the veteran Bob Fitzsimmons, then in his 41st year, outpointed Gardner in San Francisco.

There were doubts about the authenticity of the victory which made Fitzsimmons (the former heavyweight and middleweight champion) the first man to rule at three weights, but there were none at all about the fight in which he lost the title. Philadelphia Jack O'Brien, whose parents (real name O'Hagan) came from County Derry, knocked out Fitzsimmons in 13 rounds in December 1905 but, within two years, he had published a signed

Jack Root (above) *was the first light-heavyweight champion – hardly surprising, as his manager Lou Houseman had created the division. But Root held the title for only three months before George Gardner* (right)*, from County Clare, knocked him out in 12 rounds.*

Philadelphia Jack O'Brien (left) *actually scaled under the modern light-middleweight limit when he challenged for the heavyweight title. He later claimed that both his heavyweight title bids were fixed, as was the fight in which he won the light-heavyweight title. O'Brien was succeeded as champion by Jack Dillon* (above), *one of the busiest top-grade boxers in history.*

statement in a San Francisco newspaper declaring that not only had the fight been fixed, but that so had most of his previous 150 or so contests, including his two meetings with Tommy Burns for the heavyweight title. (In the first, a 20-round draw, O'Brien weighed only 10 st 13½ lb (153½ lb) while Burns himself was 5 lb under the *light*-heavyweight limit at 12 st 2 lb (170 lb).

It was perhaps just as well that O'Brien never defended the title, for the seven-year hiatus before the division's next title fight allowed time for the scandal to fade away. O'Brien's successor was another Irish-American, a short but pugnacious individual called Jack Dillon, whose frequent victories over full-blown heavyweights earned him the nickname of 'Jack the Giantkiller'. Dillon, at only 5 ft 7½ in and 11 st 4 lb (158 lb) was much more suited to the new division, and claimed the vacant title after knocking out Hugo Kelly in 1912. It took him two years to earn universal recognition. Dillon was a prodigiously busy performer but, despite cramming 240 bouts into his 15-year career, he only defended the title twice before losing it to Battling Levinsky in Boston on 24 October 1916. Yet Dillon could be forgiven for losing, having retained the title in a 12-round 'no decision' fight seven days earlier, and boxed a non-decision six-rounder in Philadelphia, several hundred miles away, *the previous night.* Such a work-load is unimaginable in modern boxing, but astonishingly Levinsky bettered it.

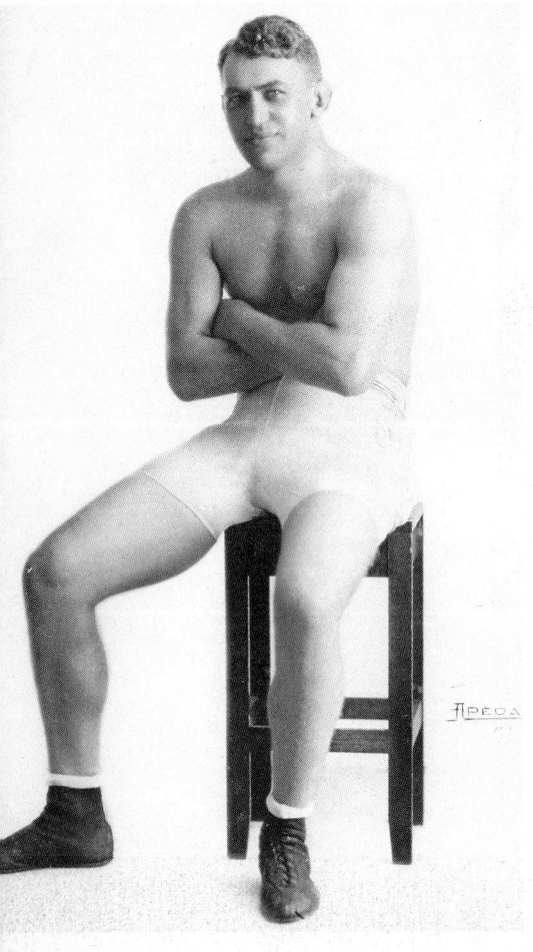

The new champion, whose real name was Barney Lebrowitz, is credited with an official total of 274 fights, but the real figure is probably nearer 400. He achieved the unique distinction of boxing three main event contests on the same day when, on New Year's Day 1915, he boxed ten rounds with Bartley Madden in Brooklyn in the morning, ten more with Soldier Kearns in New York in the afternoon, and rounded his remarkable day off with a brisk 12 rounds against Gunboat Smith at Waterbury, Connecticut, in the evening. Levinsky was no keener than Dillon on defending the championship, however, and almost four years passed before he risked it against the French war hero Georges Carpentier, who flattened him in four rounds.

Carpentier had dominated European boxing for almost a decade, winning continental titles at welterweight, middleweight, light-heavyweight and heavyweight, as well as national titles at every weight from lightweight upwards in a career which began when he was only 14 years old. When he signed in 1922 to meet another war hero, a Senegalese whose ring name was Battling Siki and who had won the *Croix de Guerre* for wiping out a machine gun post single-handedly, it was expected to be a routine defence. The African was a wild, crude brawler with no pretensions to sophistication

Battling Levinsky (above left) *once boxed three times in one day, but when he risked the title against Georges Carpentier* (left) *he lasted less than four rounds.*

Carpentier was a frequent and popular visitor to England, where his successes included his first-round knockout of Joe Beckett (below).

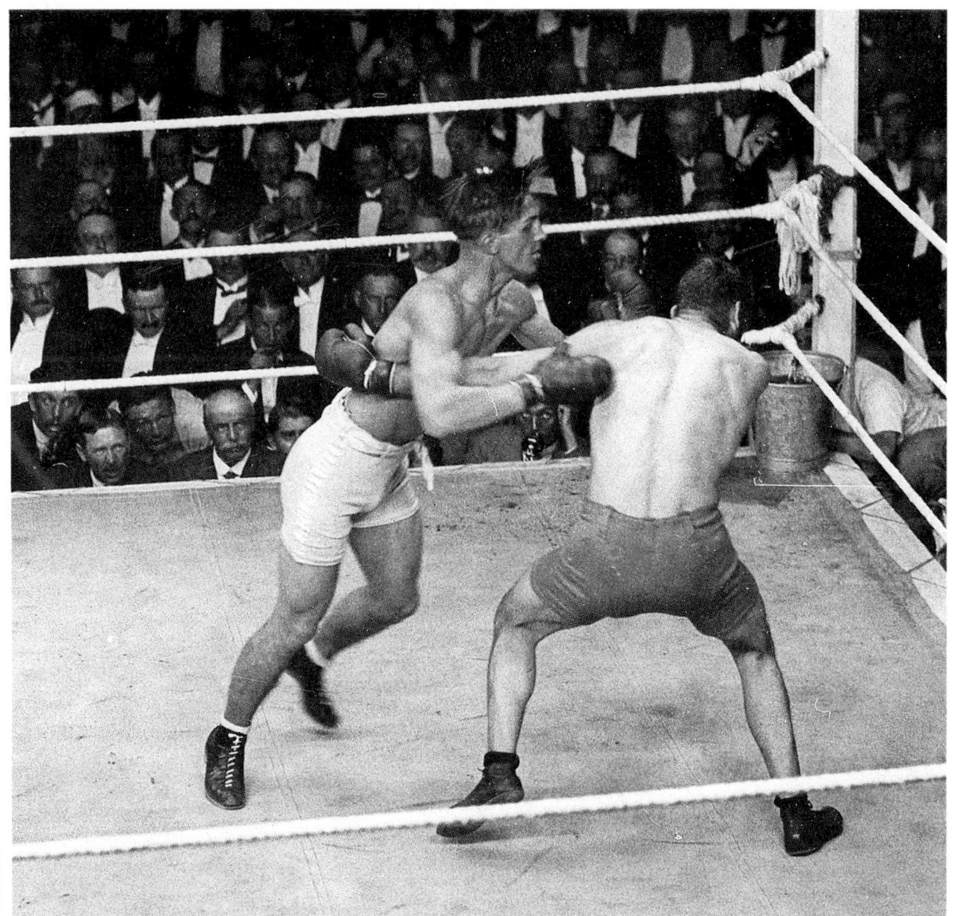

The French star's knockouts of Gunboat Smith (left) *and Billy Wells* (below) *established him as a heavyweight contender until Jack Dempsey put him in his place in 1921. A year later, Carpentier lost his light-heavyweight crown to Battling Siki* (above).

or class, although his raw power had brought him 49 wins in 57 fights. He had been held to a draw earlier that year by the London veteran Harry Reeve, who had held the British title in 1916 but who is now principally remembered as the Military Policeman whose brutal killing of a soldier, for ignoring an order to fasten his tunic button, sparked the mutiny at the British Army training camp at Etaples (France). He had boxed Reeve four times, outpointing him twice and knocking him out in six rounds in his warm-up for the Carpentier fight.

Siki had been 'adopted' as a 15-year-old in Senegal by a French society woman who, captivated by his physical attributes, gave him the name Louis Phal in honour of his most outstanding asset and brought him to Paris as her 'toy boy'.

Carpentier had secured the film rights for the fight, and intended to use it as a showcase for his histrionic talents as well as his pugilistic qualities. An early finish would devalue the film's attraction, so when Siki went over in the first round from a blow which landed on his gloves (which the African had cupped in front of his face) Carpentier stood back and sparred his way carefully through the rest of the round. The same thing happened at the start of the second: Siki fell without a blow being struck, took a count of six, but then suddenly leapt to his feet and charged the champion, catching him completely unprepared and flooring him for two. It was all that Carpentier could do to survive the round, but he recovered in the interval and came out for the third looking to dispose of his unexpectedly troublesome challenger. A right hook put Siki down, but he bounced up without a count and once more charged at Carpentier, who side-stepped but slipped and fell.

Siki helped him to his feet and was rewarded with a left, full in the face. By now the crowd were swinging to Siki's side, and Carpentier infuriated them further at the end of the round when he hit him after the bell. It was, effectively, the last decent punch he landed. For the next three rounds Siki gave him an unmerciful hammering, smashing his nose, closing one eye and gashing the other, until he finally put him down and out in the sixth. The Frenchman's seconds carried the beaten champion to his corner, while Siki was paraded around the ring on the shoulders of his supporters.

Then came sensation – it was announced that the referee, Henri Bernstein, had disqualified Siki for tripping Carpentier. The crowd was so incensed that both the referee and Carpentier had to be escorted back to the dressing rooms under armed guard. An hour later, the decision was reversed, and Siki was

Above: *Former British champion Harry Reeve faced Siki in Holland, Belgium and France, drawing their second meeting and losing the others.*

Carpentier, stylish and arrogant, toyed with the apprehensive Siki in the early exchanges.

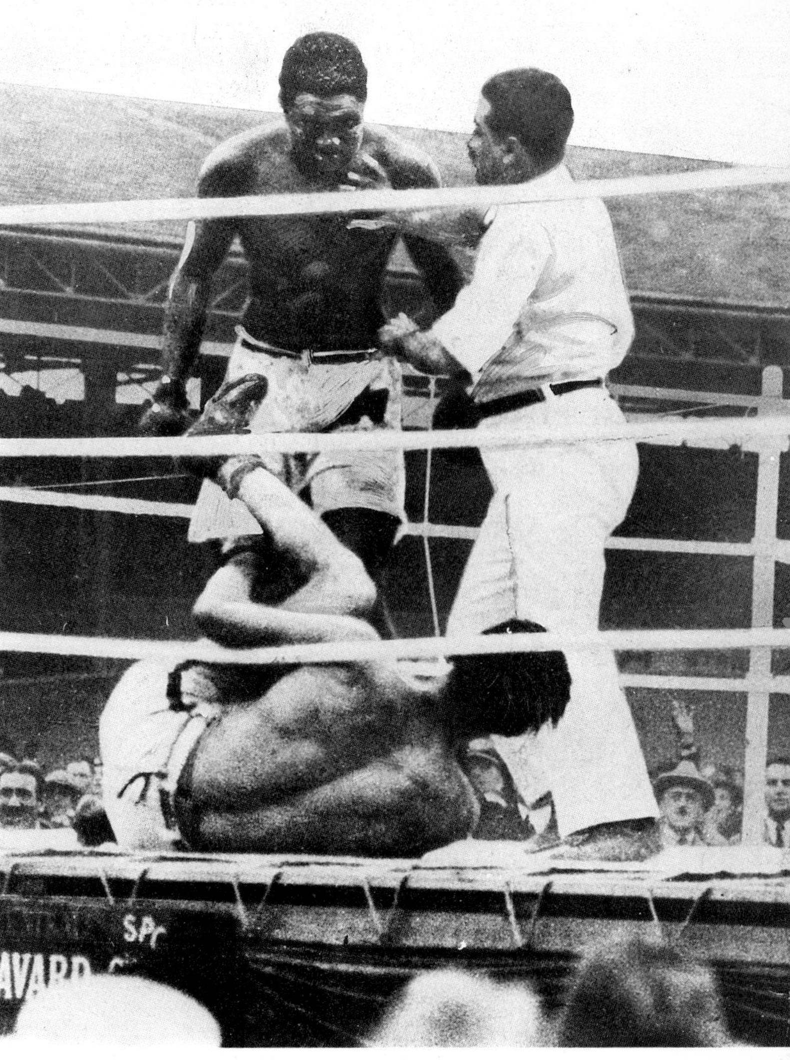

Above left and right: *The champion, Carpentier, took a fearful beating from the third round onwards, until, nose broken and eye closed, he was flattened in the sixth.*

Siki was first announced as a disqualification loser to the fury of the crowd, and had to wait a further hour before being announced as the new title holder.

belatedly proclaimed champion.

Siki was a disaster as champion, attracting the most outrageous publicity. He used to parade the streets of Paris with two lions on a leash, occasionally firing a pistol into the air when he felt he was not receiving enough attention. The British Home Office refused him permission to box Joe Beckett, on the grounds of his 'undesirability', so instead Siki made the ill-advised trip to Dublin to defend against Mike McTigue, from Ennis, County Clare, on St Patrick's Day. It was a dull affair, enlivened only by the noise of sporadic gunfire and grenade explosions from the street outside the cinema where the fight was being held. (The Irish Civil War was then at its height, making Siki's

Mike McTigue from County Clare had everything going for him: his world title chance was staged in Dublin, on St Patrick's Day.

McTigue clearly outpointed Siki (left), *but lost the title two years later in his first defence, against the former amateur wrestling star Paul Berlenbach* (above).

willingness to box there even less understandable.)

Contrary to popular myth, there was nothing wrong with the verdict that made the Irishman champion after 20 generally forgettable rounds. McTigue, a capable left-hand boxer, clearly outpointed Siki to end his career at top level. The Senegalese went to America after two easy comeback wins in France, but won only nine of his remaining 26 fights. The end came just over three years after he had shocked the boxing world by beating Carpentier. His body was found in a gutter in the notorious Hell's Kitchen area in New York. He had been shot.

McTigue, who had done all his professional fighting in America and Canada, never fought in Europe again. He lost the title in his first defence, in 1925, to a former American amateur wrestling champion called Paul Berlenbach. The new champion did not take up boxing until 1922, but won the national amateur heavyweight championship before turning professional in 1923. Nicknamed the 'Astoria Assassin', he proved a good champion with defences against the smooth-boxing Jimmy Slattery, Jack Delaney (the only man to have beaten him) and Young Stribling, before losing the title in a third fight with Delaney in 1926. They met once more, when both were ex-champions, with Delaney knocking him out in the sixth round.

Despite his Irish ring name, Delaney was actually a French-Canadian called Ovila Chapdelaine. He was an outstanding, immensely clever boxer whose style always blended perfectly with the rugged and hard-punching Berlenbach. Their four fights were all crowd-pullers, and Delaney's title win drew 49,186 to Ebbet's Field, Brooklyn. The division which had been launched under a cloud less than 25 years before was now big business.

Delaney's decision to relinquish the title in August 1927 without a defence caused some confusion. The National Boxing Association nominated Slattery to meet Maxie Rosenbloom, and recognized him as champion when he outpointed

No form-line is available on the two spar-mates (above), *but Berlenbach's 10-year career took in 50 fights with eight defeats. Tommy Loughran* (below), *crammed 172 fights into his 18 years.*

Jimmy Slattery (above) *won two versions of the light-heavyweight title. He beat Maxie Rosenbloom for the NBA title in 1927, and then lost the New York version to the same man in June 1930.*

The stylish Jack Delaney (above and right) *had a classic four-fight series with Berlenbach, winning three of them.*

Rosenbloom in a ten-rounder at Hartford, Connecticut, three weeks after Delaney's announcement. But McTigue, who had scored a brilliant four-rounds win over Berlenbach earlier in the year, reclaimed the title and received recognition from those states which were not affiliated to the NBA .

In October 1927, McTigue surrendered his version of the title to one of the division's outstanding figures – Tommy Loughran. The Philadelphian was a master boxer, who was destined to meet 13 men who held world titles, including heavyweight champions Gene Tunney, James J. Braddock, Jack Sharkey, Max Baer, and

Primo Carnera. Loughran beat the NBA champion Slattery to win the undisputed title in December 1927, and over the next two years established his authority with defences against Leo Lomski, Pete Latzo (twice), Mickey Walker, and James J. Braddock. He relinquished the championship in 1929 to compete as a heavyweight, and five years later finally got a crack at the world title, then held by the huge Italian, Primo Carnera. Loughran conceded 86 lb, which remains a record weight difference in a title fight, and lost on points.

His step up to heavyweight created a split championship at light-heavy. The powerful New York Commission recognized Jimmy Slattery as champion after his win in February 1930 over Lou Scozza, and when Maxie Rosenbloom beat Slattery four months later he was recognized by all the international bodies except the NBA. Their version

Loughran frequently took on and beat heavyweights like Maurice Strickland (left) *and Isadoro Gastanaga* (below), *but had the misfortune to make his bid for the title against the huge Primo Carnera, who outweighed him by 86 lb and beat him clearly on points.*

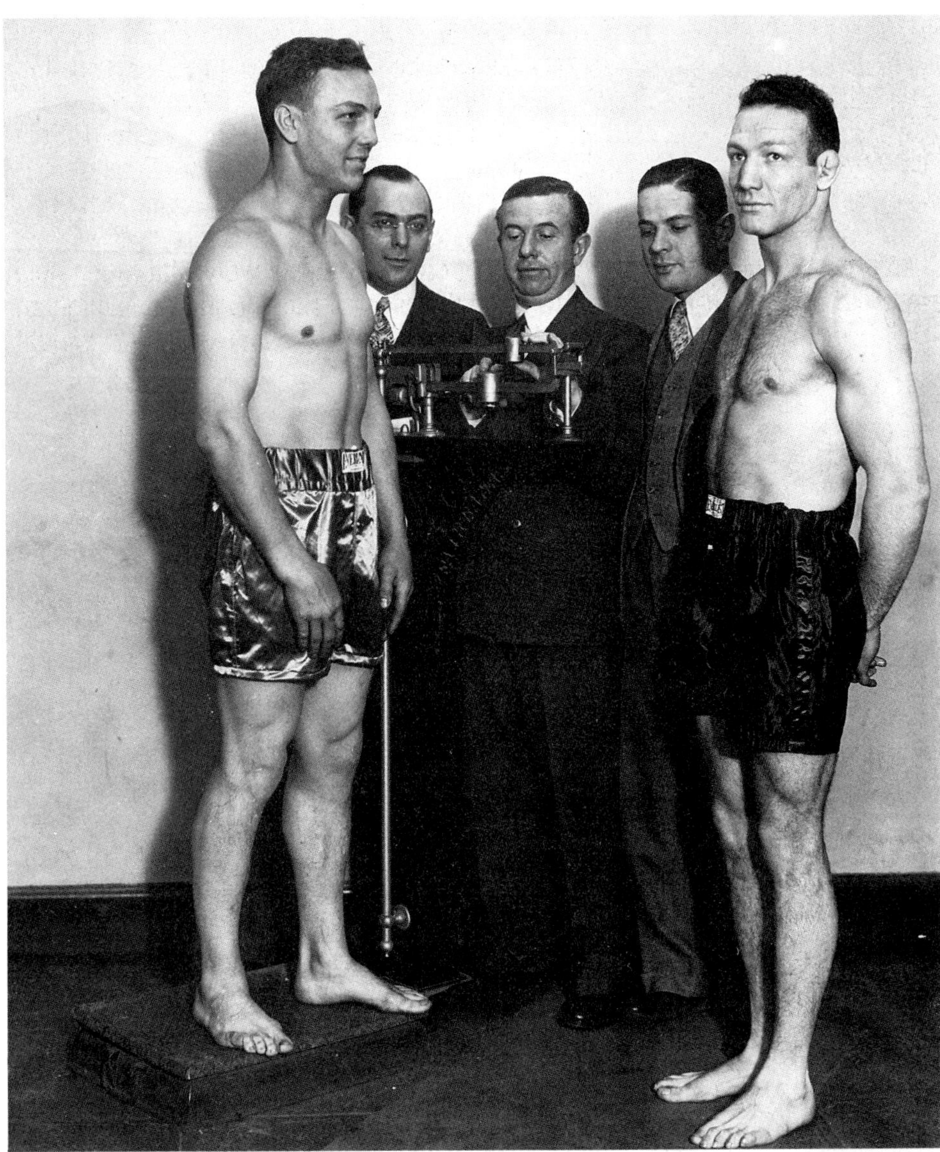

No wonder Maxie Rosenbloom looks bored by the weigh-in ritual (left, *on the right*): *he went through it 289 times. He survived this second-round knockdown* (below) *to outpoint Jimmy Adamick. But NBA light-heavyweight claimant George Nichols* (above) *was one of the few contemporaries whom Rosenbloom never met.*

of the title stayed vacant for over two years, until first George Nichols and then Lou Scozza won it in quick succession. In July 1932 Rosenbloom outpointed Scozza, and at last there was an undisputed champion again.

Rosenbloom was a colourful, clowning figure whose nickname of 'Slapsie Maxie' derived from his habit of hitting with the open glove. He was a prodigiously busy fighter, who once averaged a fight a fortnight for four and a half years, and whose career totalled 289 fights of which he won just 18 inside the distance.

Between August and December 1932 Rosenbloom managed 14 fights and won 13 of them, drawing the other. His opponents included Bob Godwin (twice) and John Henry Lewis, both of whom were future champions, and the dangerous heavyweight Leroy Haynes. But even this level of activity was not enough to satisfy the NBA, who were as prone to eccentric decisions as are their successors. They declared the title vacant, matching Bob Godwin with Joe Knight for the champion-

The effects of such a long career were etched on Rosenbloom's face (far left) *by the time he lost the title in November 1934 to the former American amateur champion Bob Olin* (left).

ship. Godwin was a strange choice: he had yet to beat Rosenbloom in three meetings (although two of them had been drawn), and had won only six of his previous 12 fights.

Initially the NBA's decision was vindicated when Godwin outpointed Knight, but within three weeks Rosenbloom had cleared up the confusion again by knocking the pretender out in four rounds. Godwin met Rosenbloom seven times in all, winning one and drawing three. He also had a ten-fight series with Knight, winning six and drawing one. This kind of series was commonplace then, with Rosenbloom, because of his extraordinary number of bouts, figuring in many. He had seven with Lou Scozza and Jimmy Slattery, six with Leo Lomski and Frankie Schoell, five with John Henry Lewis, and four each with Joe Anderson, Tommy West, Lee Ramage and Al Stillman. Rosenbloom was also in the habit of raising cash by boxing his sparring partner, under a variety of different names, in the 'hick towns' of America – a practice revived in the late 1970s by the legendary Bruce Strauss.

In November 1934 Rosenbloom was surprisingly dethroned on a controversial decision by a former American amateur champion, Bob Olin. The new champion had shaky credentials, for his five previous fights had yielded just two wins, and he had been beaten twice in 1934 by the former NBA middleweight champion Lou Brouillard. He was not much more impressive as champion, losing in 1935 to Dutch Weimer and John Henry Lewis before, in October 1935, Lewis took his title in a 15-round rematch in St Louis. (Olin went on to lose 11 of his remaining 17 fights – although in one of them, in London in 1936, he floored Tommy Farr three times but lost on points.)

Although Lewis was only 21, he had already had 58 fights with only four defeats. The losses, rather than the wins, got Lewis the title chance. He had flopped on his East Coast debut in November 1934,

Handsome and hard-hitting John Henry Lewis (left) *is still regarded as one of the division's finest title-holders.*

Previous page: *John Conteh (right), in his first appearance after being stripped of the WBC light-heavyweight title, made hard work of outpointing Joe Cokes, brother of the former welterweight champion Curtis Cokes.*

Above: *Dennis Andries, an unlikely winner of the WBC light-heavyweight title in 1986, retained it with a one-sided defeat of Tony Sibson in a rare all-British world championship. Six months later Andries was toppled by Thomas Hearns.*

Len Harvey (left, *as a 12-year-old professional) matched himself with Lewis for the world title at Wembley* (above) *in his capacity as match-maker for promoter Sir Arthur Elvin, but was outpointed.*

Harvey (on the left) on the way to a 10th-round knockout of Joe Rolfe at Holland Park, London, in 1927. The Cornishman dominated British boxing for two decades.

when James J. Braddock soundly outpointed him, and he had lost his last two fights, to Maxie Rosenbloom (for the second time) and a rough heavyweight called Abe Feldman. The losses came just seven days apart, but on opposite sides of the continent. After Rosenbloom had beaten him in Oakland, California, Lewis took a plane to New York where Feldman gave him a severe beating, cutting both his eyes. Lewis, however, had been violently airsick throughout the flight, and had not fully recovered when he faced Feldman. The form, though, was still sufficiently unimpressive to tempt Olin to choose him as a 'safe' opponent. The decision cost him dearly, for Olin had to soak up a one-sided pounding. Jack Blackburn, Joe Louis' trainer, was in the challenger's corner and was moved to tell pressmen that 'In all my years in the game, I never saw a gamer or a tougher man than Bob Olin.'

Lewis defended his title twice in 1936, both against English challengers. Jock McAvoy, who was really only a middleweight, gave him a rough 15 rounds in Madison Square Garden and then, eight months later, Lewis outpointed the marvellous Len Harvey at Wembley. Harvey was, for more than a decade, the British ring's most distinguished performer. He had been a professional since he was 12 years old, won British titles at three weights, challenged Marcel Thil for the world middleweight title, and boxed 418 times, losing a handful. The Lewis fight is probably the only time that a promoter's matchmaker paired himself with a world champion – Harvey had been hired by Sir Arthur Elvin to organize the boxing shows there, and booked himself to face Lewis as his opening attraction! The show sold out, but Harvey, after making a brilliant start, damaged his right hand in the third round and, his effectiveness greatly reduced, finished a close points loser.

The Lewis v Harvey fight was not for the undisputed title. A new organization, the International Boxing Union, had been formed in Europe and recognized the Belgian Gustave Roth as 'world champion'. But it was never more than a European concern, and after the Second World War it evolved into the present European Boxing Union. The bulk of the 'world title fights' staged under its auspices in the middle to late 1930s were in effect just European championships, but Roth made his title pay with six successful defences before losing it in 1938 to the German Adolf Heuser, who did not defend it after the outbreak of war.

Lewis was a busy champion. He knocked out Olin in the eighth round of a championship rematch in 1937, and retained the title twice in 1938, as well as boxing 18 non-title fights in 1937 and ten in 1938. But he was hiding a terrible secret: cataracts had blinded him in the left eye three years previously, and the sight was fading in the right eye also. In October 1938 he announced that he was giving up the light-heavyweight title to seek a fight with his friend Joe Louis for the heavyweight championship. Lewis' condition was an open secret in the business, and almost certainly Louis was aware of it when he knocked him out in two minutes 29 seconds at Madison Square Garden on 25 January 1939. 'I made it quick 'cos he's my friend', Joe said afterwards. Lewis never fought again. He quit with a record of 103 wins and five

Jock McAvoy (left), Harvey's arch-rival on the British scene, fared no better against John Henry Lewis than Harvey managed eight months later. Lewis outpointed him in New York in March 1936 to retain the title.

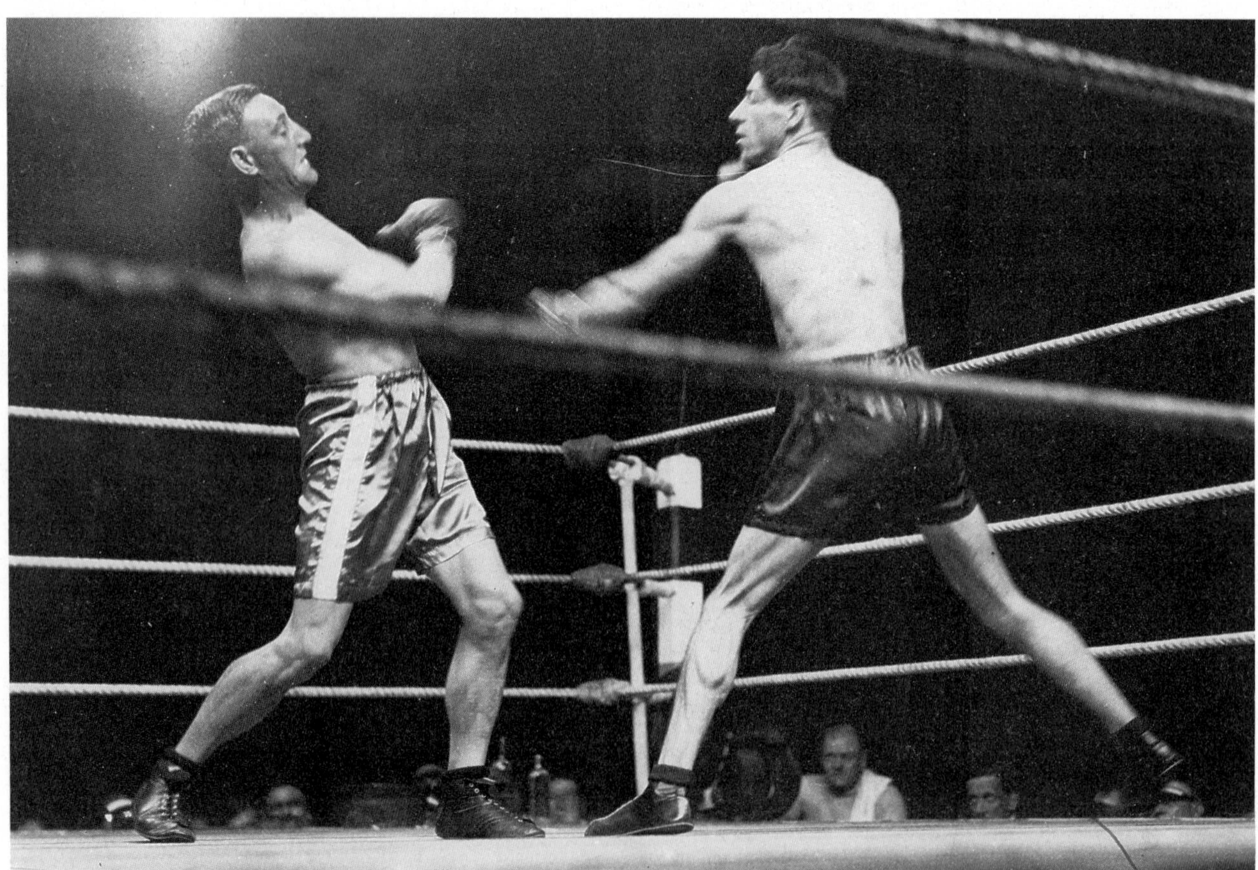

Scottish middleweight Alex Ireland (left) was kayoed in seven to give Harvey the first of his three British championships.

draws in 116 fights, and Joe Louis was the only man to beat him inside the distance.

Lewis' move into the heavyweight division caused the now-customary muddle. The British Board paired Len Harvey and Jock McAvoy for the title, and received some support in Europe (although Adolf Heuser still held the IBU version.) Harvey and McAvoy drew a British record crowd of 90,000 to the White City Stadium in London to see the veteran Cornishman outpoint McAvoy and thereby reverse one of his few defeats. But Harvey did not pursue his claim – he joined the RAF and boxed only once more, in 1942, when Freddie Mills knocked him out in two rounds at Tottenham's football ground. That fight also carried official Board of Control recognition as a world title fight, but Mills himself did not take the 'title' too seriously, nor did the British public regard him as world champion until, six years later, he beat Gus Lesnevich.

Rough, brawling Freddie Mills ended Harvey's fabulous career when he knocked him sprawling from the ring at Tottenham Hotspur Football Ground, London, in 1942. The fight was staged in the afternoon because air raid precautions prohibited the lighting necessary for an evening promotion.

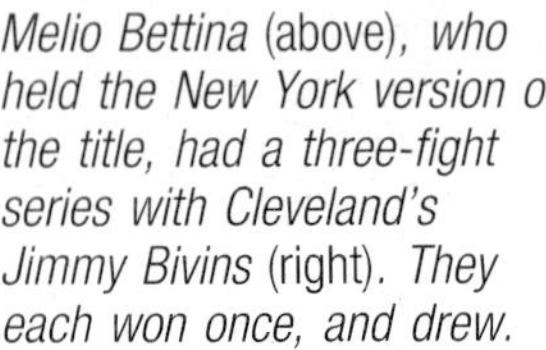

Melio Bettina (above), *who held the New York version of the title, had a three-fight series with Cleveland's Jimmy Bivins* (right). *They each won once, and drew.*

The New York version, meanwhile, had been won by Tiger Jack Fox, who held it for a little over two months until Melio Bettina stopped him in nine rounds. The NBA and the New York Commission then agreed to recognize the winner of a 15-rounder between Bettina and a handsome Irish-American called Billy Conn as the title holder. Conn duly had a unanimous win in Madison Square Garden on 13 July 1939 to launch one of the division's most colourful championship reigns.

Conn was a tall, strikingly good-looking man who, without having had a single amateur contest, turned professional as a welterweight in 1935. He was a boxer of instinctive genius who fortunately balanced his appetite for the high life with a thoroughly professional approach to training. Like Gene Tunney before him, he carried out a detailed study of the styles and records of all his leading contemporaries. Within two years Conn was at the top. In 1937 he faced five sometime world champions, and beat four of them – middleweights Babe Risko, Vince Dundee and Teddy Yarosz, and welterweight Young Corbett III. Only Solly Krieger, who had won the NBA middleweight title the following year, outpointed him – and Conn reversed that result six months later.

The Krieger win, and a pair of easy triumphs over the current middleweight champion Fred Apostoli, earned Conn his title chance against Bettina, and when he outclassed the Italian-American southpaw a second time in September 1939 he, rather than Harvey, was generally accepted as the world's best at 175 lb. A pair of points wins over Gus Lesnevich enhanced his status yet further, although Lesnevich would be heard from again.

Promoter Mike Jacobs, with an eye to a million-dollar gate, persuaded the charismatic Conn to chase a fight with Joe Louis. Conn launched his heavyweight campaign with an emphatic 13th-round win over Bob Pastor, a tricky type who had taken Louis the distance in 1937, and followed that

Billy Conn never had a single amateur contest, yet beat four champions in 1937, less than two years after turning pro.

Conn's successes in 1939–40 spanned three weight divisions. First he beat middleweight champion Fred Apostoli (here firing a left to Conn's body). Future light-heavyweight champ Gus Lesnevich (right) *was next, and then in September 1940 he defeated heavyweight Bob Pastor* (below, *on the left).*

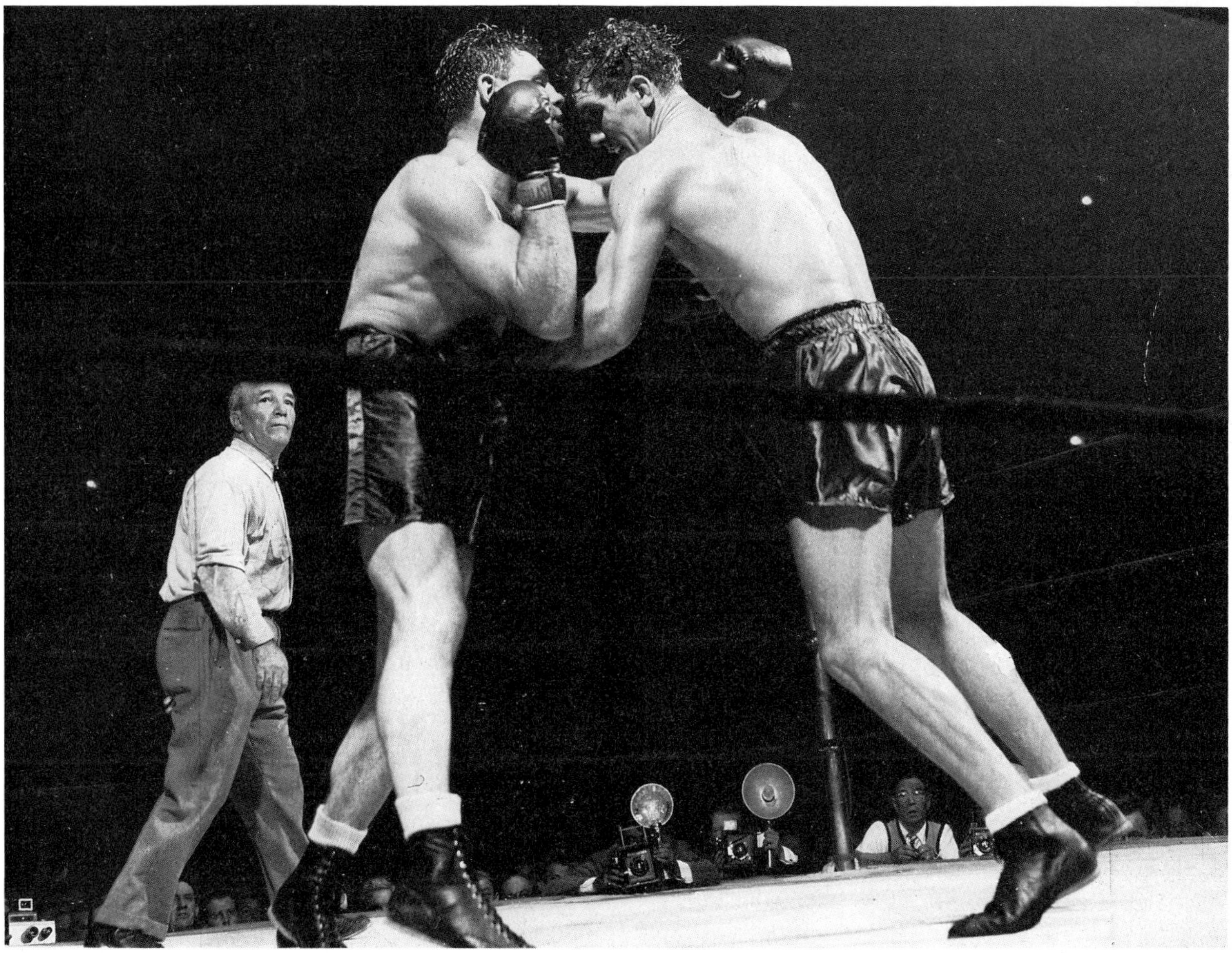

Anton Christoforidis won and lost the European middleweight title before reigning as NBA light-heavyweight champion.

with a string of six wins that included a points win over Lee Savold and an eighth-round knockout of the well respected Finn, Gunnar Barlund.

The Louis fight took place at Yankee Stadium on 18 June 1941, and for 12 rounds Conn danced his way into a wide points lead, only to neglect his boxing in his eagerness to win spectacularly. Louis only needed one chance, and when he got it he knocked Conn unconscious with a single left hook. According to Conn, he said to Louis later: 'You should have let me win. Then I could have held the title for a year and when we had a rematch, for a lot of money, you could have won it back.' Louis replied: 'How could you hold it for a year? You had it for 45 minutes and couldn't hang onto it that long!' There was a rematch, five years later, but both were past their prime and Louis knocked Conn out in the eighth round.

Conn had given up the light-heavyweight crown in late 1940, and in January it was taken over by the Greek Anton Christoforidis, who outpointed the former champion Melio Bettina to earn NBA recognition as champion.

The Greek, who had won and lost the European middleweight title before coming to America in 1940, had a short reign. Gus Lesnevich, whose two previous title bids had been thwarted by Conn, outscored him four months later and then, in August, earned champion recognition by all authorities except the British by outpointing Tami Mauriello in New York. The new titleholder was a seasoned professional of 26, who had learned his trade as a middleweight in the mid-1930s after winning the national Golden Gloves tournament. Defeats by Young Corbett III and Freddie Steele (both world title claimants) limited his progress, so he went to Australia, grew into a light-heavyweight, and established himself with a win over the former world champion Bob Olin.

Lesnevich's performances in defeat against Conn were good enough to keep him in the title picture, and the affable New Jerseyite, of Russian extraction, was a popular figure as the new champion. Like Conn, he tried to step up to heavyweight by beating Bob Pastor, but the plan went wrong when Pastor outpointed *him*, and then Jimmy Bivins, too, outscored him in what proved to be his only two fights for almost four years. With America now at last in the Second World War, Lesnevich joined the US Coastguards and the title went into storage. (The rival claimant, Freddie Mills, was also in uniform, serving with the RAF)

Lesnevich's return to the ring in 1946 was hardly encouraging – he knocked out Joe Kahut in the first round, but was then forced to retire after four rounds against heavyweight Lee Oma with severe facial cuts. When he travelled to London to

Battered winner Gus Lesnevich walks away from the fallen Freddie Mills after one of the most savage ring battles.

meet Mills for the undisputed title on 14 May 1946, the brawling Englishman was generally felt to have a great chance of taking the undisputed title. Their fight, at Harringay Arena, proved one of the most savage ever seen in a British ring. Mills was floored four times in a disastrous second round, being saved by the bell with the count at eight. Thereafter, he deserted his normal free-swinging style to box his way on top with classical but decidely uncharacteristic left jabbing. Although the American's left eye was swollen shut and bleeding, and his nose was damaged, he rallied heroically in the tenth to floor Mills twice. When Mills went down moments later for the third time, referee Eugene Henderson waved the fight over without even taking up the count. He was later subjected to a torrent of criticism from press and public when it emerged that there had only been four seconds left in the round when he stopped it.

While Lesnevich probably could not have continued for much longer, Henderson was vindicated when Mills admitted that he had been in an even worse state. He had no recollection of events after the second round, and had boxed purely on instinct.

The champion picked up some considerably easier money with two defences against the gangster-controlled Blackjack Billy Fox, who had been manoeuvred into a world title fight by a long succession of carefully pre-arranged results. Lesnevich had too much pride to accept any such arrangement, though, and gave Fox a one-sided beating, stopping him in ten rounds. Fox's management then bribed middleweight contender Jake LaMotta to 'throw' a fight with Fox in November 1947 in return for a promised crack at the middleweight title, and LaMotta duly obliged in four rounds, thus earning Fox another chance at Lesnevich. This time, Gus knocked him out in the first round.

Mills had kept active since his 1946 defeat by Lesnevich, although he had also been drastically overmatched against heavyweights Bruce Woodcock and Joe Baksi, both of whom inflicted terrible punishment on him. He had also been stopped by the American light-heavyweight Lloyd Marshall, but had won and retained the European title and thus qualified for a second fight with Lesnevich. This time, the weight-weakened, 31-year-old champion was outpointed over 15 comparatively dull rounds at White City, London on 26 July 1948.

Middleweight Jake La Motta later admitted that he had 'taken a dive' against Billy Fox in 1947 in order that Fox would qualify for a rematch with Lesnevich, who flattened him again.

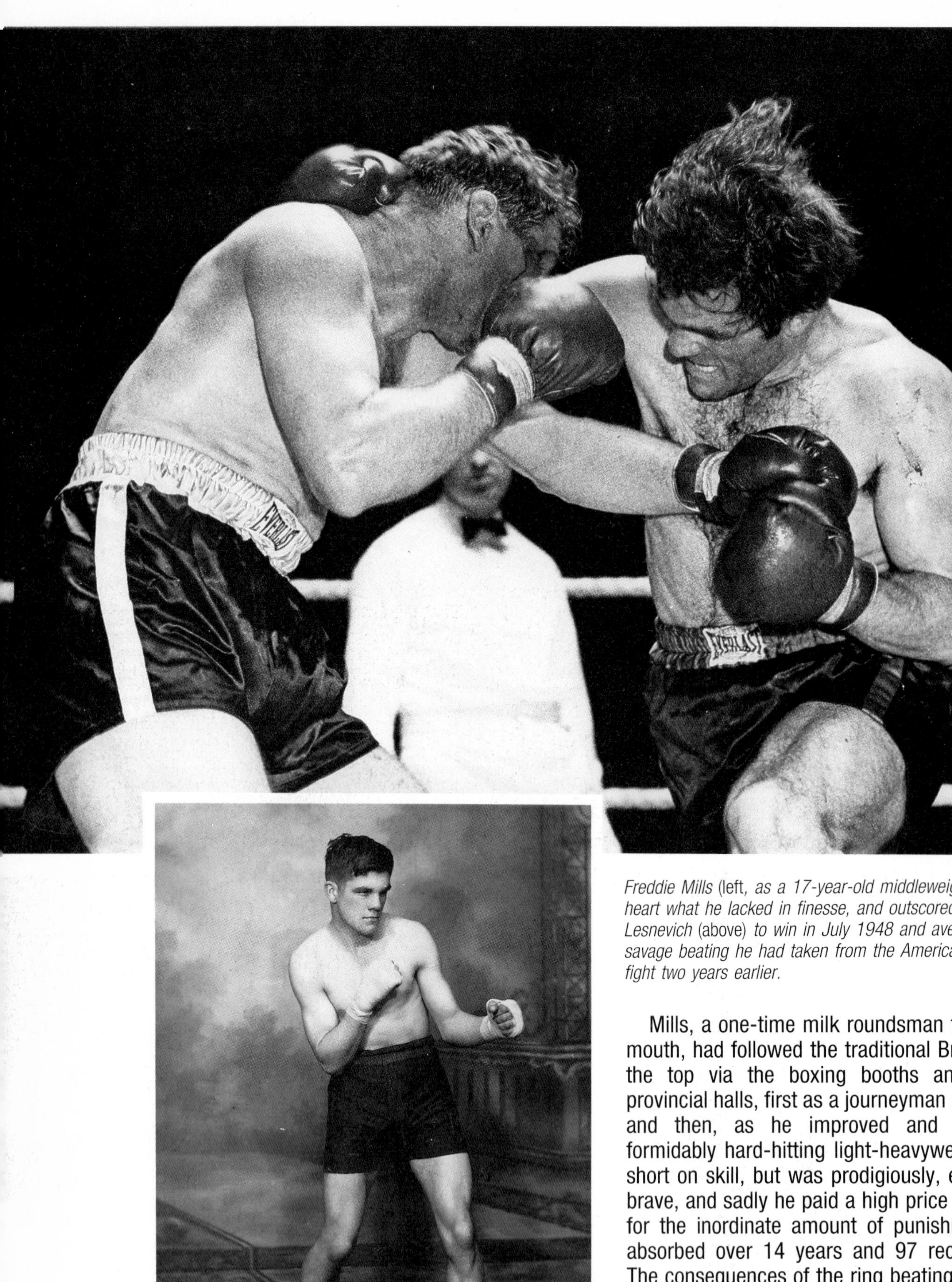

Freddie Mills (left, *as a 17-year-old middleweight) made up in heart what he lacked in finesse, and outscored a faded Lesnevich* (above) *to win in July 1948 and avenged the savage beating he had taken from the American in their first fight two years earlier.*

Mills, a one-time milk roundsman from Bournemouth, had followed the traditional British route to the top via the boxing booths and the small provincial halls, first as a journeyman middleweight and then, as he improved and grew, as a formidably hard-hitting light-heavyweight. He was short on skill, but was prodigiously, even foolishly brave, and sadly he paid a high price in later years for the inordinate amount of punishment he had absorbed over 14 years and 97 recorded fights. The consequences of the ring beatings he suffered were evident in his post-retirement problems, which culminated in his suicide in 1965.

Mills boxed only three times after beating Lesnevich. He knocked out South African heavyweight Johnny Ralph but then took yet another pounding in a challenge for Bruce Woodcock's

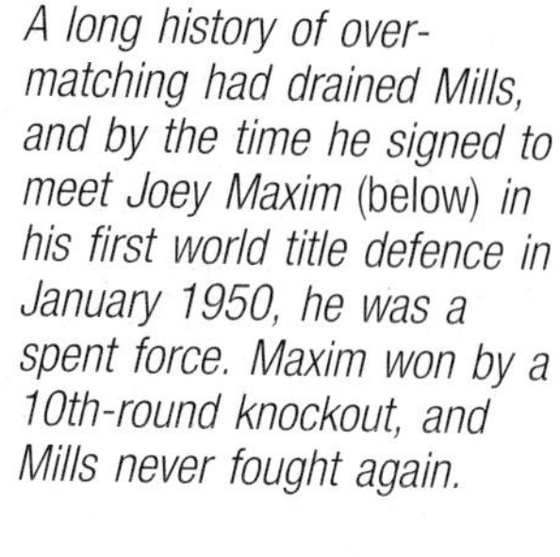

A long history of over-matching had drained Mills, and by the time he signed to meet Joey Maxim (below) *in his first world title defence in January 1950, he was a spent force. Maxim won by a 10th-round knockout, and Mills never fought again.*

By the time Maxim beat Mills (left) *he was a veteran, who had learned his trade against tough heavyweights like the Swede, Olle Tandberg* (right) *whom Maxim outpointed in New York in 1948. In all, 18 of Maxim's 115 fights were against sometime world champions.*

British and Empire heavyweight titles. Finally, in January 1950, he lost the world title to a competent if unexciting Italian-American called Joey Maxim, whose real name was Giuseppe Berardinelli.

Maxim, like most of the top fighters of that time, was already approaching the veteran stage before he got the title chance. The Mills fight was his 88th, of which he had lost 16 and drawn four. He was

managed by Jack 'Doc' Kearns, who in more prosperous times had guided ten world champions, most notably Jack Dempsey. Kearns steered him through defences against Irish Bob Murphy and Sugar Ray Robinson, who collapsed from heat exhaustion in a famous battle at Yankee Stadium in June 1952. The heat was so intense that even the referee, Ruby Goldstein, had to be replaced at the end of the tenth round. Robinson, bidding to add the light-heavyweight championship to the welter-weight and middleweight crowns he had already won, was in a commanding points lead at the end of 13 rounds but was incapable of answering the bell for the 14th.

Maxim also squeezed in a points loss to an old foe, Ezzard Charles, in a 1951 challenge for the heavyweight title, before in December 1952, he took on the superb Archie Moore. The veteran Moore, now 36, had been a leading contender for seven and a half years, ever since he had knocked out Lloyd Marshall in June 1945. But he had been avoided by Lesnevich, Mills and Maxim, until finally he got the title opportunity by agreeing to give Kearns a share of his contract. Moore outscored Maxim comfortably, but had to defend against him twice more at Kearns' insistence. He risked his title only six times between the third Maxim fight in January 1954 and 25 October 1960, when the NBA withdrew recognition from him for his failure to defend against the top-rated Philadelphian Harold Johnson, whom he had already beaten in four out of five meetings. During that period Moore spent much time in fruitless pursuit of the heavyweight championship, being beaten in nine rounds by Rocky Marciano in 1955, and in five by Floyd

Maxim's defence against Ray Robinson (above) *almost cost him his title, but heat exhaustion finally beat Robinson* (below), *and the middleweight champion could not answer the bell for the 14th.*

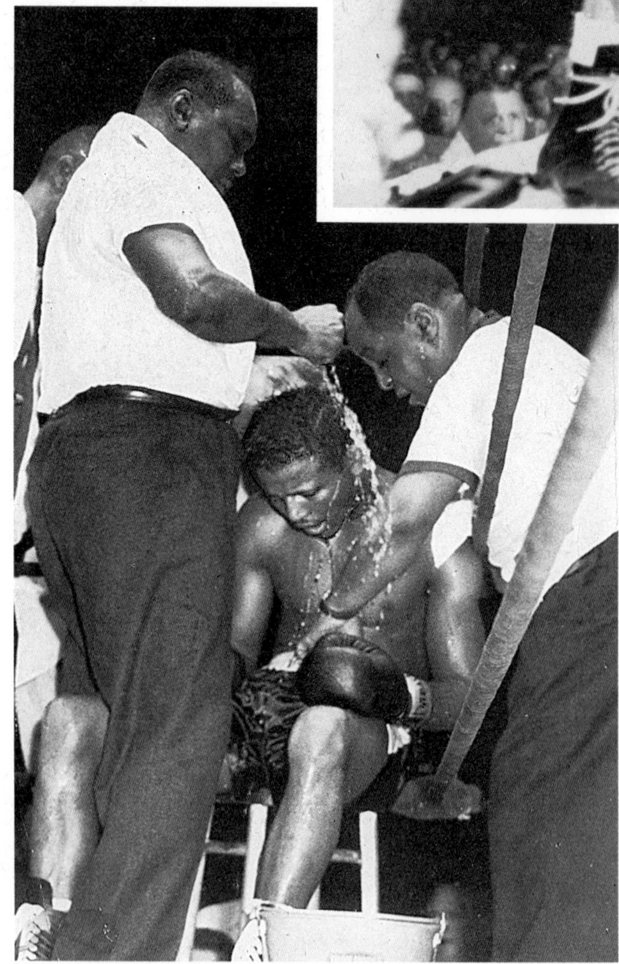

Archie Moore (left, *dethroning Maxim) had a long wait for a title chance, but once installed as champion he held the honour for nine years and nine defences, including his 1954 defeat of Harold Johnson* (below).

Patterson 14 months later.

Moore's defence against the crude but powerful Canadian Yvon Durelle in Montreal in December 1958 is remembered as his finest performance. Floored three times in the opening round, the 45-year-old champion fought back to knock Durelle out in the 11th round. In a rematch a few months later, he beat the Canadian easily in three rounds. It proved to be his last defence of the undisputed title, and the NBA recognized the 32-year-old Johnson as champion after his ninth-round retirement win over Jesse Bowdry on 7 February 1961.

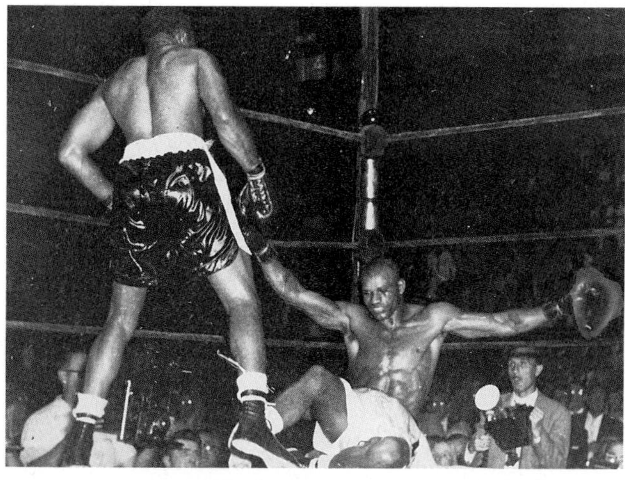

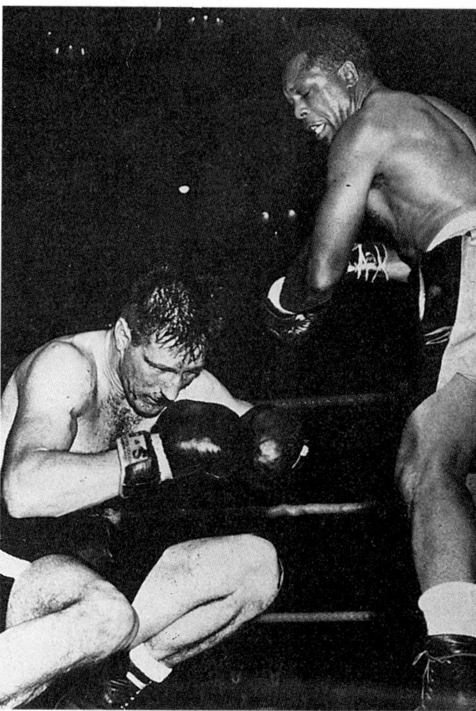

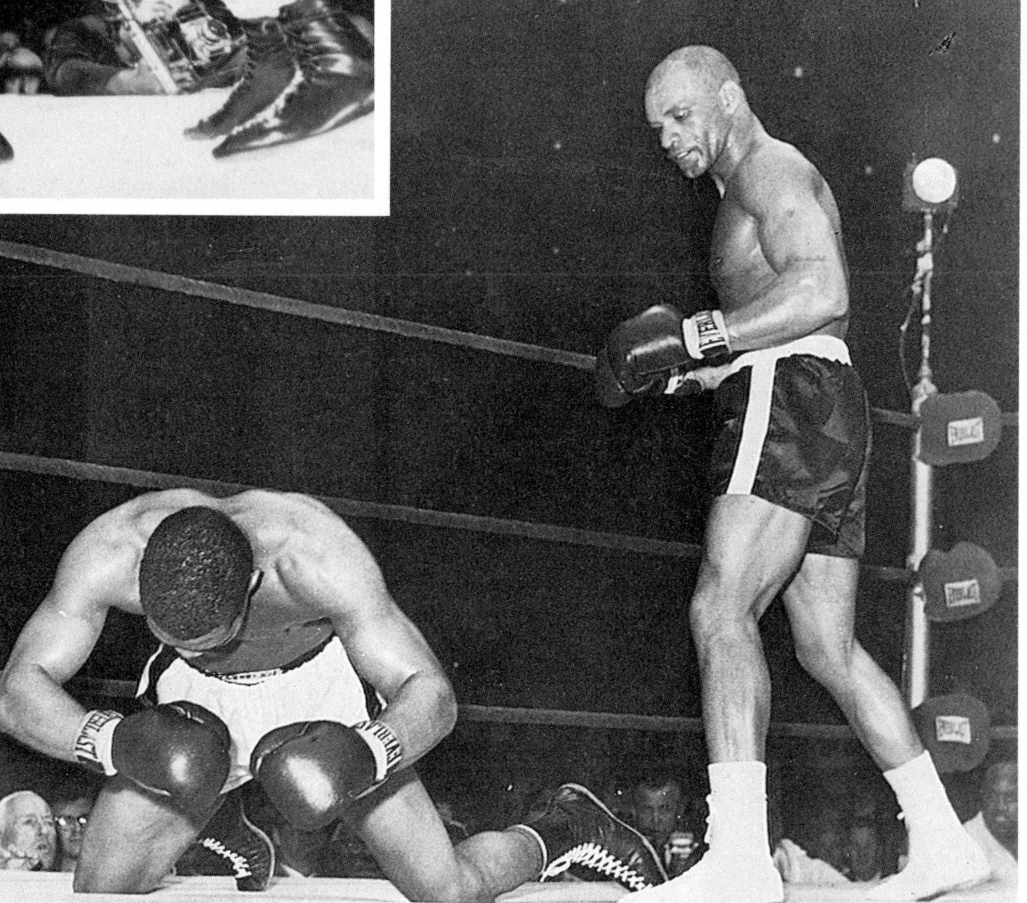

This epic knockout of Yvon Durelle of Canada (above) *was Moore's finest achievement: the 45-year-old champion was floored three times in the first, but won in the 11th round. He beat Durelle again in a rematch, but the NBA withdrew recognition from him in October 1960 and Moore's old rival Harold Johnson, whom Archie had beaten in four out of five meetings, stopped Jesse Bowdry in nine rounds* (left) *to win the vacant title.*

Moore's last defence was a points win over the European champion Guilio Rinaldi (above). *Johnson* (right, *in a 1954 win over Paul Andrews) earned universal recognition by beating Doug Jones in May 1962.*

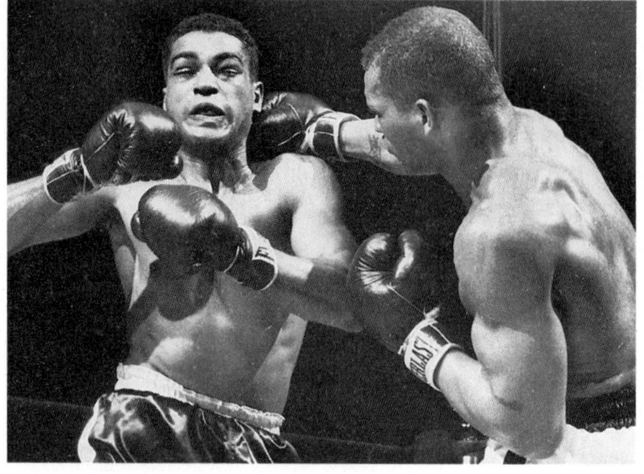

Moore had one more title fight, outpointing the Italian Guilio Rinaldi, but in February 1962 the rest of the world's governing bodies went along with the NBA and stripped him of the title, recognizing Johnson as champion after his win over Doug Jones in May 1962.

Johnson managed only one successful defence before he was dethroned, in a big upset, by the stylish Willie Pastrano from New Orleans, a clever but light-hitting boxer who vacillated between the light-heavy and heavyweight classes. The consensus was that Pastrano had been very lucky to win the split decision in Las Vegas, but he proved a solid champion who turned back challenges from Gregorio Peralta and from England's Terry Downes, who had been middleweight champion briefly in 1961-62. Pastrano had always been a popular performer in England during his heavyweight days, but he almost came unstuck against Downes at Belle Vue, Manchester, in November 1964. Downes, boxing better than he had ever done in the last fight of his career, looked poised for victory until the desperate Pastrano floored him twice for an 11th-round stoppage.

It was Pastrano's last success. Four months later the formidable José Torres, who had won a silver medal for Puerto Rico in the 1956 Olympic Games and who had lost only once in 35 fights under the guidance of Floyd Patterson's mentor Cus D'Amato, destroyed him in nine rounds at Madison Square Garden. Pastrano's answer to the Commission doctor, checking on his condition between rounds that night, is worth recording. 'Of course I know where I am', the soon-to-be ex-champion told the

Johnson's reign was ended by Willie Pastrano (on the right, above, *retaining the title against Greg Peralta). Pastrano was toppled by Jose Torres* (far left *flooring Wayne Thornton) who in turn lost to the Nigerian Dick Tiger* (left). *Tiger, the former middleweight champion, made two successful defences including this 12th-round victory* (below) *over the bloodied Roger Rouse.*

doctor. 'I'm in Madison Square Garden, getting the shit kicked out of me.'

Torres came to the title too late, aged nearly 29, to establish the sort of dominance over the division that he might have done had he been given the opportunity a few years earlier, but he retained the title three times before the remarkable 37-year-old Nigerian Dick Tiger, the former two-time middleweight champion, outpointed him in December 1966 and repeated the result when they met again six months later.

But Tiger was not destined for a long reign

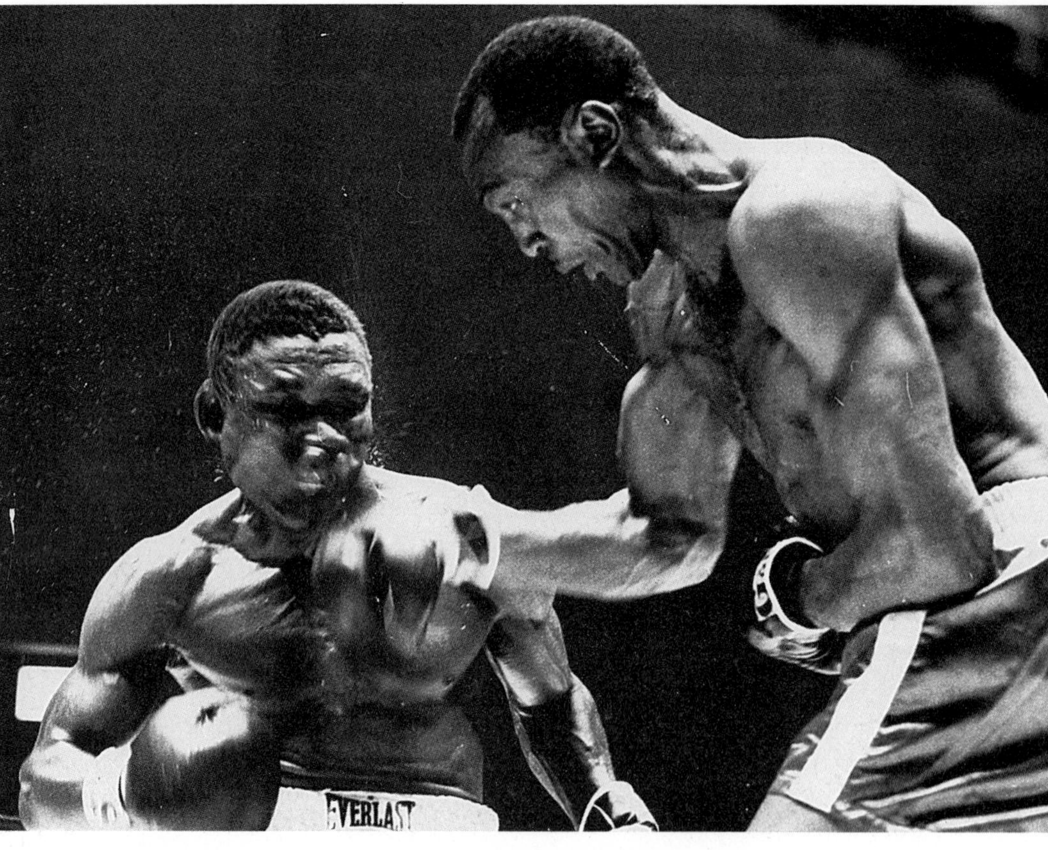

Heavy-hitting Bob Foster (above) *earned only training expenses from his title win over Dick Tiger* (right) *in 1968.*

either. Bob Foster, a gangling 6 ft 3 in deputy sheriff from Albuquerque, New Mexico, had electrified the division with his powerful punching, particularly with the left hook, and in May 1968 he managed to raise the financial backing to tempt Tiger to risk the title at Madison Square Garden. Foster flattened the African with a single left hook in the fourth round, but earned only training expenses for doing so. He earned well from the title in the years ahead, though, as he established himself as a champion worthy to stand alongside Archie Moore in the All-Time lists.

After four defences, all won inside schedule, Foster was stripped by the WBA for 'consistently failing to defend against top-rated contenders.' Vincente Rondon of Venezuela won their version of the championship in February 1971, and retained it four times before Foster outclassed him in two rounds in a unification match in April 1972. Foster made a total of 13 successful defences, including a 14th-round knockout of England's brave Chris Finnegan in a memorable clash at Wembley, but

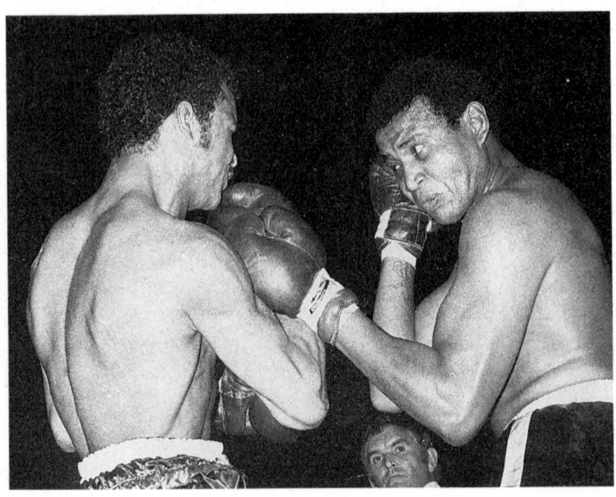

Vincente Rondon on the right, below, *losing against John Conteh, won five WBA title fights in 1971.*

Gallant Chris Finnegan (right) *stood up to Bob Foster for 14 thrilling rounds at Wembley in 1972.*

when he struggled to draw with Jorge Ahumada in June 1974 it was clearly time for him to go, aged almost 36. Foster delayed his decision until the WBC announced in August that they were stripping him for failure to meet either Ahumada again or the other leading contender, England's John Conteh.

Conteh outpointed Ahumada at Wembley in a brilliant 15-rounder on 1 October 1974 to take the vacant WBC title, while another Argentinian, Victor Galindez (who had stopped Ahumada three times in four fights) took the WBA version by stopping America's Len Hutchins two months later. Conteh and Galindez were, pound for pound, two of the finest boxers of their generation, but they were destined never to face each other. Conteh's career was plagued by promotional and managerial disputes, and by recurring hand injuries, and he had made only three defences in two-and-a-half years when the WBC stripped him for refusing to go through with a contracted defence in Monte Carlo against yet another Argentinian, Miguel Cuello. The veteran American Jesse Burnett came in at short notice but was stopped in nine rounds.

Cuello lost the title in his first defence to the

Victor Galindez (above) *was one of the finest fighters of the period, and a title unification match with WBC holder John Conteh* (below, *outscoring Alvaro Lopez*) *would have been a classic. But Conteh was stripped for failing to fulfil a contract to meet Miguel Cuello* (right), *who took the vacant title.*

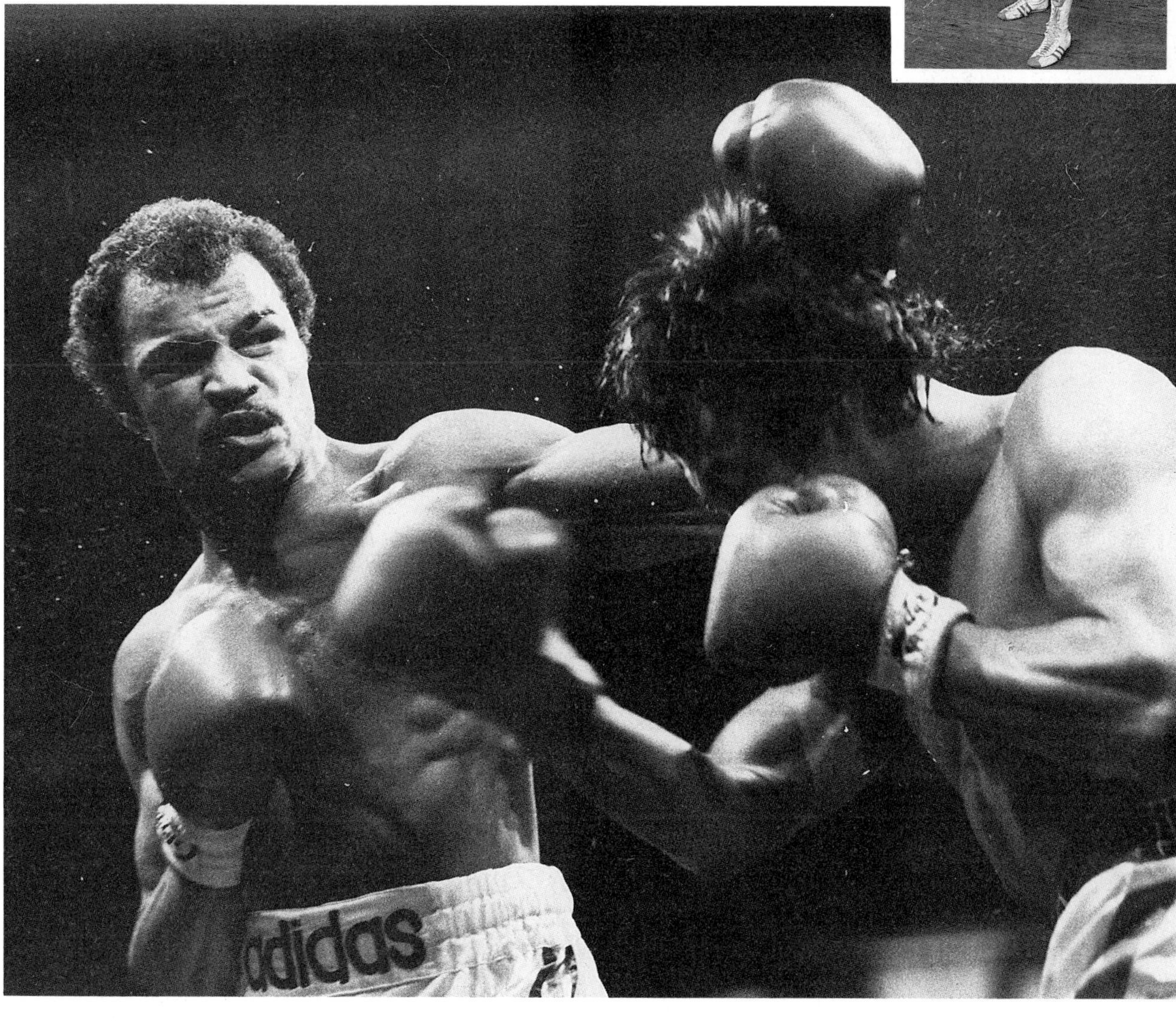

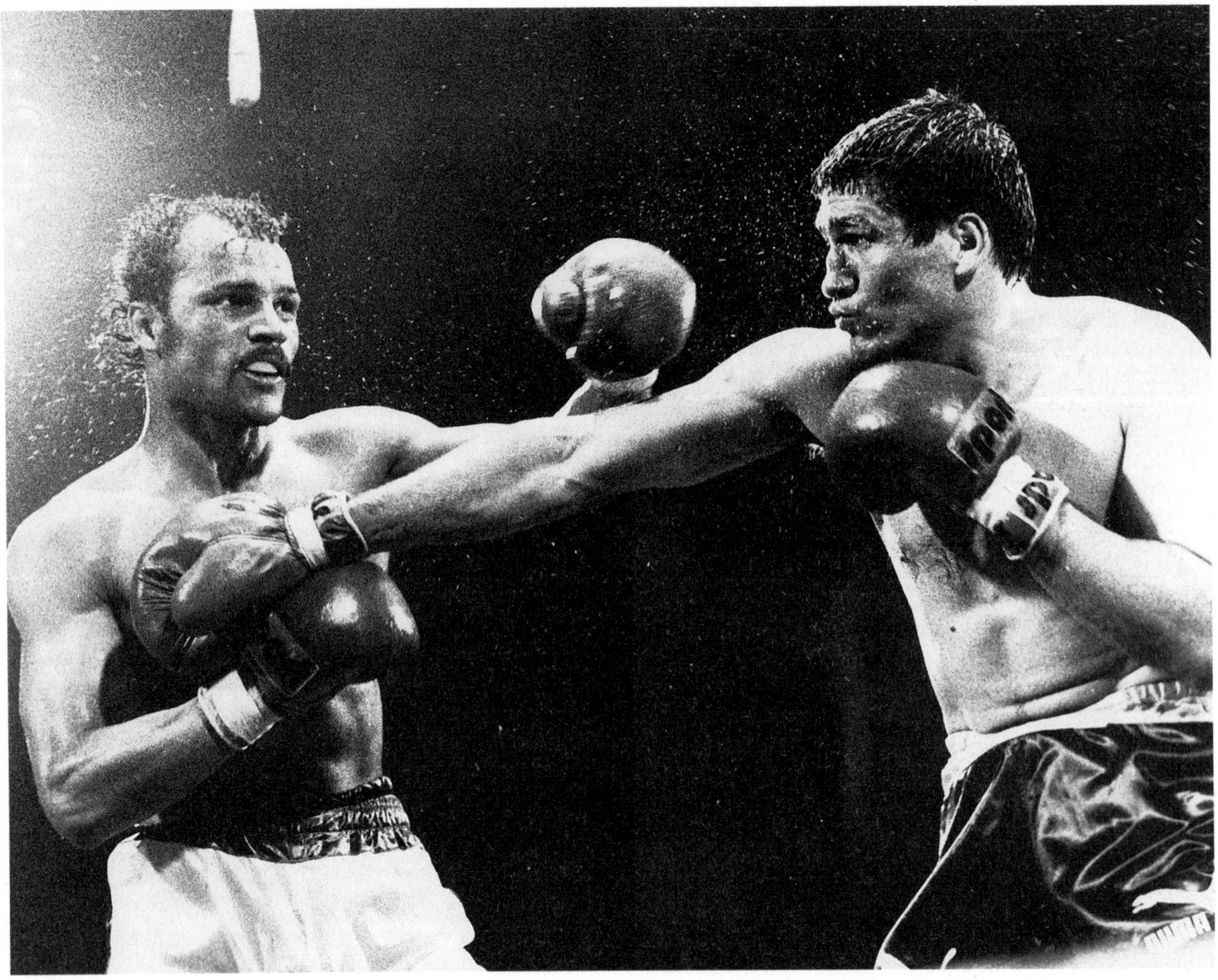

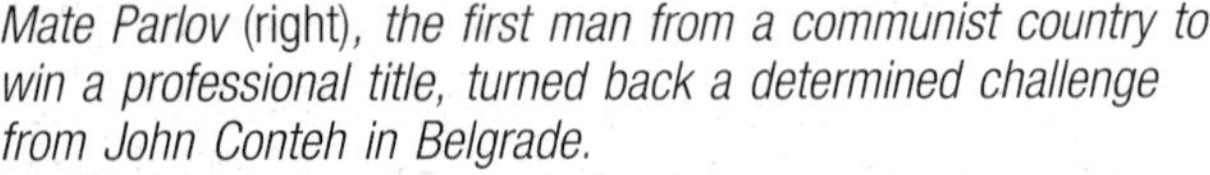

Mate Parlov (right), *the first man from a communist country to win a professional title, turned back a determined challenge from John Conteh in Belgrade.*

former Olympic champion from Yugoslavia, Mate Parlov, who thus became the first man from a Communist country to win a world professional title. Parlov held it on a split decision over Conteh in Belgrade, but then lost it to the balding American Marvin Johnson, who was himself de-throned five months later by Matt Franklin, a product of a Philadelphian orphanage and whose forte was endurance. Franklin converted to Islam, changed his name to Matthew Saad Muhammad, and earned the trade's awed respect with a succession of bitterly won title defences against the likes of Conteh (twice), Alvaro Lopez, Vonzell Johnson, and Jerry Martin. In all, Saad Muhammad successfully defended his title eight times, all except the first with Conteh ending inside the distance, before surrendering the championship to another convert to Islam, Dwight Muhammad Qawi, who had formerly boxed as Dwight Braxton. Qawi made

Matthew Saad Muhammad figured in some of the division's most exciting title fights, including an epic against John Conteh in Atlantic City (right) *and a ninth-round stoppage of rugged Scot Murray Sutherland* (left). *Saad Muhammad's courage and endurance were legendary, and carried him through eight defences of the WBC crown.*

Victor Galindez was a busy champion, defending the WBA title successfully 10 times before losing it for the first time to Mike Rossman, but he still fitted in non-title engagements like this points win over Jesse Burnett in Oslo.

three defences in 1982, but in March 1983 lost to the WBA champion Mike Spinks (brother of the former heavyweight champion) in the division's first unification match for nine years.

Galindez, meanwhile, had been a busy and worthy holder of the WBA title. His ten defences between April 1975 and May 1978 included a dramatic knockout of Richie Kates in Johannesburg, when the American was counted out with just *one second* remaining, as well as two desparately close wins over the perennial challenger Alvaro 'Yaqui' Lopez, who failed in all four attempts to become world champion and later made a fifth, again unsuccessful, attempt on the cruiserweight title.

When Galindez was surprisingly stopped by Mike Rossman of Philadelphia in September 1978, it was assumed that all those hard battles had caught up with him. However, he bounced back to beat Rossman in nine rounds in April 1979, only to lose it again to the former WBC champion Marvin Johnson seven months later. Johnson's tenure of the WBA title was no longer than his spell as WBC

Left: *Action from the second of Galindez' memorable defences against the South African Pierre Fourie. Both, ironically, died in road accidents.*

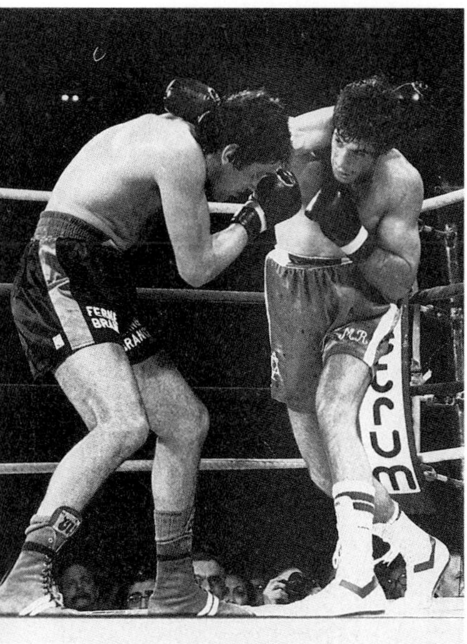

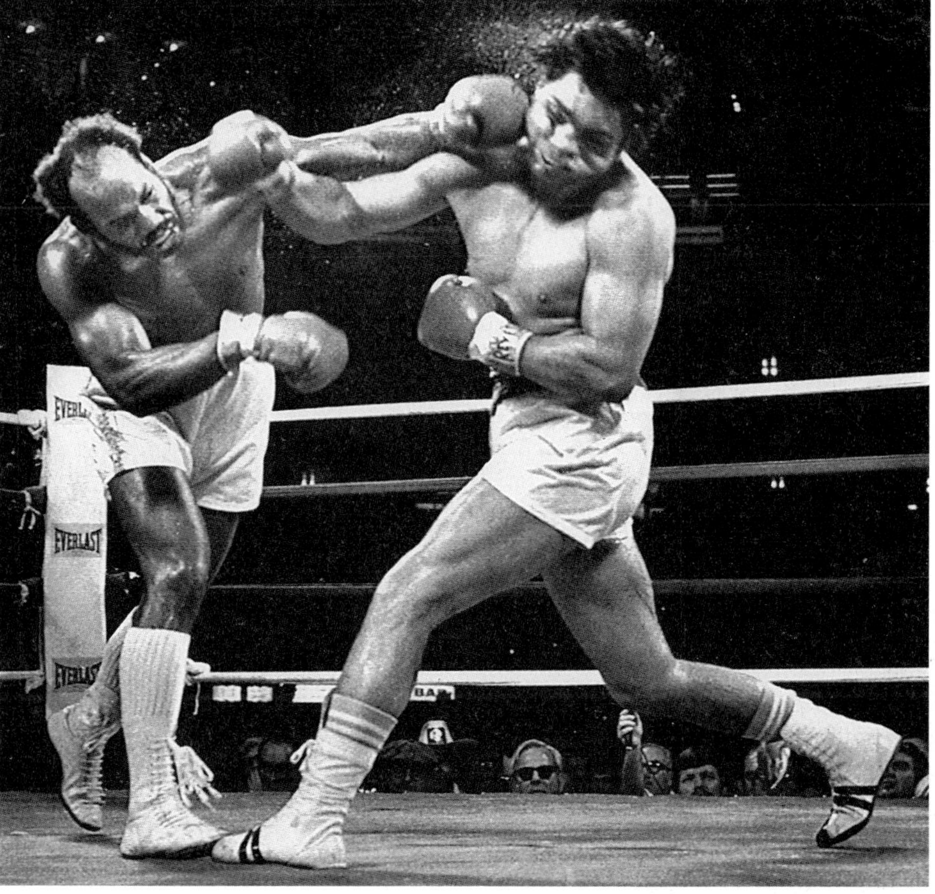

Rossman made only one winning defence, stopping Aldo Traversaro in Philadelphia (above) *before Galindez reclaimed the title. Seven months later Galindez was an ex-champ again, after this left from Marvin Johnson broke his jaw in New Orleans.*

Jerry Martin, on the wrong end of Eddie Mustafa Muhammad's jab, failed in attempts on both the WBC and WBA versions of the title in the early 1980s.

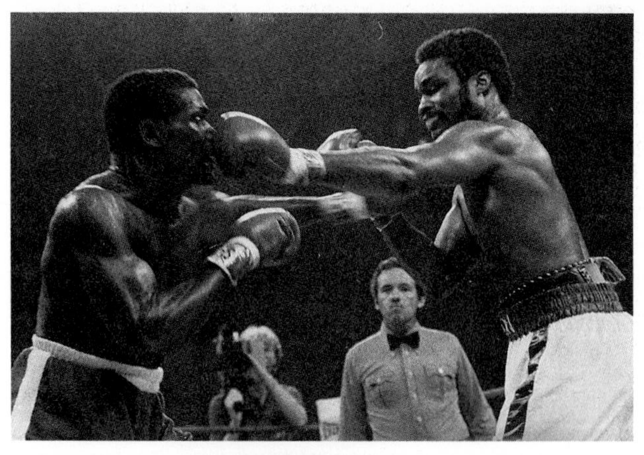

champion had been. Four months later he was stopped in 11 rounds by the talented, but often lethargic, Eddie Mustafa Muhammad, who lost the title in his third defence to the 1976 Olympic middleweight winner Mike Spinks.

Spinks soon established himself as the dominant figure in the division, with five inside-schedule defences before he unified the title by beating the WBC champion Dwight Muhammad Qawi in March 1983. Four defences later, he relinquished the title to win the IBF heavyweight crown from Larry Holmes, and inevitably the title split three ways.

J. B. Williamson, an ex-marine from Los Angeles, won the WBC version and promptly lost it to the British champion Dennis Andries, a capable but unfashionable 33-year-old whose late-career success was heart warming. Andries retained it

Mike Spinks (below, *left against Oscar Rivadeneyra in a 1983 defence of the undisputed title) became the division's most dominant figure since Bob Foster.*

Spinks' successor J. B. Williamson (right) *proved a poor replacement, and was beaten in his first defence by Britain's lightly regarded Dennis Andries.*

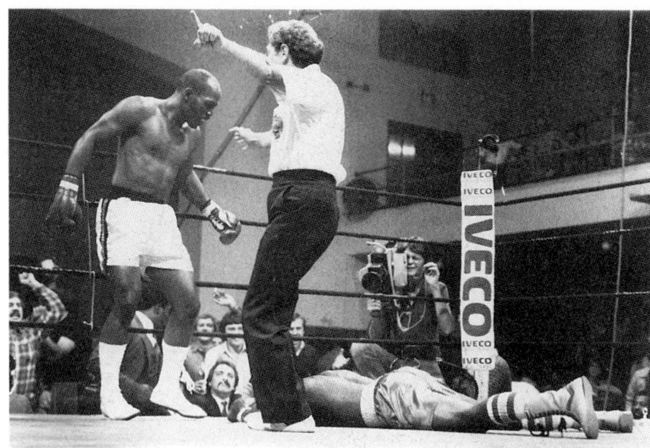

Marvin Johnson (left, *knocking out Alvin Manson) has been on the championship scene since 1978.*

Colourful Bobby Czyz (below) *at last fulfilled his early career promise by winning the IBF title.*

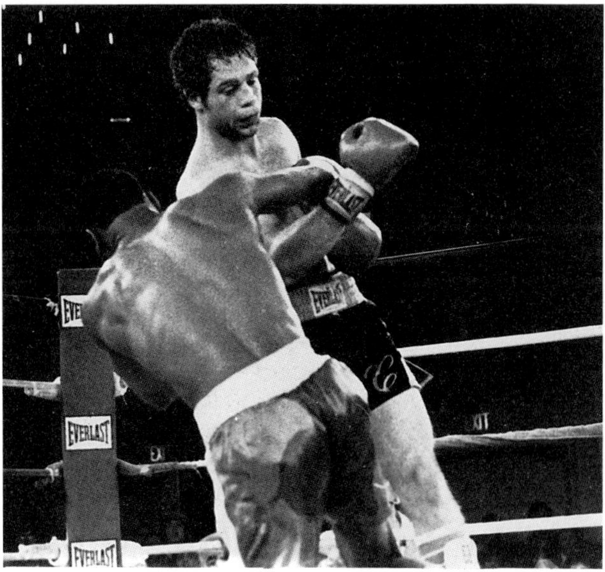

against his middleweight compatriot Tony Sibson, but in March 1987 he was dethroned by the former welterweight and light-middleweight champion Thomas Hearns, who battered him to painful tenth-round defeat in Detroit.

Marvin Johnson crowned a great comeback by taking the WBA version of the vacant title, beating Leslie Stewart of Trinidad. But in a rematch in May 1987, the gallant old veteran reached the end of a long road when Stewart battered him into retirement after eight one-sided rounds. The IBF version was won by the Yugoslav ex-amateur Slobodan Kacar, who lost it in September 1986 to the colourful American Bobby Czyz, who had made three quick defences by mid-1987. There are not, at present, any moves to unify the title, so the light-heavyweight division – one of boxing's classic eight categories – looks like being saddled with three 'champions' for the foreseeable future.

HOW THE LIGHT-HEAVYWEIGHT TITLE HAS CHANGED HANDS

22 Apr 03	Jack Root w.pts.10 Kid McCoy at Detroit
04 Jul 03	George Gardner w.ko.12 Jack Root at Fort Erie
25 Oct 03	Bob Fitzsimmons w.pts.20 George Gardner at San Francisco
20 Dec 05	Philadelphia Jack O'Brien w.ko.13 Bob Fitzsimmons at San Francisco
28 May 12	Jack Dillon w.ko.3 Hugo Kelly at Indianapolis
24 Oct 16	Battling Levinsky w.pts.12 Jack Dillon at Boston
12 Oct 20	Georges Carpentier w.ko.4 Battling Levinsky at New York
24 Sep 22	Battling Siki w.ko.6 Georges Carpentier at Paris
17 Mar 23	Mike McTigue w.pts.20 Battling Siki at Dublin
31 May 25	Paul Berlenbach w.pts.15 Mike McTigue at New York
16 Jul 26	Jack Delaney w.pts.15 Paul Berlenbach at Brooklyn
30 Aug 27	Jimmy Slattery w.pts.10 Maxie Rosenbloom at Hartford, Conn. *(For vacant NBA title)*
07 Oct 27	Tommy Loughran w.pts.15 Mike McTigue at New York
12 Dec 27	Tommy Loughran w.pts.15 Jimmy Slattery at New York *(For undisputed title)*
10 Feb 30	Maxie Rosenbloom w.pts.15 Jimmy Slattery in New York *(Rosenbloom won recognition as champion by all except the NBA)*
08 Mar 32	George Nichols w.pts.10 Dave Maier in Chicago *(NBA version of title)*
31 May 32	Lou Scozza w.pts.10 George Nichols in Buffalo *(NBA title)*
14 Jul 32	Maxie Rosenbloom w.pts.15 Lou Scozza in Buffalo *(For undisputed title)*
01 Mar 33	Bob Godwin w.pts.10 Joe Knight at Palm Beach *(For vacant NBA title)*
24 Mar 33	Maxie Rosenbloom w.ko.4 Bob Godwin in New York *(For undisputed title)*
16 Nov 34	Bob Olin w.pts.15 Maxie Rosenbloom at New York
11 Oct 35	John Henry Lewis w.pts.15 Bob Olin in St Louis
Oct 38	*Lewis vacated title to challenge Joe Louis for heavyweight championship*
28 Nov 38	Tiger Jack Fox w.pts.15 Al Gainer at New York
03 Feb 39	Melio Bettina w.rsf.9 Tiger Jack Fox at New York
30 Jul 39	Billy Conn w.pts.15 Melio Bettina at Pittsburgh
13 Jan 41	Anton Christoforidis w.pts.15 Melio Bettina at Cleveland
22 May 41	Gus Lesnevich w.pts.15 Anton Christoforidis at New York
14 May 46	Gus Lesnevich w.rsf.10 Freddie Mills at London
26 Jul 48	Freddie Mills w.pts.15 Gus Lesnevich at London
24 Jan 50	Joey Maxim w.ko.10 Freddie Mills at London
17 Dec 52	Archie Moore w.pts.15 Joey Maxim at St. Louis
25 Oct 60	*Moore stripped of NBA title for failing to defend)*
12 May 62	Harold Johnson w.pts.15 Doug Jones at Philadelphia *(Undisputed title)*
01 Jun 63	Willie Pastrano w.pts.15 Harold Johnson at Las Vegas
30 Mar 65	Jose Torres w.rsf.9 Willie Pastrano at New York
16 Dec 66	Dick Tiger w.pts.15 Jose Torres at New York
24 May 68	Bob Foster w.ko.4 Dick Tiger at New York
09 Dec 70	*Foster Stripped of title by WBA for refusing to meet their deadline for defence against No. 1 WBA challenger, Jimmy Dupree*
22 Feb 71	Vicente Rondon w.rsf.6 Jimmy Dupree at Caracas *(Vacant WBA version of title)*
07 Apr 72	Bob Foster w.ko.2 Vicente Rondon at Miami Beach *(Undisputed title)*
Aug 74	*World Boxing Council withdrew recognition of Foster as world champion for failure to sign for a title defence against John Conteh or Jorge Ahumada. Foster later announced retirement*
01 Oct 74	John Conteh w.pts.15 Jorge Ahumada at Wembley *(Vacant WBC title)*
07 Dec 74	Victor Galindez w.rtd.12 Len Hutchins in Buenos Aires *(Vacant WBA title)*
May 77	*John Conteh stripped of his title by the WBC for failure to go through with a contracted defence against Miguel Angel Cuello*
21 May 77	Miguel Cuello w.ko.9 Jesse Burnett at Monte Carlo *(Vacant WBC version of title)*
07 Jan 78	Mate Parlov w.ko.9 Miguel Cuello in Milan
15 Sep 78	Mike Rossman w.rsf.13 Victor Galindez in New Orleans
02 Dec 78	Marvin Johnson w.rsf.10 Mate Parlov at Marsala, Italy
14 Apr 79	Victor Galindez w.rtd.9 Mike Rossman in New Orleans *(WBA title)*
22 Apr 79	Matthew Saad Muhammad (formerly Matt Franklin) w.rsf.8 Marvin Johnson at Indianapolis *(WBC title)*
30 Nov 79	Marvin Johnson w.rsf.11 Victor Galindez in New Orleans *(WBA title)*
31 Mar 80	Eddie Mustafa Muhammad (formerly Eddie Gregory) w.rsf.11 Marvin Johnson in Knoxville *(WBA title)*
18 Jul 81	Mike Spinks w.pts.15 Eddie Mustafa Muhammad at Las Vegas
19 Dec 81	Dwight Braxton w.rsf.10 Matthew Saad Muhammad at Atlantic City *(WBC title)*
18 Mar 83	Mike Spinks w.pts.15 Dwight Muhammad Qawi (formerly Dwight Braxton) at Atlantic City *(For undisputed title)*
Sep 85	*Spinks relinquished the title on becoming IBF world heavyweight champion*
10 Dec 85	J.B. Williamson w.pts.12 Prince Mamah Mohammed at Los Angeles *(Vacant WBC title)*
21 Dec 85	Slobodan Kacar w.pts.15 Eddie Mustafa Muhammad at Pesaro *(Vacant IBF title)*
09 Feb 86	Marvin Johnson w.rsf.7 Leslie Stewart at Indianapolis *(Vacant WBA title)*
30 Apr 86	Dennis Andries w.pts.12 J.B. Williamson at London *(WBC title)*
06 Sep 86	Bobby Czyz w.rsf.5 Slobodan Kacar at Las Vegas *(IBF title)*
07 Mar 87	Thomas Hearns w.rsf.10 Dennis Andries at Detroit
23 May 87	Leslie Stewart w.rtd.8 Marvin Johnson at Port of Spain, Trinidad

MIDDLEWEIGHTS

THE MIDDLEWEIGHTS are boxing's thoroughbreds, combining the power of the heavyweights with the speed and skill of the lighter men. The division has produced more of the sport's genuine heroes than any of the other, ever-proliferating weight categories. It has given us the grace and genius of Sugar Ray Robinson, the ferocity of Stanley Ketchel, Harry Greb, and Mickey Walker, the cool technique of Tony Zale, the charisma of Marcel Cerdan, the elemental violence of Jake LaMotta and Rocky Graziano, the courage – and the wit – of Terry Downes, and the professional perfection of Marvin Hagler. Carlos Monzon would merit inclusion on any list of the dozen greatest pound-for-pound fighters of all time, and the elegant Italian Nino Benvenuti would command a similar ranking on any European Roll of Honour.

The middleweights have sometimes been muddled, but always marvellous. In common with all boxing's divisions, its championship has been frequently fragmented, but even then it was usually shared by men of high quality, who produced some of the game's most cherished memories.

The weight class had been recognized since Tom Chandler beat Dooney Harris in 23 rounds at San Francisco on 13 April 1867, but the first generally accepted international championship fight was between 'Nonpareil' Jack Dempsey (an Irishman from Kildare whose real name was John Kelly) and George Fulljames from Toronto.

Dempsey knocked Fulljames out in 22 rounds at Great Kills, New York, on 30 July 1884, and held the title for seven years, defending it successfully four times. One of these, his 45-round knockout of

The unforgettable Harry Greb, whose combination of fierce fighting and wild living made him a middleweight legend.

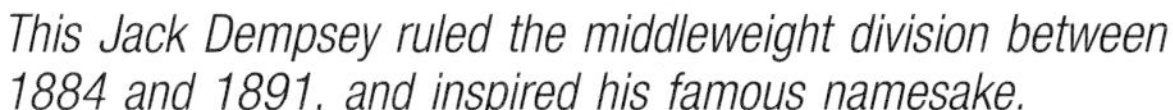

This Jack Dempsey ruled the middleweight division between 1884 and 1891, and inspired his famous namesake.

Kid McCoy (above) *staked a claim to the title in 1896, but was not universally accepted until the following year. A decade later, the title had passed to the rough and rugged Stanley Ketchel* (right).

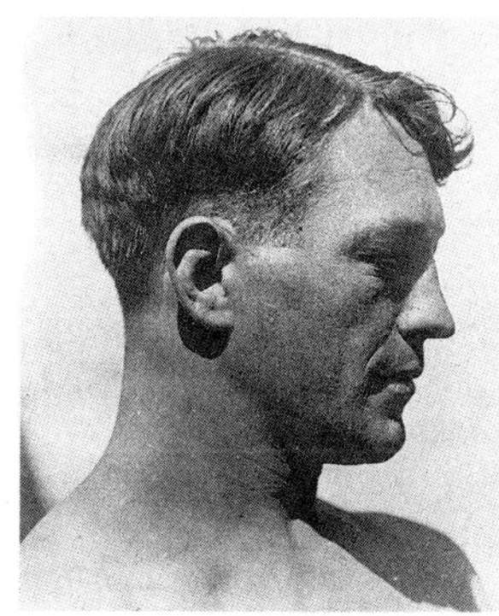

Johnny Reagen in 1887, is the only title fight ever to have been held in *two* rings. When the first became waterlogged, the fighters and their entourage boarded a passing river barge to conclude their business some 20 miles upstream.

Two years later Dempsey suffered one of his only three defeats when George LaBlanche knocked him out in 32 rounds at San Francisco. LaBlanche had weighed in at 161 lb – seven pounds over the limit then operative – but still claimed the title. However, since he had flattened Dempsey with an illegal 'pivot blow' his claim was unsympathetically received.

Dempsey was finally toppled by Bob Fitzsimmons, who was winning the first of his three world titles, in January 1891. It was a painful experience for the Irishman, who was floored 13 times, until Fitzsimmons himself pleaded with him to quit. 'A champion never quits', Dempsey replied. 'You'll have to knock me out'. Fitzsimmons duly did so in the 13th round. The Cornishman made only one defence, knocking out his fellow-Englishman Dan Creedon in two rounds in 1894. He raised the limit from 154 lb to 158 lb to suit himself, but gave up the title in 1895 to compete as a heavyweight.

Kid McCoy became the new champion almost by accident in 1896, knocking out Tommy Ryan in the 15th round. The fight had been billed as being for Ryan's welterweight championship, but since both men scaled within the middleweight limit that title was automatically at stake. McCoy defended it once in South Africa in 1896, and earned general acceptance as champion by outpointing Fitzsimmons' old challenger, Dan Creedon, in 1897. He, too, relinquished the title to box as a heavyweight, and Ryan took it over in 1898, defending it six times before retiring in 1907.

Hugo Kelly, who despite his Irish ring name was actually Italian, proclaimed himself champion on Ryan's departure, but a stronger claimant soon emerged. Stanley Ketchel, the son of a Russian

Hugo Kelly (left) *proclaimed himself champion in 1907, but Ketchel took only three rounds to expose Kelly's limitations in this 1908 clash in San Francisco.*

Billy Papke (above, *on the left) fouled his way to the title against Ketchel in September 1908, but Ketchel won their other three fights, including the title rematch.*

father and Polish mother, knocked out the respected Joe Thomas in 32 rounds in September 1907. He beat Thomas in a rematch, and then earned universal recognition with successive knockouts of the Sullivan twins, Mike and Jack, and Kelly. But only three weeks after he had demonstrated his superiority over Joe Thomas yet again, this time with a two-round knockout, Ketchel lost the title. Billy Papke, as rough and mean a fighter as the ring ever produced, smashed Ketchel in the throat as the referee completed his pre-fight instructions. He should have been thrown out, but the fight went ahead and Ketchel, who had not recovered properly from the foul, was knocked out in the 12th round.

Two months later Ketchel exacted savage revenge, pounding Papke mercilessly before kayoing him in the 11th round. Ketchel announced in January 1910 that he was giving up the title, following his defeat by Jack Johnson in a heavyweight title bid. Papke immediately reclaimed the championship, but the situation became confused when Ketchel apparently changed his mind and made three more defences in 1910. These wins – over Frank Klaus, Willie Lewis, and Jim Smith – were all billed as title fights, as was Papke's third-round win over Lewis in Paris in March 1910. Seven months later Ketchel was shot and killed in an argument over a woman – but it would be six years before the world again had an undisputed champion.

Papke took his version of the title to Europe, where he retained it against Jim Sullivan in London, and Marcel Moreau, Georges Carpentier, and George Bernard in Paris. The Bernard fight was a strange affair. The Frenchman fell asleep in his corner at the end of six evenly contested rounds and could not be revived in time for the seventh, thus giving Papke a retirement win. Bernard subsequently alleged that he had been drugged, which in those free-and-easy times was perfectly possible.

Ketchel squares off with heavyweight champion Jack Johnson before their 1909 title clash. Johnson knocked him out in the 12th, but the smaller man scored a shock knockdown.

Two other title claimants emerged around this period. Frank Mantell, who had been born in Brandenburg, Germany, but now lived in America, outpointed Papke in Sacramento, California, in February 1912 and claimed the title. But since Papke argued that he had not regarded it as a title defence, Mantell received only limited recognition.

He defended his version against Jack Henrick in California, and a New Yorker, Jeff Smith, in Paris, but was then outpointed over 20 rounds at the Ring, Blackfriars, in London, by Pat O'Keefe. This esoteric version of the championship disappeared when O'Keefe stepped up to heavyweight to challenge Billy Wells for the British title.

Frank Klaus, a German-American from Pittsburgh, had a more substantial claim. He outpointed Jack Dillon in California in March 1912, just two months before Dillon himself claimed the light-heavyweight championship after beating Hugo

Papke knocked out Jim Sullivan in London (left). *His luck ran out, though, when he was disqualified against Frank Klaus* (right) *in 1913. Papke had a four-fight series with Hugo Kelly: the pair are pictured* (below) *before their final meeting, won by Papke (right) in the first round.*

Kelly. Klaus took his title to Paris, which was Mecca to American boxers in those days, and retained it on a 19th-round disqualification against Georges Carpentier. The Frenchman's manager, Francois Descamps, jumped into the ring to protest about Klaus' illegal use of the elbows and thereby incurred automatic disqualification for his man.

Although Klaus was 3 lb over the championship weight, which by then had stabilized at the 11 st 6 lb limit set in 1909 by the National Sporting Club, the win earned him recognition in Europe as champion. Klaus was a rough fighter, but not a vicious one. The report in *Boxing* of the Carpentier fight in Dieppe records that, after Klaus had fouled the Frenchman again:

> Another howl went up, but even before this had started Klaus was clearly sorry for his action, and held out his hand in meek apology. The referee went on with his reprimand, and Carpentier seemed to be deeply hurt, as he refused to accept Klaus' proffered mitt. Klaus was determined that Carpentier should realise that he was genuinely sorry for his transgression, and so he proffered his unprotected face as a target for retaliation, saying 'Strike!' as he did so. This chivalrous action completely disarmed the French boy. A smile flickered over his battered features, and he at once acknowledged his rival's contrition by grasping his right hand and shaking it cordially.

Since Papke was still based in Paris, and continuing to claim the title himself, Klaus fought him in the French capital in March 1913 to settle the issue, with Papke being disqualified for repeated butting in the 15th round. This, effectively, was the end of Papke's career. He had only three more minor contests, winning just one, and his life as an ex-champion was unhappy and unsuccessful. In 1936 he killed his wife (from whom he had recently been divorced), and then shot himself. Klaus' newly won championship did not bring him much luck either, for he never won another fight. In October he was knocked out in six rounds by George Chip (real name Chipulonis), a Lithuanian from Pennsylvania; Chip repeated the result in five a few months later.

However, any hope that Chip might bring some consistency to the troubled division disappeared when, in April 1914, he fell victim to a drastic managerial miscalculation. The champion's brother, Joe, had been matched with a southpaw of modest accomplishment called Al McCoy. Shortly before the fight at Broadway Arena, in Brooklyn, Joe was taken ill and pulled out of the fight. Charley

Defeat by Klaus on a disqualification marked the end of the championship road for Papke (above).

George Chip (below) *substituted for his brother Joe against Al McCoy – and it cost him his world title.*

Al McCoy (above) *became champion with a first-round body punch in one of boxing's biggest upsets.*

Mike O'Dowd (below) *took the title from McCoy in 1917, and did not defend it for two years.*

Goldman, later famous for his association with Rocky Marciano, was then managing McCoy and he persuaded Chip's manager to allow George to face McCoy in a no-decision fight (i.e., one in which a winner could be found only by a knockout). Since McCoy was not really in the champion's class Chip saw little risk in accepting, but instead he was knocked out in the first round by a left to the stomach, and had to wait seven years for a chance to regain the title.

McCoy's record was so indifferent that yet another crop of rival claimants disputed his right to call himself champion. They included the Americans Jeff Smith (who had drawn with Mantell and beaten Chip), Eddie McGoorty and Jimmy Clabby, who all went to Australia where they competed for something called the 'Australian world middleweight title'. This was won in succession by McGoorty, Smith, Mick King of Sydney, Smith again, and Les Darcy.

Darcy strengthed his claim to the title by beating off challenges from King, McGoorty, Fred Dyer, Clabby (twice), and George Chip, in what proved, tragically, to be the Australian's last fight. He had travelled to America to seek a fight with McCoy for the undisputed title, but developed pneumonia and died in Memphis on 24 May 1917. Darcy's death at least had the effect of leaving the championship firmly in McCoy's hands, but he promptly lost it in his first defence, three and a half years after he had surprised Chip, to a former soldier from St Paul called Mike O'Dowd. The Irish-American's sixth-round knockout merits a footnote in history as the last bout held under the Frawley Law, which prohibited the giving of points decisions in New York.

O'Dowd kayoed McCoy in a rematch, but was outpointed in May 1920 by a New Yorker, Johnny Wilson, whose real name was John Panica. The verdict was rumoured to owe more to Wilson's underworld connections than it did to what transpired in the ring at Boston that night, and certainly Wilson never disguised his friendship with

Johnny Wilson (left) *was a tough guy in and out of the ring, who boasted of his gangster connections.*

Left: *Wilson, on the left, had been conned into believing that Greb had trained in night clubs.*

gangsters. After his retirement he ran the Silver Slipper nightclub in New York, which was a haven for the leading underworld figures of the day. Shortly before he died at 92 (he was the oldest surviving world champion) in December 1985, Wilson told an American newspaper 'Tough guys like Legs Diamond were gentlemen in my place. Everybody came to the Slipper. I knew Al Capone – he had class'.

Wilson was a competent enough fighter, as he proved by retaining the title against the veteran George Chip, and then winning a clear decision over O'Dowd in a rematch in March 1921. However, the whiff of scandal was noticed again in July of that year when he defended against a local fighter, Bryan Downey, in Cleveland, Ohio. Wilson

Greb broke all the rules about how a fighter should live, but rarely allowed himself to get out of condition.

Greb's greatest victory was this 1922 win over future heavyweight champion Gene Tunney, who was reduced to mauling and clinching to survive the 15 rounds. It made Greb the American light-heavyweight champion.

was floored three times in the seventh round, but referee Jimmy Gardner disqualified Downey for 'attempting to hit Wilson while he was down'. The Cleveland Boxing Commission refused to accept Gardner's verdict and declared Downey the new champion by a knockout, as did the Ohio Boxing Federation. Wilson and Downey boxed a no-decision rematch in September 1921, and the championship once more entered one of its periodic spells of confusion and turmoil.

In August 1922 the New York Commission declared the title vacant and recognised Dave Rosenberg as champion after his points win over Phil Krug. Downey, meanwhile, had been defending his portion of the title against Frank Carbone and Mike O'Dowd, before losing it in September 1922 to Jock Malone. O'Dowd bounced back from his defeat by Downey to win the New York title from Rosenberg in November 1922, but then lost that on a first-round knockout to Malone in March 1923. Malone now had a strong claim to recognition, but he allowed it to lapse and in fact never defended it.

Wilson, meanwhile, had signed to defend against one of the most extraordinary fighters of all – Harry Greb. Boxing has never seen anyone quite like Greb. He defied all the rules of training and conditioning, and his appetite for drink, women, and high-living was awe-inspiring even in those free-spending Prohibition days. He showed a similar disregard for the rules of boxing, and gloried in his reputation as the dirtiest fighter of the day. He frequently fought light-heavyweights and even heavyweights, and in a career that began in 1913 he had boxed world champions and title claimants such as Battling Levinsky (six times), Jeff Smith (five), George Chip (four), Mike McTigue and Tommy Loughran (three times each), Al McCoy, Frank Klaus and Mike O'Dowd. He had also boxed heavyweight title challengers Tommy Gibbons four times and Billy Miske thrice.

Greb's most famous victory was on 23 May 1922, when he inflicted the only defeat ever suffered by Gene Tunney in a 15-rounder for the vacant American light-heavyweight title. Although Greb weighed only 11 st 8¼ lb (162¼ lb) against Tunney's 12 st 6½ lb (174½ lb) that night, he gave the future heavyweight champion a savage beating. Tunney subsequently won two decisions over him, and had the better of two other no-decision fights, but Greb's feat is none the less remarkable for that. By the time he met Wilson, Greb had already had 233 fights, losing just three. One was to Tunney, in the fight prior to facing Wilson, and another had been eight years previously when he had his arm broken in the second round by Kid Graves. Even more astonishing was the fact that Greb had been blind in his right eye ever since he was thumbed by 'Kid' Norfolk during a no-decision 10-rounder in 1921. (The vast majority of Greb's engagements were no-decision affairs, and of the 294 fights which he amassed in his 12-year career, 170 were of this nature.)

Even with all that experience behind him, though, Greb took no chances. He led the Wilson camp to believe that he was not taking the fight too seriously, and made a point of visiting one of New York's many speakeasies (drinking clubs) each day after training. Wilson expected an ill-conditioned and debauched challenger, but instead Greb (whose speakeasy glasses had held water rather than gin) was superbly prepared and easily took the title with a 15-round decision at the Polo Grounds. Greb removed any doubts about his right to the championship by outpointing Downey in December 1923 and beating Wilson, again on points, in

Middleweight champions Tiger Flowers (above) *and Mickey Walker offered a contrast in every way. Flowers, a church deacon, was a clever, thoughtful boxer while Walker, a confirmed playboy, loved a punch-up . . . in and out of the ring. Like Greb, Flowers had a short life, dying when he was 42.*

January 1924. Fay Kaiser and the Englishman Ted Moore from Plymouth failed to dislodge him in 1924, as did another of the middleweight division's playboys, Mickey Walker, in July 1925.

Greb and Walker fought a magnificent 15-rounder at the Polo Grounds and, according to legend, met after the fight in a local night club. As fighters are prone to do, they started joking with each other about the fight. The discussion got a little out of hand and, as the pair adjourned from that club for Johnny Wilson's establishment, the Silver Slipper, Walker said to Greb 'If you hadn't thumbed me, I'd have knocked you out.' Greb replied 'Come on up the street, and we'll see who knocks out who'. But that unofficial, unscheduled, and unpaid rematch was quickly broken up by the police and the result went unrecorded.

Greb had only one more successful defence, against Tony Marullo of New Orleans, before in February 1926 he was surprisingly outpointed by Theodore 'Tiger' Flowers, a church deacon from Georgia, who thus became the division's first black champion. They had a rematch a few months later, but Greb was again outpointed. The years of high living, and the strain of 294 battles – 92 of them fought with one eye – had caught up with him. A month after the second fight with Flowers, he had the right eye removed and replaced with a glass substitute, and before the year was out he was dead. Early in October Greb was involved in a car accident in which he suffered a minor fracture of the nose. He required an operation to improve his breathing, but following a cardiac arrest on the operating table he never regained consciousness.

Flowers lost the title to Mickey Walker in December 1926 just over six weeks after Greb's death and, in an eerie echo of Greb's fate, also had less than 12 months to live as ex-champion. He went into hospital for the removal of scar tissue after he had knocked out a New York heavyweight, Leo Gates, in four rounds. Four days later, on 16 November, he died of cardiac arrest on the operating table. Like Greb, he was just 32 years old.

The new champion, Mickey Walker, was a fiercely pugnacious Irish-American whose ring style fully justified his nickname 'The Toy Bulldog'. He had begun fighting professionally as a 17-year-old welterweight, and by the time he was 21 had dethroned the veteran world champion Jack Britton. He shared Greb's tastes for the good life, to such an extent that he was even rumoured to have been under the influence when he lost his welterweight

title in his eighth defence, against Pete Latzo, in Scranton on 20 May 1926.

His appetite for women matched his fondness for a drink. He was married seven times, but to only four women, prompting the wisecrack that he not only had return fights, but return weddings. Walker had been steered to the welterweight title by Jack Bulger, but when Bulger died shortly after the win over Britton the ubiquitous Jack Kearns took over his management. Kearns' hunger for money matched Walker's love of fighting, so they had a thoroughly compatible partnership: Kearns ensured that his fighter was both busy and well-paid.

His first defence was against the British champion, Tommy Milligan of Edinburgh, who had been a leading contender for Walker's welterweight title. Milligan even went to America to strengthen his case for a title chance, but lost two of his three fights there and, on his return to Britain, stepped up to middleweight and twice thrashed the former world title challenger Ted Moore.

The impresario C.B. Cochran, whose previous world title promotion had been Freddie Welsh's lightweight championship win over Willie Ritchie in 1914, arranged the fight for London's Olympia on 30 June 1927. It was an expensive venture – Walker insisted on a £20,000 purse, a large percentage of which had first to be paid to the champion's nominated representative in Paris, and

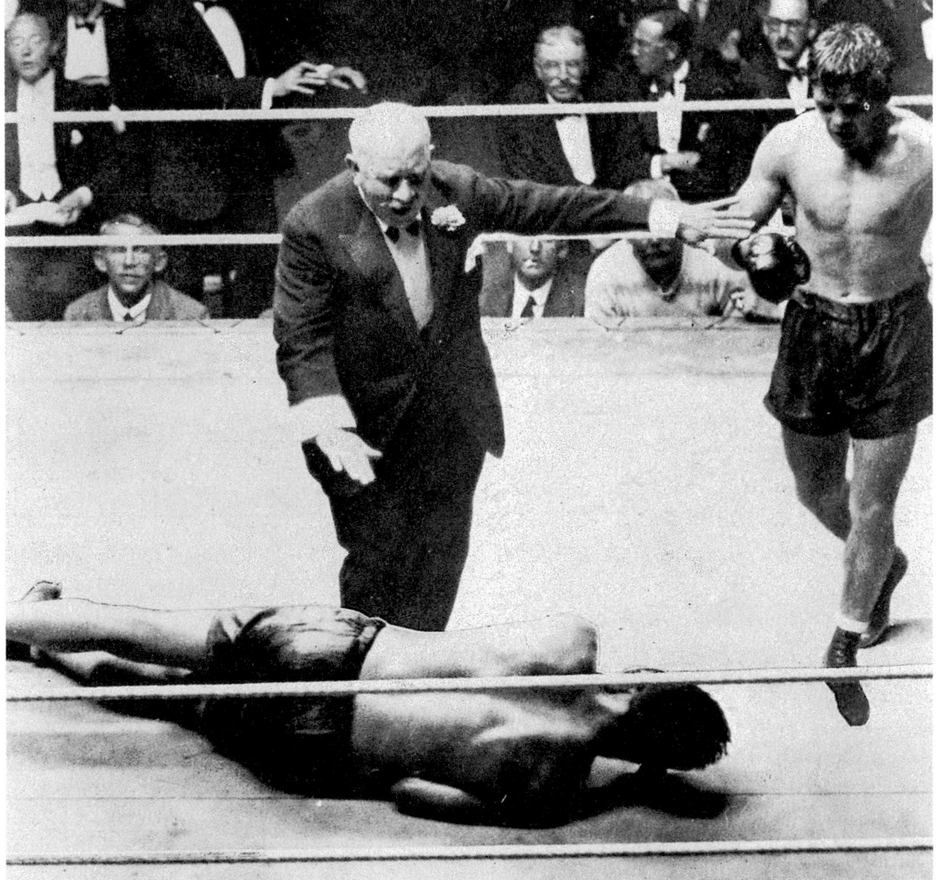

Walker (above) *and manager Jack Kearns bet the American's total £20,000 purse on him to beat Scottish challenger Tommy Milligan at London's Olympia in 1927, and even nominated the Prince of Wales as referee. Royal patronage was not forthcoming, but Walker was not too distressed . . . at the exchange rate then current, his 10th-round knockout win* (right) *earned him $300,000.*

then caused more problems with the choice of referee. Walker and Kearns suggested that Georges Carpentier should officiate, but Milligan objected strongly and nominated Eugene Corri instead. Walker refused Corri, and the situation then became utterly absurd when the Americans proposed the Prince of Wales for the job.

This was too much for Cochran, who threatened to cancel the show entirely if Corri was not accepted. Walker backed down, but his anxiety over the choice of official was understandable – since he and Kearns had bet the entire purse on the fight they were taking no chances. When the gallant but outgunned Scot was counted out in the tenth round, the Americans walked away with winnings which, at the exchange rate then current, totalled around $300,000. Walker defended his title three more times, beating Ace Hudkins twice on points, and knocking out Willie Oster in three

Big-hearted Walker frequently fought out of his weight class, even taking on heavyweights like Max Schmelling. The German gave him a bad eight-round beating (below). *After his retirement, Walker pursued an unlikely second career . . . as an artist* (right).

rounds (although this is not always recorded as a title defence.) He also found time, between the Hudkins fights, to challenge Tommy Loughran for the light-heavyweight title, losing on points.

On 19 June 1931, Walker relinquished his middleweight crown to pursue the heavyweight championship. It seemed a rather Quixotic task for a man who rarely weighed more than 12 st (168 lb) and who was only 5 ft 7 in tall, but his extraordinary grit and heart carried him to victories over good heavyweights such as 'Kingfish' Levinsky, Paolino Uzcudun, and Johnny Risko. He also boxed a 15-round draw with Jack Sharkey in July 1931, less than a year before Sharkey won the title. Not even a brutal beating from another heavyweight champion, Max Schmeling, in 1932, could discourage Walker. He went the distance with Maxie Rosenbloom in 1933 for the light-heavyweight title, and a year later beat Rosenbloom in a non-title fight. He also drew twice with Bob Godwin, the former NBA light-heavyweight claimant, before retiring in 1935 (although he made a meaningless one-fight comeback in 1939.) Walker quit with an overall record of 163 fights, of which he had won 94 and drawn four, boxing 45 no-decision contests.

Like so many 'high energy' fighters, Walker was not a particularly heavy puncher and won only three of his 18 championship fights inside the distance. After his retirement, Walker became an artist of note and had several exhibitions of his paintings.

Walker's decision to relinquish the title threw the division into turmoil, and for the next dismal decade there would be two, and sometimes even three, rival champions at any one time, with the various governing bodies constantly switching recognition from one to the other. Unravelling the strands of the championship during the period 1931-1941 is a Herculean task, as even the contemporary publications often conflict as to who held which version of the title at what time.

The NBA were first in the field, nominating William 'Gorilla' Jones, a southpaw from Tennessee, to meet 'Tiger' Thomas for their version of the vacant championship. Jones outpointed him, and retained the title twice before throwing it away on a low-blow disqualification against the balding Frenchman, Marcel Thil, in Paris in 1932. Thil's victory earned him European and NBA recognition, and he defended both these versions against the Englishman Len Harvey in London in July 1932.

Gorilla Jones (left) *and Marcel Thil* (below) *held versions of the title during the division's most confused decade, between 1931 and 1941, when there were many claimants to the crown.*

Marcel Thil was not a glamorous champion, but he was hard to beat. His brawling, mauling style carried him to victory over Len Harvey (above). *He won three championship fights on disqualification, including this 1936 meeting* (below) *with Lou Brouillard.*

In October 1932 the New York Commission put forward Ben Jeby and Chick Devlin to contest their version, which Jeby (real name Morris Jebaltowski) won on points. The NBA briefly withdrew recognition from Thil in 1933 (although he continued to be recognized in Europe) and instead they nominated Jones again as their champion, after he had knocked out Sammy Slaughter in seven rounds in Chicago in January 1933. But Jones never defended the title, which he gave up in 1934, and the NBA subsequently reinstated Thil as their representative. Between his win over Harvey in July 1932 and his disqualification win over Lou Brouillard in Paris in January 1936, Thil made six defences. In 1936, however, the NBA again withdrew recognition from him and put forward Jones, yet again, to contest the vacancy with Freddie Steele.

Europe, meanwhile, continued to regard Thil as champion. Steele outpointed Jones to win the vacant NBA title and retain the New York title he already held. In September 1937 Thil was stopped on a cut by Fred Apostoli, of San Francisco, at New York. The New York Commission ordered Freddie Steele, who by now was recognized by both them and the NBA as champion, to defend against Apostoli, whose defeat of Thil had earned *him* recognition in Europe. When Steele refused to comply with their order, the Commission recognized Apostoli as champion.

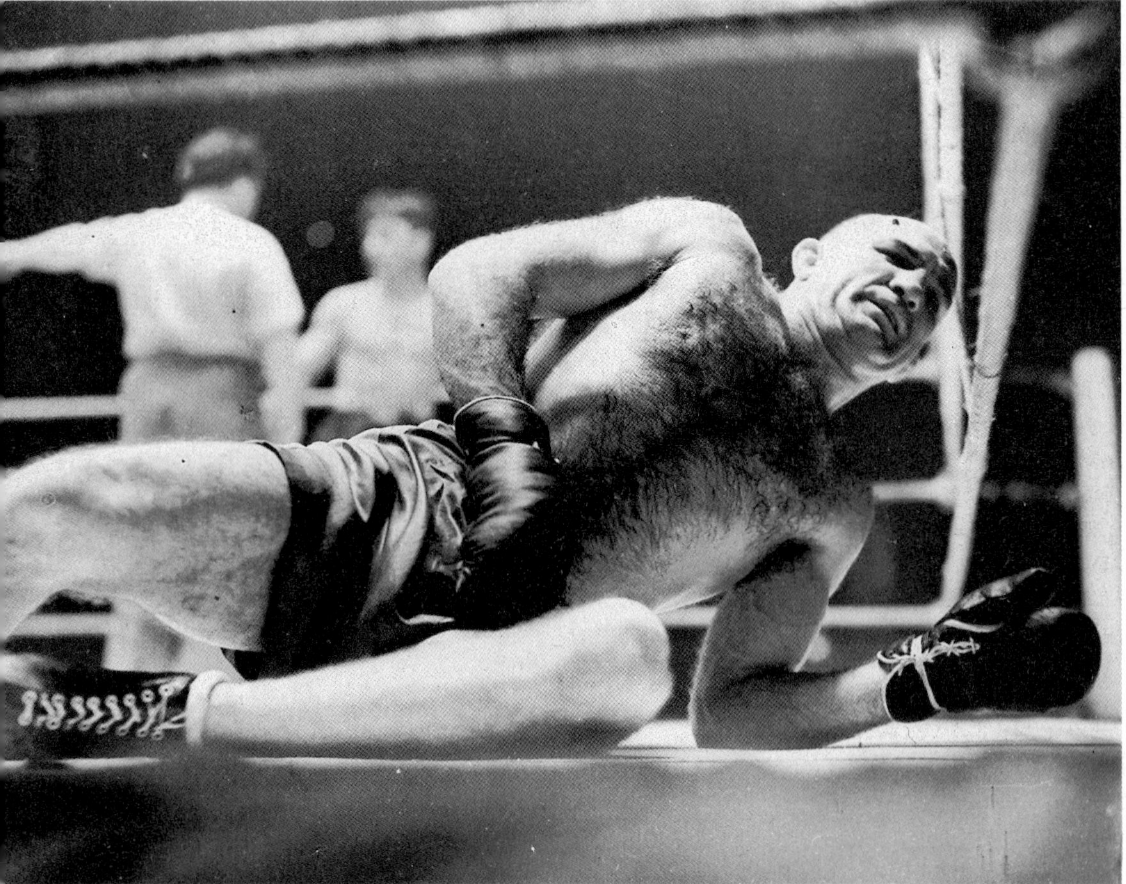

Fred Apostoli (below) *ended Thil's career with a 10th-round stoppage in New York in 1937.*

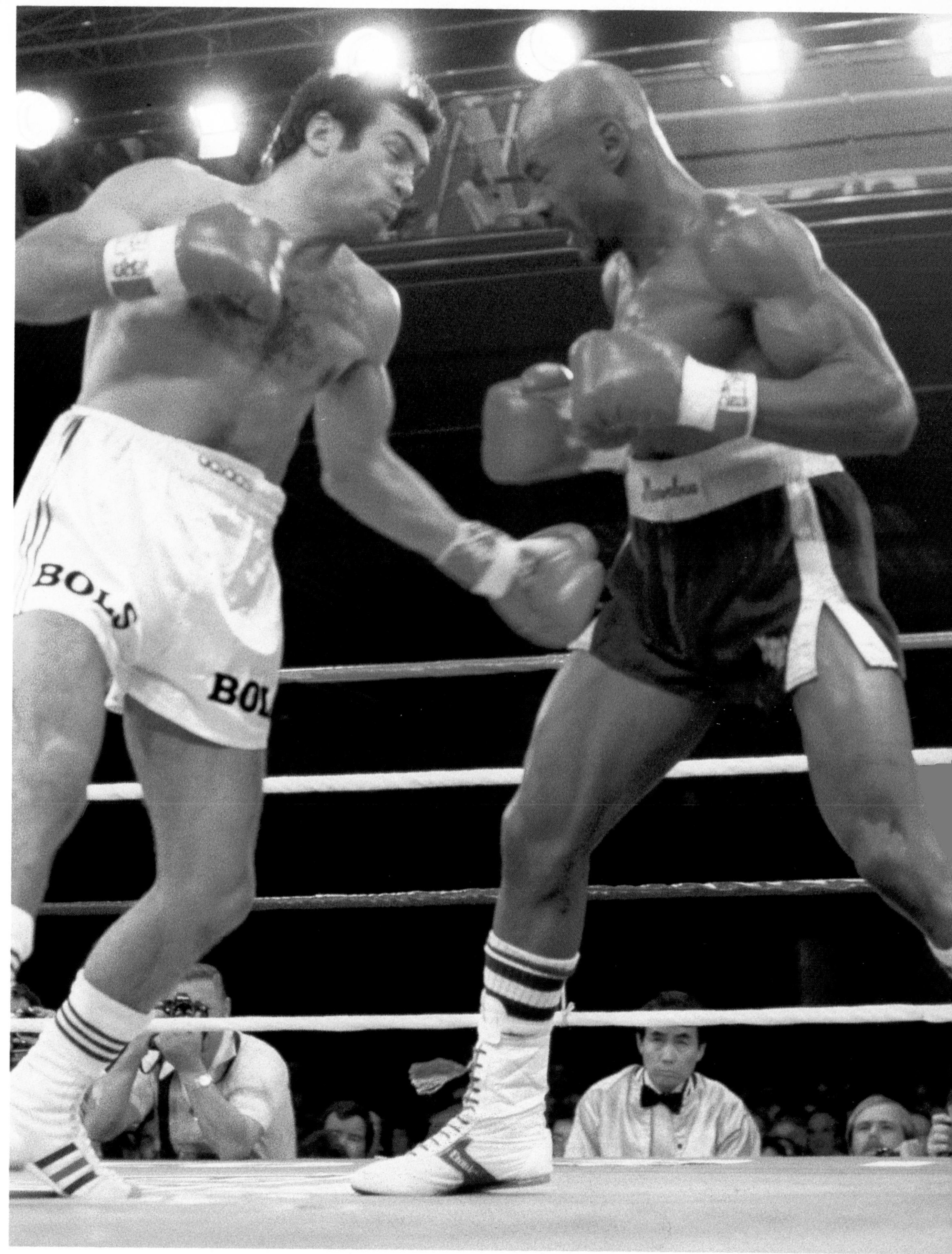
BOLS
BOLS

Juan Roldan (previous page) *and Roberto Duran* (above) *gave Marvin Hagler two of his most difficult middleweight title defences. Roldan even floored Hagler briefly before losing on an eye injury, while Duran took him to a close points decision in Las Vegas.* Right: *British southpaw Maurice Hope against the Italian-Australian Rocky Mattioli, whom he twice defeated for the WBC light-middleweight title.*

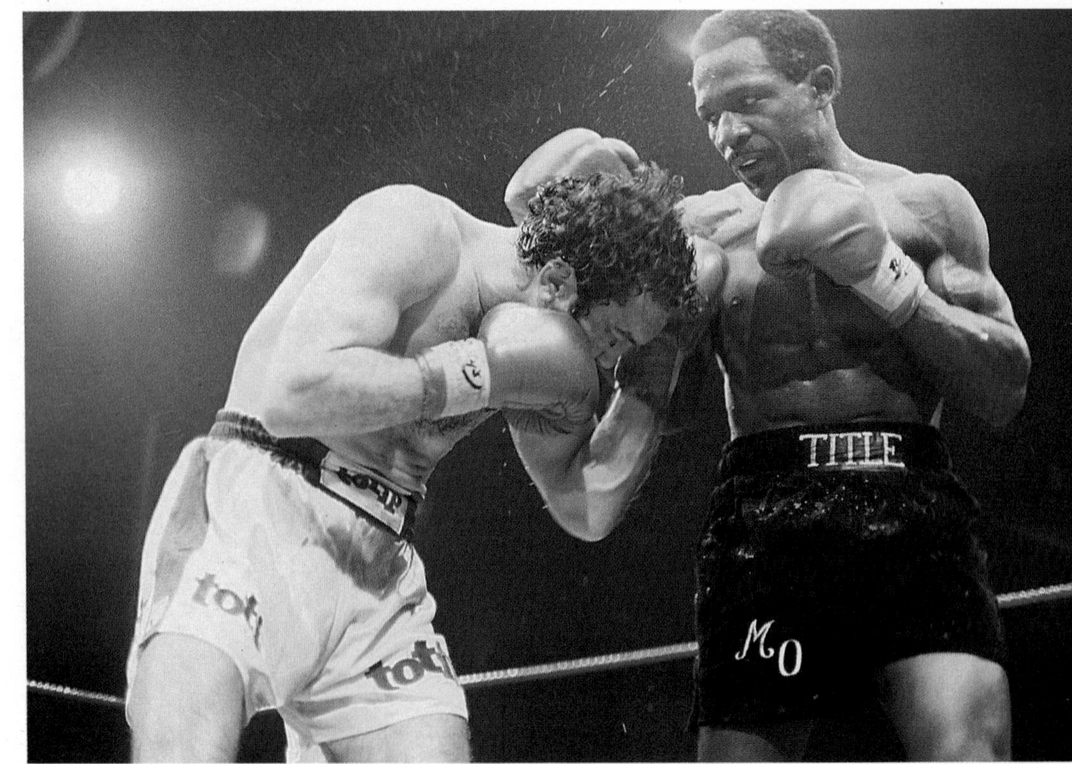

Ben Jeby (above) *and Vince Dundee* (right) *had short tenures of the New York version of the disputed championship in the early 1930s. The Dundee brothers (Vince and welterweight Joe) were first to win world titles.*

The New York version of the title had changed hands with bewildering rapidity since Ben Jeby had outpointed Chick Devlin in November 1932. Jeby managed three quick defences before he was knocked out in seven rounds by Lou Brouillard in August 1933, but the French-Canadian was champion for less than three months, being outscored in October by Vince Dundee, younger brother of the former welterweight champion Joe Dundee (the family name was actually Lazzaro, and Joe had been born in Rome). However, Dundee lost the title in his third defence to Teddy Yarosz, a clever but light-hitting Pennsylvanian, who outpointed him in Pittsburgh.

Two sometime-champions faced each other when Teddy Yarosz, on the right, outpointed Solly Kreiger in a New York 10-rounder in January 1937.

Yarosz had a short and undistinguished reign as champion, losing the title in his first defence to Ed 'Babe' Risko, who had beaten him in seven rounds in a non-title match earlier in 1935. Risko's reign was even more unimpressive. After three ten-round points wins, he was flattened inside a round in a non-title fight by British puncher Jock McAvoy (who was unable to secure a fight for *any* version of the title). Risko retained it on a points verdict over Tony Fisher in February 1936, but then lost ten-rounders to both Fred Apostoli and Freddie Steele before Steele finally dethroned him in July 1936.

Ed 'Babe' Risko (right, *celebrating his title win over Teddy Yarosz) was champion for only 10 months before Freddie Steele* (below, *on the left) dethroned him in 1936.*

Stylish Fred Apostoli (left) *outscores Solly Kreiger in February 1937 in defence of the New York and European versions.*

In January 1937 Steele outpointed Gorilla Jones to win the vacant NBA version and retain the New York title, and he retained both titles in a rematch with Risko in February 1937. Risko's career, which had never been outstanding, nose-dived after that when he lost nine of his remaining 12 fights, eight of them inside the distance. Steele retained the titles against Frank Battaglia, Ken Overlin and Carmen Barth, and when he was stripped of the New York title for refusing to meet Fred Apostoli, he continued to claim the NBA title until Al Hostak knocked him out in the first round at Seattle in July 1938. Hostak promptly lost it to Solly Kreiger of New York, but regained it from him on a fourth-round stoppage in June 1939 and held onto it in a December 1939 defence against Eric Seelig of Germany. Seelig's third-round knockout marked Germany's last world championship involvement until June 1962, when Gustav Scholz challenged Harold Johnson for the light-heavyweight title.

In July 1940 Tony Zale, from the steel town of Gary, Indiana, stopped Hostak in the 13th round in Chicago and, at last, put the championship back on the road to respectability.

Al Hostak (below) *won and lost the NBA title twice in a colourful 15-year career, each time inside the scheduled distance.*

Tony Zale (below), *one of the great middleweight champions, took the title from Hostak in 1940, and ruled for eight years.*

The New York and European versions, meanwhile, had been retained twice by Apostoli, but the San Franciscan, who never viewed the rigours of training with much enthusiasm, was then stopped in seven rounds by Ceferino Garcia, a left-hooking Filipino, in October 1939. Garcia knocked out Glen Lee of Nebraska in 13 rounds two months later, in the first world title fight ever held in the Philippines, and then in March 1940 spoiled Henry Armstrong's bid to become history's only four-weight world champion when he battled him to a draw in Los Angeles. Armstrong, who had already won the featherweight, lightweight, and welterweight titles, weighed only 10 st 2 lb (142 lb) and conceded 11½ lb to the champion.

Ken Overlin, a former sailor from Decatur, Illinois, ended Garcia's short spell at the top with a points win in Madison Square Garden in May 1940. He retained the title twice in six weeks against Steve Belloise, a strong puncher from New York, but lost it in May 1941 to Billy Soose, a one-time college boy from Pennsylvania, who had beaten Overlin and Tony Zale in successive non-title fights in the summer of 1940. Soose retained it on a technical draw against Ceferino Garcia in September 1941, but then abdicated to compete as a light-heavyweight. Tony Zale outpointed Georgie Abrams to win the New York and European versions of the vacant title at Madison Square Garden on 2 November 1941, a fight which was also a defence of his NBA title. After a decade of unrelieved mediocrity and unprecedented confusion, the middleweights at last had a single, undisputed champion. The lean times were over, and the division was about to enter one of the most colourful, exciting and vivid periods in its history.

Ceferino Garcia (right, *on the right in a losing bid for Barney Ross' welterweight title) moved up to claim a share of the middleweight championship, which he lost in May 1940 to Ken Overlin* (above).

Rocky and the Man of Steel

TONY Zale (real name Anthony Florian Zaleski) had first caught the eye of the American boxing experts in 1934 when, in the Golden Gloves national finals in New York, he substituted for a Detroit competitor called Joe Louis. (Zale was narrowly beaten by Melio Bettina, who later won the world light-heavyweight title.) He turned professional in June of that year, but after a promising beginning, during which he won his first nine fights, he seemed to lose his way, winning only eight of his next 18.

Zale retired for over a year but returned to action in 1937, under the joint management of Sam Pian and Art Winch, who guided him through a series of carefully chosen matches, all of them in Chicago, into contender status. By July 1940 he held half a title, having taken the NBA version from the crude but dangerous Al Hostak of Minneapolis, whom he had beaten in a non-title fight earlier in the year. By the time Zale had outpointed Abrams for the undisputed championship, he had become a hard, mature 28-year-old with a deserved reputation for courage, stamina and durability which was reflected in his nickname 'Man of Steel'. But just as he looked poised for a long and prosperous reign at the top the War intervened, and robbed him of what should have been his peak years.

Between February 1942, when Zale was outpointed by light-heavyweight Billy Conn, and January 1946, he was inactive. By the time he was released from the Navy, and resumed his career with a fourth round knockout of Bobby Giles in January 1946, the champion was nearly 33 years old. But he quickly picked up where he had left off, and knocked out another five opponets of mixed quality before, in September 1946, he faced the man with whom his name is forever linked – Rocky Graziano. Zale and Graziano would meet three times, with the first two contests meriting inclusion with the classic battles of a division which has produced more than its share of ring epics.

Graziano, then 24 years old, was the antithesis of the clean-living, religious, exemplary ex-Serviceman Zale. He had spent his childhood running wild in the slums of New York, earning spells in reformatories and remand homes. He had been dishonourably discharged from the forces, served a term in an army prison and, in 1947, had

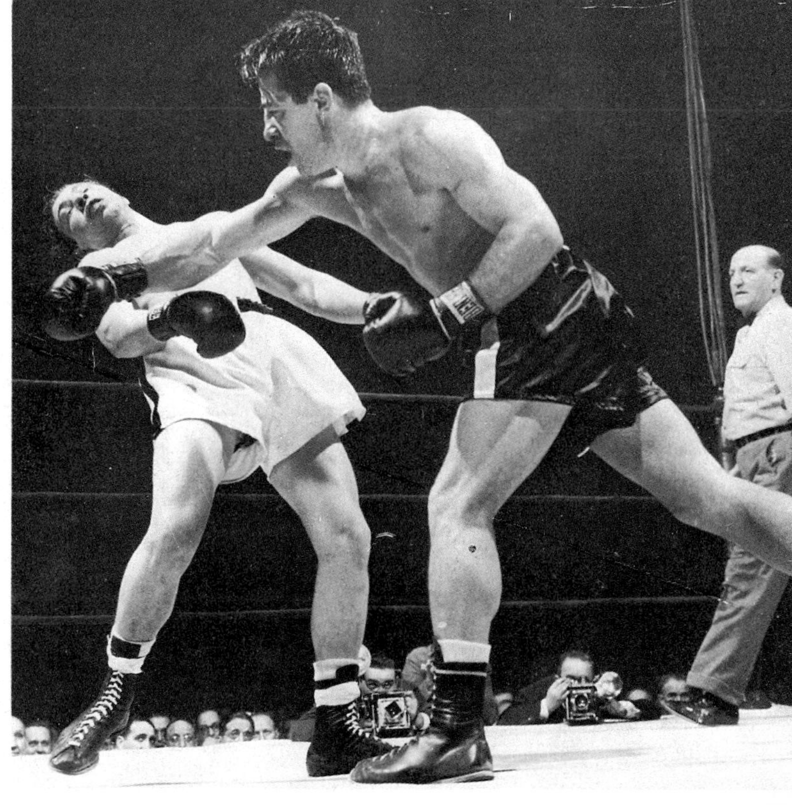

The exciting Rocky Graziano (above), *pictured* (right) *in typical slugging action against Tony Janiro, electrified the division in the late 1940s.*

When Graziano stopped Harold Green in three rounds (below) *and thus avenged two earlier points losses, demand grew for him to face Zale. The fight lived up to expectations, with Zale scoring a thrilling sixth-round knockout* (right). *It was not the end of their rivalry.*

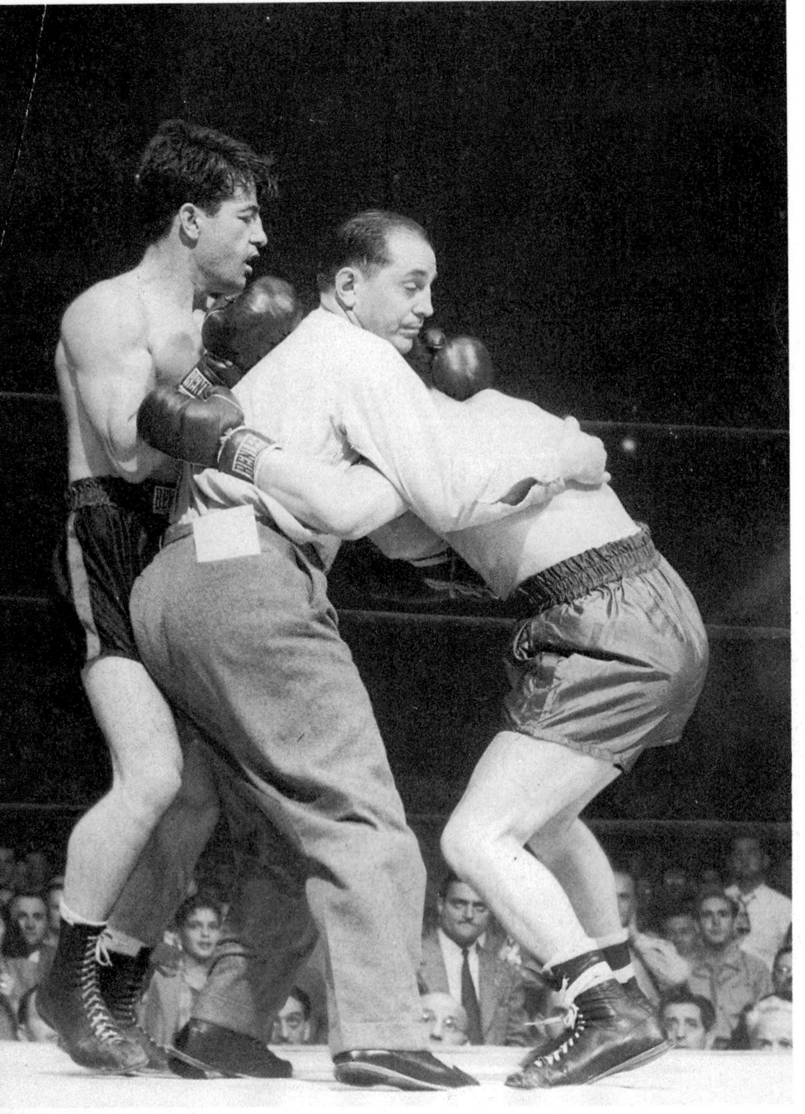

his licence revoked in New York for failing to report an attempted bribe.

Zale v Graziano was the perfect match: boxing's 'Bad Boy' pitted against its 'Ideal Citizen'; Graziano's powerful punching, representing the irresistible force, against Zale's legendary endurance and iron chin, the immovable object. Forty thousand fans packed the Yankee Stadium on 27 September 1946, when the pair shared receipts of $350,000. The challenger was a 3-1 favourite, but the veteran Zale had him on the floor inside a minute. Yet Graziano slammed back so effectively that Zale ended the opening round on the canvas, badly dazed. Calling on all his astonishing powers of recuperation, Zale hauled himself back into the fight, walking through the New Yorker's fierce right-hand hitting, and ignoring cuts on the mouth and eye, to knock him out in the sixth round.

They met again in July 1947, this time in Chicago since the fight had been thrown out of New York when the Commission revoked Graziano's licence for failing to report an attempt to bribe him to lose to Cowboy Reuben Shank – a fight which never actually took place. The receipts at Chicago Stadium were $414,000, an indoor record, and once again Graziano started favourite despite having been knocked out in their last meeting. This time the action was even more ferocious. Graziano recalled in his autobiography *Somebody Up There Likes Me:*

> This was no boxing match. It was a war and if there wasn't a referee, one of the two of us would have wound up dead. Today I still can't look at the pictures of that Chicago Stadium fight without it hurts me and I get nightmares that I am back in the ring on that hot July night and I am looking out through a red film of blood.

Zale dominated the early stages, cutting Graziano's left eye and almost closing it in the first round, and flooring him in the third. The challenger's cornerman, Whitey Bimstein, pleaded with referee Johnny Behr not to stop the fight at the end of the round, and Graziano responded to his reprieve with an attack of a sustained intensity rarely witnessed before.

> I was an animal in a cage of ropes, a bleeding, cornered, half-blind, aching, sweating snarling animal who had to kill or be killed. I don't remember no bells ringing or no

crowd or no referee. The figure of Zale was a blur sometimes, then the blood got wiped off my good eye and he was sharp and splotched with red and moving slower and slower under the hot lights and in the steam-bath air of the arena.

It went on like that until the sixth round, when referee Behr leapt between them and hauled Graziano off the beaten and battered champion.

There had to be a third instalment, and it took place at Ruppert Stadium, Newark, on 10 June 1948. Graziano, who was paid $120,000, again started favourite but Zale, now 35 years old, had

Zale and Graziano provided one of the ring's great rivalries: Graziano won the rematch (right) *but Zale recaptured the title* (below) *with a superb third-round knockout.*

Marcel Cerdan (left) *was the finest European fighter of his time, and he made a stunning impression on American fans with his second-round knockout* (below) *of Harold Green in 1947.*

whipped himself into superb shape for the last great performance of his fighting life. He dropped Graziano twice in the third round, and the second knockdown was the end. Zale fought only once more, and it cost him his championship at the hands of France's greatest ring hero since Georges Carpentier – Marcel Cerdan.

The handsome, curly-haired Cerdan, the son of a pork butcher, had been born at the French Foreign Legion town of Sidi Bel-Abbes in Algeria on 22 July 1916. He turned professional at 18 encouraged by his father and three brothers, and commenced building what remains one of the finest records ever compiled by a European. Between his debut, on 14 November 1934, and his

Above: *Cerdan (left) and Lavern Roach in a fight which featured a 24-second 'knockdown'.*

world title fight with Zale in September 1948, Cerdan had fought 112 times and lost just three – and two of those were on disqualification. He was virtually unbeatable in Europe, winning French and European titles at both welterweight and middleweight, and earning a special place in the affections of the ever-romantic French with his long-running and very public affair with the singer Edith Piaf. The intervention of the Second World War meant that Cerdan was 30 before he made his American debut in September 1946, outpointing the former world title challenger Georgie Abrams at Madison Square Garden, New York.

The fight established him as a contender, and he followed up that win with a stunning second-round knockout of Harold Green (who had twice outpointed Rocky Graziano) in 1947. An eighth-round knockout of Lavern Roach was remarkable as much for a 24-second knockdown as for Cerdan's performance. Roach was dropped in the second round, but the referee, instead of taking up the count, engaged in a heated debate with the timekeeper as to whether the New Yorker had been punched or tripped. Roach took full advantage of the confusion to remain sitting on the canvas until the referee at last started the count, getting up at 'nine'.

Such was the Frenchman's appeal that 20,000 fans paid almost $250,000 to watch him challenge Zale at Roosevelt Stadium, Jersey City, on 21 September 1948. Zale was a 2-1 favourite, but apart from one moment in the fourth round when he rocked Cerdan with a right, it was the Frenchman's fight all the way. The 11th round ended with Zale propped against the ropes, and as Cerdan turned away towards his corner Zale's legs

Below: *The finish of a great career for Tony Zale, as he collapses at the end of the 11th round against Cerdan.*

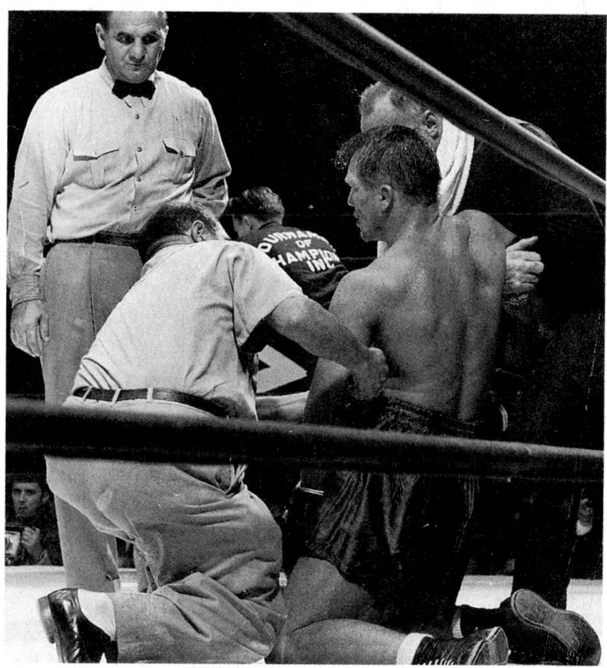

gave way and he collapsed into the referee's arms. It was the old champion's last fight ... and, tragically, Cerdan's last championship victory.

He had two non-title wins over Dick Turpin, in London, and Lucien Krawsyck, in Casablanca, but then lost the title in his first defence, in Detroit on 16 June 1949, to Jake LaMotta, a rough brawler from New York. Cerdan dislocated his shoulder in the third round, but battled on until, after ten rounds, he could go no further. On 27 October, the plane carrying Cerdan back to America for the rematch crashed into a mountain in the Azores, killing all 46 people on board.

LaMotta was very much in the mould of his childhood acquaintance Rocky Graziano, a petty thief and delinquent who, fortunately, settled on boxing instead of crime as his escape route from the slums. By the time he had beaten Cerdan he

'Bronx Bull' Jake LaMotta (left) *took the title from Cerdan in June 1949, but the champion dislocated his shoulder in the third round of their fight* (below). *There was to be a rematch, but Cerdan died in a plane crash.*

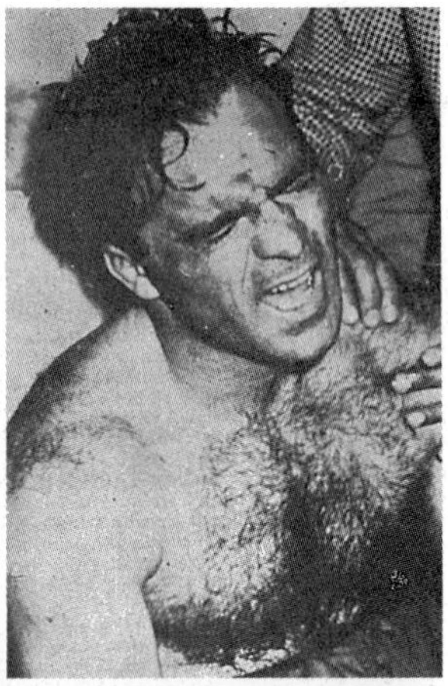

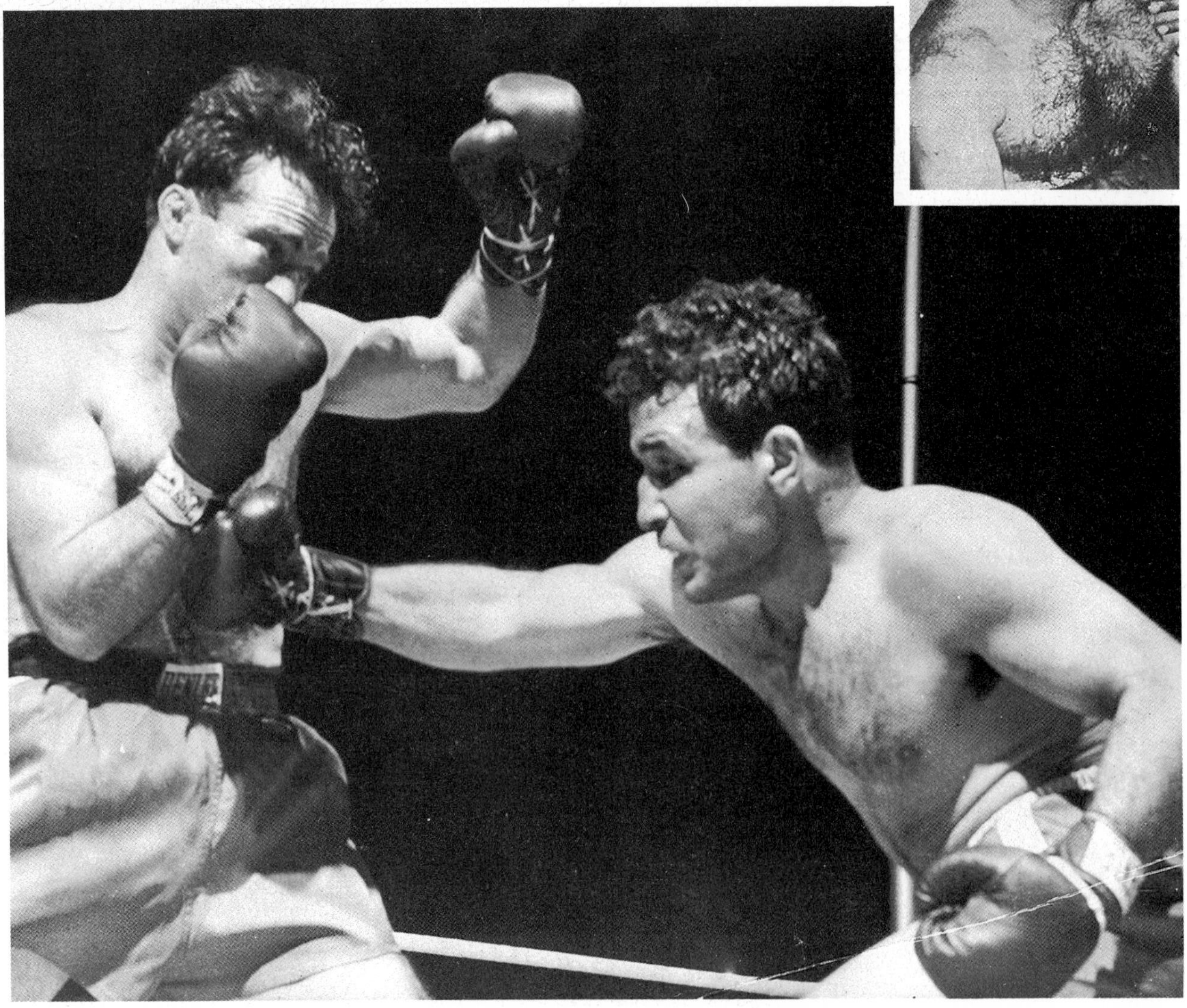

LaMotta fought anyone, anywhere, from middleweights like George Kochan (above, *whom he beat in nine rounds) to light-heavyweight contenders like Bob Murphy* (right). *LaMotta and Murphy met twice, for a win apiece.*

Dick Wagner (above, *on the left), who later went the distance with Floyd Patterson, was stopped in nine rounds by LaMotta in 1950.*

was a veteran of 87 professional fights, and had been a ranked contender for many years. He had also beaten Ray Robinson, the first man to do so in 41 fights (Robinson went another *91* fights before he lost again). LaMotta had also beaten the former welterweight champion Fritzie Zivic in three out of four meetings, but according to his version of events the 'Mob' then controlling boxing refused to give him a title chance because he would not take on their nominee as his manager.

Finally, LaMotta agreed to 'throw' a fight with the gangster-controlled light-heavyweight Blackjack Billy Fox in New York in 1947 in return for a guaranteed title chance, and he obliged in four rounds. LaMotta defended his action to author Pete Heller in an interview in 1970:

> Today, it's a little different: If a fellow deserves a chance at the title the people will argue for it, they will speak up, the newspaper people will speak up. But in my time there was a lot of guys that deserved chances to fight for the title. There were a lot of uncrowned champs around at that time that didn't get the shot. And those are the guys I had to fight because nobody else wanted to fight 'em. There were a lot of good fighters around at that time, but because they weren't on the 'in' they were left out.

The 'Mob' took nearly two years to give LaMotta his chance, and even then he had to make an undercover payment of $20,000 to ensure that the fight took place. But having at last won the title, LaMotta made it pay with defences against European opponents Tibero Mitri of Italy, who was outpointed, and Laurent Dauthille of France, who was knocked out with 13 seconds left in the last round of a fight which Dauthille could not have lost on points. It was, perhaps, the most dramatic ending ever seen in a championship fight.

While LaMotta was consolidating his hold on his hard-won title, his old rival Sugar Ray Robinson was campaigning for a chance to take it off him...and having beaten LaMotta in four of their

Sugar Ray Robinson (above) *was LaMotta's arch-rival. 'I fought him so often I got diabetes', LaMotta joked.*

Both LaMotta's successful defences were against Europeans, Tiberio Mitri of Italy (above) *and Laurent Dauthille of France* (right), *who was beaten 13 seconds from the end of the 15th round of a fight in which the challenger held a clear points lead.*

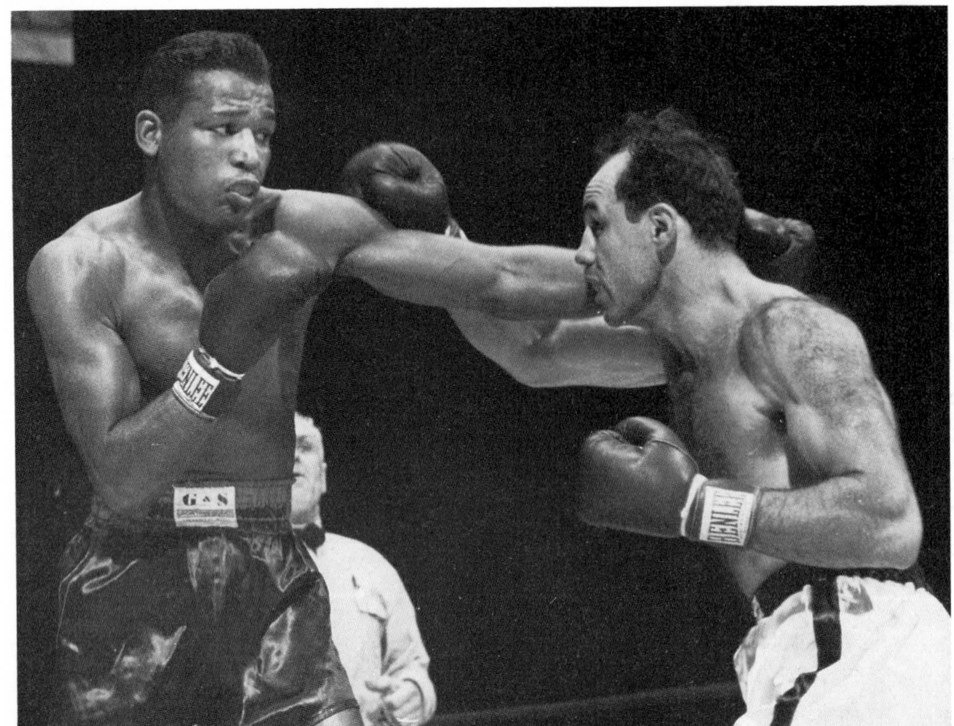

Robinson had been unbeatable as a welterweight before he moved up to middleweight and stopped Steve Belloise (left) *in seven rounds in August 1949. He earned Pennsylvania recognition as champion ten months later, and retained the 'title' twice, including this 12th-round knockout of Carl 'Bobo' Olson* (below).

five meetings, he had every reason to feel confident. At 29, Robinson was as close to perfection as any fighter the sport has known, a supremely graceful yet powerful box-fighter with dazzling hand and foot speed, and the ability to knock opponents out with either hand. The statistics of his career are staggering: as an amateur he was unbeaten in 85 fights, of which he won 69 inside the distance, 40 in the first round. Turning professional in 1940, he won his first 40 fights in a row before LaMotta outpointed him, but he reversed that loss just three weeks later. Inside his first 12 months as a professional Robinson beat three world champions – Sammy Angott, Marty Servo, and Fritzie Zivic, and he beat them again in 1942. In 1946 he won the vacant welter weight title, which he defended five times between then and 1950.

Robinson started his pursuit of the middleweight title in 1950, and on 5 June won recognition from the Pennsylvania Commission as world champion by outpointing the Frenchman Robert Villemain. He retained the 'title' twice that year against Jose Basora and Carl 'Bobo' Olson, a man who would figure prominently in his future.

Robinson's wildly extravagant life style delighted gossip columnists. He employed a retinue of 'personal assistants', including hair-dressers, masseurs, shoe-shiners, and even a dwarf who acted as court jester, and his exotic taste in clothes, cars, and women made him the most instantly recognizable face in Harlem, where he owned bars and a night club.

When the LaMotta fight was arranged for 14 February 1951 in Chicago, Robinson's record stood at one loss and two draws in 123 fights, of which he had won 78 inside the distance. LaMotta had boxed 94 times, winning 78 and drawing four. Inevitably, given the fight's date and location, it has

The incredibly courageous LaMotta took a fearful beating from Robinson, in the most one-sided of their six meetings.

passed into history as boxing's St. Valentine's Day Massacre. Robinson drew the weight-weakened champion's strength with skilful, evasive boxing in the first ten rounds, and then stepped up the pace as LaMotta faded until, in the 13th, he punched LaMotta to a standstill and forced referee Frank Sikora to intervene. The fight was stopped with the defiant champion leaning against the ropes, arms dangling, but refusing to fall.

Robinson became even more extravagant as middleweight champion, and undertook a whistle-stop European tour to earn some ready cash. He lined up seven fights between 21 May and 10 July in Paris, Zurich, Antwerp, Liege, Berlin, Turin, and London, aiming to round off the tour with an undemanding defence against the British champion Randolph Turpin. Turpin was a former navy cook whose unorthodox style had brought him 40 wins and one draw in 43 fights, but he was not thought to pose any real threat to the dazzling American. The fight captured the imagination of the British public whose excessive patriotism, added to Robinson's personality, ensured a full house of 18,000 at the Exhibition Hall, Earl's Court, London.

They were not disappointed: Robinson, scaling only half a pound over the modern light-middleweight limit, could not fathom out Turpin's peculiar lean-back-then-lunge style, nor did the blows which had brought him so many quick wins have any noticeable effect on the challenger.

Referee Frank Sikora rescues the battered but still defiantly upright LaMotta in the 13th round (above). *The new champion seemed set for a long reign . . . but former Navy cook Randolph Turpin* (right, *beating Pete Mead in four rounds) had a surprise lined up for him.*

Robinson could never quite solve Turpin's awkward, crouching style, and was caught repeatedly by the Englishman's lunging left jab. At the start of the last round, the crowd were so confident of a Turpin victory that they broke into 'For He's A Jolly Good Fellow'. It was an unforgettable night for British boxing.

Turpin's lead increased as the rounds slipped by, and when Robinson's left eyebrow was cut in the seventh round he was forced to concentrate on protecting the injury, thus letting Turpin jab his way even further in front. By the time the bell sent them out for the 15th and final round, the crowd knew that they were witnessing the biggest middleweight upset in decades, and throughout the round sang *For he's a Jolly Good Fellow* as Turpin carefully boxed his way to the title.

But Turpin's glory was short-lived – he held the title for just 64 days, the shortest reign in the division's history. The rematch took place at the Polo Grounds, New York, on 10 September,

The scene at the Polo Grounds, New York (below) *as 61,370 watch Robinson attempt to regain the title just 64 days after losing it. For nine rounds they had little to cheer about, as Turpin pecked away with jabs while Robinson struggled* (right).

attracting a crowd of 61,370, which paid record receipts for a non-heavyweight fight of $767,626. Robinson's preparations were much better this time, but he still had trouble with Turpin's peculiar style, particularly his jab, which A.J. Liebling described as being 'like a man starting his run for the pole vault.' After nine rounds, which had been devoid of any real excitement, there was nothing much between them – but then Robinson's left eyebrow split open again and, as referee Ruby Goldstein peered at the injury, Robinson retaliated with a blistering attack.

He feinted a jab to Turpin's head and, as the champion jerked his head backwards, stepped in with a smashing right. Turpin fell into a clinch, but Robinson shrugged him off and dropped him with a left to the body and a right to the jaw for a count of seven. Gilbert Odd, who was at ringside that night, recalled what happened next in his book *Cruisers to Mighty Atoms:*

> Then was seen some of the fiercest, fastest, and most accurate punching ever thrown. Blows were rained in on Randy from every conceivable angle. Hooks, uppercuts, swings, the lot. Leaning back on the hemp, the Briton did his best to ride the torrent of tossed leather, but some were bound to connect and after taking telling shots on either side of the jaw, Turpin doubled up into a cover.
>
> As he did so, Robinson switched his attack to the body, clubbing rights to Turpin's ribs and then, as his guard came down, ripping in a flurry of

Robinson reclaims his crown with 'some of the fiercest, fastest, and most accurate punching ever seen.'

Above: *Former champion Rocky Graziano fell in three rounds when he tried to regain the title.*

Right: *Carl 'Bobo' Olson pins Randolph Turpin to the ropes in their clash for the vacant title.*

blindingly fast hooks to the head. Referee Goldstein moved in to stop it just as Turpin started to pitch forward. Since there had been just eight seconds it must have been doubtful whether he could have continued. Some even claimed that he had been panicked into the stoppage by the death that had occurred a short time previously in a fight at St Nick's Arena in New York, but considering Robinson's proven record of destructive power, Goldstein's action was humane and fully justified.

Robinson made two defences, outpointing Bobo Olson and knocking out Rocky Graziano, and then retired in December 1952 after his abortive attempt, six months previously, to take the light-heavyweight title from Joey Maxim. Predictably, the championship split once more. Olson outpointed Paddy Young to win American recognition, while Turpin won the British and European version by outpointing the Frenchman Charles Humez.

The rival claimants met for the undisputed title in Madison Square Garden in October 1953, but Turpin's preparations were plagued by scandal, rows, and crises, culminating in his arrest on a sex charge. He fought so badly, losing on points, that even his mother was moved to say: 'I hate to say this, but I don't think he had any intention of winning'. The defeat marked the end of Turpin as a world-class fighter. He was destroyed in a round by Tibero Mitri for the European title in 1954 and, although he won a Lonsdale Belt outright when he moved up to light-heavyweight, a bad knockout by

left in the round Goldstein came in for much criticism for intervening so late in the round, especially as Robinson's eye was so badly cut that Yolande Pompey in 1958 ended his career. His money gone, he turned to wrestling and even unlicensed boxing, and finally shot himself in May 1966, at the age of 37.

Olson was a busy champion, making three

Turpin had raised British hopes by outscoring the Frenchman Charles Humez (right) *for the European version of the title, but fought listlessly against Olson and was trounced. The new champion's first defence was against the former welterweight champion Kid Gavilan* (below), *whom he outpointed.*

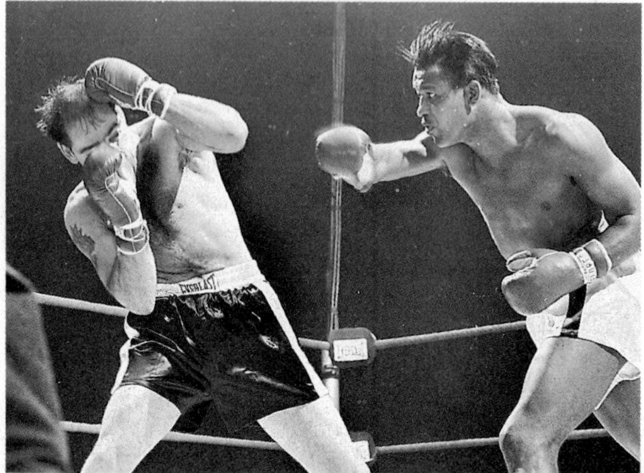

Robinson's comeback received a setback when the unranked Ralph 'Tiger' Jones (left) *outpointed him in January 1955 – but before the year was over, Sugar Ray was champion again after an easy second-round win over Olson* (below left).

defences in 1954 and trying unsuccessfully for the light-heavyweight crown against Archie Moore in 1955. But Robinson, meanwhile, had not been prospering in retirement. A series of ill-advised business ventures prompted him to launch a comeback, and after a shaky start he regained the title for the second time by knocking Olson out in two rounds in December 1955.

But Robinson was now in his mid-30s and his skills, although still magnificent, were beginning to fade. Gene Fullmer, a brawling Mormon from Utah, took the title on a unanimous decision in Madison Square Garden in January 1957, although Robinson flattened him with a single left hook in the fifth round of their rematch, four months later, to become champion for the fourth time.

The welterweight title, once held by Robinson, had passed to Carmen Basilio, a rugged one-time onion farmer from Canastota, New York. Like Robinson, he fancied his chances in the heavier division and when he got his opportunity in Yankee Stadium, in September 1957 he outlasted the aging champion to win a desperately close split

Above: *A brilliant left hook in the fifth round flattened Gene Fullmer and made Robinson champion for the fourth time, but less than five months later he was an ex-champ again.* Right: *Carmen Basilio (left, beating Pierre Langlois) took the title in a classic 15-rounder in New York.*

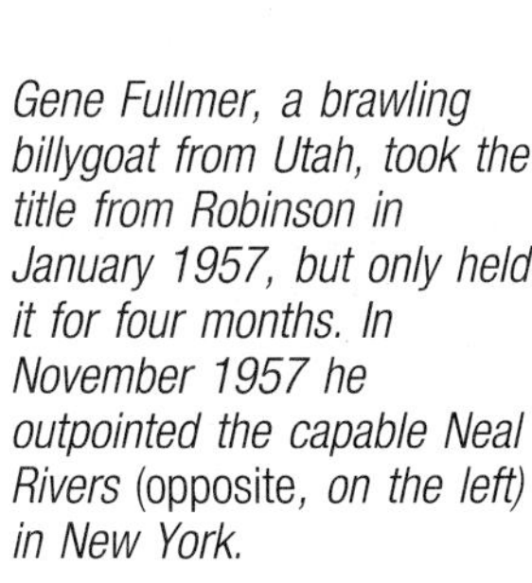

Gene Fullmer, a brawling billygoat from Utah, took the title from Robinson in January 1957, but only held it for four months. In November 1957 he outpointed the capable Neal Rivers (opposite, on the left) *in New York.*

decision. It looked like the end for Robinson, but the most remarkable fighter in the division's history regained the championship yet again in another bitterly fought 15-rounder at Chicago, in 1958. Robinson was now 37, although some sources had him two years older, but even at that advanced age it was officialdom rather than a fellow-performer who claimed at least half his title. The NBA stripped

It seems unthinkable that any fighter could have completed 15 rounds against Ray Robinson with such a horribly injured eye, but Basilio did.

Basilio and Robinson were bitter rivals who also disliked each other intensely, and their two title clashes (left, above *and* right) *were both epics of skill, endurance and savagery.*

him in May 1959 for his failure to defend, and Fullmer won the vacant title by stopping Basilio in 14 rounds.

Robinson defended the remaining share of the title in Boston in January 1960 against a local ex-fireman, Paul Pender, but lost it on a split decision, a result which Pender repeated six months later. Two months later, the amazing Sugar Ray dredged up one last great performance when he held Fullmer to a draw in Las Vegas for the NBA title, a result observers thought favoured the champion.

There was one more title shot, but this time Fullmer clearly outpointed him. Robinson fought on for another four years, and finished his career with a ten-rounder against the then No. 1 contender, Joey Archer, who beat him on points. Robinson was 44, and having his 201st fight (he won 174).

The New York and European version passed briefly from Pender to Terry Downes, a wise-cracking, all-action, superbly brave Londoner who had spent his teenage years in America, served in the US Marines, and even qualified for the

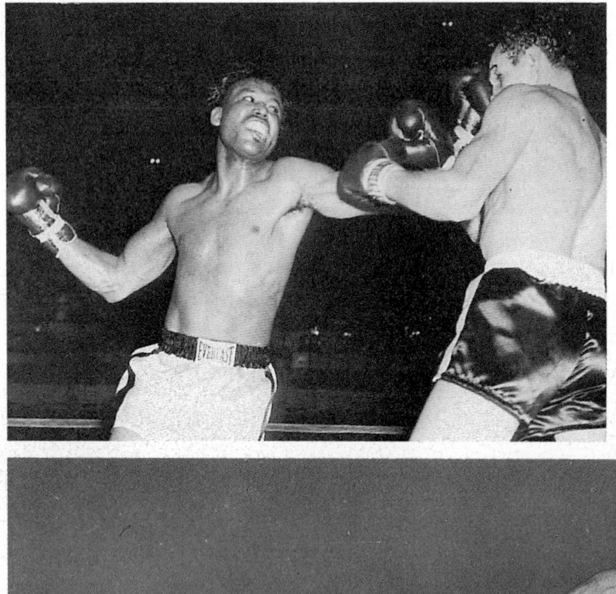

Left: *Paul Pender, an obscure ex-fireman from Boston, ends Robinson's reign with a points win in January 1960. It was a split decision, and Pender later repeated it.*

Below: *Terry Downes, a world champion in the making, sent British title-holder Pat McAteer (right) into retirement with this points defeat in a 1958 eight-rounder.*

American Olympic team before it was realized that he was British. Downes was as entertaining outside the ring as inside it, and was shrewd enough to get into the bookmaking business when street betting was legalized in Britain, thus making a fortune.

Downes had been stopped on cuts by Pender in their first meeting in Boston in January 1961, but forced the American to retire after nine rounds of their Wembley rematch six months later. He held the title for only nine months and Pender reclaimed it on a unanimous decision in Boston, in April 1962. It was Pender's last fight: in November 1962 he was stripped of the title for failing to defend it.

Gene Fullmer had proved himself a worthy NBA

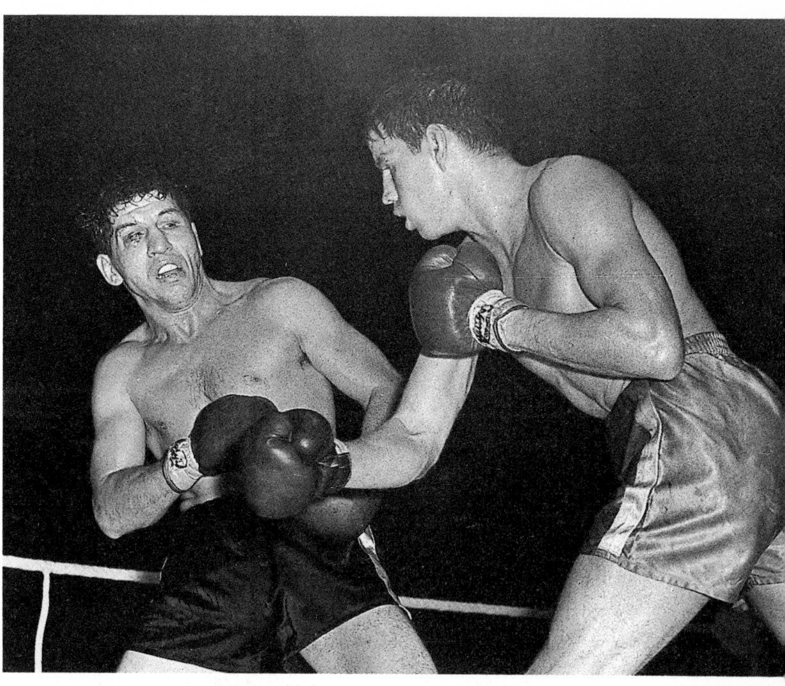

Downes (right, *on the right) outpointed future champ Joey Giardello to earn a shot at Pender's title, but the American won on cuts in seven rounds. There was a rematch at Wembley six months later, in July 1961* (below), *and this time Downes forced Pender to retire on his stool after nine rounds.*

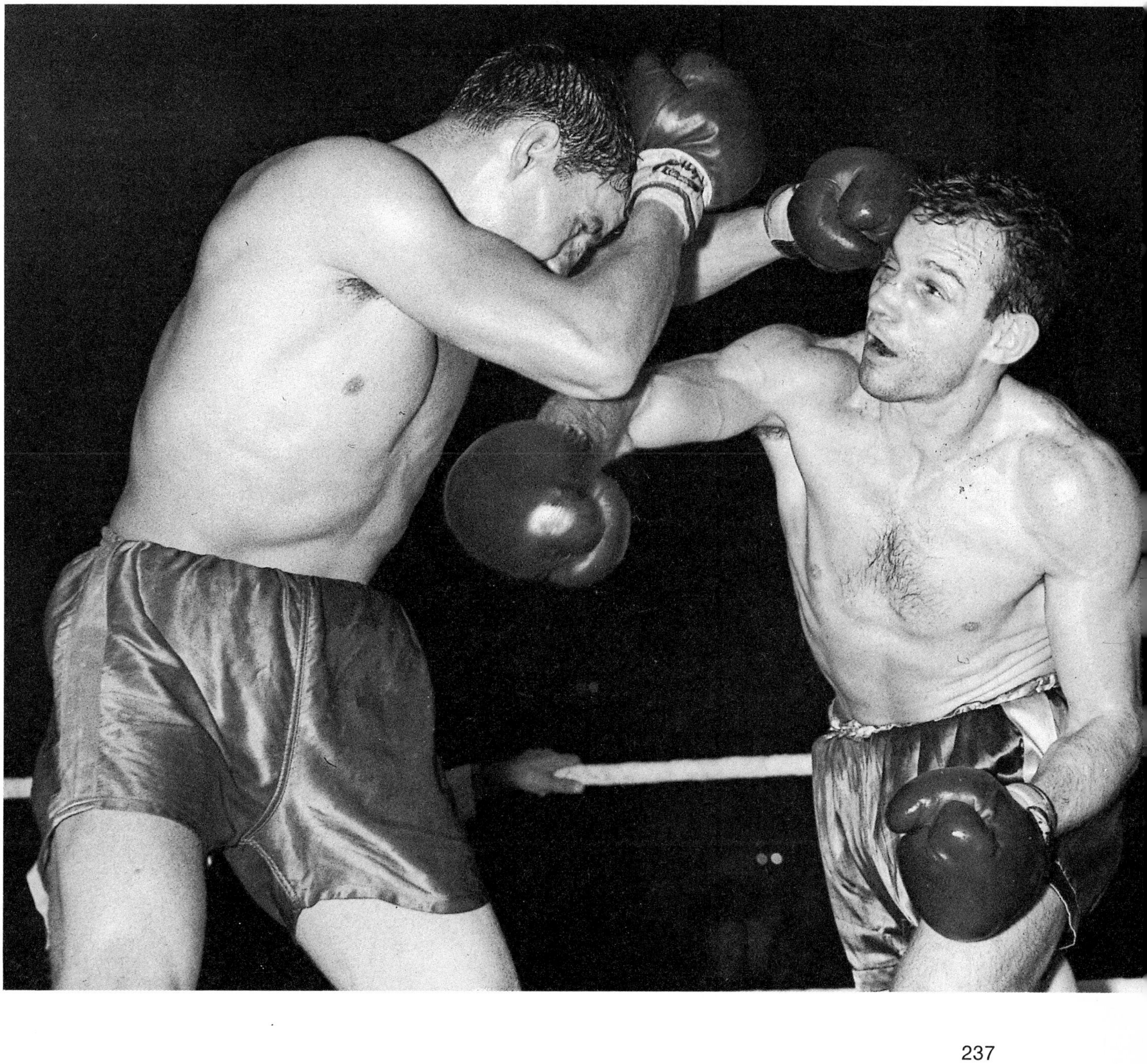

champion with defences against Spider Webb, Joey Giardello (a draw), Robinson (a draw and a win), Florentino Fernandez, and the tragic welterweight champion Benny Paret, who died after his next fight. In October 1962, however, he was outpointed by a Nigerian, Dick Tiger, who had learned his trade in losing six and eight-rounders in Liverpool and London, before winning the Empire title and moving to America, where his career blossomed. In November, Tiger was accorded universal recognition following Pender's stripping, and he retained the title in two rematches with Fullmer, drawing with him in Las Vegas and then stopping him in seven rounds in West Africa's first world title fight, at Ibadan, Nigeria, in August 1963.

Joey Giardello, a Philadelphia veteran who had

Below: *this 10th-round knockout of welterweight champion Benny Paret in December 1961 was Gene Fullmer's last victory. Paret died after* his *next fight, against Emile Griffith.*

Right: *Paul Pender (left) reclaims the title from Terry Downes in Boston. He never fought again, but Downes went on to challenge for the light-heavyweight title against Willie Pastrano in 1964.*

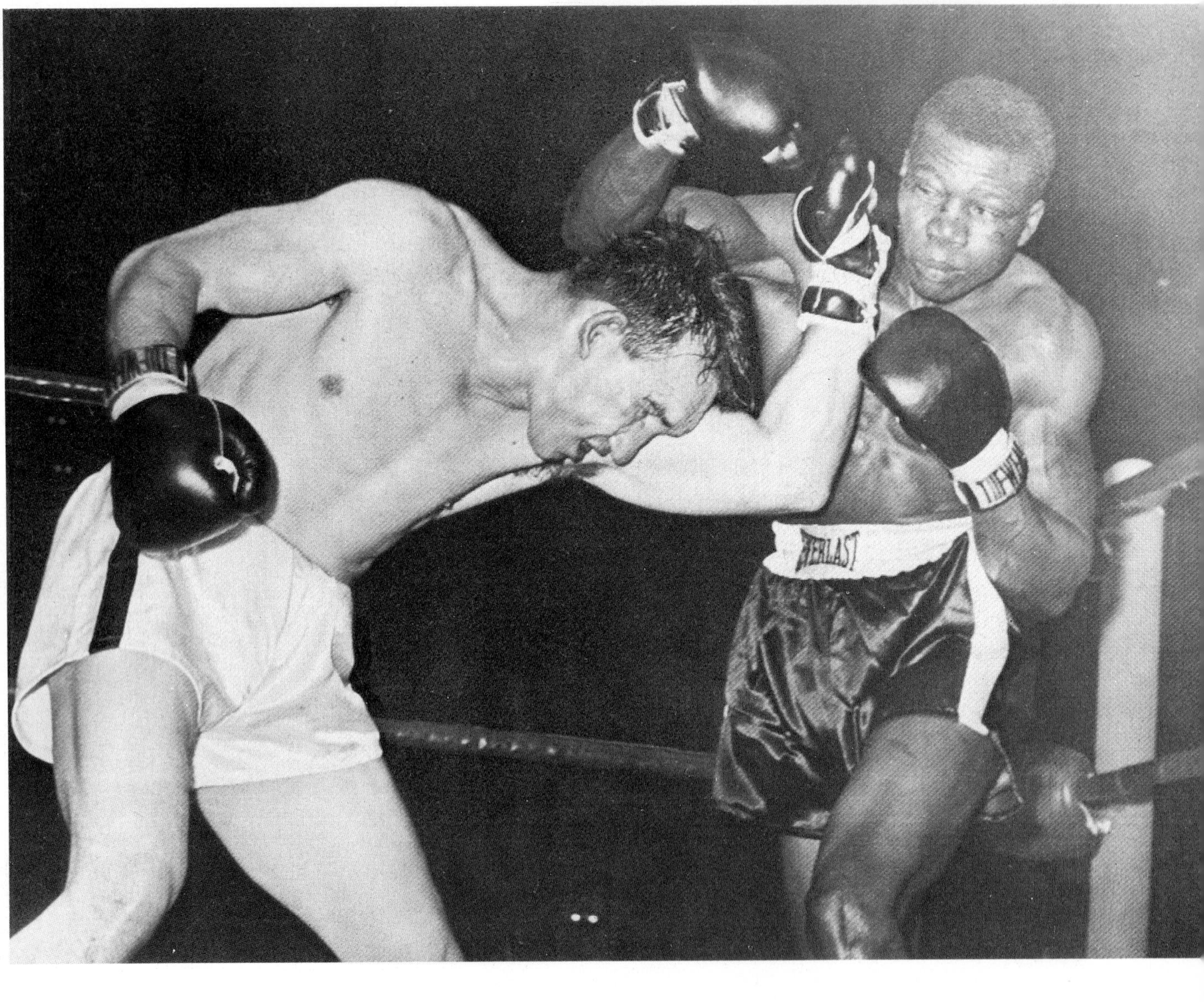

Dick Tiger was an unheralded preliminary fighter when he stopped Terry Downes in this early-career clash (left) *in Shoreditch Town Hall. It must have been inconceivable to the fans in the famous old London fight hall that both winner and loser would go on to world titles. Tiger's career blossomed when he went to America after winning the Empire title, and victories like this decision over Detroit's classy Henry Hank* (below, *on the left*) *secured him his title chance against Gene Fullmer.*

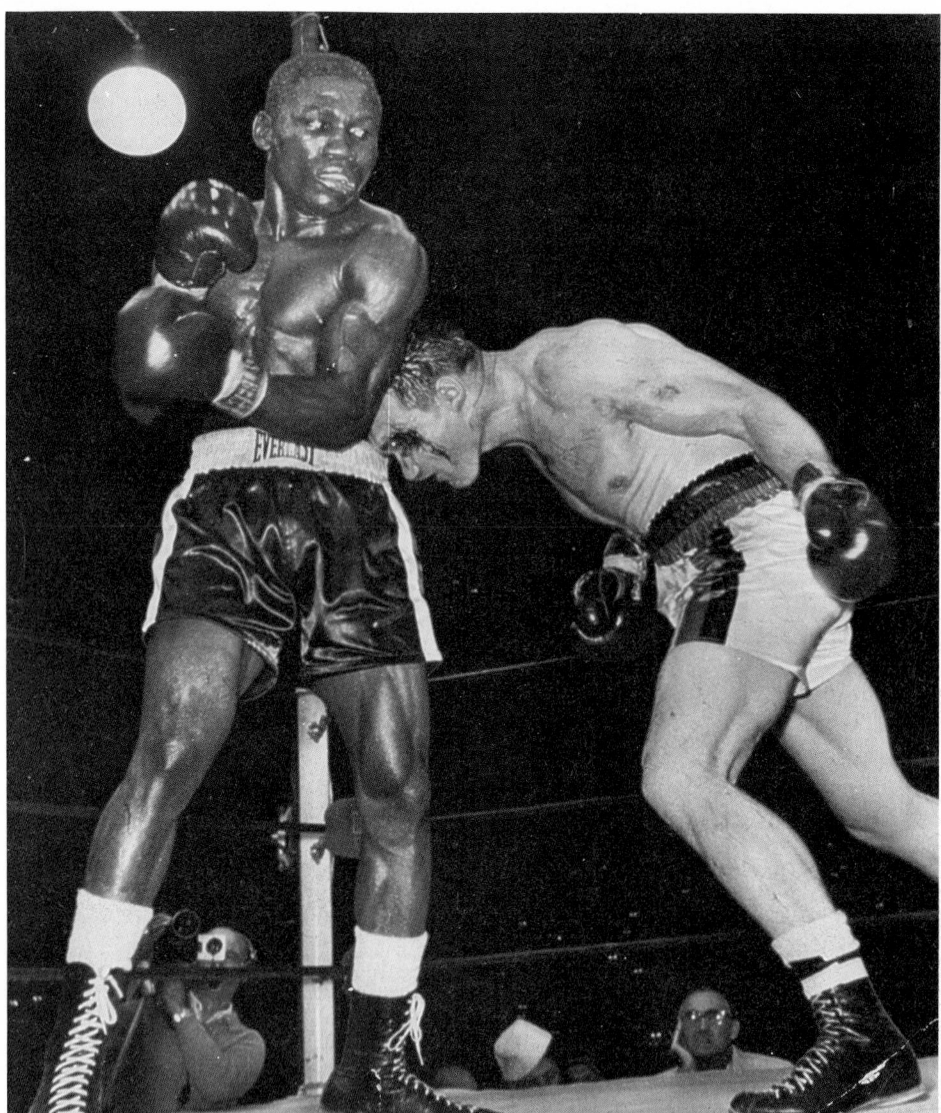

Tiger stopped Fullmer in Nigeria (left), *then lost the title in an upset to veteran Joey Giardello* (below). *Giardello (seen* above *knocking out Willie Troy in 1954) retained it against Rubin Carter* (facing page, top) *then was outscored by Tiger in a return fight.*

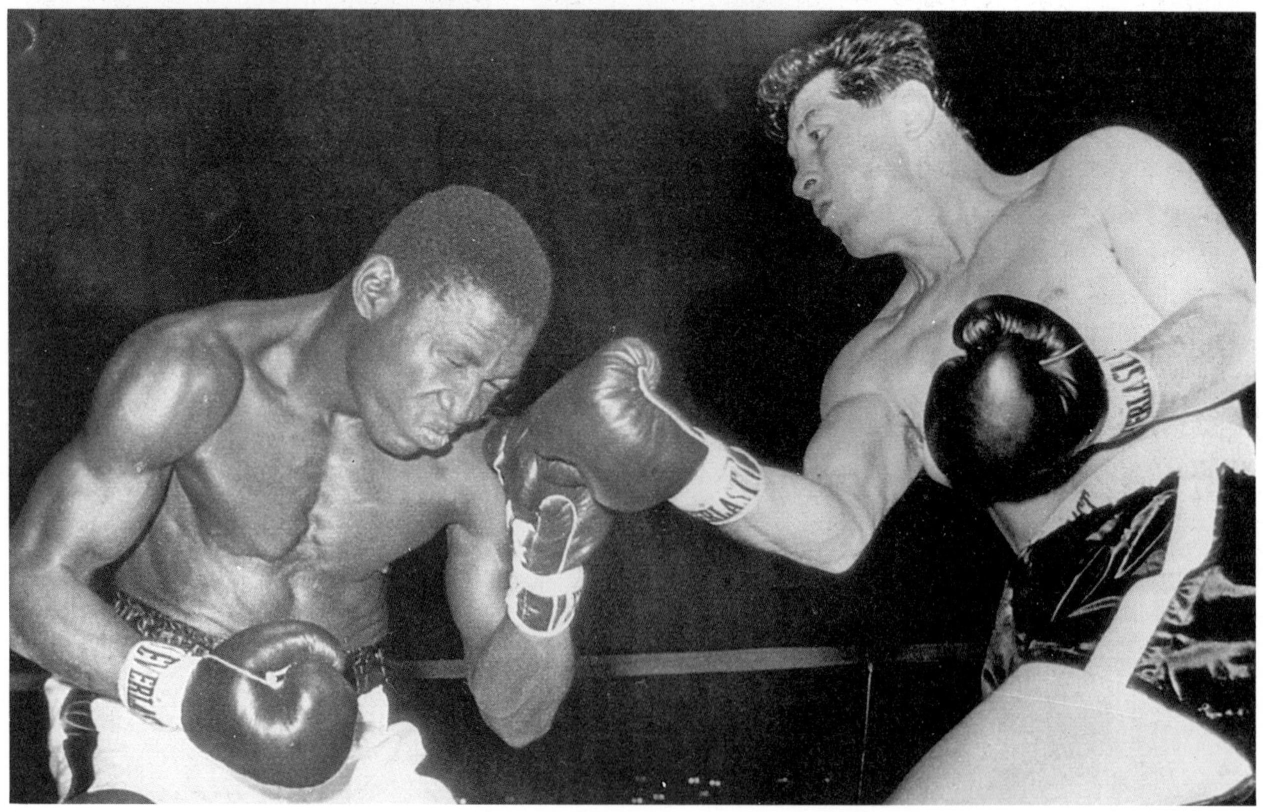

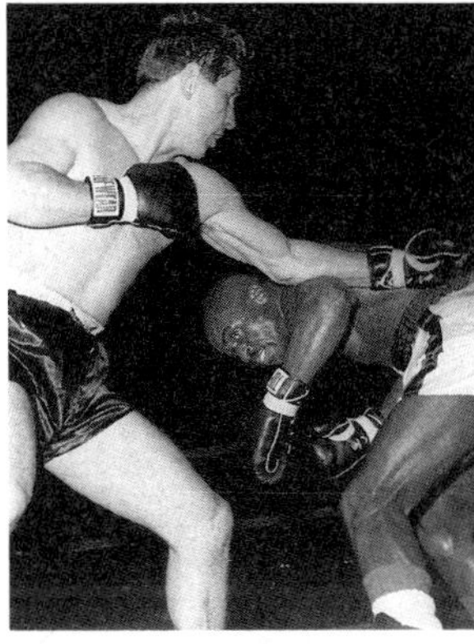

Below: *Welterweight champion Emile Griffith stepped up a division to outscore Tiger in this 1966 encounter.*

been a top contender for a decade but had only had one title chance, when he drew with Fullmer, counter-punched his way to the title on an upset decision in Atlantic City in December 1963. He retained it against Rubin 'Hurricane' Carter, who later became a *cause célebre* after his conviction for triple murder. Tiger took it back from Giardello on a unanimous verdict in October 1965, but then lost it to another upwardly mobile welterweight champion, Emile Griffith, in April 1966.

Griffith had won the welterweight title three times and lost it twice. He retained the middleweight crown twice against the New York Irishman Joey Archer, each time on the narrowest of split decisions, and then lost it to the Italian Nino Benvenuti, who had formerly held the light-

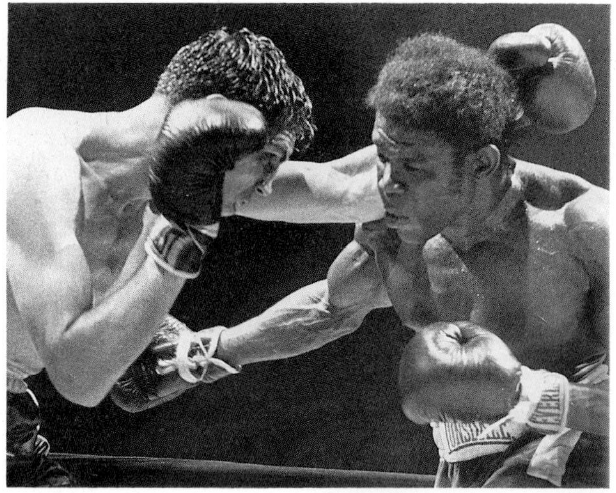

middleweight title and whose record of one loss in 72 fights was the finest of any European since Marcel Cerdan. Griffith reclaimed it five months later, but Benvenuti won it again in March 1968 and held onto it for four defences, including one against an American, Tom Bethea, at Umag, Yugoslavia, which was the first world title fight to be held in a Communist country.

The handsome Italian's reign was ended on a 12th-round knockout in Rome on 7 November, 1970 by an Argentinian who was destined to dominate the division as no middleweight had done since Robinson – Carlos Monzon. His record of 14 successful defences still stands, and included all

Griffith retained the championship twice against Joey Archer (above) *before losing it in the first of a three-fight series with Nino Benvenuti* (below)*. The Italian had lost only once in 72 fights, including this 1965 points win* (right) *over the useful American Rip Randall.*

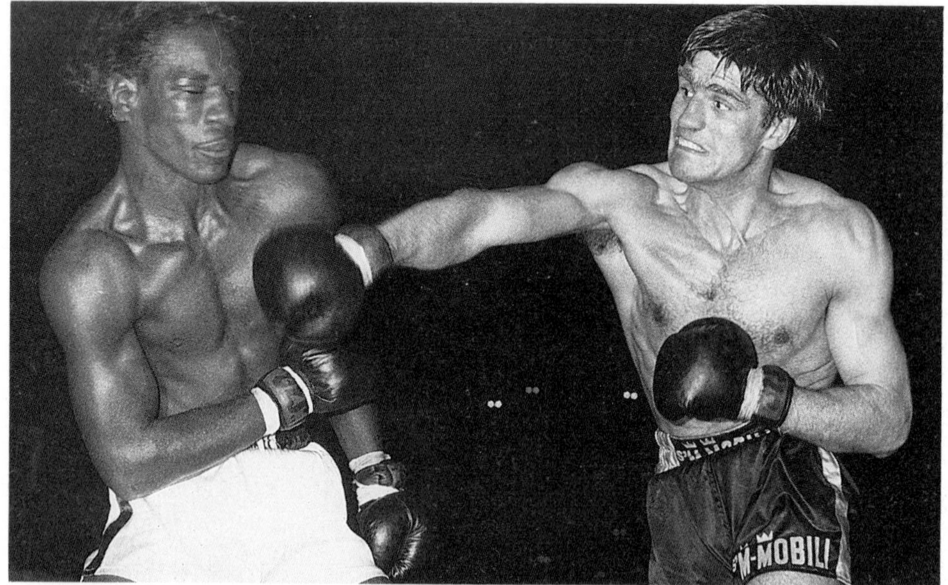

Previous page: *action from the most exciting middleweight championship of recent years, as Marvin Hagler stops Thomas Hearns in three explosive rounds at Caesars Palace.*
Right: *Wilfred Benitez, a three-weight world champion, retains the WBC light-middleweight title against Carlos Santos (on the right).*
Below: *the mighty Thomas Hearns, in his last appearance as a light-middleweight, stops the former IBF champion Mark Medal at Caesars Palace.*

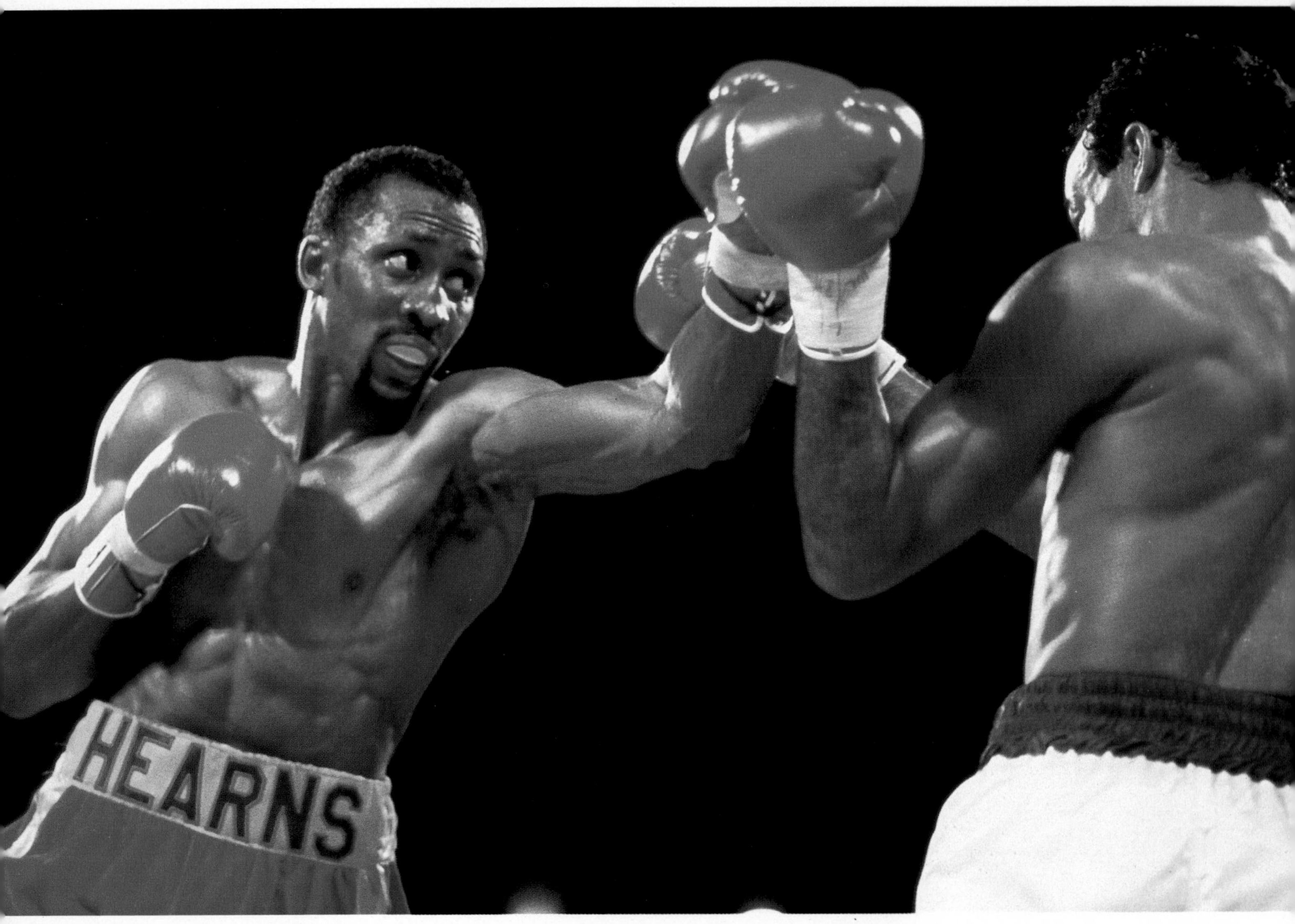

The magnificent Carlos Monzon (above) *floors ex-champ Nino Benvenuti in their return fight in 1971* (right). *The Argentinian made a record 14 defences, and retired at the top with just three defeats in 102 fights, and an unbeaten run stretching back over 82 appearances.*

the outstanding contenders of his time. He was extraordinarily tall for a middleweight, at marginally under 6 ft, and used his height and reach to full effect. Opponents of the standard middleweight size found it difficult to get past his long and accurate left jab, and if they did manage to do so they would invariably be stopped short by crunching rights. In all, Monzon won 89, drew nine, and lost just three of his 102 fights (one No contest), with 61 of them ending inside the schedule, including ten of his championship fights.

He risked his title wherever there was a payday to be had – against Benvenuti in Monte Carlo, Griffith in Buenos Aires, Denny Moyer in Rome, Jean-Claude Bouttier (twice) in Paris, Tom Bogs in Copenhagen, Bennie Briscoe in Buenos Aires, Griffith (again) in Monte Carlo, and the brilliant Cuban-born welterweight champion Jose Napoles in Paris. However, in April 1974 the WBC stripped him for his failure to defend against their top challenger, Rodrigo Valdes of Colombia, who won their version of the title by knocking out Briscoe in a brutal slugging match in Monte Carlo.

Monzon retained the WBA title against the Australian Tony Mundine in Buenos Aires, Tony Licata of America in New York, and European

champion Gratien Tonna in Paris, while Valdes busied himself with WBC defences against Tonna, Ramon Mendez, Rudy Robles, and Max Cohen. The Colombian was a classy and hard-hitting fighter who, in an era not dominated by Monzon, would probably have been a respected and long-reigning champion. As it was Monzon unified the title by beating him on a unanimous decision in Monte Carlo, in June 1976, and retained it in a return fight there one year later before retiring as unbeaten, and even unbeatable, champion.

Valdes won the vacant championship by outscoring the shaven-skulled Philadelphian Bennie Briscoe, another outstanding middleweight who would have graced the title in a different time. But the hard battles caught up with the Colombian, and he lost the undisputed title in his first defence to Hugo Corro, a neat-boxing but unspectacular Argentinian, who retained it against the American Olympic champion Ronnie Harris, and against Valdes in a rematch, before being outscored by the former European light-middleweight champion, Vito Antuofermo of Italy.

The New York-based Antuofermo was a stocky, short-armed and light-hitting fighter who got to the

Anyone who deserved it got a crack at the title when Monzon was champion, including Jean-Claude Bouttier of France (above) *and Tom Bogs of Denmark* (left). *Ten of Monzon's defences were staged in Europe.*

Rodrigo Valdes (inset) *won the WBC title when it was stripped from Monzon, and stopped the erratic but dangerous Frenchman Gratien Tonna* (right) *in his first defence.*

top with a mixture of stubborness, durability, courage, and a willingness to shed apparently limitless amounts of blood. Antuofermo made only one successful defence, and in retrospect it was an astonishing result: he battled to a draw with the man who was already regarded as the uncrowned champion, Marvin Hagler. Antuofermo was undoubtedly favoured by the draw in Caesars Palace, Las Vegas, in November 1979 but it was the best result the big-hearted Antuofermo ever achieved.

He was dethroned in his next defence at Caesars Palace by the southpaw Englishman Alan Minter, who shared Antuofermo's propensity to bleed but had the redeeming asset of a finishing punch, which had brought him 22 inside-the-distance wins in his 42 fights. Minter, in common with most British world title winners, tends to be dismissed as a 'lightweight' by American writers, but he was a

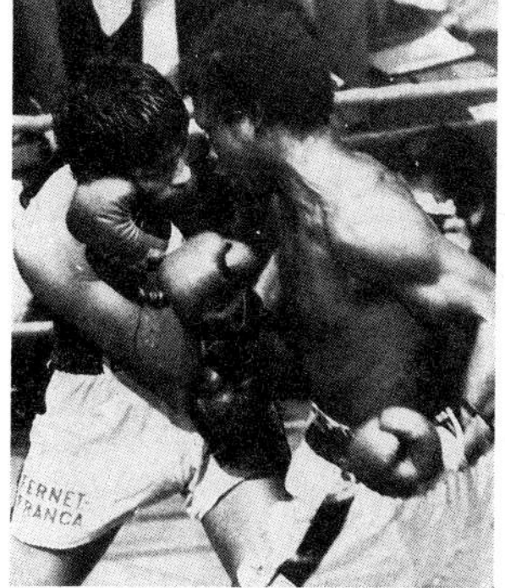

Hugo Corro (left) *ended Valdes' second spell as champion with a points win in San Remo, but lost the title in his second defence to the rough, durable Italian Vito Antuofermo* (below).

Antuofermo had spent most of his career in New York, where performances like this bruising win over Willie Classen (below) *made him a popular attraction.*

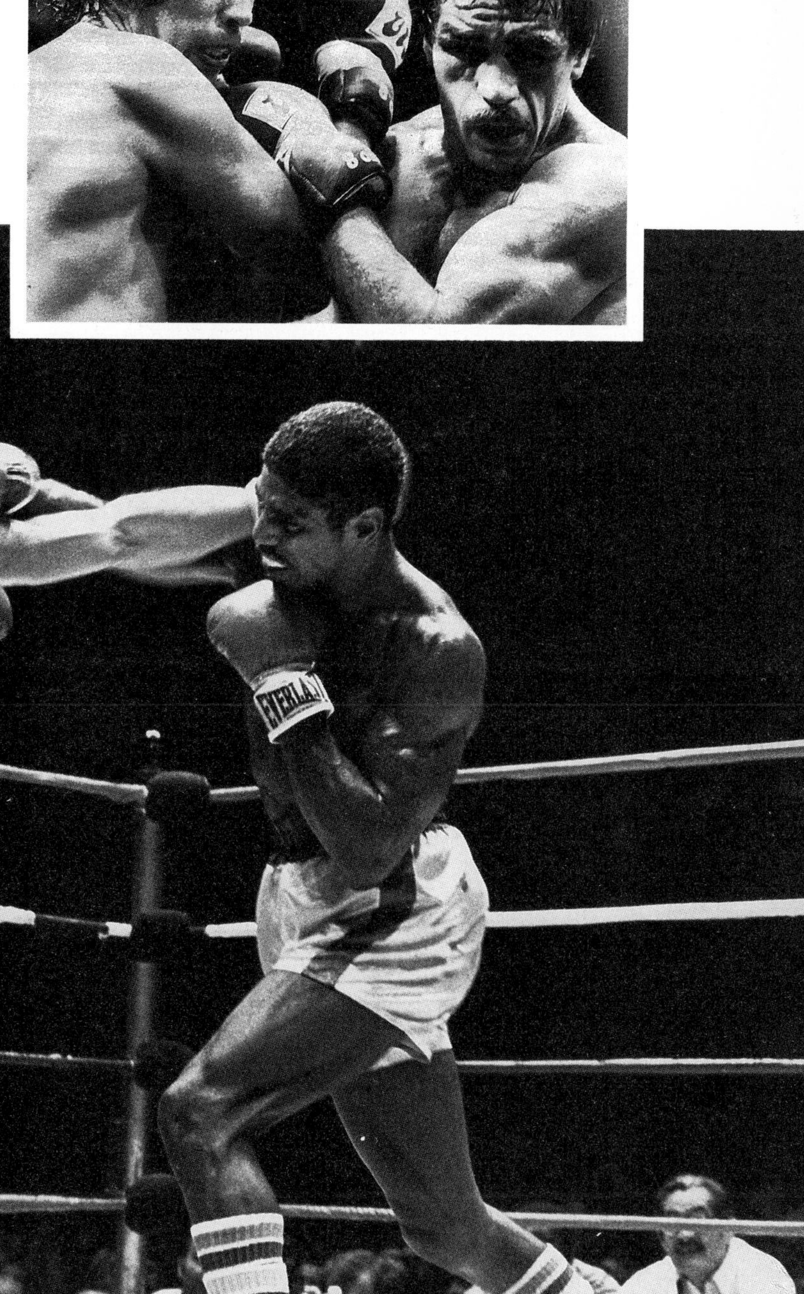

worthy champion who had beaten quality opponents such as Kevin Finnegan (three times), Tony Licata, Sugar Ray Seales, and (in his 112th and final fight) Emile Griffith. The absurd American method of recording any fight ending inside the distance as a 'knockout' is largely responsible for their low regard for Minter – although the Englishman had been stopped six times before becoming champion, it was always because of facial damage.

Minter had won the European and British titles, and had also been an outstanding amateur, taking a bronze medal at the 1972 Olympic Games. He kept the title for one defence, cutting up Antuofermo in eight rounds at Wembley, but then in September 1980 he met his mandatory challenger, Marvin Hagler of Brockton, Massachusetts, at Wembley. It was a night which lives in infamy in British sporting history. An unsavoury, racist element amongst Minter's supporters whipped up a jingoistic, flag-waving, anti-black fervour that permeated and soured the Wembley atmosphere. Hagler was too powerful for Minter, though the champion had not been off his feet when severe cuts forced the third-round stoppage.

For the first time in living memory, a new world champion could not be proclaimed the winner in a British ring. The hooligans threw beer cans into the ring, one of them bouncing off Hagler's cornerman as he shielded the crouching champion and others showering ringside reporters and commentators. Racist abuse was hurled at Hagler, who needed a police escort to get him to the safety of the dressing room.

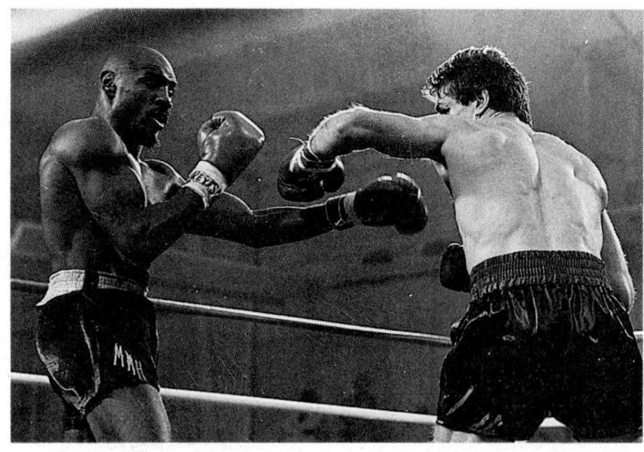

Marvin Hagler's first attempt on the title was foiled by the draw awarded to Antuofermo in Las Vegas (above), *but Vito's luck ran out in the same ring four months later, in March 1980, when Alan Minter outscored him* (below).

Minter had an epic three-fight series (below) *with Kevin Finnegan, winning all by minimum margins.*

The unpredictable Gratien Tonna (below, *on the right*) *is about to surrender to Minter at Wembley.*

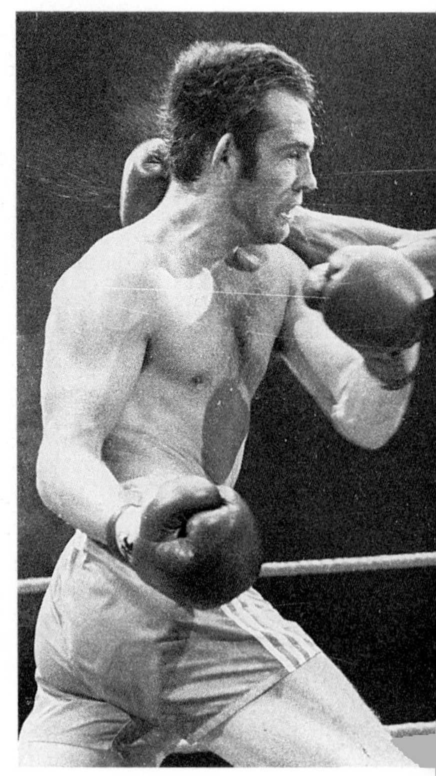

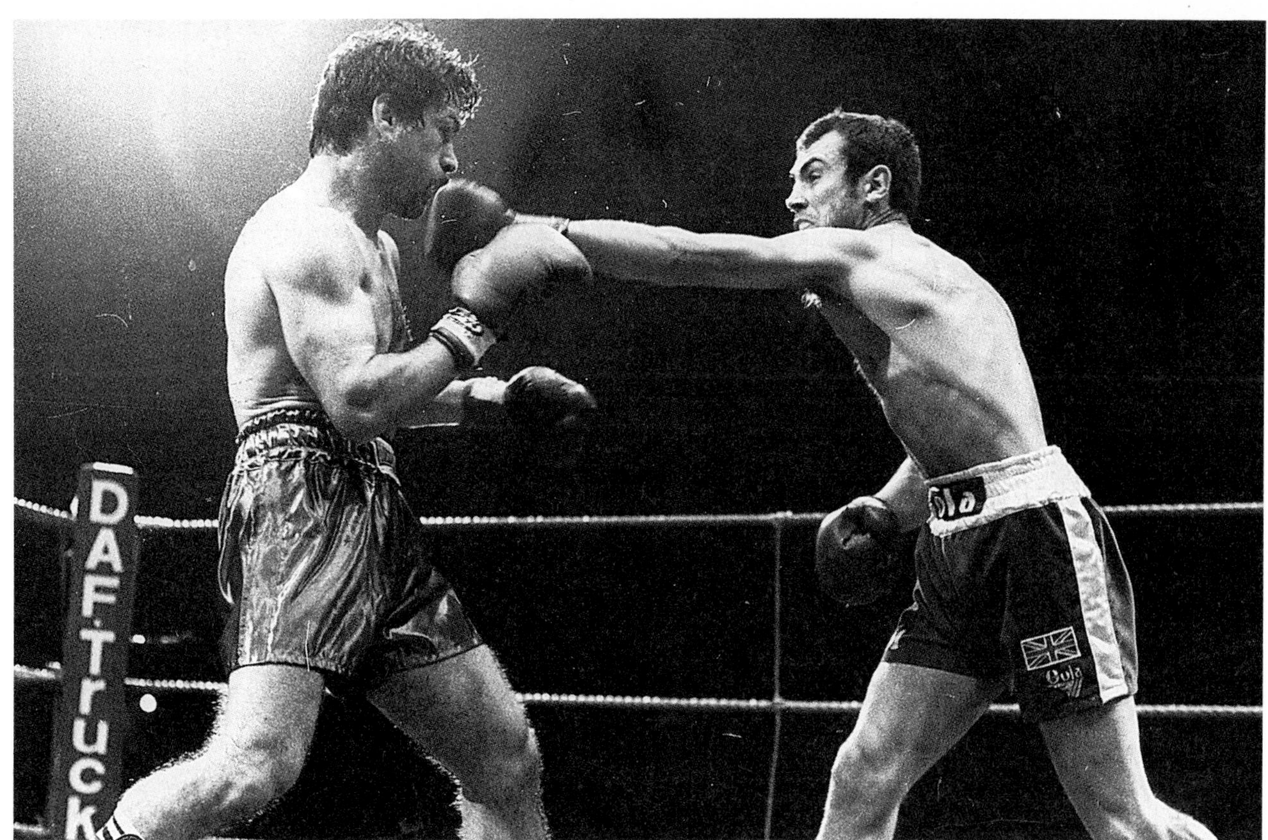

Antuofermo came to England for a rematch with Minter, but this time Minter handled him easily.

It was a shameful beginning to a glorious reign, one that stood comparison with any of his predecessors as champion. Hagler dominated the division for six years and 12 successful defences, and it took a genius like Sugar Ray Leonard to unseat him. In the tradition of the great champions, the shaven-skulled Hagler gave a title fight to any man who deserved it. He accounted for all styles of challenger: left-hookers like England's Tony Sibson, tall boxers like Fulgencio Obelmejias, brawlers like Mustafa Hamsho and Juan Roldan, and cagey box-fighters like the veteran triple champion Roberto Duran.

Beer cans shower the ring at Wembley (below) as Hagler becomes world champion.

Hagler's wins over top contenders like Gene 'Cyclone' Hart (right) had led the fans to regard him as the uncrowned champion for several years before Marvin made it official.

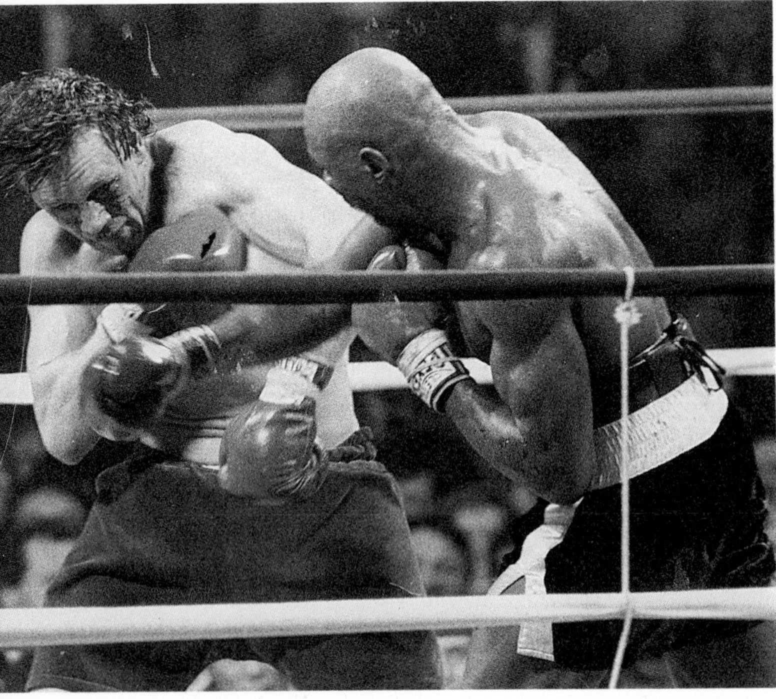

His greatest performances were in Caesars Palace, Las Vegas, where he crushed light-middleweight champion Thomas Hearns in three of the most exciting rounds ever seen and then, a year later in April 1986, outlasted the unbeaten Ugandan puncher John 'The Beast' Mugabi for an 11th round knockout. Ironically, his reign also ended at Caesars, in April 1987.

Below: *Thomas Hearns and Hagler staged three rounds of breathtaking violence at Caesars Palace, Las Vegas. It was a fight to match Zale v Graziano, or Robinson v Basilio.*

Above: *English left-hooker Tony Sibson was battered to a painful six-round defeat in Worcester, Mass.*

Below: *The amazing Roberto Duran went closer than anyone when he held Hagler to a tight points verdict.*

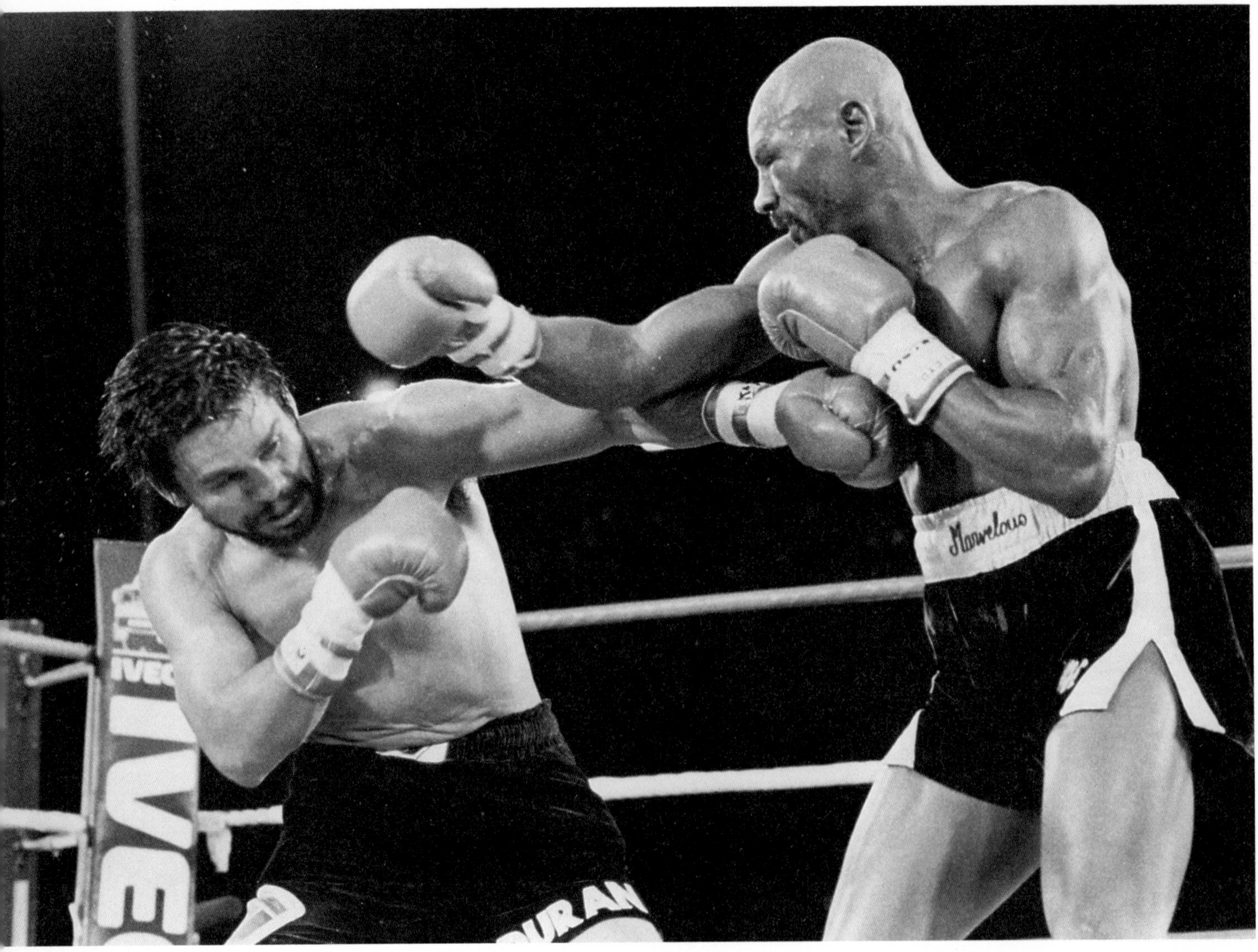

John 'The Beast' Mugabi (above) *provided Hagler* (right) *with his last championship victory, and one of his greatest fights, in Las Vegas in 1986.*

Ray Leonard, inactive for three years, finally yielded to the demands of his ego, his public, and an $11m guarantee and signed to face Hagler in a bid for a third world title. Hagler (who earned an estimated $19m) conceded that they meet over the shorter WBC distance of 12 rounds, and that concession may have cost him the championship. Leonard edged home on the closest of split decisions, and finished in a state of near exhaustion at the end of 12 absorbing, gruelling, and sometimes brilliant rounds.

There was a case for a rematch, but instead Leonard – unpredictable to the last – announced his retirement and walked away from a fortune. Arguments about the merits of that verdict will now never be resolved, but it would be a shame if it were to deny Hagler his place with the legends. By any yardstick, he had already achieved enough to deserve that status, and he may yet come to be acknowledged as the finest champion ever to grace what is, in the eyes of those who know, understand and love their sport the finest division of them all – the marvellous middleweights.

HOW THE MIDDLEWEIGHT TITLE HAS CHANGED HANDS

1884-1900
30 Jul 84 Nonparile Jack Dempsey w.ko.22 George Fulljames at Toronto
14 Jan 91 Bob Fitzsimmons w.ko.12 Jack Dempsey at New Orleans
02 Mar 96 Kid McCoy w.ko.15 Tommy Ryan at Long Island, New York
25 Feb 98 Tommy Ryan w.ko.18 George Green in San Francisco
1900-
02 Sep 07 Stanley Ketchel w.ko.32 Joe Thomas at San Francisco
07 Sep 08 Billy Papke w.ko.12 Stanley Ketchel at Los Angeles
26 Nov 08 Stanley Ketchel w.ko.11 Billy Papke in San Francisco
19 Mar 10 Billy Papke w.ko.3 Willie Lewis at Paris
11 Feb 11 Cyclone Johnny Thompson w.pts.20 Billy Papke in Sydney
Thompson relinqished the title without defending it. There were various claimants including Papke, Frank Mantell, and Frank Klaus, but Papke's claim was generally regarded as the strongest
08 Jun 11 Billy Papke w.rtd.9 Jim Sullivan in London
05 Mar 13 Frank Klaus w.dis.15 Billy Papke at Paris
11 Oct 13 George Chip w.ko.6 Frank Klaus at Pittsburgh
07 Apr 14 Al McCoy w.ko.1 George Chip at Brooklyn
14 Nov 17 Mike O'Dowd w.ko.6 Al McCoy at New York
06 May 20 Johnny Wilson w.pts.12 Mike O'Dowd at Boston
14 Aug 22 Dave Rosenberg w.pts.15 Phil Krug in New York
(New York version of title)
02 Dec 22 Mike O'Dowd w.dis.8 Dave Rosenberg in New York
16 Mar 23 Jock Malone w.ko.1 Mike O'Dowd in St. Paul
(Malone never defended the title and Harry Greb was universally recognised as champion after his wins over Johnny Wilson and Bryan Downey in 1923)
31 Aug 23 Harry Greb w.pts.15 Johnny Wilson at New York
26 Feb 26 Tiger Flowers w.pts.15 Harry Greb at New York
03 Dec 26 Mickey Walker w.pts.10 Tiger Flowers at Chicago
25 Aug 31 Gorilla Jones w.pts.10 Tiger Thomas at Milwaukee
11 Jun 32 Marcel Thil w.dis.11 Gorilla Jones at Paris
11 Nov 32 Ben Jeby w.pts.15 Chuck Devlin at New York
(For New York title)
09 Aug 33 Lou Brouillard w.ko.7 Ben Jeby at New York
30 Oct 33 Vince Dundee w.pts.15 Lou Brouillard at Boston
11 Sep 34 Teddy Yarosz w.pts.15 Vince Dundee at Pittsburgh
19 Sep 35 Ed (Babe) Risko w.pts.15 Teddy Yarosz at New York
11 Jul 36 Freddie Steele w.pts.15 Ed (Babe) Risko at New York
01 Jan 37 Freddie Steele w.pts.10 Gorilla Jones at Milwaukee
(For NY and vacant NBA titles)
The NY Commission vacated Steele's title for his failure to defend against Fred Apostoli, whom they proclaimed champion. Apostoli strengthened his claim by stopping Marcel Thil—recognised in Europe as champion—in 10 rounds on 23.9.37 in New York
26 Jul 38 Al Hostak w.ko.1 Freddie Steele at Seattle
(Vacant NBA title)
01 Nov 38 Solly Kreiger w.pts.15 Al Hostak at Seattle
27 Jun 39 Al Hostak w.rsf.4 Solly Kreiger at Seattle
02 Oct 39 Ceferino Garcia w.rsf.7 Fred Apostoli in New York
(NY title)
23 May 40 Ken Overlin w.pts.15 Ceferino Garcia in New York
19 Jul 40 Tony Zale w.ko.13 Al Hostak in Chicago *(NBA title)*
09 May 41 Billy Soose w.pts.15 Ken Overlin in New York
(NY title)
Soose relinquished the title and Zale was universally regarded as champion after his 15-rounds points win over Georgie Abrams in New York on 28 Nov 41
16 Jul 47 Rocky Graziano w.rsf.6 Tony Zale at Chicago
10 Jun 48 Tony Zale w.ko.3 Rocky Graziano at Newark
21 Sep 48 Marcel Cerdan w.rtd.11 Tony Zale at Jersey City
16 Jun 49 Jake LaMotta w.rtd.10 Marcel Cerdan at Detroit
14 Feb 51 Ray Robinson w.rsf.13 Jake LaMotta at Chicago
10 Jul 51 Randolph Turpin w.pts.15 Ray Robinson at London
12 Sep 51 Ray Robinson w.rsf.10 Randolph Turpin at New York
18 Dec 52 *Robinson retired*
21 Oct 53 Carl (Bobo) Olson w.pts.15 Randolph Turpin at New York
09 Dec 55 Ray Robinson w.ko.2 Carl (Bobo) Olson at Chicago
02 Jan 57 Gene Fullmer w.pts.15 Ray Robinson at New York
01 May 57 Ray Robinson w.ko.5 Gene Fullmer at Chicago
23 Sep 57 Carmen Basilio w.pts.15 Ray Robinson at New York
25 Mar 58 Ray Robinson w.pts.15 Carmen Basilio at Chicago
28 Aug 59 Gene Fullmer w.rsf.14 Carmen Basilio at San Francisco
(For vacant NBA title)
22 Jan 60 Paul Pender w.pts.15 Ray Robinson at Boston
11 Jul 61 Terry Downes w.rtd.9 Paul Pender at London
07 Apr 62 Paul Pender w.pts.15 Terry Downes at Boston
23 Oct 62 Dick Tiger w.pts.15 Gene Fullmer at San Francisco
09 Nov 62 *New York and Europe withdrew recognition of Pender as champion because of his failure to defend title in stipulated period. Both bodies joined WBA (formerly NBA) in recognising Tiger as world champion*
07 Dec 63 Joey Giardello w.pts.15 Dick Tiger at Atlantic City
22 Oct 65 Dick Tiger w.pts.15 Joey Giardello at New York
25 Apr 66 Emile Griffith w.pts.15 Dick Tiger at New York
17 Apr 67 Nino Benvenuti w.pts.15 Emile Griffith at New York
29 Sep 67 Emile Griffith w.pts.15 Nino Benvenuti at New York
04 Mar 68 Nino Benvenuti w.pts.15 Emile Griffith at New York
07 Nov 70 Carlos Monzon w.ko.12 Nino Benvenuti at Rome
Apr 74 *World Boxing Council withdrew recognition of Carlos Monzon as champion for failure to defend against their official contender, Rodrigo Valdes*
25 May 74 Rodrigo Valdes w.ko.7 Bennie Briscoe in Monte Carlo
(Vacant WBC title)
26 Jun 76 Carlos Monzon w.pts.15 Rodrigo Valdes in Monte Carlo
(For undisputed title)
30 Jul 77 *Carlo Monzon retired as champion after outpointing Valdes over 15 rounds in a title defence in Monte Carlo*
5 Nov 77 Rodrigo Valdes w.pts.15 Bennie Briscoe at Campione d'Italia
(For vacant undisputed title)
22 Apr 78 Hugo Corro w.pts.15 Rodrigo Valdes in Buenos Aires
30 Jun 79 Vito Antuofermo w.pts.15 Hugo Corro in Monaco
16 Mar 80 Alan Minter w.pts.15 Vito Antuofermo in Las Vegas
27 Sep 80 Marvin Hagler w.rsf.3 Alan Minter at Wembley
06 Apr 87 Sugar Ray Leonard w.pts.12 Marvin Hagler at Las Vegas
(For WBC title only—WBA and IBF had stripped Hagler of their titles for fighting the unranked Leonard instead of their designated contenders)

LIGHT MIDDLEWEIGHTS

THE INTRODUCTION of the 11 st (154 lb) division, known variously as the light-middleweight, junior middleweight, or super-welterweight, came marginally too late to benefit Sugar Ray Robinson, who might otherwise have joined the exclusive list of men who have won three world titles.

Robinson was the prototype light-middleweight – too big to compete comfortably at the welterweight limit of 10 st 7 lb (147 lb) but invariably having to concede weight to full-blown middleweights who fought at the divison's limit of 11 st 6 lb (160 lb). A year before Denny Moyer of Portland, Oregon, had won the inaugural title (created by the NBA in 1962), he had been outpointed by Robinson. Moyer lost the title in his second defence to Ralph Dupas, in April 1963 – three months after Sugar Ray, then almost 42 years old, had outpointed Dupas in a ten-rounder at Miami Beach.

Since a 13 lb weight difference was too much for men such as Robinson, and was a greater gap than existed between any other two weight categories, the NBA's decision to introduce the new division was welcomed in most quarters. The European Boxing Union held their first title fight at the new weight in 1964, although the arch-conservatives of the British Boxing Board of Control held out until 1973.

The first world champion, Denny Moyer, had challenged Don Jordan for the welterweight title as a 19-year-old in 1959, and after losing the 154 lb title to Ralph Dupas of New Orleans in his second defence, he moved up to full middleweight and enjoyed a long and successful career, even meeting Carlos Monzon for the world title in Rome in 1972. Dupas, similarly, worked his way through the divisions. He started his career as a 14-year-

Above: *Denny Moyer, the division's first champion, celebrates his 100th fight by outpointing Gerhard Piaskowy in Berlin.*

Below: *Sandro Mazzinghi of Italy was too powerful for Ralph Dupas, knocking him out in nine rounds in the American's second defence.*

New Orleans veteran Ralph Dupas (above, on the right) *takes the title from Moyer in April 1963. It was Dupas' third title bid, at different weights.*

The title passed from Mazzinghi (above) *to Nino Benvenuti, and then to Korea's first world champion Kim Si Koo* (right).

old lightweight in 1950, and lost title fights at lightweight (to Joe Brown in 1958) and welterweight (to Emile Griffith in 1962) before outpointing Moyer in New Orleans in April 1963.

Dupas won the title in his 122nd fight, but made only one successful defence (outscoring Moyer in a rematch) before being knocked out in nine rounds in Milan by the crew-cut, crude, and tremendously powerful Italian Sandro Mazzinghi, who had lost only once in 30 fights. Mazzinghi made three winning defences (including a victory over Fortunato Manca, in the first all-Italian world championship) but was then knocked out in six rounds by another compatriot, Nino Benvenuti, who later won the middleweight title twice. Benvenuti outpointed him in a return, but then made the mistake of taking the title to Korea where Kim Si Koo won a unanimous decision. This was Benvenuti's first loss in 66 professional fights and 120 amateur contests, but it reversed the only defeat Koo had ever suffered (as an amateur), making him the first of his country's many subsequent world champions.

Mazzinghi reclaimed the title for Italy by outpointing Koo in Milan, but then figured in the division's most controversial title fight when, on 25 October 1968, he did not answer the bell for the start of the ninth round of a defence in Rome against a part-time school teacher from Las Vegas, Freddie Little. Mazzinghi was badly cut, and had taken a pounding, but the referee, Herbert Tomser of Germany, ruled that in accordance with EBU provisions the fight was a no-contest, since the fight had been ended by injury in its first half. (Herr Tomser considered the end of the eighth round to represent a 15-rounder's halfway mark.) The decision was patently absurd, and two days later

Right: *Part-time school teacher Freddie Little should have been crowned champion in his controversial 1968 fight with Mazzinghi in Rome, but had to wait until March 1969 before getting another chance. After his retirement, Little became a world-class referee and a member of the Nevada State Athletic Commission.*

Carmelo Bossi (left, *beating Jean Josselin for the European welterweight title) dethroned Little, but lost the title to Koichi Wajima, whose five defences included a draw with Miguel de Oliveira* (right) *before he was beaten in a brutal battle by Oscar Albarado* (above). *The Texan knocked him out in the 15th round.*

the title was declared vacant.

Little won the vacant championship by beating Stan Hayward of Philadelphia in Las Vegas in March 1969, and twice retained it. Somewhat surprisingly, in the light of his previous experience, he returned to Italy in July 1970 and duly surrendered the title to Carmelo Bossi, who had won a silver medal in the 1960 Olympic Games. Bossi retained it on a draw against Jose Hernandez of Spain, but then lost it to the division's first outstanding champion – Koichi Wajima of Japan. Wajima, who made six successful defences (all in Japan), was briefly dislodged by Oscar 'Shotgun' Albarado, but after the Texan had retained the championship for one defence, against Ryu Sorimachi in Tokyo, Wajima reclaimed it on a unanimous decision in January 1975. That was the division's last contest for an undisputed title. One month later the WBC stripped him for failing to defend against a Brazilian, Miguel de Oliveira, whom he had already met twice in title fights, drawing in 1973 and outpointing him in February 1974.

Wajima lost the WBA version to a Korean, Jae Do Yuh, in June 1975, but won it back with a dramatic last-round knockout in February 1976. He then lost it for the final time to Spain's Jose Duran on a 14th-round knockout in May 1976, but Duran held it for only five months, being outscored by Miguel Castellini of Argentina in Madrid. The Argentinian was dethroned by Nicaragua's Eddie Gazo in his first defence in March 1977, and Gazo at least managed to make three defences – all in the Orient – in 1977. His luck ran out on his fourth trip, when Masashi Kudo of Japan took his title on a split verdict in Akita on 9 August 1978.

Kudo made three defences before surrendering the title, in October 1979, to arguably the finest stylist the division had yet produced – Ayub Kalule, a brilliant Ugandan southpaw who was based in Denmark. Kalule, the former world amateur champion, would probably have made more than just four successful defences had not the fabulous Sugar Ray Leonard decided to move up from welterweight to take Kalule's title on a hard-earned, ninth-round stoppage in June 1981. Leonard never defended the title, and Tadeshi Mihara of Japan won the vacant championship by outpointing the American Rocky Fratto. However, Mihara lost the title in his first defence to Davey

Wajima, a three-time world champion, outpointed de Oliveira (above) *in 1974, but two years after his defeat by Jose Duran the WBA title was regained for Japan* (left) *by Masashi Kudo, who outpointed Eddie Gazo (on the left). But the brilliant Ugandan Ayub Kalule (on the right,* below, *outpointing Kevin Finnegan) took over from Kudo, beating him on points in 1979.*

Inset left: *Tadashi Mihara, briefly WBA champion in 1981–2, knocks out Katsuhiro Sawada in five rounds to retain his Japanese title.*

Below: *Charlie Weir, a colourful South African, found Davey Moore too hot to handle in their Johannesburg clash for the WBA title in 1982.*

Mike McCallum, the future WBA champion, scored this 1983 points win over Manuel Jiminez in Atlantic City.

Moore of New York, who was having only his ninth fight. Despite his inexperience, Moore proved a good champion, making three defences before the veteran Panamanian Roberto Duran knocked him out in eight rounds to win his third world title, in Madison Square Garden on 16 June 1983, his 32nd birthday. Duran never defended the championship, relinquishing it in June 1984 on the eve of meeting Thomas Hearns for the WBC title. Hearn's second-round knockout should, logically, have earned him universal recognition but instead the WBA ordered Mike McCallum of Jamaica to meet Ireland's Sean Mannion for the vacant title, which McCallum won. The Jamacian made four defences up to the end of 1986.

The WBC title has had seven holders since Miguel de Oliveira outpointed Jose Duran to take over from Wajima on 7 May 1975. The Brazilian lost it six months later to Elisha Obed of the Bahamas, who made two defences before suffering his first defeat in 68 fights, when Eckhard Dagge of

Elisha Obed (above) *flattered to deceive with a long winning run, but lost his WBC title when forced to retire against the German Eckhard Dagge* (above right). *Dagge held it for a year and successfully defended against Emile Griffith before passing it on to Rocky Mattioli, who in turn was beaten* (below) *by big-hearted British southpaw Maurice Hope (on the right).*

Germany beat him on a 10th-round retirement in Berlin in June 1976. Dagge held it on an unpopular split verdict over 38-year-old Emile Griffith and a fortunate draw against British champion Maurice Hope, but was then knocked out by the globe-trotting Italian Rocky Mattioli. Mattioli had started his career in Australia, won the title in Germany, defended it in Melbourne and Pescara, and finished with four wins in America.

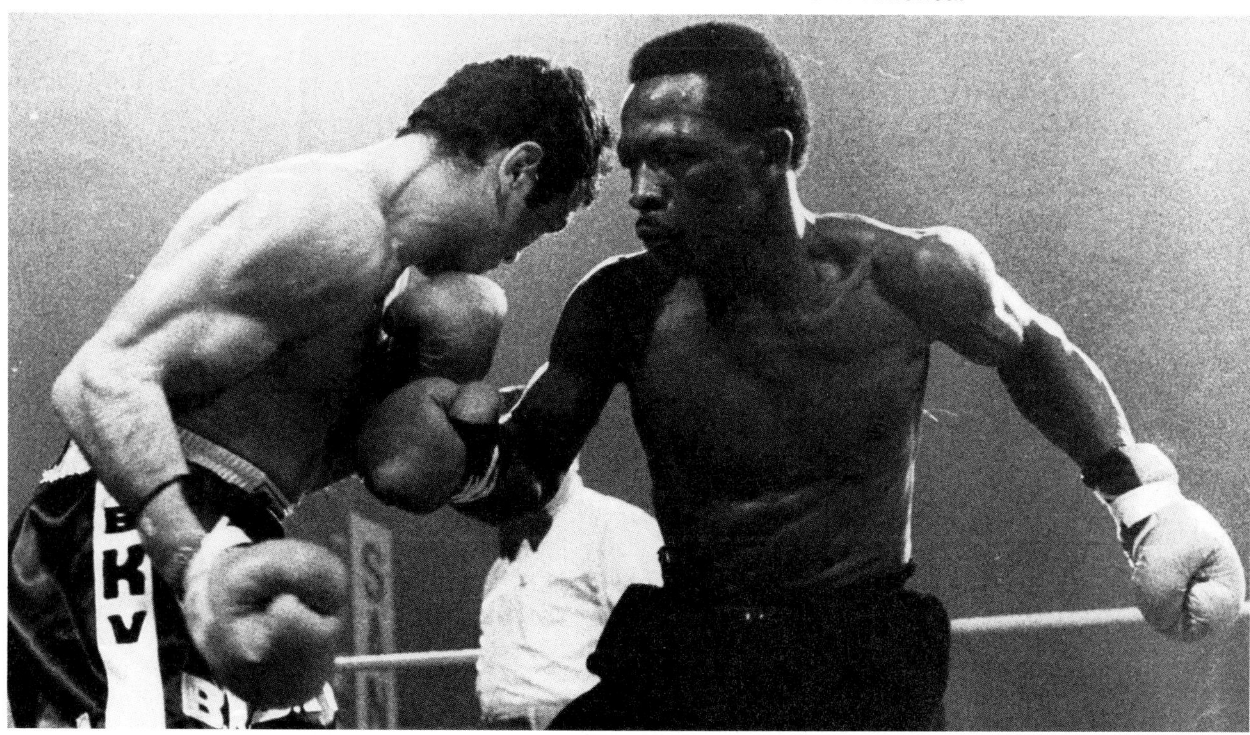

Two Latin legends clashed in Las Vegas when Wilfred Benitez (above, *on the right) outpointed Roberto Duran. Benitez was eventually beaten by Thomas Hearns* (below, *on the left, defeating Luigi Minchillo), and when Hearns relinquished the WBC title it was taken over by his stablemate Duane Thomas* (right, *against Nino Gonzalez).*

Mattioli was forced to retire after eight rounds by Antigua-born, British-based Maurice Hope in March 1979, who – along with his contemporary, WBA champion Ayub Kalule – was perhaps the division's outstanding title holder. The southpaw Hope made three defences, but was then knocked out in 12 rounds by the former light-welter and welterweight champion Wilfred Benitez, who retained the title against Carlos Santos and Roberto Duran before losing to Thomas Hearns.

Hearns, also a former welterweight champion, retained it four times until relinquishing it in 1986. The title was then won in a big upset by his Detroit stablemate Duane Thomas, who stopped the hotly favoured John Mugabi in three rounds in December.

The IBF version was inaugurated in 1984 and has been held by, successively, Mark Medal, Carlos Santos, and Buster Drayton, who was dethroned in June 1987 by Canada's Matthew Hilton, one of a family of four boxing brothers.

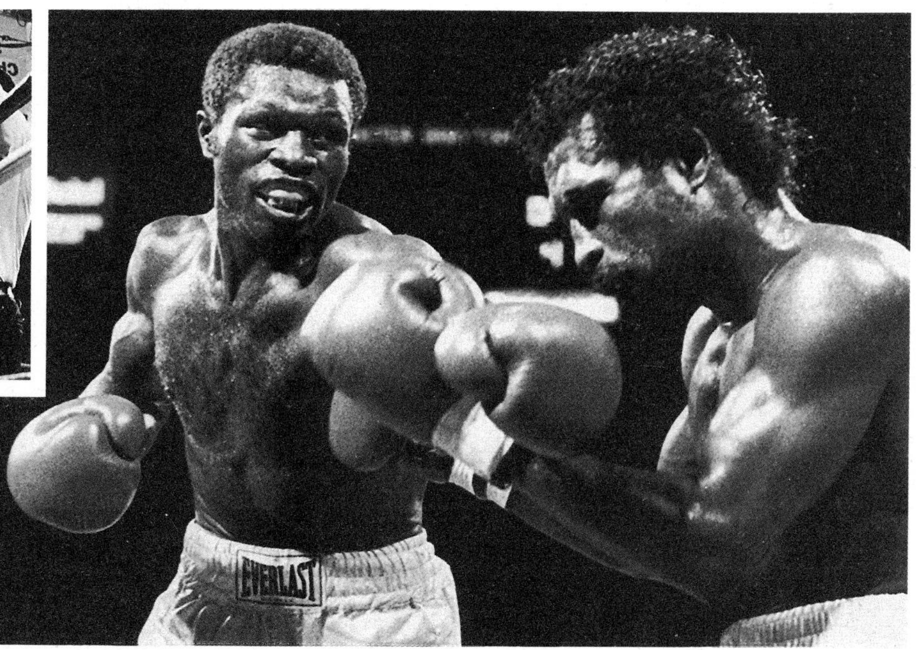

Two other stablemates, John Mugabi and Buster Drayton, had mixed luck in 1986. Mugabi (above) *surrendered against Duane Thomas for the WBC title, while Drayton outpointed Carlos Santos* (right) *to become IBF king.*

HOW THE LIGHT-MIDDLEWEIGHT TITLE HAS CHANGED HANDS

20 Oct 62	Denny Moyer w.pts.15 Joey Giambra at Portland, Oregon *(For vacant title)*
29 Apr 63	Ralph Dupas w.pts.15 Denny Moyer at New Orleans
07 Sep 63	Sandro Mazzinghi w.ko.9 Ralph Dupas at Milan
18 Jun 65	Nino Benvenuti w.ko.6 Sandro Mazzinghi at Milan
25 Jun 66	Kim Ki-Soo w.pts.15 Nino Benvenuti in Seoul.
26 May 68	Sandro Mazzinghi w.pts.15 Kim Ki-Soo at Milan. *Mazzinghi stripped of title for failure to defend*
17 Mar 69	Freddie Little w.pts.15 Stan Hayward at Las Vegas
09 Jul 70	Carmelo Bossi w.pts.15 Freddie Little at Monza
31 Oct 71	Koichi Wajima w.pts.15 Carmelo Bossi in Tokyo
04 Jun 74	Oscar Albarado w.ko.15 Koichi Wajima in Tokyo
21 Jan 75	Koichi Wajima w.pts.15 Oscar Albarado in Tokyo. *WBC withdrew recognition from Koichi Wajima as champion for failing to agree to a title defence against their top contender, Miguel DeOliveira*
10 May 75	Miguel DeOliveira w.pts.15 Jose Duran in Monte Carlo *(Vacant WBC title)*
07 Jun 75	Jae Do Yuh w.ko.7 Koichi Wajima at Kitsakyushu, Japan. *(WBA title)*
13 Nov 75	Elisha Obed w.rtd.10 Miguel DeOliveira in Paris
17 Feb 76	Koichi Wajima w.ko.15 Jae Do Yuh in Tokyo
18 May 76	Jose Duran w.ko.14 Koichi Wajima in Tokyo
18 Jun 76	Eckhard Dagge w.rtd.10 Elisha Obed in Berlin
08 Oct 76	Miguel Angel Castellini w.pts.15 Jose Duran in Madrid
06 Mar 77	Eddie Gazo w.pts.15 Miguel Angel Castellini at Managua
06 Aug 77	Rocky Mattioli w.ko.5 Eckhard Dagge in Berlin
09 Aug 78	Masashi Kudo w.pts.15 Eddie Gazo at Akita
04 Mar 79	Maurice Hope w.rtd.8 Rocky Mattioli at San Remo
24 Oct 79	Ayub Kalule w.pts.15 Masashi Kudo at Akita
24 May 81	Wilfred Benitez w.ko.12 Maurice Hope at Las Vegas
25 Jun 81	Sugar Ray Leonard w.rsf.9 Ayub Kalule at Houston
Jul 81	*Leonard vacated title to concentrate on welterweight division*
07 Nov 81	Tadashi Mihara w.pts.15 Rocky Fratto at Rochester, NY *(Vacant WBA title)*
02 Feb 82	Davey Moore w.rsf.6 Tadashi Mihara in Tokyo *(WBA title)*
03 Dec 82	Thomas Hearns w.pts.15 Wilfred Benitez in New Orleans *(WBC title)*
16 Jun 83	Roberto Duran w.rsf.8 Davey Moore in New York
11 Mar 84	Mark Medal w.rsf.5 Earl Hargrove at Atlantic City *(Vacant IBF title)*
Jun 84	*Duran relinquished WBA title*
19 Oct 84	Mike McCallum w.pts.15 Sean Mannion at New York *(Vacant WBA title)*
02 Nov 84	Carlos Santos w.pts.15 Mark Medal at New York
Feb 86	*Carlos Santos stripped of IBF title when injury prevented him from defending it on time*
04 Jun 86	Buster Drayton w.pts.15 Carlos Santos at East Rutherford, New Jersey *(Vacant IBF title)*
Oct 86	*Thomas Hearns relinquished WBC title to fight in higher divisions*
05 Dec 86	Duane Thomas w.rsf.3 John 'The Beast' Mugabi at Las Vegas *(Vacant WBC title)*
27 Jun 87	Matthew Hilton w.pts.15 Buster Drayton in Montreal

WELTERWEIGHTS

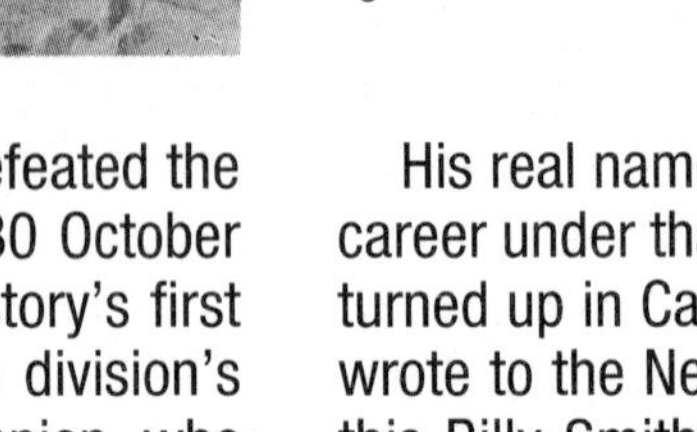

Left: *Mysterious Billy Smith, a rough fighter who was disqualified 11 times in 82 fights.*

Above: *Tommy Ryan, champion from 1894–96, spars with Jim Dineen (on the right).*

PADDY DUFFY, an Irish-American who defeated the English champion William McMillan on 30 October 1888, claims the distinction of being history's first world welterweight title holder. But the division's first real *character* was its second champion, who claimed the title in 1892 after Duffy had retired without a defence, and who held it, on and off, until the turn of the century. He was the romantically named 'Mysterious' Billy Smith.

His real name was Amos Smith. He launched his career under that name on the East Coast, and then turned up in California, boxing as Billy Smith. A fan wrote to the New York *Police News* asking 'Who is this Billy Smith?' The editor, a Captain Cook, duly dubbed him 'Mysterious' Billy Smith, and the nickname stuck.

Smith knocked out the Australian, Tom Williams, in two rounds in 1893, so adding authority to his

Three legendary names from the welterweight division's early days: left *to* right – *Barbados Joe Walcott, Dixie Kid and Honey Mellody. Their careers, collectively, spanned 51 years in the ring.*

world title claim in the division whose weight limit then was 10 st 2 lb (142 lb). His first reign was ended by Tommy Ryan, who outpointed him in 1894, and held onto the title in a return fight when the police stopped it in the 18th round. Ryan's sparring partner for the first Smith fight had been Norman Selby, who boxed as Kid McCoy. In March 1896 McCoy contacted his former employer, begging for a title fight. He convinced Ryan that he was ill and weak, but turned up in prime condition and floored the champion 12 times before knocking him out in the 15th round.

When McCoy relinquished the title to concentrate on the middleweight division, Smith reclaimed it. He held onto it with a string of impressive results, including a win over 'Barbados' Joe Walcott, a gifted Barbadian with whom he had a bitter six-fight series. Their meetings were so foul-filled that before one of them Smith was actually required to lodge a 'good behaviour' bond of $250. Given Smith's appalling record of 11 disqualification defeats, it is appropriate that it was a foul that cost him his championship to Jim 'Rube' Ferns in the 21st round at Buffalo on 15 January 1900. Ferns held it for only nine months, losing to William 'Matty' Matthews an Irish-American from New York, the man whom Smith had defeated to reclaim the title in August 1898.

Ferns regained the title from Matthews in May 1901, but in December that year Walcott at last became champion, knocking out Ferns in five rounds. Dixie Kid, whose real name was Aaron Brown, took Walcott's title on a 20th-round foul in 1904 and retained it in a drawn rematch one month later, but when Kid outgrew the division later that year Walcott reclaimed the title after a draw with lightweight champion Joe Gans.

Billy 'Honey' Mellody dethroned Walcott in his first defence in October 1906, but then lost it in his first defence to Mike 'Twin' Sullivan, who promptly gave it up. Harry Lewis, a Jew whose real name was Henry Besterman, claimed it after knocking out Mellody in four rounds in April 1908, and raised the limit to the British standard of 10 st 7 lb (147 lb). He took the championship to Europe, defending it four times, twice in Paris and twice in London during 1910-11.

During his absence in Europe various Americans claimed the title, including Jimmy Gardner, Jimmy Clabby, Ray Bronson, and Mike Gibbons, among others. John Murray, editor of the trade paper *Boxing*, commented caustically in the 31 January 1914 edition that 'All that any American boxer needs to do to win a recognized world championship is to go around night and day shouting that he is THE champion, and he will soon gather all the necessary adherents'. The situation was further complicated by Lewis' continued reluctance to risk his portion of the title, which he did not defend from 1911 until his retirement (having spent the rest of his career in Europe) in 1913.

But at last a credible champion emerged from the pack. Waldemar Holberg, a short-armed Dane with a tendency to foul which cost him eight disqualification defeats, beat the American claimant Ray Bronson in Melbourne, but then threw it away on a foul three weeks later in the same city to an Irishman from Dundalk, Co Louth, called Tom McCormick. The three-time ABA champion, Matt Wells of Walworth, had moved to Australia after losing his British lightweight title to Freddie Welsh, and on 21 March 1914 took over McCormick's claim to the world title by outpointing him in Sydney. (McCormick returned to Britain to rejoin the army, and died in action in France two years later.)

Wells took the title to America and lost it to Mike Glover, yet another Irish-American (whose real name was Michael Cavanagh) but Glover's reign was the shortest on record. He won it on 1 June 1915 in Boston and lost it 21 days later, also in Boston, to Jack Britton. Britton (real name William Breslin) then inaugurated the greatest rivalry in boxing history by losing the title in August that year to a Jew from London's East End, Gershon Mendeloff, who boxed as Ted 'Kid' Lewis. It was the first of 20 meetings between them, spread over six years, with Britton taking the series by winning four against Lewis' three, with one draw, and 12 no-decision fights. They bounced the title back and

Denmark's Waldemar Holberg (seated) was champion of the world in 1914 . . . for three whole weeks.

Londoner Matt Wells (below, *in 1919) won two and lost two against Australian Hughie Mehegan. He came out on top in this 1913 encounter in London* (right), *outscoring Mehegan (on the right) over 20 rounds.*

forth over the next few years – Lewis to Britton in 1916, back to Lewis in 1917, and finishing with Britton champion again in 1919, when the Irish-American outpointed the Englishman on St Patrick's Day and promptly despatched a jubilant telegram...to Buckingham Palace!

Britton retained the title five times, until the 21-year-old Mickey Walker outpointed the 37-year-old veteran in November 1922. Britton, though, went

Jack Britton (right and far right, *with Benny Leonard) had* twenty *battles with the Englishman, Ted 'Kid' Lewis, four of them involving the world title. Lewis, whose free-hitting style is captured in this shot of him in action* (below) *against Johnny Basham in 1921, made a fortune in America between 1914 and 1919.*

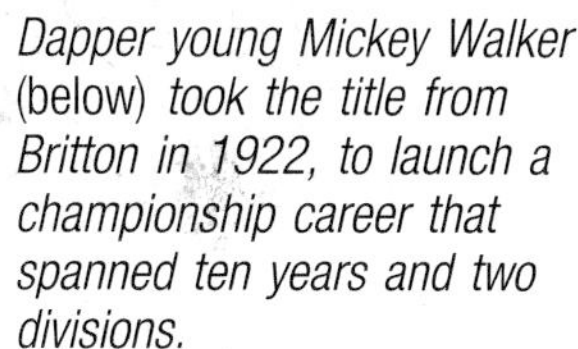

Dapper young Mickey Walker (below) *took the title from Britton in 1922, to launch a championship career that spanned ten years and two divisions.*

Lewis fought at every weight from feather to light-heavy, and this 1921 defeat of Noel 'Boy' McCormick (left) *earned him a match with Georges Carpentier for the world title in that division. Lewis did not survive the opening round. Pete Latzo* (below), *who took the welterweight title from Walker, also challenged unsuccessfully for the light-heavyweight crown.*

Years after his retirement, Lewis, an East End Jew, oddly became a 'minder' for the British fascist leader Oswald Mosley: they are pictured at a fundraising dinner.

on boxing for another eight years, retiring at almost 45 after 327 fights. His arch-rival Lewis, whose array of titles included British and European titles at featherweight, welterweight, and middleweight, as well as Empire championships at welterweight and middleweight, also challenged Georges Carpentier for the world light-heavyweight title in 1922. He retired in 1929 after 279 fights, and – curiously, for someone of his racial origins – became involved with Oswald Mosley's Fascists in the 1930s.

Walker retained the title against Pete Latzo, Lew Tendler, Bobby Barrett and Dave Shade (who had held Britton to a draw in a 1922 title bid) but then lost it on a ten-round decision to Latzo in May 1926. Latzo made two successful defences but then, although so tight at the welterweight limit that he had to fast for 24 hours before the weigh-in, risked it for the third time against the Italian-born Joe Dundee, whose brother Vince later won a share of the disputed middleweight title. He

Below: *Joe Dundee took Latzo's title on a disputed points verdict in June 1927, and failed to distinguish himself as champion.*

Right: *Jackie Fields beat Dundee by disqualification in 1929, but lost the title a year later to Young Jack Thompson (on the left).*

seemed to have comfortably outpointed Dundee in their New York 15-rounder in June 1927, but the decision went against him.

Dundee proved a reluctant champion who staked his title only once, knocking out Hilario Martinez of Spain in eight rounds. The NBA stripped him for his continued failure to defend it, and matched Jackie Fields of Chicago with Young Jack Thompson of Los Angeles for the vacant crown. They met in Chicago in March 1929, when Fields took a 10-rounds points win in a fight which provoked such fierce rioting in the crowd that 150 people were treated in hospital, one of whom died the following day. Fields and Dundee met for the undisputed title on 25 July 1929, and Dundee was floored twice before being disqualified in the second for a low blow. Fields (real name Jacob Finkelstein) had won the Olympic featherweight title in 1924, and had lost only three of his 53 fights prior to beating Dundee.

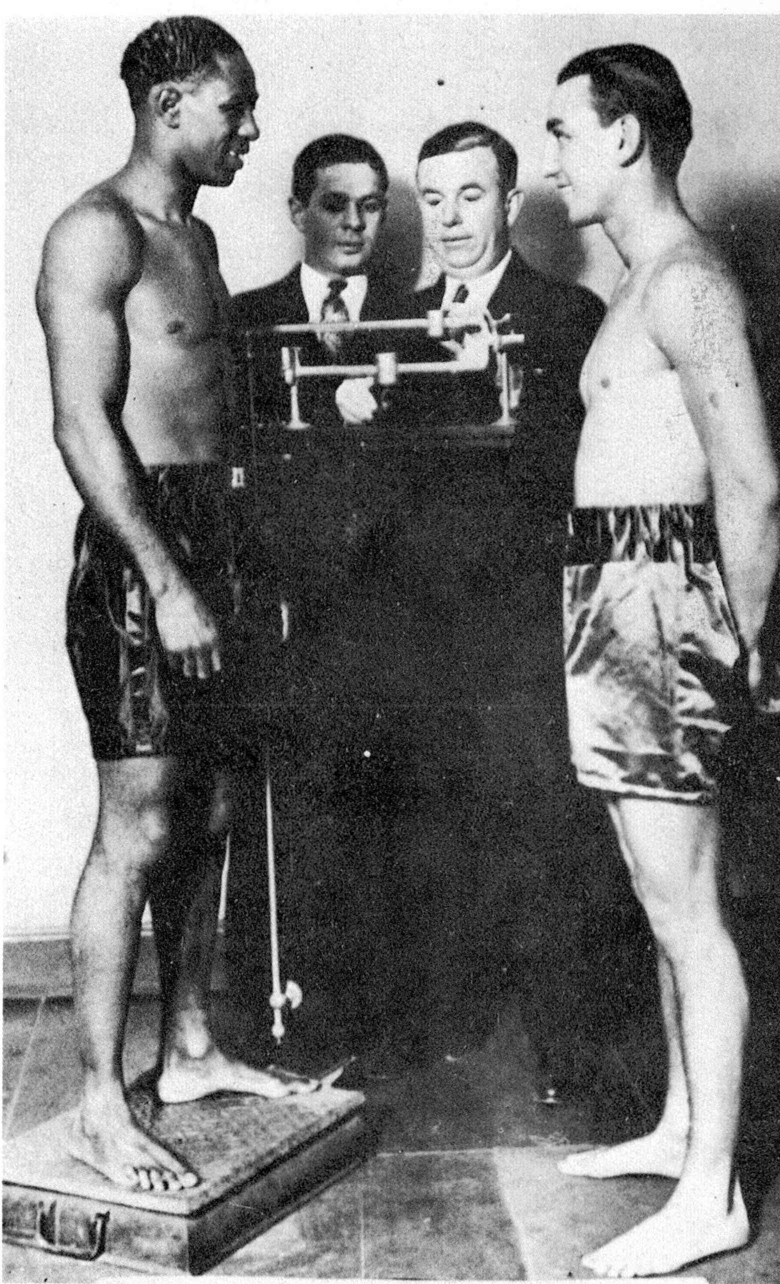

Fields (right, weighing in with Baby Joe Gans) won the featherweight gold medal for America in the 1924 Olympic Games in Paris.

Lou Brouillard (above *and* right, *outpointing southpaw Young Corbett III) later won a version of the middleweight title. Young Corbett III later took the welterweight title from Jackie Fields.*

Belfast-born Jimmy McLarnin (below) *built his reputation by beating a string of top Jewish fighters, at a time when ethnic rivalry, particularly in the fight game, was intense.*

Fields' first outing as champion, oddly, was against Dundee's brother Vince, whom he outpointed in Chicago, and 19 days later in 1929 he outscored another sometime middleweight title claimant, Gorilla Jones. But in May 1930 Thompson reversed the 1929 result and took the title on points in Detroit. He had overcome an indifferent start to his career, in which he had won just 14 of his first 30 fights, to become one of the outstanding performers of his day. He had beaten Joe Dundee in two rounds in 1928, but the champion insisted that Thompson come in over-weight so he could not claim the title.

Tommy Freeman, a 10-year veteran from Hot Springs, Arkansas, took Thompson's title in September 1930 and cashed in on it with six defences between January and April 1931, losing it on 14 April in a rematch with Thompson, who stopped him in 12 rounds. The title then passed briskly from

Above: *McLarnin ended the career of the great Benny Leonard at 211 fights with this sixth-round stoppage.*

Below: *McLarnin did not share Leonard's fate – his last fight brought him a win over Lou Ambers (left).*

Thompson to Lou Brouillard of Canada, back to Jackie Fields, and then to Young Corbett III, an Italian-born southpaw from San Francisco. On 29 May 1933, the division entered its Golden Era when Belfast-born Jimmy McLarnin knocked out Corbett in the first round in Los Angeles, and for the next eight years the championship was held by four outstanding fighters – McLarnin, Barney Ross, Henry Armstrong, and Fritzie Zivic.

McLarnin had turned professional as a 17-year-old under the management of Charles 'Pop' Foster, with whom he spent his whole career. The pair enjoyed a life-long friendship, and when Foster died in 1956 he left McLarnin his fortune of around $200,000.

McLarnin grew up in Vancouver where he had emigrated as a youngster. He was an instant sensation as a professional. In his second year in the game he beat Fidel LaBarba, a future flyweight title claimant, and in 1925 beat three more champions in the space of five months – flyweight Pancho Villa, welterweight Jackie Fields, and bantamweight Bud Taylor. McLarnin built his reputation by beating Jewish fighters, in a period when ethnic rivalry was strong, and he accounted for most of the leading Jewish stars like Sid Terris, Joe Glick, Sgt Sammy Baker, Ruby Goldstein, Al Singer and Benny Leonard. Although he was outpointed by Sammy Mandell in a lightweight title bid in 1928, he moved up to welterweight to beat Young Jack Thompson to establish himself in the heavier class.

Jimmy McLarnin and Barney Ross personified the Irish v Jewish ethnic rivalry that dominated American boxing in the early 1930s. They met three times for the welterweight title, with Ross winning the first (above) *and the third* (right).

McLarnin held the title for one day short of a year, losing it on 28 May 1934 in the first of three classic encounters with Chicago's Barney Ross, whose hard-earned split-decision win restored some Jewish pride. The scoring was peculiar: the two votes for Ross, from referee Harry Forbes and judge Harold Barnes, were respectively 13-1-1 and 12-2-1, while the vote for McLarnin by judge Tom O'Rourke was 9-1-5 in rounds. They were rematched on 17 September 1934, and this time the Irishman reversed the result on a split vote.

Ross lost the title to McLarnin (left, *off balance) but regained it eight months later and retained the championship twice, including this points win over Izzy Jannazzo* (right, *on the canvas.*

Exactly a year after their first meeting, Ross ended the series with a unanimous verdict at the Polo Grounds, New York. McLarnin fought just three more times, losing to and beating Tony Canzoneri, and ending his career with a win over Lou Ambers, of whom both were world champions.

The European-based IBU eccentrically declared the title vacant and, in the only contest for their version, Felix Wouters outpointed Gustav Eder on 16 February 1938.

Ross defended the title twice, outpointing Izzy Jannazzo and Ceferino Garcia (who later won a version of the middleweight title) before losing it in 1938 to perhaps the greatest champion in boxing history – Henry Armstrong. Matching Ross with Armstrong, the world featherweight champion, was a master-stroke by promoter Mike Jacobs. Armstrong's extraordinary all-action style, which brought him the nickname 'Hammerin' Hank', derived from his low pulse rate. He was also an astonishingly busy fighter – in 1937, for example, he boxed 27 times, winning all but one inside the distance, and in his 23rd fight of the year he beat Petey Sarron in six rounds to become featherweight champion.

The contract for the Ross fight, at Madison Square Bowl on Long Island, required Ross to weigh not more than 142 lb and Armstrong not less

Barney Ross (below) *had two thrilling battles with Billy Petrolle* (above, *on the left*), *winning both on points. Petrolle retired after their second fight, in January 1934, but despite his outstanding record, Petrolle only got one crack at a world title, when he was outpointed (in his 151st fight) by Canzoneri for the lightweight title in November 1932.*

than 138 lb. The latter clause was inserted at the insistence of Al Weill, manager of the lightweight champion Lou Ambers who was keen to defend his 135 lb title against Armstrong later that year. Armstrong scaled 138 lb at the weigh-in on 26 May, but bad weather caused a postponement until 31 May. It was the end for the 29-year-old Ross, after 81 fights. He could not keep Armstrong out, and the blown-up featherweight swarmed all over him for 12 rounds and then, apparently, eased off to allow Ross the professional satisfaction of finishing on his feet.

Armstrong's autobiography *Gloves, Glory, and God*, written, unusually, in the third person, records:

> It isn't known yet, and probably will be denied, but Henry 'carried' Ross for the last

When Henry Armstrong hammered Barney Ross into retirement with this 15-round points beating in 1938 (right), *he scored the first of a record 20 victories in welterweight title bouts, a run which included a points win over Ernie Roderick* (below) *in London in 1939.*

three rounds. He faked his punches at Ross, swinging rights and left hooks that looked good, but that weren't carrying any steam and that landed on Ross's gloves. It was done almost by silent agreement. Henry's manager caught a signal from the Ross corner that Barney was through, but wouldn't quit. So Eddie Mead (Armstrong's manager) whispered to Henry 'Quit trying for a knockout. Let him stay'. And that's the way it was.

Henry never regretted doing that. He still admires Ross as the biggest-hearted opponent he ever faced. Courage was written all over him, and Henry respected that.

The amazing Armstrong duly won the lightweight title as well, on 17 August 1938, thereby becoming the only man in history to hold three world titles simultaneously. There have been other triple winners since then, but most of them held disputed titles and none of them won their championships over such a big weight span (21 lb).

Armstrong became the most active welterweight champion ever, making 20 defences between November 1938 and September 1940. In his eighth title engagement of 1940, he finally reached the end of the championship road when Fritzie Zivic, the youngest of five boxing brothers from Pittsburgh, closed both the champion's eyes and, with the last punch of the fight, floored him for the first time in his 26 title bouts. Armstrong was saved by the bell to end the 15th, but he had been widely outpointed.

They had a rematch in January 1941, which attracted a new indoor attendance record of 23,306 to Madison Square Garden, but once again Armstrong took a brutal beating. His right eye was cut and closed, and his left eye almost shut. He rallied, with one last flourish in the 11th, but could not maintain the effort and Zivic was back on top in the 12th round when referee Arthur Donovan led Armstrong to his corner. Armstrong retired, but made a comeback in 1942 and had a further 49 fights. However, he never again got close to the title, even though he defeated Juan Zurita, Leo Rodak, Zivic (when both were ex-champions), Tippy Larkin, Sammy Angott, and Mike Belloise, all sometime world champions, during his comeback.

Zivic lost the title in a big upset in July 1941 to the 8-1 underdog Freddie 'Red' Cochrane, a 26-year-old from Elizabeth, New Jersey. Cochrane had one of the least impressive records of any world challenger: he had lost 30 fights and drawn another nine when he beat Zivic at Newark. When America joined the Second World War, Cochrane enlisted in the US Navy and the title went into cold storage

Pedro Montanez of Puerto Rico falls to defeat in the ninth round of his 1940 bid for Armstrong's title in New York.

Freddie 'Red' Cochrane had lost 30 fights and drawn another nine before he became world champion in a 1941 upset.

Marty Servo lost money by becoming champion: his purse came to less than the $50,000 he had guaranteed to Cochrane.

from July 1941 until February 1946. When Cochrane returned to action his logical contender was Sugar Ray Robinson, but instead Marty Servo of New York bought himself a title fight by guaranteeing the champion $50,000. Servo, a cousin of the former lightweight king Lou Ambers, had also been kept inactive by the war. He did not box from May 1942, when he was outpointed by Robinson, until December 1945, but he easily kayoed Cochrane in four rounds to take the title.

His purse for the fight did not even cover the

$50,000 guarantee he had been obliged to give Cochrane, but he looked forward to a well-paid defence against Robinson to recoup that outlay. (Both Cochrane and Servo had first been required to give an undertaking to meet Robinson within six months.) But only seven weeks after becoming champion, Servo was overmatched against the fierce-hitting middleweight Rocky Graziano and was badly beaten in two rounds. Graziano injured Servo's nose so severely that he was forced to announce his retirement just a week before the Robinson bout was due to take place. He tried a brief comeback the following year, but had only two fights and quit for good after being knocked out inside a round by Joe DiMartino in August 1947.

The list of candidates to meet Robinson for the vacant title was so short that the New York Commission was even unable to hold an elimination tournament. Tommy Bell, a lanky fighter from Youngstown, Ohio, who had taken Robinson the distance in 1945, was therefore allowed to face him again for the title at Madison Square Garden on 20 December 1946, and justified the match with a stubborn performance, although he was soundly outpointed. Robinson had been the *real* world champion since 1941, a year in which he beat both Zivic and Servo. In August 1943 he had also outpointed another ex-champion, Henry Armstrong.

He held the welterweight title for over four years, but such was his superiority over the rest of the field that he made only five defences. The first of these ended tragically when Jimmy Doyle, from Cleveland, died after being knocked out in the eighth round. It was the first fatality in a world title bout since the English bantamweight Walter Croot died after being knocked out in the 20th round by Jimmy Barry of America in 1897.

Robinson relinquished the title on beating Jake LaMotta to become middleweight champion on 14 February 1951. The NBA recognized a well-connected Chicago fighter, Johnny Bratton, as champion after he had outpointed Charlie Fusari on a split decision in March 1951. (Fusari had lasted the distance with Robinson in a title challenge seven months previously, although winning only one of the 15 rounds.) Bratton's record was modest – he had lost 16 times, including three of his previous seven fights. It was no surprise when, on 18 May 1951, he was beaten by another of Robinson's title victims, Kid Gavilan of Cuba.

Gavilan (real name Geraldo Gonzalez) was a busy and colourful boxer who had perfected a

Even the mighty Sugar Ray Robinson could have his bad nights, as in this 1949 draw with the useful but long-forgotten Henry Brimm (left, *on the left*). *But when the welterweight title was at stake, as in his points win* (below) *over Kid Gavilan in July of that year, Robinson was unbeatable.*

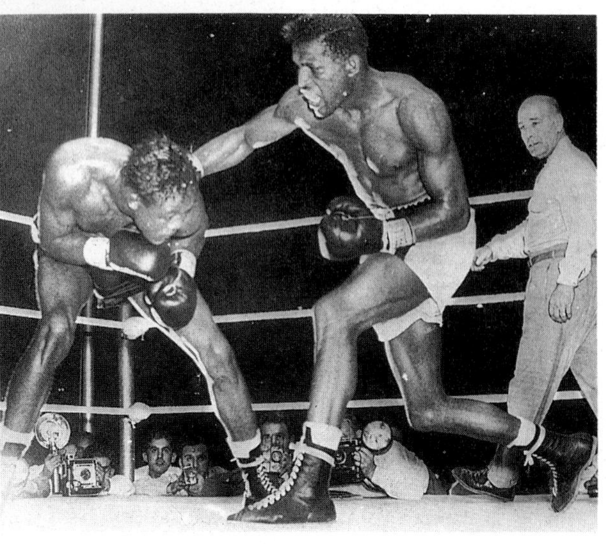

Below: *challenger Bernard Docusen of New Orleans took Robinson the full 15 rounds in this June 1948 title bid in Chicago.*

The lunging right was a distinctive feature of the ring style of Johnny Bratton, who held the NBA version of the title for just over two months in 1951. Bobby Jones (on the receiving end, right) *was beaten in five rounds in March 1953, but Del Flanagan* (below) *ended Bratton's 86-fight career with a ninth-round stoppage two years later.*

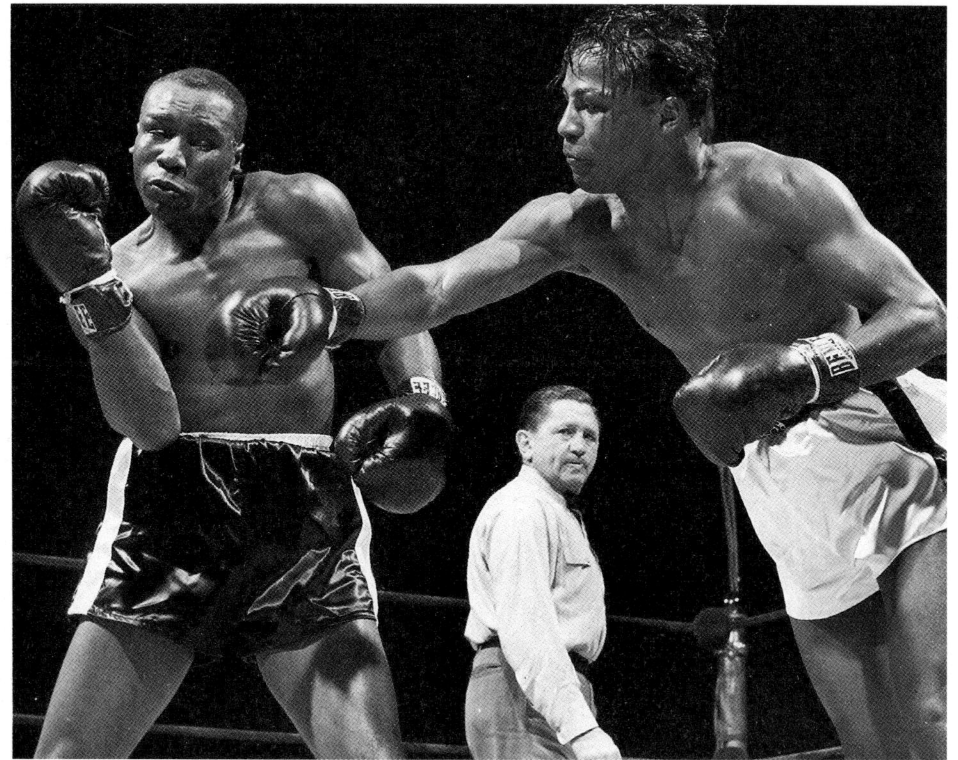

whipping half-hook, half-uppercut, which he called a 'bolo' punch. He based it on the action employed in cutting sugar cane with a machete, as used in his homeland. When Gavilan won a bitterly fought and controversial verdict over New Yorker Billy Graham in Madison Square Garden, in August 1951, he earned universal recognition when the EBU went along with the NBA and New York (who had recognized him after beating Bratton). He became an active champion, who had more than his share of luck.

Gavilan's second defence, like the first, was won on a split decision, this time over Bobby Dykes of San Antonio. His third, against the popular Gil Turner, drew 39,025 people to the Municipal Stadium in Philadelphia, paying a welterweight championship record of $269,667. Gavilan confirmed the win over Graham with a unanimous decision in Havana in October 1952, and this time there were no arguments from the New Yorker, but after an easy defence against Chuck Davey, a white college student from Lansing, Michigan, he had another close call. Carmen Basilio, a big underdog in the betting, floored Gavilan for the first time in his career for 'nine' in the second round, and dominated the rest of the fight – yet the Cuban's luck held as he got yet another split decision.

He retained the title in a rematch with Bratton, but then was, for once, on the wrong end of a bad verdict when Johnny Saxton, whose manager was the underworld boss Blinky Palermo, was given the decision over him in Philadelphia in October 1954.

Left: *Kid Gavilan, still three years away from the title, outpoints Roman Alvarez in a 1948 ten-rounder.*

Below: *When Gavilan beat Gaspar Ortega of Mexico in 1957, the Cuban was close to retirement.*

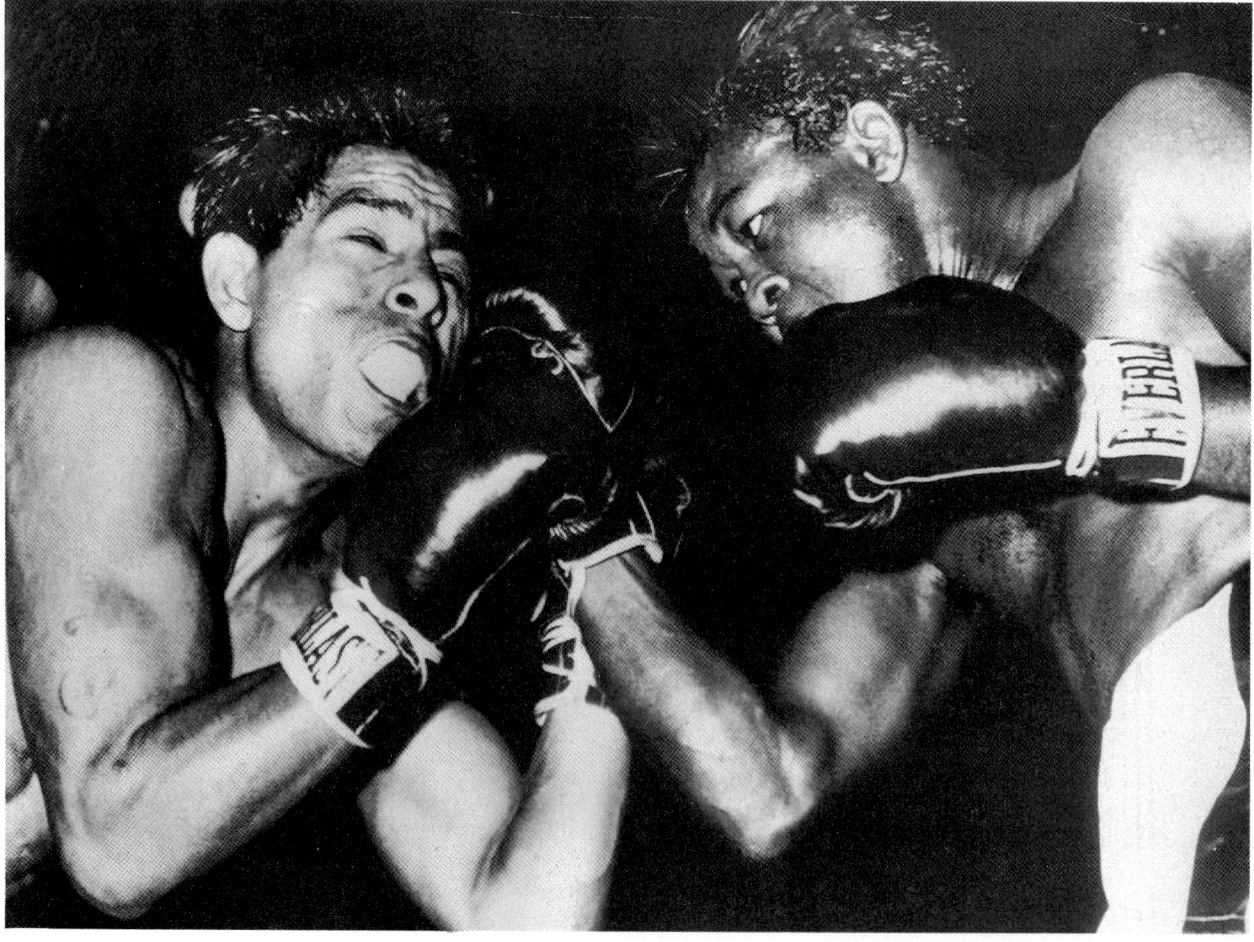

Gavilan frequently took on good middleweights, as with this 10th round stoppage of Walter Cartier in 1951 (above). *In his next fight he trounced Bobby Dykes in a welterweight defence* (right), *and gave the college boy from Michigan, Chuck Davey, a 10-round hiding in 1953* (below) *before losing the title on a bad verdict to Johnny Saxton* (below right *seen being hoisted by his sinister underworld-figure manager Blinky Palermo). Gavilan had enjoyed some close verdicts himself, but never recovered top class after losing his title.*

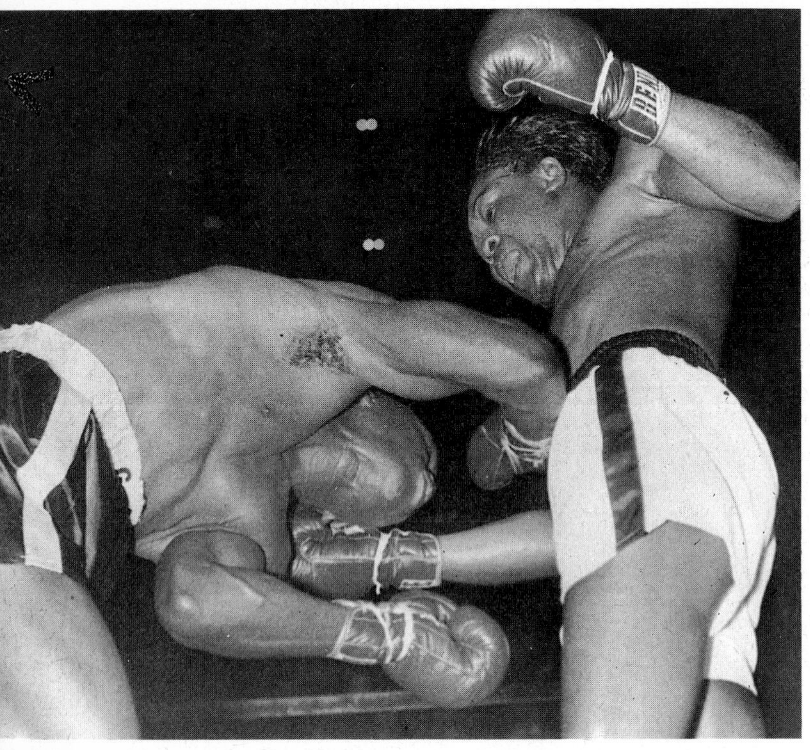

Gavilan's form slumped after that, and he won just nine of his remaining 26 fights, which included two well-remembered meetings in London with European champion Peter Waterman.

Saxton was dethroned after only five months by Tony DeMarco, an exciting left-hooker from Boston, who beat him in 14 rounds in April 1955. Nine weeks later, the patient Basilio finally got his second chance at the title. This time he left nothing in the hands of the judges, battering DeMarco to defeat in the 12th round at Syracuse.

Their rematch in Boston five months later produced an identical finish – it actually lasted two seconds longer than the first – but was even more

Johnny Saxton was rumoured to have had underworld 'help' in taking the title from Gavilan (above), *but he was on his own against Tony DeMarco* (right), *who stopped him in 14 rounds five months later. DeMarco's reign was even briefer, lasting just nine weeks before Carmen Basilio* (below) *battered him to 12th-round defeat.*

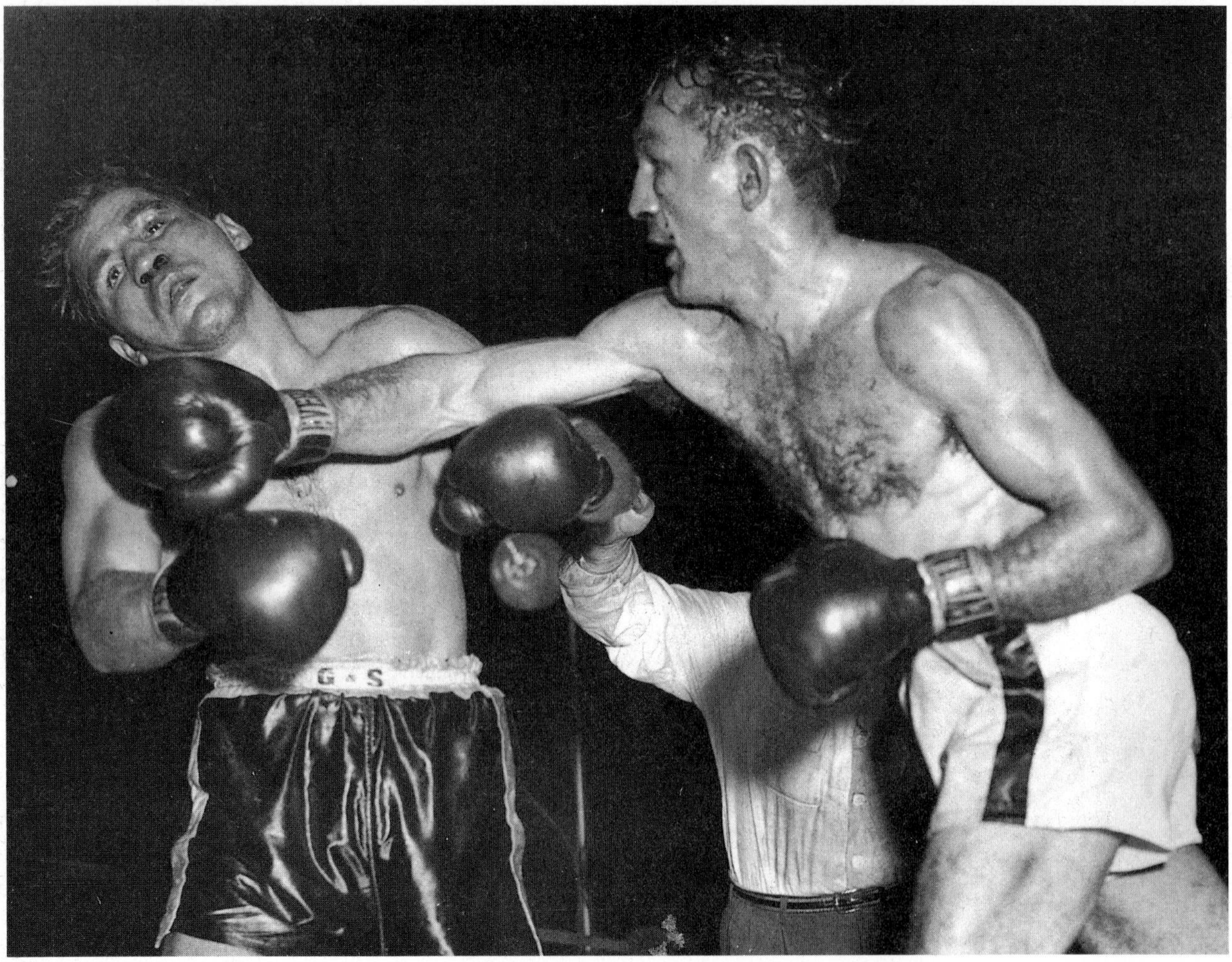

T.H.

Previous page: *Thomas Hearns was ahead on points when Ray Leonard launched this savage attack to win their welterweight title unification match in the 14th round of a classic showdown at Caesars Palace.*

Above: *Milton McCrory was expected to provide stiff opposition for Don Curry when they contested the undisputed welterweight title, but Curry swept him aside in two rounds. Currie looked destined for greatness, but Lloyd Honeyghan had other ideas.*

Left: *The Basilio v DeMarco rematch was perhaps the decade's most exciting title fight at the weight.*

exciting, with the rock-hard Basilio being badly hurt and almost kayoed in the seventh round. Basilio recalled the experience vividly in an interview with Pete Heller, quoted in *In This Corner:*

> I got hit on the point of the chin. It was a left hook that hit the right point of my chin. What happens is it pulls your jawbone out of your socket from the right side and jams into the left side and the nerve there paralyzed the whole left side of my body, especially my leg. My left knee buckled and I almost went down, but when I got back to my corner the bottom of my foot felt like it had needles about six inches high and I just kept stamping my foot on the floor, trying to bring it back. And by the time the bell rang for the eighth round it was all right.

Johnny Saxton had allowed Basilio to go through with the DeMarco rematch, but on 14 March 1956 he got his chance to regain the title. It was, once again, a very controversial decision. The near-unanimous opinion of the 12,145 fans in Chicago Stadium was that Basilio had easily outscored the negative, ultra-defensive Saxton, but the judges ruled otherwise. Public opinion forced a rematch,

'It paralyzed the whole left side of my body . . . the bottom of my foot felt like it had needles about six inches high.' That was Basilio's graphic description of the moment (above) *when DeMarco almost kayoed him. Basilio lost the title in his next defence* (right), *when the well-connected Johnny Saxton once more became champion on a controversial decision.*

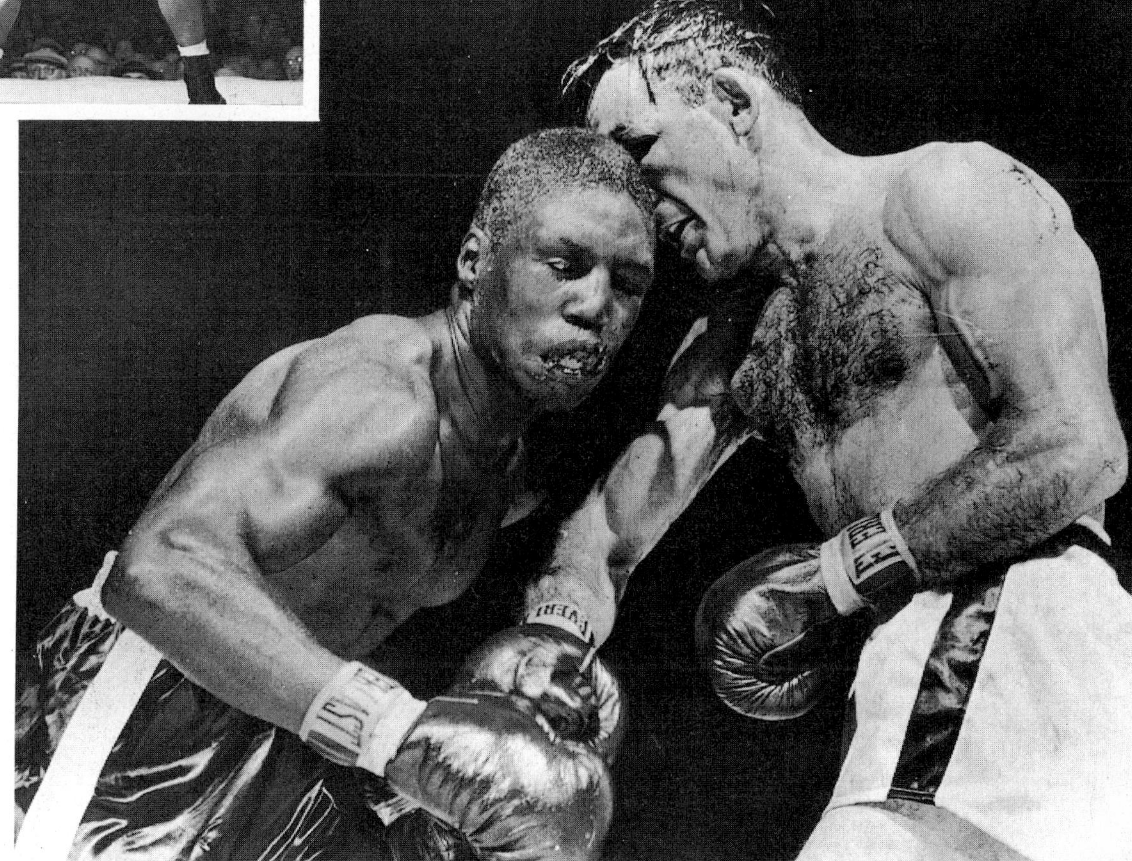

which took place six months later. This time Basilio won in nine rounds, and then settled the issue for good by knocking Saxton out in two rounds of a third meeting, in February 1957. Basilio relinquished the title on becoming middleweight champion in September 1957, and Virgil Akins from St Louis won the elimination tournament by stopping New Jersey's Vince Martinez in the fourth round.

Akins won a non-title fight with Charlie 'Tombstone' Smith, but then lost his way hopelessly. He won only one of his next nine fights, and the second of those defeats cost him his world title, against Don Jordan, one of a family of 11 boys and eight girls. Jordan, originally from the Dominican Republic, was a strange individual who claimed to have been a professional assassin before settling in California. He boasted of once having killed 30 people in a month, mostly using poisoned darts shot from a blowpipe.

But Jordan was an uninspiring champion, making only one successful defence (against Denny Moyer) before losing the title to a Cuban, Benny 'Kid' Paret, in Las Vegas on 27 May 1960. Given that Las Vegas is now the boxing capital of

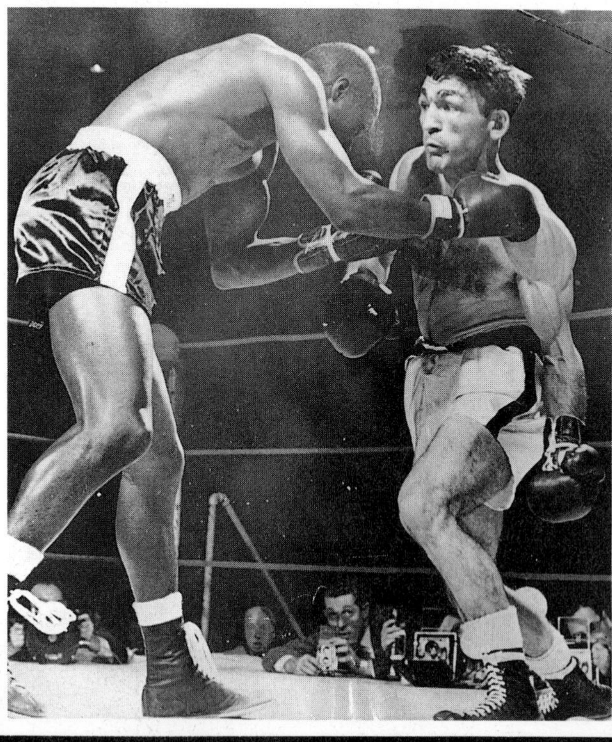

Basilio moved up to middleweight after this second-round knockout of Saxton (right), *clearing the way for Virgil Akins* (below, *on the left) to take the title by stopping Vince Martinez.*

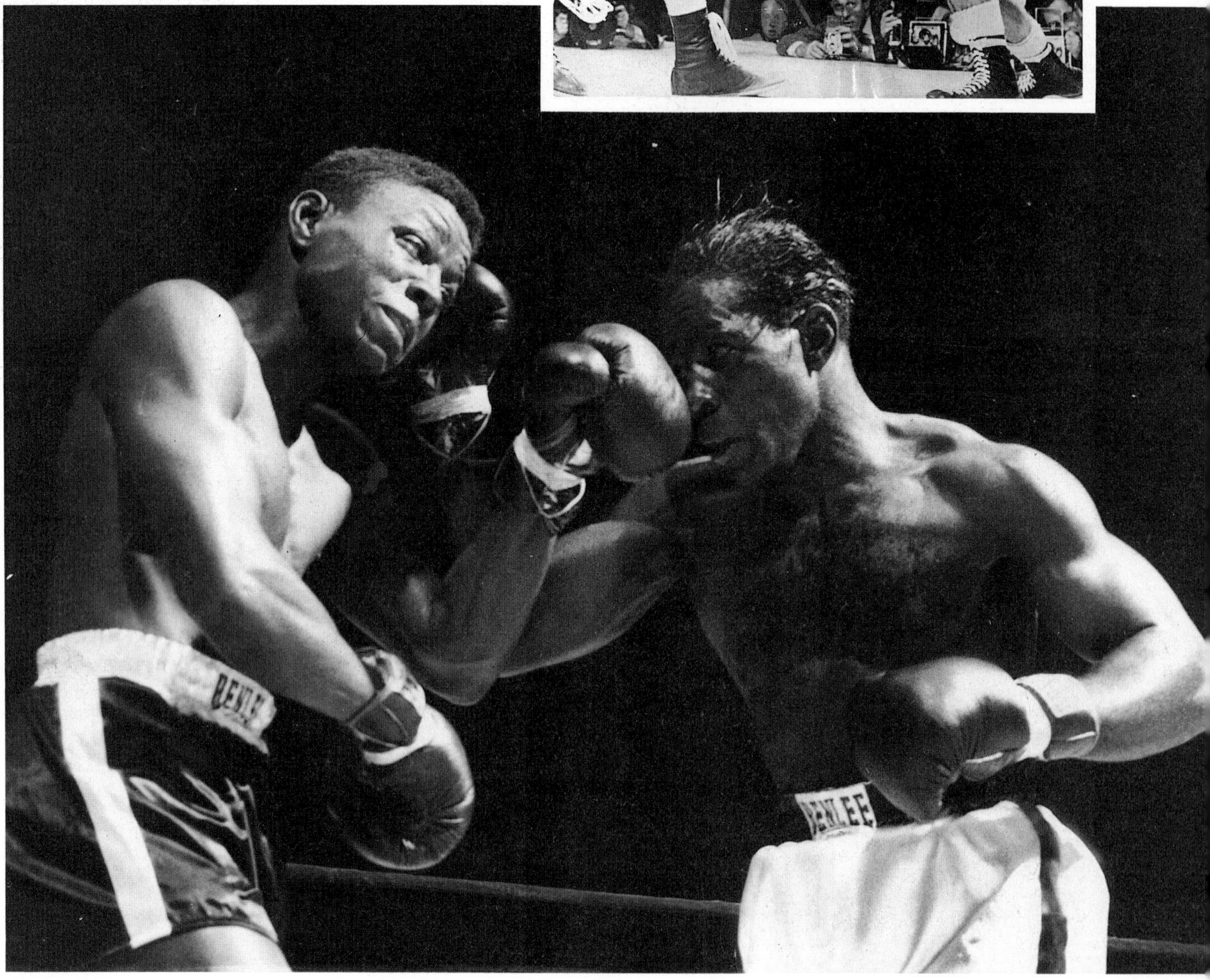

the world, it is strange to reflect that this was the first championship fight ever staged in the city. Paret, like Gavilan, was a one-time sugar cane cutter who had switched his fighting base to America after Fidel Castro's new government outlawed professional boxing. He was a strong, rather than skilful fighter, and he did not hold the title for long. He outpointed the veteran Argentinian Federico Thompson in his only successful defence, lost a couple of non-title ten-rounders to Denny Moyer and Gaspar Ortega, and was then knocked out in the 13th round at Miami Beach on 1 April 1961 by Emile Griffith.

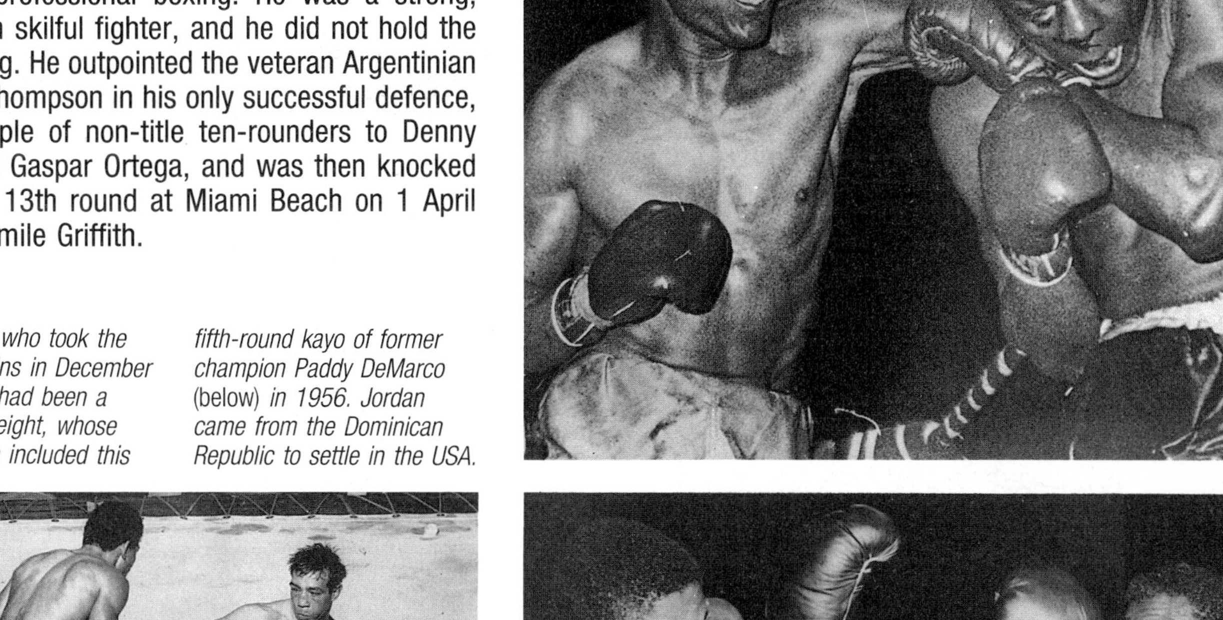

Don Jordan, who took the title from Akins in December 1958 (right) *had been a useful lightweight, whose better results included this fifth-round kayo of former champion Paddy DeMarco* (below) *in 1956. Jordan came from the Dominican Republic to settle in the USA.*

Benny 'Kid' Paret, a Cuban expatriate who fought out of New York, took the title from Jordan (above) *in May 1960. It was the first world title fight ever staged in Las Vegas, a city which is now the capital of world boxing. A year later Emile Griffith, a part-time hat maker from the Virgin Islands, kayoed Paret in the first of their three title meetings* (left).

Griffith was originally from the Virgin Islands, but the family moved to New York where he worked in the millinery business owned by one of his co-managers, Howie Albert. Aided by the regular television exposure which by that time was a major factor in American boxing, Griffith had progressed rapidly to contender status in less than three years, under the astute guidance of Albert and his partner Gil Clancy. Wins over established contenders like Ortega, Moyer, Jorge Fernandez, Florentino Fernandez, Willie Toweel and Luis Rodriguez moved him into the fight with Paret. Although he was never regarded as a particularly heavy puncher, he still managed to knock out the usually durable Paret with a brilliant left hook in the 13th round.

Griffith retained his title against Gaspar Ortega, but then Paret took the championship on a split decision in September 1961. They fought again in New York in March 1962, and Griffith (whom Paret had taunted with accusations of homosexuality, a much more damaging jibe in those days than many

Left: *Willie Toweel took such a mauling from Griffith in this 1960 meeting in New York that he never fought again.*

Below: *Paret regained the title from Griffifth in September 1961, thus setting up their third fight.*

Harry Gibbs, Britain's best post-war referee, orders Griffith to a neutral corner before taking up a count over British champion Brian Curvis at Wembley. The Welshman took a bad beating, but lasted the 15 rounds.

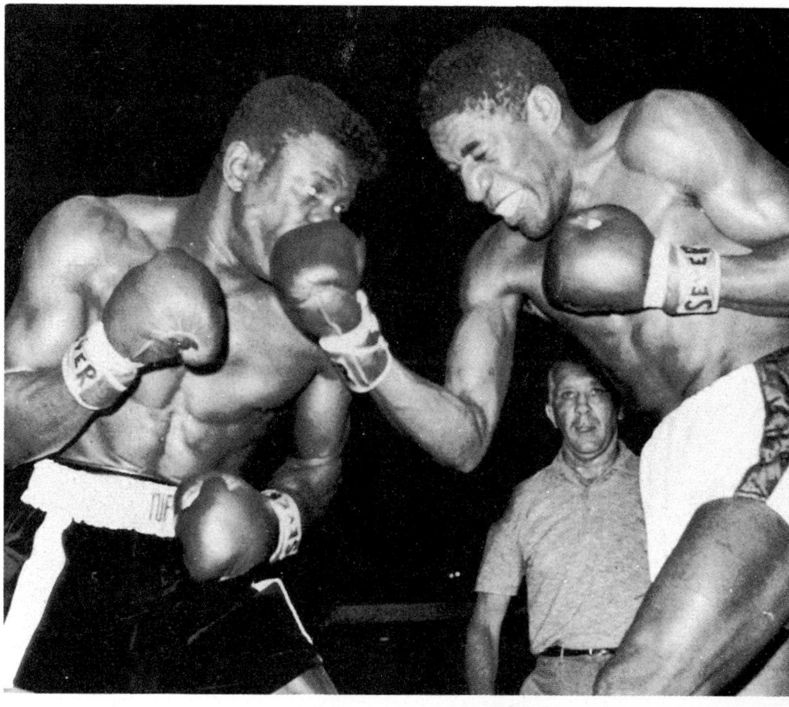

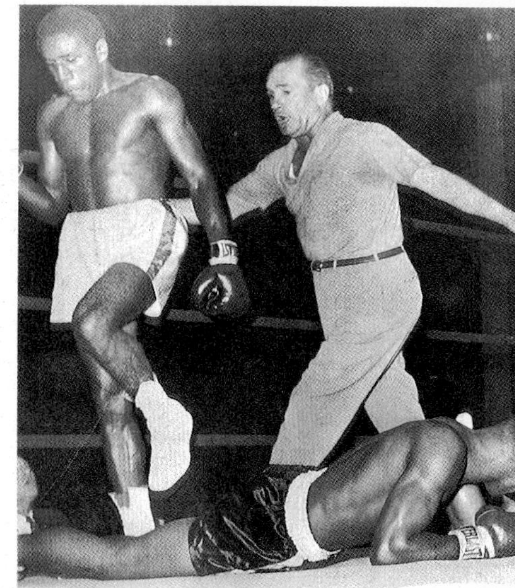

Luis Rodriguez (right, *in an early win over Carl Hubbard) had a three-fight championship series with Griffith* (above). *All were settled by split decisions, with Rodriguez winning the first and Griffith the next two. The Cuban's first outing after losing the title was a ninth-round stoppage of Denny Moyer* (below), *and Rodriguez remained a top-level competitor to the end of his 121-fight career.*

would regard it now) pounded the Cuban to a savage defeat in the 12th round. Paret never regained consciousness, and died on 3 April.

The fight had been shown live on American television and, coming less than a fortnight after the death in similar circumstances of featherweight champion Davey Moore, provoked international calls for boxing to be outlawed. Paret had taken an ill-advised match against Gene Fullmer for the NBA middleweight title three months previously, and had been severely beaten in ten rounds. It was generally felt that this had been very much a contributory factor to his death.

Griffith put the appalling affair behind him, defending against top contenders Ralph Dupas and Jorge Fernandez. He also won two fights in Europe against Teddy Wright and Chris Christensen, which though billed in Vienna and Copenhagen respectively as being for the 'world junior middleweight title' were never recognized elsewhere. In March 1963, Griffith lost the welterweight crown to yet another Cuban, the flashy and extrovert Luis Rodriguez whom he had outpointed in a 1960 ten-rounder.

Rodriguez had joined the post-Castro exodus to Miami, where Angelo Dundee turned him into a world contender with wins over stars such as Virgil Akins, Isaac Logart, Garnet Hart, Federico Thompson and Joey Giambra. In June 1963 Rodriguez took on Griffith for the third time, but on Griffith's home ground at Madison Square Garden.

Left: *Curtis Cokes outscores European champion Jean Josselin of France to become undisputed champion.*

Above: *Willie Ludick, a useful South African, was stopped in five rounds in this 1968 bid for Cokes' title.*

Like their first title clash, it went to a split decision, but this time Griffith got it. A fourth fight, in Las Vegas a year later, was no more conclusive – it too produced a controversial split verdict, which again went to Griffith.

After three more defences, including a win in London over the British champion Brian Curvis of Wales, Griffith won the middleweight championship from Dick Tiger on 23 April 1966. He wanted to hold on to both titles, but first the New York Commission ruled that he had to choose between them, and he opted for the middleweight, and then on 10 June the WBA stripped him for failing to defend the welterweight title within the statutory six month period.

The WBA elimination tournament was won by a Texan, Curtis Cokes, who had surprisingly stopped former champion Luis Rodriguez in the semi-final. Cokes then gained New York and European recognition by beating the European champion Jean Josselin of France on a unanimous decision in his home town of Dallas on 28 November 1966. Charley Shipes, the California champion, won recognition as world champion in his home state by stopping Percy Manning in ten rounds in December

1966, but Cokes cleared up this last minor complication by beating Shipes in eight rounds in October 1967. In all, Cokes made five successful defences, but on 18 April 1969 he surrendered his title after 13 rounds to the last of the great Cuban emigrés, Jose Napoles.

Unlike his compatriots, most of whom settled in Miami, Napoles went to Mexico where, between 1962 and 1969, he built a formidable reputation first as a light-welterweight, beating former world champion Eddie Perkins in 1965, and then as a welterweight. He became a magnificent champion, perhaps the best the division had known since Ray Robinson. He retained the title against Cokes, Griffith, and the tough Californian Ernie Lopez before losing it briefly on a cut to the 9-1 outsider Billy Backus of Canastota, a nephew of Carmen Basilio. Napoles regained it six months later, stopping Backus in eight rounds in June 1971, and made nine more defences against the best available contenders until in May 1975 he relinquished the WBA version to concentrate on defending the WBC title. His nine defences took

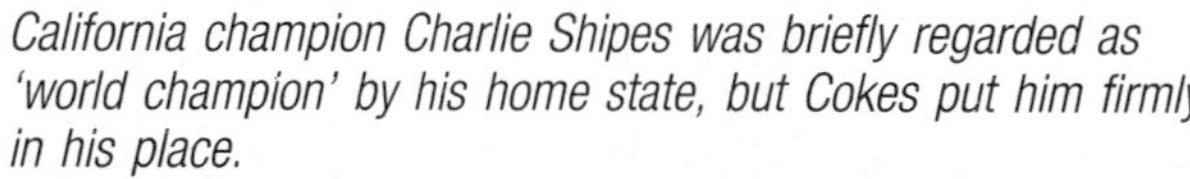

California champion Charlie Shipes was briefly regarded as 'world champion' by his home state, but Cokes put him firmly in his place.

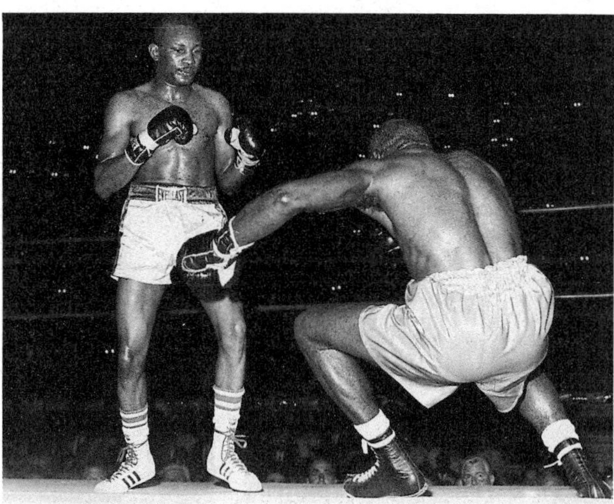

Carmen Basilio's nephew Billy Backus (right, *flooring Frenchman Robert Gallois in a non-title fight) had a short spell at the top in 1971.*

Two of the greats faced each other in Los Angeles in October 1969, when Jose Napoles (below, *on the left) beat Emile Griffith.*

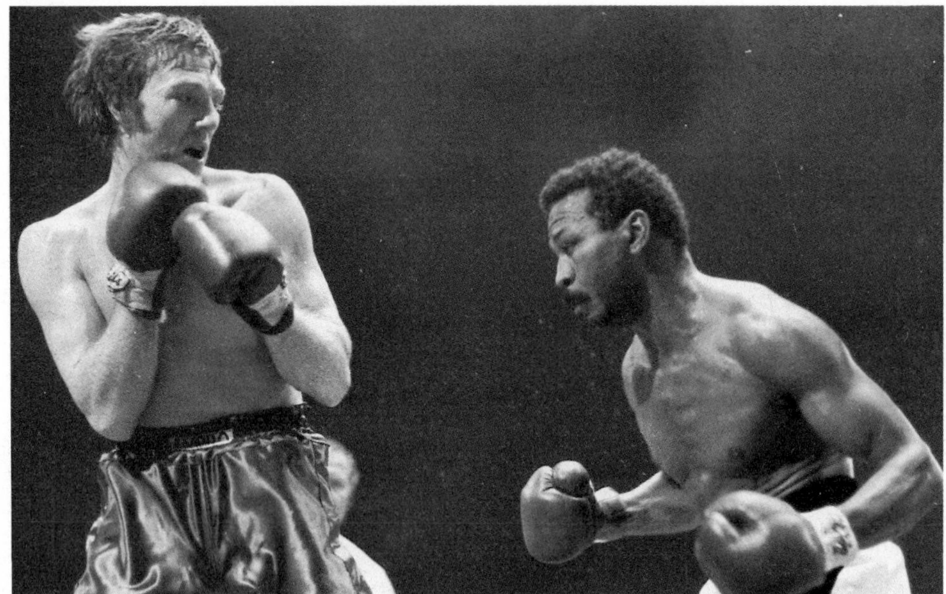

him to London (where he knocked out European champion Ralph Charles), Grenoble, Toronto, California and Mexico City.

Hedgemon Lewis, a classy black stylist who was born in Alabama but boxed out of Los Angeles, earned New York recognition briefly in 1972, when he twice outpointed Billy Backus over 15 rounds. But that unconvincing claim vanished with his ninth-round stoppage by Napoles in August 1974.

The closest Napoles came to defeat by a welterweight during this period was in his last defence of the undisputed title in March 1975, when Armando Muniz, a Los Angeles-based Mexican, cut the champion so badly over both eyes that the ringside doctor ordered the fight to be stopped at the end of the 12th round. Yet the referee awarded Napoles a 'technical decision' because, he said, the cuts were caused by butts. Napoles gave Muniz a return fight four months later, when he won a unanimous decision in Mexico City.

But, at 35 years of age, Napoles' superb skills were waning, and the rate of deterioration was accelerated by the beating he took from middleweight champion Carlos Monzon in their title fight in Paris, in February 1974. Ten months later, time ran out for him. John H. Stracey, a courageous, aggressive and well-managed Englishman, got off the floor in the first round to hammer Napoles into a sixth-round defeat. Napoles never boxed again.

Stracey had been an outstanding amateur, who won an ABA title and boxed for Britain in the 1968 Olympic Games. He won the British title in 1973 and the European a year later, and had been manoeuvered up the rankings by manager Terry Lawless and matchmaker Mickey Duff. They matched him brilliantly with a series of once formidable but still highly rated opponents, none of whom ever boxed again, including Roger Menetrey, Ernie Lopez, and Jackie Tillman. The pattern continued when Stracey won the title. His first defence was against the fading Hedgemon Lewis, whom he sent into retirement with a tenth-round stoppage.

Napoles became a touring champion, who would defend his title wherever there was a payday on offer. British and European champion Ralph Charles (above, *on the left*) *got his chance in London but was kayoed in seven, while Commonwealth title-holder Clyde Gray was outpointed in Toronto* (below). *Napoles scored a knockdown* (above) *in the eighth round of his second fight with Armando Muniz.*

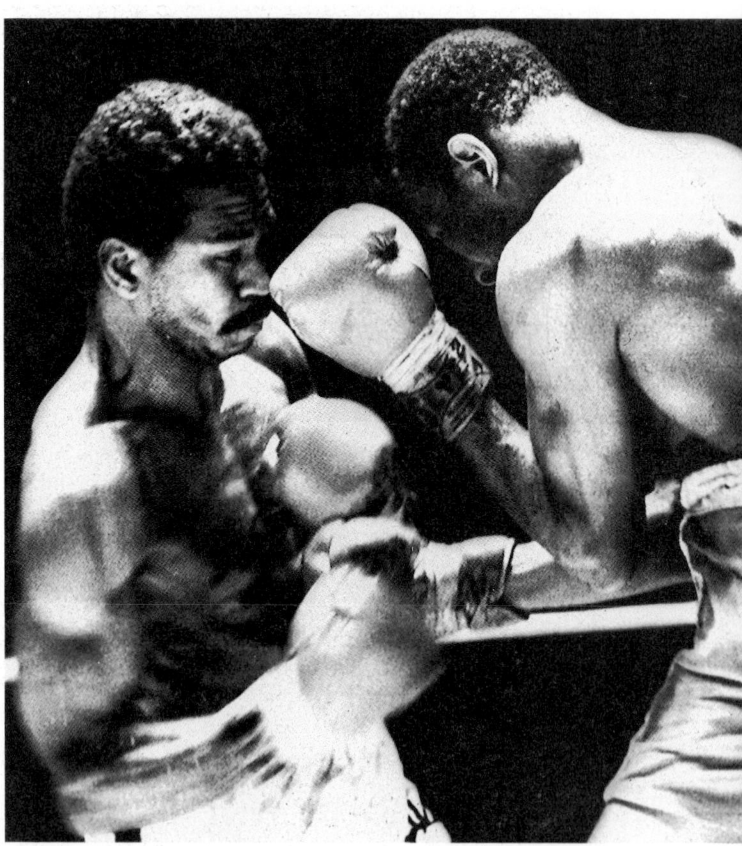

Napoles was pounded into sixth-round defeat by the gutsy Londoner John H. Stracey (right), *who had earlier stopped Switzerland's Max Heibesen* (below).

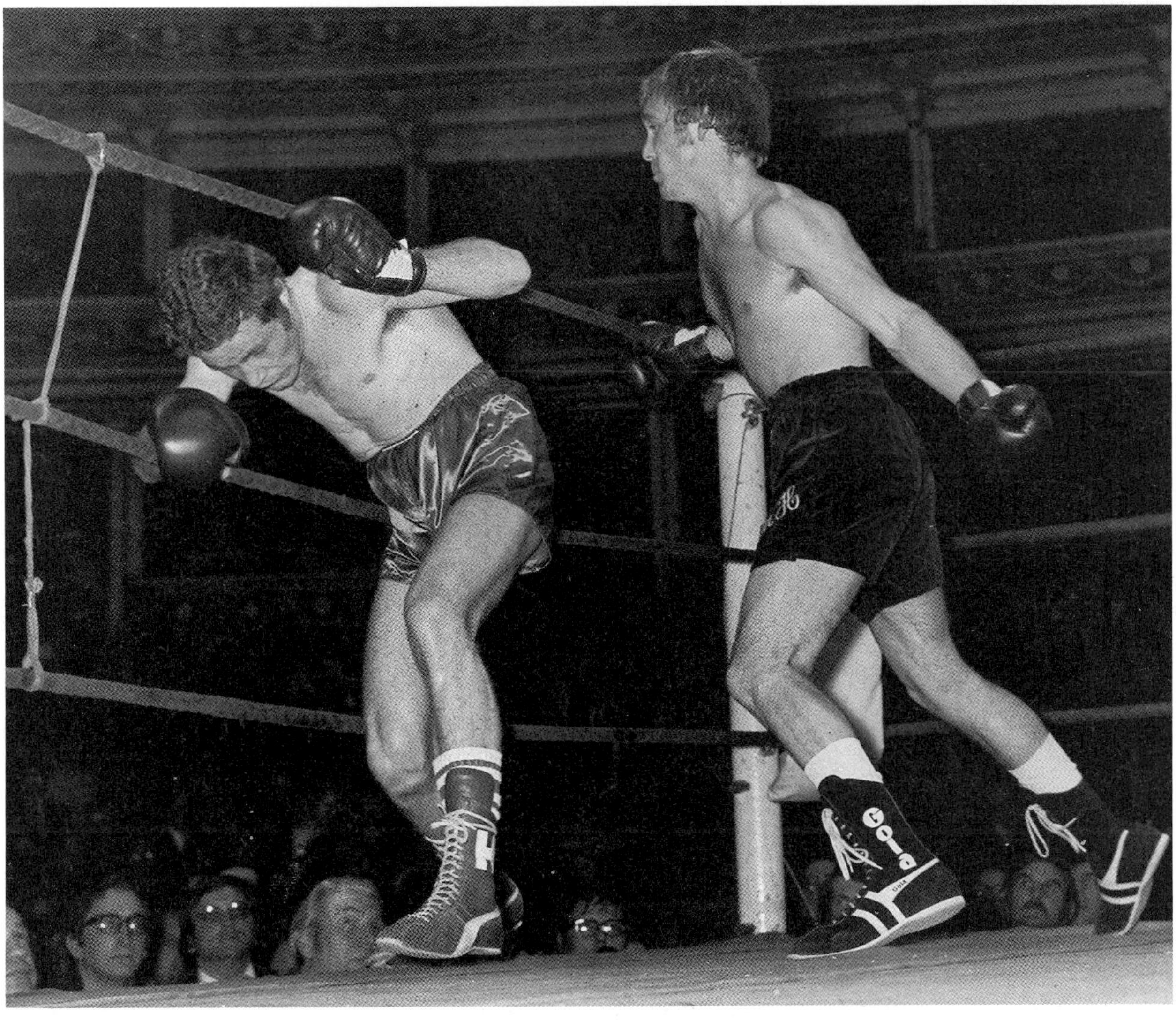

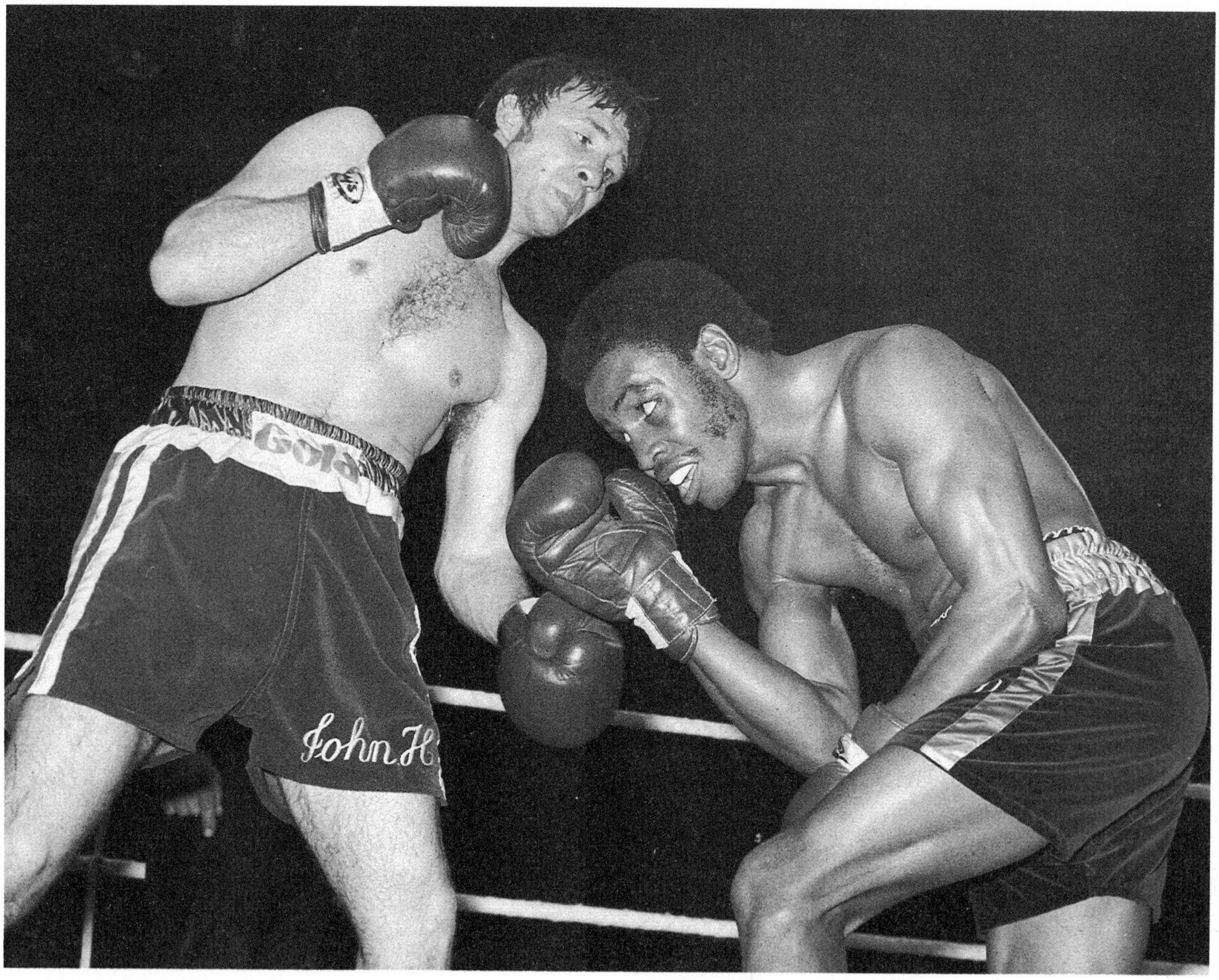

The Londoner's reign ended after only six months when Carlos Palomino, a California-Mexican with a decent but not awe-inspiring record, destroyed him in 12 rounds with body punches. Palomino became an active, well-paid, but under-estimated champion. He came through two desperately tough defences against Armando Muniz, whom he stopped with 36 seconds remaining in the last round of a fight where the points were exactly even, and Englishman Dave Green, whom he kayoed in the 11th with one dramatic left hook. His five subsequent defences were less demanding, although they included a fourth and last title attempt by the indefatigable Muniz, who since his retirement has become a successful politician in Los Angeles. Palomino's sixth defence was his last, when the brilliant Puerto Rican prodigy Wilfred Benitez, only three months after his 20th birthday, beat him on a split decision in San Juan on 14 January 1979.

Benitez had become the youngest world champion in history when he outpointed Antonio Cervantes for the WBA light-welterweight title in March 1976, when he was just 17½ years old. He should, under normal circumstances, have had a

Stracey survived his first challenge, from veteran Hedgemon Lewis (above), *but came to grief second time around* (below) *against the classy Californian Carlos Palomino, whose body punches stopped Stracey in the twelfth round.*

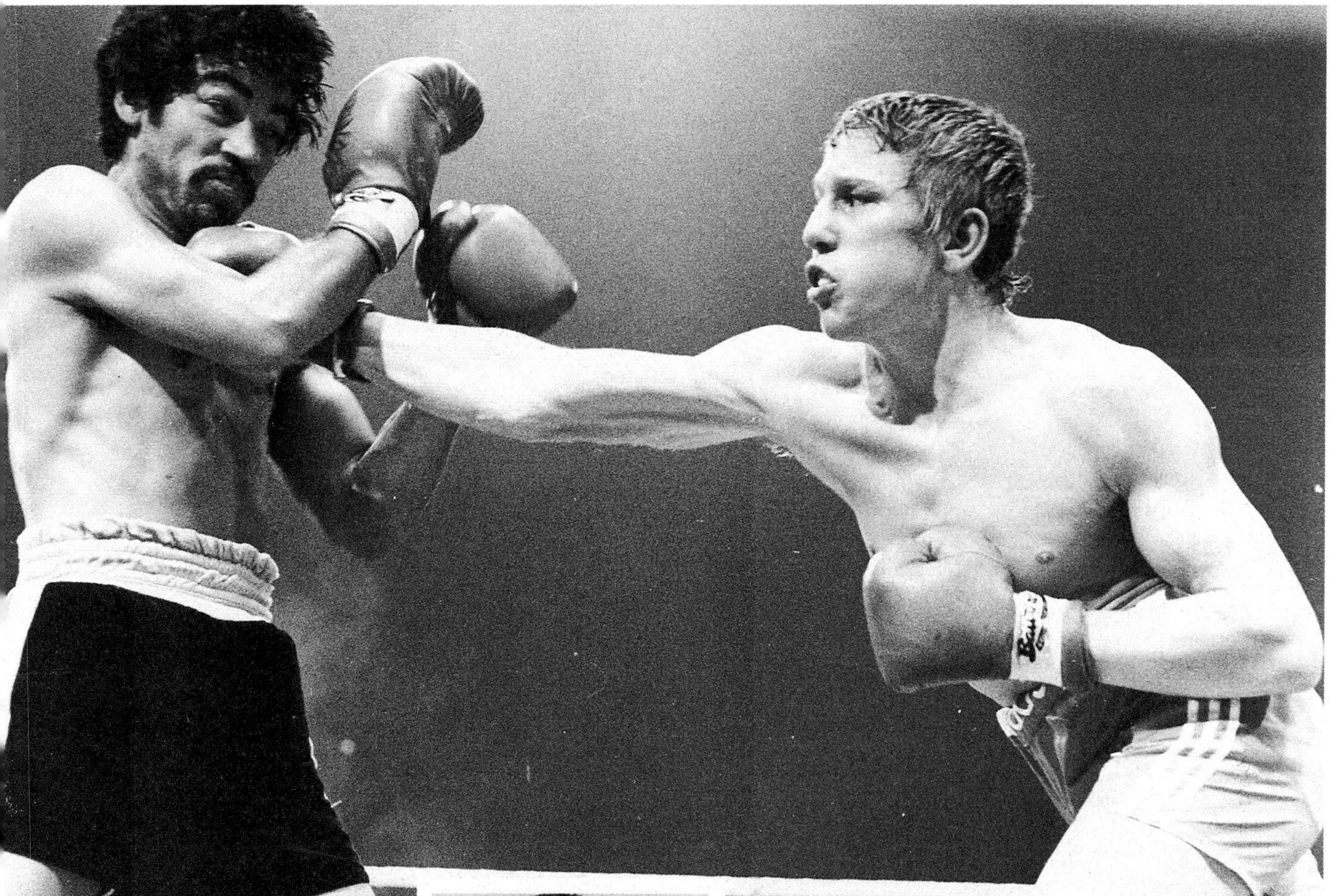

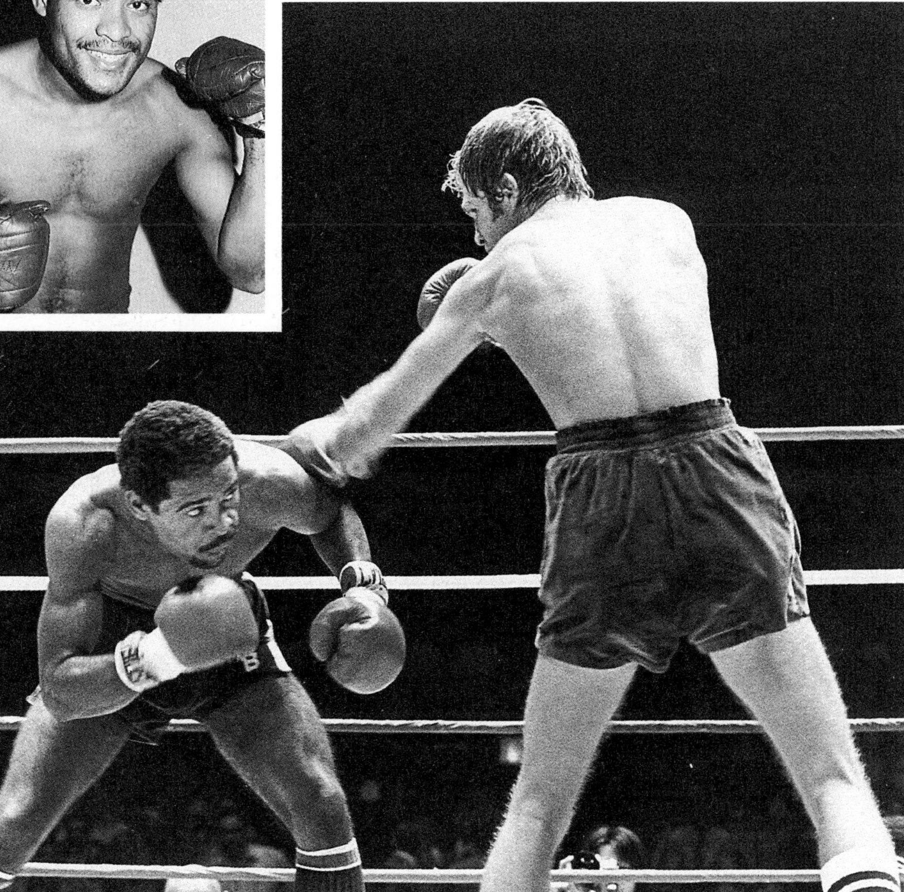

Palomino's run of seven successful defences included a thrilling 11th-round knockout of English challenger Dave Green (above), *before he was toppled on a split decision by the former light-welterweight champion Wilfred Benitez* (inset *and,* right, *in action against Randy Shields).*

long spell at the top of the welterweight division, but he had the misfortune to be a contemporary of the 1976 Olympic light-welterweight champion, Sugar Ray Leonard. It took Leonard only two years and eight months to earn a fight with Benitez, and such was the challenger's charisma, crowd appeal, and television 'bankability' that he was paid a record $1m against Benitez's $1·2m for their fight at Caesars Palace on 30 November 1979. They were worth it: in a thrilling battle, Benitez fought back from a third-round knockdown and a sixth-round head clash, which split open a cut on his forehead, to come within six seconds of lasting the full distance. In the dying moments, the Puerto Rican's legs betrayed him and he fell for an 'eight' count, and referee Carlos Padilla jumped between them as Leonard moved in to finish it.

But Leonard, too, was not destined for a long reign. He made a quick and easy defence against Dave Green three months later, knocking out the Englishman in four rounds, but then faced a much more formidable challenge. Roberto Duran, having fought himself out of opposition as an unbeaten 12-defence lightweight champion, staked his claim to a welterweight title fight by outpointing Carlos Palomino in the former champion's farewell fight in Madison Square Garden in June 1979 and scored three more wins at his new poundage to earn a fight with Leonard. On a rain-swept night in

Above: *Angelo Dundee's coaching and Ray Leonard's ring genius produced the game's outstanding personality since Ali.*

Below: *Leonard claimed the first of his world titles by stopping Benitez in the last round of a thriller at Caesars Palace.*

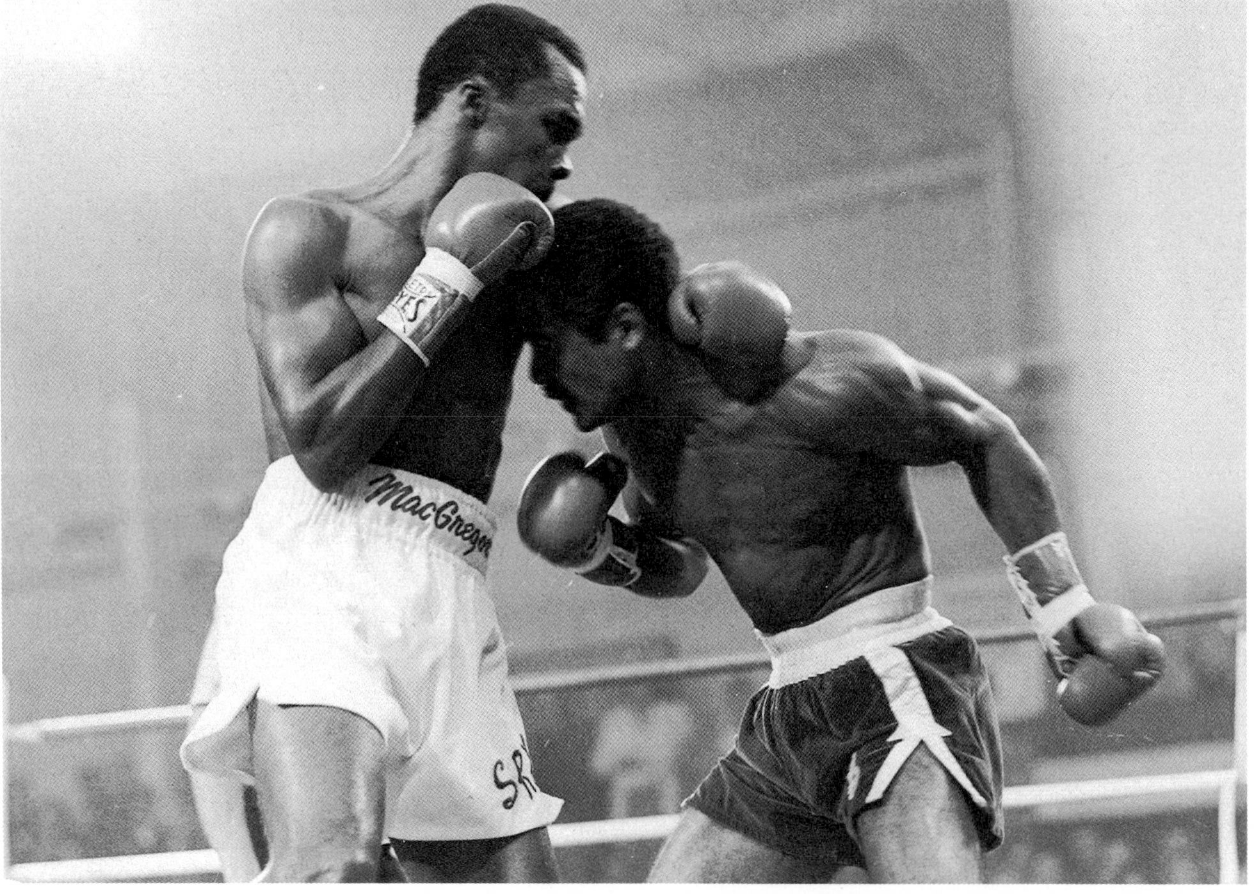

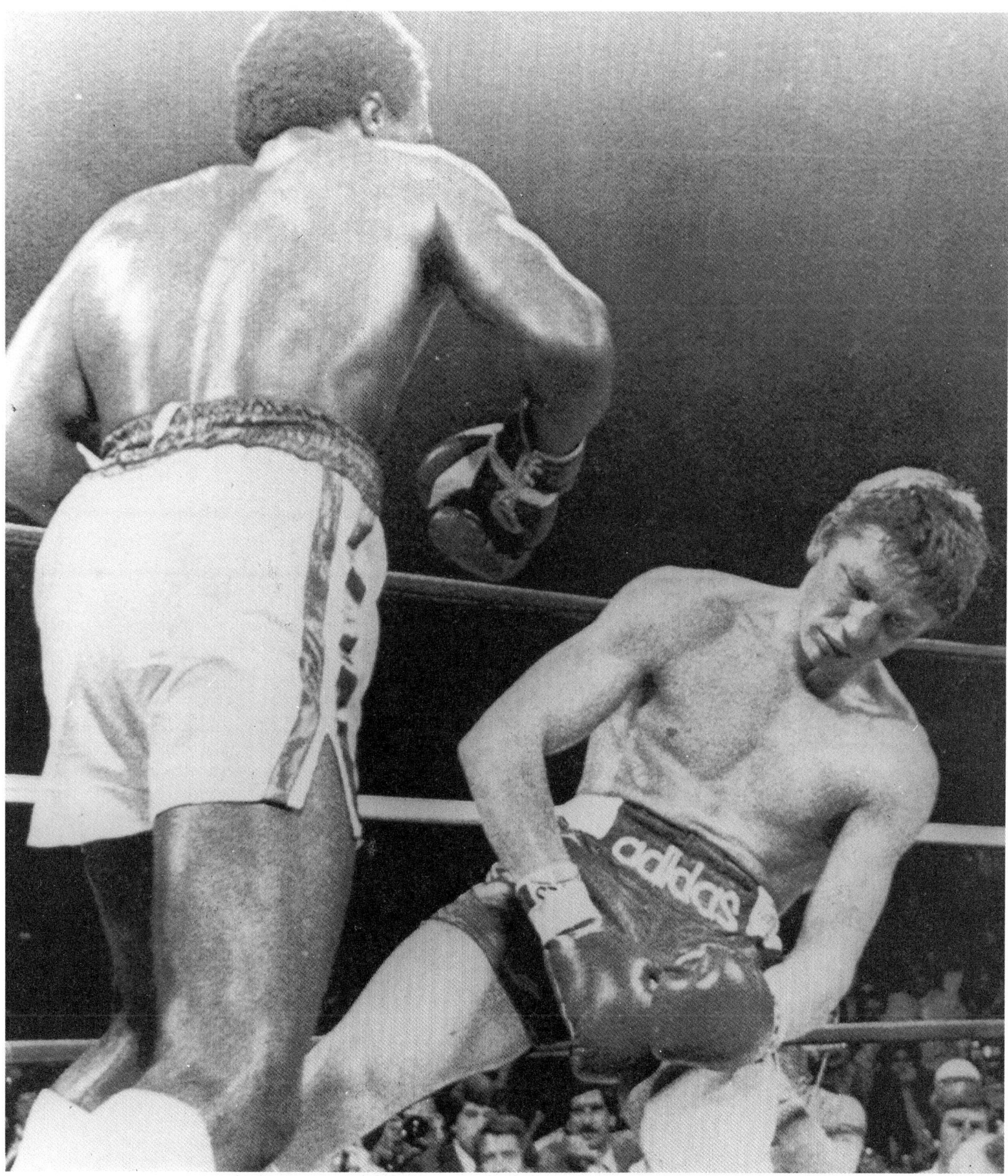

The brave Dave Green was badly overmatched against Leonard in the new champion's first defence, and was kayoed in four rounds.

Montreal on 20 June 1980, the pair provided one of the most bitterly fought and relentlessly exciting fights in the division's history, in front of a crowd of 46,317 people.

Ringside commentator Reg Gutteridge recalled in *The Big Punchers* that:

> With total disregard for danger, their bodies steaming heavily, they fought with a fire that stamped the championship a great one long before it had finished...At the end of each round Duran snarled at Leonard, trying to mouth through his gumshield, and swaggered back to his corner, excited by the wild joy of his own vitality...By constantly attacking, shoving Leonard into the ropes, Duran shaped the fight and gave it momentum.

It was a desperately close finish, with Duran scraping a unanimous win with scores of 145-144, 146-144 and 148-147. The last score was wrongly totalled, and was announced as 147 each before being corrected an hour later.

They were rematched for a reported total of $13m five months later, in the New Orleans Superdome. Duran, the man who had elevated machismo to an art form, threw away the reputation it had taken him 13 years and 71 fights to acquire when he turned his back on Leonard in the eighth round and walked to his corner in surrender. But it was not an act of cowardice: Leonard's tactics had confused and bewildered Duran, to the point where the champion was not prepared to carry on fighting on terms which he neither accepted nor recognized. Duran probably regretted the words *'no mas'* ('no more') as soon as he had uttered them; he had to win the WBA light-

Roberto Duran and Ray Leonard provided 15 unforgettable rounds in their first meeting – and a chaotic anti-climax in the rematch.

Wicked-hitting Mexican Pipino Cuevas (above) *made 11 successful defences of the WBA title, including this sixth-round knockout of Shoji Tsujimoto* (left) *before Thomas Hearns* (below) *flattened him in two rounds in Detroit and set up one of the division's 'superfights' ... Leonard v Hearns at Caesars Palace.*

middleweight title and, unbelieveably, hold Marvin Hagler to a close decision for the middleweight championship before he could live them down. It was a less expensive loss – the Panamanian government revoked the special tax-exempt status which Duran had enjoyed in recognition of his role as national hero.

The WBA version of the championship had, in the meantime, passed from Angel Espada, a Puerto Rican who won the vacant title in June 1975 and retained it twice, to Pipino Cuevas, a thunderous-punching Mexican who destroyed 11 challengers (ten inside the distance) and finally to Thomas Hearns, a 6 ft 1 in puncher from Detroit who kayoed Cuevas in two rounds in August 1980. Hearns retained his title with three stunning performances, and the demand for a showdown between him and Leonard grew until the match was at last made for Caesars Palace, Las Vegas, in September 1981, with Leonard taking an $8 million guarantee against Hearns' $5 million. However, the WBA light-middleweight title, which Leonard had won from Ayub Kalule three months earlier, was not at stake.

For once, in an age of hype and overkill, a fight did live up to its billing. It was an unforgettable clash of champions, with Leonard, his left eye almost closed and trailing on points, launching a

SUGAR

thrilling 13th-round rally that broke Hearns' resistance. Hearns was floored twice – although the first was ruled a slip – and Leonard finished it mercilessly in one minute 45 seconds of the 14th round.

Leonard made just one more defence, an easy three-round win over the journeyman Bruce Finch in Reno, before his career was cruelly cut short by a detached retina in the left eye. He retired undefeated, had a solitary and undistinguished comeback win two years later, and quit for the second time. But the lure of a fight with Marvin Hagler proved too strong, and on 6 April 1987, in a remarkable one-fight comeback, he took Hagler's middleweight crown on a close and controversial decision at Caesars Palace, Las Vegas.

With Leonard's retirement the title split again. The WBA version was won by Don Curry, a sleek and stylish box-fighter from Houston, while the WBC's new champion was Hearns' stablemate Milton McCrory, who had won his title in two bitter 12-rounders with Colin Jones of Wales. They first met at Reno in March 1983, when McCrory seemed to have won but got a draw, and when they were rematched on a sweltering Las Vegas afternoon three months later Jones looked to have done enough, but McCrory won by a split decision.

The two rival champions developed impressively, Curry with five defences (four won inside the distance, including a cuts stoppage of Jones in Birmingham) and McCrory with four (three inside the distance). They each brought undefeated records into the ring for their unification match in Las Vegas on 6 December 1985. Curry was

Below: *Don Curry, WBA champion* (left) *and his WBC rival Milton McCrory* (right) *were both unbeatean when they met in a unification match in Las Vegas in 1985, but Curry crushed his rival in two rounds.*

Leonard and Hearns were paid a combined $13m for their showdown at Caesars Palace in September 1981 (opposite page).

Welshman Colin Jones (below, *on the left against Don Curry) was unlucky in three world title attempts especially against McCrory.*

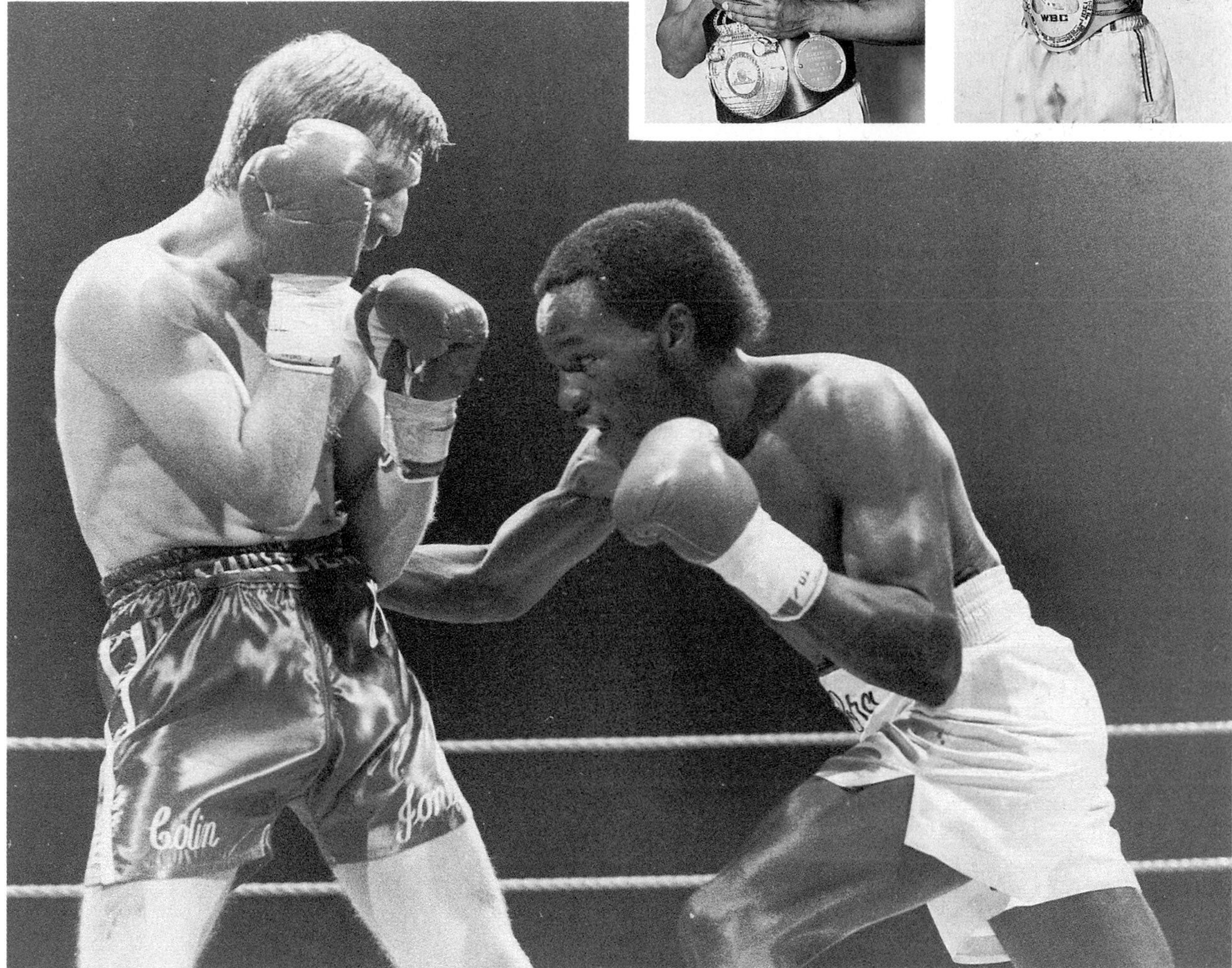

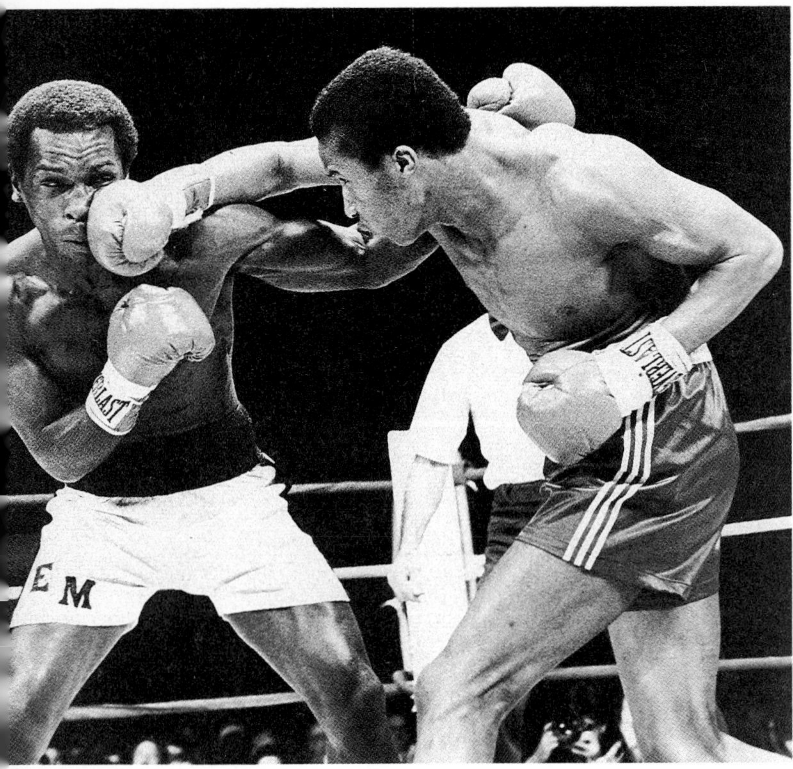

McCrory (right) started his career with a string of 17 inside-the-distance wins, including this second round knockout of Eddie Marcelle.

Roger Stafford (right) took McCrory the full 10 rounds at Phoenix in April 1982, only the second man to take McCrory the distance at the time.

unbeaten in 22 fights, 18 won inside the distance, while McCrory had 27 wins and a draw, with 22 opponents knocked out or stopped. It should have been a competitive match, but Curry overpowered him in less than five minutes. McCrory was floored twice, and was counted out after one minute 53 seconds of the second round.

Curry dismissed his next challenger, Eduardo Rodriguez, in two rounds and looked destined for greatness – until Lloyd Honeyghan, a 26-year-old Jamacian-born Londoner, showed how elusive that quality is with a stunning surprise win over the American in Atlantic City on 27 September 1986. Curry was reportedly weight-drained, and took a steady pounding before retiring on his stool at the end of the sixth round. It was British boxing's biggest moment since Randolph Turpin had trounced Sugar Ray Robinson 35 years before.

Victory made Honeyghan and Marvin Hagler the only men to hold all three titles (WBA, WBC, and IBF), but in December Honeyghan announced that he was relinquishing the WBA version as a protest

Curry's two-round destruction of McCrory (right) was a devastating performance that seemed to mark the Texan as a man destined for greatness . . . but then along came Lloyd Honeyghan, and that opinion had to be hastily revised.

Few gave Honeyghan a chance against the supposedly unbeatable Curry, but the Londoner's fierce aggression, along with Curry's weight-weakened condition, forced the American to quit after six rounds.

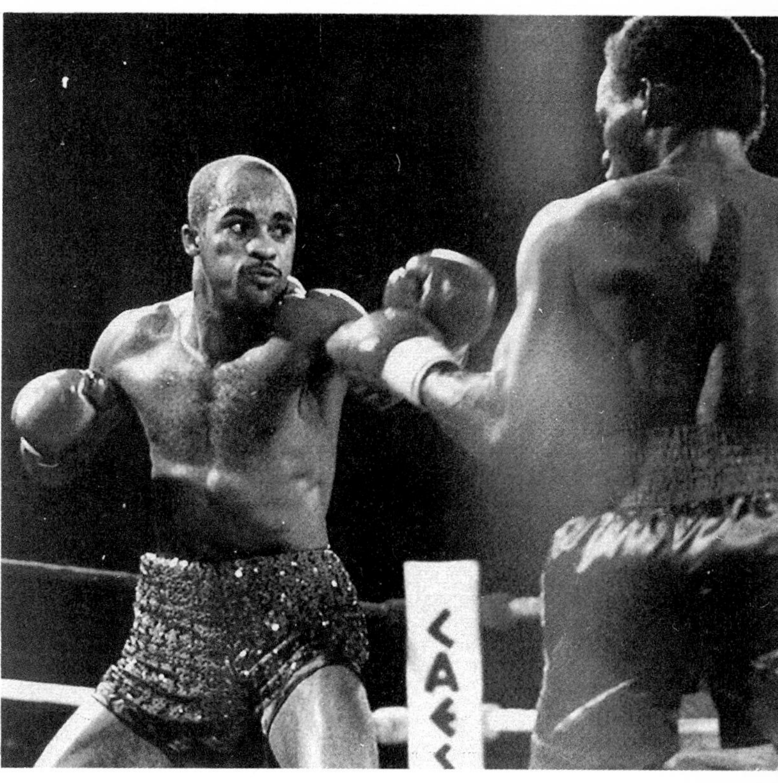

against apartheid (the WBA had arranged an eliminator between a South African, Harold Volbrecht, and the unbeaten ex-Olympic champion Mark Breland).

Breland easily defeated the outclassed Volbrecht to take the vacant WBA title in Atlantic City on 6 February 1987, and 16 days later Honeyghan battered the former WBA light-welterweight champion Johnny Bumphus to a second-round defeat at Wembley to retain the IBF portion of the championship.

A reunification match between the gifted and colourful pair cannot, officially, take place for at least two years, as Breland has been suspended for that period by the WBC for meeting a South African. But money talks loudest when the matches are most attractive, and few in the business expect the inevitable showdown to be deferred for so long.

HOW THE WELTERWEIGHT TITLE HAS CHANGED HANDS

1888–1900

30 Oct 88 Paddy Duffy w.ko.17 William McMillan at Fort Foote, Virginia
(Division became dormant)
14 Dec 92 Mysterious Billy Smith w.ko.14 Danny Needham at San Francisco
26 Jul 94 Tommy Ryan w.pts.20 Mysterious Billy Smith at Minneapolis
02 Mar 96 Charles 'Kid' McCoy w.ko.15 Tommy Ryan at Maspeth, Long Island
(McCoy vacated the title and Mysterious Billy Smith reclaimed it)

1900–

15 Jan 00 Rube Ferns w.dis.21 Mysterious Billy Smith at Buffalo
16 Oct 00 Matty Matthews w.pts.15 Rube Ferns at Detroit
24 May 01 Rube Ferns w.ko.10 Matty Matthews at Toronto
18 Dec 01 Joe Walcott w.ko.5 Rube Ferns at Fort Erie
30 Apr 04 Dixie Kid w.dis.20 Joe Walcott at San Francisco
12 May 04 Dixie Kid drew 20 Joe Walcott at San Francisco
(Dixie Kid outgrew the division, and Walcott reclaimed the title)
16 Oct 06 Honey Mellody w.pts.15 Joe Walcott at Chelsea (USA)
23 Apr 07 Mike (Twin) Sullivan w.pts.20 Honey Mellody at Los Angeles
(Sullivan relinquished title)
20 Apr 08 Harry Lewis w.ko.4 Honey Mellody at Boston
The title fell into dispute, and there was no recognised champion until Ted 'Kid' Lewis in 1915. Bouts advertised as being for the title in this period included:
01 Jan 14 Waldemar Holberg w.pts.20 Ray Bronson at Melbourne
24 Jan 14 Tom McCormick w.dis.6 Waldemar Holberg at Melbourne
21 Mar 14 Matt Wells w.pts.20 Tom McCormick at Sydney
06 Jun 15 Mike Glover w.pts.12 Matt Wells at Boston
22 Jun 15 Jack Britton w.pts.12 Mike Glover at Boston
01 Aug 15 Ted 'Kid' Lewis w.pts.12 Jack Britton in Boston
24 Apr 16 Jack Britton w.pts.20 Ted 'Kid' Lewis in New Orleans
25 Jun 17 Ted 'Kid' Lewis w.pts.20 Jack Britton at Dayton
17 Mar 19 Jack Britton w.ko.9 Ted 'Kid' Lewis at Canton
01 Nov 22 Mickey Walker w.pts.15 Jack Britton at New York
20 May 26 Pete Latzo w.pts.10 Mickey Walker at Scranton
03 Jun 27 Joe Dundee w.pts.15 Pete Latzo at New York
25 Mar 29 Jackie Fields w.pts.10 Young Jack Thompson at Chicago
(For NBA recognition, Dundee having been stripped because of his failure to defend the title)
25 Jul 29 Jackie Fields w.disq.2 Joe Dundee at Detroit
(For undisputed title)
09 May 30 Young Jack Thompson w.pts.15 Jackie Fields at Detroit
05 Sep 30 Tommy Freeman w.pts.15 Young Jack Thompson at Cleveland
14 Mar 31 Young Jack Thompson w.ko.12 Tommy Freeman at Cleveland
23 Oct 31 Lou Brouillard w.pts.15 Young Jack Thompson at Boston
28 Jan 32 Jackie Fields w.pts.10 Lou Brouillard at Chicago
22 Feb 33 Young Corbett III w.pts.10 Jackie Fields at San Francisco
29 May 33 Jimmy McLarnin w.ko.1 Young Corbett III at Los Angeles
28 May 34 Barney Ross w.pts.15 Jimmy McLarnin at New York
17 Sep 34 Jimmy McLarnin w.pts.15 Barney Ross at New York
28 May 35 Barney Ross w.pts.15 Jimmy McLarnin at New York
31 May 38 Henry Armstrong w.pts.15 Barney Ross at New York
04 Oct 40 Fritzie Zivic w.pts.15 Henry Armstrong at New York
21 Jul 41 Freddie (Red) Cochrane w.pts.15 Fritzie Zivic at Newark
01 Feb 46 Marty Servo w.ko.4 Freddie (Red) Cochrane at New York
20 Dec 46 Ray Robinson w.pts.15 Tommy Bell at New York
Robinson vacated title to box as a middleweight
14 Mar 51 Johnny Bratton w.pts.15 Charlie Fusari at Chicago
(Vacant NBA title)
18 May 51 Kid Gavilan w.pts.15 Johnny Bratton at New York.
(Undisputed title)
20 Oct 54 Johnny Saxton w.pts.15 Kid Gavilan at Philadelphia
01 Apr 55 Tony DeMarco w.rsf.14 Johnny Saxton at Boston
10 Jun 55 Carmen Basilio w.rsf.12 Tony DeMarco at Syracuse
14 Mar 56 Johnny Saxton w.pts.15 Carmen Basilio at Chicago
12 Sep 56 Carmen Basilio w.rsf.9 Johnny Saxton at Syracuse
(Basilio then relinquished title to box as a middleweight)
06 Jun 58 Virgil Akins w.rsf.4 Vince Martinez at St Louis
(For vacant title)
05 Dec 58 Don Jordan w.pts.15 Virgil Akins at Los Angeles
27 May 60 Benny (Kid) Paret w.pts.15 Don Jordan at Las Vegas
01 Apr 61 Emile Griffith w.ko.13 Benny (Kid) Paret at Miami
30 Sep 61 Benny (Kid) Paret w.pts.15 Emile Griffith at New York
24 Mar 62 Emile Griffith w.rsf.12 Benny (Kid) Paret at New York
21 Mar 63 Luis Rodriguez w.pts.15 Emile Griffith at Los Angeles
08 Jun 63 Emile Griffith w.pts.15 Luis Rodriguez at New York
1966 *(Griffith relinquished title on winning middleweight championship)*
24 Aug 66 Curtis Cokes w.pts.15 Manny Gonzalez at New Orleans
(Vacant WBA title)
28 Nov 66 Curtis Cokes w.pts.15 Jean Josselin at Dallas for undisputed title
18 Apr 69 Jose Napoles w.rsf.13 Curtis Cokes at Inglewood
03 Dec 70 Billy Backus w.rsf.4 Jose Napoles at Syracuse
04 Jun 71 Jose Napoles w.rsf.8 Billy Backus at Inglewood
14 May 75 *Jose Napoles announced he would relinquish WBA title to concentrate on defending the WBC version*
28 Jun 75 Angel Espada w.pts.15 Clyde Gray in San Juan
(Vacant WBA title)
06 Dec 75 John H. Stracey w.rsf.6 Jose Napoles in Mexico City
(WBC title)
22 Jun 76 Carlos Palomino w.rsf.12 John H. Stracey at Wembley
17 Jul 76 Jose Pipino Cuevas w.ko.2 Angel Espada at Mexicali
(WBA title)
14 Jan 79 Wilfred Benitez w.pts.15 Carlos Palomino at San Juan
30 Nov 79 Sugar Ray Leonard w.rsf.15 Wilfred Benitez at Las Vegas
20 Jun 80 Roberto Duran w.pts.15 Sugar Ray Leonard in Montreal
(WBC title)
02 Aug 80 Thomas Hearns w.rsf.2 Pipino Cuevas in Detroit
(WBA title)
26 Nov 80 Sugar Ray Leonard w.rtd.8 Roberto Duran at New Orleans
16 Sep 81 Sugar Ray Leonard w.rsf.14 Thomas Hearns at Las Vegas
(For undisputed title)
1982 *(Leonard retired as undisputed champion)*
13 Feb 83 Don Curry w.pts.15 Junsok Hwang at Fort Worth
(Vacant WBA title)
19 Mar 83 Milton McCrory drew 12 Colin Jones at Reno
(Vacant WBC title)
13 Aug 83 Milton McCrory w.pts.12 Colin Jones at Las Vegas
(Vacant WBC title)
06 Dec 85 Don Curry w.ko.2 Milton McCrory at Las Vegas
(Undisputed title)
27 Sep 86 Lloyd Honeyghan w.rtd.6 Don Curry at Atlantic City
Jan 87 *Lloyd Honeyghan relinquished WBA title rather than face a possible defence against their number one contender, Harold Volbrecht of South Africa*
06 Feb 87 Mark Breland w.ko.7 Harold Volbrecht at Atlantic City
(Vacant WBA title)

LIGHT WELTERWEIGHTS

PINKEY MITCHELL of Milwaukee can claim the dual distinction of being the first world champion at 10 st (140 lb) and the only man ever to win his world title in a popularity poll. The division (known variously as light-welterweight, junior welter-weight, or super-lightweight) was the brain-child of Mike Collins, publisher of a Minneapolis weekly called *The Boxing Blade.* In 1922, Collins was also managing Mitchell, who could not comfortably make the lightweight limit but who was reluctant to concede weight to fully blown welterweights.

Collins announced the creation of the new category, and invited his readers to select its first champion. To the surprise of absolutely nobody, Mitchell topped the voting and was officially proclaimed world champion – at least in the eyes of *The Boxing Blade* – on 15 November 1922. He risked his new title only twice, boxing a no-decision with Nate Goldman in 1923 and then losing to Mushy Callahan, a West Coast-based New Yorker, in September 1926. Mitchell's record after becoming champion was appalling – he won just three of his remaining 35 fights, and even though 20 were no-decision affairs he still managed to lose ten times.

Callahan probably only got the chance because he had lost his two previous fights, to Jack Silver and Baby Joe Gans, thus leading the ultra-cautious Mitchell to choose him as a 'safe' defence. Callahan, to his credit, did not apply the same policy himself, defending the title in London, in February 1930, against perhaps the finest fighter England ever sent across the Atlantic, Jack 'Kid' Berg – who had already outscored him six months previously. Berg, nicknamed the 'Whitechapel Whirlwind' because of his all-action style, had been a sensation in America in 1929. He was unbeaten in 15 fights in New York and Chicago, and, only four weeks before meeting Callahan, outpointed the former featherweight champion Tony Canzoneri in the first of three classic clashes between the bitter and well-matched pair.

Pinkey Mitchell is the only world champion ever to have been elected to the job.

Although Jack 'Kid' Berg outpointed Mushy Callahan (left) *in a fight billed as for the world title, he did not win the championship belt* (above) *until his defeat of Goldie Hess in January 1931.*

The NBA stripped Callahan of the title in January 1930, perhaps as a ploy to ensure that the championship did not leave America. If that was the case, though, they need not have bothered – Britain did not recognize the division, as Lord Lonsdale forcibly reminded the MC at the Albert Hall when he announced the fight as being for the 'Junior Welterweight Championship of the World'. Lonsdale leapt to his feet, waving his programme to attract the MC's attention, and shouted 'Don't be absurd. There's no such thing as a junior championship!'

Berg battered Callahan into a 10th-round retirement, and headed back to America to consolidate his claim to the title. Although New York recognized him, the NBA withheld their approval until his points win over Goldie Hess in Chicago in January 1931. By that time the busy Berg had already defended the title six times, although only two of them were actually billed as defences. On the other four occasions, both Berg and his opponent scaled within the championship weight, thus automatically putting his title at risk.

Berg lost the title in similar circumstances: when he challenged Canzoneri for the lightweight title in April 1931. His own championship was forfeited when Canzoneri knocked him out in the third round. Berg continued to claim the title, and his fifth-round retirement win over Marius Baudry of France at the Albert Hall, London, in December

Berg's knockout by Tony Canzoneri (right *and* below) *cost him his world title even though the match officially involved only Canzoneri's lightweight title.*

1931 was billed as a championship defence. But the American authorities, quite rightly, recognized Canzoneri as champion until he was defeated on points by the lightly regarded Philadelphian, Johnny Jadick in 1932. Jadick confirmed his superiority by outpointing Canzoneri in a rematch six months later, but was dethroned by the first Mexican to hold the 140 lb title – Jose Perez Flores, whose professional name was Battling Shaw. (Jadick's post-championship career followed the unhappy trend set by his predecessors – he won only 15 of his remaining 56 fights, and retired in 1937 having won four of his previous 33 contests.)

Shaw reigned for only three months, losing his title to Canzoneri in May 1933 and, in the grand tradition, losing all his subsequent eight fights. Canzoneri's stay at the top was even shorter – Barney Ross took both his titles less than five weeks later, and defended the heavier title six times until he relinquished it in June 1935, after he had regained the welterweight title from McLarnin.

Thereafter the title fell into disuse. It was revived briefly in 1946, mainly for the benefit of the stylish New Jersey lightweight Tippy Larkin, who outpointed Willie Joyce in a Boston 12-rounder which the New York and Massachusetts Commissions recognized as being for the vacant title. Larkin was a 117-fight veteran with a long string of wins, punctuated by knockout defeats by class opponents

Johnny Jadick (left) *and Barney Ross* (below left) *both held the 140-lb title until it fell into disuse in the mid-1930s. The division was revived briefly by Tippy Larkin* (right) *in 1946, but then lapsed again until Carlos Ortiz* (below, *in action against Duilio Loi) exhumed it in 1959.*

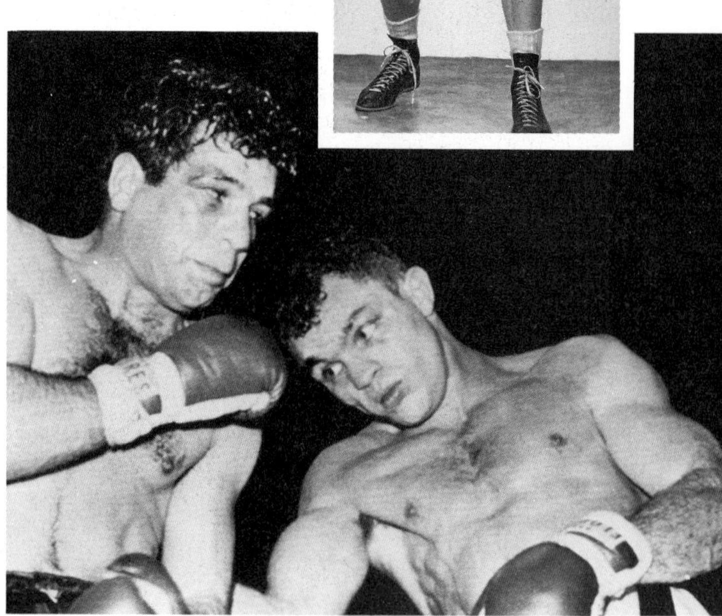

such as Al Davis, Lew Jenkins, Beau Jack (for the vacant New York version of the lightweight title) and Henry Armstrong. He made only one defence, beating Joyce in a New York rematch five months later, but then weight problems forced him into the welterweight division and the title stagnated again until 1959.

An enterprising matchmaker at Madison Square Garden revived it by pairing Carlos Ortiz, a popular New York-based Puerto Rican who was having trouble landing a match against lightweight champion Joe Brown, with Kenny Lane, a southpaw from Michigan with a similar complaint. The fight was an anti-climax, Ortiz winning on a second-round cut, but the quality of his next two defences, against Battling Torres and the stylish Italian Duilio Loi, gave the title some credibility. Loi failed in his first attempt at the title, in San Francisco in June 1960, but outpointed Ortiz in the rematch in Milan three months later. It was the 31-year-old Loi's 112th fight – and the win over Ortiz meant that the remarkable Italian had now beaten the only two men to have beaten *him*. (The other was the Dane, Jorgen Johansen, who won and lost against Loi in European lightweight title fights.)

Loi won the 'rubber' match with Ortiz, and then had a three-fight series with Eddie Perkins, a smooth-boxing craftsman from Chicago, who drew their first fight, won the second, and lost the title to Loi in the third.

Loi retired as undefeated champion on 23

Chicago stylist Eddie Perkins (below, *landing a jab on Mexican champion Baby Vasquez) was a world-ranked lightweight before he moved into the higher division for a three-fight world title series against the classy Italian Duilio Loi* (right).

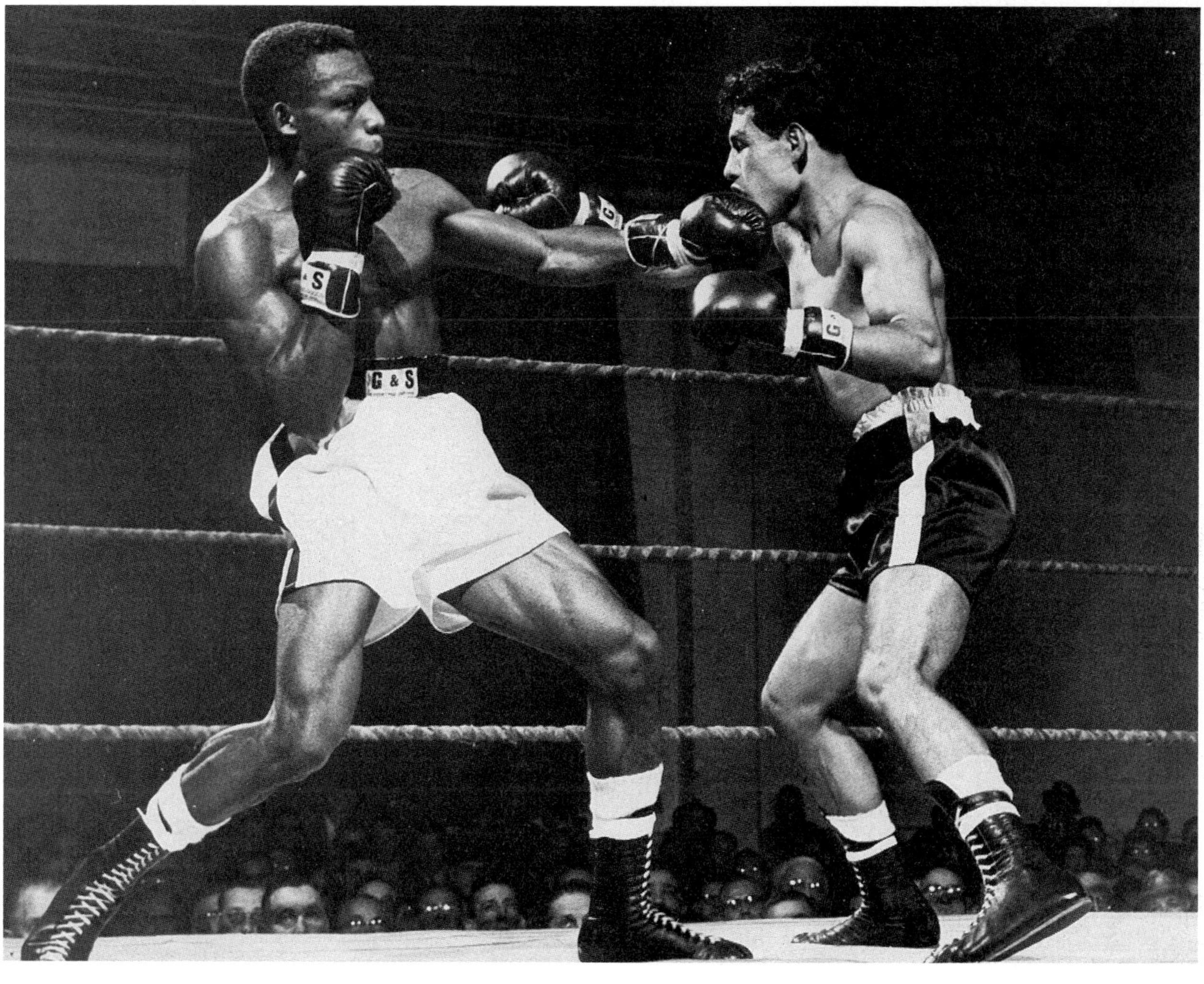

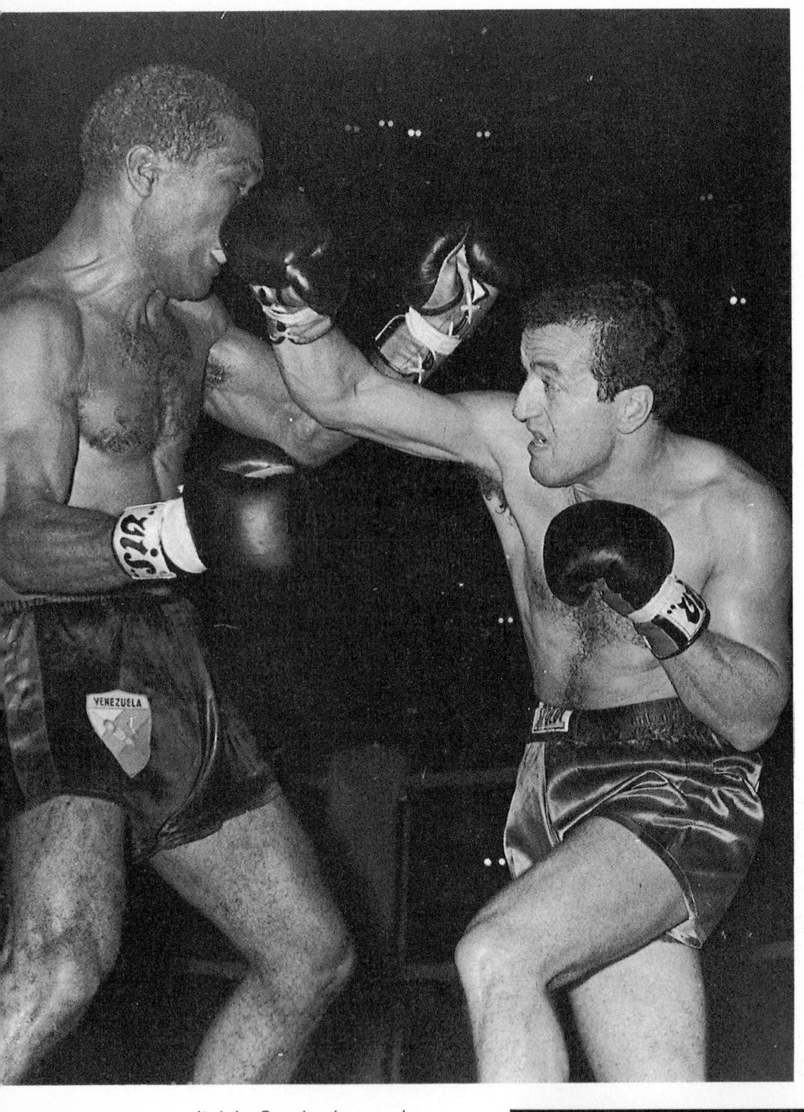

January 1963. The WBA, which by then had evolved from the old NBA, recognized Roberto Cruz of the Philippines as champion after his one-round knockout of Battling Torres, but the rest of the world waited until Perkins had outpointed Cruz in June 1963. Perkins was a globe-trotter who fought anywhere he could earn a purse, defending his title in Japan, Jamaica, and Venezuela, and stopping off for non-title fights in America, Mexico,and Colombia. The Venezuelan stop cost him the championship, when Carlos Hernandez outpointed him, and the hard-punching Latin made two quick defences before losing it to another Italian Sandro Lopopolo.

Lopopolo was beaten in his second defence by Paul Fuji of Japan, who was himself training for a scheduled second defence, against Pedro Adigue of the Philippines in August 1968, when he suddenly retired, only two weeks before the fight. He changed his mind just as suddenly, signing to meet Nicolino Loche of Argentina, a 105-fight veteran who had beaten Lopopolo and Perkins, and drawn with Carlos Ortiz. In the meantime, though, the WBC had matched Adigue with Adolph Pruitt of St Louis for their version of the title, thus initiating a split which has lasted into 1987.

The WBA title has, on balance, produced better

Nicolino Loche was already a veteran with 105 fights behind him when he took the title from Japan's Paul Fuji (below), *but the Argentinian went on to record five defences and held the title for over three years.*

Italy's Sandro Lopopolo (below) *held the title for a year in 1966–67, but his only successful defence was an eight-round win over Vicente Rivas* (above), *who had outpointed him in a non-title 10-rounder three months earlier.*

A spectacular illustration of the hitting power possessed by the legendary 'Kid Pambele' – Antonio Cervantes.

quality champions than the rival versions. Loche beat Fuji in nine rounds and made five defences, including wins over Carlos Hernandez and Antonio Cervantes, before Alfonso 'Peppermint' Frazer of Panama dislodged him in March 1972. Frazer lost it on his second defence to Cervantes, who went on to become one of the division's finest champions. The Colombian, known as 'Kid Pambele', made 11 defences before being dethroned on a split decision by the youngest man ever to win a world title – Wilfred Benitez of Puerto Rico, who was still six months away from his 18th birthday. The brilliant Benitez (who went on to win world titles at welterweight and light-middleweight) made two defences, but was then stripped by the WBA for failing to meet Cervantes in a rematch.

Cervantes stopped Carlos Maria Giminez to take the vacant title, and made a further six defences. His championship career was ended by the remarkable Aaron Pryor, an ex-amateur star who fought like a throwback to Henry Armstrong. Pryor risked the title eight times, including two classic confrontations with Alexis Arguello of Nicaragua, who was bidding for his fourth world title. In December 1983 he relinquished the WBA title and accepted recognition from the IBF but after defending the championship twice he drifted away from boxing, battling unsuccessfully against a serious drugs problem. He had had 36 fights, winning them all, 33 inside the distance.

The WBA crown passed from Pryor to Johnny Bumphus, Gene Hatcher and Ubaldo Sacco, honest performers of no great distinction, to Patrizio Oliva

Below: *Cervantes records yet another knockout ... in all, 12 of his world title fights ended like this, and the Colombian is deservedly remembered as one of the division's greatest champions.*

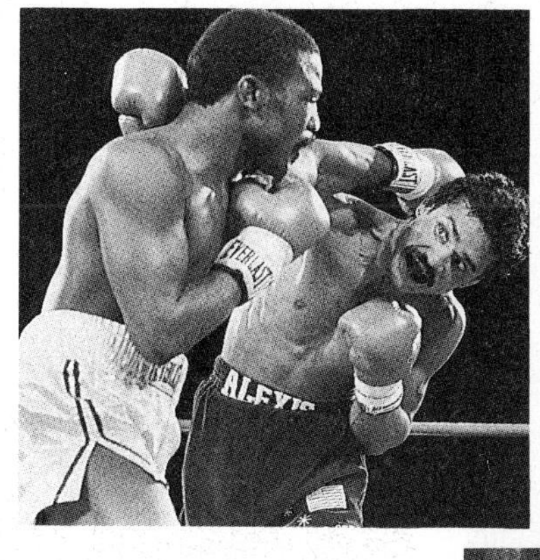

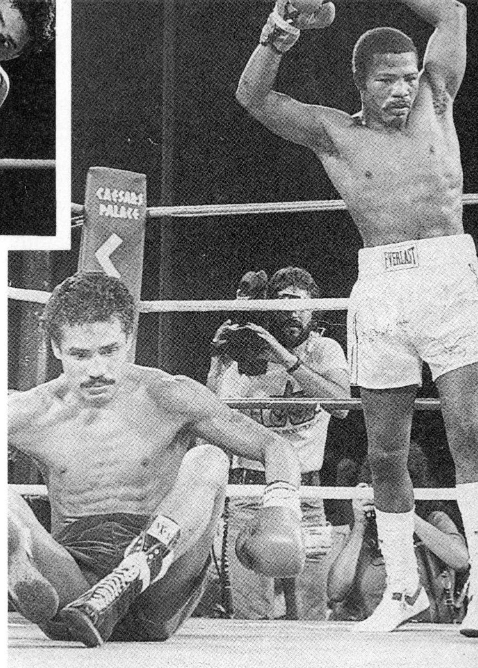

Aaron Pryor won two marvellous battles with Alexis Arguello (above and right), who was bidding for an unprecedented fourth world championship. But Pryor's career was derailed by a drugs problem, and he drifted away from the sport with a perfect 36–0 record.

of Italy. The former Olympic winner was unbeaten in 48 fights going into 1987.

Pedro Adigue of the Philippines outpointed Adolph Pruitt for the vacant WBC title in December 1968, lost a non-title rematch with Pruitt in five rounds two months later, and then scored a one-round win over Koichi Wajima – who went on to be a three-times world light-middleweight champion. Adigue was beaten in his first defence by Italy's Bruno Arcari, a tough southpaw who made nine defences and then relinquished the title because of weight problems. Arcari boxed on until 1978, retiring with a superb record of only two defeats in 73 fights – and one of the losses was on his professional debut.

Arcari was succeeded by another European, Perico Fernandez of Spain, but he managed only one successful defence before Saensak Muangsurin, a Thai kick-boxer who was having only his third Western-style fight, beat him in eight rounds.

Below: *There have been few better champions than Italian southpaw Bruno Arcari, who lost only twice in 73 fights.*

Right: *Johnny Bumphus had a superb amateur record, but lacked the ruggedness and durability for the pro game.*

Muangsurin was briefly inconvenienced by Fernandez' compatriot Miguel Velasquez, who took his title on a four-rounds disqualification in June 1976 but lost it back to him four months later. The Thai made another seven winning defences, including a 1977 points win over Saoul Mamby in Bangkok which was watched by a crowd of 35,000, a record for the division.

Muangsurin was the last WBC champion to command significant respect. He was beaten by Kim Sang Hyun of Korea in 1978, and the title since then has been held with varying degrees of authority by Saoul Mamby of New York (five successful defences); Leroy Haley of Las Vegas (two defences); Bruce Curry, elder of the two champion brothers from Fort Worth (two defences); Bill Costello of New York (three defences); Lonnie Smith of Denver (no successful defences); Rene Arredondo of Mexico, brother of the former junior lightweight champion Ricardo (no successful defences); and Tsuyoshi Hamada of Japan, who had made one successful defence up to 1987.

The IBF version passed from Pryor to Gary Hinton and then to Joe Louis Manley from Atlantic City. Manley was dethroned by Terry Marsh, a part-time fighter and full-time fireman, on an unforgettable night in March 1987. The stylish Marsh, an ex-Marine who won three ABA titles in five finals, battered the American to a tenth-round defeat in the improbable setting of a specially imported circus tent in Basildon, Essex.

After a hazy beginning and a couple of false starts, the division is here to stay – but this is not one of its more memorable eras, and it sorely needs a colourful champion of the quality of Cervantes or Pryor to boost its flagging prestige.

Saensak Muangsurin (above) *won the WBC title in only his third Western-style bout, after making his reputation in Thai kick-boxing. But he compiled an outstanding record that included nine successful defences. The Orient's standard is presently carried by Tsuyoshi Hamada of Japan* (right), *who holds the WBC title.*

HOW THE LIGHT-WELTERWEIGHT TITLE HAS CHANGED HANDS

1922 *The New York State Athletic Commission introduced junior welterweight division and Pinkey Mitchell was recognised as world champion by popular consensus of opinion*
21 Sep 26 Mushy Callahan w.pts.10 Pinkey Mitchell at Vernon, California
Jan 30 *Callahan was stripped of the title by the NBA after he had signed to defend against Jack 'Kid' Berg in London*
18 Feb 30 Jack 'Kid' Berg w.rtd.10 Mushy Callahan in London
23 Jan 31 Jack 'Kid' Berg w.pts.10 Goldie Hess in Chicago *(Berg won NBA recognition as champion)*
21 Mar 31 Tony Canzoneri w.ko.3 Jack 'Kid' Berg in Chicago *(Billed as a lightweight title defence by Canzoneri, but as both were within the light-welterweight limit that title was automatically at stake)*
18 Jan 32 Johnny Jadick w.pts.10 Tony Canzoneri in Philadelphia
20 Feb 33 Battling Shaw w.pts.10 Johnny Jadick at New Orleans
21 May 33 Tony Canzoneri w.pts.10 Battling Shaw at New Orleans
23 Jun 33 Barney Ross w.pts.10 Tony Canzoneri at Chicago *(Title fell into disuse)*
29 Apr 46 Tippy Larkin w.pts.12 Willie Joyce in Boston *(For revived title, as recognised by NY Commission and the NBA. Larkin made only one defence, and the title again fell into disuse)*
12 Jun 59 Carlos Ortiz w.rsf.2 Kenny Lane in New York *(for revived title)*
01 Sep 60 Duilio Loi w.pts.15 Carlos Ortiz in Milan
14 Sep 62 Eddie Perkins w.pts.15 Duilio Loi at Milan
15 Dec 62 Duilio Loi w.pts.15 Eddie Perkins at Milan *(Loi announced retirement in January, 1963)*
21 Mar 63 Roberto Cruz w.ko.1 Battling Torres in Los Angeles *(For vacant title)*
15 Jun 63 Eddie Perkins w.pts.15 Roberto Cruz at Manila
18 Jan 65 Carlos Hernandez w.pts.15 Eddie Perkins at Caracas
29 Apr 66 Sandro Lopopolo w.pts.15 Carlos Hernandez in Rome
30 Sep 67 Paul Fuji w.rtd.2 Sandro Lopopolo in Tokyo *(WBC stripped Fuji of title for failure to defend against their No. 1 challenger Pedro Adigue)*
12 Dec 68 Nicolino Loche w.rtd.9 Paul Fuji in Tokyo *(WBA title)*
14 Dec 68 Pedro Adigue w.pts.15 Adolph Pruitt in Manila *(Vacant WBC title)*
31 Jan 70 Bruno Arcari w.pts.15 Pedro Adigue in Rome
10 Mar 72 Alfonso Frazer w.pts.15 Nicolino Loche in Panama City
29 Oct 72 Antonio Cervantes w.ko.10 Alfonso Frazer in Panama City *(Bruno Arcari gave up WBC title due to weight-making difficulties.)*
21 Sep 74 Perico Fernandez w.pts.15 Lion Furuyama in Rome *(Vacant WBC title)*
15 Jul 75 Saensak Muangsurin w.rtd.8 Perico Fernandez in Bangkok
06 Mar 76 Wilfredo Benitez w.pts.15 Antonio Cervantes in San Juan
30 Jun 76 Miguel Velasquez w.dis.4 Saensak Muangsurin in Madrid
29 Oct 76 Saensak Muangsurin w.rsf.2 Miguel Velasquez at Segovia
Dec 76 *Benitez stripped of WBA title for failing to defend against Antonio Cervantes*
25 Jun 77 Antonio Cervantes w.rsf.5 Carlos Gimenez at Maracaibo *(Vacant WBA title)*
30 Dec 78 Kim Sang Hyun w.rsf.13 Saensak Muangsurin at Seoul
23 Feb 80 Saoul Mamby w.ko.14 Kim Sang Hyun in Seoul *(WBC title)*
02 Aug 80 Aaron Pryor w.ko.4 Antonio Cervantes in Cincinnati
26 Jun 82 Leroy Haley w.pts.15 Saoul Mamby at Cleveland
20 May 83 Bruce Curry w.pts.12 Leroy Haley at Las Vegas
1983 *Pryor relinquished his WBA title, but retained recognition by the IBF*
29 Jan 84 Bill Costello w.rsf.10 Bruce Curry at Beaumont, Texas
01 Jun 84 Gene Hatcher w.rsf.11 Johnny Bumphus at Buffalo, NY
21 Jul 85 Ubaldo Sacco w.rsf.9 Gene Hatcher at Campione D'Italia
21 Aug 85 Lonnie Smith w.ko.8 Bill Costello at Kingston, New York
Feb 86 *Aaron Pryor stripped of IBF title for failure to defend on time*
15 Mar 86 Patrizio Oliva w.pts.15 Ubaldo Sacco at Monte Carlo *(WBA title)*
26 Apr 86 Gary Hinton w.pts.15 Antonio Reyes Cruz at Lucca, Italy *(Vacant IBF title)*
05 May 86 Rene Arredondo w.ko.5 Lonnie Smith at Los Angeles *(WBC title)*
24 Jul 86 Tsuyoshi Hamada w.ko.1 Rene Arredondo at Tokyo
30 Oct 86 Joe Louis Manley w.ko.10 Gary Hinton at Hartford, Connecticut
04 Mar 87 Terry Marsh w.rsf.10 Joe Louis Manley at Basildon
04 Jul 87 Juan Martin Coggi w.ko.3 Patrizio Oliva at Ribera, Italy

LIGHTWEIGHTS

George 'Kid' Lavigne (left) *and Dick Burge* (below) *met for the title in 1896, Lavigne winning on a 17th-round knockout. Burge joined the British Army on the outbreak of the First World War, although he was then past 50, and served as a Sergeant until his death in an air raid in 1917.*

DICK ROCHE does not appear in any of the record books, but he played a significant role in the early history of the lightweight division. Roche was a gambler from St Louis who had a substantial financial interest in the outcome of the first international championship in this division, held at Revere, Massachusetts, on 16 November 1887.

Jack McAuliffe, who was born in Cork but fought out of New York, claimed the American title, and his fight with English champion Jem Carney of Birmingham was accepted on both sides of the Atlantic as being for the world title. As was the custom in those brutal days, it was a fight to the finish. In the 74th round, with McAuliffe fading fast and his principal backer Roche facing a heavy loss, the gambler made his historic intervention. He and his friends invaded the ring, forcing the referee to call the fight a draw.

The scandal was such that nine years elapsed before there was another fight for the world title, and when that took place the chances of a similar occurrence were non-existent: it was staged in that cathedral of propriety, the National Sporting Club (NSC) in London. Once again, it featured the American champion against his British counterpart – George 'Kid' Lavigne, a French-Canadian based in Michigan, against Dick Burge of London. Lavigne had started his career as a bare-knuckle fighter, but by 1896 had established himself as America's best lightweight with performances that included a 20-round draw with Young Griffo and a points win over Joe Walcott.

Lavigne met Burge at the NSC on 1 June 1896, and knocked him out in the 17th round of a gruelling fight. (Burge had a chequered career thereafter, spending a period in jail and, with his wife Bella, promoting shows at The Ring,

Blackfriars.) Lavigne made seven defences, losing eventually to Switzerland's only world title winner, Frank Erne of Zurich. Erne had drawn with Lavigne for the title in 1898, and his first defence against Jack O'Brien also ended all-square. Erne then retained his crown with a 12th-round retirement win over the Old Master, Joe Gans, when he split open a cut over the challenger's left eye. Gans bent double to signal his retirement.

Erne's subsequent career was erratic. He dropped his weight to 128 lb to meet the brilliant Terry McGovern but took a bad beating in three rounds, and then, in 1901, stepped up to welterweight to try for Rube Ferns' world title, this time being knocked out in the ninth round. When he gave Gans a rematch in May 1902, he lasted precisely 50 seconds.

Gans had served his apprenticeship in the savage 'Battle Royals' in his home town, Baltimore, when six fighters – almost invariably black – were put in the ring together and the last man standing was the winner. He was a boxer of rare genius, but like all the black fighters of the time was required to 'throw' contests which he could easily have won. His two-round loss to Terry McGovern in December 1900 was a particularly ill-executed fake, with Gans going down four times from crude and sometimes non-existent punches, and being pelted with newspapers and cigar stubs as he left the ring to the jeers of the furious fans.

But that ignominious episode was Gans' last defeat for almost eight years, during which time he became one of the finest ringmen of his generation, building a reputation that has endured. He dominated the division so thoroughly that his white rivals scuffled amongst themselves instead for the

Three great names from the division's early days: Frank Erne (below), *Joe Gans* (right) *and Ad Wolgast, pictured* (bottom) *squaring off with Anton Legrave before their 1911 title fight.*

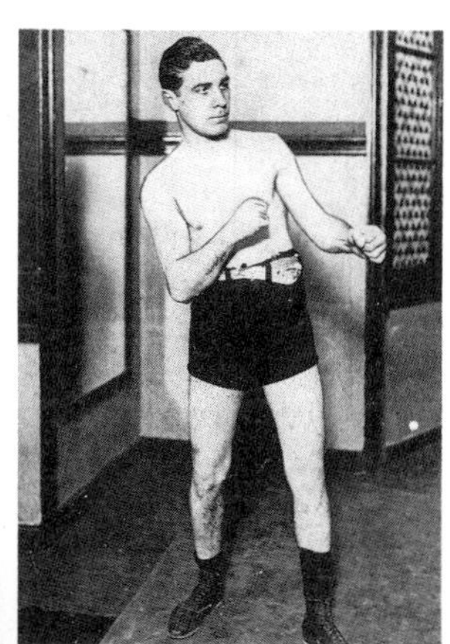

'White Lightweight Championship', which Jimmy Britt of San Francisco won by stopping Frank Erne in seven rounds in November 1902 and defended six times before losing to Gans in 1907.

By 1906, though, the strain of 15 years at the top was telling on the 32-year-old champion. He accepted an offer of $11,000 from Tex Rickard – staging his first promotion – to meet Battling Nelson, an aggresive, hard-hitting Dane, at Goldfield, Nevada. Although Gans was champion, the white challenger dictated the terms and his purse – $23,000 – was more than double Gans'. Nelson's manager, Billy Nolan, insisted that the champion make the division limit – then 133 lb – at the weigh-in at the ringside.

Battling Nelson (left) *was one of the toughest men ever to hold the lightweight title, as he proved in three memorable clashes with Joe Gans* (below).

Above: *The mining town of Goldfield, Nevada as it looked when Tex Rickard matched Gans with Nelson.*

Below: *Nelson kayoes Gans in the 17th round of their rematch, two years after their battle at Goldfield.*

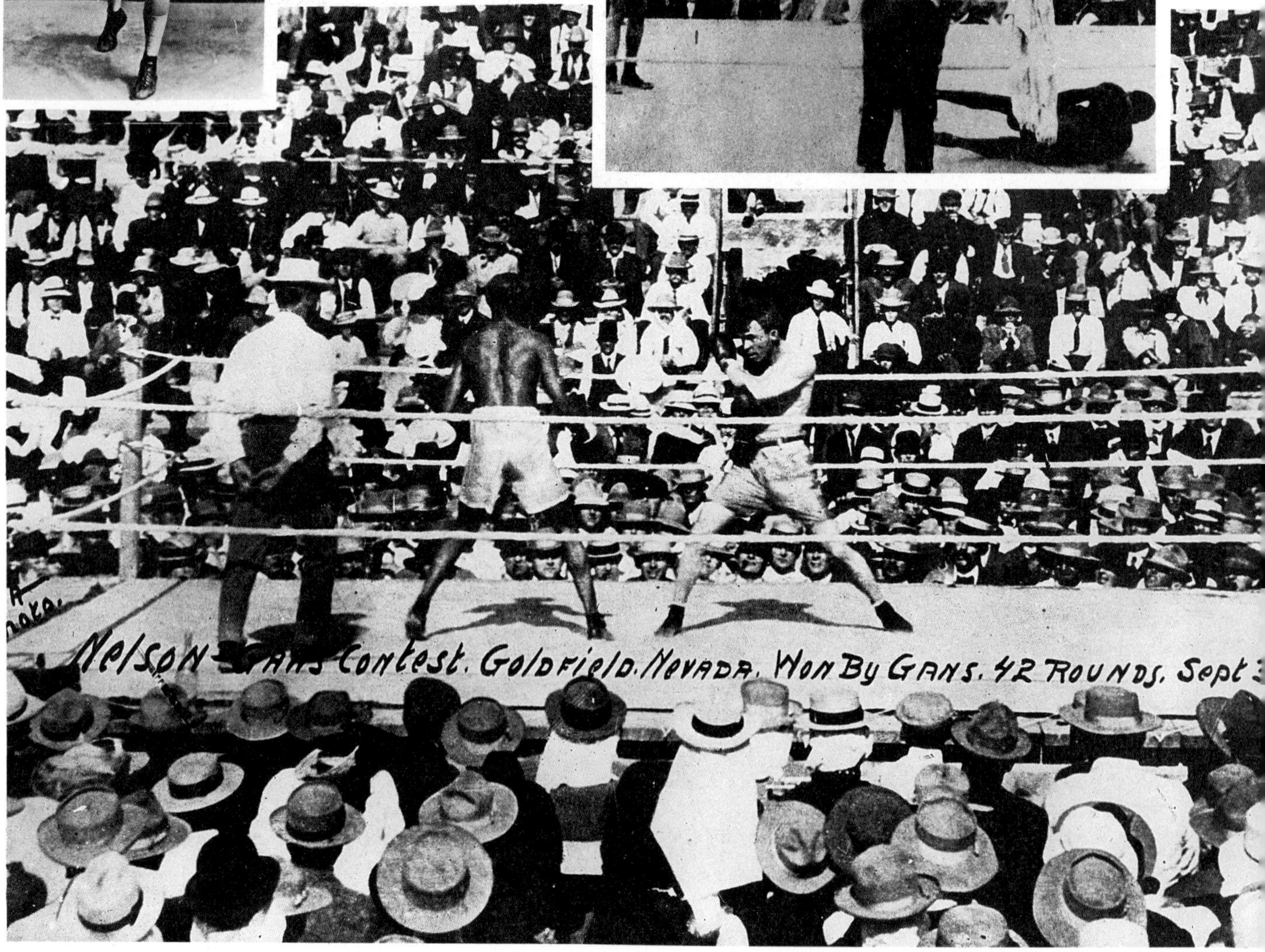

Boxing under a fierce Nevada sun, Gans outclassed the Dane for 32 rounds, but then in the 33rd broke his hand and was forced to try to hold off Nelson one-handed. Nelson pounded him in the body so severely that, at one point, Gans vomited over the top rope. Even under such difficulties Gans' skill was so consummate that, in the 42nd round, the increasingly frustrated Nelson deliberately hit him low and was disqualified.

Gans made four more successful defences, but he was living on borrowed time, and was already in the grip of the consumption that would eventually kill him.

Nelson finally got a second chance at the title in July 1908, and this time knocked Gans out in 17 rounds. They met for the third time two months later when Gans held the edge for 20 rounds, but was knocked out in the 21st. Less than two years later, he was dead.

Nelson, known as the 'Durable Dane', was born in Copenhagen on 5 June 1882. He was a savagely aggressive fighter who met his match in his third defence when Ad Wolgast, of Michigan, stopped

Ad Wolgast (above, *on the left, before his 13th-round win over Owen Moran) came out on top in perhaps the most savage lightweight fight of all time when he stopped Battling Nelson* (below) *in 40 rounds.*

The incredible finale to Wolgast's 'double knockout' defence against Mexican Joe Rivers.

him in the 40th round of a brawl that was so foul-filled that, in the seventh, Nelson asked the referee 'Don't we have any rules at all?' Although he fought on for another seven years, he never got a chance to regain the title.

Wolgast figured in the most controversial and sensational finish in boxing history when, in July 1912, in the 12th round of a thrilling battle with Mexican Joe Rivers, the pair connected simultaneously and scored a rare double knockdown. Referee Jack Welch helped Wolgast to his feet and, propping him up with one arm, counted out the prostrate challenger with the other. However, Wolgast's tendency to foul eventually cost him his title in November 1912, when Willie Ritchie (whom Wolgast had outfought in a no-decision affair a few months previously) beat him on a 16th-round disqualification.

British champion Freddie Welsh, from Pontypridd, was a leading contender who had boxed a 20-rounds draw at the NSC in 1910 against Packy McFarland of America, which was announced as a world title fight. He had also outpointed Ritchie in 1911, and so in British eyes had at least as good a claim to the title as the American.

Welsh outpointed Australia's Hughie Mehegan over 20 rounds at Olympia, London, three weeks after Ritchie's win over Wolgast, and was acclaimed in Britain as world champion. Ritchie made two impressive defences of his share of the

Rival title claimants Willie Ritchie (left) *and Freddie Welsh* (below) *were both stylish boxers, unlike their tearaway predecessors Nelson and Wolgast, and their championship unification match in London on 7 July 1914 lived up to the fans' expectations.*

Lloyd Honeyghan and Terry Marsh provided Britain with two unexpected world titles when Honeyghan (left) *pounded the hitherto-unbeatable Don Curry into sixth-round submission in Atlantic City, and Marsh* (below) *took the IBF light-welterweight title from Joe Louis Manley in a circus tent in Basildon.*
Following page: *Aaron Pryor and Alexis Arguello had two fierce battles for Pryor's WBA light-welterweight crown, with the black American winning them both.*

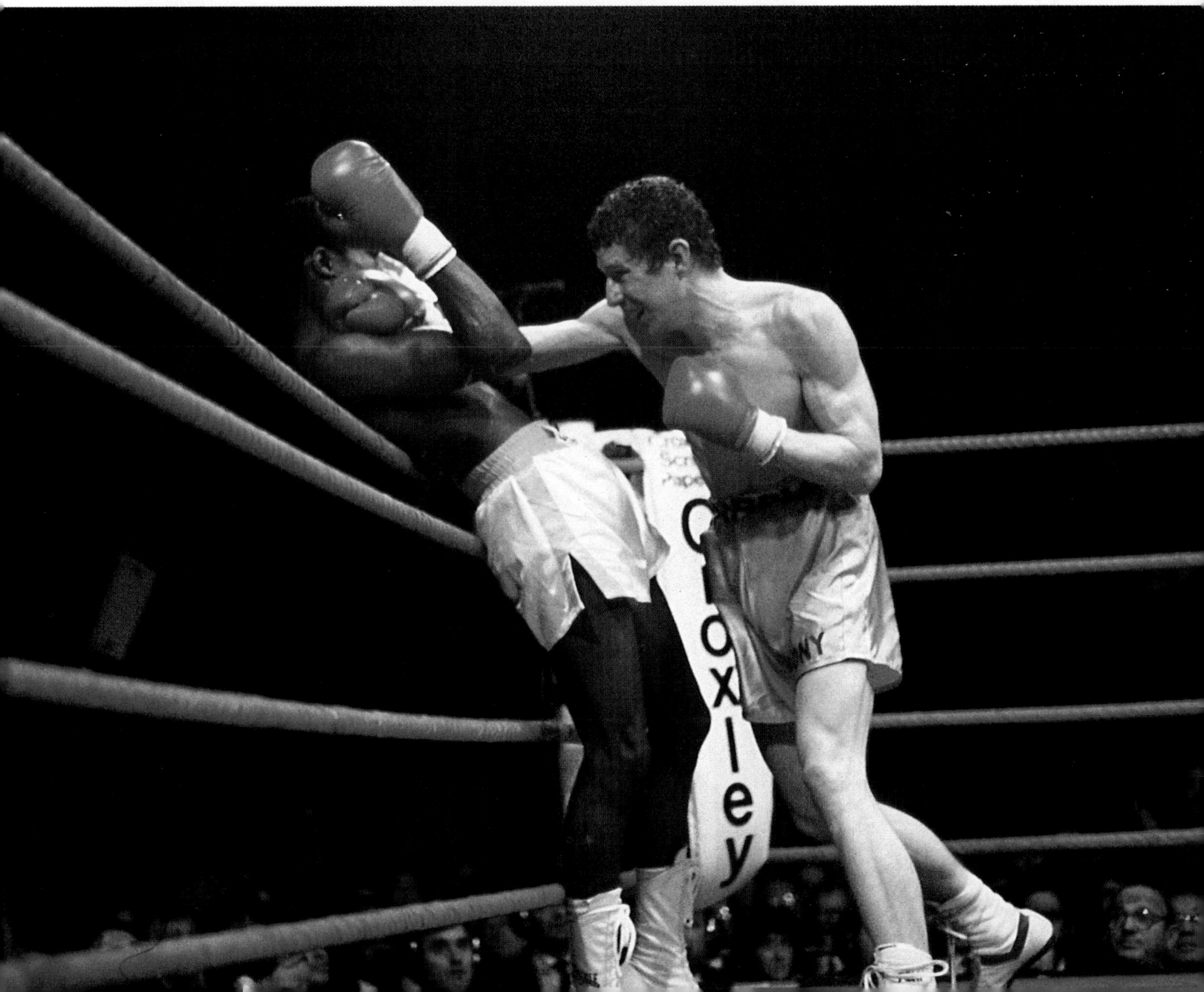

EVERLAST
OF TIME

Ritchie's win over the respected Harlem Tommy Murphy (left) *enhanced public interest in his title unification match with Welsh to the point where the trade paper* Boxing *(which still exists as* Boxing News*) produced a special souvenir poster* (below) *to mark the event.*

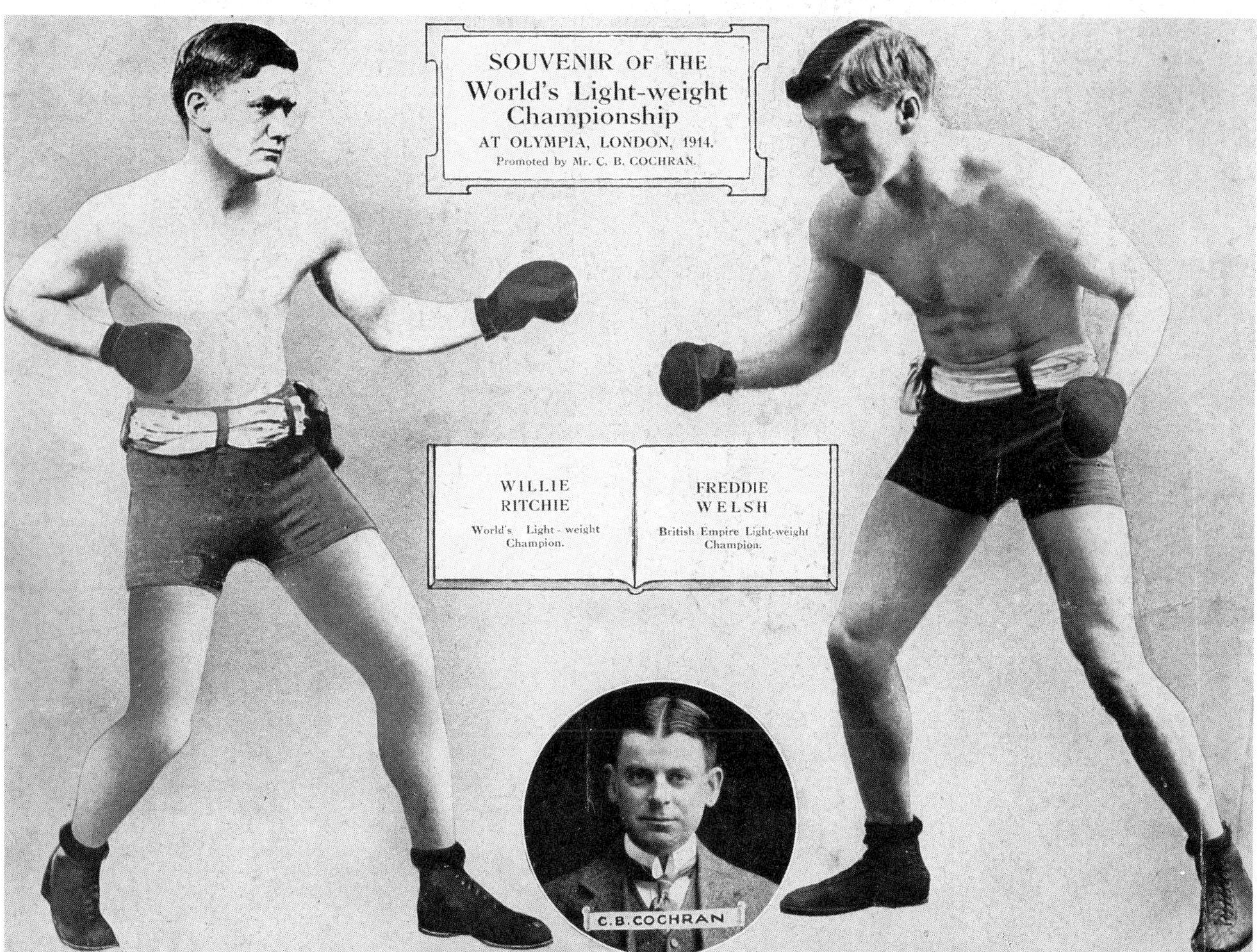

title, knocking out Joe Rivers and outpointing Harlem Tommy Murphy, and then, on 7 July 1914, met Welsh at Olympia for the undisputed title. It was the first universally accepted lightweight title fight to be contested at the modern poundage of 135 lb. The American limit had been 133 lb, but the NSC set the maximum at 135 lb in 1909, insisting that this weight should apply in future . . . and since Welsh became champion with a comfortable points

Welsh, although on the defensive here, comfortably outpointed the American to become the undisputed champion.

win, the Americans were in no position to argue.

Welsh's real name was Frederick Hall Thomas, but at his first six-rounder in Philadelphia, in 1905, he was merely announced as 'Freddie Welsh', since the MC could not be bothered to ascertain his correct name. By the end of his first year in the business, Welsh had boxed an astonishing 26 times and had reached 20-round main event status. He returned to Britain in 1907, and two years later won the first Lonsdale Belt by outpointing Johnny Summers for the British title, which he retained a year later with a famous disqualification victory over the other Welsh idol, Jim Driscoll. His world title win over Ritchie was, curiously, the last time that he was seen in a British

Freddie Welsh (left) *displaying the Lonsdale Belt which he retained with a famous defeat* (below) *of the other idol of Wales, Jim Driscoll (taking a count)*

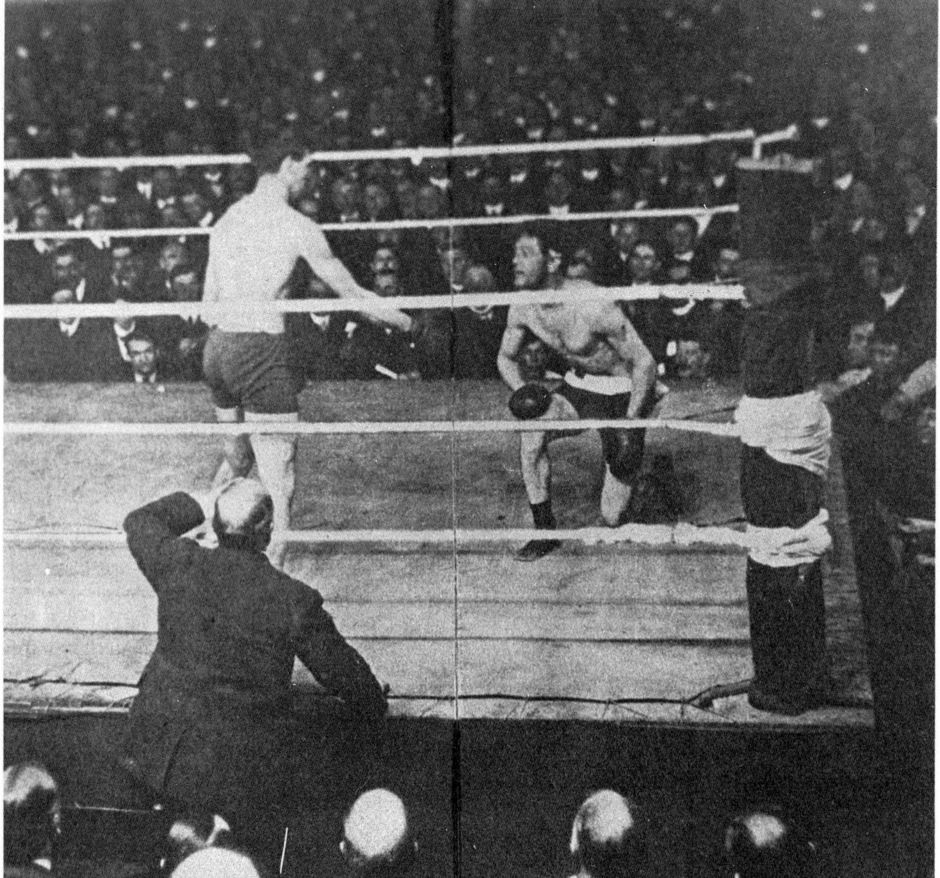

English-born Charlie White (top) *and Ad Wolgast* (above) *both failed to take the world title from the skilful Welsh.*

ring. He immediately went back to America where, although he met some outstanding fighters such as Wolgast, Joe Shugrue, Charlie White, and Ritchie again (in no-decision fights), he only actually defended the title twice. Wolgast was disqualified in the 11th round for repeated low blows, and the Liverpool-born White was out-pointed following a 30-minute interval when Welsh had been unable to continue after being hit low in the third round.

Welsh's career ended ingloriously in May 1917 when he was stopped in the ninth round by Benny Leonard, whom he had previously met twice in no-decision bouts. The beaten champion did not make a penny from the fight since his manager had bet the entire $4,000 purse on him.

Leonard is accepted as the greatest Jewish fighter of all time. He was a stylish and skilful ring-master whose dazzling footwork, precise timing, and hitting power had carried him into the Welsh fight on a run of four consecutive knockout victories, including a seventh-round win over Richie Mitchell, whose brother Pinkey was the first junior welterweight champion. Leonard went on to dominate the division as comprehensively as Gans had done a decade earlier. Between the Welsh fight in 1917 and his 13th-round disqualification against Jack Britton, in a welterweight title bid in June 1922, he boxed 79 times and was never beaten. Many, of course, were no-decision affairs but invariably the newspaper verdict – which was how bets were settled in these circumstances – favoured Leonard.

Leonard defended against the best challengers available – Johnny Kilbane, Charlie White (who floored him for 'nine'), Richie Mitchell, Rocky Kansas (twice), Joe Welling, and Lew Tendler (twice), quitting as unbeaten champion in January 1925. He had made a fortune, but lost the lot in the Wall Street Crash of 1929 and was forced to comeback, at 35.

Benny Leonard (left *and* below, *in the traditional pre-fight pose with Jack Britton) was the greatest Jewish boxer of all time, with an unbeaten run of 79 after taking the title from Freddie Welsh.*

Even at that advanced age Leonard was still good enough to stay unbeaten for 19 fights, until Jimmy McLarnin knocked him into permanent retirement in the sixth round in the old champion's 211th fight. He had lost just 20. Leonard became a respected referee, but died of a heart attack while officiating at a fight in St Nick's Arena, New York, on 18 April 1947.

He was succeeded by Jimmy Goodrich, who had surprisingly changed his name from James Edward Moran at a time when it was fashionable for non-Irish fighters to adopt Irish names. (His heavy weight contemporary Joseph Cukoschay, for example, is better remembered as Jack Sharkey.) Goodrich won his title in peculiar circumstances: boxing Stanislaus Loayza of Chile in the final of the New York Commission's tournament to fill the vacancy, Goodrich was presented with the title in the second round after Loayza had broken his ankle in the first and was unable to continue.

The new champion, who was managed by Freddie Welsh, held the title for only five months. He was outpointed in December 1925 by Leonard's old opponent Rocky Kansas, who was in the twilight of a long, 15-year career. Kansas won the title in his 161st fight, but retired on losing it four fights later, in Chicago, to Sammy Mandell. History has not been kind to Mandell. *Aficionados* recall Jimmy McLarnin and Tony Canzoneri with awe,

Leonard hit hard times after his retirement, and was forced to return to the ring. He was still good enough, at 35, to stay unbeaten for 19 fights before Jimmy McLarnin (left) *ended Benny's fabulous career with a sixth-round knockout* (below).

Rocky Kansas (right) *was only five fights away from retirement when he took the title from Freddie Welsh's protégé Jimmy Goodrich. Kansas quit after losing it to the under-rated Sammy Mandell* (below).

Al Singer (above) *occupies a curious spot in the record books: he is the only champion at any weight to have won and lost his title in the first round. Singer took it from Sammy Mandell, and lost to Tony Canzoneri* (below) *four months later.*

and rank them with the division's outstanding champions, yet Mandell beat them both, in title defences, outpointing McLarnin in 1928 and Canzoneri a year later. His reign ended abruptly when Al Singer of New York knocked him out in 106 seconds at the Yankee Stadium in July 1930.

Singer became the only champion ever to win *and* lose his title inside a round, when Canzoneri knocked him out in 66 seconds at Madison Square Garden four months later. Between the two title fights, Singer had taken a three-rounds beating from Jimmy McLarnin in a non-title match.

Canzoneri, who was born in the small town of Slidell, Louisiana, but boxed out of New York, had worked his way up through the divisions to star in them all. He had fought twice for the NBA

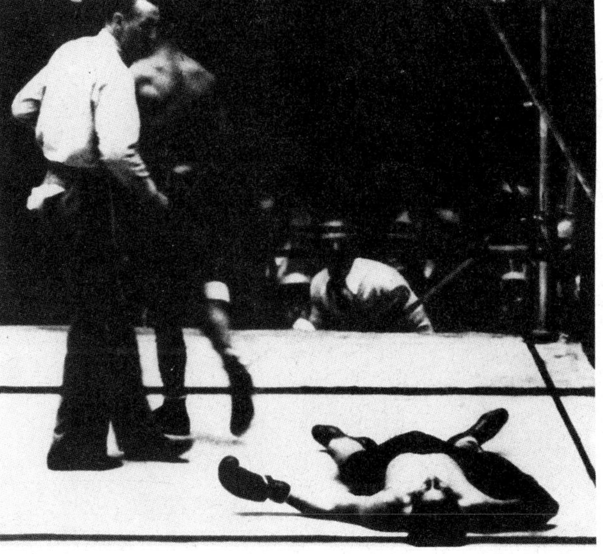

Tony Canzoneri (below) *and the all-action Londoner Jack 'Kid' Berg* (right) *met three times, twice in contests involving both the lightweight and junior welterweight titles. Berg took a 10-round decision over him in January 1930, but Canzoneri won the two that mattered.*

bantamweight title in 1927, drawing with and being outpointed by Bud Taylor, and had won the vacant featherweight championship later that year by outpointing Johnny Dundee. He moved up to lightweight after Andre Routis took his 9 st (126 lb) title in September 1928, and in December 1928 he boxed a ten-rounds draw with Al Singer to establish himself as a contender in that division also. His first challenge for the lightweight title failed when Mandell outpointed him in Chicago, but he stayed in contention despite losing to Jack 'Kid' Berg and Billy Petrolle. His second chance, against Singer in November 1930, he took spectacularly.

When he kayoed 'Kid' Berg in three rounds in his first defence in April 1931, he became a dual world champion, taking Berg's junior welterweight title. For the rest of the year he kept both titles active, risking the junior welterweight crown twice and having two other contests, with Berg and the reigning junior lightweight champion Kid Chocolate, in which both titles were at stake. Eventually he lost the junior welterweight title to Johnny Jadick in 1932, but he regained it from Battling Shaw a year later and also reversed one of his rare defeats by outpointing Billy Petrolle in a lightweight defence in November 1932.

Canzoneri's first spell as lightweight champion was ended by Barney Ross, who outpointed him in Chicago in June 1933 to take both his titles, and he repeated the result with a 15-rounds win in New York three months later. But Canzoneri kept himself

Canzoneri (above, *outpointing Jimmy McLarnin and* below, *outscoring Leo Rodak) lost the lightweight title to Barney Ross* (left), *seen blocking a left from Billy Petrolle on the way to a points win over the 'Fargo Express'.*

firmly in the championship picture with wins over class men like Frankie Klick, Kid Chocolate, Baby Arizmendi, Leo Rodak and Eddie Zivic, so that when Ross relinquished the title in 1934 to concentrate on the welterweight division, Canzoneri regained it by beating his one-time sparring partner Lou Ambers, from Herkimer, New York.

This was the first in a series of three meetings between the pair. Canzoneri retained the cham-

pionship against Al Roth, but then was outpointed by Ambers in Madison Square Garden in September 1936 and again, in a final championship meeting, in May 1937. It was Canzoneri's 22nd title fight, spanning four weight divisions, and it was his last appearance in big-time boxing. He fought 23 more times, losing five, and retired after his only knockout in 175 contests, when Al 'Bummy' Davis left-hooked him to defeat in three rounds in November 1939.

Ambers (real name Luigi D'Ambrosio) was one of ten children born to first-generation Italian immigrants who had settled in New York. He had a whirlwind style, developed in 136 semi-professional 'bootleg' fights before making his official debut in 1932. Two years later Al Weill, who later guided Rocky Marciano to the heavyweight championship, became Ambers' manager and, within 12 months, got him his first chance at the world title.

Although he was floored three times on the way to a painful points defeat by his one-time employer, Canzoneri, he stayed unbeaten in his next 14 fights against opponents of the calibre of Fritzie Zivic (the future welterweight champion), Klick, and Arizmendi. By the time he got his rematch with Canzoneri he was, at 22, in his prime. Ambers easily outpointed the veteran, but his form slumped inexplicably on becoming champion. He won only one of his next four outings, being beaten by Eddie Cool and Jimmy McLarnin and held to a draw by Enrico Venturi, but he was still too young for Canzoneri in their final meeting, taking a

Lou Ambers (left) *once worked as a sparmate for Tony Canzoneri, but later trounced his one-time boss in two world title fights* (below). *He also retained the championship on a split decision over Pedro Montanez* (above, on the right), *a Puerto Rican who had never lost in 61 fights.*

The amazing Henry Armstrong (above) *already held the featherweight and welterweight titles when he took Ambers' lightweight championship on a split decision* (below) *and completed an historic treble. Armstrong's achievement can never be equalled, as modern rules require a man winning a second title to relinquish one or the other. None of Armstrong's titles were at the 'in-between' weights, a remarkable feat.*

convincing points win.

Three fights later Ambers retained the title on Mike Jacobs' famous Carnival of Champions show at the Polo Grounds, New York, in September 1937, when in one of four title fights on the same promotion he won a split decision over Pedro Montanez. The Puerto Rican had beaten Ambers in a non-title fight in April 1937, and was unbeaten in 61 fights. Ambers' purse was $82,500, the highest ever paid to a lightweight.

In August 1938 he lost the title to the history-making Henry Armstrong, who thereby became the only man ever to hold three world championships simultaneously (he already ruled the featherweight and welterweight divisions). Ambers survived two knockdowns to hold Armstrong to a split decision with scores of 8-6-1, 7-6-2, and 7-8 (in rounds). They were rematched 370 days later, and 30,000 fans came to Yankee Stadium to watch Armstrong, fighting with uncharacteristic disregard for the rules, hit Ambers low so often that he was penalized five of the first 11 rounds.

Ambers, with that sort of advantage, was a unanimous points winner, thereby snapping Armstrong's unbeaten run at 46. In April 1940 Ambers was under pressure from the NBA to defend against their leading contender Davey Day of Chicago, whom he had outpointed three years

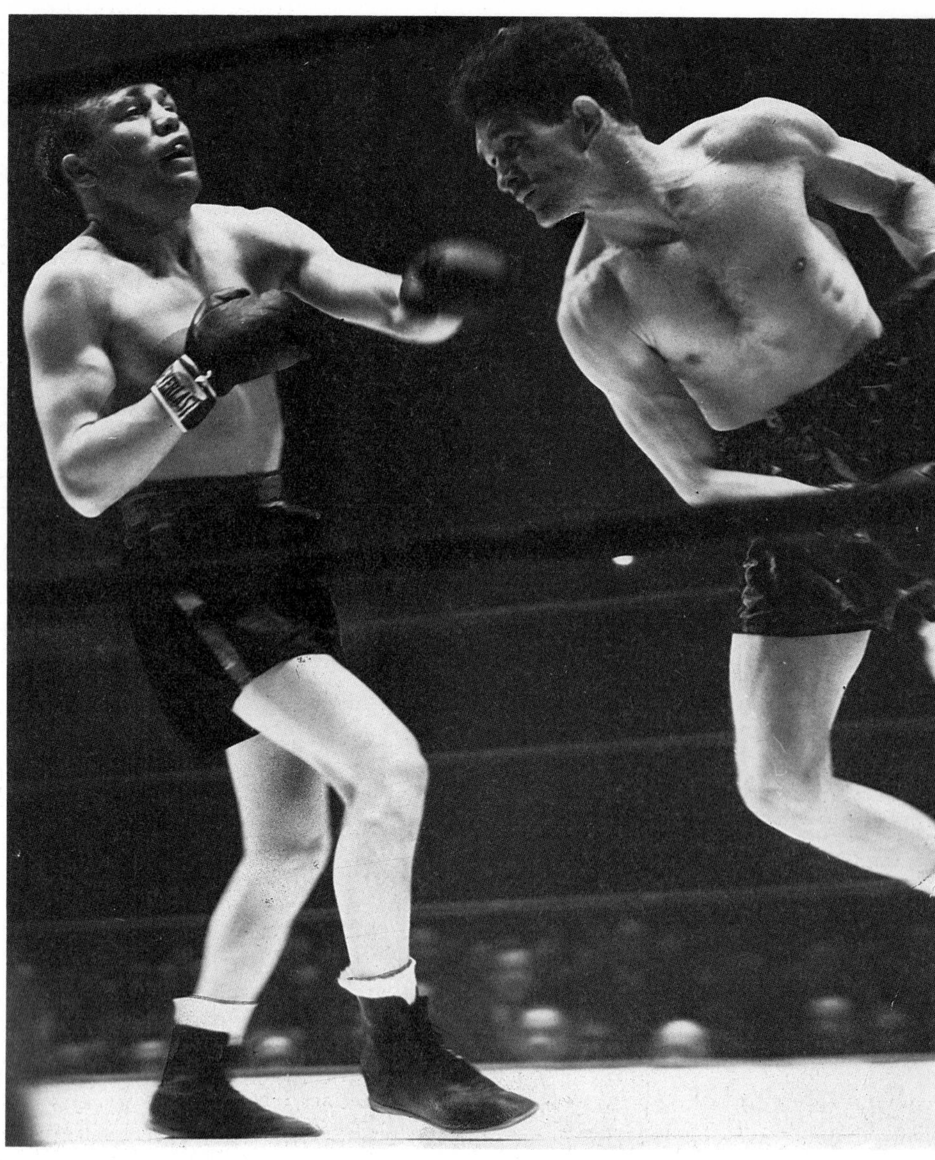

The lightweight division started the 1940s with a split at the top: Sammy Angott (above) *won the vacant NBA version of the title, while the unpredictable Texan Lew Jenkins* (right, *on the right) took the remainder from Lou Ambers exactly a week later, on 10 May.*

previously. When Ambers refused to meet him the NBA took away his title, and matched Day with Sammy Angott of Washington. Angott won the vacant title, on points, in May 1940.

Meanwhile Ambers agreed to defend against an erratic, eccentric Texan, with the 'Good Ol' Boy' name of Elmer Verlin Jenks, who boxed as Lew Jenkins. He was wildly undisciplined, with a weakness for drink and women that was matched only by his reluctance to train. His poor condition cost him 12 inside-the-distance defeats in 107 contests, but of his 63 victories 46 were achieved inside the distance. Ambers, too, fell victim to Jenkins' punching, taking five counts on the way to a three-round defeat at Madison Square Garden in May 1940.

Ambers was overwhelmed by Jenkins' fierce hitting, and was floored five times in three rounds.

Two months after winning the title Jenkins was in the ring with Henry Armstrong in a battle of champions, but the welterweight king stopped him in six rounds. He then outpointed future champion Bob Montgomery in a non-title fight, and stopped Pedro Lello in two rounds in his first defence, but in December 1941 Angott easily outpointed him to become the undisputed champion. Jenkins won only one of his subsequent ten fights, and retired at the end of 1942. He returned to action in 1946 and fought on for another four years, quitting for good after successive defeats by Carmen Basilio and Beau Jack.

Angott was an unexciting performer, whose nickname 'The Clutch' was an accurate reflection of his style. He defended the undisputed title once, surviving a knockdown to take a split decision over Allie Stolz in 1942, and then surprisingly announced his retirement on 13 November 1942.

Below: *Free-swinging Jenkins attacks Fritzie Zivic, who stopped him in 10 rounds in 1942 after drawing with him two years earlier.*

Right: *Jenkins does not look like a winner here, but he recovered to stop Pedro Lello in two rounds in his only successful defence.*

Sammy Angott's nickname was 'The Clutch', and Beau Jack found out why when they fought a mauling draw in 1944 (above). *Jack's fights were usually much more exciting affairs, like this points win over Willie Joyce* (below) *in 1945 and he was particularly popular at Madison Square Garden.*

The title divided again: New York recognized Beau Jack, a former shoe-shine boy from Georgia, after his three-round knockout of Tippy Larkin in December 1942, but the state of Maryland – hardly a major force in world boxing – recognized Luther 'Slugger' White, who outpointed Willie Joyce of Indiana in January 1943. (The two losers went on to meet in 1946 for the revived junior welterweight title, with Larkin twice outpointing Joyce.)

Jack was a crowd-pleaser who rapidly became a favourite at Madison Square Garden, where he had more main events than anyone else. He grossed $1.5 million, a vast amount in those days, but lost the lot. When last heard of he was, ironically, once more working as a shoe-shine boy in the same Miami hotel that had employed him all those years before.

Jack, whose real name was Sidney Walker, was beaten five months later by Bob Montgomery, a stylish, fast-handed boxer from South Carolina. He

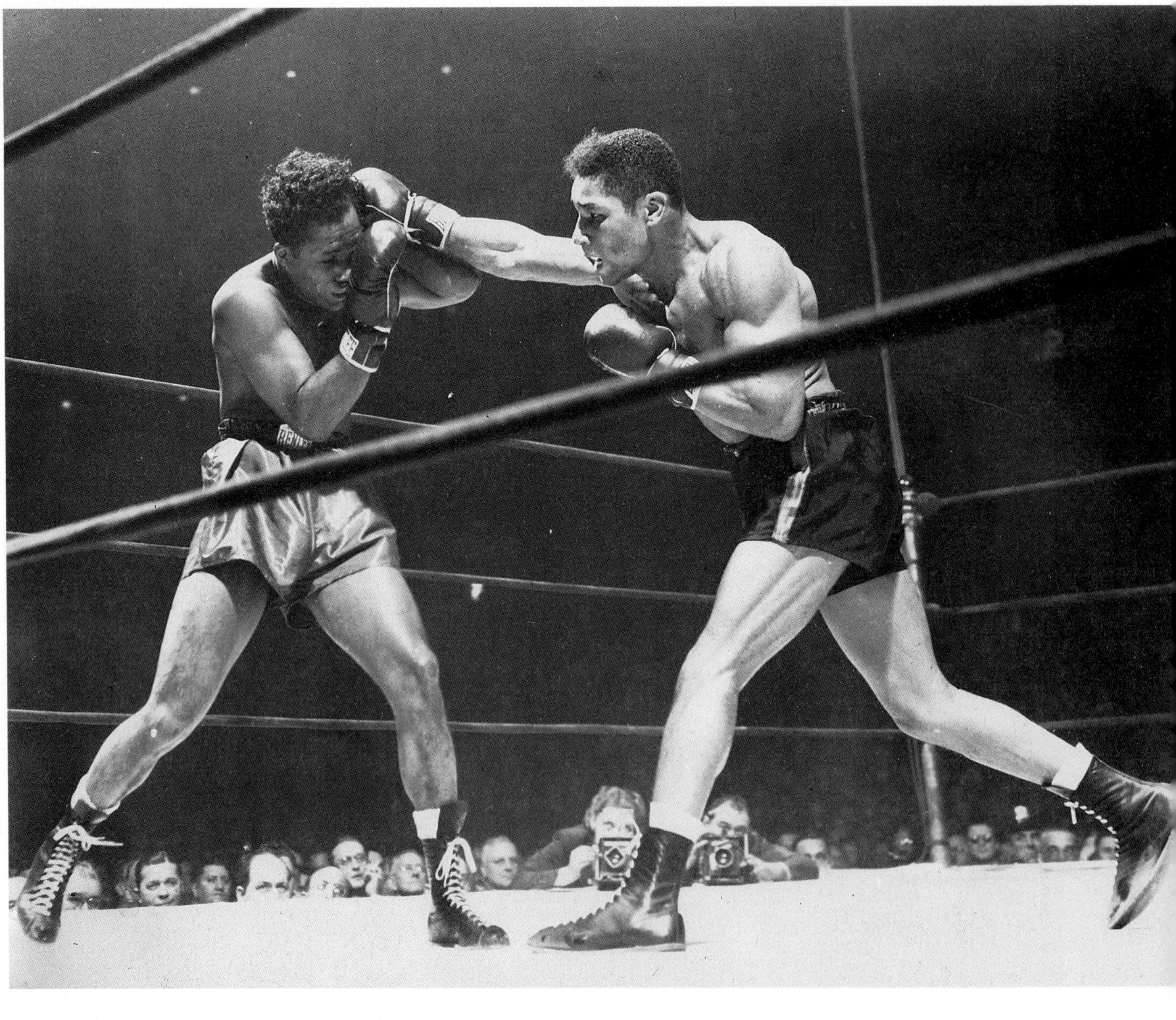

In his prime, Beau Jack grossed $1.5m, a phenomenal figure for the 1940s ... but the good times were sadly short-lived.

The one-time shoe-shine boy back working in the same hotel that had employed him nearly 50 years previously.

regained the title from Montgomery in November 1943, but lost it to him in their third meeting in March 1944. They met for the fourth time in August 1944 and, although Jack won the ten-rounder on points, the title was not at stake. In all, these bitter rivals boxed 55 rounds.

Montgomery made two defences in 1946, knocking out Allie Stolz in 13 rounds, and then reversing a surprise two-round, non-title loss to Wesley Mouzon by kayoing him in eight rounds in November 1946. Nine months later he faced Ike Williams for the undisputed title.

Bob Montgomery (left) *knocked out Ike Williams* (right) *in 1944. When they met again three years later they were both world champions, and Williams' sixth-round kayo victory reunified the title.*

Williams, from Brunswick, Georgia, had become NBA champion through a line of succession reaching back to October 1943. Angott, realizing that his original retirement decision had been hasty and ill-advised, reclaimed at least the NBA half of the championship by outpointing the Maryland

entrant, Slugger White, in Los Angeles. However, he was beaten five months later by Juan Zurita, the first Mexican holder of the lightweight title. Zurita was in the veteran stage, becoming champion in his 130th fight, and he retired after Williams had knocked him out in two rounds in his first defence, in Mexico City, in April 1945.

The new champion, whose family had moved north when he was a boy, had been fighting professionally since he was 16 years old. He had suffered his share of setbacks, notably a 12th-round knockout by Bob Montgomery in 1944, but he came back from that with wins over Sammy Angott (twice), Slugger White, Freddie Dawson, and many of the other leading lightweights of the period. He defended the title twice in 1946, stopping Enrique Bolanos in eight rounds in Los Angeles, and (in the first NBA title fight to be staged in Britain) knocking out the Welshman Ronnie James in nine rounds at Ninian Park, Cardiff.

Williams' sixth-round victory over Montgomery at Philadelphia on 4 August 1947 reunited the championship, and he kept a firm grip on it for the next four years, turning back challenges from Enrique Bolanos (twice), Beau Jack, Jesse Flores, and Freddie Dawson. He was dethroned in the 137th fight of an 11-year career when, drained by the effort of losing 21 lb to make the lightweight limit, he was floored and stopped in 14 rounds by yet another product of the Deep South – Jimmy Carter from Aiken, South Carolina.

Carter was a competent but unfashionable fighter. His title win attracted the smallest crowd ever to attend a championship fight in Madison Square Garden, with just 3,594 fans paying a mere $13,260. Carter's purse was precisely $3,627.63, and without television revenue it would have been $1,377.63. Having spent most of his career in the New York area, Carter now departed for the West Coast as champion and at last started to earn what he was worth. He defeated perennial title challenger Enrique Bolanos (in a non-title fight), and then lost on points to the biggest drawing card in California, the colourful Art Aragon. They were rematched for the title three months later, in November 1951, and this time the Los Angeles crowd paid $109,463. Carter won on points, and earned his biggest purse, $32,000. Five months later he went back to California to defend his title, when he outpointed a rugged Mexican, Lauro Salas, but six weeks later the championship changed hands in a rematch.

They met for a third time in Chicago in October of that year, and once again Carter had the sad distinction of attracting the smallest championship crowd on record to the Chicago Stadium – 5,283.

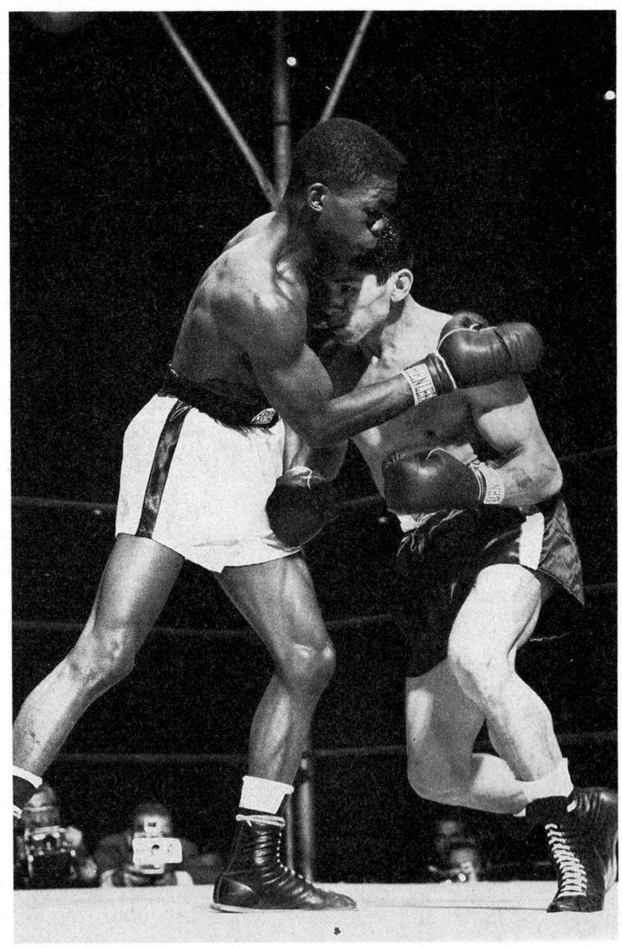

Jesse Flores (above, *on the right) lasted into the 10th round in this 1948 challenge for Ike Williams' title but was floored six times.*

Jimmy Carter (below, *on the right) took 13 rounds to catch up with the elusive George Araujo in a title defence in 1953.*

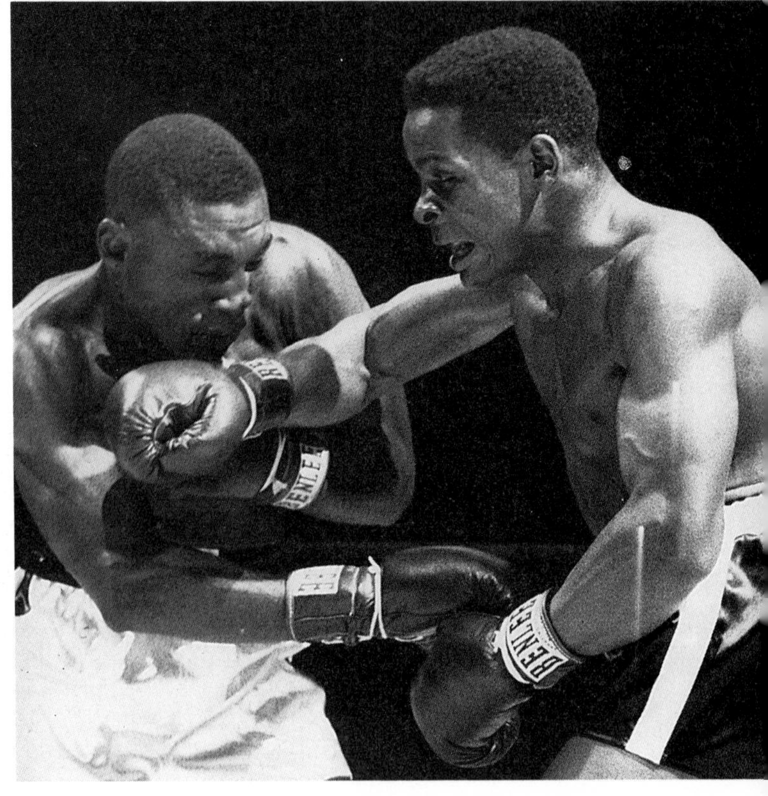

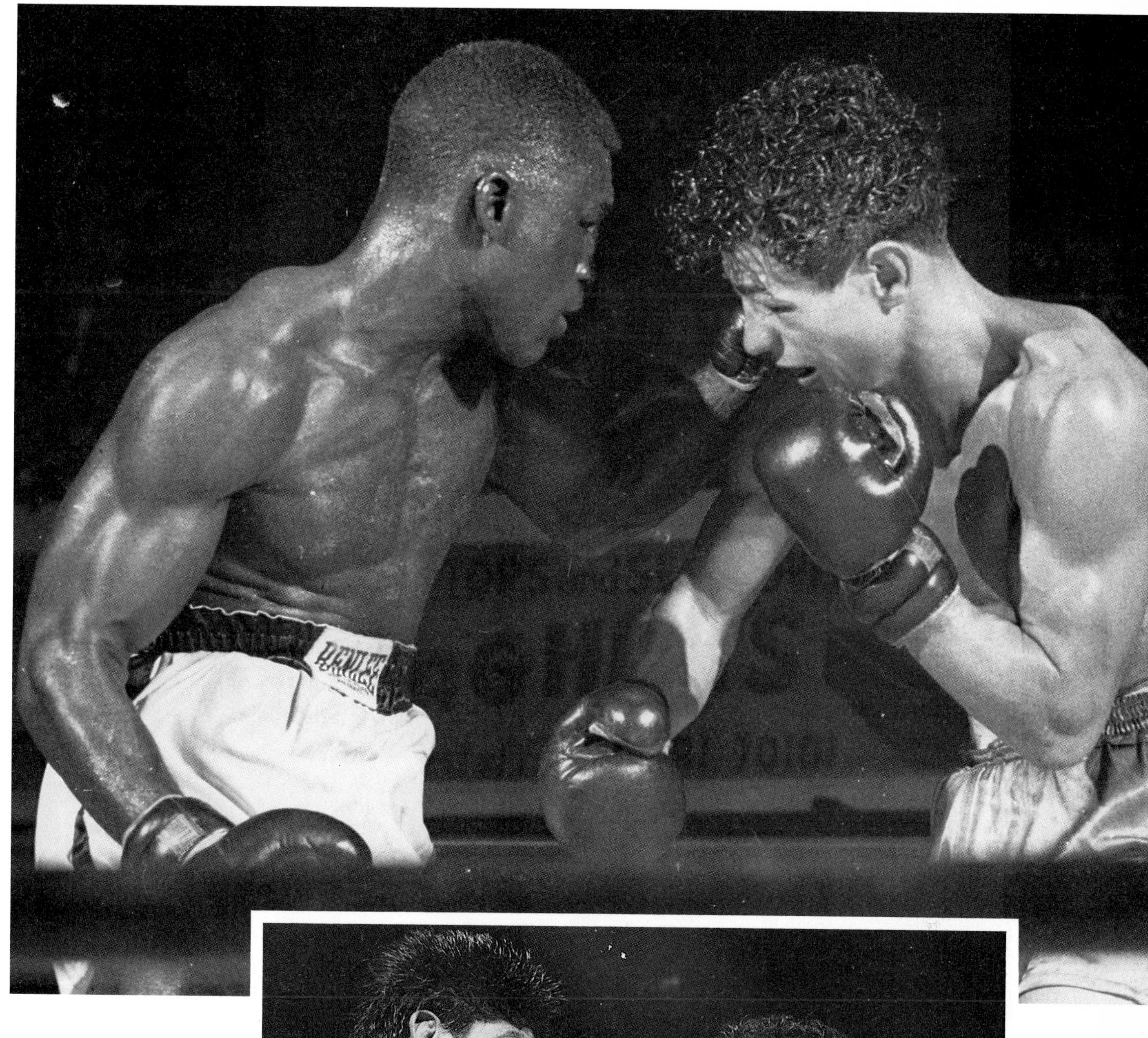

California produced a crop of colourful lightweights in the 1950s, notably Art Aragon (above, in a losing title bid against Carter) and Lauro Salas, who won and lost the title against Carter and, four months after becoming an ex-champion, was outscored in New York by Pat Marcune (below, on the right).

Carter (below) *was an in-and-out performer who was capable of disappointing displays such as this title loss to Lauro Salas* (right) *or surprisingly easy victories, like this knockout of his former conqueror Armand Savoie* (bottom).

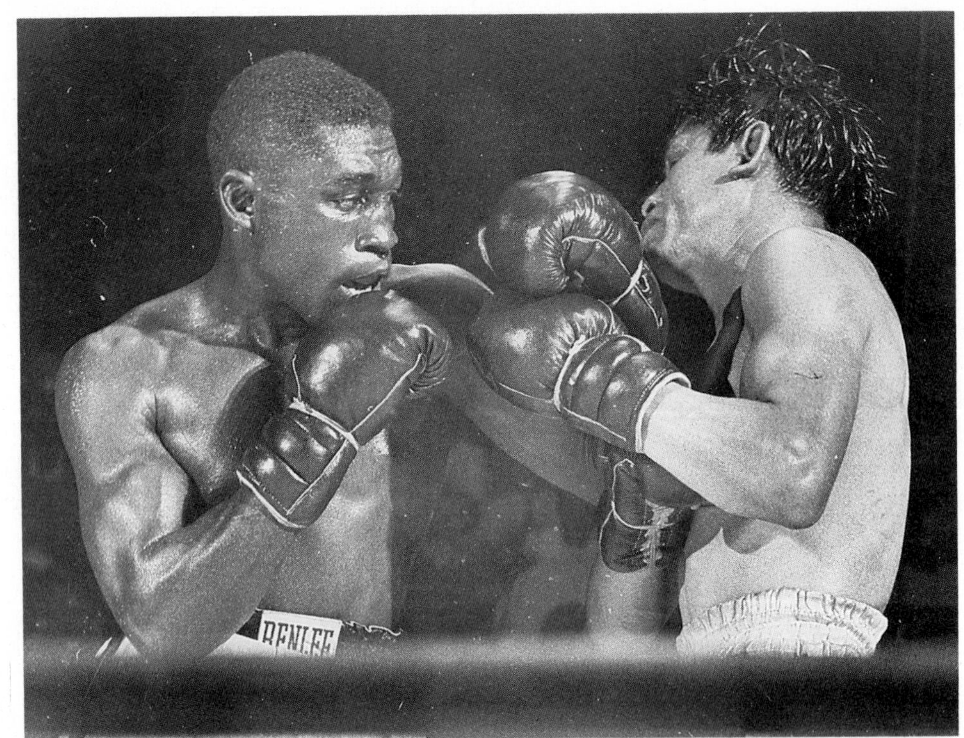

But Carter regained the title on an easy 15-round decision and, after 79 fights, had long since become resigned to the public's indifference to his talents. He was thought to be ready for the taking when he defended against Tommy Collins, a white Irish-American crowd-puller from Boston in April 1953. The champion was without a win in his last three fights, while Collins was unbeaten. But Carter outclassed his over-matched challenger, flooring him ten times in four savage rounds, and four months later the veteran again upset the odds by knocking out George Araujo in 13 rounds.

Wallace 'Bud' Smith (above) *ended Carter's interest in the championship by beating him twice in 1955* (below), *recording points wins in Boston and Cincinnati.*

After another easy victory, over the Canadian Armand Savoie (who had beaten him in a non-title fight), Carter was surprisingly dethroned by Paddy DeMarco from Brooklyn, a fighter with an inconsistent record who had won only six of his 13 fights prior to meeting Carter. But the title was only on loan to the New York Italian, for Carter stopped him in the 15th round of their San Francisco rematch in November 1954. DeMarco won only six of his remaining 22 fights.

Carter's luck finally ran out when Wallace 'Bud' Smith beat him on a close decision in Boston, in June 1955, and when Smith repeated the result in November of that year Carter's championship days were over. Smith, like DeMarco, had a decidedly modest record and ended his career with only 31 wins in 60 fights. He lost the title in his first defence to the best champion since the glory days of Ross and Canzoneri – Joe Brown of New Orleans. Brown had, with self-deprecating humour, chosen the nickname 'Old Bones' in tribute to his

Left: *Ralph Dupas failed in this attempt on Joe Brown's lightweight title, but later won the light-middleweight title.*

Above: *Joey Lopes (right) held Joe Brown to a draw in August 1957, but was stopped in a rematch.*

professional longevity. He had turned professional in 1943, had a solitary fight, and then retired for two and a half years before resuming his career in 1946. For the next decade he met the best that the lightweight and welterweight divisions could offer, but although his long record showed wins over men of the quality of Arthur King, Arthur Persley (twice), Teddy 'Red Top' Davis, Virgil Akins (twice) Isaac Logart, and 'Bud' Smith himself, he was past 30 before he finally got his chance at the title.

No one expected the veteran to hold it for long, but over the next six years he made a remarkable 12 defences. He risked the title, in the old tradition, wherever there was a payday. Frequently, as against Kenny Lane, Ralph Dupas, or Dave Charnley (whom he twice beat) the challenger was the favourite to win, but Brown, a marvellously

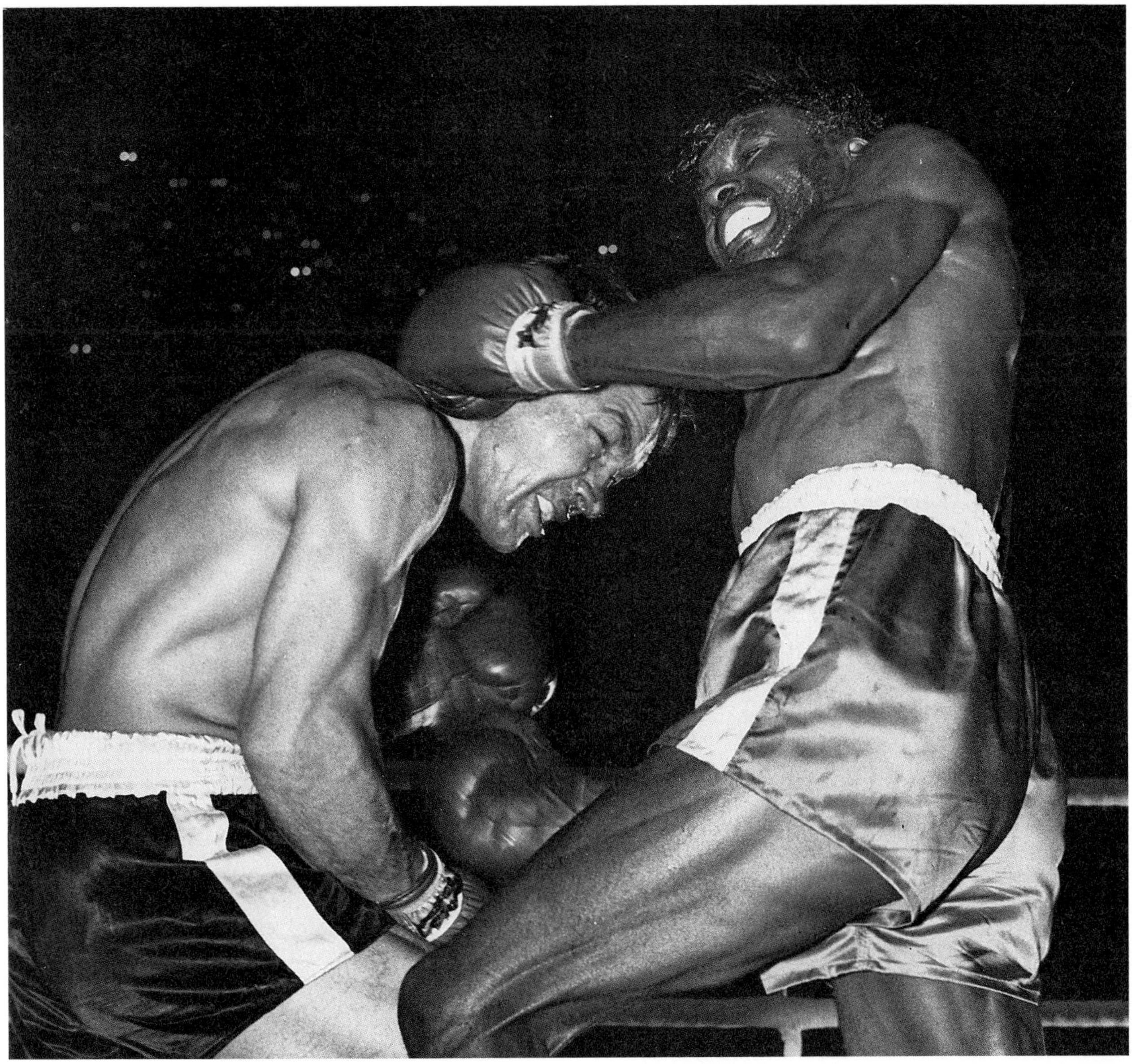

Above: *Brown came close to defeat against Englishman Dave Charnley, one of the best lightweights of his time.*

Right: *Carlos Ortiz won 14 of the 15 rounds when he ended Brown's long championship reign.*

clever performer with a stinging right, always managed to pull out that intangible extra that separates the champions from the challengers. But advancing years, as much as the unquestioned ability of his opponent Carlos Ortiz, finally ended his superb championship reign in Las Vegas, in April 1962. Ortiz, a New York-based Puerto Rican, won a massive points victory, and although the amazing Brown fought on until April 1970 – when he was 44 years old – he lost 23 of his remaining 45 fights.

Ortiz, who had won and lost the 140 lb championship, risked his title in Tokyo, Puerto Rico, and Manila against tough opponents such as Doug Vailliant, Flash Elorde (the marvellous junior lightweight champion) and his former junior welter-weight title opponent, Kenny Lane (who had been briefly recognized as world champion by his home state of Michigan, after outpointing Paul Armstead over 15 rounds at Saginaw, on 19 August 1963). Ortiz was dethroned on a split decision by a speedy, smart-boxing Panamanian called Ismael Laguna in Panama City in April 1965, but he regained the title with a unanimous win in Puerto Rico seven months later.

Ortiz went on to defend the title five times, although for a brief period the WBC withdrew recognition from him after a controversial and confused fight with the former featherweight champion, Sugar Ramos of Cuba. They met at Mexico City on 22 October 1966, when referee Billy Conn (the former light-heavyweight champion) stopped the fight in the fifth round with Ramos cut on the left eyelid. The crowd rioted and Ramon Velasquez, the WBC Secretary, ordered Ortiz to return to the ring to resume the fight. When he quite rightly refused to do so, Velasquez declared Ramos the new champion. Two days later the WBC President, Luis Spota, announced that the title was now vacant and ordered a rematch. This duly took

Ortiz proved an outstanding champion, retaining the title against worthy challengers like Doug Vailliant (above) *and Flash Elorde* (left) *before losing it for the first time to Ismael Laguna* (below, *on the left, outpointing Rafiu King of Nigeria in Paris in 1963).*

place in Mexico City (the Cuban's adopted hometown) on 1 July 1967, and this time Ortiz won easily in four rounds to regain universal recognition.

The Puerto Rican's long reign ended in June 1968, when Carlos 'Teo' Cruz of the Dominican Republic took a unanimous points decision in Santo Domingo. Cruz was a journeyman professional whose record was spotted with losses. He made only one successful defence, outpointing the colourful Californian Mando Ramos in Los Angeles in September 1968, but was stopped in 11 rounds in a rematch in February 1969 with a badly cut left eye. Cruz won four more fights to put himself in line for a third meeting with Ramos, but then on 15 February 1970 he was tragically killed in an air crash, along with his wife and two children.

The 20-year-old Ramos, the division's youngest champion, was also destined for a short reign. He retained the title once, knocking out the Japanese Yoshiaki Numata in six rounds, but was then forced to retire after nine rounds with cuts over both eyes

Above: *Ismael Laguna faced Ortiz three times for the title, winning the first but losing the other two, all being points decisions.*

Below: *There have been few more exciting champions than Mando Ramos (left), but Carlos Cruz was too good in this 1968 clash.*

against the Panamanian, Ismael Laguna. Laguna, likewise, managed one defence, stopping Ishimatsu Suzuki in 13 rounds in Panama, but on 16 September 1970 the WBA stripped him of his title for failing to honour a contract for a Los Angeles rematch with Ramos. The WBA, however, did approve a match between Laguna and the lightly regarded (at least on the American side of the Atlantic) Ken Buchanan for the title. On 26 September the Edinburgh stylist scored a brilliant split-decision victory in the afternoon heat in San Juan, Puerto Rico, to become Britain's first world lightweight champion since Freddie Welsh.

But since Britain was not at that time affiliated to the WBA, Buchanan was not accepted as champion by the British Boxing Board of Control until, on 12 February 1971, he outpointed Ruben Navarro (who substituted at short notice for Ramos) in Los Angeles to earn universal recognition. A mere four months later, though, the WBC stripped him for

Above: *Laguna only won three of his seven title fights, but was one of the division's dominant figures.*

Below: *Laguna never fought again after this unsuccessful attempt to regain the title from Buchanan in 1971.*

Right: *Ken Buchanan faced Laguna in the Puerto Rican heat, and the Scot pulled off a shock win.*

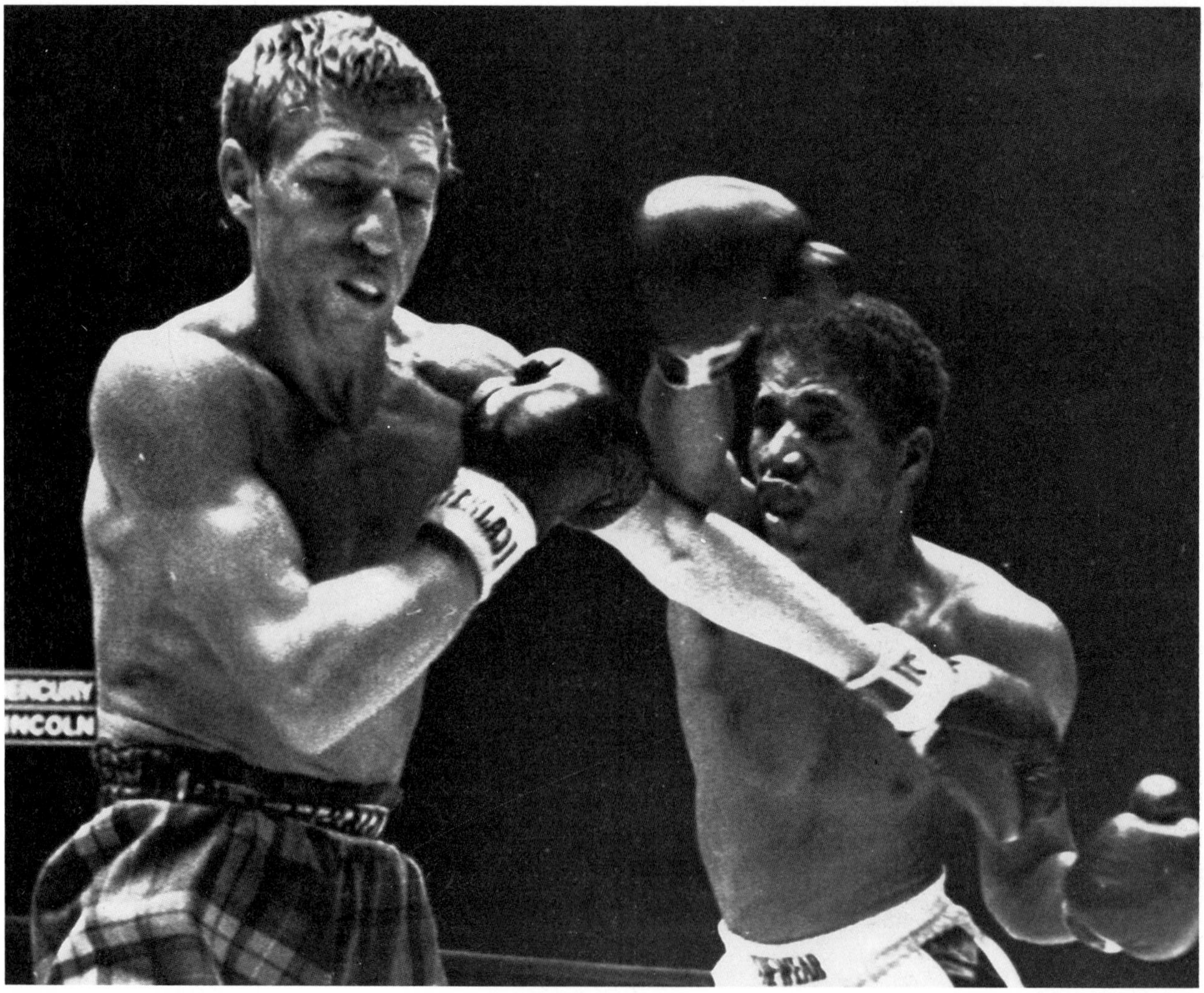

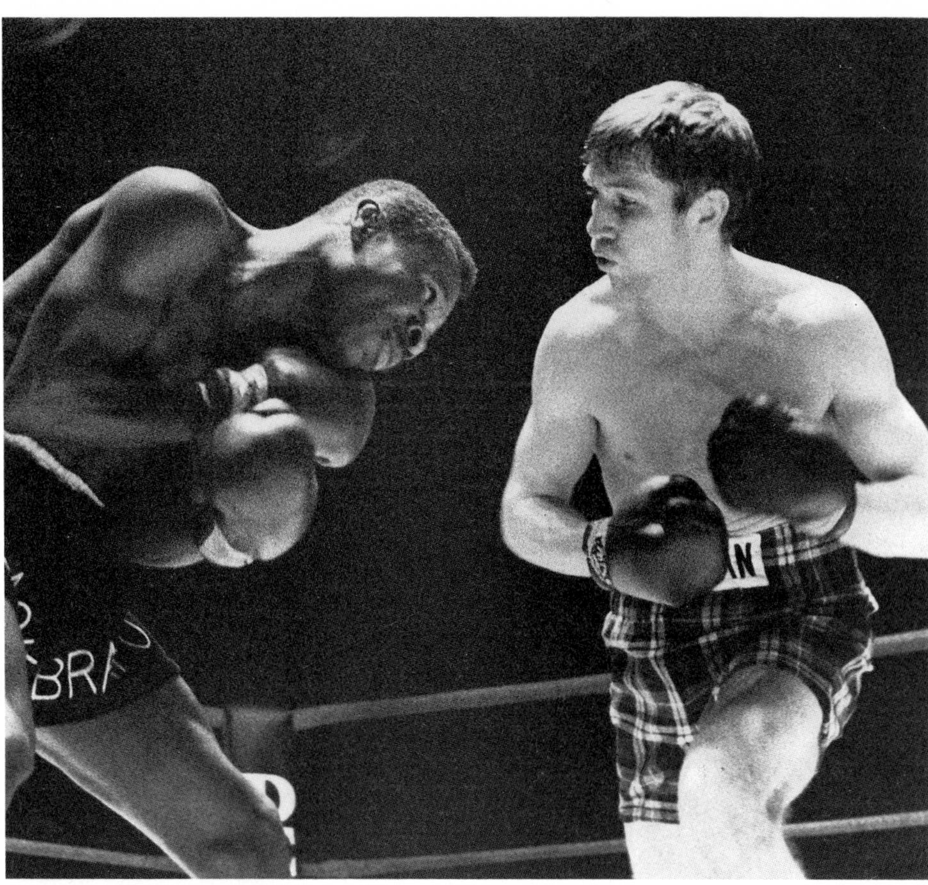

Buchanan was always a popular performer in Denmark, where he boxed seven times. He ended former Commonwealth champion Joe Tetteh's long career with a third-round win in 1974 (above) *and then chose Randers as the venue for his 34th birthday comeback in 1979, when he outpointed Benny Benitez* (left).

signing for a rematch with Laguna instead of meeting their top challenger, Pedro Carrasco of Spain. But this time the British Board stayed loyal to their man, despite their involvement with the WBC, and continued to regard the Scot as champion. Buchanan survived a badly cut eye to win a unanimous decision over Laguna in Madison Square Garden in September 1971. It was probably the finest performance of his long career – but it was also the last world title fight he would win. Ironically, the man who, nine months later, ended his reign had preceded him that night into the Garden ring to stop Benny Huertas, a useful Puerto Rican, inside a round.

Roberto Duran was not yet 21 years old but he had been a pro since he was 15, and the win over Huertas was his 25th in a row, all but five inside the distance. The explosive Panamanian, full of swaggering, arrogant, exuberant aggression, had hit the lightweight division with the kind of impact the young Cassius Clay had had on the heavyweights a decade previously. His impact on the unfortunate Buchanan was just as dramatic, although much of Duran's work in the Madison

Square Garden ring on that June evening in 1972 strayed well beyond the bounds of legality. The referee finally stopped the fight at the end of the 13th round, with the Scot clutching his groin in agony after taking a viciously low right. The receipts of $223,901 was an indoor record for a lightweight fight, which was as much a tribute to Buchanan's drawing power as Duran's: he had made a tremendous impression on the New York public in beating Laguna, and in a 1970 points win over a previously undefeated Canadian welterweight, Donato Paduano.

Significantly, Duran never gave Buchanan a second chance, and a decade later described him as the toughest and most difficult opponent he had ever faced. Duran became a magnificent champion, even an unbeatable one. He defended the WBA title 12 times, including a brilliant revenge victory over the only man to have beaten him – Esteban DeJesus of Puerto Rico. He overcame challengers from Australia, Japan, Mexico, Costa Rica, the Dominican Republic, Puerto Rico, and, of

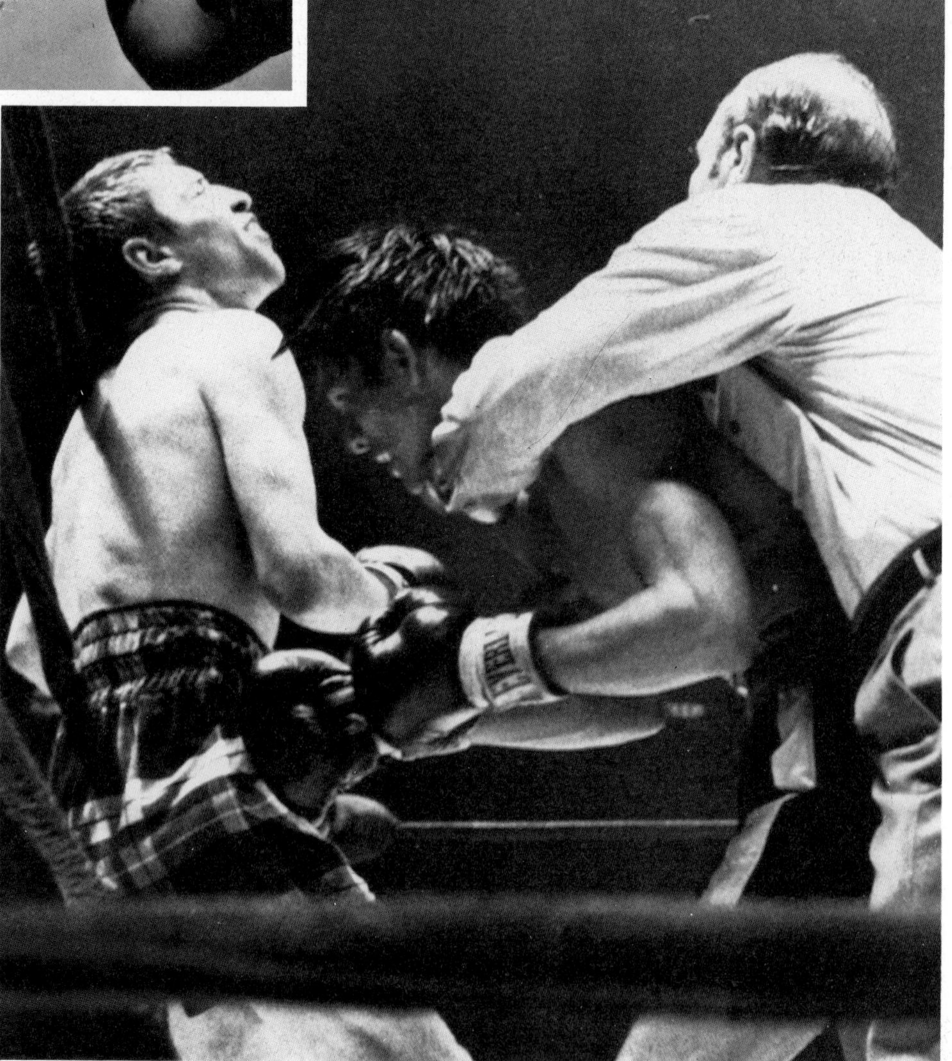

The exuberant, uninhibited aggression of Panama's Roberto Duran (above) *made him arguably the greatest pound for pound fighter in the game's history – but he was also one of the roughest, as this savagely low blow* (right) *demonstrated. It ended Ken Buchanan's reign: the Scot, understandably, could not answer the bell for the 14th round.*

course, America. (His American victims included Lou Bizzaro, whose brother Johnny had challenged Carlos Ortiz for the title in 1966.) Even though he had to wait until his final appearance in the lightweight division (when he knocked out WBC champion Esteban DeJesus again in 12 rounds) to earn undisputed recognition, no one could seriously argue that he was not the world's best lightweight during the 1972-1979 period.

Duran was only taken the distance once in his 12 defences, by the Puerto Rican Edwin Viruet, in 1977. He had a feud with the Viruet brothers, Edwin and Adolph, who were amongst his most troublesome opponents. Edwin took him the distance twice, in a non-title ten-rounder in September 1975, and in their Philadelphia title fight two years later, while Adolph had a bitter ten-rounder with him in New York, in 1978. There was nothing forgiving or magnanimous in Duran's nature: having beaten Adolph, he swaggered into Viruet's dressing room where the loser was being consoled by brother Edwin and snarled 'Next time, your father'!

Left: *Duran twice defeated the only man to claim a victory over him as a lightweight – Esteban DeJesus.*

Below: *Edwin Viruet lasted the distance twice against Duran, who had a long-running feud with the family.*

Pedro Carrasco (above) *was world champion for a fortnight until the WBC annulled his win over Mando Ramos.*

Eight of his 13 championship contests ended on clean countouts, evidence of the hitting power which earned him his *'manos de piedra'* (hands of stone) nickname. His supremacy was so unchallengeable that it seems almost an irrelevance to chronicle the chequered history of the WBC title during the Duran era.

Buchanan's immediate successor as WBC champion, Pedro Carrasco of Spain, was crowned in extraordinary circumstances by Nigerian referee Samuel Ahubota. He disqualified the ex-champion Mando Ramos for 'hitting on top of the head and below the belt' after Carrasco had been floored four times in 11 rounds in Madrid, on 5 November 1971. The verdict was so outrageous that two weeks later the WBC declared it 'null and void' and ordered a rematch, which took place in Los Angeles in February 1972. Carrasco fought much better than he had done on his home ground, and pushed Ramos to a split decision. But the farce continued when the WBC then withdrew championship recognition of the fight because the decision

Carrasco's brilliant record of 105 wins in 110 fights (with two draws) included this points win (above) *over another Spanish star, the future WBC light-welterweight champion Miguel Velasquez, in defence of his European title in 1969. He was floored four times by Mando Ramos* (left) *but given the title on a disqualification in November, 1971, a decision later annulled.*

had been 'locally influenced.'

They ordered a third meeting, which took place in Madrid in June 1972, and it resulted in another split-decision win for the American. But the controversy was not over yet – the Spanish Boxing Federation claimed that a post-fight drug test showed Ramos to have been under the influence of amphetamines. The crowd of 12,000 at the Madrid Sports Palace booed, jeered, and whistled the verdict, and hundreds of seat cushions were hurled at the ring. The Spaniards pressed hard for a fourth meeting, but to no avail. Three months later the issue became academic when Chango Carmona, of Mexico smashed Ramos to a brutal eight-round defeat in Los Angeles before 20,000 fans at the Coliseum. The former champion was rushed into intensive care, and it was generally assumed that his short but dazzling career was over. But he reappeared a year later and had another ten fights, winning just four of them. He retired for good after his second-round loss to the obscure Wayne Beale in Las Vegas, in October 1975, shortly before his 27th birthday.

Carmona held the title for less than two months, being forced to retire at the end of 12 rounds against another Mexican, Rodolfo Gonzalez, in Los Angeles on 10 November 1972. Carrasco, by now disillusioned with boxing and despairing of ever getting another title fight, retired a month later even though he was still ranked No. 1. He quit with a superb record of only three defeats in 110 fights, two of them against Ramos.

Gonzalez was a long-serving professional whose career stretched back to 1959. He had turned professional at 14 years of age, and was an instant sensation with 31 consecutive wins, 29 of them inside the distance. But he drifted away from boxing after a points loss in February 1963, and did not reappear for almost three years. It took him a long time to recapture his early fire, and he lost three of his first seven comeback fights. He proved a worthy champion, however, stopping Buchanan's former rival Ruben Navarro in nine rounds and the Italian, Antonio Puddu, in ten. In April 1974 he lost the title on an eighth-round kayo to Guts Ishimatsu of Japan, who in his previous incarnation as Ishimatsu Suzuki had failed in title bids against Ramos and Duran.

Ishimatsu retained it twice against Arturo Pineda (once on a draw), Gonzalez in a rematch, Alvaro Rojas, and Buchanan, whom he narrowly out-pointed in Tokyo in February 1975. But in May

Rodolfo Gonzalez slips European champion Antonio Puddu's left and counters with a right on the way to a 10th-round stoppage in defence of the WBC title in 1973.

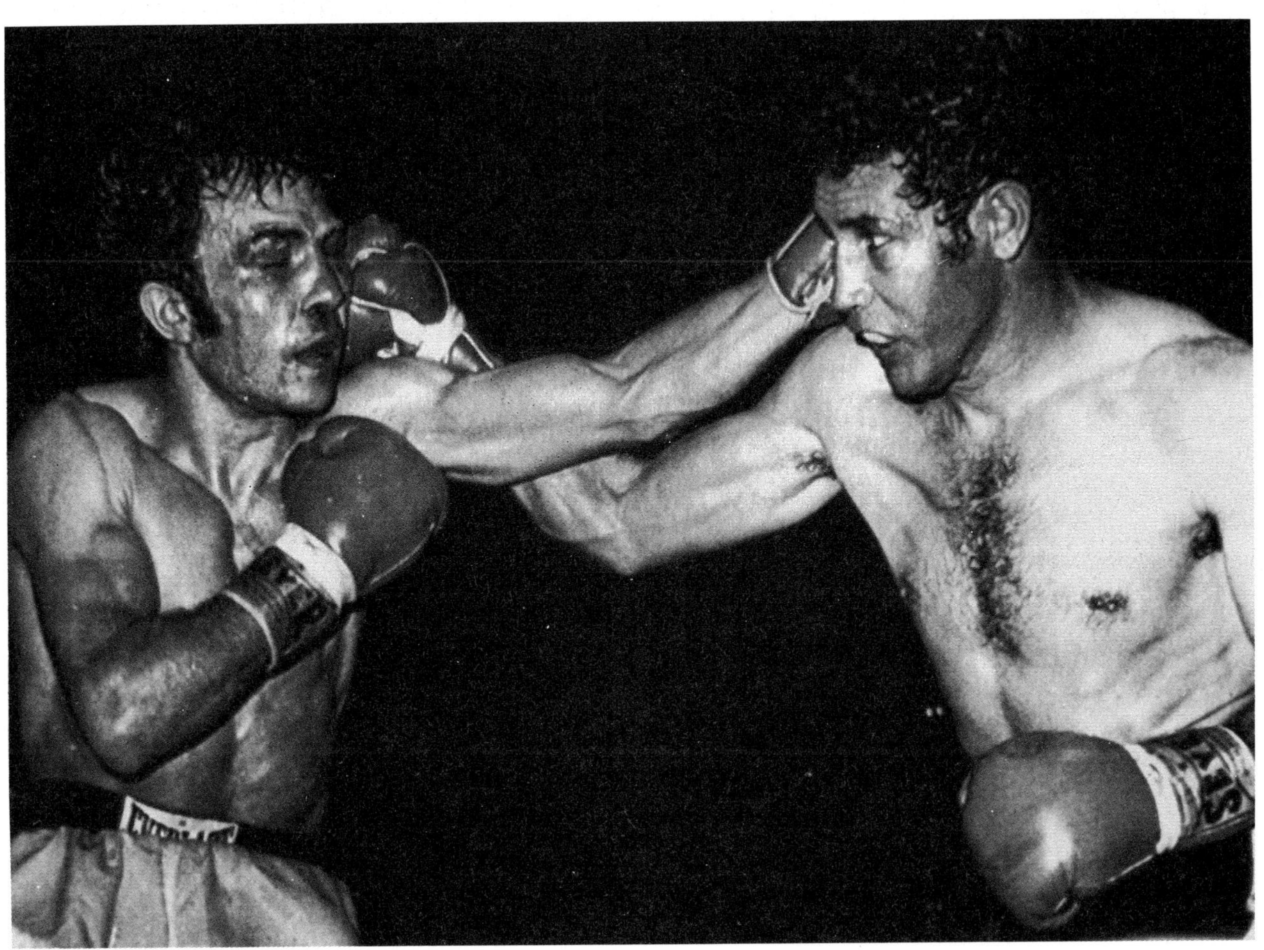

1976 Ishimatsu's reign was ended by Esteban DeJesus, a gifted stylist from Puerto Rico who, had it not been for the towering presence of Roberto Duran, would surely have had a long spell as undisputed champion. He was an idol in his homeland, drawing a crowd of 17,000 to watch him stop the Japanese Buzzsaw Yamabe in four rounds, at Bayamon in 1977. He made two other successful defences, against Hector Medina and Vicente Saldivar Mijares, but then on 21 January 1978 the incomparable Duran knocked him out in 12 rounds, at Las Vegas, to reunify the championship.

Increasing weight problems forced Duran to relinquish the title in February 1979, when once more the championship split. The European title holder, Jim Watt from Glasgow, a capable but unspectacular southpaw, was steered into top contender status by his shrewd manager Terry Lawless and the London matchmaker-promoter Mickey Duff. He was paired with Alfredo Pitalua of Colombia for the vacant WBC title in Glasgow on 17 April 1979. The Colombian was the half-brother of the former middleweight champion Rodrigo Valdes, and the one-time super-bantamweight challenger Ruben Valdes. Urged on by a capacity crowd, on an emotional night at the Kelvin Hall, Watt boxed brilliantly to stop Pitalua in the 12th round.

Watt may have been lucky to get the title, but there was nothing fortunate about his performances as champion. Watt became Britain's most successful and best-paid world champion at any weight for years, stopping Roberto Vasquez (nine rounds), local rival Charlie Nash of Ireland (four rounds) and, in his career peak, outpointing the former Olympic star and unbeaten professional Howard Davis of America, on a rainy night at Ibrox Park, Glasgow. The win over Davis forced the American 'experts' to take Watt seriously. Initially, they had viewed the Davis fight as a formality for the challenger, but that result, followed by Watt's bloody 12th-round stoppage of another American,

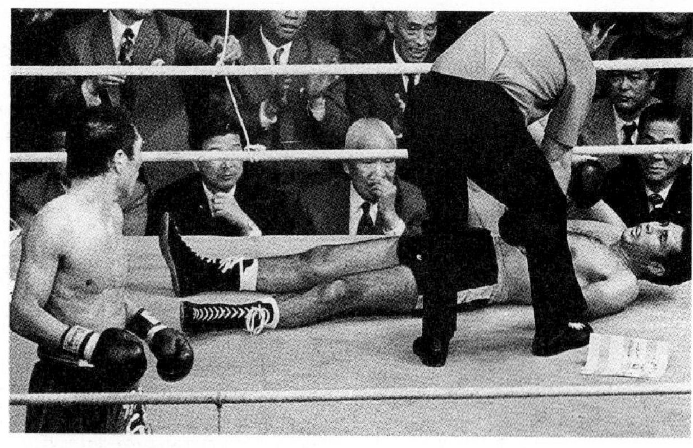

Guts Ishimatsu found his name change (from Ishimatsu Suzuki) worked wonders as he flattened Rodolfo Gonzalez to take the WBC title.

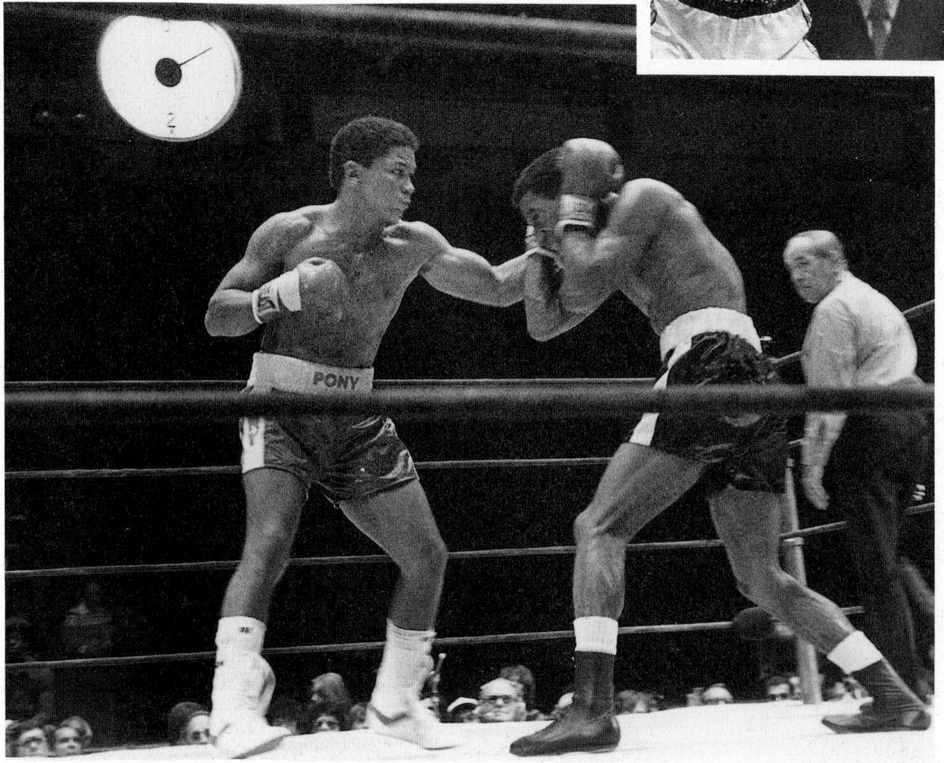

Ishimatsu turned back five challengers, including Ken Buchanan (above) *before Esteban DeJesus* (left, *outpointing Jimmy Blevins)* *dethroned him in 1976.*

Glasgow southpaw Jim Watt provided some of the most emotional nights in British boxing history with his WBC title wins over Alfredo Pitalua (right) *and Roberto Vasquez* (below) *in the atmospheric Kelvin Hall.*

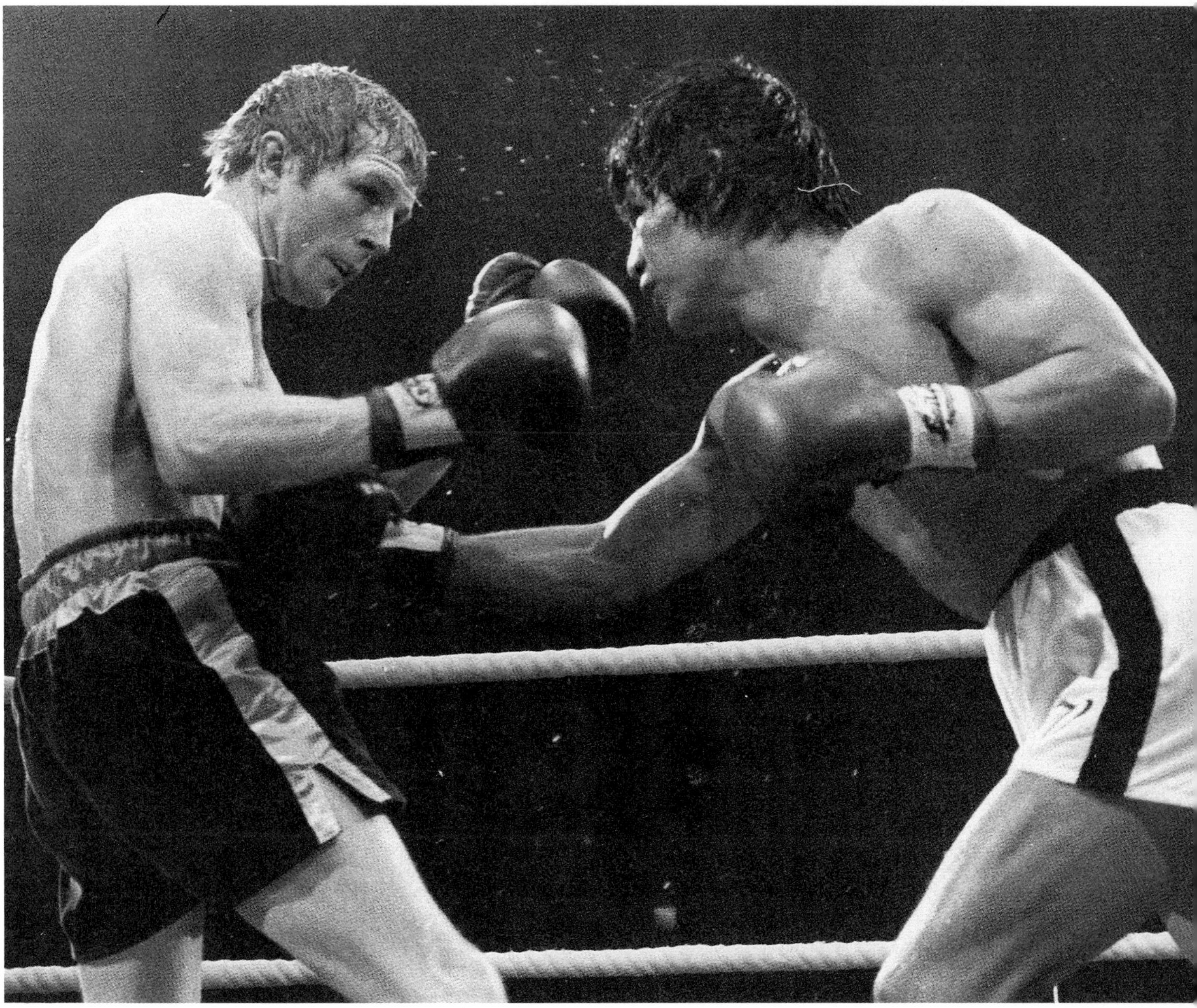

Sean O'Grady, established his worth in America as well as at home.

But the combination of advancing years (he was almost 33) and the brilliant talent of the formidable Nicaraguan Alexis Arguello was too much for Watt on his final appearance, at Wembley on 20 June 1981. Arguello floored and convincingly outpointed him, thereby becoming one of the few men to have won world titles at three weights (he had previously been featherweight and junior-lightweight champion.) Arguello brought his own flair and style to the title, and when Ray Mancini – whom Arguello stopped in 14 rounds in his first defence – went on to win the WBA title, the Nicaraguan's position as the world's best lightweight was beyond dispute.

He retained the WBC title against Robert Elizondo (in the seven rounds), James Busceme (six rounds) and Andy Ganigan (five rounds). However, after his marvellous but losing challenge for Aaron Pryor's WBA light-welterweight title, in 1982, he relinquished the lightweight championship title.

The crown was taken up by Edwin Rosario of Puerto Rico, a hard-hitting and unbeaten stylist who had won 16 of his 18 fights inside the distance. Rosario knocked out Elizondo in the first round to retain the title in March 1984, and then took a desperately close and hard-won points win over Howard Davis in June. In November 1984 he was battered to a shock fourth-round defeat by the man whom he had outpointed for the vacant title – Jose Luis Ramirez of Mexico. Ramirez won the title in his 93rd fight, of which he had lost only four.

Left: *Ireland's Charlie Nash (on the left) dropped Watt in the opening round but was stopped in the fourth.*

Below: *Olympic champion Howard Davis was expected by some to outclass Watt, but was soundly outpointed.*

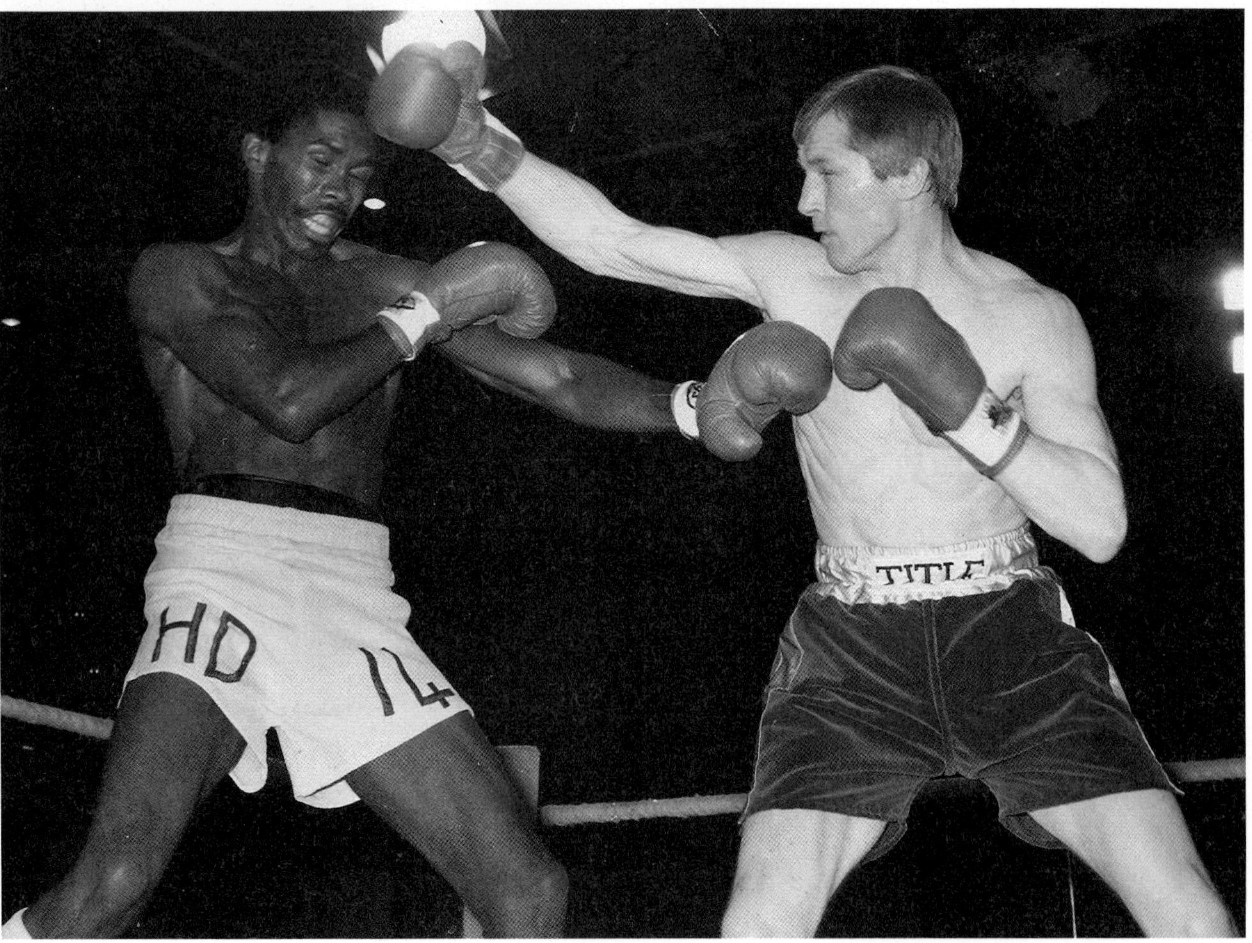

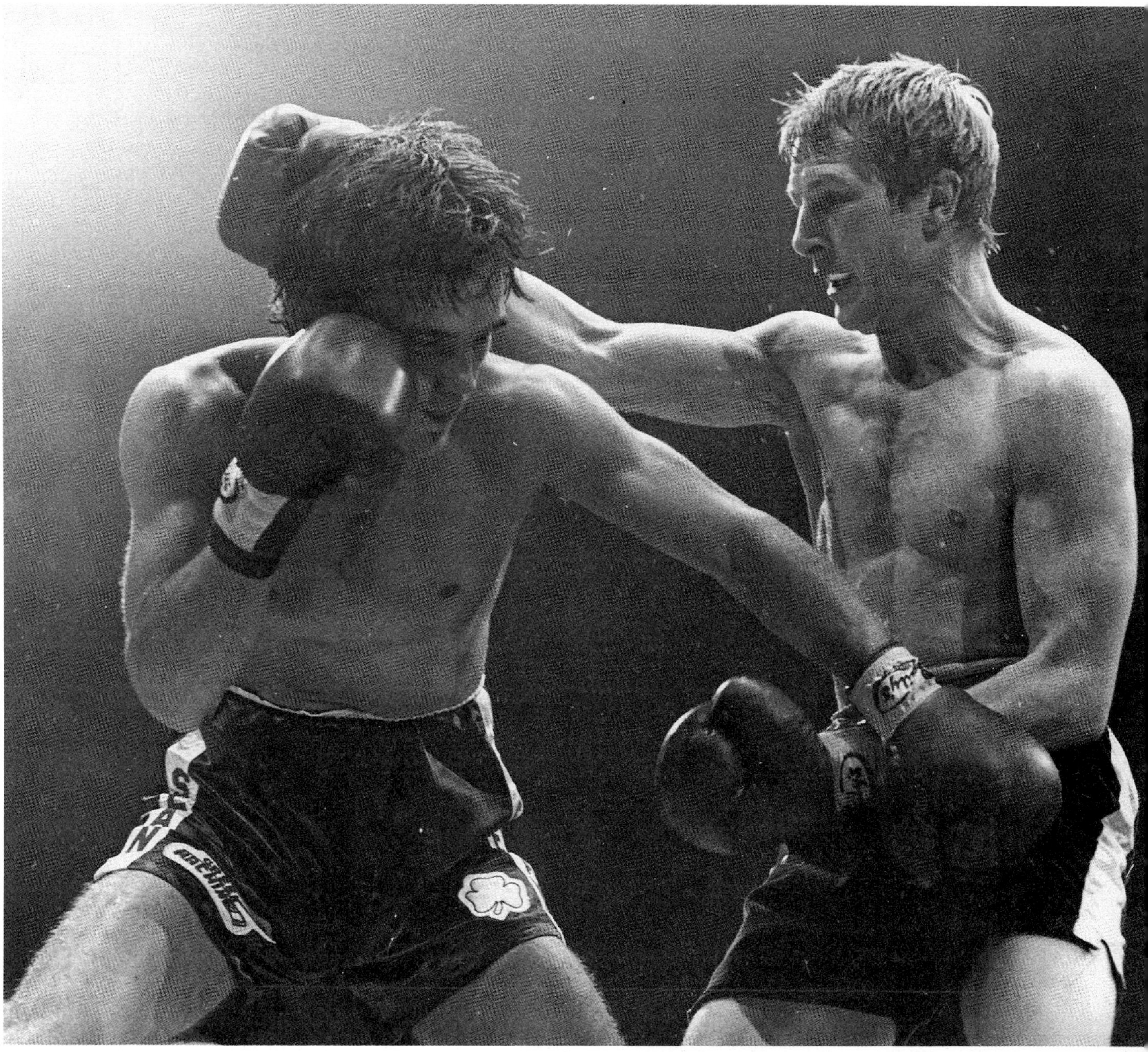

Sean O'Grady, himself a future holder of the WBA title, was stopped on cuts in Watt's last successful defence (above). *Seven months later, Alexis Arguello* (left) *beat Watt at Wembley and went on to defend the title twice before 1981 was out, including this seventh-round stoppage of Roberto Elizondo* (right).

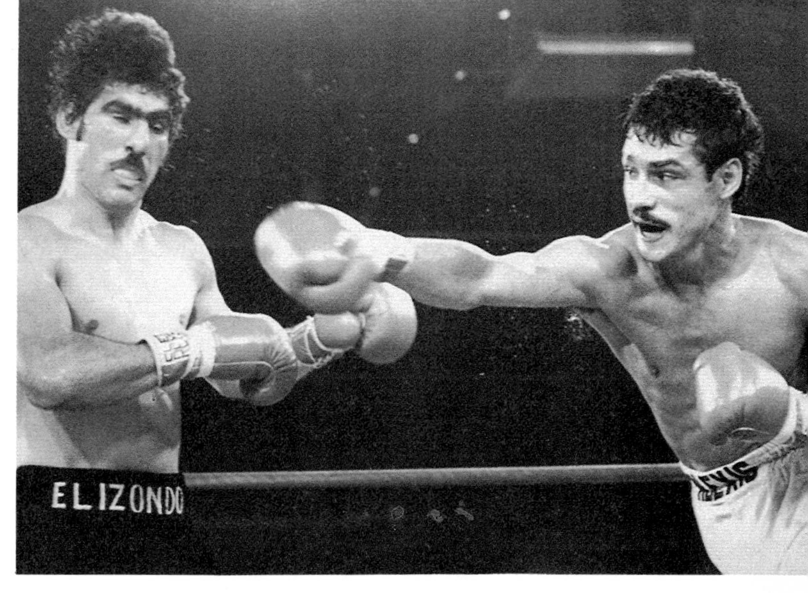

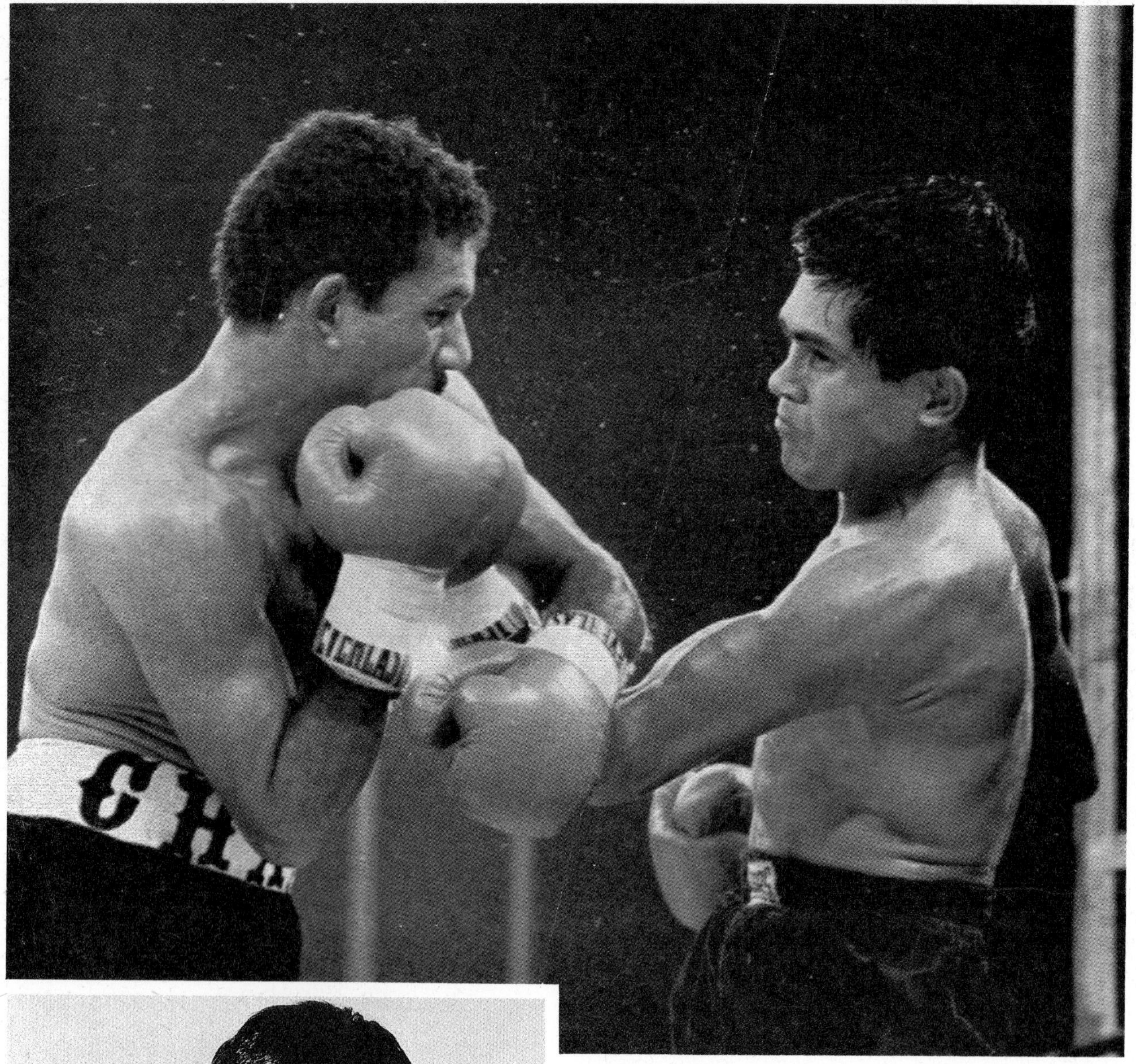

Left: *Jose Luis Ramirez turned pro when he was just 14 years old.*

Above: *Edwin Rosario (on the left) loses the WBC title in a major upset to Ramirez.*

Although he had been a professional since he was 14 years old, and had an outstanding record which featured 74 inside-the-distance wins, he had rarely been able to land any significant fights in America – and when he did, as against Arguello in 1980 and Mancini in 1981 – he lost.

Ramirez' reign lasted only until Hector Camacho, the former junior-lightweight champion from Puerto Rico, outpointed him in his first defence in Las Vegas on 10 August 1985. Camacho retained the title against Rosario, whom he beat on a bitterly disputed split decision in New York, in June 1986, and the former WBC junior-lightweight champion Cornelius Boza-Edwards, whom he outscored in Miami in September.

The WBA title was won on Duran's abdication by Ernesto Espana of Venezuela, who knocked out the

Alexis Arguello (right, *on the left) crowned a fabulous career by taking Jim Watt's WBC lightweight title. It was the Nicaraguan's third championship, and he went on to establish himself as one of the division's best title-holders. Livingstone Bramble* (below, *battering Tyrone Crawley into a 14th round defeat) threatened to do likewise, until he was surprisingly dethroned by Edwin Rosario.*

Two great Latin champions . . . Lupe Pintor (left, *on the left) retaining the bantamweight title against Jose Uziga in 1981, and* (below) *Alexis Arguello on the way to a fifth round knockout of southpaw Andy Ganigan in 1982.*

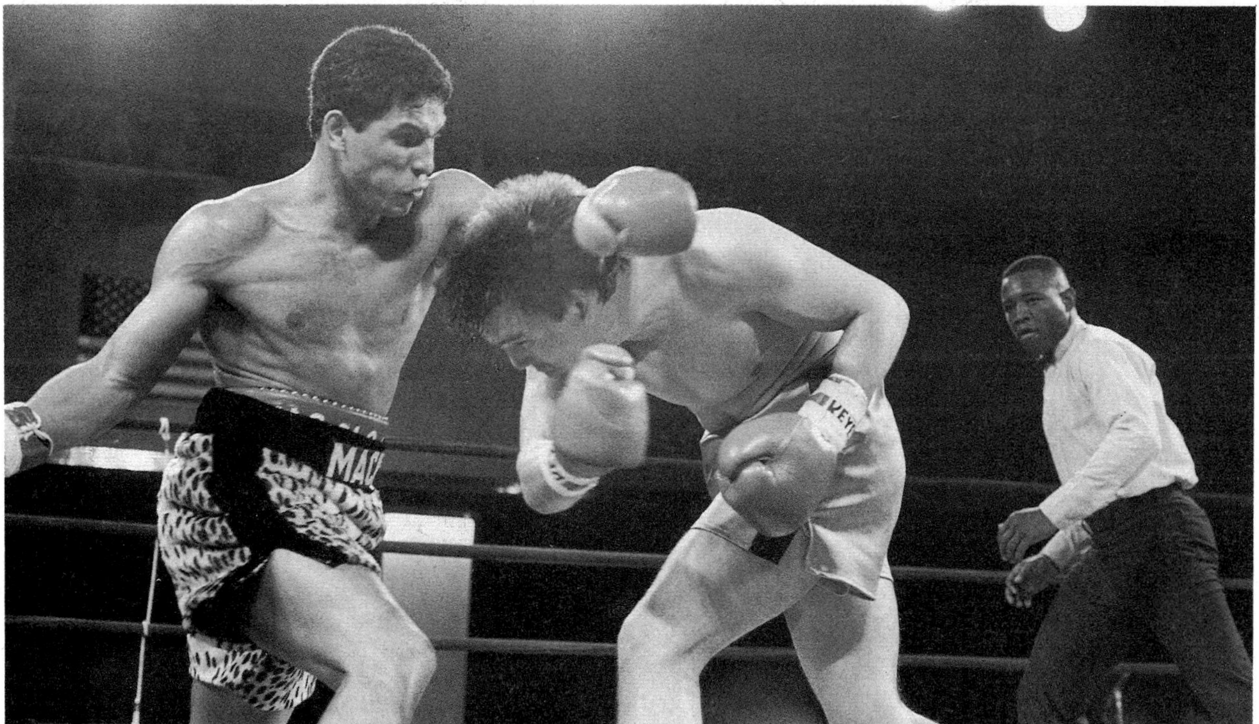

Above: *The extravagantly talented 'Macho' Camacho (on the left) stops Louie Burke in a non-title affair.*

Commonwealth champion Claude Noel of Trinidad in the 13th round at San Juan, on 16 June 1979. They had originally been matched in a 12-round final eliminator, but the fight was upgraded to full championship status the day before it took place. Espana retained it against Johnny Lira of Chicago, in August 1979, but three months later was dethroned by yet another product of Emmanuel Steward's famous Kronk Gym in Detroit, Hilmer Kenty.

Kenty, the gym-mate of welterweight and light-middleweight champion Thomas Hearns, had a memorable 1980. He retained the title three times, against Young Ho-Oh, Espana and Vilomar Fernandez, but was surprisingly outpointed in April 1981 by Jim Watt's former challenger, Sean O'Grady of Oklahoma City. O'Grady's record was remarkable. Managed and promoted by his father Pat – a colourful, garrulous figure – O'Grady had launched his professional career shortly before his 15th birthday. The win over Kenty was his 75th

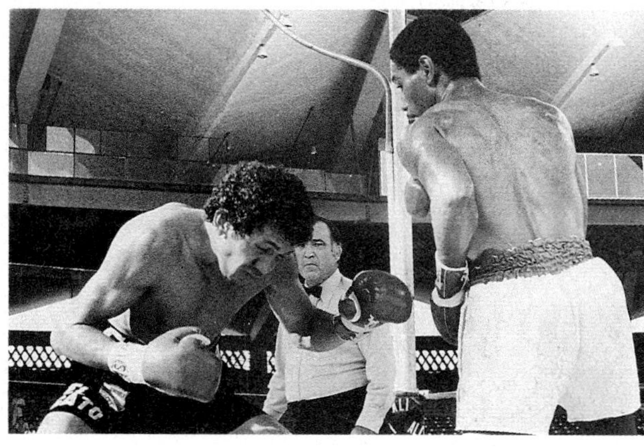

Above: *Camacho's last defence of the WBC title: a win over the former junior lightweight champ Cornelius Boza-Edwards.*

Left: *Hilmer Kenty brought the first title to the Kronk gym when he defeated WBA champ Ernesto Espana in 1979.*

Kenty (left) *beat three good challengers in 1980, including Vilomar Fernandez* (below), *the New York veteran who had once beaten Alexis Arguello.*

victory in 77 fights, and was only the tenth time that he had been taken the distance. His spectacular run of victories undoubtedly owed much to his father's match-making, but he proved against Watt and Kenty that he was a genuinely good fighter.

Pat O'Grady was a strong-minded and independent type, who did not take kindly to being given edicts by the WBA concerning title defences. Since he ignored their defence deadlines, the WBA promptly stripped Sean of his title and paired Claude Noel with Rodolfo Gonzalez (not the former champion of that name) for the vacant title, which

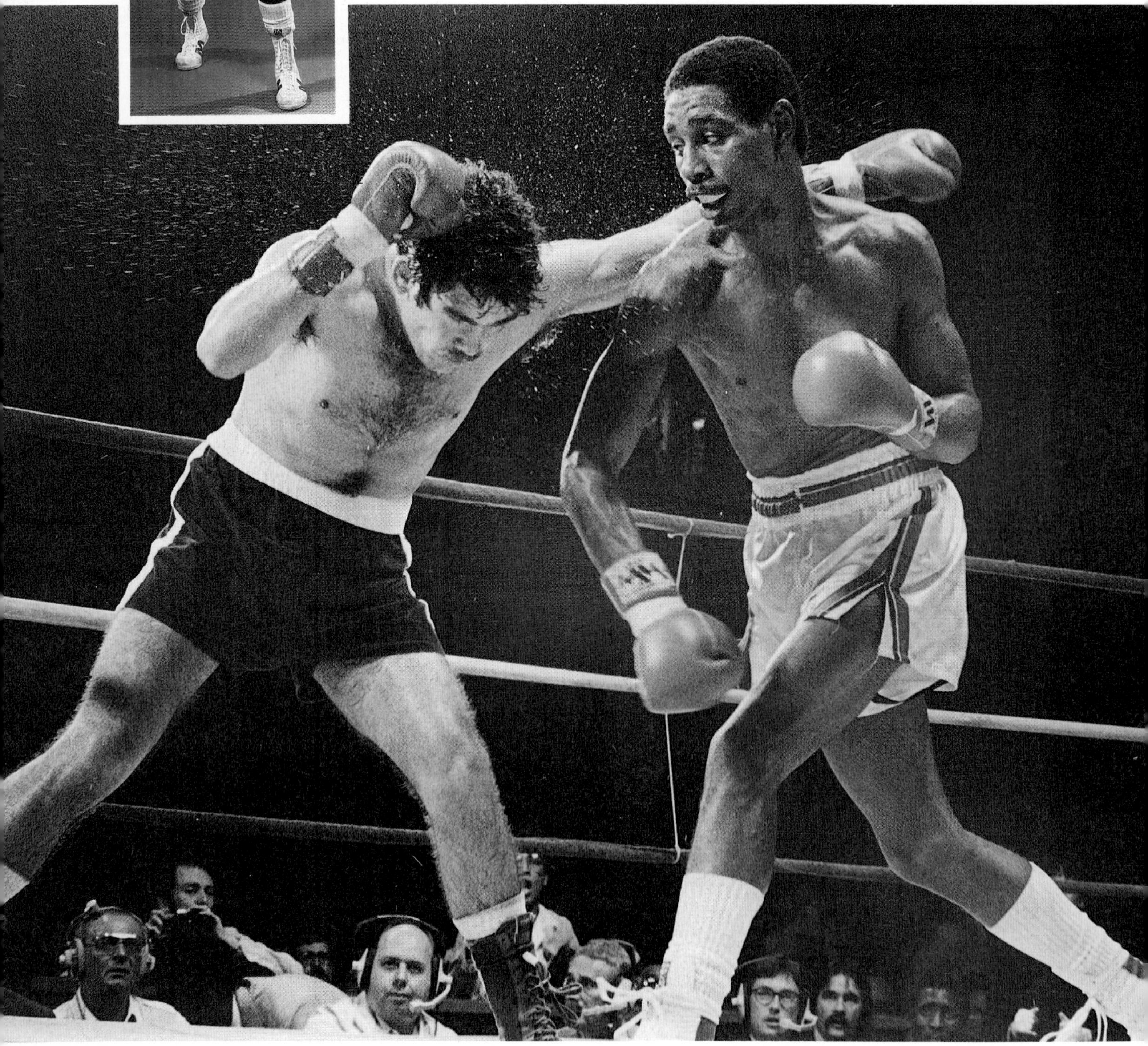

Noel won on a 15-round decision in Atlantic City on 12 September 1981. (The irrepressible O'Grady then launched his own organization, the World Athletic Association, which proclaimed Sean the lightweight champion. However, he lost the 'title' in his first defence, to Andy Ganigan, and had just seven more fights – five of them wins – before retiring at 24.)

Noel lost the WBA championship in his first defence to Arturo Frias, a hard-punching but vulnerable Californian, who retained it on an injury stoppage of Espana, but was then beaten by Ray Mancini in what was described as the year's most exciting one-round fight. Mancini's victory, in Las Vegas on 8 May 1982, was some measure of compensation for the failure of his father, Lenny Mancini, to secure a title fight during his peak career years in the 1940s. The new champion, who was superbly 'packaged' by his manager David Wolf, became the darling of the American media,

Above: *Esteban Olvera was an early-career knockout victim of O'Grady's, who went the distance only ten times before winning the title.*

Below: *Ray Mancini's WBA title win over Art Frias lasted less than a round, but was packed with action before Frias was kayoed.*

Above: *Esteban Olvera was an early-career knockout victim of O'Grady's, who went the distance only ten times in 76 fights before winning the title.*

Below: *Ray Mancini's WBA title win over Art Frias lasted less than a round, with both being rocked, before Frias was kayoed with six seconds left in the round.*

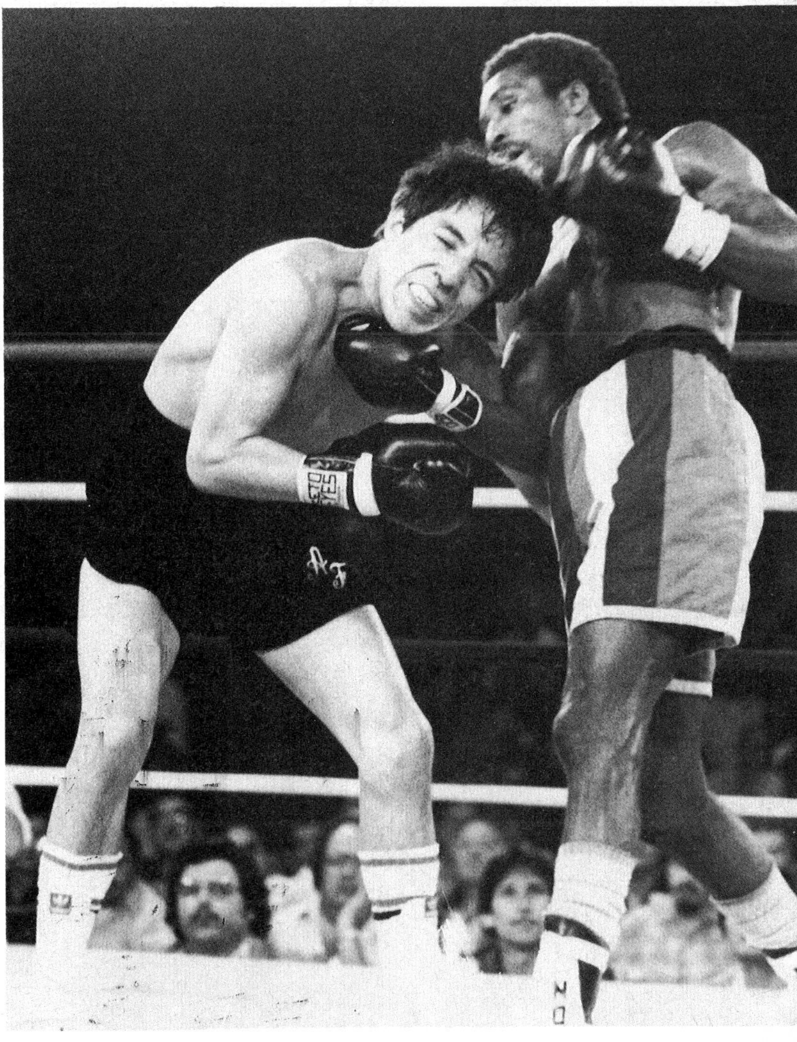

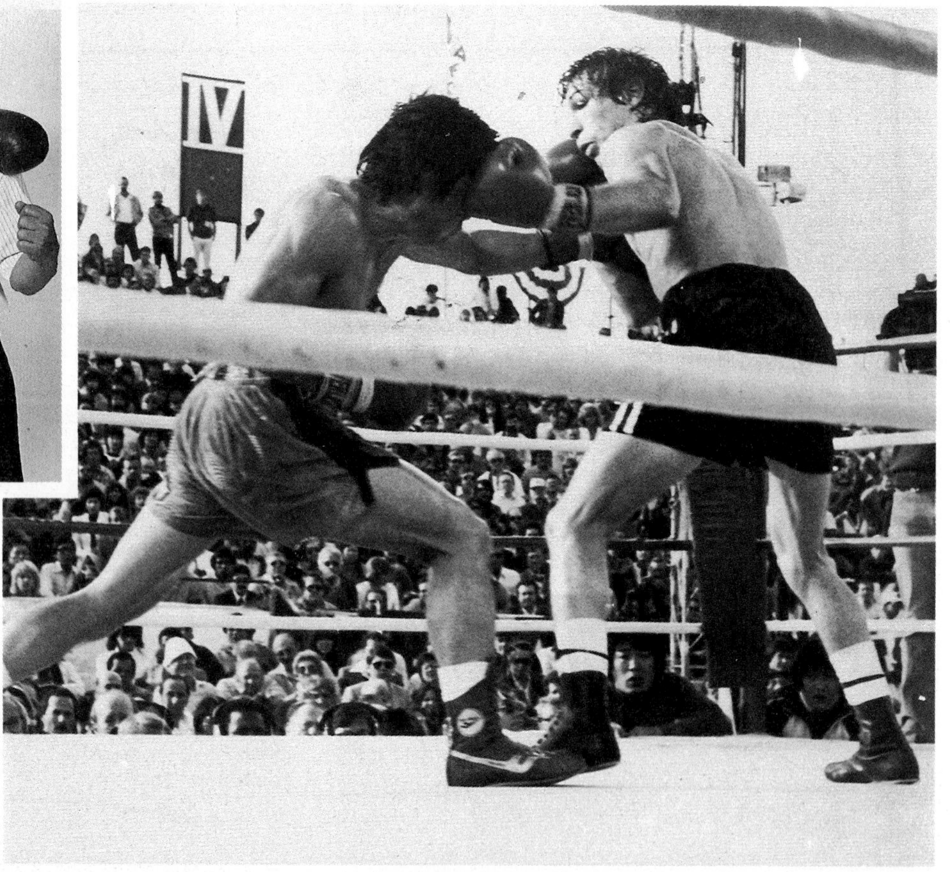

Mancini's father Lennie (above) *had been a ranked lightweight contender in the 1940s, but never got a title shot. His son was a busy champion, whose successful defences included a tragic knockout of the Korean Duk-Koo Kim* (right), *and the former featherweight and junior lightweight champ Bobby Chacon* (below).

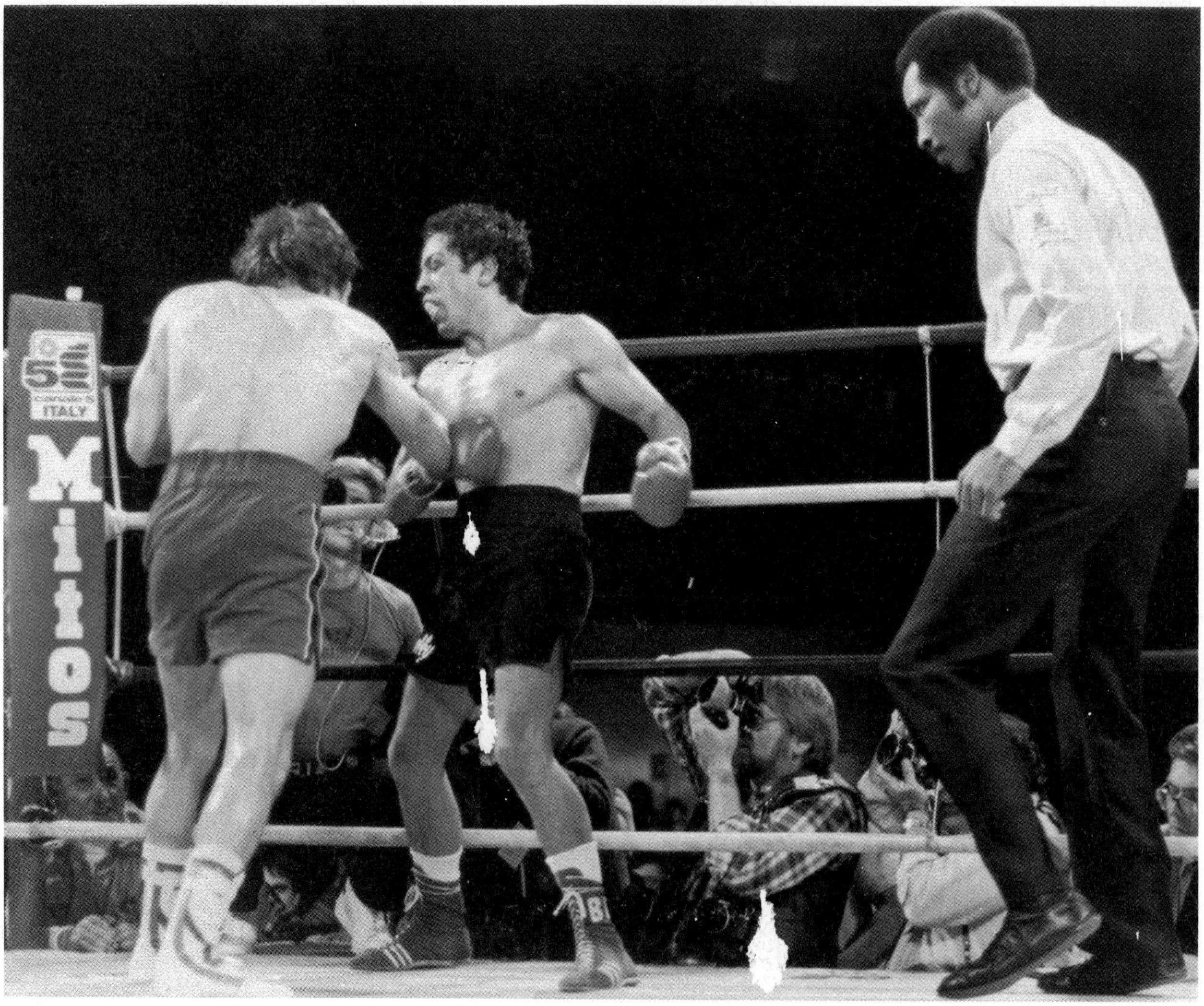

which was reflected in his earnings. Yet he was not a mere media creation, but a very capable, courageous and rugged fighter who stopped challengers Espana, Duk Koo Kim (who tragically did not regain consciousness), Orlando Romero and Bobby Chacon.

Mancini's defences were all thrill-a-second affairs, and his style destined him for a short career. Livingstone Bramble, a West Indian who fought out of Atlantic City, ended his brief but exciting reign with a 14th-round stoppage in Buffalo in June 1984, and outpointed him in a rematch in February 1985. The dread-locked Bramble stopped Tyrone Crawley impressively in his second defence but, just as interest was building in a unification match with WBC champion Hector Camacho, he was the victim of a stunning two-round upset by the former WBC champion Edwin Rosario.

The IBF appeared on the lightweight scene in January 1984, when Charlie 'Choo Choo' Brown outpointed Melvin Paul in their inaugural title fight, but he lost the championship three months later to Harry Arroyo, who came from Mancini's hometown of Youngstown, Ohio. Arroyo retained it against Charlie 'White Lightning' Brown and Terrence Alli,

Livingstone Bramble (right), *a classy box-fighter who stopped Mancini in 14 rounds in June 1984* (below), *looked set for a long reign until he was surprisingly crushed by Edwin Rosario in the second round.*

before losing it to another Kronk Gym product, Jimmy Paul, who outpointed him at Atlantic City on 6 April 1985.

The smart-boxing Paul, who trounced another American television favourite Robin Blake in a defence, was regarded as being at least as good as

Below: *Jimmy Paul takes the IBF title from Harry Arroyo, thus removing the possibility of a showdown between Arroyo and his fellow native of Youngstown, Ohio – Ray Mancini.*

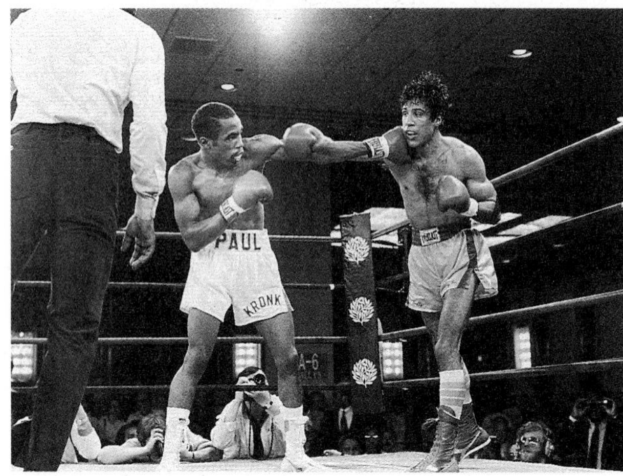

Below: *This sixth-round win over Andy Ganigan for the USBA title was Paul's big breakthrough.*

Right: *Paul retained the USBA title with an impressive sixth-round kayo of the flashy Alvin 'Too Sweet' Hayes.*

the two rival claimants, but in December 1986 he was surprisingly outpointed by Greg Haugen from Alaska. Haugen had got into boxing through the notorious 'Tough Guy' all-comers tournaments that were popular in America in the early 1980s. He was a rugged, brawling type, whose career took off after he moved to Las Vegas and began to get regular television exposure.

Haugen's title-winning weekend was memorable for him on several counts: he had bet $2,000 on himself, at odds of 3–1 against, and two days after becoming champion married the mother of his two children. Haugen was dethroned on his first defence by a colourful Italian-American, Vinnie Pazienza, who outpointed him in a magnificent 15-rounder in June 1987. Pazienza v Camacho would have been a hugely attractive match, but increasing weight problems forced the Macho Man to relinquish the WBC title and seek his third championship in the 140 lb division.

IBF champion Greg Haugen learned his trade by taking on all comers in 'Tough Guy' tournaments in Alaska.

HOW THE LIGHTWEIGHT TITLE HAS CHANGED HANDS

1872–1900

06 Oct 72 Arthur Chambers w.dis.35 Billy Edwards at Squirrel Is., USA
27 Feb 86 Jack McAuliffe w.pts.17 Jack Hopper at New York
14 Dec 94 George (Kid) Lavigne w.ko.18 Andy Bowen at New Orleans
03 Jul 99 Frank Erne w.pts.20 George (Kid) Lavigne at Buffalo

1900–

12 May 02 Joe Gans w.ko.1 Frank Erne at Fort Erie
04 Jul 08 Battling Nelson w.ko.17 Joe Gans at San Francisco
22 Feb 10 Ad Wolgast w.ko.40 Battling Nelson at Port Richmond
28 Nov 12 Willie Ritchie w.dis.16 Ad Wolgast at Daly City, Calif
07 Jul 14 Freddie Welsh w.pts.20 Willie Ritchie at Olympia London
28 May 17 Benny Leonard w.ko.9 Freddie Welsh at New York
15 Jun 25 *Leonard retired as undefeated champion*
03 Jul 25 Jimmy Goodrich w.ko.2 Stanislaus Loayza at Long Island, New York *(For vacant title)*
08 Dec 25 Rocky Kansas w.pts.15 Jimmy Goodrich at New York
03 Jul 26 Sammy Mandell w.pts.10 Rocky Kansas in Chicago
17 Jul 30 Al Singer w.ko.1 Sammy Mandell at New York
14 Nov 30 Tony Canzoneri w.ko.1 Al Singer at New York
23 Jun 33 Barney Ross w.pts.10 Tony Canzoneri at Chicago
34 *Ross relinquished title*
10 May 35 Tony Canzoneri w.pts.15 Lou Ambers at New York
03 Sep 36 Lou Ambers w.pts.15 Tony Canzoneri at New York
17 Aug 38 Henry Armstrong w.pts.15 Lou Ambers at New York
22 Aug 39 Lou Ambers w.pts.15 Henry Armstrong at New York
10 May 40 Lew Jenkins w.rsf.3 Lou Ambers at New York
19 Dec 41 Sammy Angott w.pts.15 Lew Jenkins at New York
13 Nov 42 *Angott announced his retirement*
18 Dec 42 Beau Jack w.ko.3 Tippy Larkin at New York *(For vacant NY title)*
21 May 43 Bob Montgomery w.pts.15 Beau Jack at New York
27 Oct 43 Sammy Angott w.pts.15 Luther White at Los Angeles *(For vacant NBA title)*
19 Nov 43 Beau Jack w.pts.15 Bob Montgomery at New York
03 Mar 44 Bob Montgomery w.pts.15 Beau Jack at New York
08 Mar 44 Juan Zurita w.pts.15 Sammy Angott at Hollywood
18 Apr 45 Ike Williams w.ko.2 Juan Zurita at Mexico City
04 Aug 47 Ike Williams w.ko.6 Bob Montgomery at Philadelphia *(For undisputed title)*
25 May 51 Jimmy Carter w.rsf.14 Ike Williams at New York
14 May 52 Lauro Salas w.pts.15 Jimmy Carter at Los Angeles
15 Oct 52 Jimmy Carter w.pts.15 Lauro Salas at Chicago
05 Mar 54 Paddy DeMarco w.pts.15 Jimmy Carter at New York
17 Nov 54 Jimmy Carter w.rsf.15 Paddy DeMarco at San Francisco
29 Jun 55 Wallace (Bud) Smith w.pts. 15 Jimmy Carter at Boston
24 Aug 56 Joe Brown w.pts.15 Wallace (Bud) Smith at New Orleans
21 Apr 62 Carlos Ortiz w.pts.15 Joe Brown at Las Vagas
10 Apr 65 Ismael Laguna w.pts.15 Carlos Ortiz at Panama City
13 Nov 65 Carlos Ortiz w.pts.15 Ismael Laguna at San Juan, Puerto Rico
29 Jun 68 Carlos Teo Cruz w.pts.15 Carlos Ortiz at Santo Domingo
18 Feb 69 Mando Ramos w.rsf.11 Carlos Teo Cruz at Los Angeles
03 Mar 70 Ismael Laguna w.rtd.9 Mando Ramos at Los Angeles. *(WBC stripped Laguna of title for allegedly breaking contract to make his first defence in Los Angeles for promoter Mrs Aileen Eaton. Mando Ramos had won California 'final eliminator' by outpointing Sugar Ramos on 6 Aug 70 to earn title fight with Laguna)*
26 Sep 70 Ken Buchanan w.pts.15 Ismael Laguna at San Juan *(WBA title)*
12 Feb 71 Ken Buchanan w.pts.15 Ruben Navarro as Los Angeles *(Undisputed title)*
13 Sep 71 Ken Buchanan w.pts.15 Ismael Laguna in New York *(WBC stripped Buchanan of title for signing to meet Laguna in Madison Square Garden, New York instead of meeting their No. 1 challenger, Pedro Carrasco. British Boxing Board, although affiliated to WBC, upheld Buchanan as world champion)*
05 Nov 71 Pedro Carrasco w.dis.11 Mando Ramos in Madrid. *(Vacant WBC title—verdict declared 'null and void' at WBC meeting in Mexico City on 20 Nov 71 due to controversy surrounding Ramos' disqualification. WBC ordered a return fight)*
18 Feb 72 Mando Ramos w.pts.15 Pedro Carrasco in Los Angeles *(Vacant WBC title—WBC later withdrew recognition of the fight as a world championship because the decision was 'locally influenced')*
26 Jun 72 Roberto Duran w.rsf.13 Ken Buchanan in New York. *(WBA—British and New York title).* *(Britain and New York withdrew recognition of Roberto Duran in September 1973, for failing to honour Madison Square Garden contract to defend against Ken Buchanan)*
28 Jun 72 Mando Ramos w.pts.15 Pedro Carrasco in Madrid. *(Vacant WBC title)*
15 Sep 72 Chango Carmona w.rsf.8 Mando Ramos in Los Angeles
10 Nov 72 Rodolfo Gonzalez w.rtd.12 Chango Carmona at Los Angeles
11 Apr 74 Guts Ishimatsu w.ko.8 Rodolfo Gonzalez in Tokyo
08 May 76 Esteban De Jesus w.pts.15 Guts Ishimatsu in San Juan
21 Jan 78 Roberto Duran w.ko.12 Esteban De Jesus in Las Vegas *(For undisputed title)*
Jan 79 *Duran relinquished the title because of his difficulty in making the weight*
17 Apr 79 Jim Watt w.rsf.12 Alfredo Pitalua in Glasgow *(Vacant WBC title)*
16 Jun 79 Ernesto Espana w.ko.13 Claude Noel in San Juan *(Vacant WBA title)*
02 Mar 80 Hilmer Kenty w.rsf.9 Ernesto Espana in Detroit
12 Apr 81 Sean O'Grady w.pts.15 Hilmer Kenty in Atlantic City
20 Jun 81 Alexis Arguello w.pts.15 Jim Watt at Wembley
12 Sep 81 Claude Noel w.pts.15 Rodolfo Gonzalez at Atlantic City *(For vacant WBA title. The WBA had vacated O'Grady's title because of a contractual dispute).*
05 Dec 81 Arturo Frias w.ko.8 Claude Noel at Las Vegas
08 May 82 Ray Mancini w.rsf.1 Arturo Frias at Las Vegas
01 May 83 Edwin Rosario w.pts.12 Jose Luis Ramirez at San Juan *(For WBC title vacated by Arguello)*
30 Jan 84 Charlie 'Choo Choo' Brown w.pts.15 Melvin Paul in Atlantic City *(For vacant IBF title)*
15 Apr 84 Harry Arroyo, w.rsf.14 Charlie 'Choo Choo' Brown in Atlantic City
01 Jun 84 Livingstone Bramble w.rsf.14 Ray Mancini at Buffalo
03 Nov 84 Jose Luis Ramirez w.rsf.4 Edwin Rosario at Bayamon
06 Apr 85 Jimmy Paul w.pts.15 Harry Arroyo in Atlantic City
10 Aug 85 Hector Camacho w.pts.12 Jose Luis Ramirez at Las Vegas
26 Sep 86 Edwin Rosario w.ko.2 Livingstone Bramble at Miami Beach *(WBA title)*
05 Dec 86 Greg Haugen w.pts.15 Jimmy Paul at Las Vegas *(IBF title)*
Apr 87 *Hector Camacho relinquished WBC title because of weight problems*
07 Jun 87 Vinney Pazienza w.pts.15 Greg Hogan at Providence, Rhode Island

JUNIOR LIGHTWEIGHTS

THE JUNIOR lightweight (or super featherweight) division was instituted by the New York State Athletic Commission in 1920, for the benefit of fighters who found the gap between featherweight (126 lb) and lightweight (135 lb) too wide to bridge. Although it was a sensible innovation, the new division took a long time to win acceptance – Britain did not adopt it until 1968, and the first European championship at the weight (130 lb) was not held until 1971.

Promoter Tex Rickard was the moving spirit behind this division, and the first world champion, Johnny Dundee, was crowned on a Rickard show in New York on 18 November 1921. Dundee's fifth-round disqualification win over George 'KO' Chaney earned him the vacant title and a $2,500 belt. His real name was Giuseppe Carrora, and his choice of a Scottish *nom de guerre* brought him the vaguely offensive nickname 'The Scotch Wop'. Dundee was born in Sciacca, Italy, but was brought to America as a child and grew up in New York's West Side. His name change occurred when his manager, Scotty Monteith, saw the 16-year-old Carrora in a street fight and decided that 'anyone who can fight like that can't be a Wop – he's got to be a Scot.'

Dundee's career extended over 22 years, from 1910 to 1932, and took in 321 contests of which he lost only 31. By the time he had won the junior lightweight title, he had already had 257 fights. He made successful defences against Little Jack Sharkey, Vincent 'Pepper' Martin and Elino Flores, before being briefly unseated by Jack Bernstein, at the Velodrome, New York.

The loss did not seriously inconvenience Dundee: two fights later he won the featherweight title from Eugene Criqui, and became a dual champion by regaining the junior lightweight title

Johnny Dundee, the division's first champion, shapes up with flyweight champion Jimmy Wilde (right) in 1921.

from Bernstein in December 1923. Within eight months, though, both titles were gone. Brooklyn's Steve 'Kid' Sullivan outpointed him in June for the junior lightweight championship, and in August he relinquished the featherweight title. He got a surprise chance to regain the featherweight championship in 1927, despite having only two wins in his previous 12 fights, but was outpointed by Tony Canzoneri.

Sullivan's credentials were equally shaky. His record showed eight defeats in the 11 fights before he beat Dundee, but at least his form improved. As champion he managed two defences, against Pepper Martin and Mike Ballerino, before Ballerino outpointed him in a rematch in Philadelphia in April 1925. Ballerino made only one defence, outpointing the persistent Pepper Martin, and was dethroned in December 1925 by the division's first really outstanding champion, Tod Morgan. His real name

Left: *Kid Chocolate, the brilliant Cuban who went 160 fights without defeat before losing to 'Kid' Berg.*

Above left: *Tommy Paul, the former NBA featherweight champion, held Chocolate to a draw in a 1934 ten-rounder.*

Above right: *Frankie Klick (right, in a losing 12-rounder with Tony Canzoneri) never defended his title.*

was the mundane-sounding Bert Pilkington, which he changed on launching his professional career in 1920 when he was 17 years old. Morgan's apprenticeship was abnormally long – his first 53 fights were all over the novice four-round distance, and he did not reach ten-rounds status until his 73rd outing. He became a busy champion, participating in 12 fights which were billed as being for the 9 st 4 lb (130 lb) title, although they are not all officially recorded as such.

Morgan fought all over America, and also risked the title in Vancouver. He had a peculiar record during his four years as champion, losing almost as many of his non-title fights as he won, but he could always be relied on to find his true form when the championship was at stake. His reign ended in scandal when the Russian-born Benny Bass, having his 23rd fight of the year, knocked him out in two rounds in Madison Square Garden in December 1929. Both fighters' purses were suspended while the Commission investigated a possible betting coup: Bass, the NBA featherweight champion in 1927-28, had been made a 5-1 on favourite, despite Morgan's fine record as champion. Bass, whose nickname was, inevitably, 'The Fish', was stopped with a cut left eye in seven rounds in his second defence by the brilliant Cuban, Kid Chocolate, when they met in Philadelphia in July 1931.

The Kid, whose real name was Eligio Sardinias, went through 160 fights (including 100 as an amateur) before he lost for the first time to the Englishman, Jack 'Kid' Berg, in 1930. He tried unsuccessfully for the featherweight title in December 1930, being outpointed by Battling Battalino, and four months after beating Bass he challenged for Tony Canzoneri's lightweight and light-welterweight titles, losing on points. He eventually won the New York version of the featherweight title, knocking out Lew Feldman in 1932, and retained it against Fidel LaBarba (one of the four men to have beaten him), and England's Tommy Watson. But he had such a taste for high living that he squandered an estimated $500,000 during his years at the top. By 1933, when Frankie Klick of San Francisco knocked him out in seven rounds to take the junior lightweight title, he was riddled with syphilis.

Two months later, in February 1934, the Kid relinquished his claim to the featherweight title, although he boxed on for another four years and 49 fights, losing just three of them. His overall record on retirement, in 1938, was a remarkable 132 wins and six draws out of 148 fights.

Klick never defended the junior lightweight title. He could no longer make the weight, and within three months of winning the 130 lb title he was challenging Barney Ross, unsuccessfully, for the 147 lb crown. Becoming champion did nothing for his career, and he won only five of his remaining 24 fights.

The title fell into disuse thereafter, although it resurfaced briefly in 1949 when Sandy Saddler, who had lost the featherweight title earlier in the

Featherweight champion Sandy Saddler claimed a version of the 130-lb title in 1949, but nobody took it too seriously and the division lapsed back into disuse for another decade.

Harold Gomes (left, *stopping Lulu Perez on a cut in 1957) revived the division two years later, but lost the title in his first defence to the superb Filipino southpaw Flash Elorde* (right). *Elorde (seen* below *landing a classic jab on Miguel Berrios) became the division's first* great *champion.*

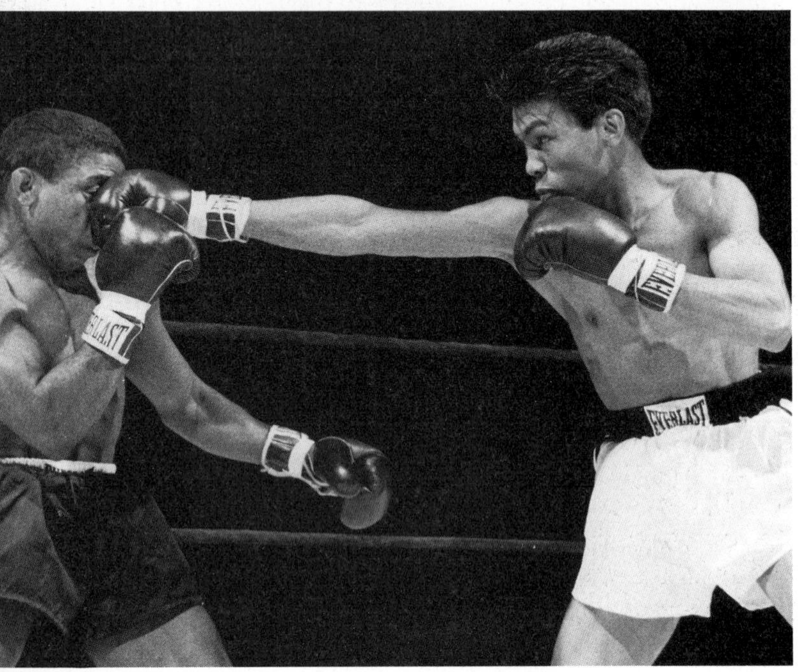

year to Willie Pep, won a ten-rounder in Cleveland over the Cuban, Orlando Zulueta, that was billed locally as being for the junior lightweight championship. His two-round knockout of Diego Sosa in Havana, in March 1951, was also billed as a 130 lb title fight, although neither contest carried any kind of official endorsement. Saddler needed a police escort from the ring after the win over Sosa, when the crowd of 10,000 pelted the ring with bottles and cushions, claiming that their man had been knocked out by a foul blow.

Saddler himself does not appear to have taken his 'championship' very seriously, and never again defended it. The division remained inactive until July 1959 when Harold Gomes of Providence, Rhode Island, outpointed a Texan called Paul Jorgensen over 15 rounds, in his home town for the vacant title, with NBA approval. Gomes lost the championship in his first defence to a superb Filipino, who is unquestionably the finest fighter that country has produced, and arguably the greatest champion in the division's history – Gabriel 'Flash' Elorde.

He had won Oriental bantamweight, featherweight, and lightweight titles, and had lost a fierce 13-round war with Sandy Saddler (whom he had previously outpointed) for the world featherweight title. By the time Elorde became junior lightweight champion, stopping Gomes in seven rounds in Manila on 16 March 1960, he was already a veteran of 71 fights. Yet he ruled the world at 130 lb for the next six years and, in fact, had his final fight in May 1971, by which time he had been a professional for more than 20 years. Elorde deserves the credit for ensuring the division's future. He defended the title so many times, against worldwide opposition, that he became one of the best-known fighters of his generation.

Elorde made 11 successful defences, against contenders from America, Italy, Ghana, Korea, and Argentina, and also made two brave attempts on Carlos Ortiz' world lightweight title, being stopped in 14 rounds in 1964, and again in 1966. He was beaten at last on a split decision by Yoshiaki Numata of Japan, on 15 June 1967 in Tokyo. Including Filipino, Oriental, and world championships, this was his 44th title fight.

Numata lost his first defence to his compatriot Hiroshi Kobayashi, who knocked him out in 12 rounds in Tokyo in December 1967. The new champion made two defences of the undisputed title, drawing with Rene Barrientos and outpointing Jaime Valladares, but then in January 1969 he was stripped by the WBC for failing to meet Valladares in a rematch. The title has remained split ever since, with no prospect of unification.

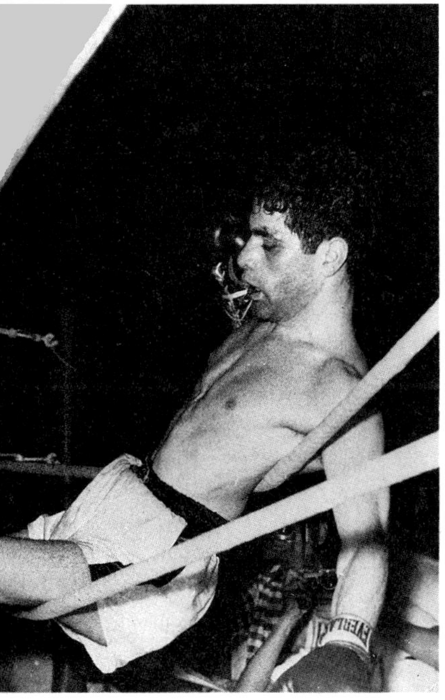

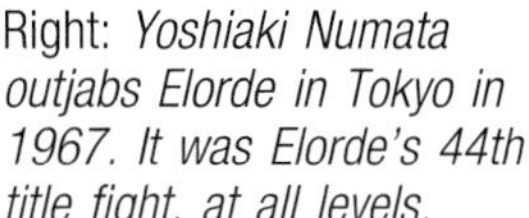

Right: *Yoshiaki Numata outjabs Elorde in Tokyo in 1967. It was Elorde's 44th title fight, at all levels.*

Kobayashi managed four defences of the WBA share of the championship, but was forced to retire after ten rounds in his fifth defence by the Venezuelan, Alfredo Marcano. Marcano, in turn, lost the title in his second defence to Ben Villaflor of the Philippines, in Villaflor's adopted hometown of Honolulu. Villaflor drew his first defence, but was then dethroned by yet another Japanese, Kuniaki Shibata, in March 1973. Shibata's reign was even shorter – he outpointed Victor Echegary of Argentina (who had drawn with Villaflor) but lasted less than a round in a rematch with Villaflor in October 1973.

The Filipino, in his second spell as champion, at last brought some continuity to the WBA title, which he held for three years and five defences. He had a considerable share of luck, though, drawing with Apollo Yoshio and Sam Serrano, and winning a split decision over a Korean, Hyun Chi Kim. When he lost the title in a rematch with Serrano, in San Juan on 16 October 1976, he made sure that he was well compensated: his purse of $150,000 was a record

Hiroshi Kobayashi (left, *outpointing Jaime Valladares) maintained the Orient's interest in the title, as did another Japanese Kuniaki Shibata* (below).

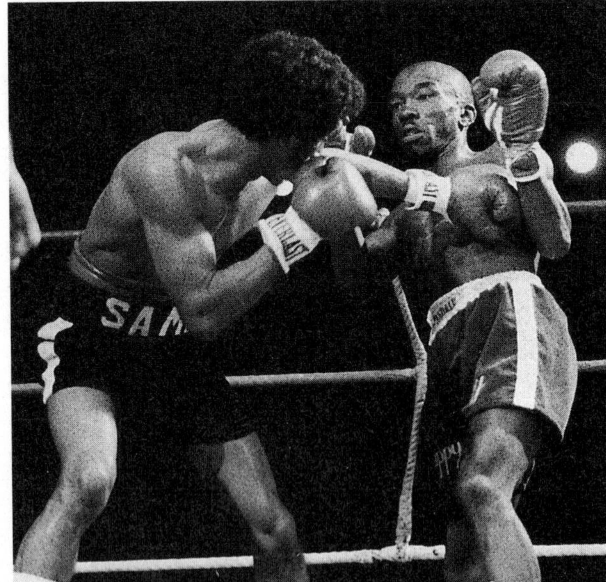

Sam Serrano (left) *was a dominant figure in the division's history with a string of defences, including this South African win over the unpronounceable Nkosana Mgxaji. He later lost the title to Yasutsune Uehara* (below), *and regained it from him eight months later.*

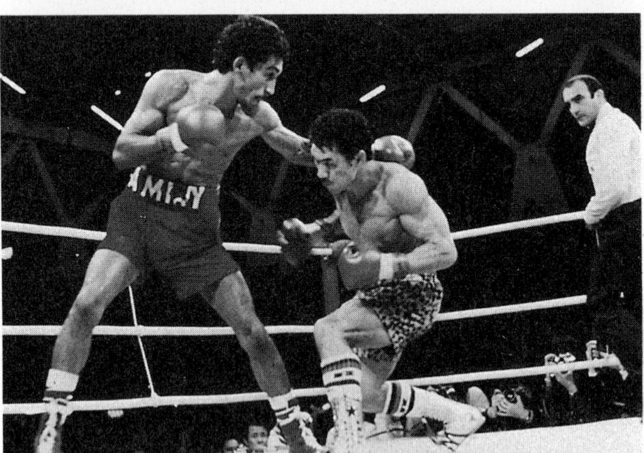

for the hitherto modestly paid division.

Serrano was a tricky southpaw who, for the next seven years, would be one of the dominant figures in the division. In his first reign he made ten successful defences, five inside the distance, but was surprisingly knocked out in the sixth round of his 11th defence in Detroit by a Japanese, Yasutsune Uehara, in August 1980. Uehara had been knocked out in two rounds by Villaflor in a 1974 title bid, in what was only his 12th fight. He retained the title against the classy Venezuelan, Leonel Hernandez, but then lost it back to Serrano in Wakayama, in April 1981. He never fought again.

The Puerto Rican held the title until January 1983, although he made only three defences in that time. He appeared to have been beaten by the Chilean Benedicto Villablanca in Santiago, in June 1982, when the referee stopped the fight in the 11th round because Serrano was badly cut, but even as Villablanca celebrated his coronation, ringside officials over-ruled the verdict and declared it a no-contest. Serrano's luck ran out in January 1983 when Roger Mayweather, a lanky puncher from Michigan who boxed out of Las Vegas, stopped him in eight rounds in San Juan.

Right: *This points win over former bantamweight champ Lionel Rose (on the right) was the last victory of Yoshiaki Numata's career.* Below: *a champion of later vintage, South Africa's Brian Mitchell, taking the title from Alfredo Layne of Panama.*

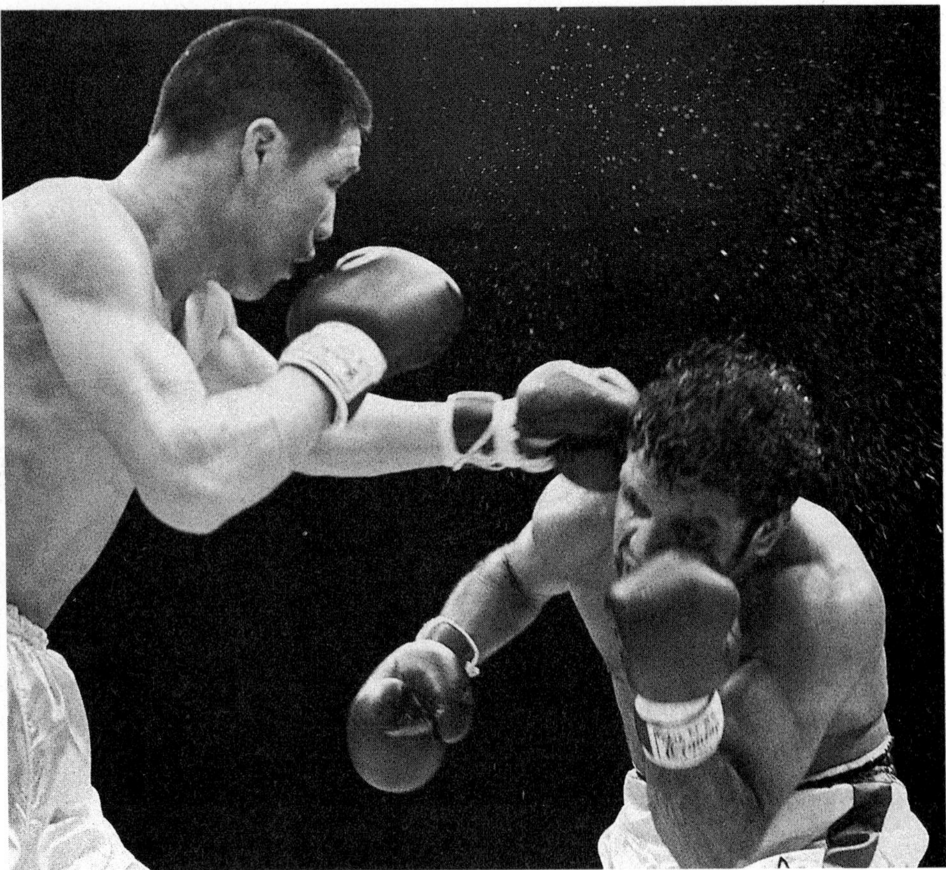

Mayweather, nicknamed the 'Black Mamba', initially looked impressive with defences against Jorge Alvarado and the unfortunate Villablanca, whom he knocked out in a round. However, he was dramatically beaten inside a round in his third defence by Rocky Lockridge, a Texan who had been outpointed by Eusebio Pedroza less than a year previously in a WBA featherweight title bid.

Lockridge defended against Tae Jin Moon of Korea and the outclassed Kamel Bou-Ali, but in May 1985 lost what most impartial observers felt was a biased home-town decision, in San Juan, to the Puerto Rican Wilfredo Gomez, the former super-bantamweight champion. Since then the title has passed from Gomez to Alfredo Layne from Panama, who lost it in his first defence to Brian Mitchell of South Africa.

The WBC championship, taken from Kobayashi in January 1969, was won a month later by the Filipino Rene Barrientos, with whom Kobayashi had drawn in March 1968. Barrientos outpointed Ruben Navarro, later to challenge for the lightweight title, but then lost it in his first defence to the former champion Yoshiaki Numata, on a split decision in Tokyo. Numata retained it against the ex-WBA featherweight champion Raul Rojas, Barrientos again, and the former bantamweight champion Lionel Rose of Australia, but his reign was ended in October 1971 by the Mexican, Ricardo Arredondo, whose brother Rene was briefly WBC light-welterweight champion in 1986.

Arredondo was a good champion, holding the title for two and a half years and five defences. He was eventually dethroned in February 1974 by the former WBA champion Kuniaki Shibata, who retained it three times before being knocked out in two rounds, in July 1975, by the outstanding Puerto Rican Alfredo 'Snakeman' Escalera.

Escalera built up a record to rival Serrano's, cramming in ten defences between July 1975 and September 1977. He was considered lucky to get a split verdict over the Philadelphian, Tyrone Everett, in the American's home town in November 1976, and had also been involved in a controversial ending in Japan, earlier in the year when his sixth round stoppage of Buzzsaw Yamabe was changed to a 'No Decision' by the Japanese Commission because the referee had failed either to count Yamabe out, or to consult with the ringside doctor.

Escalera's reign was ended in January 1978 by the brilliant Alexis Arguello, when the former featherweight champion stopped him in 13 rounds in San Juan. The Nicaraguan was unbeatable at this weight, making eight defences of which only one, against Arturo Leon, lasted the distance. It is a measure of his superiority over his contemporaries that Rafael Limon, Bobby Chacon, and Rolando Navarette all became champions after unsuccessful challenges against Arguello, as did Cornelius Boza-Edwards, whom Arguello stopped in a non-title fight.

Limon, a rugged southpaw from Mexico City, won the vacant title in December 1980 (when Arguello moved up to lightweight) by stopping Idelfonso Betelmy in the last round in Los Angeles, but he surprisingly lost it three months later to the

Below: *Kuniaki Shibata regains the WBC title against the Mexican Ricardo Arredondo, whose brother Rene later won the WBC light-welter title.*

Right: *Bazooka Limon's defeat by Cornelius Boza-Edwards (on the left) was a shock but the Ugandan became a key figure in the division in the early 1980s.*

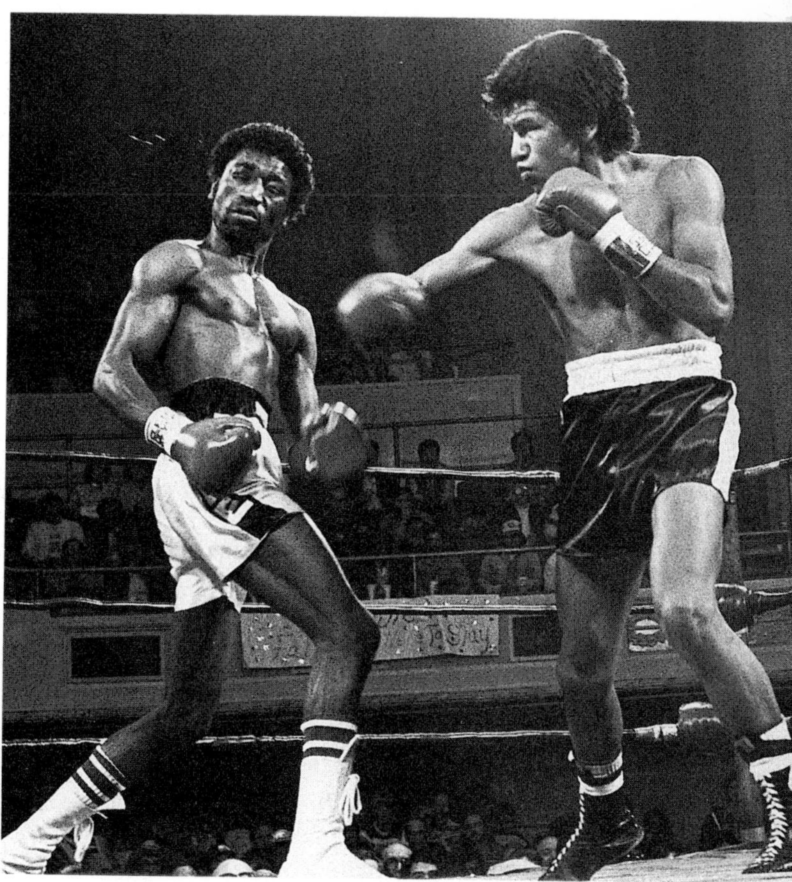

Ugandan, Boza-Edwards. The new champion, whose family name was Boza, had adopted the hyphenated 'Edwards' in tribute to an Englishman, Jack Edwards, who had looked after him in Uganda and later in London, where the youngster settled. Boza-Edwards moved permanently to America in 1980, establishing himself with a gallant performance against Arguello. He kept the title with a savage 13th-round stoppage of Bobby Chacon, the former featherweight champion, in May 1981. It was one of the most thrilling fights in the division's history but, together with the demands of the Limon fight, contributed to his listless display when losing the title on a fifth-round knockout to a crude Filipino, Rolando Navarette, three months later.

The Filipino southpaw made just one successful defence, then lost it on a 12th-round stoppage to Limon in Las Vegas in May 1982. Limon was beaten in his second defence by Chacon, in yet another of the thrilling championship fights which were a feature of this division in the early 1980s. However, Chacon was stripped of his title in controversial circumstances by the WBC, after a long-running saga involving American promoter

The former featherweight champion Bobby Chacon figured in some of the most thrilling battles in junior lightweight history, such as his two wars with Boza-Edwards (above *and* below) *and his three with Bazooka Limon* (left).

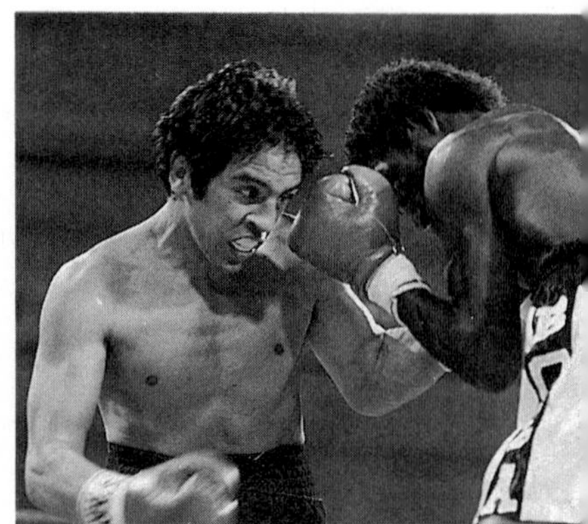

Don King, Boza-Edwards and his manager Mickey Duff, and Duff's Californian associate Don Chargin. King and Duff each claimed to have a contract for Chacon's first defence. Duff wanted to match him with Boza-Edwards, King with the Puerto Rican sensation Hector Camacho.

The California Commission found in King's favour, but a compromise was worked out which allowed Chacon to meet, and outpoint, Boza-Edwards in a 12-rounder which did not carry WBC recognition as a title fight. The dispute cost Chacon the title a month later, when he was stripped for refusing to meet Camacho for King when offered $450,000, since Chargin had offered him $1,000,000 for the same fight. Camacho stopped Limon in five rounds for the vacant title, which he defended once before relinquishing it in 1984 to chase the lightweight title, which he duly won.

Julio Cesar Chavez of Mexico stopped Mario Martinez in eight rounds to succeed Camacho in September 1984, and retained it with a series of stunning performances which made him clearly the division's outstanding fighter. His only defeat, going into 1987, was an early career disqualification.

The IBF championship was inaugurated in 1984, when Hwan-Kil Yuh of Korea outpointed Rod Sequenan of the Philippines. The title passed from the Korean to Lester Ellis of Australia, who retained it twice before being beaten by his compatriot Barry Michael. Michael was already a veteran when he became champion, but has made three defences, including Britain's first IBF title fight when he outpointed the Moroccan-born, Manchester-based Najib Daho, in August 1986.

Julio Cesar Chavez (right), *a dazzling Mexican who won the WBC title in 1984, proved unbeatable at the weight. His IBF contemporary, Australia's Barry Michael* (below, *retaining against Najib Daho) was a tough and rugged veteran who had fought his way through the weights, even beating the Australian welterweight champion.*

HOW THE JUNIOR LIGHTWEIGHT TITLE HAS CHANGED HANDS

18 Nov 21	Johnny Dundee w.dis.5 George Chaney in New York *(Vacant title)*
30 May 23	Jack Bernstein w.pts.15 Johnny Dundee in New York
17 Dec 23	Johnny Dundee w.pts.15 Jack Bernstein in New York
20 Jun 24	Steve Kid Sullivan w.pts.15 Johnny Dundee at Brooklyn
01 Apr 25	Mike Ballerino w.pts.10 Steve Kid Sullivan at Philadelphia
02 Dec 25	Tod Morgan w.ko.10 Mike Ballerino at Los Angeles
19 Dec 29	Benny Bass w.ko.2 Tod Morgan in New York
15 Jul 31	Kid Chocolate w.rsf.7 Benny Bass at Philadelphia
26 Dec 33	Frankie Klick w.ko.7 Kid Chocolate at Philadelphia *(Title fell into disuse)*
20 Jul 59	Harold Gomes w.pts.15 Paul Jorgenson at Providence *(To win revived title)*
16 Mar 60	Flash Elorde w.rsf.7 Harold Gomes at Manila
15 Jun 67	Yoshiaki Numata w.pts.15 Flash Elorde in Tokyo
14 Dec 67	Hiroshi Kobayashi w.ko.12 Yoshiaki Numata in Tokyo *(Title taken from Kobayashi by WBC for failure to defend against Rene Barrientos)*
15 Feb 69	Rene Barrientos w.pts.15 Rueben Navarro at Manila *(Vacant WBC title)*
05 Apr 70	Yoshiaki Numata w.pts.15 Rene Barrientos at Tokyo
10 Oct 71	Ricardo Arredondo w.ko.10 Yoshiaki Numata at Sendai
29 Jul 71	Alfredo Marcano w.rsf.10 Hiroshi Kobayashi at Aomari, Japan *(WBA title)*
25 Apr 72	Ben Villaflor w.pts.15 Alfredo Marcano at Honolulu
12 Mar 73	Kuniaki Shibata w.pts.15 Ben Villaflor at Honolulu
17 Oct 73	Ben Villaflor w.ko.1 Kuniaki Shibata in Honolulu
28 Feb 74	Kuniaki Shibata w.pts.15 Ricardo Arredondo in Tokyo *(WBC title)*
05 Jul 75	Alfredo Escalera w.ko.2 Kuniaki Shibata at Mito, Japan *(WBC title)*
16 Oct 76	Sam Serrano w.pts.15 Ben Villaflor in San Juan
28 Jan 78	Alexis Arguello w.rsf.13 Alfredo Escalera in San Juan
02 Aug 80	Yasutsune Uehara w.ko.6 Sam Serrano in Detroit *(WBA title)*
Oct. 1980	*Arguello relinquished WBC title to campaign as a lightweight*
11 Dec 80	Rafael Limon w.rsf.15 Idelfonso Bethelmi at Los Angeles *(Vacant WBC title)*
08 Mar 81	Cornelius Boza-Edwards w.pts.15 Rafael Limon at Stockton
09 Apr 81	Sam Serrano w.pts. 15 Yasutsune Uehara at Wakayama
29 Aug 81	Rolando Navarette w.ko.5 Cornelius Boza-Edwards at Via Reggio
29 May 82	Rafael Limon w.ko.12 Rolando Navarette at Las Vegas
11 Dec 82	Bobby Chacon w.pts.15 Rafael Limon at Sacramento
19 Jan 83	Roger Mayweather w.ko.8 Sam Serrano at San Juan *(WBA title)*
Jun 1983	*WBC stripped Chacon of the title because of a contractual dispute*
07 Aug 83	Hector Camacho w.rsf.5 Rafael Limon at San Juan *(Vacant WBC title)*
26 Feb 84	Rocky Lockridge w.ko.1 Roger Mayweather at Beaumont, Texas
22 Apr 84	Hwan-Kil Yuh w.pts.15 Rod Sequenan in Seoul *(For vacant IBF title)*
13 Sep 84	Julio Cesar Chavez w.rsf.8 Mario Martinez at Los Angeles *(For vacant WBC title: Camacho had relinquished it to box as lightweight)*
15 Feb 85	Lester Ellis w.pts.15 Hwan-Kil Yuh in Melbourne
19 May 85	Wilfredo Gomez w.pts.15 Rocky Lockridge in San Juan
12 Jul 85	Barry Michael w.pts.15 Lester Ellis in Melbourne
24 May 86	Alfredo Layne w.rsf.9 Wilfredo Gomez at San Juan *(WBA title)*
27 Sep 86	Brian Mitchell w.rsf. 10 Alfredo Layne at Sun City, Bophuthatswana

FEATHERWEIGHTS

THE FEATHERWEIGHTS have always been a cosmopolitan crowd. The 126 lb division has had champions from Kiev and Clones, Merthyr and Mexico City, Bermondsey and Brooklyn. Before the turn of the century the title had been held in succession by a New Zealander, an Australian, a Canadian, an American, an Irishman, and an Englishman, and the tradition continues. Champions and claimants have also come from France, Sicily, Cuba, Mexico, Nigeria, Japan, Venezuela, Panama, Brazil, Spain, Puerto Rico, and Ghana.

The division became active around 1860, with the fight between Nobby Clark and Jim Elliott at Weehawken, New Jersey, on 28 May 1860, sometimes being listed as the first world title match. Clark won on a 34th-round knockout but never pursued the claim, and almost 30 years elapsed before there was another attempt to find a champion when Ike O'Neill Weir, from Lurgan, Co. Armagh, met England's Frank Murphy at Kouts, Indiana, on 31 March 1889. Weir, who was based in Boston, was generally considered to be having the best of it in the 80th round when the police intervened, leaving the official result a draw. Weir got a second chance at the San Francisco Athletic Club in January 1890, but was knocked out in 14 rounds by 'Torpedo' Billy Murphy from Auckland, New Zealand.

'Little Chocolate' – George Dixon, the first universally accepted featherweight champion.

The Americans were reluctant to see the championship leave the country, and when Murphy returned home and promptly lost the title to the Australian, Young Griffo, the new champion was not recognized outside the Antipodes. As far as the Americans were concerned Murphy's two title fights were for the British Empire title, even though the Weir fight had actually taken place in San Francisco. Instead, they acclaimed the unbeaten bantamweight champion George Dixon as the new featherweight king, after the Canadian's 22nd-round stoppage of Cal McCarthy of Pennsylvania at Troy, New York, on 31 March 1891. But he was not universally accepted as the title holder until his 14th-round knockout of Fred Johnson of England, in June 1892, by which time Griffo had outgrown the division anyway.

Dixon was a busy, colourful, and well-paid

Terry McGovern (right) *figured in his share of controversial contests, including this highly suspicious knockout of Joe Gans in 1900* (above).

champion. He won a side bet of $5,000 and a purse of $7,500 for knocking out the ex-amateur star Jack Skelly (who was having his first professional fight) in eight rounds, on the famous Carnival of Champions show in New Orleans in September 1892, when James J. Corbett changed the course of boxing history by beating John L. Sullivan for the heavyweight title. The Canadian, whose diminutive size (5 ft 3½ in) and dark skin earned him the nickname 'Little Chocolate', dominated the class for five years. He was thrice held to a draw during this period, but the first man to defeat him was the Swiss-born Frank Erne (later to become lightweight champion) in 1896. Dixon reversed the result a year later, but was then outpointed by Solly Smith from Los Angeles, whom he had knocked out in an 1893 title fight.

Since Dixon claimed that the title was not at stake when he lost to Smith, he continued to bill himself as world champion. Smith did likewise, defending his title twice before Dave Sullivan, a rugged brawler who had been born in Cork, Ireland forced him to retire in five rounds. Dixon, meanwhile, had been outscored decisively at the championship weight (then 122 lb) by Ben Jordan of Bermondsey in New York on 1 July 1898, so that when Dixon beat Sullivan on a 10th-round disqualification in November, he regained only partial recognition as champion.

Jordan took his share of the championship back to London, retaining it against Harry Greenfield in the National Sporting Club in May 1899, but he lost it when Eddie Santry of Aurora, Illinois, knocked him out in 16 rounds in New York on 10 October 1899. Santry had drawn with Dixon two months previously, so there was nothing to choose between the rival claims.

The Canadian had been active in defence of his portion of the title, having seven title fights in 1899, but the youthful ferocity of the unbeaten bantamweight champion, Terry McGovern, was too much for him in his 23rd and final appearance as featherweight king. Tom O'Rourke, the veteran champion's manager, threw in the sponge in the eighth round of a punishing battle at the Broadway Athletic Club in New York on 9 January 1900. His man had been floored six times in the round, and he wanted to spare him the last indignity of being counted out.

Dixon was finished as a top-class performer, but since he had squandered his earnings he had to fight on for another seven years, campaigning in Britain from September 1902 until April 1905. He had 57 fights after losing to McGovern, but won only 11 of them.

McGovern, from Johnstown, Pennsylvania, cleared up the confusion by knocking out his rival claimant Eddie Santry in five rounds in Chicago, on 1 February 1900. However, he ran into trouble in his third championship fight in three months when he took on Oscar Gardner, of Omaha, at the Broadway Athletic Club in New York. McGovern, as was then the custom, had his 'own' referee who could usually be depended upon to give the champion every assistance, and he earned his wages when Gardner flattened McGovern with a

Young Corbett (left) *exploited McGovern's bad temper to take the title from him* (above). *Corbett eventually gave up the battle with the scales and relinquished the championship, which was claimed by Abe Attell* (right, *who is on the left, squaring off with Tommy Sullivan before their 1908 title encounter).*

mighty right in the second round. The referee took up the count at such a leisurely pace that McGovern had been on the floor for 12 seconds before the official count had reached 'three', and 20 seconds had elapsed when the groggy champion at last got up. He was then permitted to spend the rest of the round with his arms firmly wrapped around Gardner's waist, but his powers of recovery were such that the unfortunate challenger did not survive the third round.

The heavy-hitting McGovern knocked out four more aspirants (including Gardner again, this time in the fourth round) before his Irish temper cost him the title at Hartford, in November 1901, against a westerner from Denver whose real name was William Rothwell, but who boxed as Young Corbett. Rothwell had adopted the ring name in tribute to his idol, James J. Corbett, whose tactics for his fight with John L. Sullivan had been designed to provoke and irritate the hot-headed Sullivan to the point where he would make silly mistakes, so becoming an easy target for the cool challenger's punches. Young Corbett adopted the same strategy, insulting the champion in a restaurant on the afternoon of the fight, humiliating him in front of his friends and entourage, and, in the first clinch of the opening round, airing his views on the moral standards of McGovern's wife and mother. And these tactics worked – the infuriated McGovern hurled himself into the attack, scorning defence, and Corbett smashed him down twice for a second-round knockout.

Since Corbett had difficulty in making the weight, which McGovern had set at its present limit of 126 lb, he relinquished the title in December 1902 and moved up to lightweight. Abe Attell, a stylish Jew from San Francisco who had beaten George Dixon in 1901, now claimed the title. There were, as always, other claimants, but Attell was generally accepted after he had knocked out Harry Forbes of Chicago in the fifth round at St Louis, in 1904.

Attell's great weakness was gambling, and years after his retirement he was involved in a notorious betting coup involving baseball matches. The habit was with him in his championship days, too – Forbes had outpointed him in 1901, and he was favoured to do so again. Attell won $40,000 on the rematch by betting that Forbes would not last five rounds.

Attell held the title until 1912, although with different referees and scoring systems he would

Abe Attell was a notorious gambler, and he certainly had luck on his side in some of his title defences.

Above: *Owen Moran (right, shaking hands with Attell) seemed to have clearly outpointed the American twice, but had to settle for a draw each time.*

have been dethroned long before then. He was the beneficiary of two drawn verdicts against Owen Moran of Birmingham in January and September 1908, when the Englishman seemed to have won clearly each time. Their second fight was over the unprecedented distance of 23 rounds, reduced from 25 at Attell's insistence. The New York newspapers failed to give him one of the ten rounds against British champion Jim Driscoll of Cardiff, on 19 February 1909, but he kept the title since official decisions were prohibited in the city at that time. Driscoll, however, billed himself as the new champion, and his win over Jean Poesy of France in 1912 and draw with Moran in 1913 were both reported as title defences. The Welshman retired in July 1913, although he made an ill-advised, three-fight comeback six years later, when he was 38.

In all, Attell made 13 defences of the title, although some sources credit him with as many as

Even in the last fight of a long career, when Charles Ledoux stopped him in 16 rounds just months before the Welshman's 40th birthday, Driscoll could still land a perfect straight left.

21. He was beaten at last on 22 February 1912 at Vernon, California, by Johnny Kilbane, an Irish-American from Cleveland whom Attell had outpointed in a ten-rounder two years previously. The one-time clerk in the Pennsylvania Railways office had been obsessively interested in boxing long before he took the sport up at 18, and he went

Right: *Johnny Kilbane held the title for 11 years, having taken it from another long-serving champion in Abe Attell.*

Eugene Criqui, a French war hero who had challenged unsuccessfully for the flyweight title nine years previously, knocked out Kilbane for the featherweight title in 1923.

on to rule the division for 11 years. His reign coincided with the 'no-decision' era when many American states prohibited points verdicts, and a champion could therefore only lose his title if he was beaten inside the distance in a contest in which both men had scaled within the division's weight limit. His rare inside-the-distance wins are sometimes recorded as defences, since the title would have been forfeited had he been beaten in similar circumstances. But as far as can be determined, his 11-year reign embraced only four 'formal' championship matches. However, the New York Commission stripped Kilbane of the title in 1922 for his failure to meet Johnny Dundee, the junior lightweight champion (with whom Kilbane had drawn in a 1913 defence). Dundee was matched with another of Kilbane's unsuccessful challengers, Danny Frush of Aldgate, and knocked out the Londoner in nine rounds at Abbott's Field, Brooklyn, on 15 August 1922.

Kilbane was tempted out of his semi-retirement to meet Eugene Criqui, of France, at the Polo Grounds on 2 June 1923, in defence of what remained of his championship. The Frenchman, who had lost a flyweight title bid to Percy Jones nine years previously, had been wounded in the jaw by a German sniper during his army service and a steel plate had been inserted into the jawbone which, he claimed, gave him extra punch resistance. His only setbacks since resuming his career in 1917 were against Memphis Pal Moore and Bermondsey's Tommy Noble, whom promoter Tex Rickard had designated 'world champion' after the Londoner's points win over Johnny Murray in New York on 7 October 1920.

Memphis Pal Moore (left) on the way to a 14th-round win over Criqui in London in 1919.

Rickard even presented Noble with a diamond-studded 'championship belt', but no one took the affair too seriously and Noble, the former British bantamweight champion, did not have any further 'world title' contests. The Londoner had earned a £60,000 fortune during his few years in America, but soon lost it. Historian Gilbert Odd recalls meeting him many years later, when Noble was living in a single room in Streatham, London. The old champion proudly showed him Rickard's belt, but all that remained of it was a wide band of leather studded with holes where the inscribed plaque and the 36 diamonds had once been.

Criqui compiled a long and impressive record,

This trio of featherweight champions between them amassed a total of 387 recorded fights, although their actual career totals may have been even higher. Left to right*: Russia's first world champion, Louis 'Kid' Kaplan, Tony Canzoneri and Andre Routis.*

winning the European title in July 1922 and retaining it three times before the end of the year. He went into the Kilbane fight with a string of 14 consecutive wins inside the distance, and the 34-year-old veteran was duly despatched in the sixth round. The Frenchman's reign lasted 54 days, as he was outpointed by Dundee for the undisputed title at the Polo Grounds on 26 July. Increasing weight problems forced Dundee to give up the title on 10 August 1924, and the vacancy was filled by Russia's first world champion, Louis 'Kid' Kaplan, who beat Philadelphia's Danny Kramer on a ninth-round retirement in New York, on 2 January 1925.

Kaplan retained the title twice against a California-based Portuguese, Babe Herman, but he abdicated in March 1927, also because of weight problems, without any further defences. He was succeeded, curiously, by Russia's only other champion, Benny Bass, who boxed out of Philadelphia. But Bass' ten-round points win over Red Chapman in Philadelphia, on 19 September 1927, earned him only NBA recognition. Tony Canzoneri outpointed Dundee (who was making one last attempt to succeed as a featherweight) for the New York version a month later, and then won the undisputed title with a unanimous points defeat of Bass in Madison Square Garden, in February 1928.

Seven months later, the title was back in France after the 28-year-old André Routis of Bordeaux (whom Canzoneri had outpointed in a 1926 12-rounder) was awarded a bitterly disputed verdict over Canzoneri in New York. Routis retained it with a three-round knockout of Buster Brown in the challenger's home town of Baltimore, but he was plagued by eye trouble and, indeed, lost all his remaining six fights. His penultimate defeat, by Christopher 'Battling' Battalino, saw the title change hands in September 1929. The new champion, from Hartford, had been a leading amateur. He had won the national AAU title in 1927 and, in his fight before meeting Routis, had outpointed the superb bantamweight champion Panama Al Brown.

Battalino made five defences, including wins over Kid Chocolate, Fidel LaBarba (the former flyweight champion) and Freddie Miller, but his reign ended ignominiously in January 1932 in a farcical rematch with Miller, who was also his stablemate. The fight, in Miller's home town of

Battling Battalino (left) *lost his title in such suspicious circumstances to Freddie Miller* (below)*, that it was declared vacant.*

Miller lost this non-title fight to Tommy Paul (above, *on the left) on disqualification, but crammed in nine defences (including two against Nel Tarleton* (below, *kneeling) before losing the title to Petey Sarron* (left).

Cincinnati, had been scheduled as a title defence, but Battalino came in 3 lb overweight and performed abominably.

The referee stopped the fight in the third round after Battalino had gone down from an apparently harmless punch, and declared Miller the winner. Both the NBA and the New York Commission, however, ruled it a 'no contest' and declared the title vacant.

The NBA version was won in May 1932 by Tommy Paul of Buffalo, New York, who ironically had been AAU bantamweight champion in the same year (1927) that Battalino had won the featherweight competition. Paul, whose real name was Gaetano Alfonso Pappa, had lost only seven of his 70 fights prior to outpointing San Francisco's Johnny Pena for the title, and had beaten men such as Frankie Genaro, Bushy Graham, Maurice Holtzer, and Freddie Miller. But he was unimpressive as champion, losing non-title fights to Fidel LaBarba (who had beaten him twice previously), Lew Feldman and Baby Arizmendi. Finally, in January 1933, he lost the title, in his first defence, to Freddie Miller.

Miller was a masterly performer, who shrugged off the scandal surrounding his 1932 meeting with

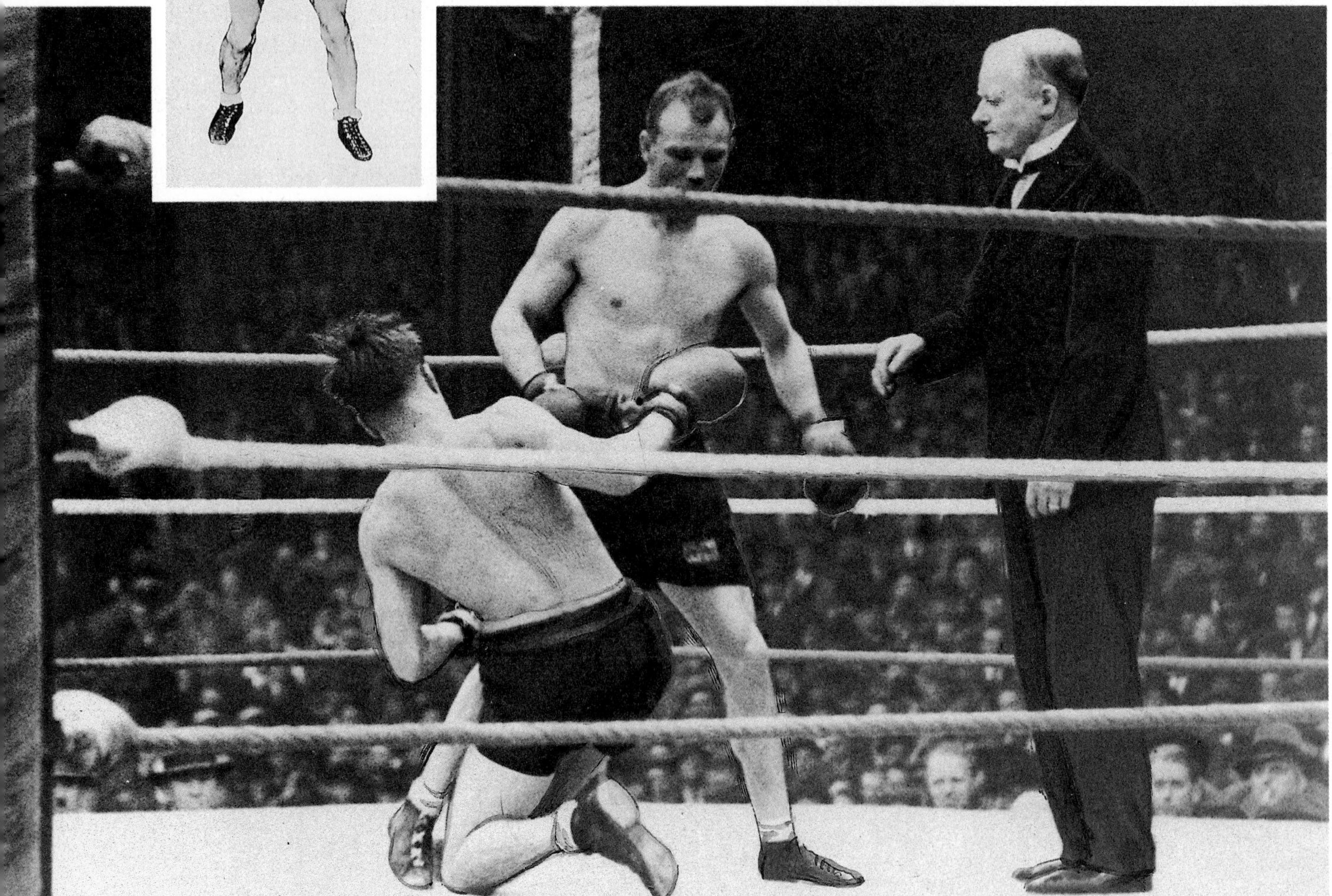

Battalino to become one of the great names in the division's history. Over the next four years the Cincinnati southpaw made nine successful defences, including two in Liverpool against the British champion Nel Tarleton. Their first fight, at Anfield in September 1934, added International Boxing Union endorsement to Miller's NBA title.

Miller was the busiest top-flight boxer of his day. He had 19 fights in 1933, 28 in 1934, and an astounding 35 in 1935. However, his work-rate dropped in 1936, and when he lost to Petey Sarron in Washington on 11 May it was only his ninth outing and his third defence of the year.

Sarron's victory was a triumph for persistence. The 29-year-old from Birmingham, Alabama, of part-Syrian extraction, had been a professional since 1925 (when he suffered a broken jaw on his debut) and he had lost three previous meetings with Miller, once for the championship in March 1936. He had had 115 fights, and had spent several years in Australia and New Zealand, where he drew the largest crowd in the island's boxing history – 39,500 – for his 1930 fight with Tommy Donovan, who beat him three times that year.

Henry Armstrong had beaten most of the top featherweights (including Mike Belloise, below) *before he took the championship from Petey Sarron* (above) *in 1937. Within ten months, he added the welterweight and lightweight titles.*

Sarron retained the title against Baby Manuel and then spent most of 1937 in South Africa. He had six fights there, including two more with Miller: the ex-champion won a non-title ten rounder on points, but lost the rematch (over the by then unusual distance of 12 rounds) fairly decisively. He also boxed twice in London, outpointing Harry Mizler in May and being disqualified against Dave Crowley a month later. He was disqualified again in a Johannesburg rematch with Mizler, in the first round, on 20 June. Then, in October, he accepted a $12,000 offer from Mike Jacobs to defend against Henry Armstrong in Madison Square Garden.

The New York Commission, doubtful of Armstrong's ability to make the weight, forced him to have a test weigh ten days before the 29 October date, and another on the eve of the fight, but he made the weight safely and, although Sarron fought well, the title changed hands on a sixth-round knockout. Armstrong's victory, giving him the first of his three world championships, reunited the title. The New York version, taken from Battling Battalino, had been won in August 1932 by the brilliant Cuban Kid Chocolate, who outpointed Chicago's Eddie Shea and retained it three times, against Lew Feldman, Fidel LaBarba, and the Englishman, Seaman Tommy Watson of Newcastle. In March 1934 the New York Commission stripped him for his failure to defend against Frankie Klick, who had been junior lightweight champion the previous year.

Klick, predictably, could no longer make featherweight, so the Commission matched Baby Arizmendi of Torreon, Mexico, with Mike Belloise of the Bronx, New York, the Mexican taking the vacant title on a unanimous decision. Arizmendi outgrew the division without defending the title, but he was a much under-rated fighter whose record included wins over Tommy Paul, Freddie Miller (who also outpointed him in an NBA title bid in 1933) Henry Armstrong (twice), Chalky Wright (twice), and draws with lightweight champions Lou Ambers and Sammy Angott.

Belloise had re-established himself with a 13th-round stoppage of Claude Varner of California in New York on 8 January 1936, and a 14th-round knockout of Everett Rightmire of Sioux City, Iowa, also in New York, on 3 April. Although both these are sometimes listed as title fights, they were

Mike Belloise (left) *and Joey Archibald* (right) *each held the New York version of the title in the 1930s. In fact, Archibald outpointed Belloise to win the vacant title in 1938.*

merely eliminators. Belloise did not gain official recognition from the New York Commission as champion until May 1936, and he defended the title only once, knocking out the Londoner Dave Crowley of Clerkenwell in Madison Square Garden in September. (Crowley had held him to a non-title draw in May, on Belloise's first appearance as champion.) After their standard-bearer had been beaten in overweight matches by Armstrong (twice) and Jackie Wilson, the Commission revoked his title on 10 August 1937, and awarded it to Armstrong for his sixth-round knockout of Petey Sarron.

The title, sadly, did not remain united for long. Armstrong occupied himself by winning world titles at lightweight and welterweight, and relinquished the 126 lb championship without a defence in September 1938. The NBA and the New York Commission nominated rival contenders. Leo Rodak of Chicago, who had eliminated Freddie Miller with a 15-rounds points win in Washington on 24 October, won the NBA title by beating Leone Efrati in Chicago on 29 December. But New York recognized Joey Archibald, a former medical student from Providence, Rhode Island, after his win over the ex-champion Mike Belloise (whom he had also beaten in July 1938). Archibald outpointed Rodak in Providence on 18 April 1939 to reunite the title, and retained it against the former bantamweight champion Harry Jeffra five months later.

In April 1940, however, the NBA withdrew recognition from Archibald for his failure to meet Petey Scalzo of Brooklyn, who had knocked him out in two rounds of a non-title fight in 1938. They took the unusual step of proclaiming Scalzo champion, and the title remained divided for the next six years. (The European-based International Boxing Union had created their own champion in October 1937, Maurice Holtzer of France earning the title by beating Belgium's Phil Dolhem in Algiers. Holtzer's draw with Maurice Dubois in Geneva, in February 1938, also carried IBU recognition, but when the Frenchman relinquished the title because of ill health in July that year, the IBU transferred their allegiance to Armstrong.)

New York continued to recognize Archibald, but their confidence proved misplaced when Jeffra outpointed him in the challenger's home town of Baltimore in May 1940. Jeffra held on to the title against Canada's Spider Armstrong, but was then surprisingly outpointed in a third match with Archibald, who got the chance despite having lost seven of his previous nine fights. Archibald's second spell as champion was short-lived – he was knocked out in 11 rounds at Washington on 11 September 1941 by the Mexican-born veteran Albert 'Chalky' Wright. It was his fourth successive defeat, and after outpointing Billy Banks, a month after the Wright setback, he failed to win any of his remaining 17 fights. The statistics of Archibald's record are intriguing – of the 42 fights between his first world title victory over Mike Belloise, in October 1938, and his retirement in August 1943, he won just 11, four of them for the title.

Harry Jeffra, meanwhile, had earned recognition in Maryland as champion by outpointing Lou

Transparenti in September 1941, but Wright clarified the situation somewhat by knocking Jeffra out in June 1942 and then outpointing Charlie 'Lulu' Constantino in Madison Square Garden in September. Two months later, Wright was dethroned by the Connecticut Italian who is regarded as, pound for pound, one of the most skilful boxers the sport has ever produced – Willie Pep. The win over Wright, which made Pep the youngest world champion since Tony Canzoneri had taken the featherweight title in 1927, was his 55th in a row, and he consolidated his claim to the title by beating Wright again, Sal Bartolo of Boston, and the former NBA champion Phil Terranova before, in June 1946, he knocked out Bartolo to become undisputed champion.

Bartolo had won the NBA version of the title through an undistinguished line of succession. Petey Scalzo had been knocked out in five rounds of his third defence, by Richie Lemos in Los

Left: *Harry Jeffra, the former bantamweight champion, added the featherweight crown in 1940.*

Despite his colour and his Anglo-Saxon name, Albert 'Chalky' Wright (right) *was actually Mexican-born. His title loss to Willie Pep* (below) *inaugurated the division's Golden Era.*

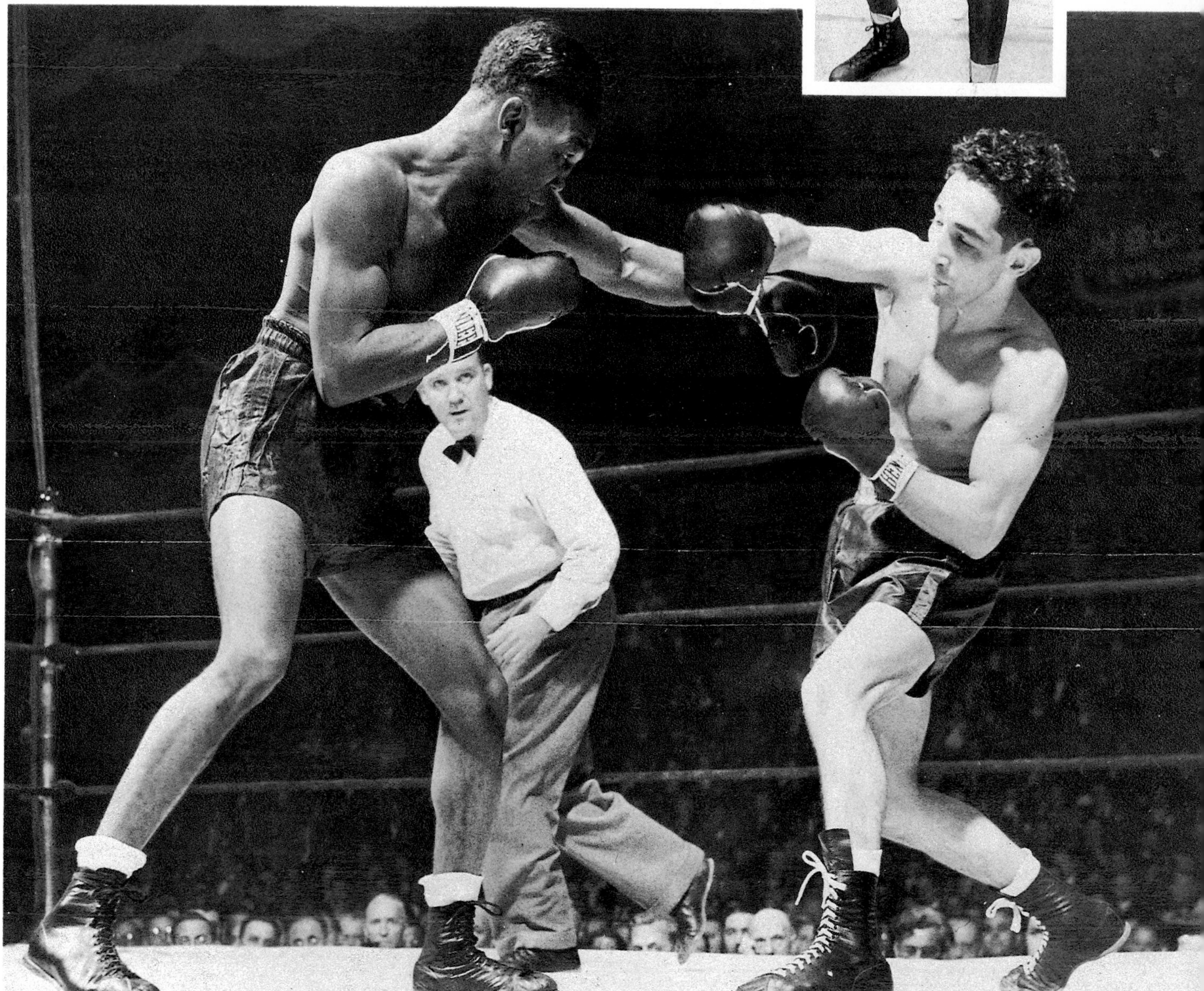

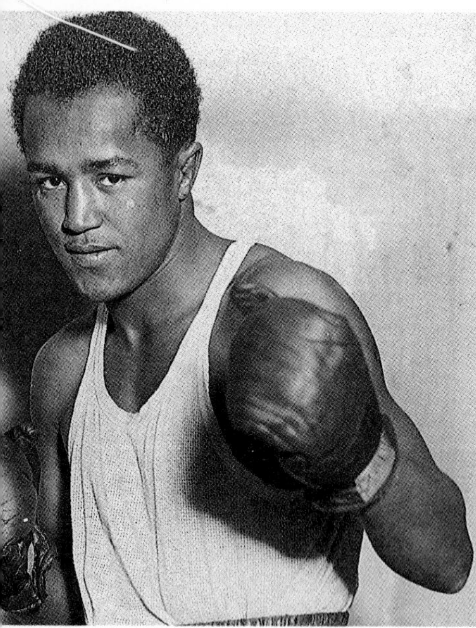

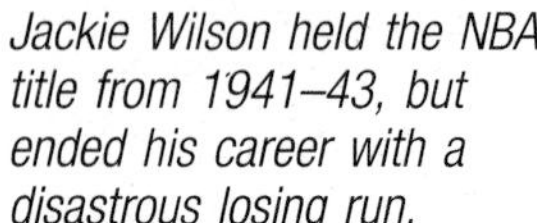

Jackie Wilson held the NBA title from 1941–43, but ended his career with a disastrous losing run.

Phil Terranova had a short-lived tenure of the NBA title, from August 1943 until losing it seven months later.

Angeles in July 1941. Lemos, a big favourite with the Hollywood set, was managed by the colourful Baron von Stumme. Although he had been beaten in seven rounds by Scalzo in 1940, he easily won the rematch.

Lemos enhanced his credibility by beating Joey Archibald, the rival champion, in an overweight ten-rounder in Los Angeles in August 1941, but then lost the NBA crown to Jackie Wilson of Arkansas in November. Wilson gave him a rematch less than a month later and repeated the result. He put the title on ice for the whole of 1942, and then lost it on 18 January 1943 in Providence on a 15-rounds decision to Jackie Callura, from Hamilton, Ontario. The Canadian outscored him again two months later, and although he subsequently achieved some good results, including wins over Lulu Constantino and ex-champion Harry Jeffra, Wilson never got another title chance. His career petered out in a miserable run of 16 defeats and one no-contest (with Chalky Wright) in his last 19 fights.

Callura held the title for only five more months, losing it in August on a eighth-round knockout to Phil Terranova of New York. Terranova kayoed him in six rounds in a rematch, but then lost it to the stylish Bostonian Sal Bartolo, whom Pep had outpointed for the rival version in 1943. Bartolo made three successful defences, but when he met Pep in the unification match in Madison Square Garden on 7 June 1946, he was knocked out in 12 rounds. It was their third meeting, and Pep's third victory.

Pep had been introduced to the sport as a youngster, when his father took him to watch Connecticut's other featherweight idol, Battling Battalino, in training. He took up the sport when he was 15 years old and was beaten only twice as an amateur – once by Ray Roberts, whose real name was Walker Smith but who is better known as Sugar Ray Robinson. Pep turned professional in July 1940, one month before his 18th birthday, and won 62 fights in a row before lightweight champion Sammy Angott outpointed him in Madison Square Garden, in March 1943. Pep won a further 73 straight, including defences of the undisputed title

Jimmy McAllister held Pep to a draw in 1945, but folded in the second round three months later (below).

Right: *Pep and Saddler were both brilliant stylists, though they look ungainly in this shot from their first fight.*

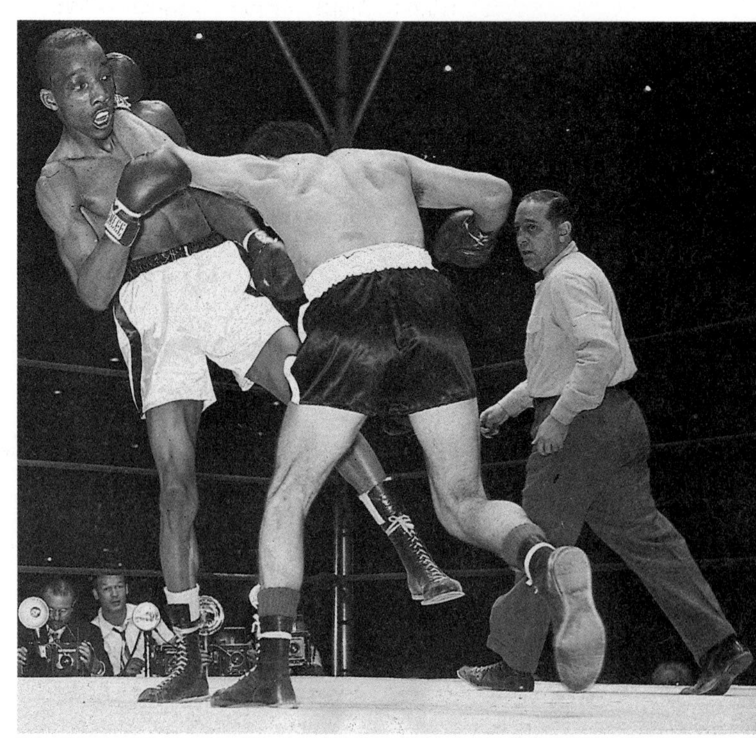

The greatest performance of Pep's 26-year career . . . his superb points win over Saddler in their classic rematch.

against Jock Leslie of Flint, Michigan, and Humberto Sierra of Havana, before his fabulous run was ended by the man who became his arch-rival, Sandy Saddler.

Saddler, from Boston, was abnormally tall for a featherweight at 5 ft 8½ in. He combined his physical advantages with fierce hitting power, which brought him 103 inside-the-distance victories in 162 fights, and a highly refined mastery of the ignobler aspects of the Noble Art. There have been few better featherweight champions, and even fewer dirtier ones. Managed by Charley Johnson, who also looked after Saddler's close friend Archie Moore, he turned professional before his 18th birthday in 1944 and was knocked out in his second fight by Jock Leslie, who went on to challenge Pep for the world title three years later. It was the only time in his 12-year career that he failed to go the distance.

Saddler fought often, learning his trade in minor arenas and small towns in the New York, Boston, and New Jersey areas. In 1944 he had 22 outings in nine months, losing just twice; in 1945 he boxed 24 times without defeat; and his only losses in the next three years and 48 fights were to Bobby McQuillar (who many years later helped train another featherweight champion, Barry McGuigan), Phil Terranova, the former NBA champion, Humberto Sierra, the former title challenger from Cuba, and Chico Rosa.

Saddler and Pep were magnificent performers whose misfortune was to be contemporaries. It was even more unfortunate that their first meeting, won by Saddler with astonishing ease in four rounds at Madison Square Garden in October 1948, should have been marred by hints of the sort of scandal which dogged Pep's later career. When the fight was announced, Pep was a 5-2 favourite, but the weight of money pouring onto the challenger swung the odds around. Pep made a feeble effort, and was on the floor three times before being knocked out by a sweeping left hook in the fourth. The rumours persisted and grew until, on the afternoon of their rematch in the Garden on 11 February 1949, the New York Commissioner Eddie Eagan summoned the pair to his private office and told them that he was 'holding them both responsible for upholding the good name of boxing'.

The attendance of 19,097 was an indoor record for the division, and the receipts of $87,563 broke the old record which Pep himself had set when he met Chalky Wright in the Garden in November 1942. Pep gave his greatest performance, in one of the finest fights in featherweight history: 15 rounds of scintillating boxing, dominated by Pep's craft, grace, and guile. But it was never one-sided and, although Pep was a wide and unanimous winner, he finished looking like a loser, with considerable facial damage. Sadler was not a champion to surrender weakly.

Pep made three defences, in one of which he outpointed the veteran European champion Ray Famechon of France, but then had two further fights with Saddler, retiring with a dislocated shoulder after seven rounds in 1950, and after nine rounds, badly battered, in 1951. Their final meeting was so outrageously foul-filled that Bob Christen berry, the newly appointed New York Commissioner, suspended Saddler for 30 days and banned Pep from ever boxing again in New York. The ban was eventually lifted, but was reimposed after Pep lost in suspicious circumstances to Lulu Perez in two rounds in 1954. Pep fought on until 1959, and then made a ten-fight comeback in 1965-66, when he was 43. His overall record showed only 11

Below: *French challenger Ray Famechon failed in his bid for Pep's title, although his nephew Johnny would win it later.*

Pep made himself persona non grata *in New York because of his foul-filled fourth meeting with Saddler* (above) *and the rumours surrounding his 1954 loss to Lulu Perez* (right).

losses in 242 fights, in a career that had spanned 26 years.

Saddler entered the American Army in 1952, and did not box at all in 1953. A 15-round fight on 9 February 1953 in Paris, between Ray Famechon and Percy Bassett of Philadelphia, was billed as being for the 'interim title'. Bassett won on a third-round retirement, but lost the 'title' on a 12-round decision to Teddy 'Red Top' Davis, from Pep's hometown of Hartford, in 1954. Saddler returned to championship action on 25 February 1955, beating Davis on a unanimous decision to clarify his status as champion. He retained it a year in a bloody 13-round battle with the Filipino Flash Elorde, later to become a great junior lightweight champion. Elorde had beaten Saddler in a non-title meeting in 1955,

Right and below: *Teddy 'Red Top' Davis (dark shorts) won something called the 'interim title' while Saddler was unable to box due to US Army service, but when he was demobbed Saddler reclaimed the disputed title by outscoring Davis on a unanimous verdict.*

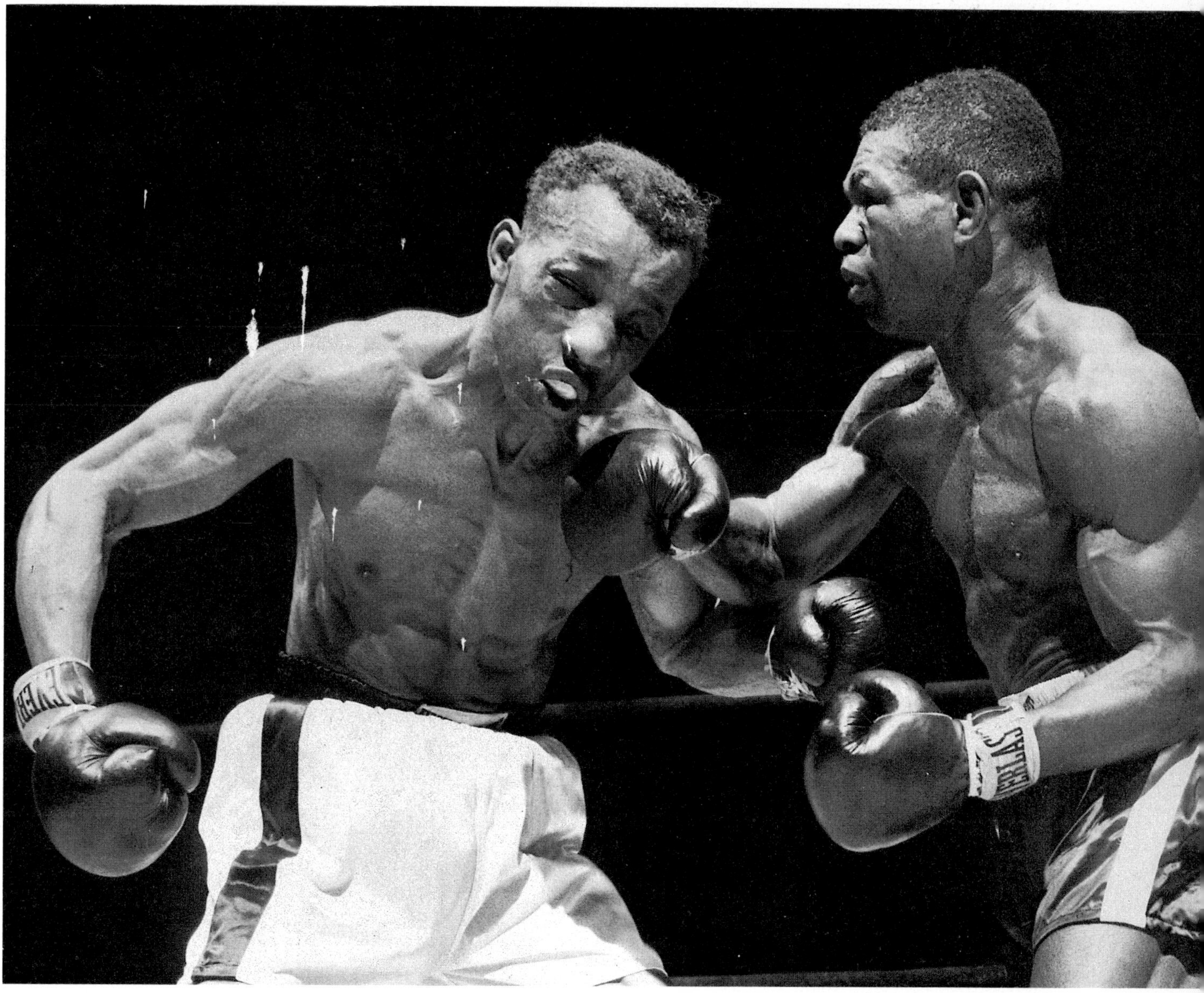

Saddler's last defence was a desperately hard-earned win over the Filipino southpaw Flash Elorde (above). *On his retirement, the vacant title was won by Nigeria's Hogan 'Kid' Bassey* (inset), *who outpointed Miguel Berrios in an eliminator* (right) *and then stopped Cherif Hamia in the tournament final.*

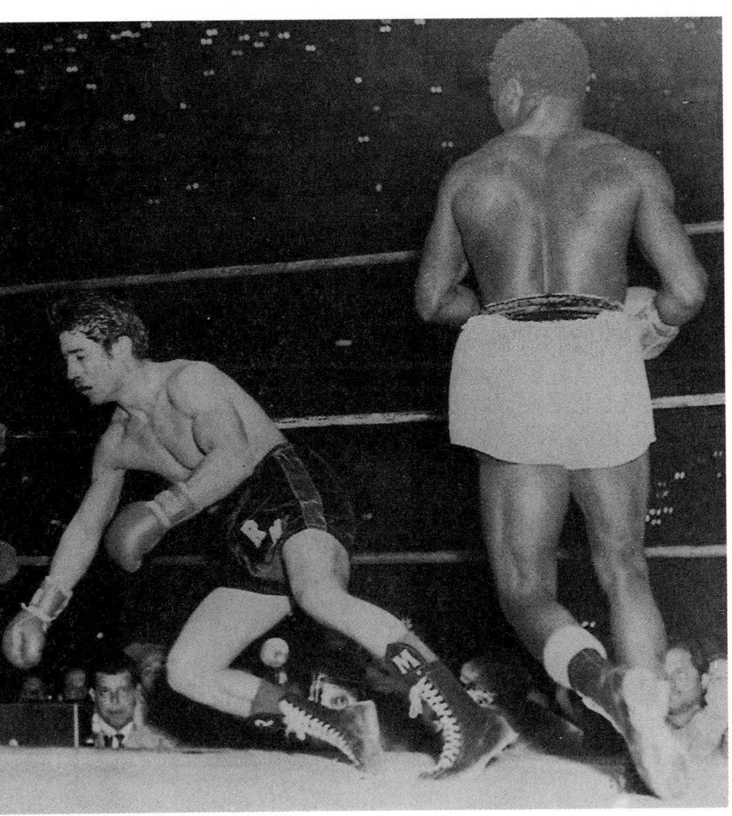

Bassey was expected to lose his first defence, against Ricardo Moreno, but retained the title in one of 1958's major surprises (above). *However, his loss to the classy Davey Moore* (below, *on the left in their rematch*) *was true to the predictions. Bassey, black Africa's first world champion since Battling Siki, then retired.*

and in their rematch was ahead by one point on all three cards when cuts forced the stoppage.

In January 1957, after being badly injured in a car accident, Saddler was forced to retire. It was a sadly anti-climactic end to a marvellous career. The tournament to fill the vacancy was won by Hogan 'Kid' Bassey of Nigeria, black Africa's first world champion since Battling Siki, light-heavyweight winner 35 years previously. Bassey had spent the major part of his career in England, and had won the Empire title in 1955 by knocking out the cagey Irishman, Billy Kelly. Bassey was not expected to survive his first challenge, which came from a heavy-fisted Mexican knockout sensation called Ricardo 'Parajito' Moreno, but the stocky Nigerian flattened Moreno in three rounds in Los Angeles, in one of the biggest upsets of 1958.

Bassey's reign was ended in his next defence, also in Los Angeles, when Davey Moore, the son of a minister from Springfield, Ohio, forced him to retire at the end of the 13th round on 18 March 1959. Moore had been a superb amateur, who quickly established himself as one of the best champions in the professional game. He defended the title successfully five times, including twice in Tokyo and once in Helsinki, and he beat good opponents in non-title matches in London, Paris, Madrid and Rome, as well as many South American capitals.

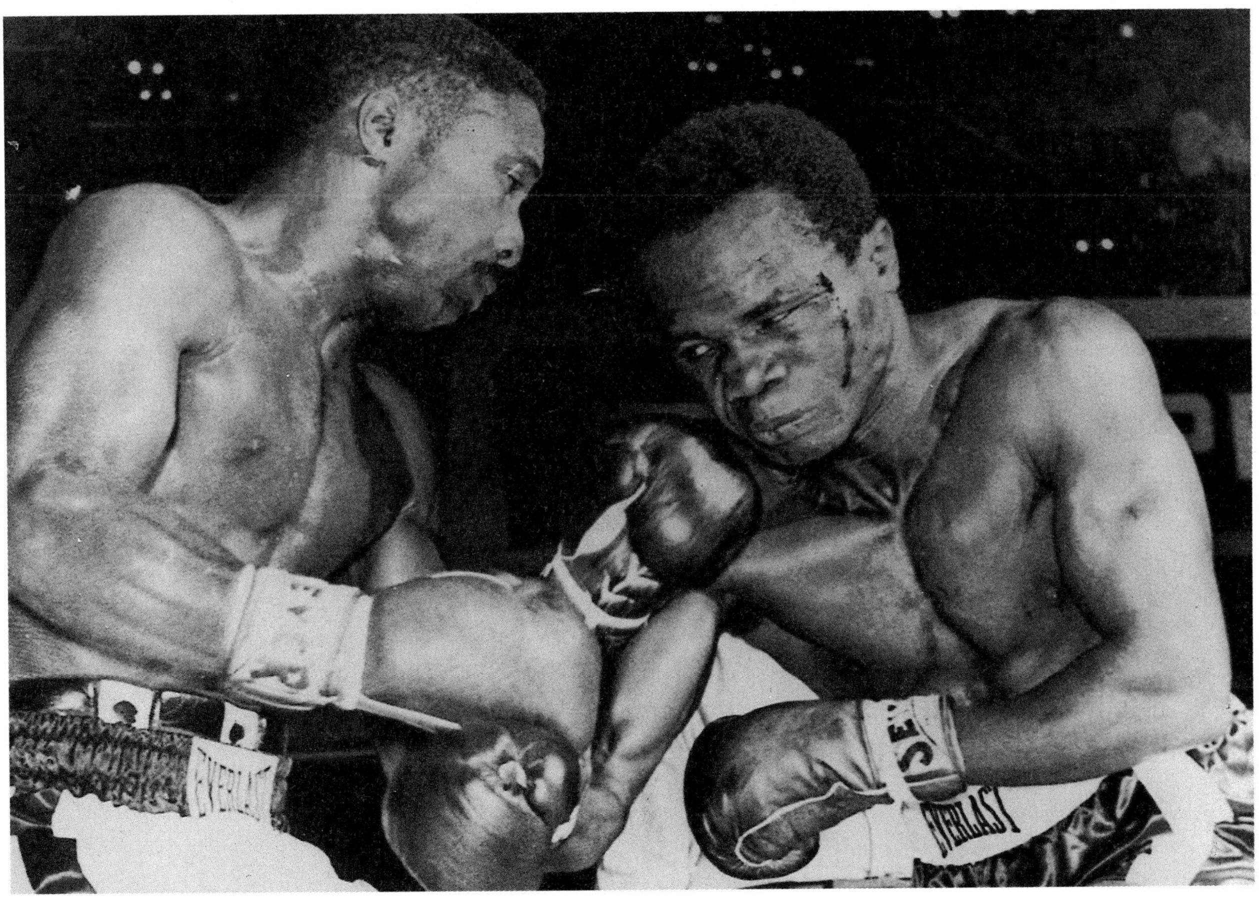

Moore was a globe-trotting champion, whose two trips to Japan included this points win over Kazuo Takayama in 1961. Takayama had also taken him the full 15 rounds a year previously.

But on 21 March 1963, defending his title on a Los Angeles show which featured three world title bouts, he retired at the end of the tenth round against a Cuban expatriate, Ultiminio 'Sugar' Ramos and when he returned to his dressing room he collapsed into a coma. He died on 23 March and the following evening welterweight champion Benny Paret was battered into a coma on live television by Emile Griffith, dying on 3 April. It was the blackest week in boxing history.

The tragic end (left) *to Moore's defence against Sugar Ramos* (below). *The battered loser lapsed into a coma, and died two days later.*

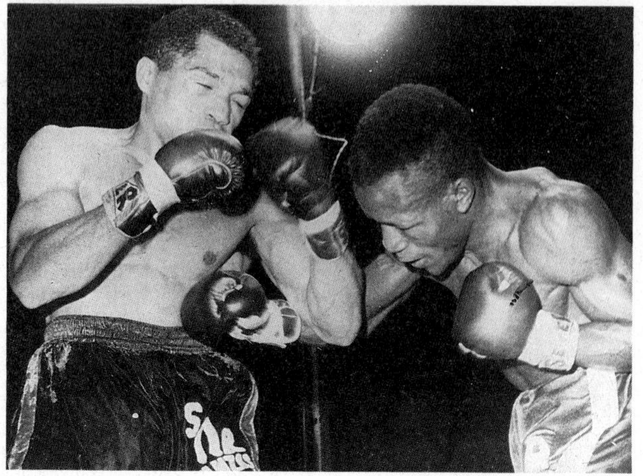

Rafiu King made a brave bid to take the featherweight title back to Nigeria when he challenged Ramos in Mexico City (left) *in the Cuban's first defence, but Ramos outpointed him.*

Ramos defended in Mexico, Tokyo, and Accra, Ghana, where he won a majority verdict over the Empire champion Floyd Robertson. The Ghana Commission, feeling (with some justification) that their man had suffered a bad deal, altered the result to 'no contest' and then, at a later hearing, to a win for Robertson. The rest of the world continued to regard Ramos as champion, and the Ghanaian's strictly local status disappeared when Ramos' successor, Vicente Saldivar, knocked him

His WBA featherweight title is slipping away irretrievably against Barry McGuigan (inset), but Eusebio Pedroza's corner remains a model of calm, quiet professionalism. McGuigan's victory, on an emotional summer evening at a London football ground, marked the end of one of the great featherweight championship reigns.

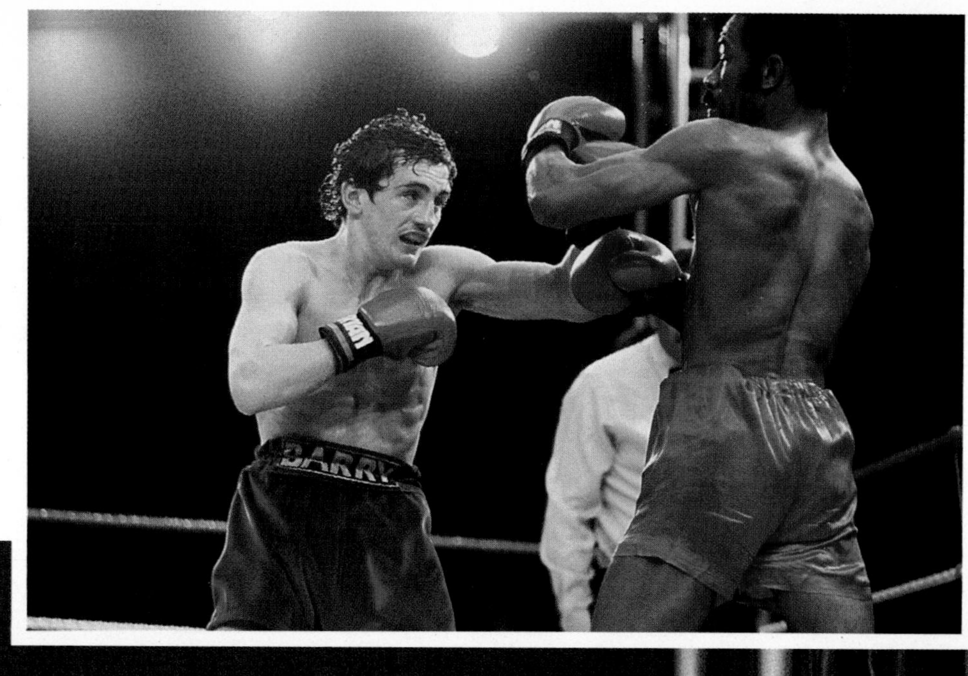

Spain's Roberto Castanon (above, on the right) was a good European champion, but the marvellous Salvador Sanchez underlined the difference between European and world status when he easily defeated the Spaniard at Caesars Palace in 1982. Mexican punchers Jaime Garza (right, on the right) and Juan Meza had a combined total of 70 inside-schedule wins in 88 fights, so it was no great surprise that their 1984 clash lasted less than a round, with Meza taking Garza's WBC super-bantamweight title on a knockout.

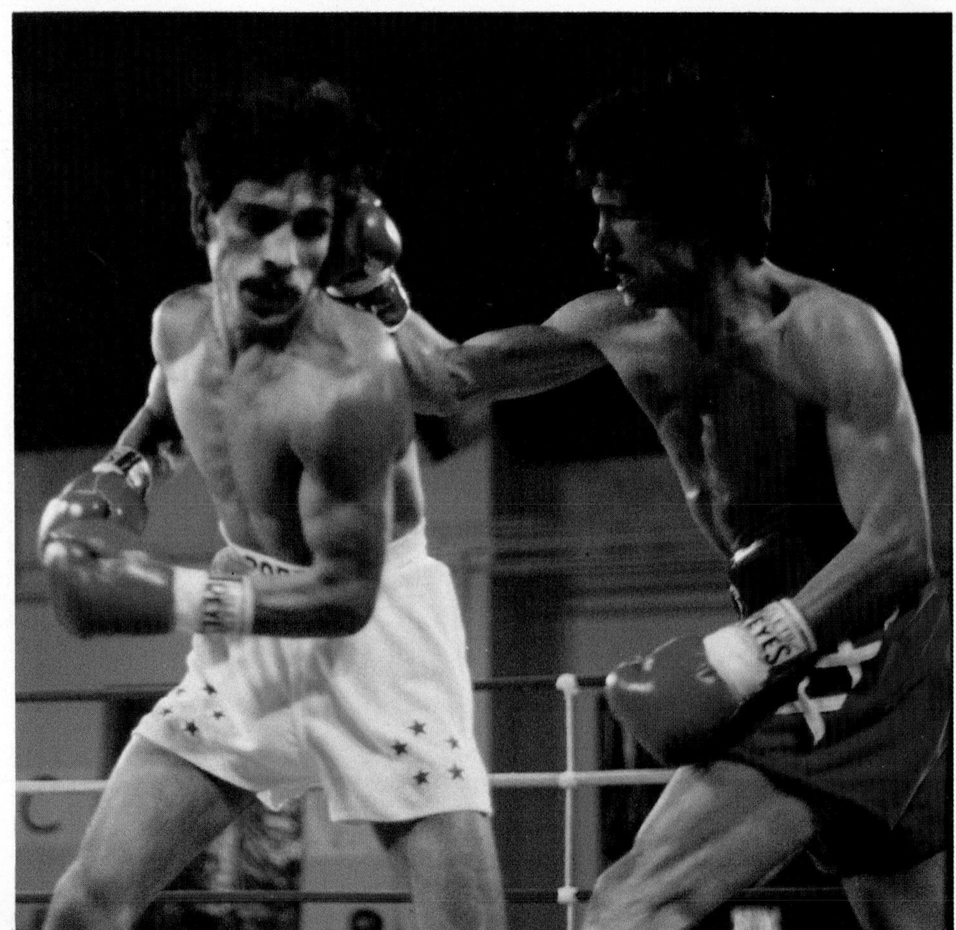

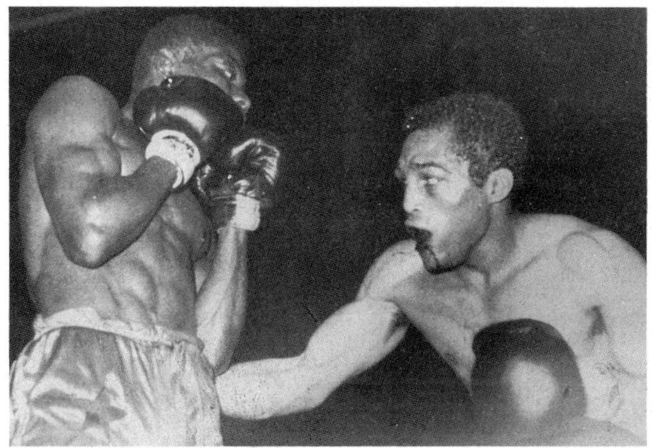

Above: *Ramos had the toughest fight of his championship reign when he got a controversial verdict over Floyd Robertson (left).*

Right: *Mexican southpaw Vicente Saldivar and Welsh stylist Howard Winstone provided three epic championship battles.*

out in two rounds in 1966.

The tough fight with Robertson left the Cuban an easy victim for Saldivar, who was his next challenger. The aggressive Mexican southpaw beat him on an 11th-round retirement in September 1964, and over the next three years he secured his ranking with the division's great champions by retaining the title seven times. He is remembered with respect in Britain for his unforgettable series with the gloriously gifted Welshman, Howard Winstone of Merthyr Tydfil. They met for the first time in London in September 1965, when Saldivar needed a tremendous late rally to save the title. The rematch, in the open air in Cardiff almost two years later, was virtually an action replay, with Winstone's elegant skill building a big points lead, which Saldivar's seemingly limitless strength and stamina chipped away until a 14th-round knock-down clinched Saldivar's win by a two-round margin.

Winstone went to Mexico City for the third fight, in October 1967, but was stopped in the 12th round. Afterwards, Saldivar took the ring mike and shocked his home fans by announcing that he would never fight again. The world's governing bodies were unable to agree on a successor, and the championship has been split ever since.

Britain and Europe backed Winstone, whom Saldivar himself had endorsed, and the WBC approved the Welshman's ninth-round win over another of Saldivar's great rivals, Mitsunori Seki of Japan in London in January 1968 as being for the vacant title. The WBA paired yet another Saldivar victim, Raul Rojas of San Pedro, California, with Enrique Higgins of Colombia for their version of the vacant title, Rojas winning on points in Los Angeles

Winstone (above) *eventually won a share of the title by stopping Mitsunori Seki on a cut* (right) *after Saldivar's retirement, but by then the superb Welshman had passed his prime.*

two months after Winstone's coronation.

But the world title success had come too late in Winstone's career, and he was beaten in his first defence in July by a long-armed, flashy Cuban expatriate, Jose Legra, at Porthcawl. He never fought again. Legra's only defeat in 83 fights since settling in Madrid in 1963 had been a ten-rounds points loss to Winstone in 1965, but he too lost the crown in his first defence to Johnny Famechon, on points at the Albert Hall, London, in February 1969. Famechon, the nephew of Willie Pep's challenger Ray, had been born in France but raised in Melbourne.

Pep was involved, controversially, in Famechon's first defence. The ex-champion refereed the fight, against the former-flyweight and bantamweight champion Fighting Harada of Japan, in Sydney Stadium in July 1969, and first awarded a draw with 71 points each, but then rechecked the card to find that Famechon had in fact won by 70-69.

Famechon knocked out Harada in 14 rounds in a rematch, but then Saldivar decided to come back and, having outpointed Legra in a 1969 ten-rounder, regained the title from Famechon by outpointing him in Rome in May 1970. He lost it seven months later to Kuniaki Shibata of Japan, who stopped him in 12 rounds in Tijuana and, effectively, ended his career. There was an ill-advised comeback in 1973 when, having been

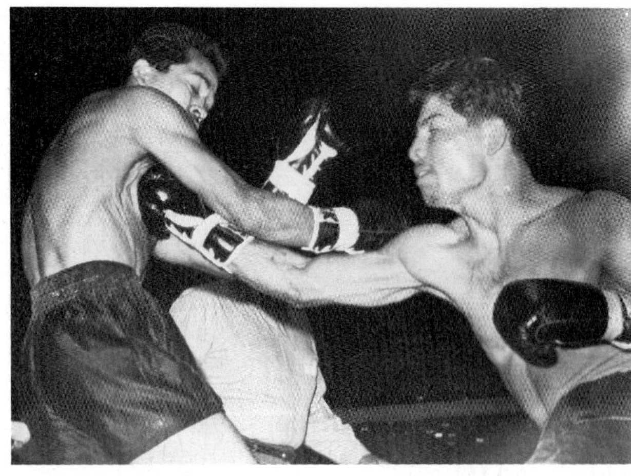

Above *Raul Rojas was stopped in the final round of a brutal battle with Saldivar (left), but won the WBA title when Saldivar retired.*

Below: *Winstone's short reign – and his career – ended with this fifth-round loss to Jose Legra at Porthcawl, Wales.*

Below: *Legra's only defeat in 83 fights since coming to Europe had been this 10-round points loss to Howard Winstone in 1965, but he took full revenge when they met again with the WBC title at stake.*

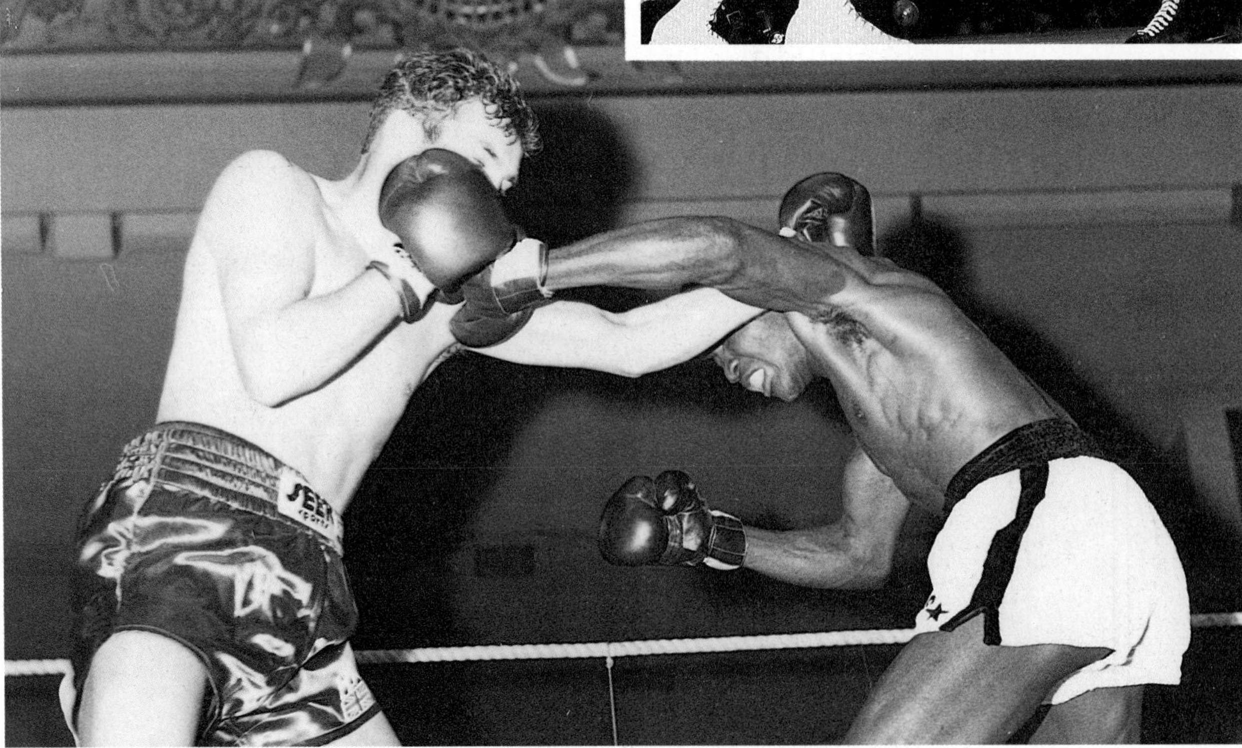

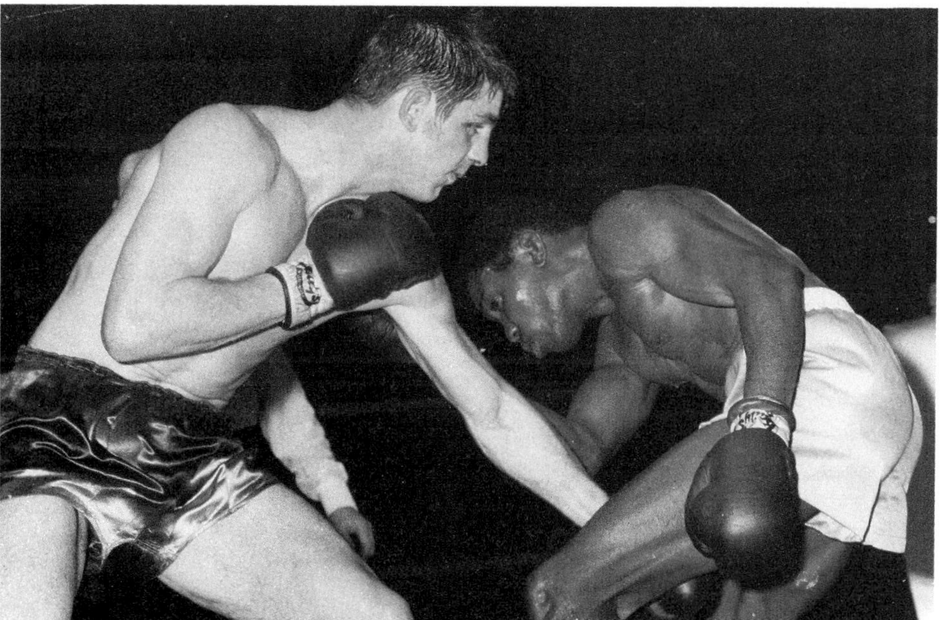

Johnny Famechon (inset) *took Legra's title in London* (left), *but the Australian travelled to Rome a year later and lost it to the former champ, Vicente Saldivar* (below). *It was Famechon's last fight.*

Three exciting champions from the early 1970s: Eder Jofre (left), *Kuniaki Shibata* (above, *knocking out Raul Cruz in a round) and Bobby Chacon* (right).

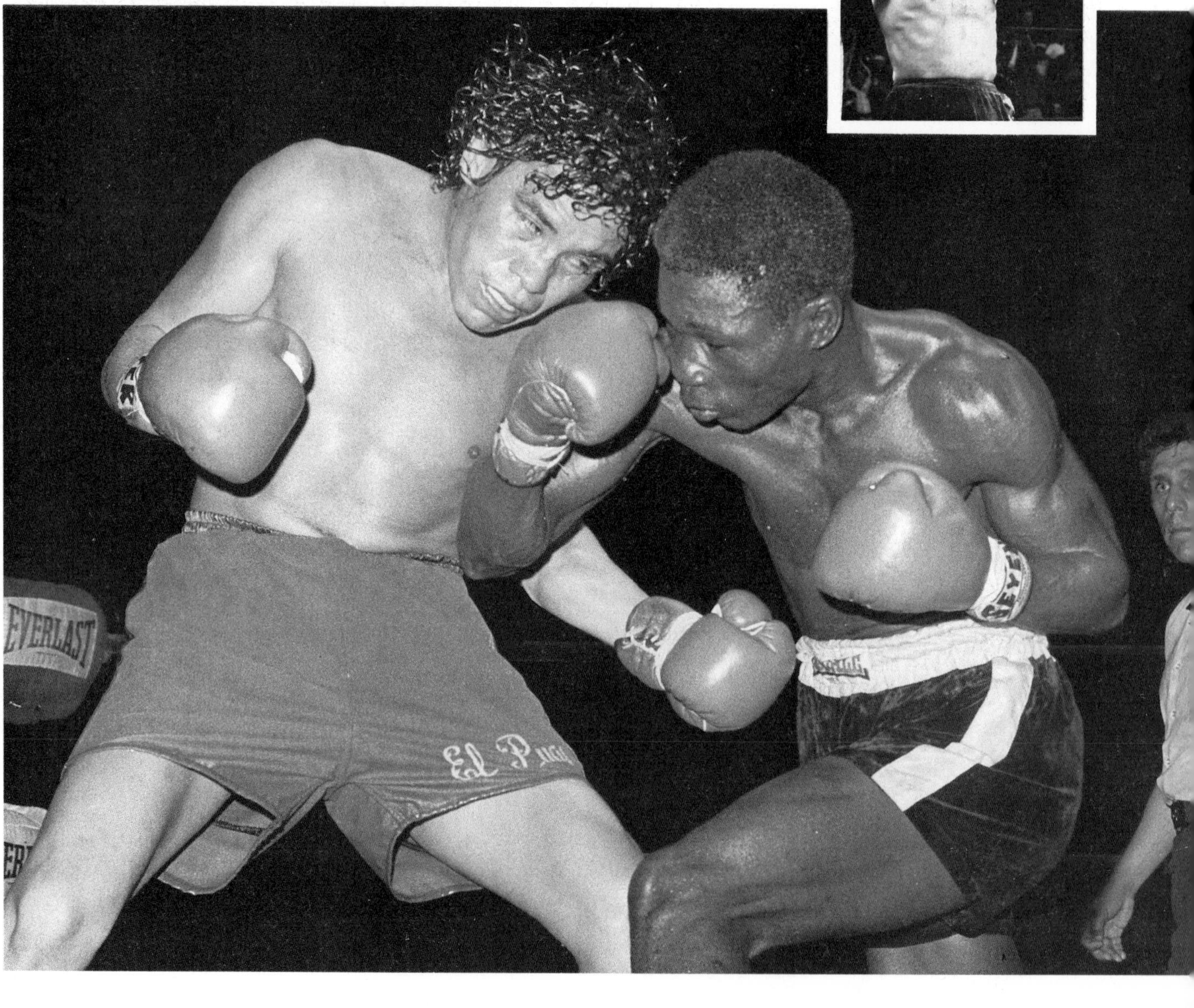

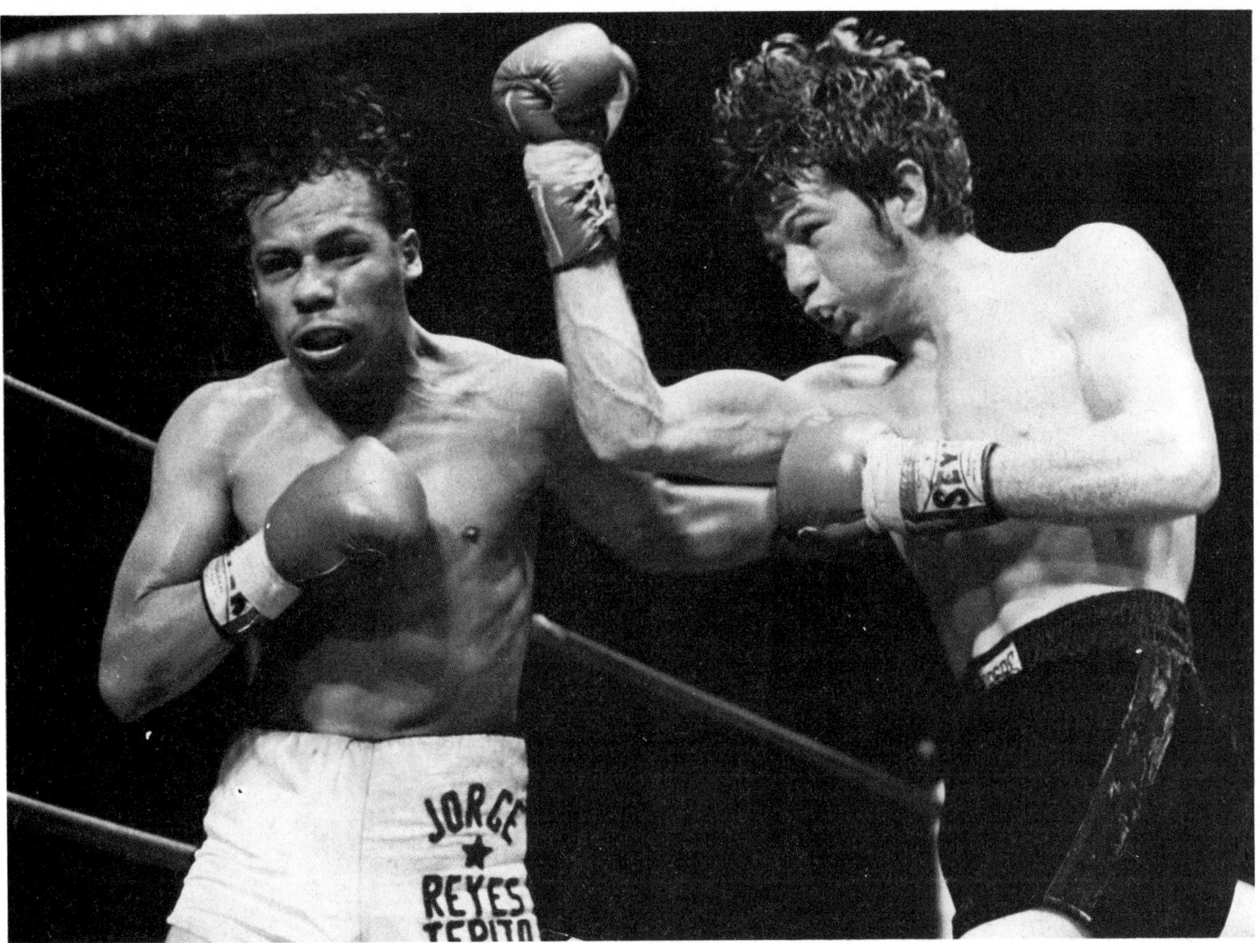

Left: *A superb action shot from David Kotei's split decision win over Ruben Olivares.*

Above: *The explosive 'Little Red' Lopez uppercuts Jorge Reyes to seventh-round defeat.*

inactive for almost two and a half years, he made one last attempt to regain the title but was badly beaten in four rounds by Eder Jofre.

Shibata, plagued by weight problems, was stopped in three rounds in his third defence by Clemente Sanchez of Monterrey, Mexico, and moved gratefully into the junior lightweight division, where he was twice champion. Sanchez lost the title in unusual circumstances: he came in 3 lb overweight for his first defence, against Jose Legra in Monterrey, in December 1972. The fight went ahead, and Sanchez was stopped in ten rounds. The WBC recognized Legra as the new champion, even though he had not won the title at championship weight. The Cuban's second reign, though, was even shorter-lived than his first – he was outpointed in May 1973 by the brilliant Eder Jofre of Brazil, the former bantamweight champion, and he retired after being knocked out in one round by Alexis Arguello in his 147th fight, in November 1973.

But Jofre, after retaining the title against Saldivar, was stripped of it for failing to defend against the former junior lightweight champion, Alfredo Marcano of Venezuela. Bobby Chacon, a glamorous but unpredictable Californian, stopped Marcano in nine rounds for the vacant title and retained it once before being dethroned by another former bantamweight great, Ruben Olivares of Mexico who, only seven months previously, had lost the WBA version of the title to Alexis Arguello. Exactly three months later, on 20 September 1975, Olivares found himself an ex-champion again when David 'Poison' Kotei of Accra, Ghana, took his title on a split decision at Inglewood Forum, California.

The Ghanaian was his country's first recognized champion, and 60,000 of his compatriots watched him retain the crown against Flipper Uehara in Accra. He defended it a second time against another Japanese, Shig Fukuyama, in Tokyo, but on 5 November 1976, in front of a featherweight record crowd of 100,000 in Accra, lost a unanimous verdict to the explosive Danny 'Little Red' Lopez. Lopez was a California-based, part-Indian from Utah, whose elder brother Ernie had challenged Jose Napoles for the welterweight title in 1970 and 1973. 'Little Red' was an all-action tearaway, whose hitting power was matched by his own vulnerability. He frequently had to get off the floor to win, and had featured in memorable battles with Bobby Chacon, Shig Fukuyama, Chuchu

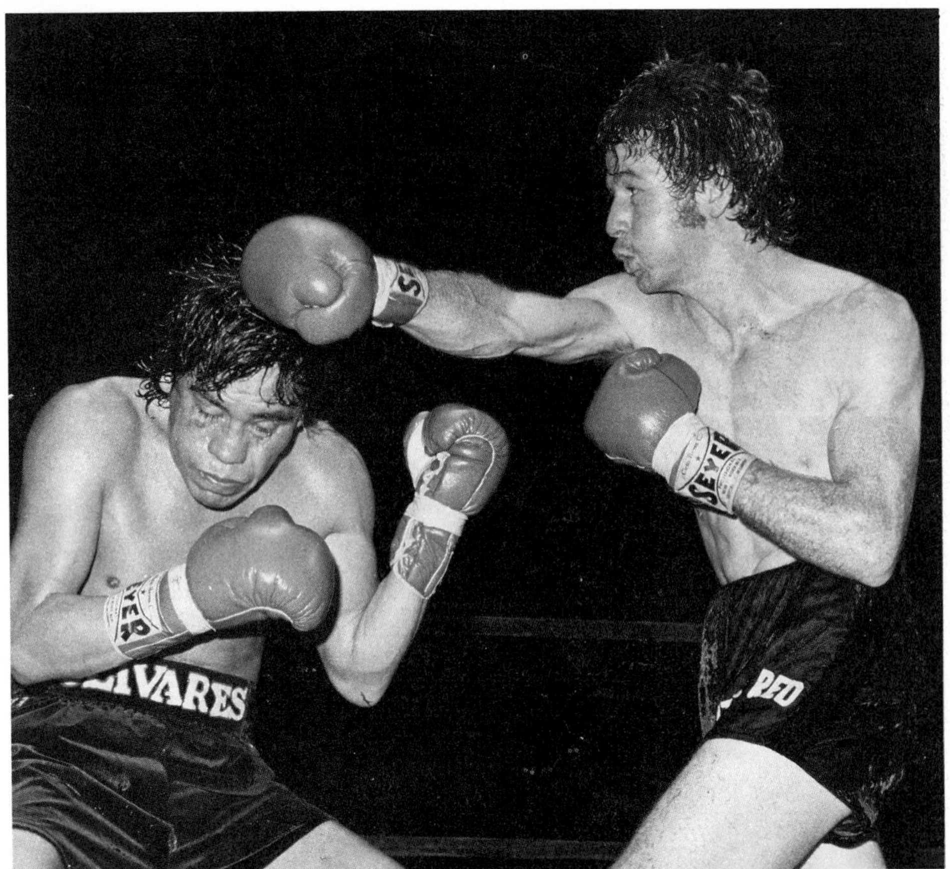

Four outstanding featherweights in action: Danny Lopez pounding Ruben Olivares to defeat in seven rounds (left), *and the classy Mexican Salvador Sanchez left-hooking Juan Laporte on the way to a points victory in defence of his WBC title* (below). *Sanchez was destined to become one of the division's best-ever champions, but he was killed in a road accident in 1982 before his full potential had been developed.*

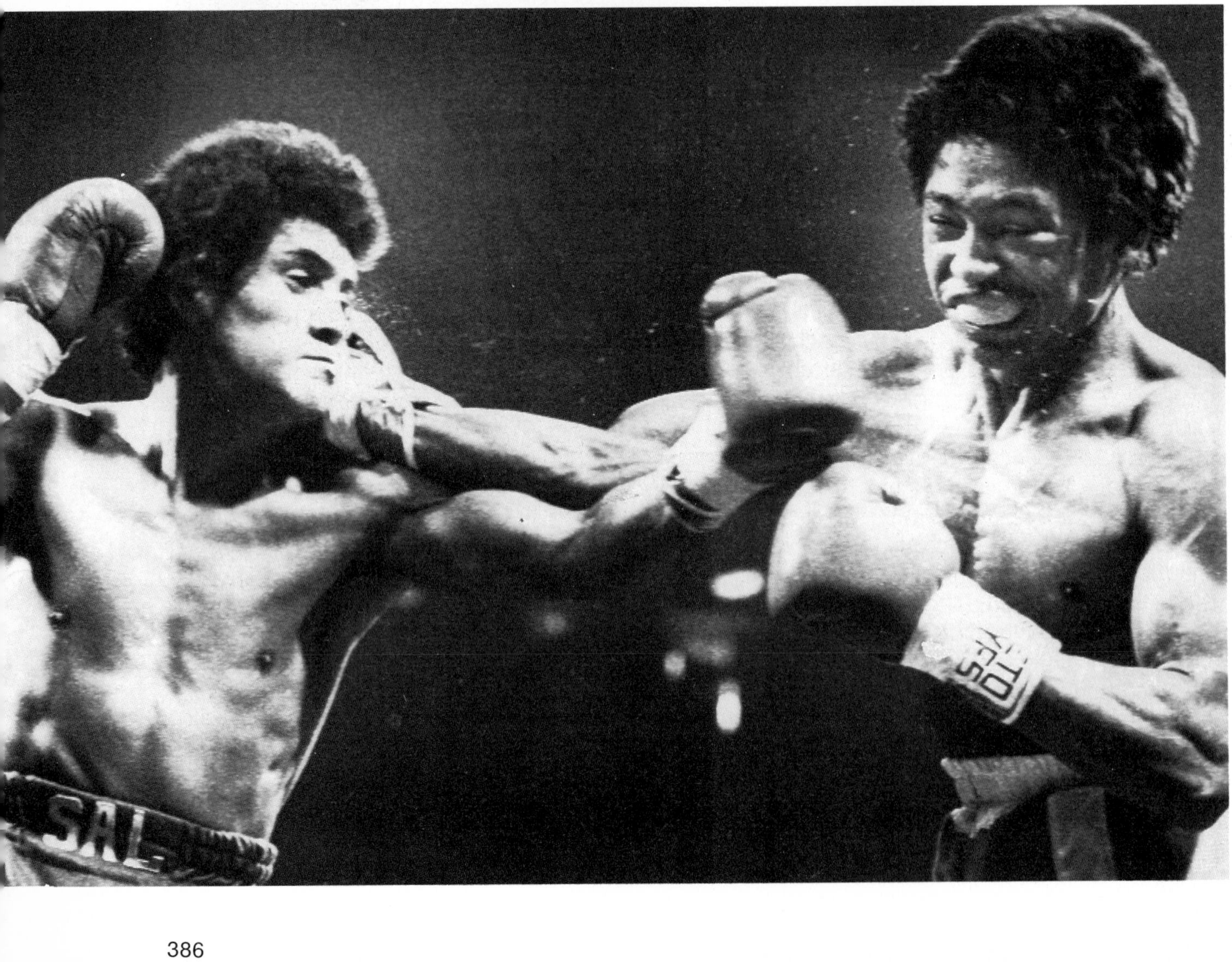

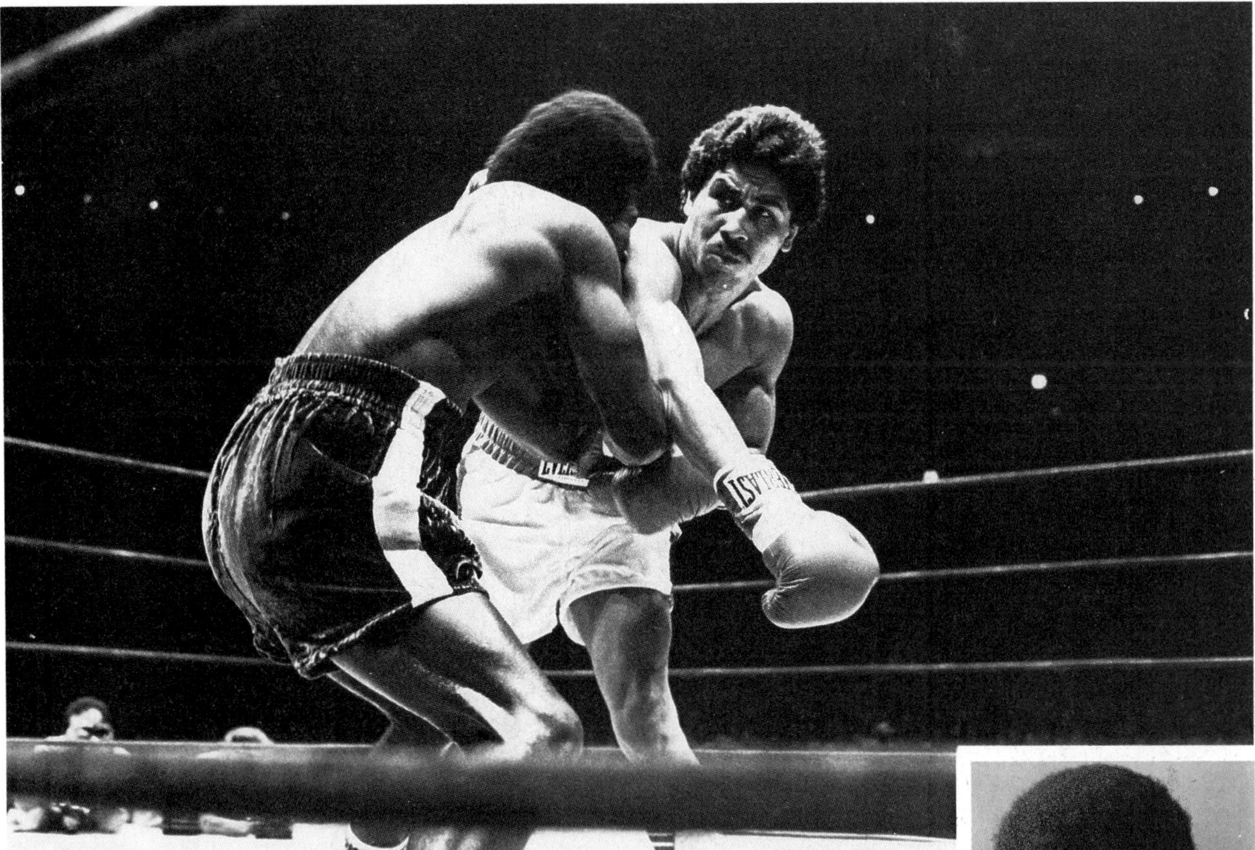

Castillo, Ruben Olivares, and Sean O'Grady before becoming champion, a pattern which continued throughout his dramatic four-year reign.

Lopez beat challengers from Mexico, Ghana, Brazil, Argentina, the Philippines, Spain, America, and the Dominican Republic, but was finally dethroned on 2 February 1980 by Salvador Sanchez, a multi-talented Mexican who, had it not been for his tragic death in a car smash in August 1982, may well have become the best champion the division has yet produced. He retained the title nine times, and it is a measure of his greatness that three of his unsuccessful challengers, Juan LaPorte, Wilfredo Gomez, and Azumah Nelson, subsequently became champions.

LaPorte, a strong Puerto Rican, stopped Mario Miranda in September 1982 for the vacant title, but lost it on his third defence to his compatriot Wilfredo Gomez, who had been unbeatable as super-bantamweight champion before moving up a weight. But Gomez held it only nine months – on 8 December 1984 he was battered into an 11th-round defeat by Nelson, an immensely powerful and hard-punching Ghanaian who has retained it five times.

The WBA title has also produced its share of outstanding champions. Its first holder, Raul Rojas, was dethroned on a unanimous decision by Sho Saijo of Japan in July 1968. Saijo survived four challenges and an episode when the WBA stripped

Wilfredo Gomez (above) *had been unbeatable at super-bantamweight, but his hold on the WBC featherweight title lasted only until he met the Ghanaian Azumah Nelson* (inset, *and,* below *beating Australia's Brian Roberts for the Commonwealth title).*

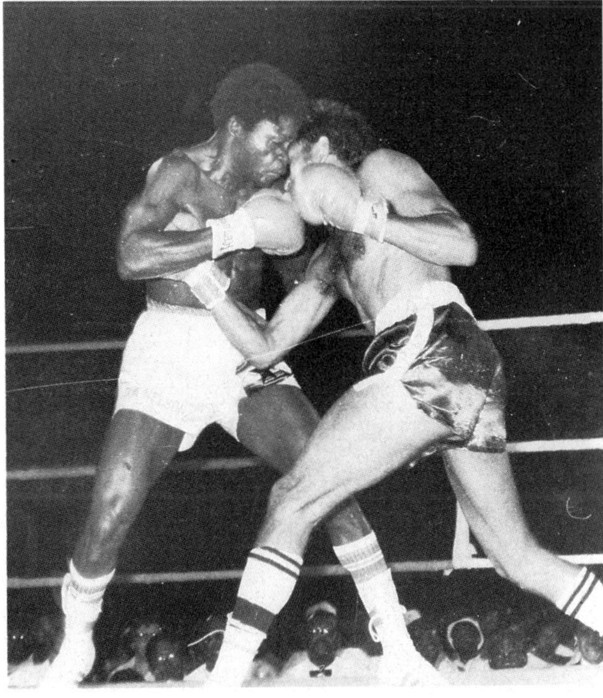

him for failing to meet Antonio Gomez of Venezuela, and then reinstated him when he signed for the fight. Gomez was the younger brother of Pedro Gomez, whom Saijo had beaten in a 1969 title fight, and he took family revenge with a fifth-round stoppage in Tokyo, in September 1971.

Gomez was beaten on his second defence by Ernesto Marcel, a competent performer who surprisingly retired after his fourth defence, a points win over Alexis Arguello (later to win world titles at three weights). Marcel was succeeded briefly by Ruben Olivares, who had been a marvellous if ill-disciplined bantamweight champion, but Olivares was knocked out in 13 rounds four months later by Arguello.

The Nicaraguan was champion for four years and four defences, but by November 1976 the struggle to make the 126 lb limit had become too great so he relinquished the title, which was won by Rafael Ortega of Panama. Ortega made one defence and then lost it Cecilio Lastra of Spain, who in turn was dethroned in his first defence by another Panamanian who, over the next seven years, earned acceptance as one of the world's great champions, pound for pound – Eusebio Pedroza. The superb Panamanian made a remarkable 20 defences. He risked his title all over the world, in Puerto Rico, Japan, America, New Guinea, Korea, Venezuela, Italy, St Vincent and finally in London where, on an unforgettable night in June 1985, at Loftus Road football ground, the youthful fire of Ireland's Barry McGuigan ended his glorious reign.

Sho Saijo outpointed Pedro Gomez (left) in this 1969 WBA title fight, then lost the championship two years later to the Venezuelan's brother Antonio.

McGuigan had, along with his manager and promoter Barney Eastwood, revived boxing in Ireland with a string of emotional, thrilling victories in the King's Hall, Belfast, which made him the most popular sportsman in his country's history. He

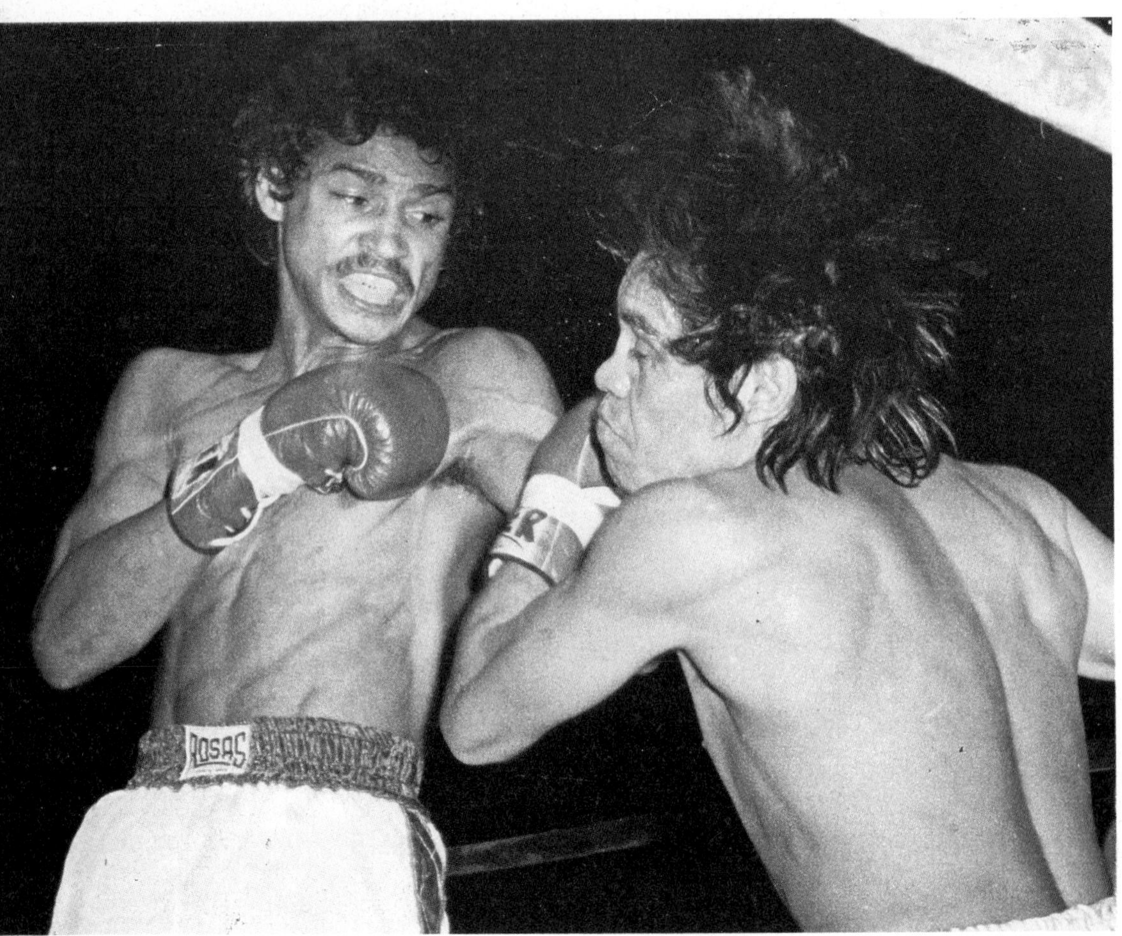

Alexis Arguello (left, *on the left) kayoes Ruben Olivares to take the first of his three world titles. He relinquished it four years later, and was succeeded by Rafael Ortega* (above, *flooring Flipper Uehara in a May 1977 defence at Okinawa).*

Eusebio Pedroza was one of the great modern champions, taking his title all over the world. He even risked it against Johnny Aba (above, on the right) *in Papua-New Guinea, but his fabulous 20-defence career was ended on an unforgettable night at a London football stadium* (below) *by the thrilling Irishman Barry McGuigan, who floored him in the seventh* (right) *and took a clear points win in front of a packed crowd.*

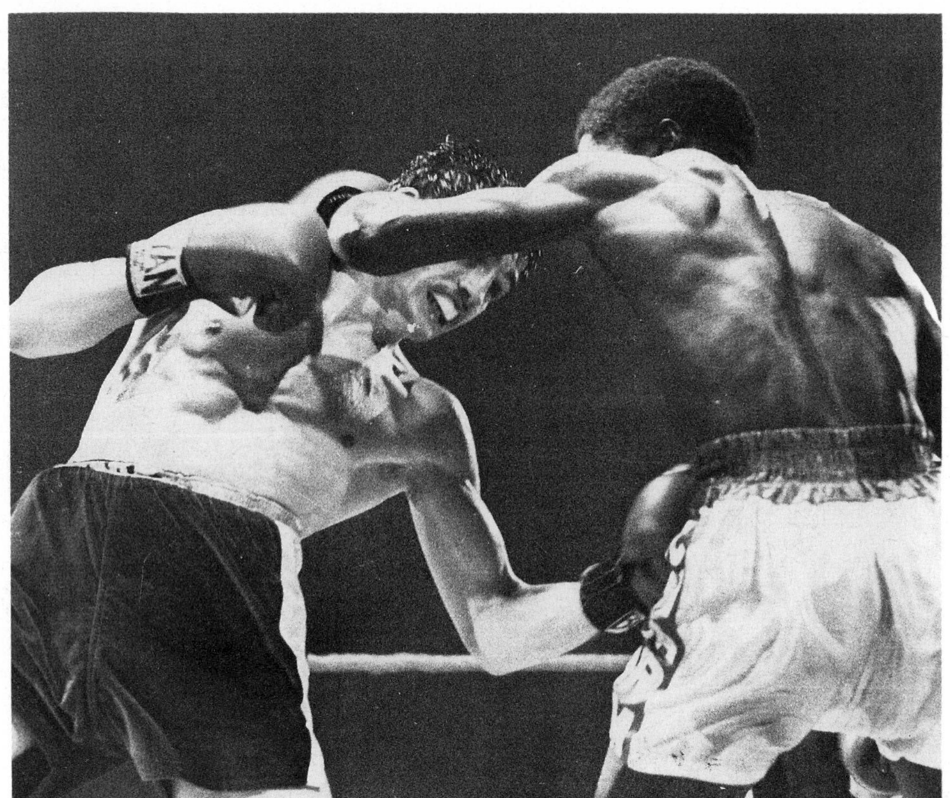

McGuigan had earned his chance at the world title with a series of thrilling victories in the King's Hall, Belfast over men like Charm Chiteule (left) *and the former WBC champion Juan Laporte* (below), *whom he outscored in his final warm-up for the challenge to Pedroza.*

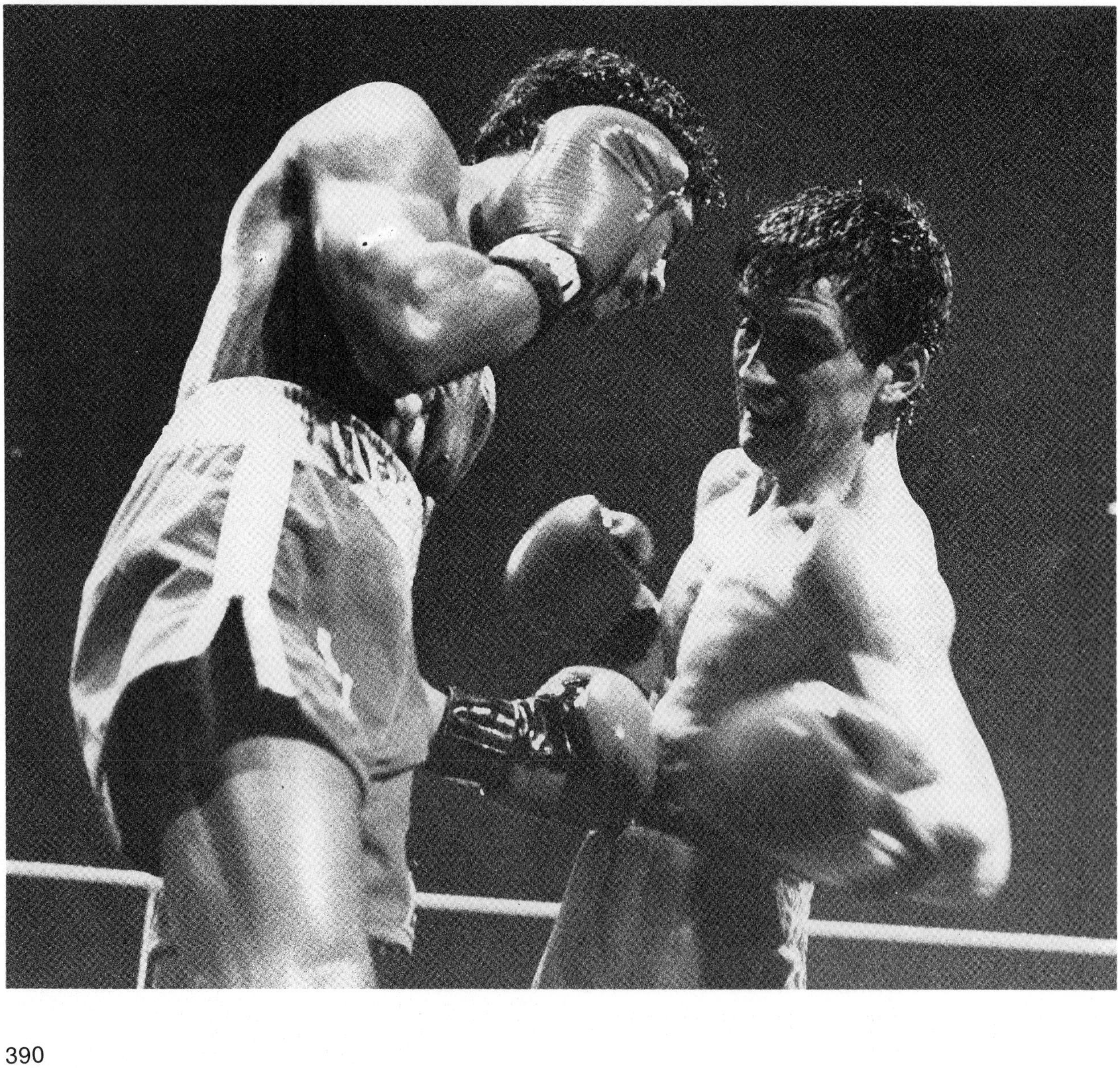

earned the title chance by beating Juan LaPorte, and he swept Pedroza off the throne with a display of exuberant aggression that recalled the Irishman's idol, Roberto Duran, at his peak. McGuigan made two defences, forcing the previously unbeaten American Bernard Taylor into retirement in Belfast, and stopping substitute challenger Danilo Cabrera in Dublin. But then, fighting in unbearable 120° F (49° C) heat on a Las Vegas afternoon in June 1986, and still suffering the effects of training injuries to his ankle and eardrum, he was floored three times and outpointed narrowly by yet another replacement challenger, Steve Cruz of San Antonio. The Texan was beaten in his first defence, in March 1987, by Antonio Esparragoza of Venezuela, who stopped him in the 12th round of a thrilling battle in Fort Worth.

The IBF version of the title, first contested on 4 March 1984, has been held by a fairly unremarkable series of champions, starting with the Korean Min-Keun Oh, who lost it to his compatriot Kee-Young Chang, who in turn lost to Antonio Rivera of Puerto Rico.

Steve Cruz, an unheralded substitute challenger from Texas, floored McGuigan three times in the desert heat of Las Vegas.

HOW THE FEATHERWEIGHT TITLE HAS CHANGED HANDS

1889–1900

31 Mar 89 Ike Weir drew 80 Frank Murphy at Kouts, Indiana
13 Jan 90 Australian Billy Murphy w.ko.14 Ike Weir at San Francisco
03 Sep 90 Young Griffo w.pts.15 Australian Billy Murphy at Sydney
06 Sep 92 George Dixon w.ko.8 Jack Skelly at New Orleans
27 Nov 96 Frank Erne w.pts.20 George Dixon at New York
07 Apr 97 George Dixon w.pts.25 Frank Erne at New York
04 Oct 97 Solly Smith w.pts.20 George Dixon in San Francisco
26 Sep 98 Dave Sullivan w.rtd.5 Solly Smith at Coney Island
11 Nov 98 George Dixon w.dis.10 Dave Sullivan in New York
(Ben Jordan of Bermondsey, London, claimed the title after outpointing Dixon over 25 rounds in New York on 1 Jul 98, Dixon having argued that his title was not at stake when he lost to Smith)
29 May 99 Ben Jordan w.ko.9 Harry Greenfield at NSC London
10 Oct 99 Eddie Santry w.ko.15 Ben Jordan in New York

1900

09 Jan 00 Terry McGovern w.ko.8 George Dixon in New York
01 Feb 00 Terry McGovern w.ko.5 Eddie Santry in Chicago *(For undisputed title)*
28 Nov 01 Young Corbett II w.ko.2 Terry McGovern at Hartford
01 Feb 04 Abe Attell w.ko.4 Harry Forbes at St. Louis
19 Feb 09 Jim Driscoll no decision 10 Abe Attell at New York
22 Feb 12 Johnny Kilbane w.pts.20 Abe Attell at Vernon, California
(NY Commission stripped Kilbane of the title for failing to defend against Johnny Dundee, and matched Dundee and Danny Frush for the vacant title).
15 Aug 22 Johnny Dundee w.ko.9 Danny Frush at Brooklyn
02 Jun 23 Eugene Criqui w.ko.6 Johnny Kilbane at New York
26 Jul 23 Johnny Dundee w.ko.6 Eugene Criqui at New York *(For undisputed title)*
10 Aug 24 *Dundee relinquished title because of weight problems*
02 Jan 25 Louis Kid Kaplan w.rtd.9 Danny Kramer in New York
Mar 27 *Kaplan relinquished the title because of weight problems*
19 Sep 27 Benny Bass w.pts.10 Red Chapman in Philadelphia
(Billed as for vacant title)
24 Oct 27 Tony Canzoneri w.pts.15 Johnny Dundee in New York
(NY version of vacant title)
10 Feb 28 Tony Canzoneri w.pts.15 Benny Bass in New York *(For undisputed title)*
28 Sep 28 Andre Routis w.pts.15 Tony Canzoneri in New York
23 Sep 29 Battling Battalino w.pts.15 Andre Routis at Hartford, Conn
Jan 32 *The NBA and NY Commission declared the title vacant after Battalino had been three lb overweight for a scheduled defence against Freddie Miller*
26 May 32 Tommy Paul w.pts.15 Johnny Pena in Detroit *(Vacant NBA title)*
04 Aug 32 Kid Chocolate w.pts.10 Eddie Shea in Chicago *(Vacant NY title)*
13 Jan 33 Freddie Miller w.pts.10 Tommy Paul at Chicago
Mar 34 *NY Commission stripped Chocolate for failing to defend against Frankie Klick*
30 Aug 34 Baby Arizmendi w.pts.15 Mike Belloise in New York *(Vacant NY title)*
11 May 36 Petey Sarron w.pts.15 Freddie Miller at Washington *(NBA title)*
May 36 *NY Commission recognised Mike Belloise as champion, Arizmendi having outgrown the division*
03 Sep 36 Mike Belloise w.ko.9 Dave Crowley in New York *(NY title)*
27 Oct 36 Henry Armstrong w.pts.10 Mike Belloise at Los Angeles
29 Oct 37 Henry Armstrong w.ko.6 Petey Sarron at New York
(For undisputed title, which Armstrong then relinquished)
17 Oct 38 Joey Archibald w.pts.15 Mike Belloise in New York *(For vacant NY title)*
29 Dec 38 Leo Rodak w.pts.10 Leone Efrati in Chicago *(For vacant NBA title)*
18 Apr 39 Joey Archibald w.pts.15 Leo Rodak at Providence R.I. *(For undisputed title)*
Apr 40 *The NBA withdrew recognition from Archibald for his failure to defend against Petey Scalzo, who had knocked him out in a non-title fight. They declared Scalzo champion)*
20 May 40 Harry Jeffra w.pts.15 Joey Archibald at Baltimore *(NY title)*
12 May 41 Joey Archibald w.pts.15 Harry Jeffra in Washington DC
01 Jul 41 Richie Lemos w.ko.5 Petey Scalzo in Los Angeles
11 Sep 41 Chalky Wright w.ko.11 Joey Archibald in Washington
18 Nov 41 Jackie Wilson w.pts.12 Richie Lemos in Los Angeles
20 Nov 42 Willie Pep w.pts.15 Chalky Wright in New York *(NY title)*
18 Jan 43 Jackie Callura w.pts.15 Jackie Wilson at Providence, R.I. *(NBA title)*
16 Aug 43 Phil Terranova w.ko.8 Jackie Callura at New Orleans
10 Mar 44 Sal Bartolo w.pts.15 Phil Terranova at Boston
07 Jun 46 Willie Pep w.ko.12 Sal Bartolo at New York. *(For undisputed title)*
29 Oct 48 Sandy Saddler w.ko.4 Willie Pep at New York
11 Feb 49 Willie Pep w.pts.15 Sandy Saddler at New York
08 Sep 50 Sandy Saddler w.rtd.7 Willie Pep in New York
Jan 57 *Saddler retired because of injuries sustained in car crash*
24 Jun 57 Hogan Bassey w.rsf.10 Cherif Hamia at Paris
18 Mar 59 Davey Moore w.ret.13 Hogan Bassey at Los Angels
21 Mar 63 Sugar Ramos w.ret.10 Davey Moore at Los Angeles
26 Sep 64 Vicente Saldivar w.ret.11 Sugar Ramos at Mexico City
14 Oct 67 *Saldivar retired as undefeated champion*
23 Jan 68 Howard Winstone w.rsf.9 Mitsunori Seki at London
(WBA refused to recognise Winstone as new champion)
28 Mar 68 Raul Rojas w.pts.15 Enrique Higgins at Los Angeles
(WBA version of vacant title)
24 Jul 68 Jose Legra w.rsf.5 Howard Winstone at Porthcawl *(WBC title)*
27 Sep 68 Shozo Saijo w.pts.15 Raul Rojas in Los Angeles *(WBA title)*
21 Jan 69 Johnny Famechon w.pts.15 Jose Legra at London
09 May 70 Vicente Saldivar w.pts.15 Johnny Famechon at Rome
11 Dec 70 Kuniaki Shibata w.rsf.12 Vicente Saldivar at Tijuana
02 Sep 71 Antonio Gomez w.rsf.5 Shozo Saijo in Tokyo *(WBA title)*
09 May 72 Clemente Sanchez w.ko.3 Kuniaki Shibata in Tokyo
19 Aug 72 Ernesto Marcel w.pts.15 Antonio Gomez at Maracay
16 Dec 72 Jose Legra w.rsf.10 Clemente Sanchez at Monterrey
(Sanchez overweight but Legra recognised as champion by WBC)
05 May 73 Eder Jofre w.pts.15 Jose Legra in Brasilia.
Ernesto Marcel retired from boxing
09 Jul 74 Ruben Olivares w.ko.7 Zensuke Utagawa at Inglewood *(Vacant WBA title)*
WBC withdrew recognition of Eder Jofre for failing to defend against their official challenger, Alfredo Marcano
09 Sep 74 Bobby Chacon w.rsf.9 Alfredo Marcano in Los Angeles
(Vacant WBC title)
23 Nov 74 Alexis Arguello w.ko.13 Ruben Olivares at Inglewood
20 Jun 75 Ruben Olivares w.rsf.2 Bobby Chacon at Inglewood *(WBC title)*
20 Sep 75 David Kotey w.pts.15 Ruben Olivares at Inglewood
06 Nov 76 Danny Lopez w.pts.15 David Kotey in Accra
Arguello gave up WBA title due to weight-making difficulties
15 Jan 77 Rafael Ortega w.pts.15 Francisco Coronado at Panama City
(Vacant WBA title)
17 Dec 77 Cecilio Lastra w.pts.15 Rafael Ortega at Torrelavega
16 Apr 78 Eusebio Pedroza w.ko.13 Cecilio Lastra in Panama City
02 Feb 80 Salvador Sanchez w.rsf.13 Danny Lopez at Phoenix
Aug 82 *Sanchez was killed in a car crash*
15 Sep 82 Juan Laporte w.rtd.10 Mario Miranda at New York *(Vacant WBC title)*
04 Mar 84 Min-Keun Oh w.ko.2 Joko Arter in Seoul *(Vacant IBF title)*
31 Mar 84 Wilfredo Gomez w.pts.12 Juan Laporte at San Juan
08 Dec 84 Azumah Nelson w.rsf.11 Wilfredo Gomez at San Juan
08 Jun 85 Barry McGuigan w.pts.15 Eusebio Pedroza in London *(WBA title)*
29 Nov 85 Kee-Young Chung w.ko.15 Min-Keun Oh in Seoul
23 Jun 86 Steve Cruz w.pts.15 Barry McGuigan in Las Vegas
31 Aug 86 Antonio Rivera w.rsf.10 Kee-Young Chung in Seoul
06 Mar 87 Antonio Esparragoza w.rsf.12 Steve Cruz at Fort Worth

SUPER BANTAMWEIGHTS

MANY OF boxing's weight divisions have had to survive a scandal or two before becoming established. Philadelphia Jack O'Brien's confessions, for example, did nothing for the credibility of the light-heavyweight title, while the aroma emanating from the first fight for the lightweight championship was so unpleasant that there was not another title fight at that weight for nine years.

It took the super-bantamweight (or junior featherweight) division only three fights to make its contribution to boxing's Roll of Dishonour, with perhaps the most controversial verdict in the sport's history. The division had been inaugurated by the WBC in 1976 with a weight limit of 8 st 10 lb (122 lb) and its first champion was a Panamanian, Rigoberto Riasco, who had been knocked out in two rounds by Alexis Arguello in a WBA featherweight title bid in May 1975. But Riasco bounced back to beat the former Commonwealth Games star Philip Waruinge, of Kenya, for the vacant super-bantamweight title on 3 April 1976 (Waruinge had settled in Japan and boxed professionally as Waruinge Nakayama).

Riasco retained the title against Livio Nolasco of the Dominician Republic, stopping him in ten rounds, and then went to Korea to meet Dong-Kyun Yum, who had held the national title at this weight since 1971, and the Oriental championship since 1974. They fought in driving rain in the Kuduk Stadium, Seoul, on 1 August, when the Korean's constant aggression seemed to have won him a fairly comfortable points victory after 15 rounds. But the 15,000 crowd was stunned when the scoring was announced: judge Huberto Figueroa of Panama had his compatriot ahead by 147-143, but this was cancelled out by the Korean judge Ho-Kon Kim, who gave Yum a 150-143 edge. The casting vote was by American referee Larry Rozadilla, who gave it to Riasco by 145-143. Angry fans surrounded Rozadilla as he tried to reach his dressing room, and 25 minutes later he returned to the ring to announce that he had discovered an error on his scorecard, which had become rain-sodden and blurred. His revised score had Yum ahead, and he duly raised the Korean's hand as the new champion.

When he was safely back in California, however, Rozadilla told a very different story. 'On the way to

Korea's Dong-Kyun Yum (left and below) *was at the centre of a scandal involving the third fight ever staged for the super-bantamweight title.*

the dressing room I was accosted by a group of men,' he said. 'I was physically and bodily dragged and pushed back into the ring against my will. I was then directed to raise the Korean's arm in victory and realized that if I failed to co-operate that my life, as well as the lives of other foreigners present, was in imminent danger. I was afraid of getting stabbed, shot, or stamped to death.'

The WBC, which had first confirmed Yum as the new champion after pressure from their Korean representative, reinstated Riasco after hearing Rozadilla's evidence. However, the Panamanian lost the title two months later in Tokyo to Royal Kobayashi, who had also been an unsuccessful challenger for Arguello's featherweight title. Six weeks later Yum unseated Kobayashi on a split decision in Seoul, although this time there was no hint of outside influence in the scoring.

The division's first eight months of existence had produced five title fights and three champions. But its next champion, Wilfredo Gomez, of Puerto Rico (who knocked Yum out in 12 rounds in May 1977) brought it order, continuity, and respectability.

Gomez held the title for five years and 17 defences, and won them all inside the distance. His

Royal Kobayashi (left) *maintained the Oriental interest in the new championship before losing it to Wilfredo Gomez* (right), *who went on to rule for five years and 17 defences, including this sixth-round defeat of the dangerous Juan Meza* (below, *on the right) in 1982.*

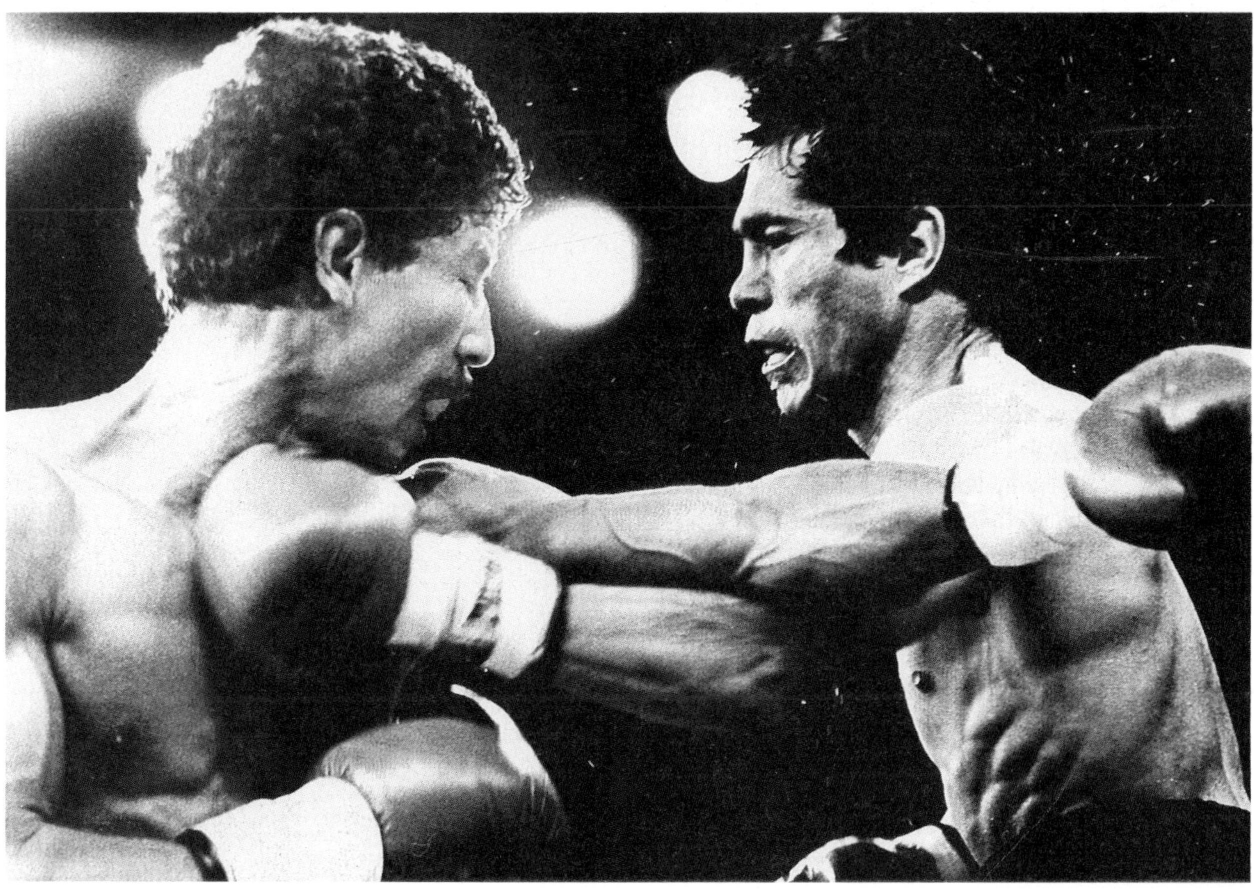

When Gomez stopped Carlos Mendoza (left) *in 10 rounds at Las Vegas in 1979, it was his 10th consecutive inside-the-distance championship win. Juan Meza* (above), *who won the title a year after Gomez had moved up to featherweight, also had an impressive knockout record, but lost in his second defence to the former bantamweight champion Lupe Pintor* (below, *on the left, outpointing Jose Uziga).*

challengers included the two best bantamweights for 20 years, Carlos Zarate and Lupe Pintor, and another hard-hitting Mexican, Juan 'Kid' Meza, who later won the super-bantamweight title. Gomez became champion five months before his 21st birthday, in his 17th fight. He had been marked for greatness since his bantamweight victory in the 1974 World Amateur Championships in Havana, where his fellow-champions included Ayub Kalule, the future WBA light-middleweight champion who won the light-welterweight division, Mate Parlov, later to be WBC light-heavyweight champion, and Howard Davis, who was beaten by Jim Watt and Edwin Rosario when he twice tried for the WBC lightweight title.

Gomez at last ran out of challengers in 1982, and moved into the featherweight division after his 14th-round defeat of Pintor in New Orleans. He took the WBC featherweight title in 1984, and the WBA junior lightweight championship a year later, but he will be remembered mainly as the man whose magnificent skills, coupled with a willingness to meet any challenger, anywhere, ensured the division's acceptance as a legitimate addition to boxing's weight classes.

His successors as WBC champion have,

Left: *Thailand's Samart Payakarun celebrates his WBC title win over Lupe Pintor, whose best days – as a bantamweight – were long behind him.* Right: *Argentina's Sergio Palma, who made five winning defences of the WBA title.*

inevitably, suffered by comparison. Jaime Garza, a Californian with a knockout record to rival Gomez', won the vacant title with his 35th quick win in 38 fights, but proved a false alarm, and lost on his second defence to Gomez' victim, Juan Meza.

Meza retained it once, stopping former featherweight challenger Mike Ayala, but was then outpointed in August 1985 by Lupe Pintor. By now the Mexican was only the shell of the great fighter he had been as a bantamweight, and was easily beaten on his first defence by Thailand's Samart Payakarun. The Thai lost it in turn to Jeff Fenech, the former IBF bantamweight champion from Australia, and promptly retired to become a Buddhist monk.

The WBA's first winner was also an ex-bantamweight champion, Soo Hwan Hong of Korea, who had briefly held the WBA title in that division in 1974-75. The Korean survived four knockdowns to kayo Panama's Hector Carrasquilla in three wildly exciting rounds for the vacant title on 26 November 1977, in Panama City. He retained it once before being stopped in 12 rounds by a Colombian who became one of the WBA's better champions – Ricardo Cardona.

Cardona, whose brother Prudencio held the WBC flyweight title briefly in 1982, made six successful defences including one against Ruben Valdes, brother of middleweight champion Rodrigo, in the first all-Colombian title fight. His reign was ended on 4 May 1980 by the first American champion, Leo Randolph, of Washington, who had won the 1976 Olympic flyweight gold medal. (To be pedantic, Randolph was actually the third American to style himself 'world super-bantamweight champion'. The New York Commission had briefly recognized the weight in 1922-1923, but abandoned it after two fights. Jack 'Kid' Wolfe of Cleveland, Ohio, outpointed Joe Lynch over 15 rounds in New York, on 22 September 1922, to claim the vacant title, but lost it over 12 rounds to Carl Duane, of New York, at Long Island City on 29 August 1923. Since Duane never defended his crown, this first attempt to establish the weight lapsed.)

Randolph was knocked out in five rounds of his first defence by Sergio Palma of Argentina, and promptly retired. America's superb 1976 Olympic team also produced world champions in Ray Leonard, the Spinks brothers Leon and Michael, and heavyweight John Tate, who was beaten in the semi-finals by Teofilio Stevenson (Randolph tends to be overlooked when that team's achievements

Benito Badilla goes down and out in the eighth round of his bid for Leonardo Cruz' WBA title in 1982.

are reviewed, but his world title was at least as valid as Tate's).

Palma, who had been outpointed by Cardona in a 1979 title bid, took his revenge by knocking out the Colombian in 12 rounds in the third of his five successful defences, which also included a points win over Leonardo Cruz of the Dominican Republic. Yet Cruz eventually took the title in Miami Beach on 12 June 1982 (at the third attempt, having also been stopped in 13 rounds by Wilfredo Gomez for the WBC version in 1978). Cruz managed three defences before losing the title to Europe's first representative, Loris Stecca of Italy, who held it for just three months. Victor Callejas of Puerto Rico

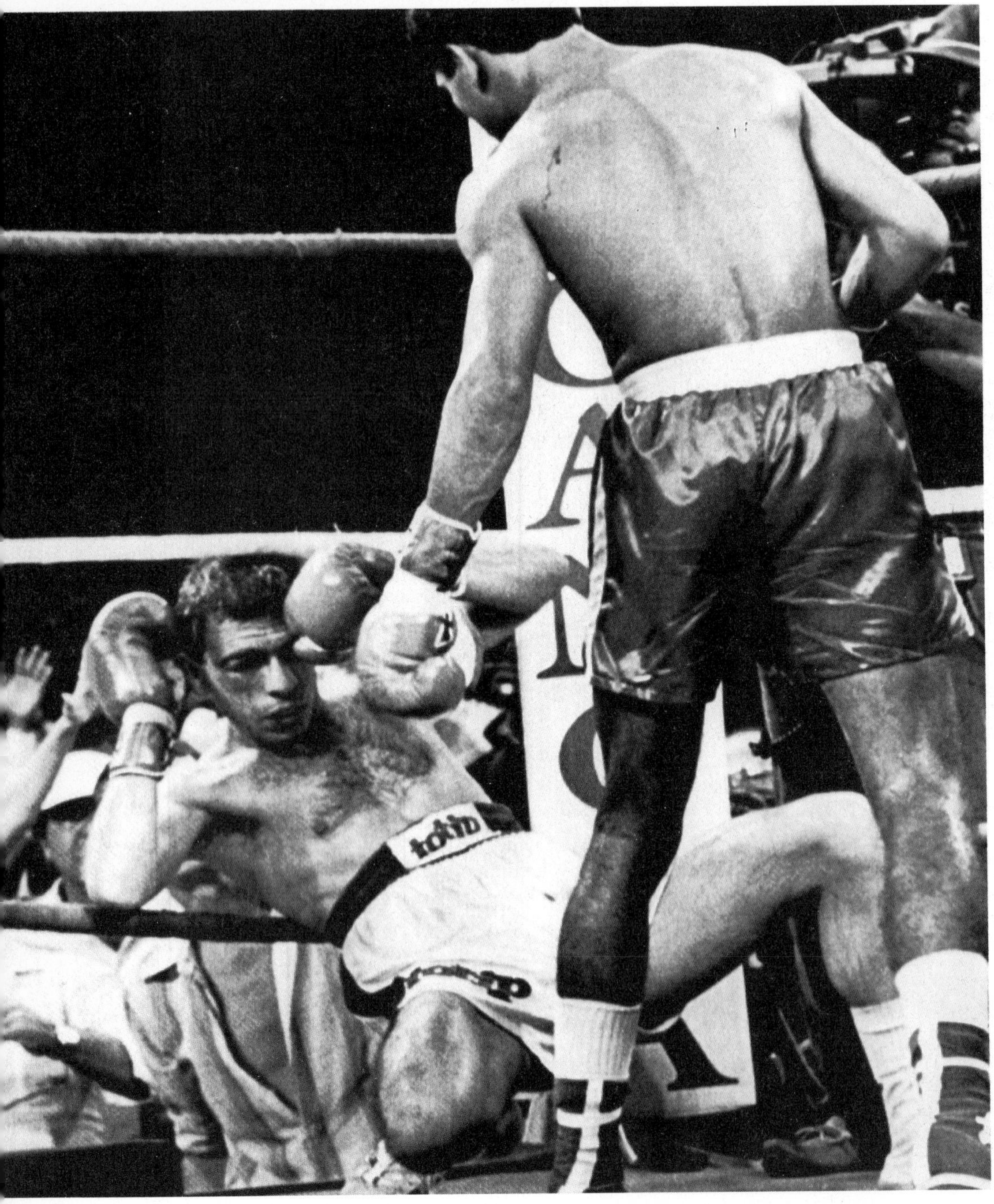

Loris Stecca's three months as champion are over (left), *as Victor Callejas crushes him in eight rounds. But Callejas made only three defences before being stripped by the WBA for inactivity, and he was succeeded by the colourful Louie Espinoza* (above).

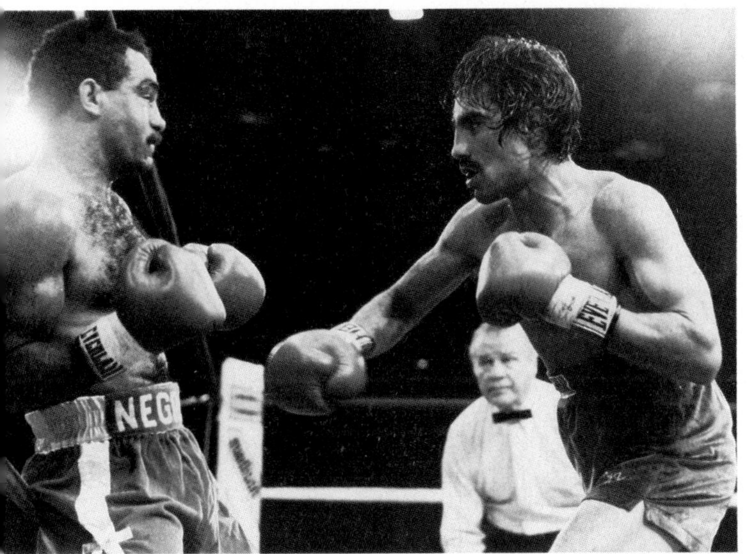

knocked him out in eight rounds in May 1984, and made three successful defences before being stripped of the title because of inactivity.

The vacancy was filled by Louie Espinoza, a colourful American from the David Wolf camp, which had also produced Ray Mancini.

The IBF's championship has been the weakest of the three versions, and has yet to be held by a fighter of genuine international merit. It was first won on 4 December 1983 by Bobby Berna, of the Philippines, since when the champions – all Koreans – have been Seung-Il Suh, Ji-Won Kim and Seung Hoon Lee, who took the vacant title after Kim had been stripped.

Espinoza's defeat of the seasoned Carmelo Negron in four rounds was a major step forward for the youngster.

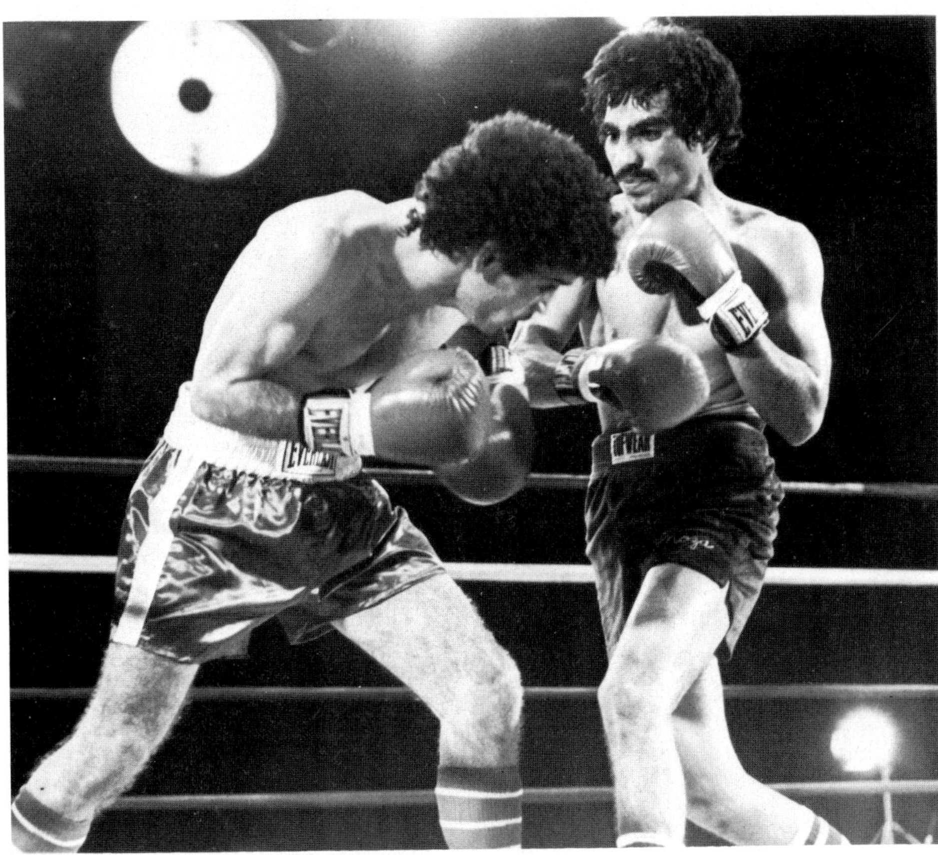

An early-career points win for Espinoza (right) over Raul Albaladejo in New York.

HOW THE SUPER-BANTAMWEIGHT TITLE HAS CHANGED HANDS

03 Apr 76	Rigoberto Riasco w.rtd.8 Waruinge Nakayama in Panama City
01 Oct 76	Royal Kobayashi w.rsf.8 Rigoberto Raisco in Seoul
24 Nov 76	Dong Kyun Yum w.pts.15 Royal Kobayashi in Seoul
21 May 77	Wilfredo Gomez w.ko.12 Dong Kyun Yum at San Juan
26 Nov 77	Soo Hwan Hong w.ko.3 Hector Carasquilla at Panama City *(Vacant WBA title)*
07 May 78	Ricardo Cardona w.rsf.12 Soo Hwan Hong in Seoul *(WBA title)*
04 May 80	Leo Randolph w.rsf.15 Ricardo Cardona in Seattle *(WBA title)*
09 Aug 80	Sergio Palma w.ko.6 Leo Randolph at Spokane *(WBA title)*
12 Jun 82	Leo Cruz w.pts.15 Sergio Palma at Miami Beach
15 Jun 83	Jaime Garza w.rsf.2 Bobby Berna at Los Angeles *(for WBC title reliquished by Wilfredo Gomez)*
04 Dec 83	Bobby Berna w.rsf.9 Seung-Il Suh in Seoul *(Vacant IBF title)*
22 Feb 84	Loris Stecca w.rtd.12 Leo Cruz at Milan
15 Apr 84	Seung-Il Suh w.rsf.10 Bobby Berna in Seoul
26 May 84	Victor Callejas w.ko.8 Loris Stecca at Guaynabo
03 Nov 84	Juan Meza w.ko.1 Jaime Garza at Kingston, N.Y.
03 Jan 85	Ji-Woon Kim w.ko.10 Seung-Il Suh in Seoul
18 Aug 85	Lupe Pintor w.pts.12 Juan Meza in Mexico City *(WBC title)*
18 Jan 86	Samart Payakarun w.ko.5 Lupe Pintor at Bangkok
Dec 86	*Callejas stripped by the WBA for failure to defend*
16 Jan 87	Louie Espinoza w.rsf.4 Tommy Valoy at Phoenix *(Vacant WBA title)*
18 Jan 87	Seung Hoon Lee w.ko.9 Payonsak Muangsurin at Pohang, Korea *(For IBF title vacated by Ji-Woon Kim's retirement)*
08 May 87	Jeff Fenech w.rsf.4 Samart Payakarun in Sydney

BANTAMWEIGHTS

THE EARLY history of the bantamweight class is a hotch-potch of disputed titles and rival claims, and since the competitors could not even agree on what was the division's weight limit, it is hardly surprising that they also frequently failed to agree on who was champion. The division had been active both in Britain and America in the second half of the nineteenth century, but the first real international title fight did not take place until 1890 when George Dixon, the brilliant black Canadian who went on to dominate the featherweight class, stopped the British representative, Nunc Wallace, in 18 rounds at the Pelican Club, London.

Dixon's authority was disputed by several rival claimants, including Tommy Kelly, Chappie Moran (who was born in Manchester) and Billy Plimmer, the British title-holder. Plimmer's claim was probably the strongest: he had beaten Kelly in a match at 110 lb in 1892, and had the better of a four-rounder with Dixon one year later, although by that time Dixon had outgrown the division and renounced his own claim. In those days there were no 'governing bodies' (unlike today, when we have several to spare) so virtually anyone could set himself up as a champion provided that he had a decent record and a good relationship with the sporting press. Thus Jimmy Barry, of Chicago, was able to proclaim himself champion after knocking out Caspar Leon, in 1894, although Thomas 'Pedlar' Palmer earned British recognition by stopping Plimmer (at 112 lb) the following year.

Palmer defended his portion of the championship five times, including a 20-round points win over future world featherweight champion Dave Sullivan in 1897, when, for the first time, the weight limit was set at the modern standard of 8 st 6 lb (118 lb). Two months after Palmer's win over

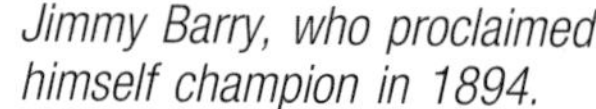

Jimmy Barry, who proclaimed himself champion in 1894.

Pedlar Palmer, who set the modern weight limit.

Sullivan, Barry knocked out Walter Croot of England in the same ring at the National Sporting Club, a fight which has a unique and tragic place in boxing history. Croot died the day after his 20th-round defeat, and Barry's acquittal on the consequent manslaughter charge established the crucial principle that death resulting from a boxing contest with gloves and fought under rules could not be other than accidental.

Barry's subsequent record was curious: he won a couple of six-rounders and then drew his last seven fights in a row, including two defences against Caspar Leon, before retiring in September 1899. He was unbeaten in 70 fights, with 59 wins, nine draws, and two no-decisions. His retirement left the field clear for Palmer, but he lost in farcical circumstances to Terry McGovern in September 1899 at Tuckahoe, New York. The timekeeper

Palmer's reign was ended unceremoniously by Terry McGovern (left), who soon moved into the featherweight class.

Above: Digger Stanley wins the first Lonsdale Belt in the bantamweight division, knocking out Joe Bowker in 1908 at the NSC.

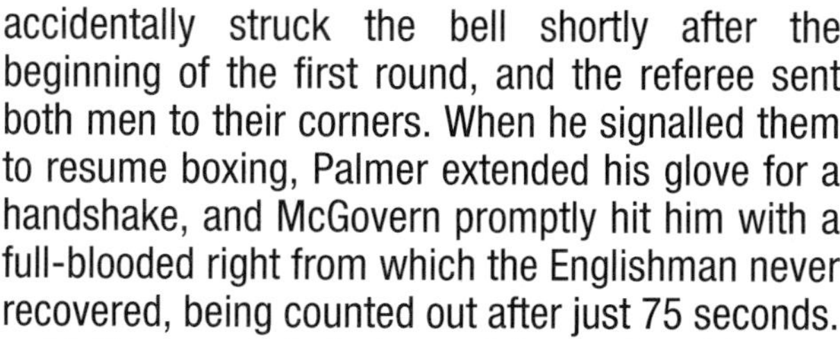

accidentally struck the bell shortly after the beginning of the first round, and the referee sent both men to their corners. When he signalled them to resume boxing, Palmer extended his glove for a handshake, and McGovern promptly hit him with a full-blooded right from which the Englishman never recovered, being counted out after just 75 seconds.

McGovern made just one defence, knocking out Harry Forbes in two rounds, and then relinquished the title on New Year's Eve 1899 to compete for, and win, the featherweight championship. Harry Harris, a skinny individual from Chicago whose unimpressive physique earned him the unflattering nickname 'The Human Hairpin', outpointed Pedlar Palmer in London for the vacant title, but gave it up because of weight problems.

Forbes, who had drawn with Caspar Leon in a vacant title match six months before Harris beat Palmer, was rematched with Leon and won on points. It was Leon's sixth unsuccessful title bid, four of which had ended in draws, three with Barry and one with Forbes.

Forbes was a busy champion, risking the title four times in 13 months, but in August 1903 he was knocked out in two rounds by Frankie Neil of San Francisco, whom he had stopped in a December 1902 title fight. Neil made three defences, including a three-round knockout of Forbes, but then left the title in London when Joe Bowker (whose real name was Tommy Mahon) outpointed him in October 1904. Bowker, a top-class fighter from Salford who had beaten Andrew Tokell and Owen Moran, relinquished it without a defence and stepped up to featherweight, where he won the British title by knocking out Pedlar Palmer.

The vacant title was claimed for Britain by George 'Digger' Stanley of Kingston-on-Thames, and for America by Jimmy Walsh, whom Stanley had beaten and drawn with in 1904. Walsh beat Stanley in October 1905, but abdicated the following year. For the next eight years there was chaos at the top, with five different versions of the title in circulation.

Stanley claimed the vacant title in 1906, Walsh returned to bantamweight title action in 1908, and

George 'Digger' Stanley claimed the world title for Britain, at a time when the championship was in a hopelessly confused state. Eight years elapsed before Kid Williams at last emerged, in 1914, as the undisputed champion.

Monte Attell (brother of featherweight champion Abe) established a tenuous claim in 1909. But the strongest claim came from Johnny Coulon, a New Orleans-based Canadian, who scored a string of good wins in so-called championship matches between 1908 and 1912. The various strands of the title were held at different times during this period by Charles Ledoux, Eddie Campi and Frank Conley, but the one who eventually emerged from the pack was Kid Williams (real name Johnny Gutenko), who was born in Copenhagen but fought out of Maryland.

In 1913 Williams kayoed Ledoux, earning universal recognition one year later with successive knockouts of Campi and Coulon. He retained the title five times, and survived a 1915 disqualification against Johnny 'Kewpie' Ertle of St Paul, Minnesota. Ertle, born in Austria, claimed the title after his fifth-round disqualification win in Ertle's hometown, but Williams argued that, since the fight had been held in a town where decisions were prohibited, he could not logically nor legally be disqualified.

Ertle's claim gained no support, nor did he ever get another chance to become champion. Williams' defences included a draw with Pete Herman of New Orleans, who had impressed in a no-decision ten-rounder against the champion a year earlier. For the rematch, Herman's manager guaranteed Williams a record purse and allowed him to bring his own referee, Billy Rocap of Philadelphia. They met again in January 1917. Once more Rocap refereed, but this time he gave the 20-year-old Herman the verdict.

Herman's first defence, a 20-round points defeat of the capable Frankie Burns in New Orleans in November 1917 was a doubly memorable occasion for the champion: he was married in the afternoon and then took ample revenge over the only man who had ever beaten him inside the distance. Herman lost the title at Madison Square Garden in December 1920 to New Yorker Joe Lynch, and three weeks later scored a famous victory in London over Jimmy Wilde. There has always been a suspicion that he had only loaned the title to Lynch to ensure that it would not leave America should Wilde beat him, and the rumours gained credibility when Herman easily won the return fight seven months later. But Herman always vehemently denied any such arrangement, and pointed out that his purse for the rematch (which drew over $100,000 at Ebbett's Field, Brooklyn) was $15,000 less than the $37,000 earned by Lynch.

By that stage, however, the smooth-boxing Herman was already blind in one eye, and less than

Kid Williams (above) *lost the title to Pete Herman, who came to London in 1921 to score a famous victory over flyweight champion Jimmy Wilde* (below). *Herman had, three weeks earlier, left his bantamweight championship in the hands of fellow-American Joe Lynch* (right).

Herman (right) knocked out British champion Jim Higgins in 11 rounds in London on 11 July 1921 and exactly a fortnight later (in the days before international air travel) regained the world title from Joe Lynch in New York.

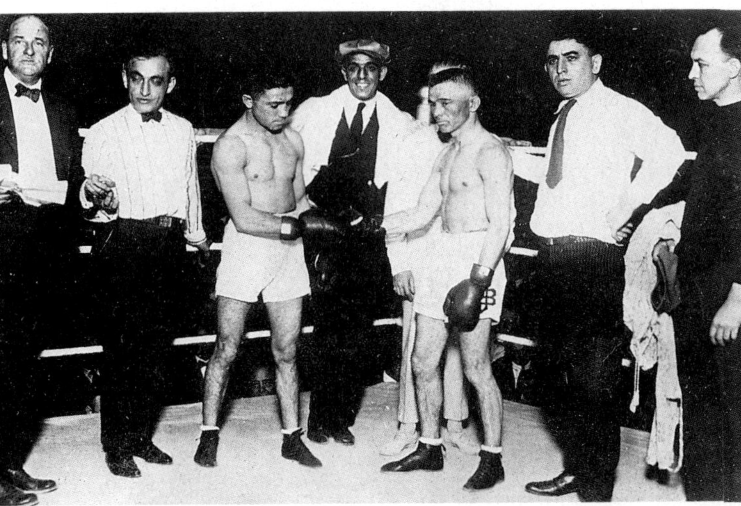

a year after he had lost the title a second time, to Johnny Buff of New Jersey in September 1921, he was completely blind. Buff, whose real name was John Lesky, was a late starter in the business, turning pro at 30 after long service in the US Navy. His career peaked in 1921 when he beat Abe Goldstein and Charles Ledoux, before taking the title from Herman and retaining it two months later against the Italian-born Little Jack Sharkey.

Lynch regained it in July 1922, forcing Buff to quit in the 14th round, and retained it against Midget Smith. He was scheduled to meet the London-born, Chicago-based Joe Burman in Madison Square Garden in October 1923, but had to withdraw after being injured in an accident. Abe Goldstein, a Harlem Jew who had boxed only four days previously, came in as substitute at less than 24 hours' notice. At the weigh-in, the New York Commission solemnly proclaimed Burman world champion, but his reign proved the shortest on record as Goldstein outpointed him that evening. He went on to win the undisputed championship by beating Lynch in March 1924, and retained it twice more that year before his fellow New Yorker, Eddie 'Cannonball' Martin, outpointed him in December 1924.

Three months later Martin gave a title shot to another New Yorker, Charley Phil Rosenberg. The

The crew-cut ex-sailor Johnny Buff poses with Herman (above) *before the fight which cost Herman the title. Less than a year later, the former champion was completely blind. Buff had won the American flyweight title earlier in 1921 by knocking out Abe Goldstein* (right) *in two rounds, but Goldstein went on to become bantamweight champion himself in 1923.*

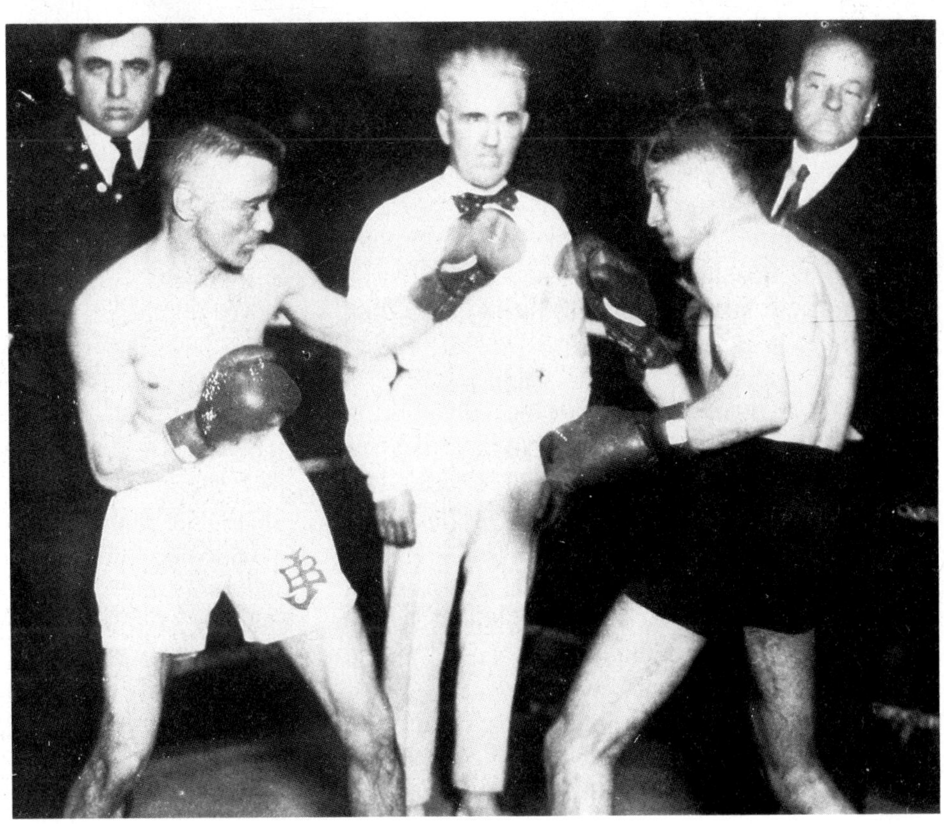

Bud Taylor (left) *outgrew the flyweight class to become NBA bantamweight champion in 1927. The disputed title was unified two years later by the lanky Panama Al Brown* (below), *a cosmopolitan oddball.*

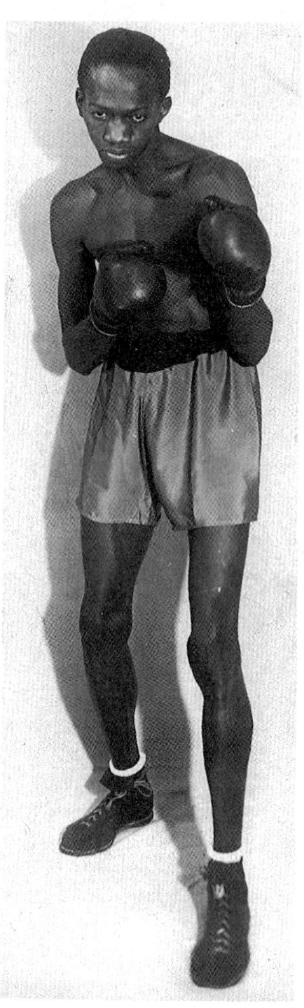

pair were old rivals, but as a draw was the best Rosenberg had managed in their three previous meetings Martin saw little risk in the match, especially as Rosenberg was scaling 11 st (154 lb) when the fight was announced, having less than two months to drop to the bantamweight limit of 118 lb.

Rosenberg made the weight by 'drying out' (denying himself liquids), and did the job so thoroughly that he actually scaled 116 lb, two pounds inside the limit. But the effort did not affect his performance, and he took Martin's championship with an easy points win. He defended it twice, knocking out Eddie Shea and outpointing George Butch, but then lost the title on the scales when he failed to make the weight for a defence against Bushy Graham (real name Angelo Geraci) in New York on 4 February 1927. Although James A. Farley, the New York Commissioner, declared the title vacant he still allowed the fight to go ahead, Rosenberg winning a 15-round verdict. But both fighters were subsequently suspended by the Commission for a year because of a secret agreement they had made concerning the percentage split of the purse money, and that effectively ended Rosenberg's career: he fought only twice more.

Less than three weeks after Rosenberg's win over Graham, Charles 'Bud' Taylor, of Indiana, outpointed Eddie Shea in Chicago to earn title recognition from four States. One month later Taylor boxed a draw with Tony Canzoneri (who went on to win three world titles) for the vacant NBA championship, while on the other side of the Atlantic Teddy Baldock of Poplar outpointed Archie Bell of Chicago in the Albert Hall, London, to win British recognition. In June, Taylor outpointed Canzoneri to become NBA champion, and four

Baltazar Sangchilli, Spain's first world champion (right), *outpointed Brown for the title in June 1935* (left). *The NBA version was held by Lou Salica, until the aggressive Sixto Escobar took it from him in November 1935* (above).

months later Baldock lost his share to the South African, Willie Smith, at the Albert Hall. Smith, who had won the 1924 Olympic gold medal, moved up to featherweight, and the British Board recognized Bushy Graham after Graham had outpointed Izzy Schwartz in May 1928 for the vacant New York version.

The rival claimants clarified the position late in 1928 when they each relinquished their titles, and on 18 June 1929 the championship was once more unified when one of its better holders, the lanky Panamanian Al Brown, outpointed Vidal Gregorio in New York. Panama Al was, at 5 ft 11 in, the tallest man ever to hold the bantamweight title. He was an 'oddball', a cosmopolitan figure who spent much of his career in Europe, spoke seven languages, enjoyed the friendship of writer Ernest Hemingway, and had a degree of sophistication that (with the notable exception of Gene Tunney) was unusual in a boxer of that period. Apart from a brief episode in 1931 when Pete Sanstol, an American-based Norwegian, was recognised in Canada (of all places) after beating Archie Bell, Panama Al held the undisputed title for five years and ten defences. (Sanstol's claim lasted only from his win over Bell, in May 1931, to his split-decision defeat by Brown in Montreal three months later.)

In May 1934 the NBA stripped Brown for his failure to defend against their leading contender, Baby Casanova of Mexico. Their vacant title was won by Sixto Escobar of Puerto Rico, who knocked Casanova out in nine rounds. The Puerto Rican lost the title on his second defence to Lou Salica of New York, but Salica held it for less than three months, Escobar outpointing him in November 1935.

The New York and IBU versions, meantime, had passed from Brown to Spain's first world champion, Baltazar Sangchilli of Valencia, who crammed in 11 non-title fights in a year before Tony Marino, of Pittsburgh, kayoed him in New York. The ill-fated Marino was champion for barely two months: he was badly beaten by Escobar when

The unfortunate Tony Marino won the title from Sangchilli in June 1936, lost it two months later, and died two days after a points defeat in January 1937.

Above: *Harry Jeffra floors Sixto Escobar on the way to a non-title points win in December 1938, one of his four wins in five meetings.*

Right: *Lou Salica was a force in the bantamweight division for almost a decade, having his first title fight in 1935 and his last in 1943.*

they met in New York on 31 August 1936 for the undisputed title, the Commission's doctor ordering the fight to be stopped at the end of the 13th round. Marino collapsed after losing an eight-rounder against Indian Quintana in Brooklyn on 30 January 1937, and died two days later. (Quintana, incidentally, had been knocked out in the first round by Escobar in a title bid in October 1936.)

Escobar was dethroned in September 1937 by Harry Jeffra of Baltimore, who went on to become featherweight champion (New York version) in 1940. Jeffra had already beaten him twice in non-title fights, so the result was hardly a major surprise. However, the irrepressible Puerto Rican bounced back to win the title a third time, outpointing Jeffra in February 1938 and then relinquishing it, after one defence, because of weight problems. (Jeffra had the last word in their long-running series, outpointing him for the fourth time in five meetings in December 1940. Escobar never fought again.)

The NBA declared Georgie Pace of Cleveland to be their champion, and Pace thus shares with WBC heavyweight champion Ken Norton the distinction of being the only men ever to have been world champions without, in their entire careers, having won a single fight which had been billed as a championship. Pace drew his first defence, against Lou Salica in Toronto in March 1940, and six months later was outpointed by Salica in the Bronx Coliseum, New York for both the NBA and New York versions of the title.

Manuel Ortiz was one of the best-ever bantamweight champions, with 19 successful defences in eight years.

Salica's win over Tommy Forte of Philadelphia in January 1941 earned him undisputed recognition, but he managed only two defences before Manuel Ortiz, a classy Californian of Mexican extraction, outpointed him over 12 rounds in Hollywood in August 1942. (Ortiz had been recognized in his home state as champion since his win over Tony Olivera in January 1942.) Ortiz became one of the finest – perhaps even *the* best – of the bantamweight champions. Apart from a short spell in 1946 when Harold Dade of Chicago, a 12-1 outsider, outpointed him in San Francisco, only to lose it back two months later, Ortiz reigned for eight years and 19 successful defences.

He never attracted the media attention which his extraordinary record merited, probably because he never appeared in New York, where most of the leading American boxing writers were based. However, he earned around $150,000 during his long stay at the top, which ended when he was outpointed in Johannesburg on 31 May 1950 by Vic Toweel, a South African of Lebanese parentage. It was Ortiz's 116th fight, and Toweel's 14th. The

Right: *Ortiz (on the left) outpoints the former European champion Theo Medina in Paris in 1951.*

Below: *South Africa's Vic Toweel (on the right) ends Ortiz's long reign with a points win in Johannesburg.*

Toweel's three successful defences included points wins over Peter Keenan (left) *and Luis Romero* (below), *before the Australian southpaw Jimmy Carruthers knocked him out in the first round* (right).

brilliant South African had lost only two of 190 amateur fights, 160 of which had been won inside the distance. He held the title for two and a half years and three successful defences, including a tenth-round retirement victory over British champion Danny O'Sullivan, who took a record 14 counts.

Above: *A ring oddity as Carruthers (right) and Chamrern Songkitrat contest the world title bare-footed.*

Below: *Robert Cohen (left) outpoints Songkitrat to win the title vacated by Carruthers.*

Toweel had been a preliminary-round loser in the 1948 Olympic Games, and in November 1952 he lost the title to another unsuccessful competitor in those Games, the Australian southpaw Jimmy Carruthers, who knocked him out in the first round. In their rematch, in March 1953, he did at least stay upright for nine more rounds. The Australian made two more defences, outpointing Henry 'Pappy' Gault of America and the Thai Chamrern Songkitrat, in that country's first world championship. It was staged in a rain-swept outdoor stadium, and as the fight progressed the boxers kept slipping in the pools of water on the canvas. Finally, they agreed to discard their ring boots and socks, and fought bare-footed. Carruthers was badly cut over both eyes, and two weeks later, on 16 May 1954, announced his retirement 'to avoid further and possible serious damage' to his eyes.

Robert Cohen of Algeria outpointed Songkitrat in Bangkok in September 1954 to win the vacant title (on a split decision) but was stripped by the NBA in January 1955 for failing to defend against Raton Macias of Mexico City. Songkitrat was given a third

Cohen (on the right) outpoints the American 'Pappy' Gault in Paris in 1953.

Above: *Songkitrat's third title bid ended in an 11th-round knockout by Raul Macias for the NBA championship.*

Below: *the Italian deaf mute Mario D'Agata (on the left) outpointing Juan Cardenas in a non-title bout in 1956.*

chance at the title, but Macias knocked him out in 11 rounds for the NBA version. Cohen retained his share with a draw against Vic Toweel's brother Willie (who later won the Empire lightweight title) but in June 1956 he was forced to retire in the sixth round of a Rome defence against Mario D'Agata, one of three deaf-mutes in a family of nine. The Italian was champion for less than one year, being outpointed in Paris in April 1957 by another Algerian, Alphonse Halimi.

Halimi lost the title in his first defence to Joe Becerra of Guadalajara, Mexico, who knocked him out in eight rounds in Los Angeles, in July 1959, and took a round longer in the rematch in February 1960. Becerra beat the first of many Japanese bantamweight challengers, Kenji Yonekura, on a split decision in May 1960 but then suddenly retired, aged 24, following his eighth-round knockout in August 1960 by Eloy Sanchez in a non-title affair.

The championship divided once more. The European Boxing Union and the British Board recognized Halimi, who won a fiercely disputed decision over the Belfast southpaw Freddie Gilroy at Wembley on 25 October 1960, and then lost it in

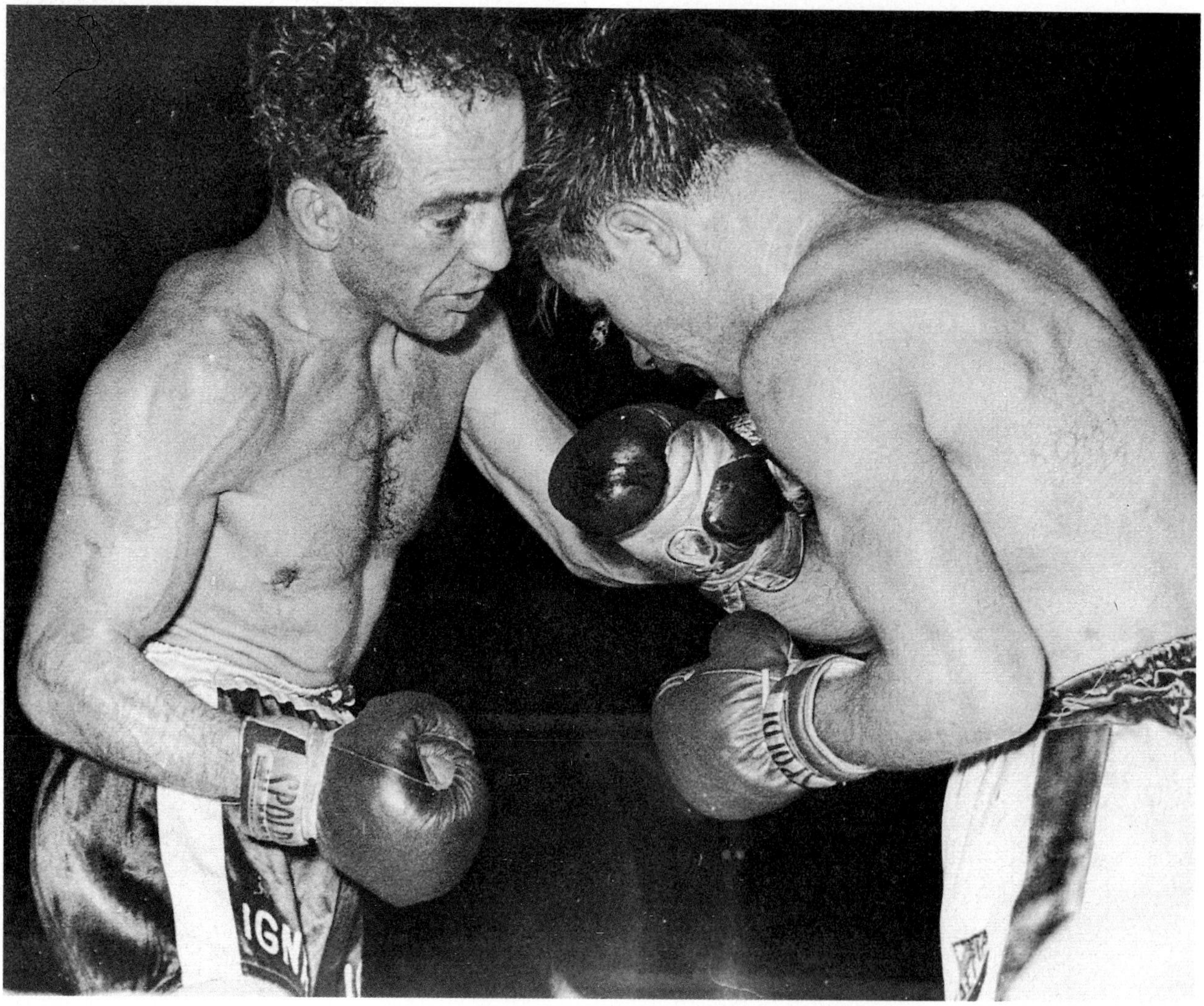

Left: *Alphonse Halimi lands an overarm right on Raul Macias as he unifies the title in Los Angeles in November 1957.*

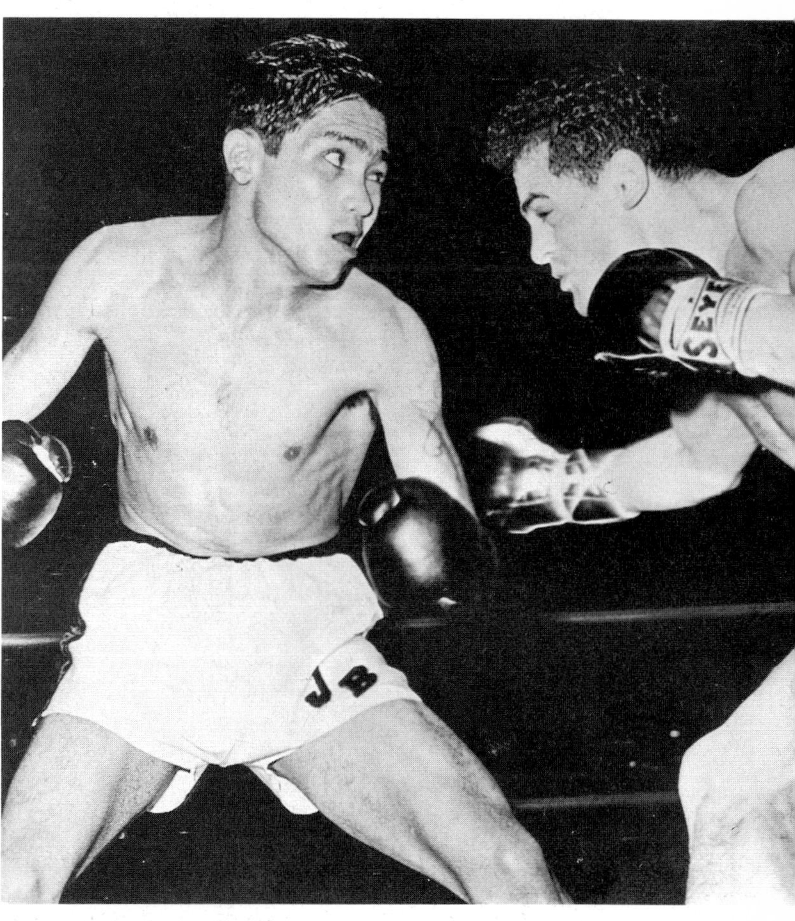

Hard-hitting Mexican Joe Becerra knocked out Halimi in eight rounds in July 1959, and repeated the result (right) *in February 1960. He retired after beating Japan's Kenji Yonekura in May 1960* (below).

Below: *Halimi regained at least European recognition as world champion with this disputed decision over Irish southpaw Freddie Gilroy (on the right) in October 1960.*

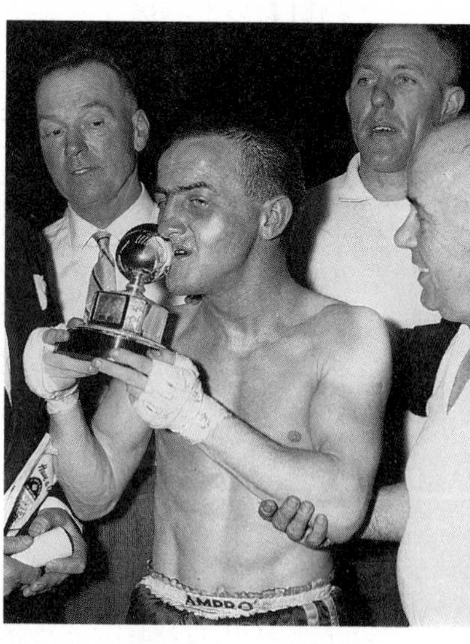

Johnny Caldwell (right, *with trophy) takes a butt in the face* (left) *from Halimi on the way to a points win for the European-version world title, but* (below, *against Frenchman Rene Libeer), the Belfastman knew a trick or two himself.*

Brazilian star Eder Jofre reunified the title by stopping Caldwell in 10 rounds (below), *and retained it four months later against Herman Marquez* (above, *on the left*). *Jofre made four more defences before being dethroned by Masahiko 'Fighting' Harada* (right).

the same ring seven months later to Gilroy's townsman and former Olympic team-mate, Johnny Caldwell, who beat him again in October 1961. The NBA version had been won by Eder Jofre, a dazzlingly talented Brazilian with a 37-fight unbeaten record. Jofre (who was one of the few vegetarians ever to win a world championship) retained it twice and then, at Sao Paulo in January 1962, in a fight which was referreed by the former featherweight champion Willie Pep, stopped Caldwell in ten rounds for the undisputed title.

Jofre was defeated for the first time in 51 fights on 18 May 1965, when Masahiko 'Fighting' Harada, the former flyweight champion, out-pointed him at Nagoya, Japan. It was the Brazilian's sixth defence of the unified title, with none of his previous challengers having lasted the distance. Harada retained it against four outstanding contenders: England's Alan Rudkin; Jofre; Joe Medel of Mexico; and Bernardo Carabello of Colombia.

His reign was ended by the pipe-smoking Australian Aborigine Lionel Rose, who won a

Below: *England's Alan Rudkin, one of the best bantamweights never to be world champion, was outscored by Harada in his first world title bid.*

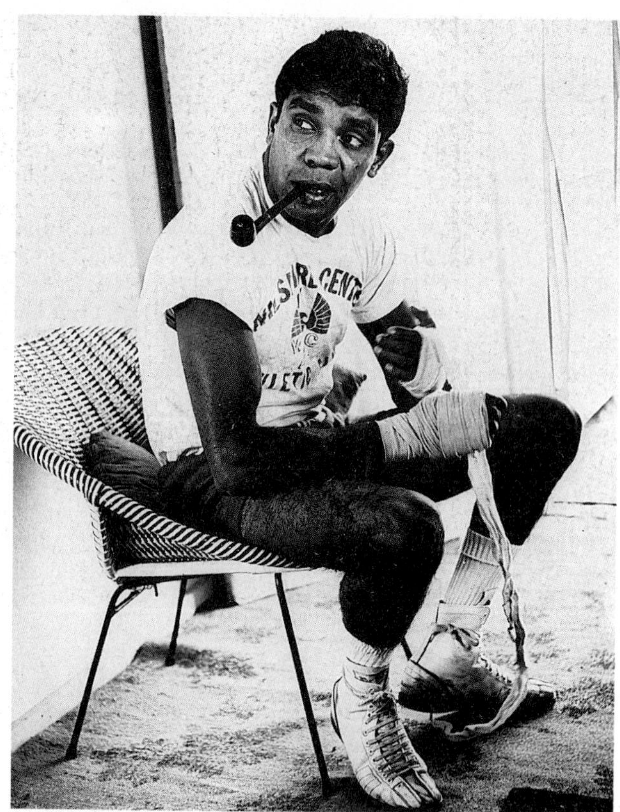

Above: *Lionel Rose's pipe was no publicity gimmick. The Australian Aborigine enjoyed a smoke.*

Below: *Jofre failed to regain the title from Harada in this 1966 rematch and retired for more than three years.*

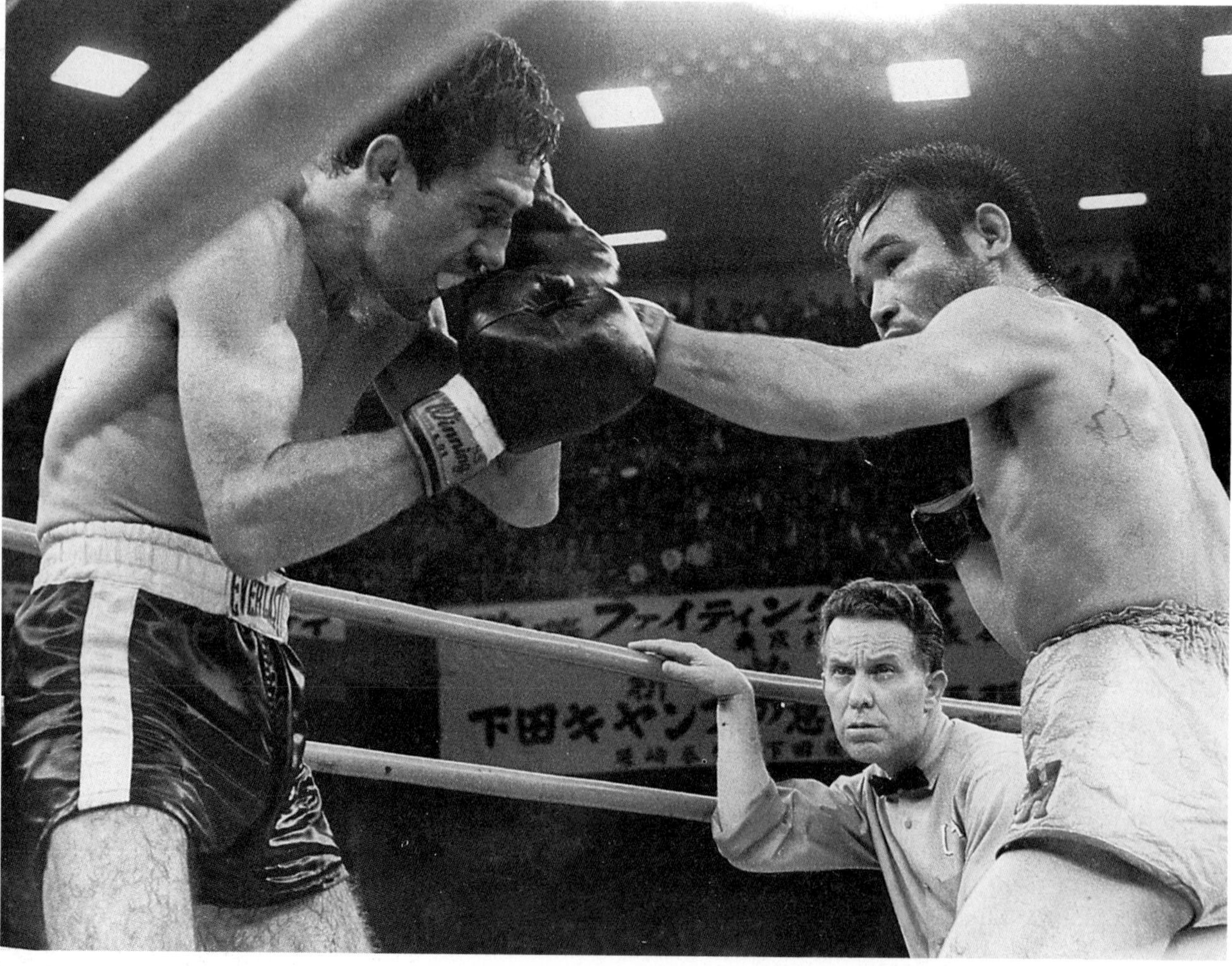

Previous page: *Carlos Zarate and Wilfredo Gomez had never been beaten in a combined 74 fights when they contested Gomez' WBC super-bantamweight title in San Juan in 1978, Gomez winning in five rounds.*

Lupe Pintor dominated the bantamweight division in the early 1980s with wins like these points verdicts over Albert Davila (right) *and Jose Uziga* (below). *The persistent Davila finally won the title, at his fourth attempt, in 1983.*

Left: *After this world title defeat by Rose, Harada moved into the featherweight division where he twice challenged for Johnny Famechon's WBC title.*

Below: *Rose's split decision win over Alan Rudkin (on the right) was notable as much for the eccentric scoring by judge Ray Mitchell as for the exciting fight itself.*

unanimous decision in Tokyo on 27 February 1968. Rose repelled three challenges, all on split decisions, from Takao Sakurai, Alan Rudkin, and Jesus 'Chuchu' Castillo. Ray Mitchell, one of the judges in the Rudkin fight, defended his scoring of 75-60 (giving Rose all 15 rounds!) by saying that he was actually able to count all the punches landed by each man during a round, an accomplishment unique amongst boxing observers.

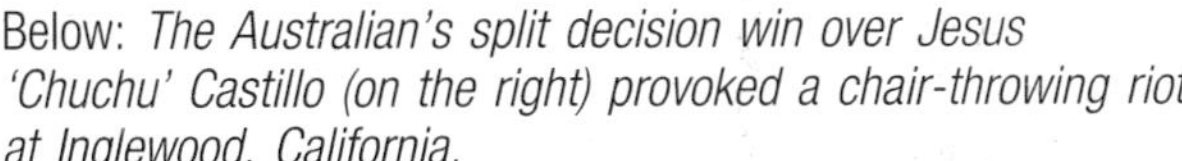

Below: *The Australian's split decision win over Jesus 'Chuchu' Castillo (on the right) provoked a chair-throwing riot at Inglewood, California.*

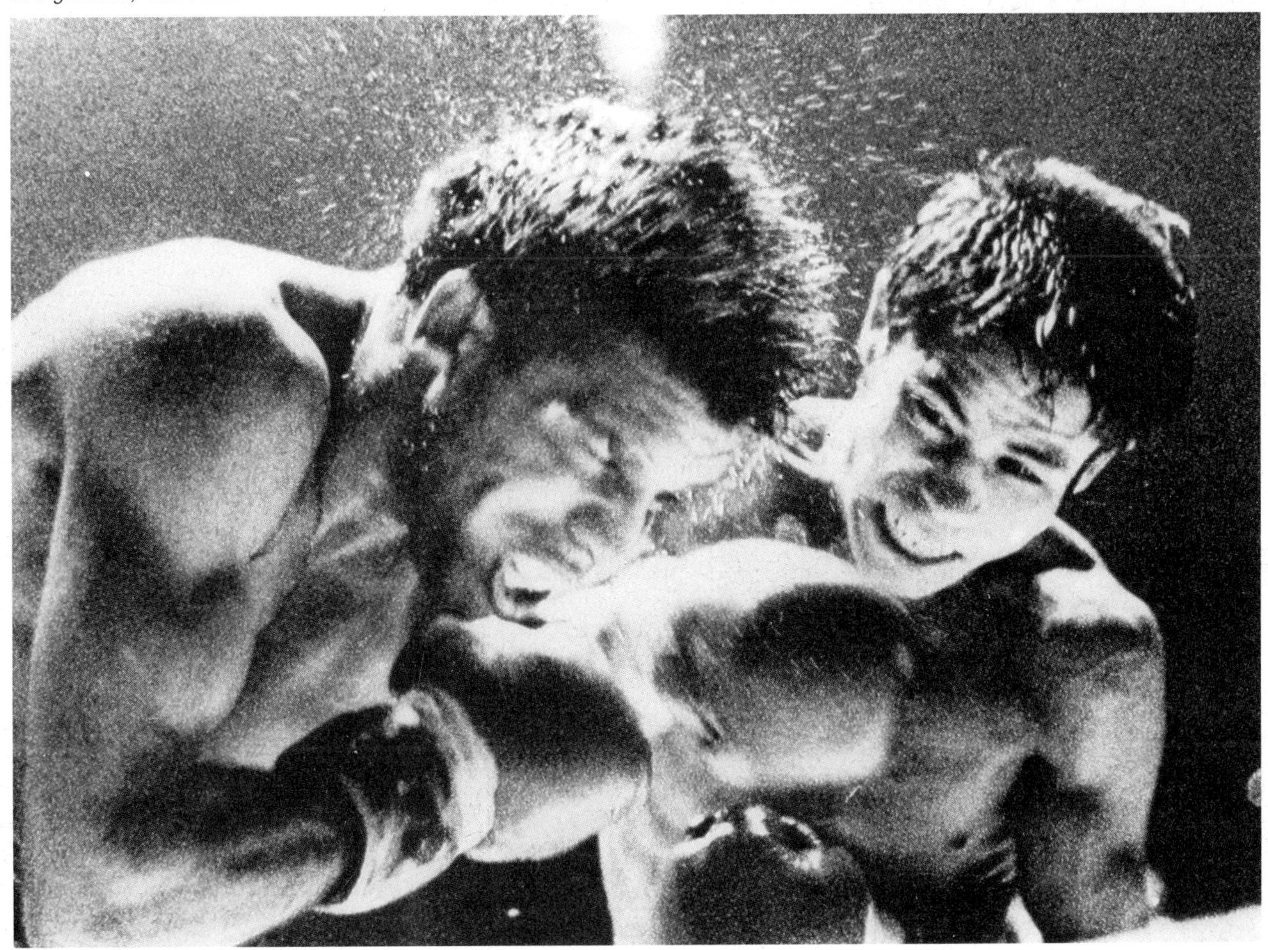

Above: *Thunderous-punching Ruben Olivares ends Rose's reign on a fifth-round knockout in August 1969.*

Below: *Rodolfo Martinez (right) outscores Japan's Yoshio Kajamoto. In his next fight he won the WBC title.*

Rose's luck ran out on 22 August 1969 when Ruben Olivares, a thunderous hitting Mexican, knocked him out in five rounds at Inglewood, California. Olivares, who had built up a phenomenal record of 49 inside-the-distance wins in an unbeaten 52-fight career, overwhelmed the persistent Alan Rudkin in two rounds on his first defence. Chuchu Castillo offered stiffer opposition: Olivares won a close 15-round decision over him in April 1970, but Castillo took the title with a 14th-round, cut eye stoppage in October. Olivares regained it on a unanimous decision in April 1971, defended it twice, but in March 1972 was knocked out in eight rounds by yet another Mexican, Rafael Herrera of Jalisco.

Herrera held it for just four months, being outpointed in July 1972 by Enrique Pinder of

Below: *Soo-Hwan Hong is forced onto the defensive against Arnold Taylor in their WBA title thriller.*

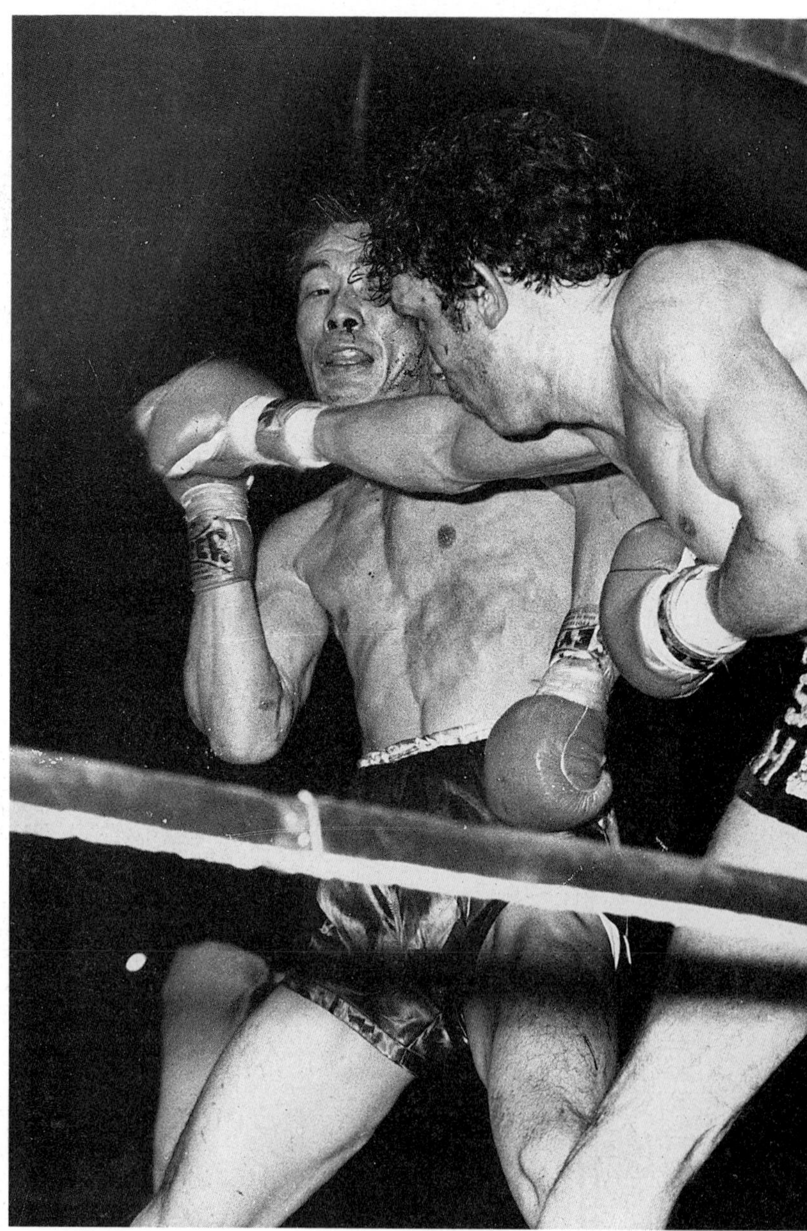

Panama. That was the last time that the undisputed bantamweight championship was contested: the WBC stripped Pinder for signing to defend against Romeo Anaya instead of their top contender, Rodolfo Martinez of Mexico, and, as in so many other categories, the split has lasted ever since.

Pinder lost the WBA version to Anaya on a third-round knockout in January 1973, and the Mexican was himself knocked out, on his third defence, by the rugged South African Arnold Taylor in Johannesburg, in November 1973. Taylor – who died tragically in a car crash in 1981 – was dethroned in July 1974 by a Korean, Soo Hwan Hong, who outpointed him in Durban. The Anaya and Hong fights were two of the most exciting battles in the division's history.

Hong was kayoed in four rounds at Inglewood, on 14 March 1975, by another of the seemingly endless stream of Mexican punchers who dominated the class in the 1970s – Alfonso Zamora, the 1972 Olympic silver medalist. Zamora

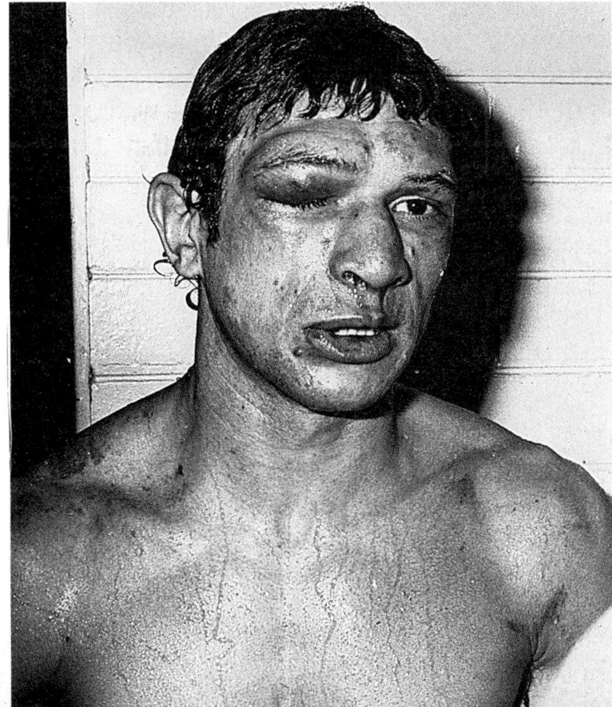

You should see the other guy . . . Arnold Taylor (left) *after his savage 15-rounder with Hong.*

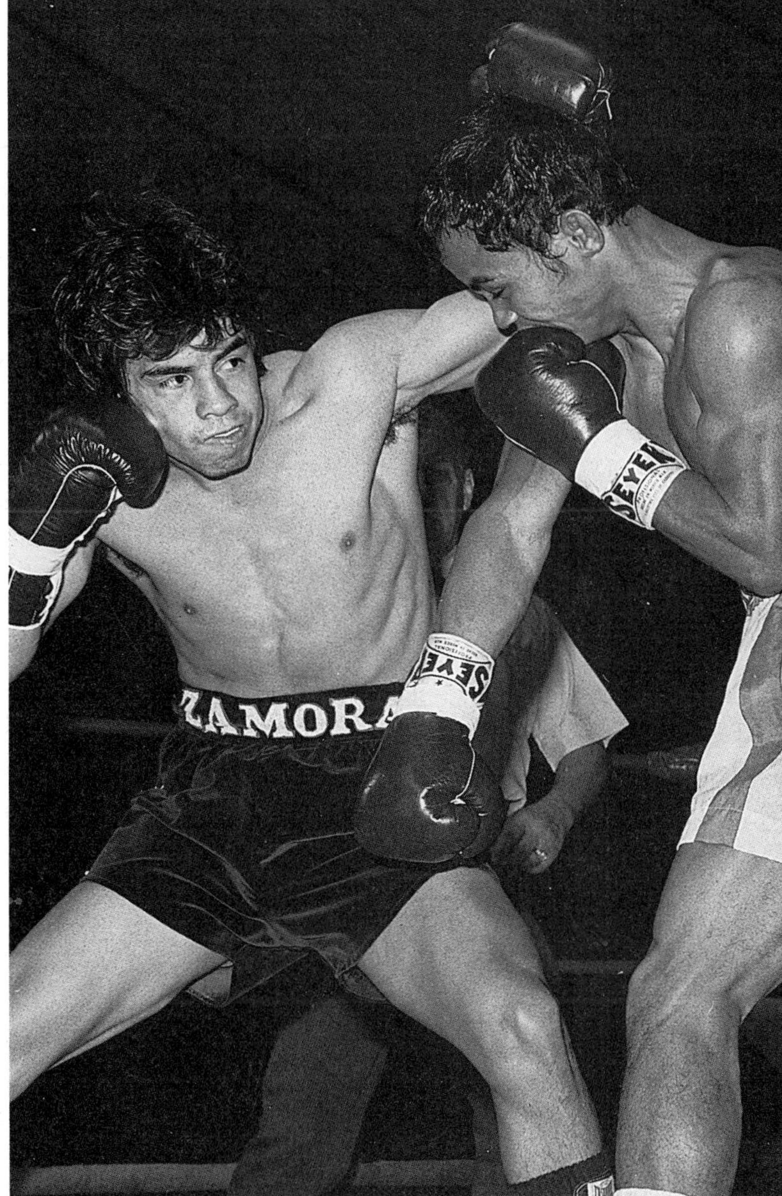

Below: *Thanomjit Sukhothai (on the right) was beaten by Alfonso Zamora in their 1975 WBA title clash.*

Carlos Zarate (on the left, stopping Alberto Davila in eight rounds in 1978) went 51 fights without defeat.

ran up a string of 29 consecutive wins inside the distance, including five world title defences, before being knocked out in four rounds by Carlos Zarate, the WBC title-holder, in a non-title clash of champions in Los Angeles on 23 April 1977.

Zarate was the third consecutive Mexican winner of the WBC version. The vacant title had been won by Rafael Herrera, who stopped Rodolfo Martinez in 12 rounds in April 1973, made one defence, and then lost it in a rematch with Martinez in December 1974. Martinez managed three defences, but on 8 May 1976 was knocked out in nine rounds by the superb Zarate. This was the new champion's 39th win inside the distance in an unbeaten 40-fight career. He went on to make nine successful defences, his first loss coming in his 51st fight when he stepped up a weight to challenge the equally gifted Puerto Rican Wilfredo Gomez for the super-bantam crown.

Zarate's reign was ended in June 1979 by his stable-mate Lupe Pintor, on a controversial split verdict in Las Vegas. Two judges scored 143-142 Pintor, while the third had Zarate in front by a massive 145-133 margin. Pintor made eight defences, one of them a 12th-round knockout of the Welshman Johnny Owen in Los Angeles, in September 1980. Owen lay in a coma for weeks, and died on 4 November.

Three years later Pintor was severely injured in a motor bike accident, and his title was declared vacant. The WBC matched Alberto Davila (who had failed in three previous title bids against Zarate, Jorge Lujan for the WBA title, and Pintor) with Francisco 'Kiko' Bejines, one of a family of three boxing brothers. They met in the same ring where Pintor had fought Owen, and in an eerie

Lupe Pintor (on the right) came close to defeat in this 1980 WBC defence against Eijiro Murata, but it was a draw.

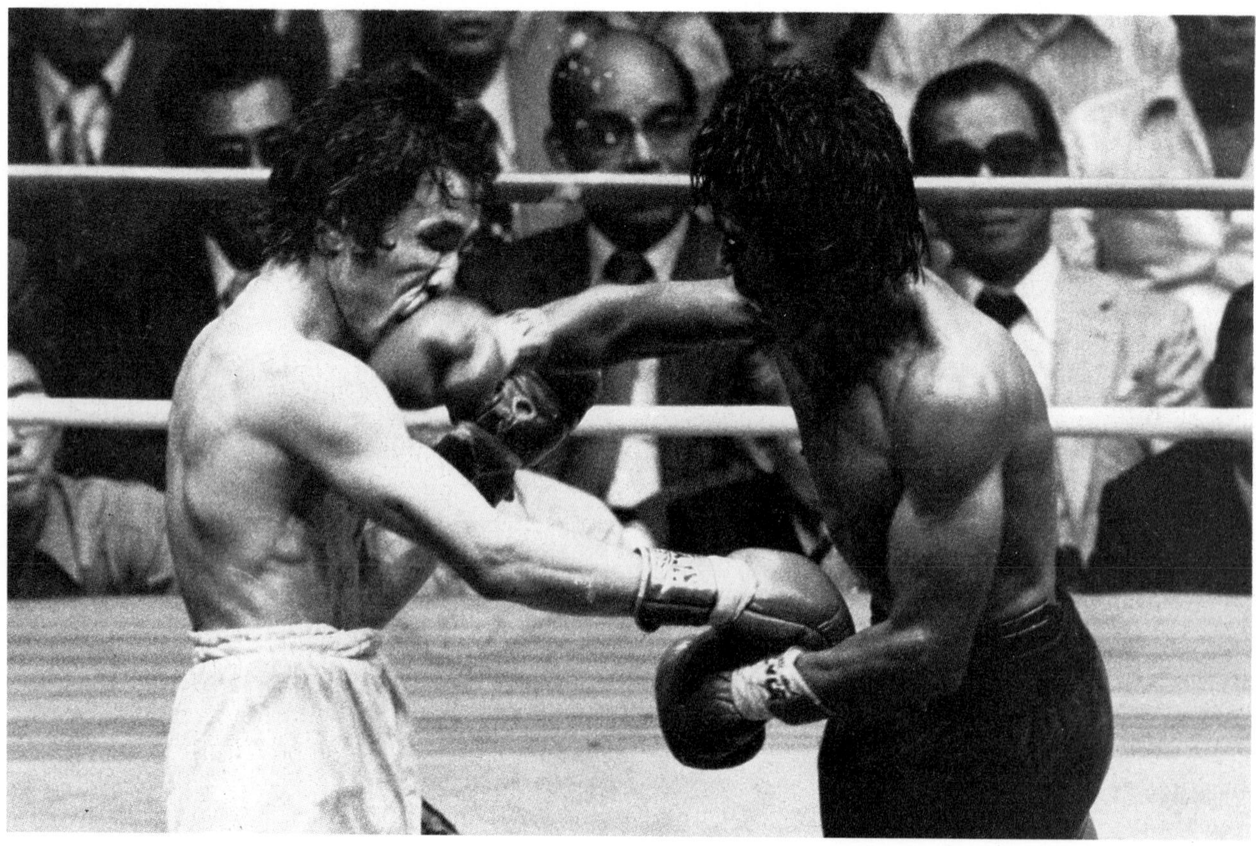

Pintor's second visit to Japan was almost as demanding, when he had to go into the 15th round before knocking out Hurricane Teru (on the right).

coincidence Bejines – ahead on two of the three official scorecards – was knocked out in the 12th and final round and later died.

Davila made only one defence, but in early 1985 was obliged to relinquish the title because of ill health. The vacancy was filled by Daniel Zaragoza of Mexico, who lost it to Miguel Lora of Colombia.

The WBA version, meanwhile, had passed from Alfonso Zamora to Jorge Lujan, a stylish and elegant Panamanian who was a 10-1 outsider when he knocked the Mexican out in ten rounds in

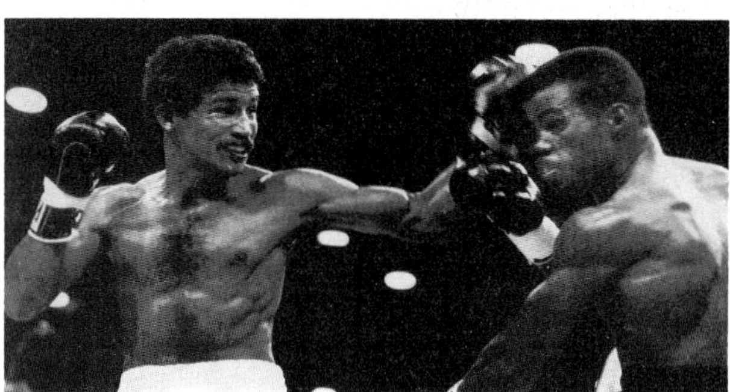

Left: *Alberto Davila kayoes Kiko Bejines for the vacant WBC title – a fight which cost Bejines his life.*
Above: *Miguel Lora (on the left) hammers Enrique Sanchez to defeat to retain the WBC title.*
Below: *Jorge Lujan stopped Cleo Garcia in the 15th in defence of the WBA title at Caesars Palace in 1979.*

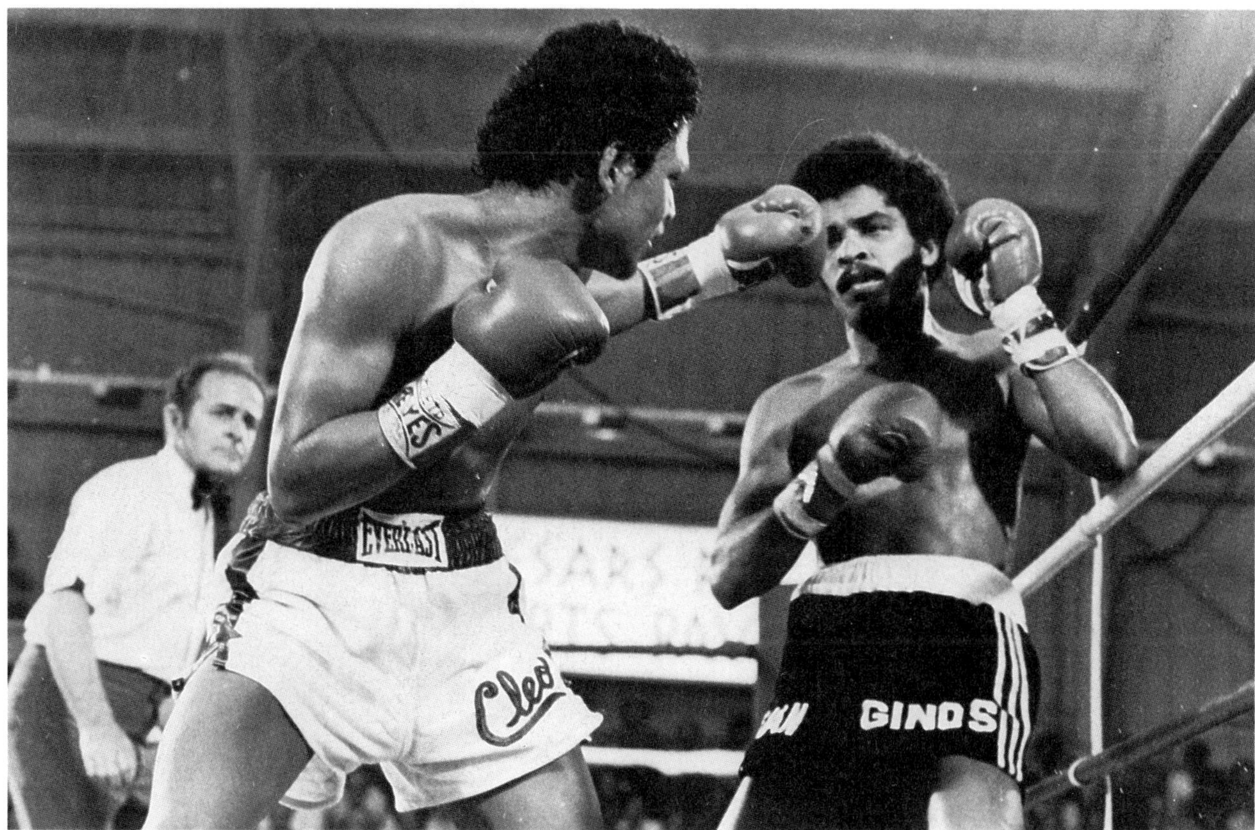

November 1977. Zamora's career petered out in a string of mediocre performances, but shortly after he had retired in 1980 he won a fortune on the Mexican national lottery.

Lujan defended the title five times, but was dethroned at Miami Beach in August 1980 by Julian Solis of Puerto Rico. Solis' first defeat in 22 fights came in his first defence, to Jeff Chandler. The unbeaten Philadelphian stopped him in 14 rounds in Miami, on 14 November 1980, and went

Jeff Chandler (left) *established himself as a contender with wins like this* (right) *over Davey Vasquez, going on to become a respected holder of the WBA title. He was beaten, after nine defences, by another American – Richard Sandoval* (below), *seen (on the left) retaining the title against Venezuela's Edgar Roman.*

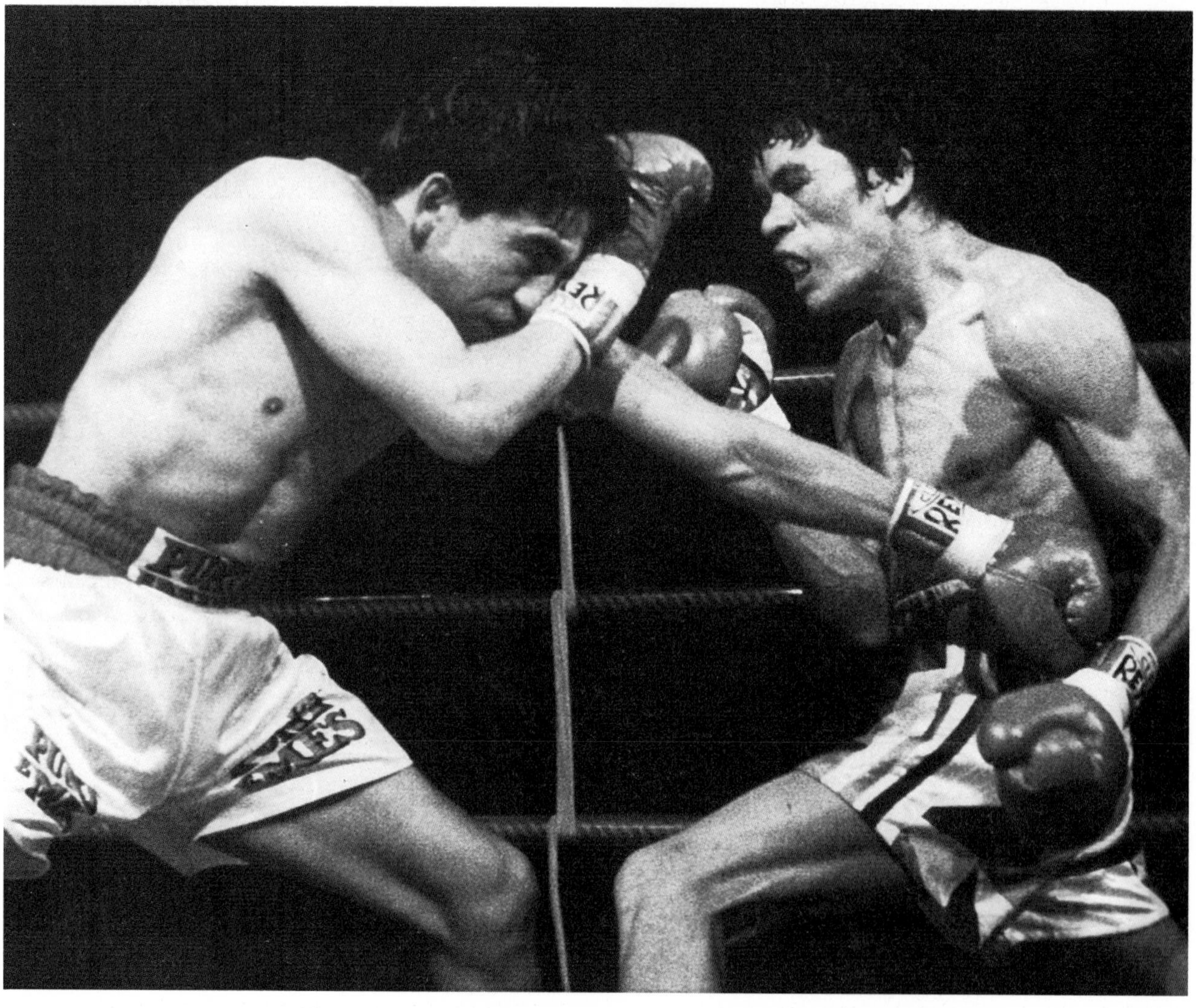

on to prove himself one of the division's better champions of recent years. He retained the title nine times before his fellow-American Richie Sandoval of California (whose brother Alberto had been beaten in 12 rounds by Pintor in a 1980 title bid) stopped him in the 15th round of a thriller at Atlantic City in April 1984.

Sandoval was toppled by a Roberto Duran lookalike, Gaby Canizales of Laredo, Texas, in his third defence. Canizales battered Sandoval so savagely, stopping him in seven rounds in Las Vegas, in March 1986, that the Californian was unconscious for 14 minutes and, although he made a full recovery, he never boxed again. Canizales surprisingly lost the title on his first defence to the Colombian Bernardo Pinango, who established himself as an effective and exciting champion.

The IBF title was inaugurated by Satoshi Shingaki of Japan, who knocked out Elmer Magallano for the vacant title at Kawashiwara on 16 April 1984, but he lost it on his second defence to Jeff Fenech of Australia. Fenech beat Shingaki in nine rounds on 26 April 1985 in Sydney, retained it four times, and then announced in early 1987 that he was relinquishing the title as he could no longer make the weight.

HOW THE BANTAMWEIGHT TITLE HAS CHANGED HANDS

1890–1900

The division became active around 1850, but George Dixon was the first generally accepted champion

27 Jun 90 George Dixon w.rsf.18 Nunc Wallace in London

1891 *Dixon relinquished the title because of difficulty in making the weight. There had been several other claimants during his reign, including Chappie Moran (GB) and Tommy Kelly. Billy Plimmer (GB) achieved partial recognition by outpointing Kelly over 10 rounds at New York on 9 May 1892, and he strengthened his claim by stopping Dixon in four rounds in New York on 22 August 1893.*

15 Sep 94 Jimmy Barry w.ko.28 Casper Leon at Lamont, Illinois *(Barry claimed the title)*

28 May 95 Billy Plimmer w.ko.7 George Corfield at London

25 Nov 95 Pedlar Palmer w.rsf.14 Billy Plimmer at London

29 Dec 98 Jimmy Barry drew 20 Casper Leon at Davenport, Iowa *(Barry retired, leaving Palmer with the strongest claim to the title)*

17 Apr 99 Pedlar Palmer w.rsf.3 Billy Rotchford at London

22 Sep 99 Terry McGovern w.ko.1 Pedlar Palmer at Tuckahoe, New York

31 Dec 99 *McGovern relinquished the title because of weight trouble*

18 Mar 01 Harry Harris w.pts.20 Pedlar Palmer in London *(Harris relinquished the title without defending it)*

02 Apr 01 Harry Forbes w.pts.15 Casper Leon in Memphis, Tennessee

13 Aug 03 Frankie Neil w.ko.2 Harry Forbes in San Francisco

17 Oct 04 Joe Bowker w.pts.20 Frankie Neil in London *Bowker relinquished the title which was claimed for America by Jimmy Walsh and for Britain by Digger Stanley*

29 Mar 05 Jimmy Walsh w.ko.6 Monte Attell in Philadelphia

20 Oct 05 Jimmy Walsh w.pts.15 Digger Stanley at Chelsea, Mass

1906 *Walsh relinquished the title due to weight problems. There followed a most confused period, with several claimants including Johnny Coulon, Digger Stanley, Monte Attell, Frankie Conley, and Walsh (on his comeback)*

13 Dec 06 Digger Stanley w.pts.20 Ike Bradley at Liverpool

08 Jan 08 Johnny Coulon w.pts.10 Kid Murphy at Preoria, Illinois

24 May 09 Jimmy Walsh drew 15 Digger Stanley in London *(Walsh vacated his claim to the title)*

22 Feb 10 Frankie Conley w.ko.42 Monte Attell at Vernon, Calif

05 Dec 10 Digger Stanley w.pts.20 Johnny Coulon at London

26 Feb 11 Johnny Coulon w.pts.20 Frankie Conley in New Orleans

23 Jun 12 Charles Ledoux w.ko.7 Digger Stanley at Dieppe

24 Jun 13 Eddie Campi w.pts.20 Charles Ledoux at Vernon, Calif

31 Jan 14 Kid Williams w.ko.3 Johnny Coulon in Los Angeles *(For undisputed title)*

10 Sep 15 Johnny 'Kewpie' Ertle w.dis.15 Kid Williams in St. Paul *(Williams argued, successfully, that as the bout had taken place in a city where decisions were prohibited he could not legally be disqualified. He continued to be regarded as champion)*

09 Jan 17 Pete Burman w.ko.7 Pete Herman at Benton Harbour *(Burman, London-born, was never recognised as champion. Herman argued that, since the bout had been scheduled as a no-decision affair, he could not lose the title)*

22 Dec 20 Joe Lynch w.pts.15 Pete Herman at New York

25 Aug 21 Pete Herman w.pts.15 Joe Lynch at New York

23 Sep 21 Johnny Buff w.pts.15 Pete Herman at New York

10 Jul 22 Joe Lynch w.rtd.14 Johnny Buff in New York *(The NY Commission stripped Lynch for withdrawing from a scheduled defence against Joe Burman. Abe Goldstein—who had boxed two days previously—substituted at less than 24 hours' notice)*

19 Oct 23 Abe Goldstein w.pts.12 Joe Burman in New York *(For NY title)*

21 Mar 24 Abe Goldstein w.pts.15 Joe Lynch in New York *(For undisputed title)*

19 Dec 24 Eddie Martin w.pts.15 Abe Goldstein at New York

30 Mar 25 Charlie Rosenberg w.pts.15 Eddie Martin at New York

Feb 27 *Rosenberg was suspended by the NY Commission for making a secret agreement with Bushy Graham concerning the percentage split of the purse money for their scheduled title fight*

24 Feb 27 Bud Taylor w.pts.10 Eddie Shea in Chicago *(Taylor won recognition in four States as champion)*

26 Mar 27 Bud Taylor drew 10 Tony Canzoneri in Chicago *(For vacant NBA title)*

05 May 27 Teddy Baldock w.pts.15 Archie Bell in London *(British version of vacant title)*

24 Jun 27 Bud Taylor w.pts.10 Tony Canzoneri in Chicago *(Vacant NBA title)*

06 Oct 27 Willie Smith w.pts.15 Teddy Baldock in London *(For British version of title. Smith never defended it, and moved up to featherweight)*

25 Feb 28 Bushy Graham w.pts.15 Cpl. Izzy Schwarz in New York *(For NY title)*

1928 *Both Taylor (NBA) and Graham (NY) relinquished their titles*

18 Jun 29 Al Brown w.pts.15 Vidal Gregorio in New York *(For vacant title)*

20 May 31 Pete Sanstol w.pts.10 Archie Bell in Montreal *(Recognised in Canada as being for the title)*

25 Aug 31 Al Brown w.pts.15 Pete Sanstol in Montreal *(For undisputed title)*

May 34 *The NBA stripped Brown for his failure to defend against Baby Casanova*

26 Jun 34 Sixto Escobar w.ko.9 Baby Casanova in Montreal *(For vacant NBA title)*

01 Jun 35 Baltazar Sangchilli w.pts.15 Al Brown at Valencia

26 Aug 35 Lou Salica w.pts.15 Sixto Escobar in New York *(NBA title)*

15 Nov 35 Sixto Escobar w.pts.15 Lou Salica in New York

29 Jun 36 Tony Marino w.ko.14 Baltazar Sangchilli in New York

31 Aug 36 Sixto Escobar w.rsf.13 Tony Marino in New York *(For undisputed title)*

23 Sep 37 Harry Jeffra w.pts.15 Sixto Escobar in New York

20 Feb 38 Sixto Escobar w.pts.15 Harry Jeffra in San Juan

Dec 39 *Escobar relinquished the title because of difficulty in making the weight. The NBA nominated Georgie Pace as champion*

24 Sep 40 Lou Salica w.pts.15 Georgie Pace in New York *(For NY and NBA titles)*

13 Jan 41 Lou Salica w.pts.15 Tommy Forte in Philadelphia *(For undisputed title)*

02 Jan 42 Manuel Ortiz w.pts.10 Tony Olivera in Oakland, Calif *(For California version of title)*

07 Aug 42 Manuel Ortiz w.pts.12 Lou Salica in Hollywood, Calif *(For undisputed title)*

06 Jan 47 Harold Dade w.pts.15 Manuel Ortiz at San Francisco

11 Mar 47 Manuel Ortiz w.pts.15 Harold Dade at Los Angeles

31 May 50 Vic Toweel w.pts.15 Manuel Ortiz Johannesburg

15 Nov 52 Jimmy Carruthers w.ko.1 Vic Toweel at Johannesburg

16 May 54 *Carruthers retired as undefeated champion*

18 Sep 54 Robert Cohen w.pts.15 Chamrern Songkitrat at Bangkok

Jan 55 *The NBA took Cohen's title because of his failure to defend against Raton Macias*

09 Mar 55 Raton Macias w.ko.11 Chamrern Songkitrat in San Francisco *(For vacant NBA title)*

29 Jun 56 Mario D'Agata w.rtd.6 Robert Cohen in Rome

01 Apr 57 Alphonse Halimi w.pts.15 Mario D'Agata in Paris

06 Nov 57 Alphonse Halimi w.pts.15 Raton Macias in Los Angeles *(For undisputed title)*

08 Jul 59 Joe Becerra w.ko.8 Alphonse Halimi in Los Angeles

30 Aug 60 *Becerra retired as undefeated champion*

25 Oct 60 Alphonse Halimi w.pts.15 Freddie Gilroy at Wembley *(For European version of vacant title)*

18 Nov 60 Eder Jofre w.ko.6 Eloy Sanchez in Los Angeles *(For NBA title)*

27 May 61 Johnny Caldwell w.pts.15 Alphonse Halimi at Wembley *(European version of title)*

18 Jan 62 Eder Jofre w.rtd.10 Johnny Caldwell in Sao Paulo *(For undisputed title)*

18 May 65 Masahiko Harada w.pts.15 Eder Jofre at Nagoya, Japan

27 Feb 68 Lionel Rose w.pts.15 Masahiko Harada in Tokyo

22 Aug 69 Ruben Olivares w.ko.5 Lionel Rose at Inglewood

16 Oct 70 Jesus Castillo w.rsf.14 Ruben Olivares at Mexico City

02 Apr 71 Ruben Olivares w.pts.15 Jesus Castillo at Inglewood

19 Mar 72 Rafael Herrera w.ko.8 Ruben Olivares at Mexico City

29 Jul 72 Enrique Pinder w.pts.15 Rafael Herrera at Panama City *(WBC stripped Pinder of title when he signed to defend against Romeo Anaya, whom they did not consider a suitable challenger)*

20 Jan 73 Romeo Anaya w.ko.3 Enrique Pinder at Panama City *(WBA title)*

14 Apr 73 Rafael Herrera w.rsf.12 Rodolfo Martinez at Monterrey *(Vacant WBC title)*

03 Nov 73 Arnold Taylor w.ko.14 Romeo Anaya in Johannesburg

03 Jul 74 Soo Hwan-Hong w.pts.15 Arnold Taylor in Durban

07 Dec 74 Rodolfo Martinez w.rsf.4 Rafael Herrera at Merida

14 Mar 75 Alfonso Zamora w.ko.4 Soo Hwan Hong at Inglewood *(WBA title)*

08 May 76 Carlos Zarate w.ko.9 Rodolfo Martinez in Inglewood

19 Nov 77 Jorge Lujan w.ko.10 Alfonso Zamora in Los Angeles

03 Jun 79 Guadalupe Pintor w.pts.15 Carlos Zarate at Las Vegas

29 Aug 80 Juilan Solis w.pts.15 Jorge Lujan at Miami

14 Nov 80 Jeff Chandler w.rsf.14 Julian Solis at Miami Beach *(WBA title)*

01 Sep 83 Alberto Davila w.ko.12 Francisco 'Kilo' Bejines at Los Angeles *(For WBC title vacated by Pintor)*

07 Apr 84 Richie Sandoval w.rsf.15 Jeff Chandler at Atlantic City

16 Apr 84 Satoshi Shingaki w.ko.8 Elmer Magallano at Kawashiwara *(Vacant IBF title)*

26 Apr 85 Jeff Fenech w.rsf.9 Satoshi Shingaki in Sydney

04 May 85 Daniel Zaragoza w. disq. 7 Freddie Jackson at Aruba, Dutch West Indies *(For WBC title vacated by Davila)*

09 Aug 85 Miguel Lora w.pts.12 Daniel Zaragoza in Miami

10 Mar 86 Gaby Canizales w.rsf.7 Richard Sandoval at Las Vegas *(WBA title)*

04 Jun 86 Bernardo Pinango w.pts.15 Gaby Canizales at East Rutherford, New Jersey

Jan 87 *Jeff Fenech relinquished IBF title due to weight problems*

Feb 87 *Bernardo Pinango retired from boxing*

29 Mar 87 Takuya Muguruma w.ko.5 Azael Moran at Moriguchi, Japan *(Vacant WBA title)*

15 May 87 Kelvin Seabrooks w.ko.5 Miguel Marturana at Cartagena *(Vacant IBF title)*

SUPER FLYWEIGHTS

THIRTY years ago, when there was no 'world governing body' in boxing, there were eight weight divisions and eight champions. At the start of 1987 there were three governing bodies, 16 weight classes (including the super-middles, recognized only by the IBF) and 43 champions . . . and even as this book was being written the WBC announced the creation of a mini-flyweight category with a limit of 105 lb. The WBC has been responsible for the proliferation in weight classes: their other creations include the cruisers, light-middleweights, super-bantamweights, super-flyweights, and light-flyweights.

Korea's Chul-Ho Kim floors Raul Valdez in their drawn battle in 1982, Kim's last successful defence of the WBC title.

The WBC inaugurated the super-flyweights (sometimes known as the junior bantams) in 1980, since when all three versions of the title have been the preserve of Latins and Orientals. The first champion in the division – whose limit is 115 lb – was Rafael Orono of Venezuela, who had been a professional for less than a year when he survived a twice-broken right hand to edge a split decision over Seung-Hoon Lee of Korea in Caracas on 1 February 1980 to take the vacant WBC title. Orono lost it in his fourth defence to another Korean, Chul-Ho Kim, in January 1981, and the busy Kim managed five defences before Orono regained it from him with a sixth-round stoppage in Seoul, in November 1982. The tall Venezuelan (5 ft 8 in) was dethroned in his fourth defence in 1983 by Payao Poontarat, a Thai with a classically English style.

Poontarat had been a star amateur, winning four national titles as well as a bantamweight gold medal in the 1980 World Military Games, silvers in the 1975 Asian Games and the 1980 World Cup, and a bronze at light-flyweight in the 1976 Olympics. A Liverpudlian, Charles Atkinson, was engaged to polish his style when Poontarat launched his professional career in October 1981, and it took the Thai only nine fights to become world champion by outscoring Orono in November 1983. He retained the title against the former WBA flyweight champion Guty Espadas, who was having his last fight, and then on 5 July 1984 met the WBA champion, Jiro Watanabe of Japan.

Their fight should, by any logical argument, have been for the undisputed title, but instead the WBA immediately stripped Watanabe – who won the 12-rounder on points – for failing to meet their top contender Khaosai Galaxi.

Watanabe had been the third holder of the WBA

Payao Poontarat (above, *and* below *with his English trainer Charles Atkinson) kept a firm grip on the WBC title until he met his WBA rival Jiro Watanabe* (right) *in 1984.*

Below: *Japan's Kazuo Katsuma was stopped in the seventh round of this 1985 bid for Watanabe's WBC title in Osaka, Japan.*

Above: *Watanabe hammered former WBA champ Gustavo Ballas to ninth-round defeat when the Argentinian tried to regain the title in 1982.*

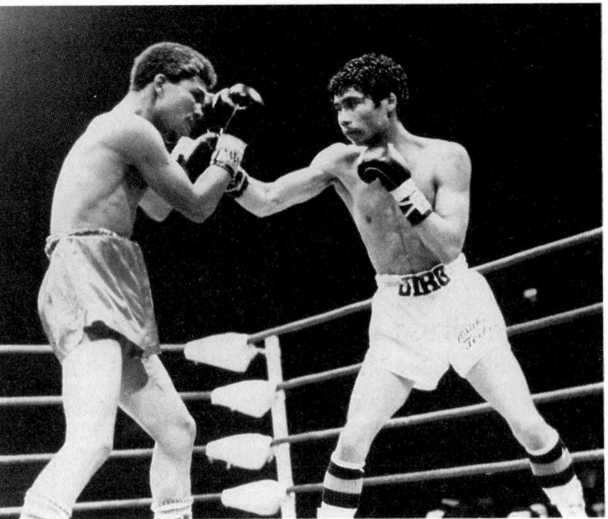

Above: *Rafael Pedroza (on the left) was clearly outpointed by Watanabe in 1982.*

title, which was won initially by Gustavo Ballas of Argentina in September 1981. Ballas was unbeaten in 54 fights, and might have been expected to enjoy a lengthy reign. In fact it lasted only three months, for he was beaten on 5 December by Rafael Pedroza of Panama, a cousin of the great featherweight champion Eusebio Pedroza. The Panamanian had been beaten for both versions of the light-flyweight title, by Luis Espada in 1977 and Yoko Gushiken in 1979, and with five defeats in his previous eight fights he was lucky to get the chance to challenge Ballas.

Pedroza, too, lost on his first defence when Watanabe outpointed him in Osaka, Japan, on 8 April 1982. The new champion came from a prosperous family – his father owned a restaurant, and Jiro (a graduate) enjoyed a comfortable life-style. He was a skilled performer at kempo (a martial art which is similar to karate) and had more than 200 contests, reaching fourth place in the world championships. He turned to boxing at the age of 22, with instant success. His hard punching, from a southpaw stance, quickly propelled him into the world rankings and brought him a title fight against WBC champion Chul-Ho Kim in April 1981. The Korean was a shade too good for him, taking a close points win, but Watanabe learned from the experience and, when his second chance came against Pedroza, he won an overwhelming points victory.

His six defences of the WBA title were all against good opposition, including two former world champions, Gustavo Ballas and Shoji Oguma. He was equally effective as WBC champion, making four defences, the first of them an 11th-round stoppage of Poontarat which sent the ex-champion into retirement. Watanabe's long reign was ended in March 1986 by the Mexican, Gilberto Roman, who retained the title five times in less than 12 months.

The WBA title, stripped from Watanabe after his win over Poontarat, was taken over by Khaosai Galaxy of Thailand, who knocked out Eusebio Espinal of the Dominican Republic (who had won all his previous 21 fights) in the sixth round in Bangkok on 21 November 1984.

Galaxy, whose real name is Sura Saenkham, won 44 out of 50 Muay Thai (kick boxing) contests before, almost by chance, turning to Western-style competition. He was attending a Muay Thai tournament in Bangkok on 17 December 1980 where, as usual, there was one international-style contest scheduled. When one of the boxers failed to show up, Galaxy was persuaded by the promoter to take his place. He knocked out his opponent in the fifth and, in less than two years, Galaxy crashed the world ratings with a stunning two-round knockout of the experienced American, Willie 'Birdlegs' Jensen (who had drawn with Rafael Orono in a 1980 WBC title bid and lasted into the 13th round against Chul-Ho Kim a year later).

The hard-punching southpaw had made five defences up to March 1987, and only two of his 30 fights had lasted the scheduled distance.

The IBF version was first contested in December 1983, when it was won by a Korean, Joo-Do Chun, who made five defences, all won by knockouts over Oriental opposition. However, Chun was himself knocked out in eight rounds in Djakarta, Indonesia, on 3 May 1985, by Elly Pical, who retained it three times.

Above: *Chul-Ho Kim turned back Jiro Watanabe's first attempt on a world title, outscoring him in 1981.*

Left: *Mexican Gilberto Roman jabs off Antoine Montero, who was stopped his WBC title challenge.*

HOW THE SUPER-FLYWEIGHT TITLE HAS CHANGED HANDS

02 Feb 80	Rafael Orono w.pts.15 Seunghun Lee in Caracas *(Vacant WBC title)*
05 Dec 81	Rafael Pedroza w.pts.15 Gustavo Ballas in Panama City
08 Apr 82	Jiro Watanabe w.pts.15 Rafael Pedroza at Osaka, Japan
24 Jan 81	Chulho Kim w.ko.9 Rafael Orono at San Cristobal
12 Sep 81	Gustavo Ballas w.rsf.8 Sukchul Bae at Buenos Aires *(Vacant WBA title)*
28 Nov 82	Rafael Orono w.rsf.6 Chulho Kim in Seoul *(WBC title)*
27 Nov 83	Payo Poontarat w.pts.12 Rafael Orono at Pattaya
09 Dec 83	Joo-Do Chun w.ko.5 Ken Kasugai at Osaka *(Vacant IBF title)*
05 Jul 84	Jiro Watanabe w.pts.12 Payo Poontarat at Osaka *(For WBC title. Watanabe was immediately stripped by the WBA for failing to defend against their leading contender, Khaosia 'Galaxy' Vangchamphoo)*
21 Nov 84	Khaosia 'Galaxy' Vangchamphoo w.ko.6 Eusebio Espinal at Bangkok *(For vacant WBA title)*
03 May 85	Ellyas Pical w.ko.8 Joo-Do Chun at Djakarta
15 Feb 86	Cesar Polanco w.pts.15 Ellyas Pical at Djakarta
30 Mar 86	Gilberto Roman w.pts.12 Jiro Watanabe at Osaka *(WBC title)*
06 Jul 86	Ellyas Pical w.ko.3 Cesar Polanco at Djakarta
28 Feb 87	Khaosai Galaxy w.ko.14 Ellyas Pical at Djakarta *(For the WBA title only—the IBF declared their title vacant)*
16 May 87	Santos Laciar w.rsf.11 Gilberto Roman at Reims

FLYWEIGHTS

THE FLYWEIGHT division was the last of boxing's eight traditional categories to become established. In the early part of this century, while the limit for the bantamweight class fluctuated anywhere between 105 and 118 lb, anyone scaling around the modern flyweight limit of 8 st (112 lb) was considered a bantamweight, regardless of the amount of weight which he might have to concede. The flyweights evolved as a separate category in 1909, at the initiative of the National Sporting Club, the body which ruled the sport in Britain with arrogant and self-invested authority until the formation of the British Boxing Board of Control. The limit was set at 112 lb, and the first British champion at the weight – Sid Smith of Bermondsey, South London – was crowned in 1911.

Two years later, on 11 April 1913, Smith crossed the Channel to outpoint Eugene Criqui (later to become featherweight champion) in Paris, in the first international title fight in the new division. His reign was amongst the shortest on record: on 2 June he was battered to an 11th-round defeat by another South Londoner, Bill Ladbury of Greenwich, at the Blackfriars Ring. It was painfully one-sided, with Smith being floored no fewer than 16 times. The title (still not recognized in America) was won in January 1914 by Percy Jones of Porth, Wales.

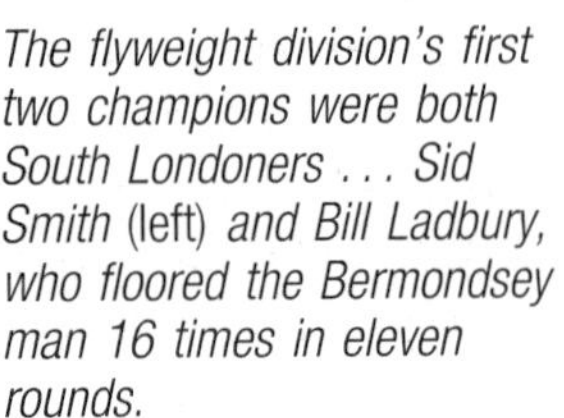

The flyweight division's first two champions were both South Londoners . . . Sid Smith (left) and Bill Ladbury, who floored the Bermondsey man 16 times in eleven rounds.

Percy Jones (left, *posing with Jim Driscoll on the right) staked a brief claim to the title, but a more lasting impression was made by his fellow-Welshman Jimmy Wilde* (right, *under pressure from American bantamweight Joe Conn). Since Wilde was a serving soldier, he could not be paid in cash for the Conn fight, so he took his purse in diamonds instead.*

Jones was knocked out in May 1914 by Joe Symonds of Plymouth, who claimed the championship even though Jones had weighed in over the limit. Symonds strengthened his claim by beating Tancy Lee in 1915, and when he was forced to retire in 12 rounds at the NSC in February 1916 by Jimmy Wilde of Tylerstown, the Welshman was generally accepted as the new world champion. Wilde was a ring phenomenon, a physical freak who never scaled more than the modern light-flyweight limit of 7 st 10 lb (108 lb) and whose appearance was so uninspiring that when after a succession of wins in Wales he was invited to appear at the Blackfriars Ring in London, the promoter was reluctant to let him fight lest he be killed.

Wilde possessed entirely disproportionate hitting power, which earned him the nickname of 'The Ghost with the Hammer in his Hand'. Although accurate records were never kept in those days, Wilde can safely be credited with more than 150 fights, of which around two-thirds ended inside the distance. He had mastered his trade in the boxing booths, taking on all-comers, and was once rumoured to have knocked out 19 men (of assorted weights) in three and a half hours, taken a 30-minute rest, and then finished off another four in 45 minutes. When Wilde stopped the New Yorker Johnny Rosner in 11 rounds at Liverpool, two months after beating Symonds, his claim to the world title was further enhanced, and his 1916 victories over Tancy Lee and Jimmy Hughes were both billed as defences.

He belatedly received American endorsement by knocking out a New York-based Italian, whose real name was Giuseppe di Melfi but who used the considerably more exotic ring name of Young Zulu Kid. They fought in a converted warehouse at Holborn, London, on 18 December 1916, Wilde winning in 11 rounds. Since the First World War was then at its height, Wilde was only able to make one defence, defeating George Clark of Bermondsey at the NSC, on a fourth-round retirement in March 1917. Wins over top Americans Joe Lynch and Memphis Pal Moore prepared the way for Wilde's American tour in 1920, during which he was unbeaten in 11 fights. However, he took an illadvised match in January 1921 at the Albert Hall, London, against Pete Herman – who only three weeks previously had lost the world bantamweight title – and was severely hammered in 17 rounds. He drifted away from boxing thereafter and was generally assumed to have retired, but in 1923 he

Scottish veteran Tancy Lee had stopped Wilde in 17 rounds when they first met, but Wilde won the rematch in 11.

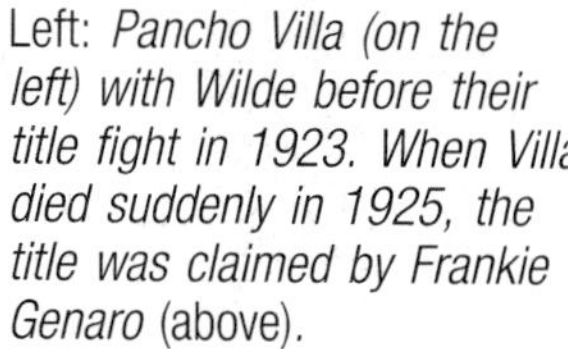

Left: *Pancho Villa (on the left) with Wilde before their title fight in 1923. When Villa died suddenly in 1925, the title was claimed by Frankie Genaro* (above).

Above: *Fidel LaBarba, like Genaro an Olympic gold medalist, is the only fighter in history to have given up a world title in order to enter university.*

was tempted back by a huge offer of $65,000 to meet a Filipino, Pancho Villa (real name Francisco Guilledo) at the Polo Grounds, New York, on 18 June. Wilde, aged 31, never had a chance and was knocked out in seven rounds.

The Filipino defended the title twice in 1924, but the following year gave away a lot of weight to the future world welterweight champion Jimmy McLarnin, and was outpointed over ten rounds at Oakland, California, on 4 July. He had gone ahead with the McLarnin fight even though he had had a wisdom tooth extracted the previous afternoon, and the punishment he took so aggravated his condition that he had to go into hospital for an operation on an abscess which developed on his jaw. Blood poisoning set in, and he died on the operating table ten days after his last fight.

Frankie Genaro of New York claimed the vacant title on the strength of his 1923 victory over Villa for the American title, but in August 1925 he was outpointed by Fidel LaBarba of New York, who had won the Olympic flyweight gold medal in 1924. LaBarba outpointed Scotland's Elky Clark in a Madison Square Garden 12-rounder in January 1927 to clinch universal recognition, but then in August of that year he retired in order to enrol at Stanford University. He resumed his boxing career a year later and fought on until 1933, challenging unsuccessfully for both the featherweight and lightweight titles.

The title split on his retirement, and remained divided for a decade. The NBA recognized the Canadian Albert 'Frenchie' Belanger after his points win over Genaro on 28 November 1927, but Genaro beat him twice for the title in 1928, only to lose it in record time – 58 seconds of the first round – in March 1929 to Emile Pladner of France, whose victory also earned him endorsement by the European-based International Boxing Union. Genaro reclaimed the title six weeks later, beating the

Emile Pladner of France kayoes Genaro in just 58 seconds of the opening round in Paris in 1929,

Frenchman on a low-blow disqualification in the fifth round in Paris. He became a busy champion, retaining the crown once in 1929 against Ernie Jarvis of Millwall, London, and three times in 1930. The third of these was a 15-rounds draw with Midget Wolgast in New York on 26 December, in what was intended to settle the championship dispute (New York recognized Wolgast as champion.)

Since there was no attempt to rematch the pair, Genaro took the title to Europe for a March 1931 defence in Barcelona, against Victor Ferrand, a fight which had a curious ending. Ferrand was four

Above: *Pladner (on the left) being outpointed by Arly Hollingsworth in Paris, when he moved up to bantamweight.*

Emile Pladner (left) *was champion for only six weeks, but the stiffly posed Midget Wolgast* (right) *held his share of the title for rather longer – from 1930 to 1935.*

points ahead at the end of their 15-round fight, but under IBU rules there had to be a winning margin of at least five points for a title to change hands, so the verdict was recorded as a draw. The American retained the title twice more in 1931, but lost it in Paris in October that year, to Victor 'Young' Perez of Tunis. The Tunisian, who was an Auschwitz concentration-camp victim in February 1943, was champion for one year and five days, being stopped in 13 rounds by Jackie Brown of Manchester in that city on 31 October 1932.

Brown made four successful defences, three of them against the same opponent, Valentin Angelmann of France, who lost the first two but drew the third. But in September 1935 the NBA/IBU championship passed to Scotland's first world-title winner, and arguably one of the most gifted performers in British boxing history – Benny Lynch. The Glaswegian floored Brown 11 times in a brutal two-rounds beating at Belle Vue, Manchester. Lynch knocked out Battersea's Pat Palmer in eight rounds in September 1936 and, on 19 January 1937, outpointed the New York title-holder, Small Montana, in a dazzling 15-rounder at Wembley to earn undisputed recognition.

The history of the New York version is rather more complicated. It was won initially by Corporal Izzy Schwartz, who outpointed the Russian-born Newsboy Brown at Madison Square Garden, on 16 December 1927, three weeks after Frenchie Belanger had been crowned as NBA champion. Schwartz retained it twice, including a points win over Belanger, but in August 1929 he was outpointed by a local fighter, Willie LaMorte, at Newark, New Jersey. The New York Commission refused to recognize LaMorte as champion, and instead set up a tournament in which the finalists were the quaintly named duo, Midget Wolgast and Black Bill. Wolgast outpointed Bill, and then cleared up the confusion by beating LaMorte in Madison Square Garden on 16 May 1930. LaMorte collapsed with a heart spasm at the end of the fifth round and

The ill-fated Young Perez, who held a share of the title in 1931–32, died in Auschwitz in 1943.

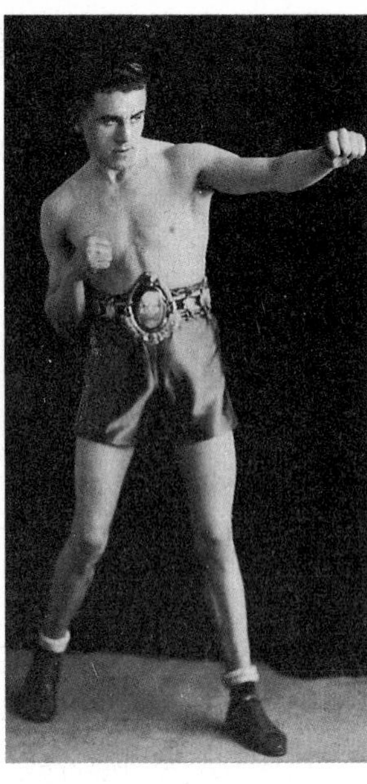

Manchester's Jackie Brown, who took the title from Perez in 1932, wearing his Lonsdale Belt.

Brown (above, *on the right) outpointed Valentin Angelmann in this Manchester 15-rounder in 1933, but when he met Benny Lynch in the same ring* (right) *two years later, it was a different story.*

Lynch gave Brown a fearful beating when they met at Belle Vue, Manchester, flooring him eleven times in two rounds (left). *It should have been the start of a glorious reign, but the brilliant little Scot* (below) *was already self-destructing on alcohol.*

boxed only three more times.

Wolgast lost the title to Small Montana of the Philippines in 1935, and Lynch's win over Montana in January 1937 at last restored order to the division. There had been other claimants during this period: Newsboy Brown was recognized in California after beating Johnny McCoy in 1928, and his 15-rounds points defeat by Edinburgh's Johnny Hill at Clapton, London, on 29 August 1928, was billed as a title fight. But Hill was knocked out in six rounds by Emile Pladner on 7 February 1929, less than a month before the Frenchman took the NBA and IBU titles from Frankie Genaro. Valentin Angelmann, the perennial challenger from France, was recognized briefly by the IBU in 1936, but they quietly allowed his claim to lapse after Angelmann had retained the title once. His record as champion, which included seven defeats in non-title fights, was too much of an embarrassment for them. Lynch, in any case, was demonstrably the world's best flyweight and had beaten Angelmann in a 1934 12-rounder.

Small Montana and Lynch embrace at the end of their Wembley 15-rounder in 1937, which is still recalled as one of the finest flyweight matches ever staged in Britain.

Lynch was a hugely popular figure in Scotland. His defence against Pat Palmer drew 32,000 to Shawfield Park in Glasgow, and what was, sadly, to be his only defence of the undisputed title – against Peter Kane of Golborne, in October 1937 – set a new Scottish attendance record of 40,000. They witnessed perhaps the finest fight ever held between flyweights. The Englishman, not yet 20 years old, had been boxing professionally since he was 16 and was unbeaten in 41 fights, all but eight of them won inside the distance. He clinched the title fight with wins over Valentin Angelmann, Ernst Weiss (Angelmann's only IBU challenger) and Jimmy Warnock, the tough Belfastman who had twice outpointed Lynch. Kane beat him in four rounds to set up the 13 October meeting with Lynch.

The fight opened sensationally, Lynch flooring his challenger with virtually his first punches. Kane fought back furiously, and for nine rounds of fierce punch exchanges there was little between them. But Kane began to tire as the fight moved into its later stages, and by the 12th he was spent. Lynch floored him once in that round and twice in the 13th to retain the title. It had been a magnificent victory, but it was also the last moment of glory the superb Scot would know.

Below: *Kane's 41 fights before facing Lynch – all wins – included this points victory in Paris over Pierre Louis (left).*

Above: *Lynch was so popular in Scotland that his defence against Peter Kane (on the right) drew 40,000 fans.*

Valentin Angelmann (on the left) dropped two decisions to Kane, in 1936 and 1937.

Lynch led a wildly undisciplined life, and was an alcoholic from an early age. He fought hard to break the habit, even at one stage going to live in a monastery in Ireland, but lacked the will-power to abstain for long. Making the flyweight limit became increasingly difficult. He was scheduled to meet Kane in a rematch five months later, but he could not make the weight and the fight went ahead as a non-title 12-rounder, ending in a draw. He finally lost the title on the scales after weighing a disgraceful 6½ lb over the limit for a defence against the American Jackie Jurich at Paisley on 29 June 1938. The championship was declared vacant, although Lynch went through with the fight and knocked Jurich out in 12 rounds. There were only two more fights to come, both inglorious defeats, and his career ended when he was only 25. Eight years later, a chronic and hopeless alcoholic, he was found dying in a Glasgow gutter.

Kane and Jurich were matched for the vacant title, Kane winning on points at Anfield football ground, Liverpool, on 22 September 1938, but almost five years elapsed before there was another title fight at the weight. The NBA proclaimed the Filipino, Little Dado, as champion on 11 December 1939 but nobody – including Dado – took the distinction very seriously and, like Angelmann's had been, his title claim was quietly allowed to lapse.

Above: *Jackie Jurich fought Lynch, and in defeat earned a match with Peter Kane for the vacant title.*

Below: *The sad and bloated Benny Lynch (third from right) back in the boxing booths, taking on all-comers.*

Above: *Six months after drawing with Lynch in their rematch, Kane was world champion: he outpointed Jurich for the title thrown away by the Scot.*

Kane was dethroned in the first round by another Scotsman, Jackie Paterson of Ayrshire, who needed only 61 seconds to kayo him at Hampden Park, Glasgow, on 19 June 1943. The Second World War, then in its fourth year, prevented Paterson from defending the title until 10 July 1946, when he drew a new Scottish record of 50,000 to Hampden Park football ground to watch him outpoint Joe Curran of Liverpool.

But Paterson, like Lynch, was plagued by weight problems. When he failed to make the weight for a defence against Dado Marino of the Philippines, in July 1947, the British Board declared the title vacant. Rinty Monaghan, an engaging Belfastman who used to serenade the crowd over the ring mike

A bewildered Kane is counted out in 61 seconds of the first round (left) *against Jackie Paterson (seen* below, *on the right, in a bantamweight win over Al Chavez in Manchester in 1947).*

Below: *Rinty Monaghan made it a practice to serenade the crowd after every fight, win or lose. He did not lose a title fight, retiring undefeated after a draw in his last defence.*

with 'When Irish Eyes Are Smiling' – outpointed Marino at Harringay Arena, London, on 20 October 1947. It was billed as a world-title fight, but was recognized as such only by the NBA and the Irish Board of Control, for Paterson had won a court injunction restraining the British Board from recognizing anyone else as world champion, and from recognizing any fight which did not involve him as being for the title.

Monaghan ended the muddle in March 1948 by knocking Paterson out in seven rounds at the King's Hall, Belfast, for the undisputed title. It was his second win over the Scotsman, whom he had also beaten in six rounds in a non-title fight in 1946. He retained it twice, before retiring undefeated in March 1950. He was succeeded, briefly, by Terry Allen of Islington, with whom he had drawn in his last fight, a title defence in the King's Hall on 30 September 1949. Allen (real name Edward Govier) outpointed Honore Pratesi of Marseilles at Harringay on 25 April 1950, but held it for less than four months before being outpointed in Honolulu by Dado Marino.

Monaghan kayoed Paterson in seven rounds (above) *to take the undisputed title, but was then outpointed in a non-title eight-rounder by Londoner Terry Allen* (below). Right: *Allen beats Eric Marsden (left) for the British title in 1952.*

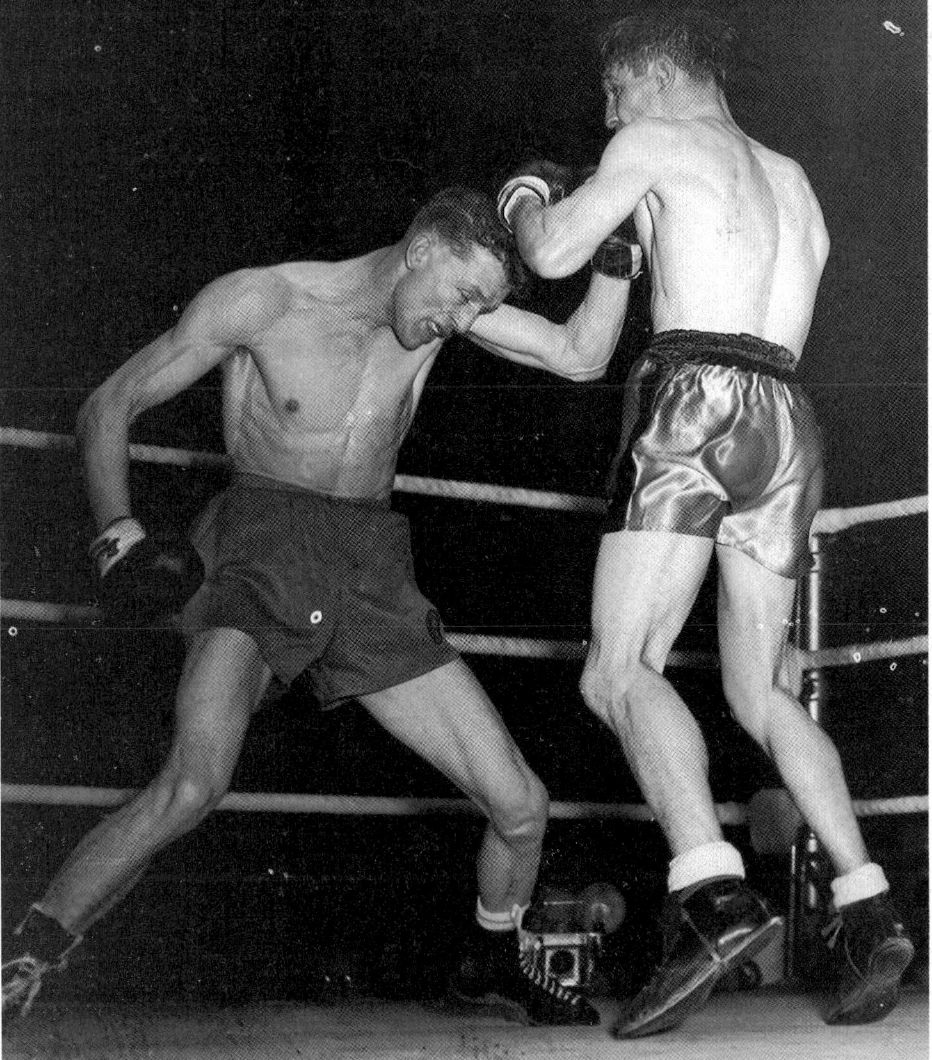

Above: *Allen, by now an ex-champ, lost this 10-rounder in London to French star Maurice Sandeyron in 1952.* Right: *Scotland's Vic Herman, who had been beaten by Allen for the vacant British title in June 1951, travelled to Tokyo in July 1953 to take on Yoshio Shirai. Herman lost the non-title 10-rounder, being stopped in the final round.*

The new champion had the double distinction of being, at 33, the oldest man to win the title and the first grandfather ever to hold a world championship at any weight. Marino retained it in a rematch with Allen in November 1951, but six months later lost it to the first of many world champions from Japan, Yoshio Shirai of Tokyo, against whom he had won and lost in non-title fights.

Shirai managed four defences, including a unanimous win over Allen in 1953, but on 26 November 1954 he lost the title to one of the division's great names, Pascual Perez of Argentina.

Left: *Yoshio Shirai, Japan's first world champion, drops Dado Marino en route to a points victory. Marino was the first grandfather to be a world champion.*

Below: *The tough little Argentinian Pascual Perez takes it on the chin from Shirai in their 1954 meeting, when the title changed hands.*

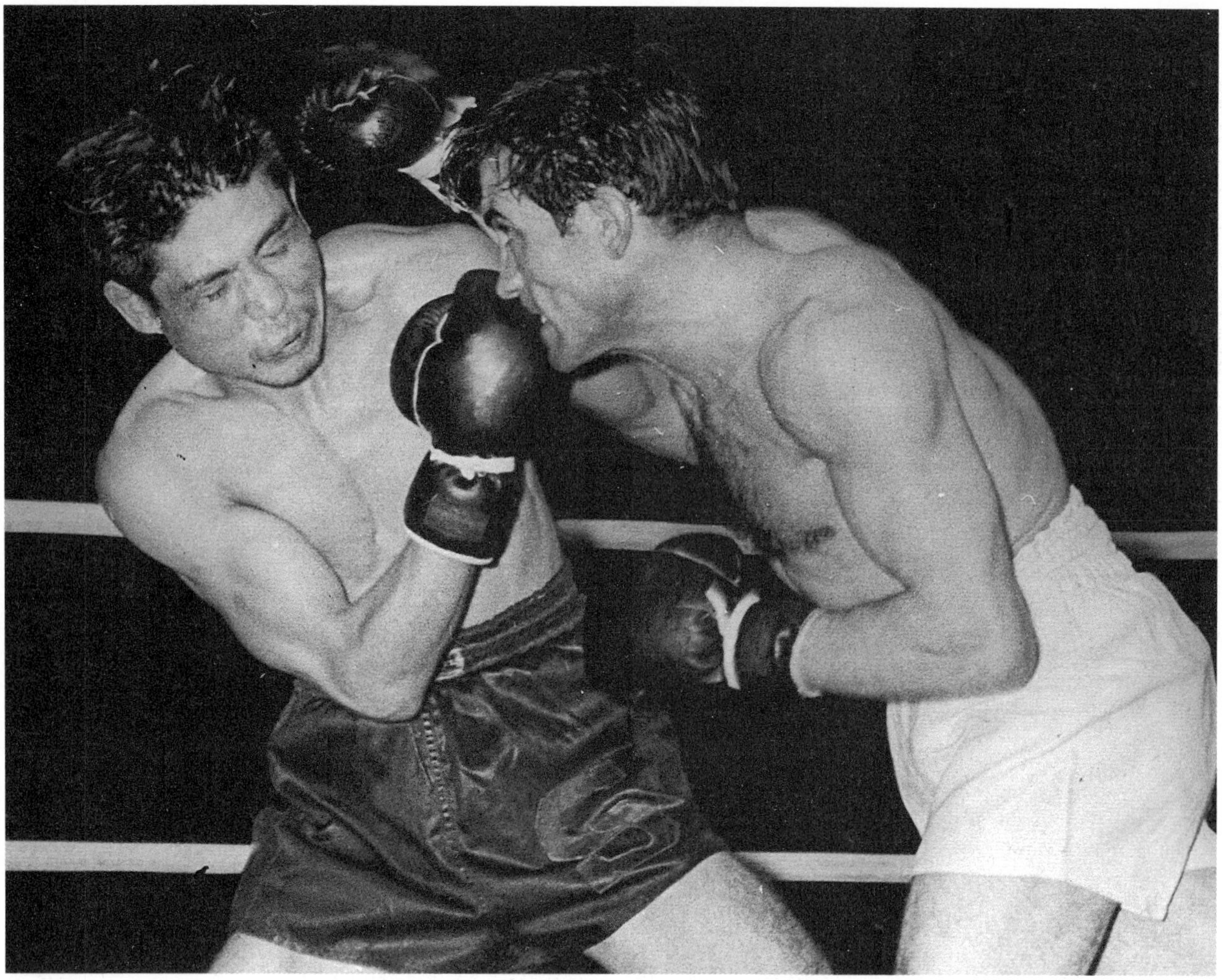

Above: *Shirai gave Perez a tough battle first time around, but lost in five rounds in the rematch.*

Below: *Perez outpoints a bloodied Leo Espinosa of the Philippines to retain the title in 1956.*

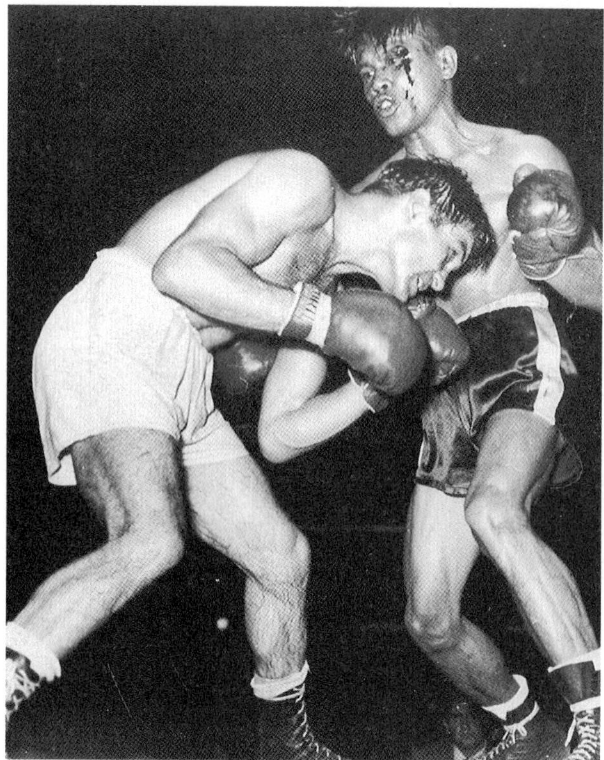

The tiny Perez, only 4 ft 10½ in, had won the 1948 Olympic flyweight title and was unbeaten in 24 fights, all but two of them won inside the distance. The Argentinian dominated the division for six years and nine successful defences against challengers from the Philippines, Cuba, Wales (Dai Dower, who was knocked out in two minutes in 1957), Spain, Venezuela, and Japan. But on 16 April 1960, a month after his 34th birthday, he was

Below: *The prostrate Dai Dower, knocked out inside a round, looks to be in danger from Perez's enthusiastic fan.*

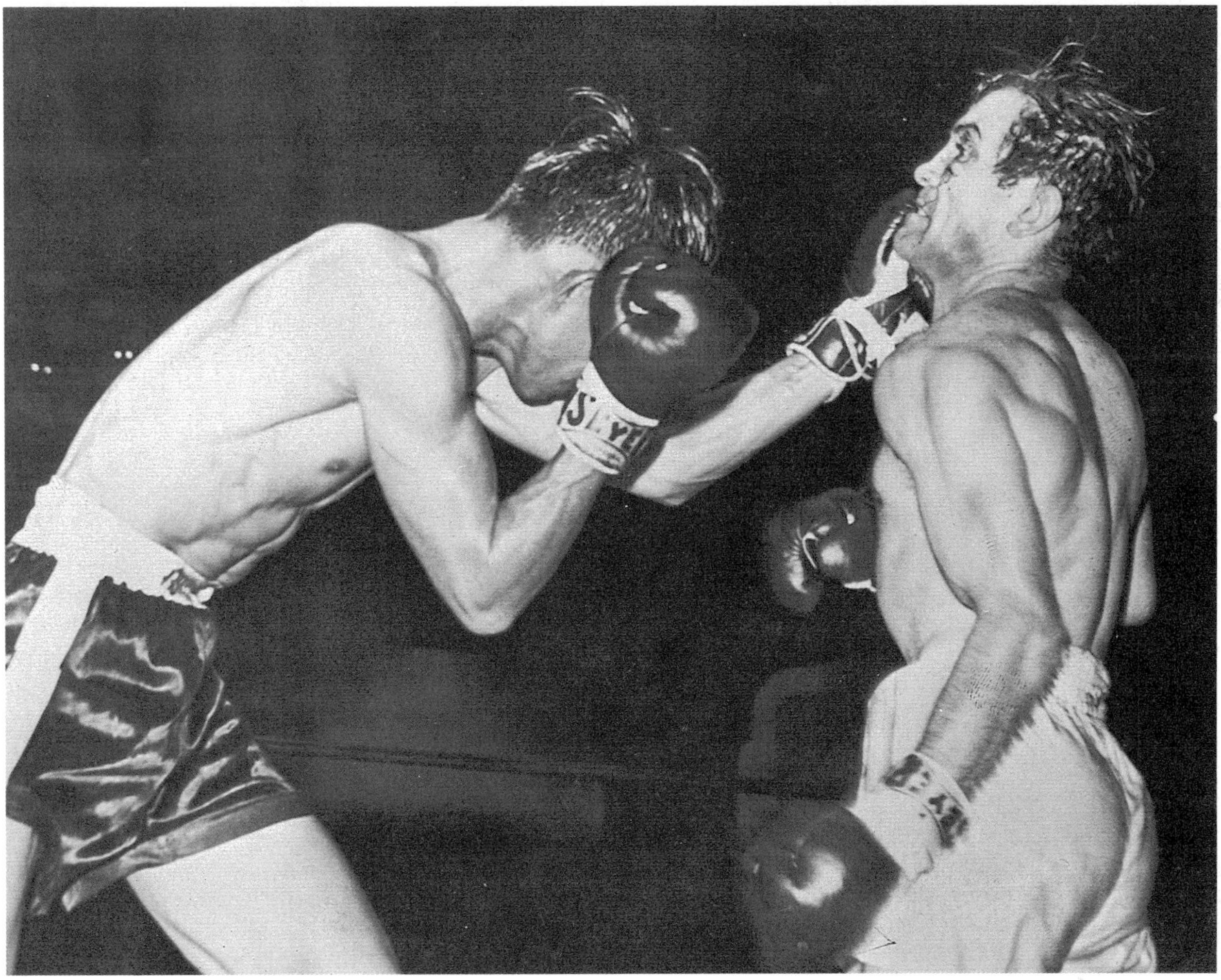

Above: *When Perez was dethroned by Pone Kingpetch in April 1960, it was only his second defeat in 56 fights.*

finally dislodged by Pone Kingpetch, of Thailand, in Bangkok. It was only his second defeat in 56 fights.

Perez failed to regain the title in a rematch in Los Angeles five months later (the first flyweight title fight to be held in America for 25 years) but he fought on for another four years, retiring on 11 April 1964. Kingpetch was knocked out in 11 rounds in his fourth defence on 10 October 1962 by Fighting Harada of Japan, who also went on to win the world bantamweight title. The Thai won it back from him in January 1963, but in September he

Kingpetch's first title came when he outpointed Danny Kidd (left) *for the Orient championship in 1957. His first world title reign was abruptly ended by another Oriental, Japan's fearsome Masahiko 'Fighting' Harada* (right).

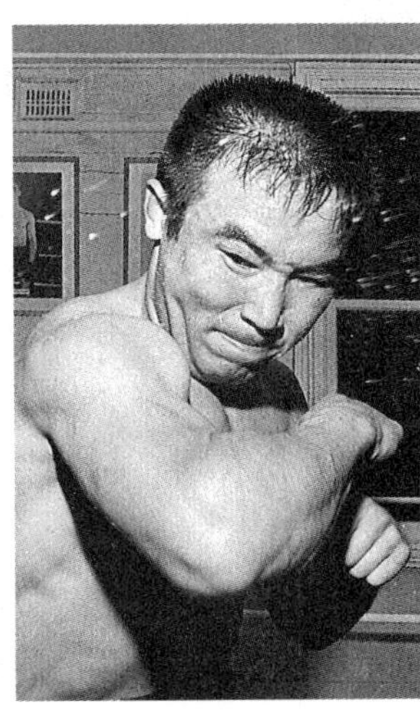

was knocked out in the opening round by another Japanese, Hiroyuki Ebihara.

The persistent Kingpetch regained the title yet again, winning a split decision over Ebihara in Bangkok in January 1964, but lost it for the final time in his next defence to Salvatore Burruni, a squat and aggressive Sardinian who outpointed him in Rome on 23 April 1965. It was the last time that the undisputed flyweight title was contested: in November 1965 the WBA stripped Burruni for his failure to defend against Ebihara, so initiating the split that has lasted up to the time of writing.

The Sardinian, who won the title 12 days after his 32nd birthday, had an outstanding record of only three losses in 81 fights when he beat Kingpetch. He had been European champion since 1961. Burruni managed only one successful defence of the WBC title, knocking out the Italian-born Australian Rocky Gattellari in Sydney, on 2 December 1965, but on 4 June 1966 he was clearly outpointed at Wembley by the brilliant young Scot, Walter McGowan.

McGowan's win gave him revenge for a points loss to Burruni in a European title bid in April 1964. The 23-year-old from Hamilton was a superb technical boxer, with blindingly fast hands and the footwork of a dancer, but he was also prone to cuts, and had to survive a bad one in his title win over Burruni. His brittle skin let him down in his

Hiroyuki Ebihara (above) *won and lost the title to Kingpetch before the Thai's five-year involvement with the world championship was finally ended by Salvatore Burruni* (right) *who was himself dethroned 14 months later by Scotland's Walter McGowan* (below).

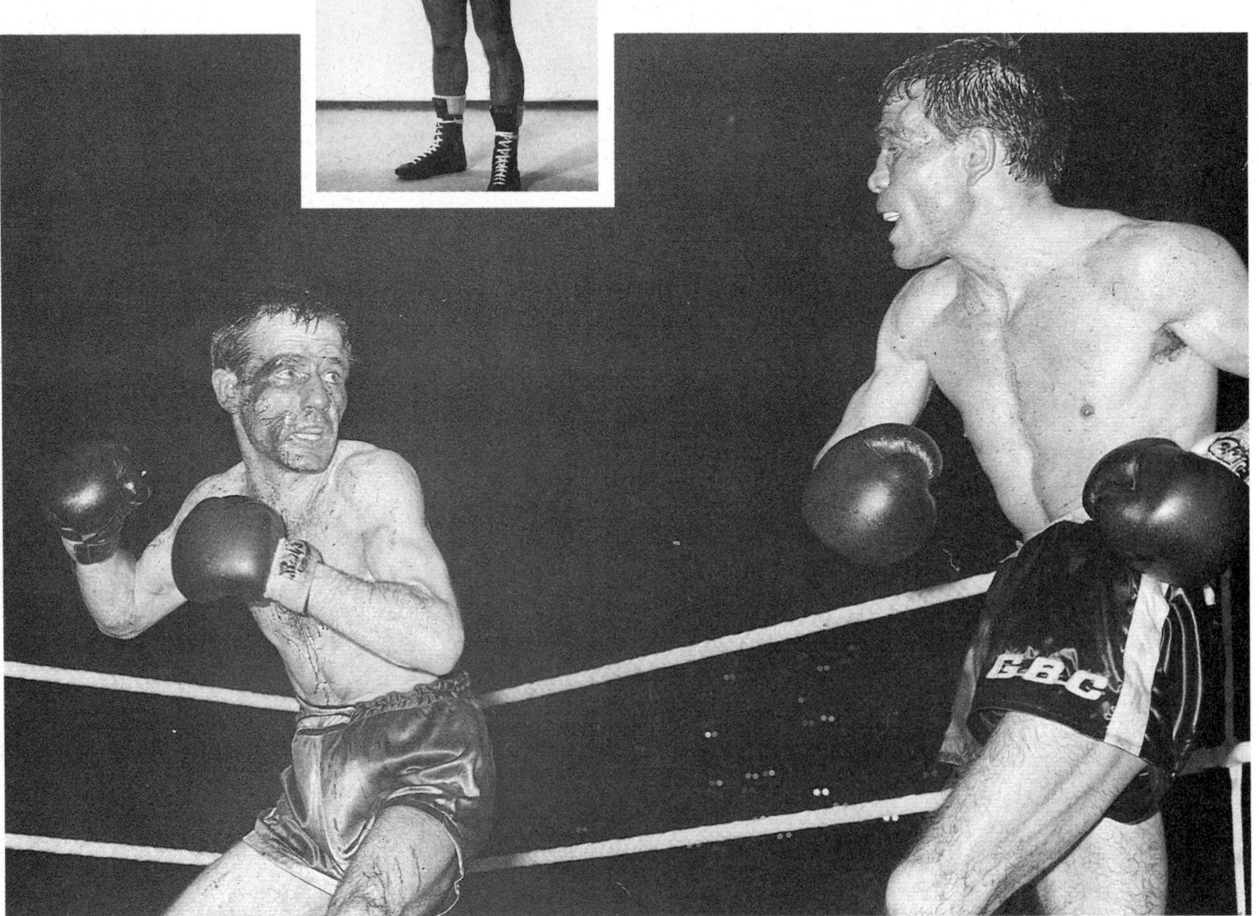

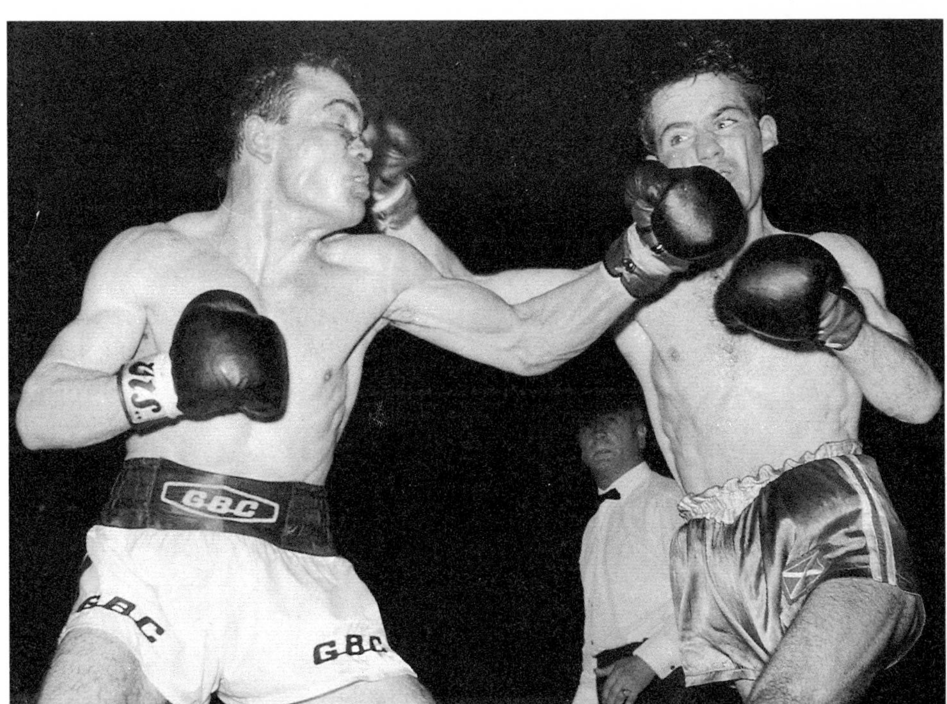

Left: *Burruni was too experienced for McGowan when they first met in Rome in 1964, with the Sardinian's European title at stake, but the Scot was a clear winner when they fought again.*

Below: *McGowan was a superb stylist with a darting left jab, which he is demonstrating on Ernesto Miranda in his final warm-up for the Burruni rematch.*

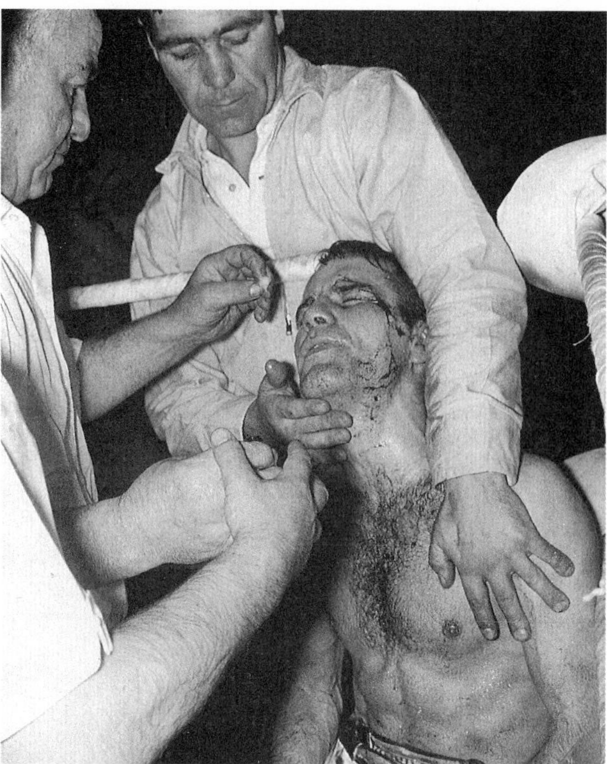

McGowan was an unlucky loser in his first defence, against Chartchai Chionoi in Bangkok (above) *and when the Thai gave him a return at Wembley nine months later the ending was just as painful* (right).

first defence, when Chartchai Chionoi of Thailand stopped him in nine rounds in Bangkok, after the Scotsman had sustained a cut nose. Chionoi gave him a rematch at Wembley in September 1967, and although McGowan's magnificent boxing had won him every round, a cut over the left eye forced the referee to stop it in the seventh. Chionoi was equally fortunate in his next defence four months later in Mexico City, when Efren Torres, who was ahead by 7-4-1 in rounds, was stopped in the 13th, also with a cut left eye. Torres, with a degree of poetic justice, won the title from the Thai in Mexico City on 23 February 1969, with the fight being stopped in the eighth round because of a cut over Chionoi's left eye.

Torres lost it back to Chionoi on his second defence, in March 1970. Erbito Salavarria of the Philippines stopped Chionoi in two rounds in Bangkok in December 1970, and made two defences, in the second of which he drew with the

Below: *Erbito Salavarria takes Chionoi's title with a surprise second-round stoppage in 1970.*

Right: *Shoji Oguma outpoints Betulio Gonzalez on a split decision for the WBC title in 1974.*

Miguel Canto (left), *on the left, outpointing Kimio Furesawa in a WBC defence in 1977) was the division's dominant figure in the second half of the 1970s. He was eventually beaten by the Korean Chan-Hee Park, who in turn lost the title to the Japanese veteran Shoji Oguma* (below, *on the right) in Seoul.*

Venezuelan, Betulio Gonzales, at Maracaibo in November 1971. However, when Salavarria was found to have used an illegal stimulant the WBC declared Gonzales champion.

Gonzalez was beaten on his second defence by Venice Borkorsor of Thailand in September 1972, but after Borkorsor had outpointed Salavarria in his sole defence, he relinquished the title to compete as a bantamweight in July 1973. The title was reclaimed by Gonzalez after his points win over Miguel Canto of Merida, Mexico, in August 1973, but his second reign was ended on a split decision in Tokyo in his third defence by Shoji Oguma, in October 1974.

The Japanese held it only until January 1975, when he lost a split decision to Canto, who went on to establish himself as one of the best champions of his generation, pound for pound.

The Mexican made an astonishing 14 successful defences, easily breaking Pascual Perez' record. His title victims included Betulio Gonzalez (twice), Oguma (three times), the former WBA champion Susumu Hanagata and Antonio Avelar, who won the title two years later, in 1981. Canto was champion until March 1979, when Chan-Hee Park of Korea outpointed him in Pusan. He made one attempt to regain the title, drawing with Park in Seoul on 19 May 1979. It was the 17th time that he had completed the full 15-round distance, an achievement that is unlikely ever to be bettered.

The Korean made five successful defences, but was then knocked out in nine rounds by Shoji Oguma in May 1980. It was an overdue win for

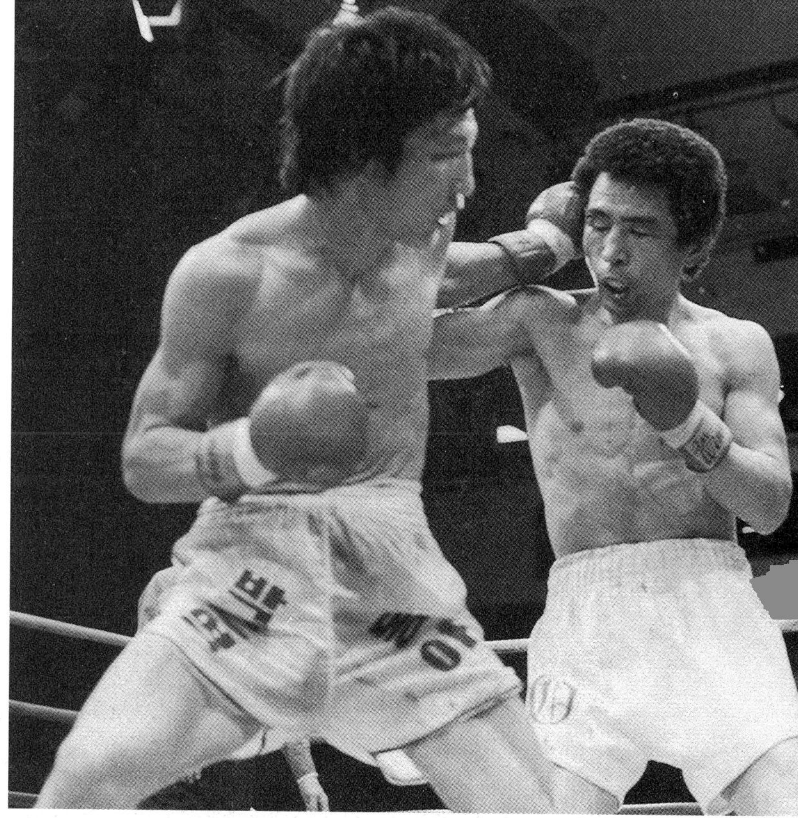

Oguma, whose five previous attempts on the several versions of the title had ended in failure. The Japanese retained it in a pair of rematches with Park, but then lost it on 12 May 1981 to Avelar. The Mexican made only one defence, knocking out the former WBA champion Tae-Shik Kim in two rounds, and thereafter the title passed in bewildering succession to Prudencio Cardona of

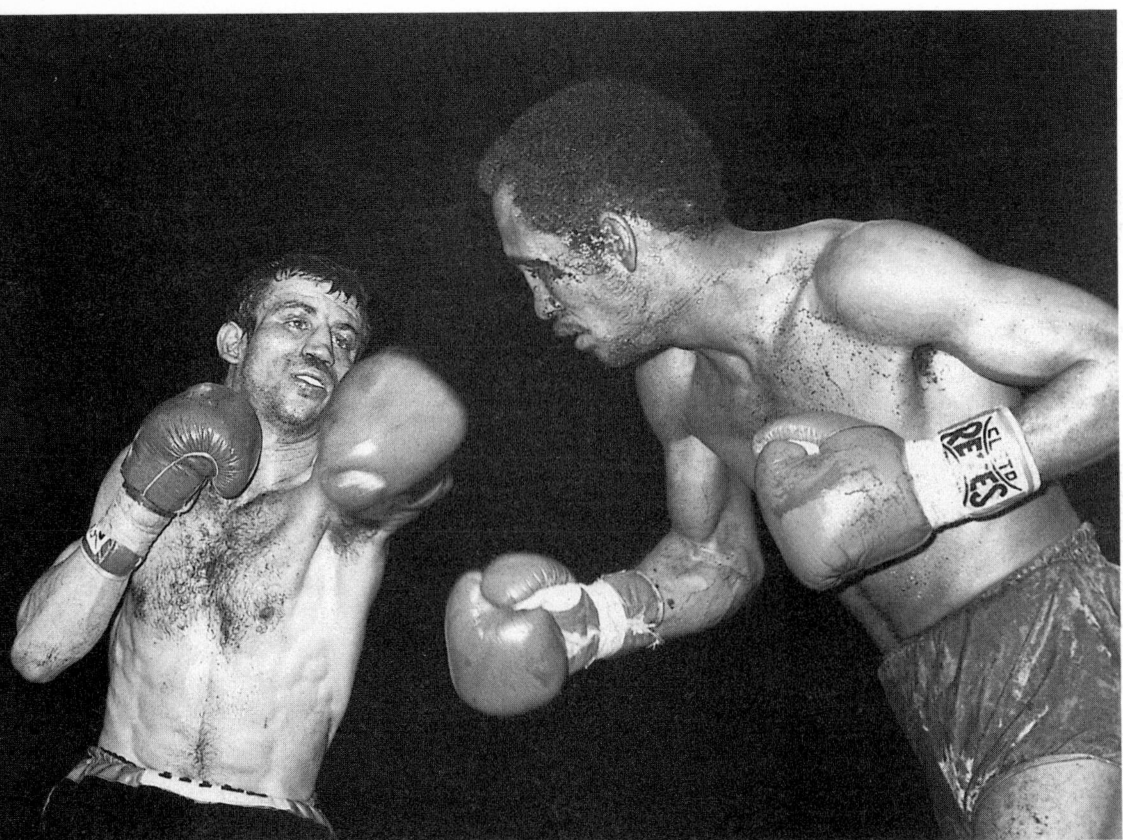

Charlie Magri, a popular and big-hearted Londoner, had a brief spell at the top in 1983, winning the WBC title on a cut from Eleoncio Mercedes (left, *on the right)* *and then losing it to Frank Cedeno* (below) *six months later.*

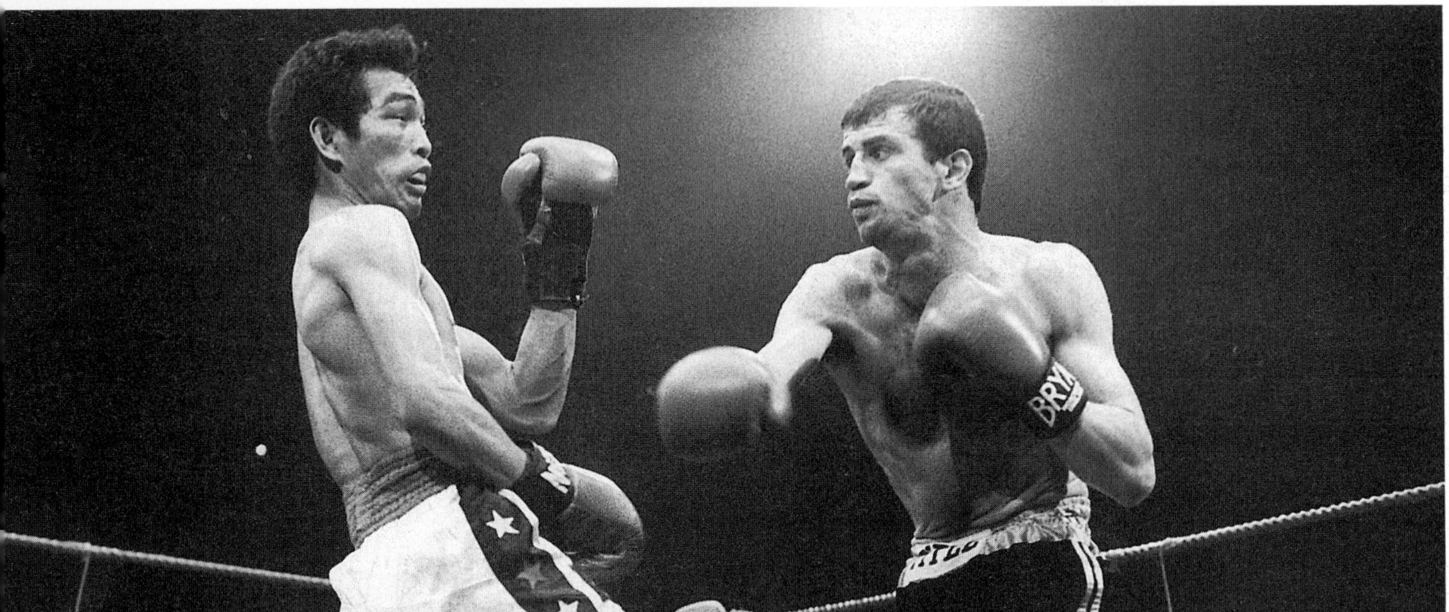

Colombia, Freddie Castillo of Mexico (the former WBC light-flyweight champion, who also came from Merida), Eleoncio Mercedes of the Dominican Republic, Charlie Magri of Stepney, London, Frank Cedeno of the Philippines, Koji Kobayashi of Japan and Gabriel Bernal of Mexico who, on 4 June 1984 at Nimes, France, made the first successful title defence for three years and six champions by beating Antoine Montero.

Bernal was dethroned on 8 October 1984 by the gifted Thai, Sot Chitalada, who to the end of 1986 made four successful defences, including a four-

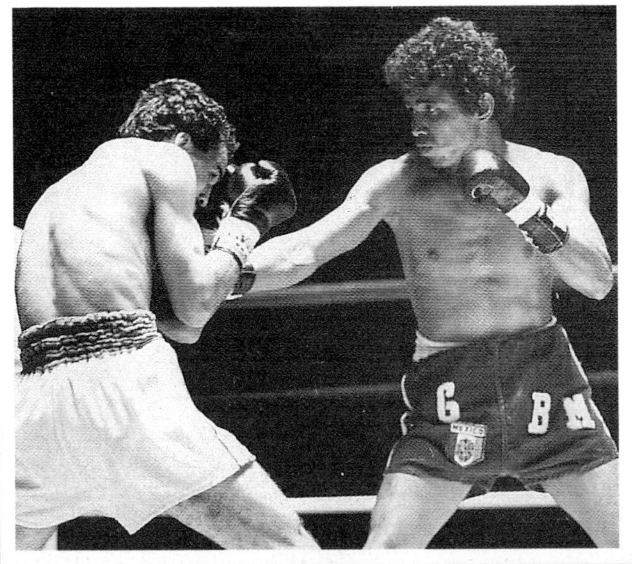

The WBC title passed briskly from Koji Kobayashi (above, *on the right, outscoring the Korean Kap-Dong Park) to Gabriel Bernal* (left, *beating Antoine Montero) and then to the Thai Sot Chitalada* (below, *on the right) who at last brought some consistency to the championship.*

The sad face of defeat: Charlie Magri with cornerman Frank Black at the end of his challenge for Sot Chitalada's WBC title in London.

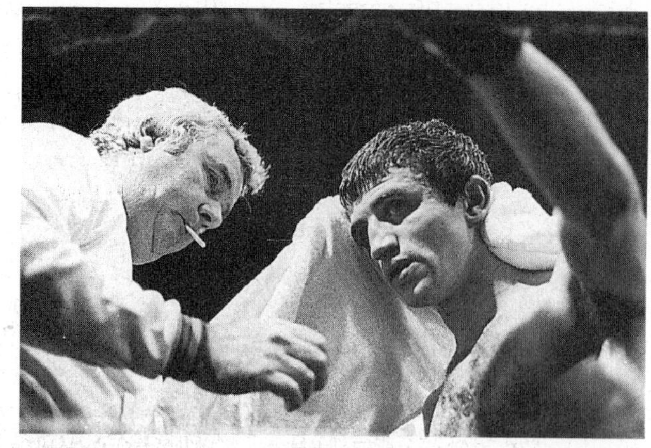

round retirement win in London over the popular, big-hearted Magri.

The WBA version of the title has been equally hotly-contested since its inception on 1 March 1966. It was first won by Horacio Accavallo of Argentina, who retired undefeated in October 1968 after three defences. Hiroyuki Ebihara, Bernabe Villacampo and Berkrerk Chartvanchai followed him inside a year, each losing it on the first defence, but Masao Ohba of Japan – who stopped Chartvancahi in 13 rounds in October 1970 – seemed set for a long reign. He made five defences, but only 23 days after his last fight (a 12th-round stoppage of ex-champion Chartchai Chionoi) he was killed in a road accident.

Chionoi won the vacant title by stopping Fritz

Below: *The joy of victory . . . Masao Ohba celebrates his 13th-round knockout of Berkrerk Chartvanchai for the WBA title in 1970.*

Right: *Horacio Accavallo (on the left), who lost only twice in 83 fights, outscores Efren Torres in defence of the WBA title in 1966.*

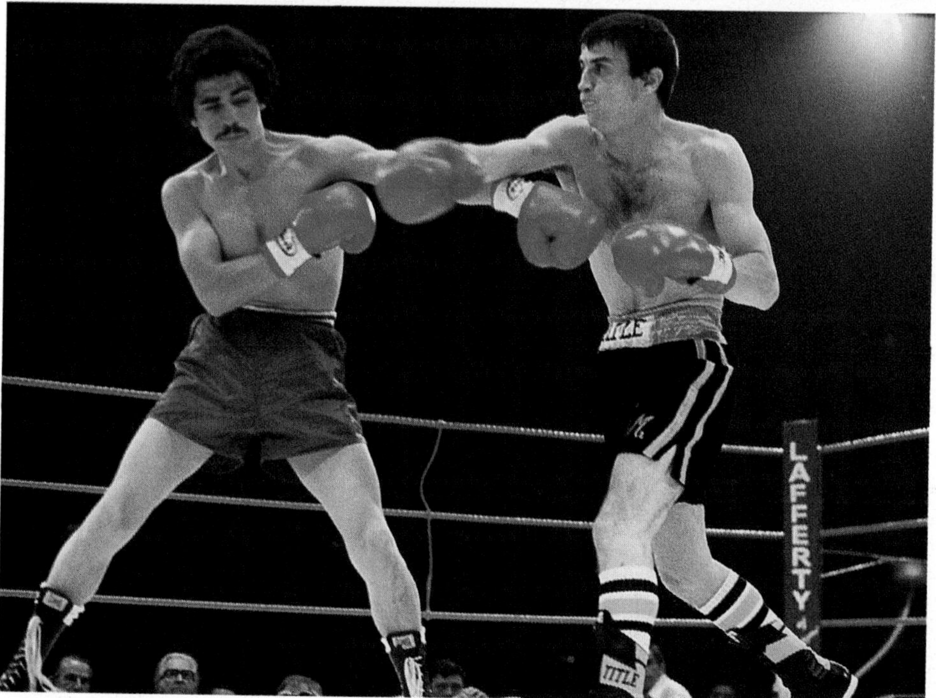

Richard Sandoval was desperately hurt by Gaby Canizales in their bantamweight title fight (above). *He made a full recovery, but never boxed again. The London fight crowd loved little Charlie Magri* (left), *whose combination of punching power and vulnerability made him the hottest flyweight attraction in British boxing for decades. His WBC title win over Eleoncio Mercedes* (following page) *was a popular if short-lived success.*

Chervet of Switzerland in four rounds and retained it twice, including a split decision over Chervet in Zurich, in Switzerland's first world title fight. The Thai's third spell as champion ended ingloriously in October 1974, when he came in 3½ lb overweight for a defence against Susumu Hanagata of Japan at Yokohama. The title was declared vacant, and awarded to Hanagata after he stopped Chionoi in six rounds. The former WBC champion Erbito Salavarria beat Hanagata on a split decision in his first defence in April 1975, but lost it in February 1976 to Alfonso Lopez, a rugged Panamanian who retained it against Oguma, but was then stopped in 13 rounds by Guty Espadas.

Espadas came from the same Mexican town, Merida, as the rival WBC champion Miguel Canto, so there was hope that Espadas' win over Lopez in Los Angeles in October 1976 might lead to a

Chartchai Chionoi can't have done quite enough of these rigorous training exercises (above)*: he came in overweight for this scheduled defence against Susumu Hanagata* (below, *on the left) and forfeited the title.*

reunification match with his neighbour. That prospect disappeared, however, when Guty was dethroned on his fifth defence, by Betulio Gonzalez, on a split decision in Maracay.

The Venezuelan veteran, champion for the third time, managed three defences before being outpointed in November 1979 by Luis Ibarra of Panama, who promptly lost it three months later to Tae-Shik Kim of Korea, who knocked him out in two rounds. Kim was outpointed on his second defence, in December 1980, by the first black South African to win a world title – Peter Mathebula from the Transvaal. Mathebula had to make the long trip to Los Angeles for his chance, but held his first defence on home ground in Soweto. It ended unhappily when Santos Laciar, of Argentina, who had come to prominence with a splendid (though losing) ten-rounder against Charlie Magri in London, knocked him out in seven rounds.

The stocky Argentinian was, surprisingly, outpointed by Luis Ibarra three months later, but Ibarra in turn lost in his first defence to Juan Herrera, yet another from the Merida production line. Herrera retained the crown against Betulio Gonzalez, but then lost it back to Laciar on a 13th-round stoppage in May 1982. This time Laciar took a firm grip on the title, making nine successful defences before relinquishing it undefeated, in 1985, to pursue the super-flyweight title.

Hilario Zapata, the former WBC light-flyweight champion, took over in October 1985 and was a busy title-holder, with five successful defences. But he was dethroned in February 1987 when Fidel Bassa of Colombia outpointed him in

Left: *Peter Mathebula went all the way to Los Angeles to take the WBA title from Tae-Shik Kim of Korea in 1980.*

Below: *Santos Laciar, later WBA champion, got his big break in this losing 10-rounder against Charlie Magri.*

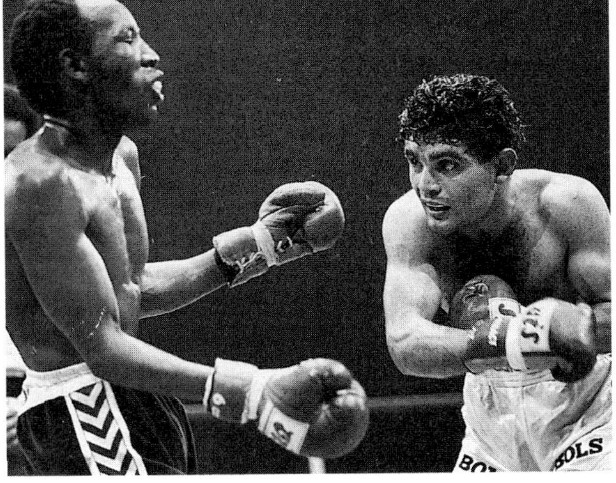

Above: *Laciar batters Commonwealth champion Steve Muchoki into ninth-round defeat in Copenhagen.*

Right: *Hilario Zapata, the former light-flyweight champion, proved a worthy successor to Laciar.*

Barranquilla. Bassa came desperately close to losing it on his first defence, when he survived a battering from Irish challenger Dave McAuley in Belfast to win in 13 thrilling rounds in April 1987.

The IBF version, first contested on 24 December 1983, has been exclusively a Korean possession. Soo-Chun Kwon won the first title fight, and made six defences before, in December 1985, he was stopped on a cut by his compatriot Chong-Kwan Chung, who in turn lost it to Hisup Shin.

HOW THE FLYWEIGHT TITLE HAS CHANGED HANDS

11 Apr 13 Sid Smith w.pts.20 Eugene Criqui in Paris *(First international flyweight bout)*
02 Jun 13 Bill Ladbury w.rsf.11 Sid Smith in London
26 Jan 14 Percy Jones w.pts.20 Bill Ladbury at London
15 May 14 Joe Symonds w.ko.18 Percy Jones at Plymouth *(Jones came in overweight but Symonds claimed the title)*
14 Feb 16 Jimmy Wilde w.rtd.12 Joe Symonds in London
18 Dec 16 Jimmy Wilde w.ko.11 Young Zulu Kid in London *(For undisputed title)*
18 Jun 23 Pancho Villa w.ko.7 Jimmy Wilde in New York
14 Jul 25 *Villa died, and Frankie Genaro claimed the title on the strength of his 1923 win over Villa for US title*
22 Aug 25 Fidel LaBarba w.pts.10 Frankie Genaro in Los Angeles *(For American recognition as champion)*
23 Aug 27 *LaBarba retired to enter university*
28 Nov 27 Albert 'Frenchie' Belanger w.pts.10 Frankie Genaro in Toronto *(For vacant NBA title)*
16 Dec 27 Cpl. Izzy Schwartz w.pts.15 Newsboy Brown in New York *(For vacant NY title)*
06 Feb 28 Frankie Genaro w.pts.10 Albert 'Frenchie' Belanger in Toronto *(NBA title)*
02 Mar 29 Emile Pladner w.ko.1 Frankie Genaro in Paris *(For NBA title. Pladner's win also earned him recognition as champion by the International Boxing Union)*
18 Apr 29 Frankie Genaro w.dis.5 Emile Pladner in Paris *(NBA and IBU title)*
22 Aug 29 Willie La Morte w.pts15 Cpl. Izzy Schwartz in Newark *(New York did not recognise La Morte as champion, but instituted a tournament in which the finalists were Midget Wolgast and Black Bill. La Morte, meanwhile, retained his share of the title with a repeat 15-rounds win over Schwartz at Newark on 3 October 1929)*
21 Mar 30 Midget Wolgast w.pts.15 Black Bill in New York *(Vacant NY title)*
16 May 30 Midget Wolgast w.rtd.5 Willie La Morte in New York
27 Oct 31 Victor Perez w.ko.2 Frankie Genaro at Paris
31 Oct 32 Jackie Brown w.rsf.13 Victor Perez at Manchester
09 Sep 35 Benny Lynch w.rtd.2 Jackie Brown in Manchester
16 Sep 35 Small Montana w.pts.10 Midget Wolgast in Oakland, Calif *(For American recognition as champion)*
19 Jan 37 Benny Lynch w.pts.15 Small Montana at Wembley *(For undisputed title)*

The fight in which British champion Johnny Hill (Edinburgh) outpointed Newsboy Brown (US) over 15 rounds at Clapton on 29 August 1928 was billed as being for the vacant world title, but Hill's claim vanished after he was knocked out in six rounds by Emile Pladner (France) in Paris on 7 February 1929. Some sources list Hill's two 1929 wins over Ernie Jarvis as world title defences, but both fights involved only the British title.

Valentin Angelmann (France) was recognised as champion by the IBU for a short period in 1937, but Benny Lynch's wins over Small Montana and Peter Kane confirmed him as undisputed champion.

13 Oct 37 Benny Lynch w.ko.13 Peter Kane in Glasgow
29 Jun 38 *Lynch forfeited the title by scaling 8st $6\frac{1}{2}$lb for a scheduled defence against Jackie Jurich*
22 Sep 38 Peter Kane w.pts.15 Jackie Jurich in Liverpool *(For vacant title)*
1940 *The NBA proclaimed Little Dado champion, but he did not defend it and his claim was never taken seriously*
19 Jun 43 Jackie Paterson w.ko.1 Peter Kane at Glasgow
31 Jul 47 *The BBBC stripped Paterson of the title because of his inability to make the weight for a planned defence against Dado Marino*
20 Oct 47 Rinty Monaghan w.pts.15 Dado Marino in London *(For NBA and Irish Board recognition as champion. Paterson had obtained a court injunction restraining the BBBC from recognising anyone else as world champion, or from recognising as a title fight any contest which did not involve him)*
23 Mar 48 Rinty Monaghan w.ko.7 Jackie Paterson in Belfast *(For undisputed title)*
30 Mar 50 *Monaghan retired as undefeated champion*
05 Apr 50 Terry Allen w.pts.15 Honore Pratesi in London *(For vacant title)*
01 Aug 50 Dado Marino w.pts.15 Terry Allen at Honolulu
19 May 52 Yoshio Shirai w.pts.15 Dado Marino at Tokyo
26 Nov 54 Pascual Perez w.pts.15 Yoshio Shirai at Tokyo
16 Apr 60 Pone Kingpetch w.pts.15 Pascual Perez at Bangkok
10 Oct 62 Masahiko Harada w.ko.11 Pone Kingpetch at Tokyo
12 Jan 63 Pone Kingpetch w.pts.15 Masahiko Harada at Bangkok
18 Sep 63 Hiroyuki Ebihara w.ko.1 Pone Kingpetch at Tokyo
23 Jan 64 Pone Kingpetch w.pts.15 Hiroyuki Ebihara at Bankok
23 Apr 65 Salvatore Burruni w.pts.15 Pone Kingpetch at Rome
Nov 65 *(Title taken from Burruni by WBA for failure to defend against Horacio Accavallo)*
01 Mar 66 Horacio Accavallo w.pts.15 Katsutoshi Takayama at Tokyo *(Vacant WBA title)*
14 Jun 66 Walter McGowan w.pts.15 Salvatore Burruni at Wembley *(WBC title)*
30 Dec 66 Chartchai Chionoi w.rsf.9 Walter McGowan at Bangkok
01 Oct 68 *Horacio Accavallo, WBA champion, retired from boxing owing to eye injuries*
23 Feb 69 Efren Torres w.rsf.8 Chartchai Chionoi at Mexico City *(WBC title)*
30 Mar 69 Hiroyuki Ebihara w.pts.15 Jose Severino at Sapporo *(Vacant WBA title)*
19 Oct 69 Bernabe Villacampo w.pts.15 Hiroyuki Ebihara at Osaka
20 Mar 70 Chartchoi Chionoi w.pts.15 Efren Torres at Bangkok *(WBC title)*
06 Apr 70 Berkrerk Chartvanchai w.pts.15 Bernabe Villacampo at Bangkok *(WBA title)*
21 Oct 70 Masao Ohba w.rsf.13 Berkrerk Chartvanchai at Tokyo
07 Dec 70 Erbito Salavarria w.rsf.2 Chartchai Chionoi at Bangkok *(WBC title)*
20 Nov 71 Erbito Salavarria drew 15 Betulio Gonzalez at Maracaibo *(Salavarria then disqualified for alledgedly using illegal stimulant, Gonzalez subsequently declared champion by WBC)*
29 Sep 72 Venice Borkorsor w.rtd.10 Betulio Gonzalez at Bangkok
25 Jan 73 *Masao Ohba, WBA champion, killed in road crash*
17 May 73 Chartchai Chionoi w.rsf.4 Fritz Chervet in Bangkok *(Vacant WBA title)*
10 Jul 73 *Venice Borkorsor, WBC champion, relinquished title to campaign as a bantamweight*
04 Aug 73 Betulio Gonzalez w.pts.15 Miguel Canto at Maracaibo *(Vacant WBC title)*
01 Oct 74 Shoji Oguma w.pts.15 Betulio Gonzalez in Tokyo
18 Oct 74 Susumu Hanagata w.rsf.6 Chartchai Chionoi at Yokohama *(Chionoi forfeited WBA title on scales when he weighed in $3\frac{1}{2}$lb over the flyweight limit after two attempts; Hanagata, who weighed in at the flyweight limit, was awarded championship when he won the fight)*
08 Jan 75 Miguel Canto w.pts.15 Shoji Oguma at Sendai *(WBC title)*
01 Apr 75 Erbito Salavarria w.pts.15 Susumu Hanagata in Toyama, Japan *(WBA title)*
27 Feb 76 Alfonso Lopez w.rsf.15 Erbito Salavarria in Manila
02 Oct 76 Guty Espadas w.rsf.13 Alfonso Lopez in Los Angeles
13 Aug 78 Betulio Gonzalez w.pts.15 Guty Espadas at Maracay
18 Mar 79 Chan Hee Park w.pts.15 Miguel Canto at Pusan *(WBC title)*
16 Nov 79 Luis Ibarra w.pts.15 Betulio Gonzalez in Maracay
16 Feb 80 Taeshik Kim w.ko.2 Luis Ibarra in Seoul
18 May 80 Shoji Oguma w.ko.9 Chan Hee Park in Seoul
13 Dec 80 Peter Mathebula w.pts.15 Taeshik Kim at Los Angeles
28 Mar 81 Santos Laciar w.ko.7 Peter Mathebula at Soweto
12 May 81 Antonio Avelar w.ko.7 Shoji Oguma at Mito
06 Jun 81 Luis Ibarra w.pts.15 Santos Laciar at Buenos Aires
26 Sep 81 Juan Herrera w.ko.11 Luis Ibarra at Merida
20 Mar 82 Prudencio Cardona w.ko.1 Antonio Avelar at Tampico *(WBC title)*
01 May 82 Santos Laciar w.rsf.13 Juan Herrera at Merida *(WBA title)*
24 Jul 82 Freddie Castillo w.pts.15 Prudencio Cardona at Merida
06 Nov 82 Eleoncio Mercedes w.pts.15 Freddie Castillo at Los Angeles
15 Mar 83 Charlie Magri w.rsf.7 Eleoncio Mercedes at Wembley
27 Sep 83 Frank Cedeno w.rsf.6 Charlie Magri at Wembley
24 Dec 83 Soo-Chun Kwon w.ko.5 Rene Busayong at Osaka *(Vacant IBF title)*
18 Jan 84 Koji Kobayashi w.rsf.2 Frank Cedeno at Tokyo
09 Apr 84 Gabriel Bernal w.ko.2 Koji Kobayashi at Tokyo
08 Oct 84 Sot Chitalada w.pts.12 Gabriel Bernal at Bangkok
05 Oct 85 Hilario Zapata w.pts.15 Alonzo Gonzalez in Panama City *(For WBA title relinquished by Laciar)*
20 Dec 85 Chong-Kwan Chung w.rsf.4 Soo-Chun Kwon at Pusan
27 Apr 86 Chung Bi Won w.pts.15 Chung Jong Kwan at Pusan
02 Aug 86 Hi Sop Shin w.ko.15 Chung Bi Won at Seoul
13 Feb 87 Fidel Bassa w.pts.15 Hilario Zapata at Barranquilla
22 Feb 87 Dodie Penalosa w.ko.5 Hi Sop Shin at Inchon

LIGHT FLYWEIGHTS

ONLY THREE men have fought for a world championship in their first professional engagement. Pete Rademacher, the 1956 Olympic heavyweight champion, was knocked out by Floyd Patterson in 1957, and Jack Skelly earned his first boxing pay cheque against featherweight champion George Dixon in 1892. Both matches were reprehensible by any standards, but at least the public were aware of the challengers' total lack of credentials. The third instance was somewhat different, and it involved the second contest ever staged for the WBC light-flyweight title.

The new division, weight limit 7 st 10 lb (108 lb) had been inaugurated by the WBC in 1975. It got off to an inauspicious start when the new champion, Franco Udella of Italy, was carried from the ring on a stretcher after being thumped in the kidneys by Valentin Martinez of Mexico, who was disqualified in the 12th round in Milan on 4 April. Udella developed health problems (which were unconnected with his unpleasant experience against Martinez) and was unable to meet a WBC deadline for a defence against the official contender, Rafael Lovera of Paraguay. The Italian was stripped of the championship in September, and the WBC matched Lovera with an ageing but dangerous Panamanian, Luis Estaba.

Estaba's qualifications were impeccable: three losses in 33 fights, even if at the age of 34, he was exceptionally old to compete for a world title. Lovera was a different case, but the WBC accepted the statistically impressive record supplied by the Paraguayan's manager and installed Rafael in the No. 1 contender position. To their intense embarrassment, Lovera performed so badly in his fourth-round knockout defeat by Estaba in Caracas on 13 September 1975 that the WBC asked a few more

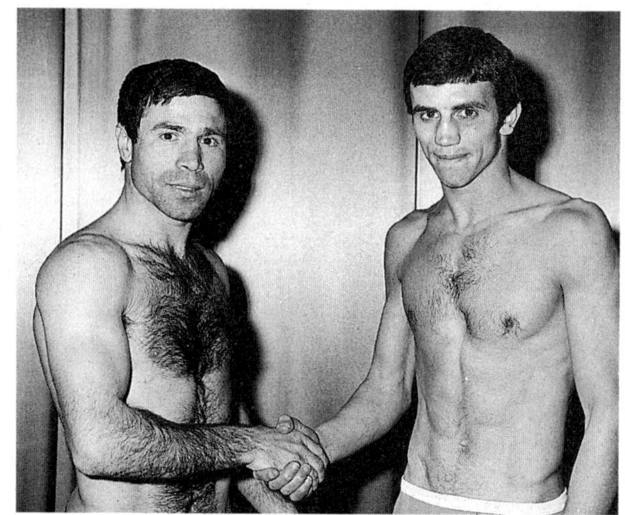

Above: *The division's first champion was an Italian, Franco Udella of Italy (left), who later lost the European flyweight title to Charlie Magri (right).*

Below: *Luis Estaba won his title in dubious circumstances, but then gave a string of good performances, including this kayo of Udella in 1976.*

probing questions, and discovered that Lovera had never had a fight in his life.

Suspensions and prosecutions ensued, but at least Estaba was allowed to keep the title he had won so easily. The veteran proved his right to it with a string of impressive defences, including a three-round knockout of Udella and a tenth-round stoppage of Martinez. In all, he retained the title 11 times, losing it on 19 February 1978 to Freddie Castillo from Merida, Mexico, in Caracas. Castillo held it for less than three months, losing a split decision in Bangkok on 6 May to Netrnoi Vorasingh, whose solitary winning defence saw him end Estaba's career with a fifth-round retirement in Caracas.

Vorasingh (who was killed in a 1982 motorbike crash) was knocked out in three rounds in Seoul in September 1978 by Kim Sung-Jun, a Korean who had won only 19 of his 29 fights. But Jun, surprisingly, turned into a decent champion who made three successful defences before Shigeo Nakajima outpointed him in Tokyo on 3 January 1980. (Jun reverted to form after losing the title, and won only three of his remaining 11 fights.)

Nakajima's reign lasted just 79 days, but his conqueror, Hilario Zapata of Panama, proved rather more enduring. In his first spell as champion, between 24 March 1980 and 6 February 1982, he made eight successful defences, risking the title in Korea, Venezuela, Japan, Panama, America, and Thailand. He lost it in an upset to Amado Ursua of Mexico, who knocked him out in two rounds, but Ursua's tenure was even more abbreviated than Nakajima's had been, lasting only 66 days. Tadashi Tomori of Japan outpointed him in Tokyo on 13 April, but Zapata reclaimed it with a points win over

Japan has had a substantial say in the destiny of boxing's lightest championship, producing stars like Shigeo Nakajima (below) *and Tadashi Tomori* (right, *struggling with the outsize trophy which the Japanese award world title winners).*

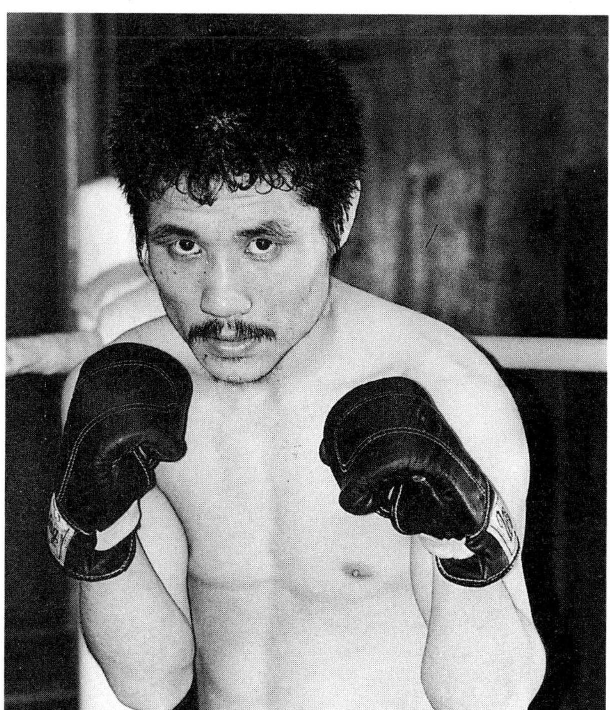

Shigeo Nakajima lands a perfect left on Sung-Jun Kim, whom he outpointed for the WBC title in 1980.

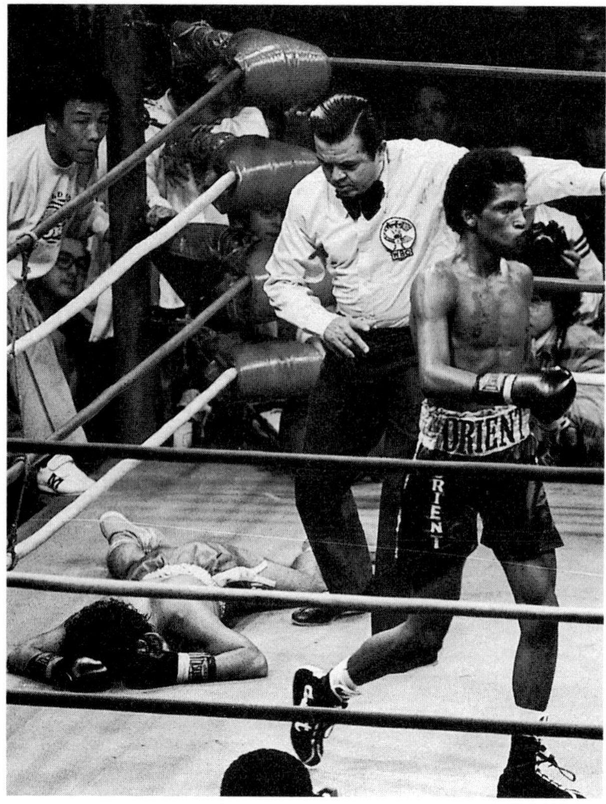

Above: *Tomori's last fight: he retired after this eighth-round knockout by Hilario Zapata in 1982 having held the title just over three months.*

the Japanese on 20 July. Zapata retained it twice – including an eighth-round knockout of Tomori – but lost it on 26 March 1983 to Jung-Koo Chang of Korea, whom Zapata had previously outpointed.

Chang's third-round knockout of Zapata launched a remarkble championship career which, to the end of 1986, embraced 11 successful

Below: *The remarkable Jung-Koo Chang, the most formidable champion the WBC division has yet produced.*

Below: *Jaime Rios (left) retains the WBA version against Kazunori Tenryu in Tokyo, his only successful defence of the title.*

defences. The points defeat by Zapata in his first world title bid in September 1982 remains his only loss in 33 fights in a career that began, with a frantic burst of activity, when he was 17: he boxed six times in 21 days.

The WBA version was first won by Jaime Rios of Panama, who outpointed Venezuela's Rigoberto Marcano in a thriller in Panama City on 23 August 1975. He made one defence before being beaten on points by Juan Jose Guzman of the Dominican Republic in Santo Domingo on 1 July 1976. Guzman held it for only three months, being knocked out in seven rounds at Kofu, Japan, on 10 October by Yoko Gushiken.

The 21-year-old southpaw from Okinawa won the title in only his ninth fight, but he kept an iron grip on it for almost five years and a record 13 successful defences. Gushiken was a protege of the Uehara brothers, Yasutsune (who held the WBA junior-lightweight title) and Flipper, who challenged for the featherweight title against David Kotei in 1976. He worked in the bath-house owned by the family, and the trio did their training after the baths

Juan Guzman (left) *held the WBA title for a mere three months before surrendering it to Yoko Gushiken* (above), *whose 13 defences included this seventh-round stoppage of Tito Abella in 1979* (below).

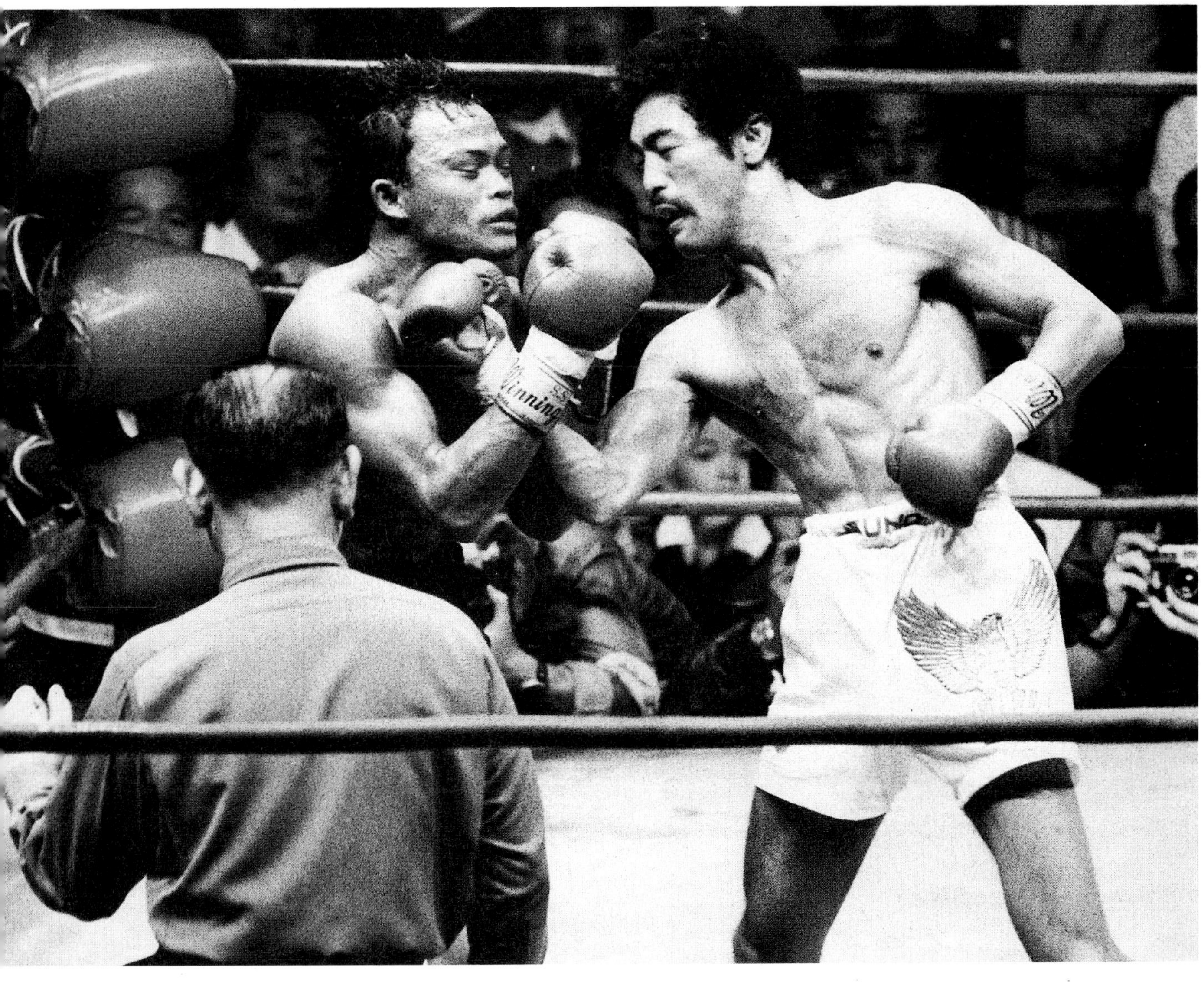

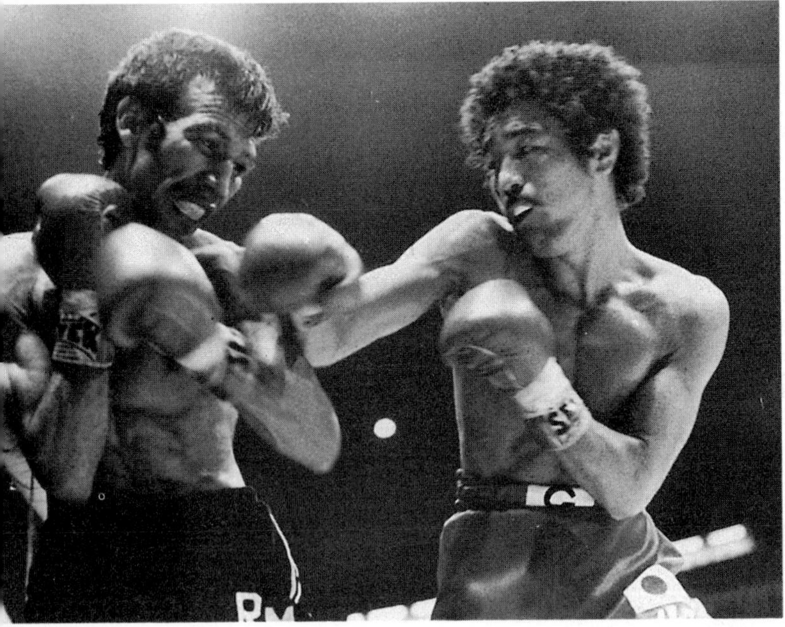

Above: *Gushiken (right) knocks out Rigoberto Marcano in the seventh in January 1979.*

Below: *Pedro Flores toppled Gushiken in March 1981, but four months later lost it in 13 rounds to Hwan-Jin Kim.*

Kim outscores the former WBA flyweight champion Alfonso Lopez in his first defence of the light-flyweight title.

closed at midnight. In return for helping to run the establishment, Gushiken lived there rent free. He was used to hard living: his father ran a 'bum boat', which is not nearly so interesting as it sounds . . . it is the term used for the small craft which ply between the island and the liners which anchor in the bay.

The hungry days were far behind him when he retired in 1981 after his only loss in 24 fights, a 12th-round knockout by Pedro Flores of Mexico, at Gushikawa, on 8 March, cost him the world title. His reputation was damaged by later allegations that several of his championship victims had been drugged or food-poisoned. (A similar accusation was made by Rene Arredondo after he had lost his WBC light-welterweight title to Tsuyoshi Hamada on a first-round knockout in Japan in 1986.)

Flores, who had lost to Gushiken in his previous fight, was dethroned on 13 July 1981 by Hwan-Jin Kim of Korea, who retained the title against Alfonso Lopez but then lost it in December 1981 to a Japanese, Katsuo Tokashiki. The stylish Tokashiki made five successful defences, the last of them a draw with Lupe Madera of Mexico. Tokashiki had outpointed Madera when they first met, drew the rematch, and then lost the title to him in bizarre circumstances in Tokyo on 10 July 1983. Madera suffered a terrible cut on the side of the head after an accidental clash of heads in the fourth round and, under WBA rules which require a points decision to be given, Madera was declared the new champion on the basis of the lead he had built in the opening three rounds. (Had the incident occurred a round earlier, the verdict would have been a technical draw, since the rule stipulates that points decisions cannot be given over the first three rounds.)

They were rematched in October 1983, and this time Madera ended the series with a convincing points win. It was the Mexican's last victory: when he lost the title to Francisco Quiroz, of the Dominican Republic, on a ninth-round knockout in May 1984, he retired from boxing. Quiroz lost his second defence to Joey Olivo of Los Angeles (America's first winner at the weight) but Olivo was in turn beaten on *his* second defence by Myung-Woo Yuh of Korea, who had retained it three times to the end of 1986.

The IBF version has yet to produce an outstanding champion and, as with so many of their lower-range titles, has been contested exclusively by Orientals. It was first won by Dodie Penalosa of the Philippines, who was stripped after

Left: *Mexico's Lupe Madera takes the WBA title from Katsuo Tokashiki on a bizarre technical decision. It was Madera's first success in three world title attempts.*
Below: *Myung-Woo Yuh, the latest of the strong Korean contingent in the light-flyweight record list, retained the WBA title with this points win in November 1986 over the Argentine, Mario DeMarco.*

three defences and, in December 1986, Jum Hwan Choi survived a knockdown to outpoint his fellow-Korean Cho Woon Park and take the vacant title.

It seems somehow appropriate that a journey which began in New Orleans in 1892 should end in Seoul in 1986. The world may have grown smaller, but the irresistible appeal of this most dramatic and heroic sport remains undiminished.

HOW THE LIGHT-FLYWEIGHT TITLE HAS CHANGED HANDS

04 Apr 75	Franco Udella w.dis.12 Valentin Martinez at Milan *(Vacant WBC title)*
23 Aug 75	Jaime Rios w.pts.15 Rigoberto Marcano at Panama City *(Vacant WBA title)*
Aug 75	*WBC withdrew recognition of Udella as champion for failing to defend on schedule against their leading contender, Rafael Lovera*
13 Sep 75	Luis Estaba w.ko.4 Rafael Lovera at Caracas *(Vacant WBC title)*
01 Jul 76	Juan Guzman w.pts.15 Jaime Rios at Santo Domingo *(WBA title)*
10 Oct 76	Yoko Gushiken w.ko.7 Juan Guzman at Kofu, Japan
19 Feb 78	Freddie Castillo w.rsf.14 Luis Estaba in Caracas *(WBC title)*
06 May 78	Netrnoi Vorasingh w.pts.15 Freddie Castillo in Bangkok
30 Sep 78	Kim Sung-Jun w.ko.3 Netrnoi Vorasingh in Seoul
03 Jan 80	Shigeo Nakajima w.pts.15 Kim Sung-Jun in Tokyo
23 Mar 80	Hilario Zapata w.pts.15 Shigeo Nakajima in Tokyo
31 Mar 81	Pedro Flores w.rtd.12 Yoko Gushiken at Naha
19 Jul 81	Hwanjin Kim w.rsf.13 Pedro Flores at Seoul
16 Dec 81	Katsuo Tokashiki w.pts.15 Hwanjin Kim at Sendai
06 Feb 82	Amado Ursua w.ko.2 Hilario Zapata in Panama City *(WBC title)*
13 Apr 82	Tadashi Tomori w.pts.15 Amado Ursua in Tokyo
20 Jul 82	Hilario Zapata w.pts.15 Tadashi Tomori at Kanazawa
26 Mar 83	Jung Koo Chang w.ko.3 Hilario Zapata at Daejon *(WBC title)*
10 Jul 83	Lupe Madera w.tech.dec.4 Katsuo Tokashiki at Tokyo *(WBA title)*
11 Dec 83	Dodie Penalosa w.rsf.12 Satoshi Shingaki at Osaka *(Vacant IBF title)*
19 May 84	Francisco Quiroz w.ko.9 Lupe Madera at Maracaibo
29 Mar 85	Joey Olivo w.pts.15 Francisco Quiroz at Miami Beach
08 Dec 85	Myung Woo Yuh w.pts.15 Joey Olivo in Seoul
Jul 86	*Dodie Penalosa stripped of IBF title for failure to defend*
07 Dec 86	Jum Hwan Choi w.pts.15 Cho Woon Park at Seoul *(Vacant IBF title)*

INDEX

Page number in *italic* refer to illustrations and captions

BIBLIOGRAPHY

Armstrong, Henry: *Gloves, Glory and God.* (Paul Davies, UK, 1957)

Dempsey, Jack & Dempsey, Barbara: *Dempsey* (W H Allen, UK, 1971; Harper & Row Pubs. Inc., New York, USA, 1977)

Fleischer, Nat and André, Sam: *A Pictorial History of Boxing.* (Hamlyn, UK, revised 1987; Citadel Press, Secaucus, USA, 1975)

Gains, Larry: *The Impossible Dream.* (Leisure Publications, London, UK, 1976)

Graziano, Rocky: *Somebody Up There Likes Me.* (World Distributors, UK, 1965)

Gutteridge, Reg: *The Big Punchers.* (Hutchinson, UK, 1983)

Heller, Peter: *'In This Corner—!': Forty World Champions Tell Their Story.* (Robson Books, UK, 1975)

Johansson, Ingemar: *Seconds Out of the Ring.* (Stanley Paul, UK, 1960)

Liebling, A.J.: *The Sweet Science.* (Gollancz, UK, 1956; Greenwood Press, Westport, USA, 1973)

Mead, Chris: *Champion— Joe Louis.* (Robson Books, UK, 1986; Charles Scritners, New York, USA)

Moore, Archie: *The Archie Moore Story.* (Kaye, UK, 1960)

Muhammad Ali: *The Greatest.* (Hart-Davis MacGibbon, UK, 1976; Random House, New York, USA, 1975)

Odd, Gilbert: *Cruisers to Mighty Atoms.* (Pelham, UK, 1974)

Pepe, Phil: *Come out Smokin': Joe Frazier, the Champ Nobody Knew.* (Woburn Press, UK, 1973)

Schulberg, Budd: *The Harder They Fall.* (White Lion Publishers, UK, 1975)

Sugar, Bert Randolph: *100 Years of Boxing.* (Windward, UK, 1981; Galley Press, New York, USA)

Tunney, Gene: *A Man Must Fight.* (Jonathan Cape, UK, 1933)